THE AMERICAN GUIDE SERIES

Military History of Kentucky

HIS EXCELLENCY, HON. ALBERT BENJAMIN CHANDLER
Governor of Kentucky
Commander-in-Chief
Kentucky National Guard

THE AMERICAN GUIDE SERIES

Military History of Kentucky

CHRONOLOGICALLY ARRANGED

Written by Workers of the Federal Writers Project of the Works Progress Administration for the State of Kentucky

---

Sponsored by

THE MILITARY DEPARTMENT OF KENTUCKY

G. LEE McCLAIN, The Adjutant General

COMMONWEALTH BOOK COMPANY
St. Martin, Ohio
2024

Copyright © 1939 by the Adjutant General of Kentucky
Copyright © 2024 by Commonwealth Book Company, Inc.

All rights reserved. No part of this book may be reproduced in any form or by any means without the prior written consent of the publisher, excepting brief quotes used in reviews.
Printed in the United States of America.

WORKS PROGRESS ADMINISTRATION

F.C. HARRINGTON, *Administrator*
FLORENCE S. KERR, *Assistant Administrator*
HENRY G. ALSBERG, *Director of the Federal Writers Project*

ISBN: 978-1-948986-80-9

COVER IMAGE: KENTUCKY MILITARY INSTITUTE, STROBRIDGE CO. CIRCA 1850, LIBRARY OF CONGRESS

FOREWORD

Frankfort, Kentucky,
January 1, 1939.

HIS EXCELLENCY, ALBERT BENJAMIN CHANDLER,
 Governor of Kentucky and
 Commander-in-Chief, Kentucky National Guard,
Frankfort, Kentucky.

SIR: I have the pleasure of submitting a report of the National Guard of Kentucky showing its origin, development and progress, chronologically arranged. This report is in the form of a history of the military units of Kentucky.

The purpose of this Military History of Kentucky is to present a written record which always will be available to the people of Kentucky relating something of the accomplishments of Kentucky soldiers. It will be observed that from the time the first settlers came to our state, down to the present day, Kentucky soldiers have been ever ready to protect the lives, homes, and property of the citizens of the state with vigor and courage.

It will be observed that the Kentucky soldier has done well his part in times of peace as well as in times of war. This history then, in truth, is a record and a story of the part that the military man, whether his organization was known as the State Militia, as the State Guard, or as the National Guard, has taken in the carving of a great state out of a vast wilderness and in maintaining its position.

The expeditions which played so prominent a part in the development of the Northwest Territory had their starting point in Kentucky. At all times the Kentucky soldier was found taking the lead in this expansion movement.

The data embodied in this history has been culled from many sources, for heretofore there have been no assembled sketches and only scattered authoritative accounts of the activities of the Kentucky Militia and its successor organizations. A chronological record of the Kentucky militiaman's major activities from 1774 to 1938 has never previously been set down in one place. Various sources have been exploited in the preparation of this work in quest for Kentucky militia data, particularly of the period prior to Kentucky's admission to statehood. The information so acquired often has been conflicting in detail. Where such conflicts have occurred, a special effort was made to separate accurate from inaccurate statements, and the final collation of facts was thus derived. Many instruments are quoted, either to preserve their quaintness of expression, or because of their conciseness. Then, too, these quoted documents, particularly of the War between the States period, serve as a safeguard against the possibility of truthful bald statements being construed as conjecture borne of sectional prejudices.

The collection of the data embodied in this book was made by members of the Kentucky Division of the Federal Writers' Project of the Works Progress Administration. The result is a collective work to which several writers and research workers have contributed. The book represents the work of a varied personnel to which consultants have generously given their services before the whole was edited in the central offices at Louisville.

The Military Department of the Commonwealth of Kentucky takes pleasure in presenting this volume to the citizens of this state, and to all who are interested in the story of Kentucky's soldiers. For the first time a true picture of the military activities in Kentucky is available in a compact form.

G. LEE MCCLAIN
The Adjutant General
State of Kentucky.

PREFACE

Kentucky has much that is not common to her sister states, among which is her militaristic spirit. From the first settlement her militia was ever willing and ready to lend assistance to a cause she deemed right, but that assistance could not be expected if the Kentuckians were to be placed under the command of "furriners" (non-Kentuckians). Assistance once pledged was zealously rendered, and even the Indians learned that Kentucky troops meant business and would "fight like devils." From pioneer days Kentucky has attracted the attention of the rest of the country by her tendency to be different to the point of developing a distinct individuality. In military, as well as political matters, she has always done the unexpected which is most strikingly illustrated by her demeanor during the reconstruction era, when it was frequently said that "Kentucky waited until after the war to secede."

More populous states may justly boast of contributing greater numbers of troops in the several wars, but none can rightfully claim troop contributions as heavy as Kentucky when proportionate state populations are taken into consideration. The Kentucky ratio has always been a source of state pride, especially because her troops have been raised chiefly as volunteers.

The goal in the preparation of this book has been to present an adequate, accurate, and interesting portrayal of the Kentucky military organization, past and present, in all its endeavors and achievements. Battles and skirmishes are dealt with briefly, for this is a history of the soldiery as a state organization rather than as a war machine.

The book could not have been completed without the voluntary assistance of many loyal Kentuckians. Especial thanks are due Gov. A. B. Chandler, Brig. Gen. G. Lee McClain, Maj. Gen. E. S. Adams, U.S.A., Maj. Robert W.

Brown, U.S.A., Lt. Col. W. S. Taylor, Col. Lucien Beckner, Mr. Otto Rothert, Col. H. J. Stites, Lt. Col. George M. Chesheir, Capt. Walter R. Calvert, Jr., Col. Thomas W. Woodyard, N.G. Ky., Rtd., Maj. J. M. Kelly, Miss Ludie Kincaid, Col. Joseph T. O'Neal, Mr. Carter Stamper, and Mr. John Wilson Townsend. Fredk. L. A. Eichelberger deserves credit for the arrangement of the material and the actual writing of the book. The Federal Writers' Project is glad of the opportunity to make this contribution to the documentary history of Kentucky.

URBAN R. BELL
State Director
Federal Writer's Project
Louisville, Kentucky

TABLE OF CONTENTS

Chapter		Page
I.	Legal Heritage	1
II.	Pioneer Period	11
III.	Statehood	65
IV.	Mexican War	121
V.	War between the States—Part I	151
V.	War between the States—Part II	193
VI.	Readjustment and Reorganization	239
VII.	War with Spain	281
VIII.	Political Turmoil and the State Guard	295
IX.	World War	327
X.	Kentucky National Guard Organization	345
XI.	Lineage of the Regiments Kentucky National Guard	371

Appendices

A.	Governors and Adjutant Generals	403
B.	Confederate Pensions	406
C.	Jerome Clarke Trial	407
D.	Military Memorials	410
E.	Biographical Sketches	417
F.	Kentucky National Guard Officers, World War	433
G.	Roster of Kentucky National Guard, 1938	442

Bibliography	475
Index	481

ILLUSTRATIONS

Governor Albert Benjamin Chandler	Frontspiece
Brigadier General G. Lee McClain, The Adjutant General	ix
Major Joseph M. Kelly, Assistant Adjutant General	x

	Faces Page
Artillery, 138th Field	272
Boone, Lt. Col. Daniel	32
Buckner, Maj. Gen. Simon Bolivar	129
Call for Volunteers, War of 1812	97
Carter, Brig. Gen. Ellerbe W.	384
Castleman, Brig. Gen. John B.	209
Cavalry, 123d	272
Clark, Maj. Gen. George Rogers	113
Confederate Mass-Burial Monument	224
Daviess, Col. Joseph Hamilton	112
Easley, Col. Roy W.	401
Guard of Honor, American Legion Convention, 1929	273
Harrison, Maj. Gen. William Henry	81
Henry, Gov. Patrick	16
Infantry, 149th	272
Johnson, Col. Richard M.	112
Kenton, Simon	32
Logan, Col. Benjamin	117
Louisville, Flood of 1937	256
Morgan, Brig. Gen. John Hunt	208
Munfordville Battlefield	225
O'Neal, Lt. Col. Joseph T.	384
Paducah, Flood of 1937	256
Perryville Battlefield	225
Reformatory Mess Line, Flood of 1937	257
Saratoga Cannon	33
Scott, Gov. Charles	96
Shelby, Gov. Isaac	80
Smith, Col. Sidney	401
State Reformatory Camp, Flood of 1937	257
Stites, Col. Henry J.	401
Taylor, Maj. Gen. Zachary	128
Wilkinson, Brig. Gen. James	113
Zollicoffer Monument	224

BRIG. GEN. G. LEE McCLAIN, KY. N. G.
The Adjutant General.

MAJOR JOSEPH M. KELLY, KY. N. G.
Assistant Adjutant General,
U. S. P. and D. O.

CHAPTER I

LEGAL HERITAGE

The Kentucky Militia as an institution was established by the laws of Virginia and continued thus until 1792, when Kentucky became a sovereign state, having theretofore been, territorially, a part of Virginia. The Virginia law was derived from the English Common Law and the Acts of the Virginia Assembly.

During this pre-statehood period the Kentucky Territory was embraced in Fincastle County, Virginia, from 1773 until October, 1776, when that county was trisected to form Montgomery, Washington, and Kentucky counties. A further division of this territory took place when Kentucky County was trisected, May, 1780, to form Fayette, Jefferson, and Lincoln counties in the District of Kentucky. Nine counties were established in Kentucky prior to statehood, in all of which the Virginia Militia law applied in general.

Minutes of the Fincastle County Court contain no particular matter dealing with the militia in the territory that became the present state of Kentucky. However, the minutes of a session of said court, held May 7, 1774, recite the receipt of the following militia commissions from Thomas Wilson, secretary of Virginia: John Byrd, colonel of the County Militia; William Christian, lieutenant colonel of the County Militia; Thomas Madison, captain of the County Militia; John Taylor, captain of the County Militia; Joseph Cloyd, captain of the County Militia; Thomas Ingles, lieutenant of the County Militia. These persons undoubtedly had jurisdiction (constructive) over any militia that might have existed in western Fincastle County until the erection of Kentucky County.

The Virginia Bill of Rights, adopted June 12, 1776, affirmed the necessity of maintaining a well regulated militia, declared against such a militia assuming the proportions of a standing army and enjoined the military to a position of subordination to the civil power. A few months later came the first Virginia State Constitution, which permitted incumbent Colonial Militia officers to retain their commissions upon taking the oath of fidelity and allegiance to the Commonwealth of Virginia. The filling of vacancies in the official ranks of the militia was made appointive in the Governor, with the advice of the Privy Council, or, upon recommendation of the county court of the county in which the vacancy occurred. However, the Governor and Privy Council were given power to remove, for just cause, any officer of the militia. Likewise the Governor and Privy Council could, jointly, call out the militia to its full strength (all able-bodied free males from eighteen to fifty years of age) and when so called it became subject to the orders of the Governor alone.

By the Act of the Assembly of Virginia of May, 1761, provision was made that, when any county lieutenant should be required to draft members of the militia, he could offer a bounty of forty shillings to every person who would voluntarily engage in the service. However, such voluntary enlistments were made with the understanding that the person so enlisting would continue in the service for any period up to one year if needed.

In 1775 Col. Richard Henderson attempted to establish a proprietary government in Fincastle County, claiming ownership of the land by purchase and grant from the Cherokee Indians. Henderson and his associates were known as the Transylvania Company, and their settlements as the Transylvania Colony. On May 23, 1775, the House of Delegates of the Transylvania Colony met at Fort Boonesborough. The journal of the proceedings of the convention relates that "May 25, 1775, on motion of Mr. Douglass, leave is given to bring in a bill for regulating a militia. Ordered that Mr. Floyd, Mr. Harrod, Mr. Cooke, Mr. Douglass, and Mr. Hite be a committee for that purpose." "May 26, 1775—Militia bill read a third time and passed." Among Colonel Henderson's first official acts as proprietor, after adjournment of the convention, was the issuance of military commissions to his appointees at the other settlements, Boiling Spring and St. Asaph's, an act to which he was empowered by the convention. However, the Transylvania acts were not countenanced by any of the old Colonies, and more than a temporary defensive organization of the militia was never accomplished. Other settlements in the Kentucky District looked to Virginia and the Carolinas for help in repulsing the Indians, but Transylvania could expect no such help, being founded upon lands claimed adversely to Virginia's previously asserted jurisdiction and recognized sovereignty.*[1]

Handbills containing the following summary of the Virginia Militia law effective in the Kentucky District, January, 1790, were distributed to the officers and men of Fayette County by County Lieutenant Levi Todd.[2]

Extracts of Virginia Militia Law

January 30, 1790.

In every company of Militia there must be a Captain, Lieutenant, Ensign, three Sergeants, three Corporals, a Drummer and Fifer and not less than forty or more than sixty-five rank and file; whenever a company exceeds this last number or decreases so as to be less than forty, it is the duty of the comanding officer of the company to report the circumstances to the commanding officer of the regiment. And here let it be observed that all the duties of a captain are incumbent on the eldest acting officer of a company, be his rank what it may.

It is the duty of the commanding officer of a company to enroll all free males above the age of 18 and under fifty (except such as are exempted by a court-martial, and also judges of Superior Courts, Members of Congress, Attorney Generals, Register and clerks of the land office, inspectors of tobacco, professors and tutors of any public seminary, all ministers of the gospel, licensed to preach according to the rules of their sect, who have taken the oath of fidelity, keepers of the public gold, millers, persons concerned in iron and lead works and persons solely employed in making or repairing fire arms and commissioners of the Tax). Every regiment shall be mustered twice a year, every company shall be mustered once in two months throughout the year, except in December and January. Every commanding officer of a company

---

*Notes, references, and sources are indicated by numerals. These refer to corresponding numbers at the end of this chapter. For notes on Chapter I see page 9.

shall notify the privates at least five days before any muster, whether of the regiment or company by himself or some of his sergeants personally or by writing left at the place of residence of such privates. Every captain and subaltern must appear at musters by eleven o'clock in the forenoon, equipped with a good musket or rifle, and have always ready a half pound of powder and one pound of lead to be produced when called upon.

Any private too poor to procure arms and ammunition, is to apply to the Court Martial and procure a certificate of his inability. Every commanding officer of a company, shall within ten days after his Regimental muster, make return of the strength and state of his company to the Commanding officer of his regiment, from whom he may receive a form and every such muster make return on oath of all delinquencies which have accrued since the last court of enquiry. In the appointment of non-commissioned officers, drummers, and fifers the approbation of the commanding officer of the Regiment must be had. Every commanding officer of a company is required at all musters under pain of arrest, to cause his men to be trained and exercised agreeable to Baron Steuben's plan of military discipline; and he is authorized to order the most expert under his command to perform this duty. Any officer who shall be guilty of disobedience or other misbehavior when on duty, or shall be any time guilty of any conduct unbecoming the character of an officer, shall be arrested by his superior in rank and tried. If any non-commissioned officer or private shall behave himself disobediently or mutinously when on duty or before any Court or Board, the commanding officer, Court or Board may either confine him for the day or cause him to be bound neck and heels for any time not exceeding five minutes. If any bystander shall interrupt, molest or insult any officer, or soldier while on duty at any muster; or shall be guilty of the like conduct before any Court or Board, such officer, Court or Board may cause him to be confined for the day. Applications for drums and fifes are to be made to the commanding officer of the County by commanding officers of companies. When property delivered to an officer on duty is lost or damaged by neglect or misconduct, the officer is liable therefor by a suit for damages. Whenever militia are called into actual service, they shall be governed by the Articles of War, which were last in force in the Continental Army, during the late War, and court martials shall be held as therein directed. When the militia are in service, the pay and rations of a Captain is forty dollars per month and three rations per day; an Ensign twenty dollars per month and two rations per day; a Lieutenant 27 dollars and two-thirds per month and two rations per day; a Sergeant eight dollars per month and one ration per day; a Corporal $7.00 per month and one ration per day; a Private $5.00 per month and one ration per day. A ration shall consist of a pound of fresh beef or pork, one pound of wheat bread or flour, one pound and a quarter of cornmeal, a gill of spiritous liquor when to be had, a quart of salt, a quart of vinegar, two pounds of soap and one pound of candles to every 100 rations. Every company shall be formed into ten classes by lot, and an exact list kept in order that there may be a regular rotation of duty. Any Captain, Lieutenant or Ensign, when called into service, neglecting or refusing to comply shall forfeit his commission and be fined, at the discretion of a court martial, not exceeding 20 pounds. Any field officer or commanding officer of a company failing to perform any duty by law prescribed for which no penalty is imposed, may be fined by a court martial or Court of Enquiry, not exceeding to a field officer 13 pounds, and to a commanding officer of a company 15 pounds. Penalties incurred by a Captain for failing to take an oath to any court, enroll his company, to appoint private musters, to give notice of musters, to attend any muster armed as the law directs, to call his roll, to examine his company and report delinquencies, to make any return by law directed, he shall forfeit for every such offense and neglect, six pounds. For failure to call forth such officers and men, as the commanding officer from time to time, shall order from his company, upon any call from the Governor, invasion of, or insurrection in the county or requisition from an adjoining county, shall forfeit and pay twelve pounds. By a subaltern officer for failure to take any oath, to attend any court, or muster, armed as directed for each offense three pounds, and moreover, the said officers shall be liable to be arrested and treated as military offenders by non-commissioned officer, or soldier, for failing to attend any muster with the arms and ammunition herein directed, shall forfeit 15 shillings. Quakers and Menonites are exempted from military duty.

This was substantially the gist of the Virginia law that governed the Kentucky District Militia until the advent of Kentucky's statehood in 1792.

Among the noteworthy special militia legislation of Virginia affecting the Kentucky District was the Act of 1775 which provided for the raising of Revolutionary troops. This act designated Fincastle as one of the counties in which rifle companies were to be formed. Fincastle was required to furnish 1 rifle company to consist of a captain, 3 lieutenants, an ensign, 4 sergeants, 2 drummers, 2 fifers, and 100 men to be stationed at posts that the Committee of Fincastle County might order. Companies from Fincastle were excused by statute from attending the general rendezvous. In the organization of the Minute Men out of the militia Fincastle belonged to that district that contained Pittsylvania, Bedford, and Botetourt counties. Every militiaman enlisted into this branch of the service was required to provide himself with a rifle, if obtainable, otherwise a tomahawk, flintlock, bayonet, pouch and three charges of powder and ball. By general statute he was compelled to keep on hand one pound of powder and four pounds of ball to be produced to his commander whenever called for. This provision had for its precedent the Statute of 1658 which made it incumbent upon officers of the militia to assure themselves "that every male citizen able to bear arms has a gun, two pounds of powder and eight pounds of shot, to be provided by every man for his family before March 31, 1659, under penalty of a fine of 50 pounds of tobacco." [3]

Another Act of 1775 directed the Fincastle Militia Committee to contact lead mine proprietors in the county for the purpose of purchasing the output of their mines, and provided that if any proprietor or operator of such mine should refuse to deliver his product, then the committee might undertake the operation of the mine to the exclusion of its owner for the duration of the war.

This act also made the entire Virginia militia subject to the orders of the Committee of Safety. All free males, sixteen to fifty years of age, were now subject to military duty except public officials and their necessary clerks, clergymen, students and their instructors of William and Mary College, overseers of plantations, millers, and iron workers. Punishment for disobedience of a soldier was fixed, at either forty shillings or to be "tied neck and heels" for any time not exceeding five minutes.[4]

In May, 1776, the Virginia Assembly empowered the commanding officer of any county to call the militia of his county into service. Then on June 12, 1776, the Virginia Bill of Rights was adopted. Section 13 provided "That a well regulated militia, composed of the body of the people trained to arms, is the proper, natural and safe defense of a free State; that standing armies in time of peace should be avoided as dangerous to liberty; and that in all cases the military should be under strict subordination to, and governed by, the Civil power."

Kentucky County was established in 1776. An Act of 1777 prescribed a draft of the militia for service in the Revolutionary Army, and directed that "free mulattoes in any companies [were] to be employed as drummers, fifers, or pioneers." Kentucky was exempted from this draft. However, further provision was made that in case of imminent danger of invasion of any county the entire militia strength could be called out and compelled to serve until relief could be given from other points. At the same time county lieutenants of the western area of Virginia were empowered to appoint scouts up to the number of ten to guard against Indian depredations.

In May, 1780, Kentucky County was trisected to form Fayette, Jefferson, and Lincoln counties. The act continued in office militia officers holding commissions at the time of trisection, and these were designated to exercise their duties in the new county embracing their residence.

In October, 1780, the assembly provided that additional troops for the Continental Army should be raised. This act levied twenty-four men from Jefferson County, eighteen from Fayette County, and forty from Lincoln County. The act met with opposition throughout the Kentucky District, the Kentuckians being opposed to rendering military services beyond their county lines.

The Virginia Legislature of May, 1781, enacted that anyone guilty of opposing the calling out of the militia in defense of the state should be considered "civilly dead," his property to descend immediately to his heirs and he "to suffer the penalties and forfeitures of praemunire."

Prior to 1781, rank played an important part in official military life, but by an act of that year the county courts were given a free hand in appointment of militia officers to the absolute disregard of seniority. Appointments were made by the county court and the commissions of such appointees issued from the state war office at Williamsburg. In November, 1781, the Virginia Assembly decreed that the pay of officers and men of the Virginia Militia should conform to the rates of pay of the Continental Army.[5]

In 1782 the Virginia Assembly provided for the organization of "Horse" units, taking every sixteenth man of the militia for the "Horse." The men entering this branch of the service voluntarily were compelled to provide their own horses, these to be not less than fourteen hands high, with saddle and bridle. The state supplied a sword, cap, pistol, and a pair of holsters.[6]

An Act of May, 1784, provided for the appointment of two Naval officers for the Kentucky District. These were stationed at the Falls of the Ohio (Louisville) and at the mouth of Limestone (Maysville) to serve as collectors of port.

During the fall session of the assembly in 1784 a revision of the militia law was undertaken. The main provisions embodied in the new code were:

(1) That the counties west of the Blue Ridge, and those below and adjoining thereto, should not be obliged to be armed with muskets, but might substitute good rifles with proper accoutrements.

(2) Field officers were made appointive with the appointment power vested in the Governor. Captains and subalterns were recommended for commission by joint action of the County Militia Committee and the senior magistrate of the county. Rank was determined by lot, the commissions all bearing the same date.

(3) Steuben's *Manual of Discipline and Formation* as used by the United States was adopted.

(4) Additional public arms were to be purchased "to the extent of money available," such arms to be purchased at home, or, if imported from Europe, such importation to be from France.[7]

The revision of 1784 further provided "that all free male persons between the ages of eighteen and forty-five years, * * * shall be enrolled or formed into companies * * *."[8] There is no record of free Negroes in Kentucky having been included in the roster of any militia company.

An act of 1787 provided for a "troop of horse" for each company. The act empowered the Governor to issue commissions for more than one troop of horse in any of the "counties on the Western Waters," where the same might be found necessary.⁹ Likewise, it authorized the Governor to order into active service as many scouts and rangers on the western frontier as might be deemed necessary, these to be paid out of the public treasury of Virginia.

Militiamen in the counties on the western waters were required by an act of December 15, 1788, to keep always ready a good musket or rifle, half a pound of good powder, and a pound of lead, to be produced to their commanding officer whenever called for, under penalty of a fine not to exceed ten shillings. The act provided that paupers were to be supplied with such arms and ammunition at public expense. This same statute substituted regimental musters for general musters.

Although these laws appeared on the statute books of Virginia, the militiaman of the Kentucky District was spurred on to duty more often by the law of self-preservation. During this early period the ever-present peril of Indian raids did more to force the settler to comply with the law defining his militia duty than any fines that might have been imposed for neglect of duty. Long before Kentucky became a state its people learned the lesson that was later embodied in the state motto: "United we stand; divided we fall."

NOTES, REFERENCES, AND SOURCES

1. See Ranck, *Boonesborough;* Lester, *The Transylvania Colony;* and "Draper MSS" 1CC21, 102.
2. See *Kentucky Gazette* of January, 1790.
3. Hening, *Statutes at Large of Virginia*, Vol. I, Act 25.
4. Though this act of 1766 was not reenacted when revisions were made, yet it was frequently invoked as a mode of punishment in aggravated cases.
5. See Hening, *Statutes at Large of Virginia*, Vol. X, p. 428.
6. *Ibid.*, Vol. XI, p. 175.
7. *Ibid.*, Vol. XI, p. 470.
8. See Section II, Act of 1784.
9. See Hening, *Statutes at Large of Virginia*, Vol. XII, p. 132.

CHAPTER II

PIONEER PERIOD

The pioneer Kentuckian saw the "Militia" of Kentucky, or rather backwoods Virginia, only as a locally organized institution, existing not so much by mandate of law as by necessity for preservation of the community. With this concept he faithfully performed his duty. From 1775 to 1792, under Virginia law, all able-bodied men were connected with some military command. The men of the settlement were one and all required to garrison the forts, cultivate the fields, build the houses, and supply the larder with meat by hunting. Although legal compulsion to the performance of military duty was seldom enforced, every man able to do so was expected to perform his full share of military service. If he failed in this, he was not only hated as a coward, but was no longer welcome in the community. Several instances are recorded of persons being "drummed out" of a fort or station for failure to respond to a militia call.

Almost every Kentucky settler during the first few decades was or had been a member of the militia of one of the Colonies, most of them in Virginia, Pennsylvania, and the Carolinas. With the exception of the Tories, almost everyone sufficiently mature had served in the Revolutionary Army. The Tories who fled to the Kentucky settlements were subjected to the same troubles that annoyed them in the East. To this was added the hostility of the Indian. The only thing left for the Tory in the West to do was to return to his old home or fight with the Kentucky settlers to maintain himself against Indian attack. To go back home was almost impossible, and very few undertook the trip. Those Tories who succumbed to the overwhelming patriotic sentiment of the backwoodsmen, and took their places at the portholes and in the forays against the enemy marauders, melted indistinguishably into the patriotic masses and rightly became known as patriots. Some Tories, like Col. John Holder, became prominent officers in the militia and successful partisan leaders as loyal and brave as the best.

The ill-kept muster rolls of the Kentucky Militia during the Revolutionary period were not preserved, although every station and fort was organized on a military basis. These men of the western frontier militia were as much a part of the Revolutionary Army as those who fought at Bunker Hill or Ticonderoga. In fact these Kentuckians faced far greater hazards than the "files of redcoats." The British soldier got his pay whether his aim was true or not, but the British-allied Indian was paid only when he brought in the Kentuckian's scalp, and few Kentuckians survived scalping. Boys from twelve years on, old men in their seventies and eighties, even women, most of whom learned to handle the rifle, all had duties assigned—perhaps a porthole to man—in case of an attack. After an Indian visitation the men of the vicinity who were liable for military duty would report to their officers for service. Pursuit would be made if there appeared to be any possibility of overtaking the Indians. The proof that an able-bodied man lived in a fort or station in Kentucky during any of the years between 1776 and 1782 is proof that he was a Revolutionary soldier.

In this early period no distinctive uniforms appeared; in fact adequate clothing of any sort was often lacking. Militia calls to repulse Indian raids usually required immediate response. Time was a material factor in repulsing such raids and did not permit preparation for departure other than the donning of the hunting shirt. The famous Kentucky hunting shirt was fashioned of linsey-woolsey, coarse linen, or dressed deerskin. The bosom was sewed as a wallet to hold a piece of bread (dodger), jerk, cloth for wiping the barrel of the rifle, and anything else the hunter or militiaman required. The belt, always tied behind, answered several purposes aside from holding the garment together. In cold weather the home-made mittens, and sometimes the shot pouch, occupied the front; to the right was suspended the tomahawk, and to the left the scalping knife in a leather sheath. Caps were made of coonskin. A pair of breeches, often made of leather, and leather leggings dressed the legs, and a pair of moccasins answered as covering for the feet.

In May, 1774, Capt. James Harrod, Abraham Hite, James and Jacob Sandusky, and thirty-seven other men, came down the Ohio River and up the Kentucky River into the area that is now Mercer County. This company was the first that came to Kentucky for the express purpose of settlement. Shortly after their arrival they laid out Harrodstown, later called Oldtown, and now Harrodsburg. Here they erected several cabins and a stockade. Indian hostilities forced the abandonment of this settlement in a few months and most of the men returned East. The following year, in May, 1775, Simon Kenton and Thomas Williams came down the Ohio River to the mouth of Limestone Creek where they cleared a patch of ground and raised a crop of corn on the site where Kenton's Station was built later. That same spring Daniel Boone served as pilot to a party of thirty persons, members of the Transylvania Company, from Rutherford County, North Carolina, to Kentucky. Col. Richard Henderson and twenty-odd associates of the Transylvania Company came with the party to an appointed place in Tennessee and there negotiated a land grant treaty with Cherokee Indians.

Boone was the Transylvania Company's agent to mark a road through the wilderness to Kentucky and there to erect a fort. In April the company arrived at the point later named Fort Boonesborough, in the present Madison County. Work on the fort was begun at once and it was completed by the middle of June after four fierce Indian attacks had been withstood.*[1]

On April 1, 1775, Boone wrote Col. Henderson as follows:

DEAR COLONEL:
After my compliments to you, I shall acquaint you of our misfortune. On the 25th of March, a party of Indians fired on my

---
* Notes, references, and sources are indicated by numerals. These refer to corresponding numbers at the end of this chapter. For notes on Chapter II see page 62.

company, about half an hour before day, and killed Mr. Twitty and his negro, and wounded Mr. Walker very deeply, but I hope he will recover. On the 28th, as we were hunting for provisions, we found Samuel Tate's son, who gave us an account that the Indians fired on their company. On the 27th my brother and I went down and found two men killed and scalped, Thomas McDowell and Jeremiah McFeeters. I have sent a man down to all the lower companies in order to gather them all at the mouth of Otter Creek. My advice to you sir, is to come or send for us as soon as possible. Your company is desired greatly, for the people are very uneasy, but are willing to stay and venture their lives with you, and now is the time to frustrate them in their intentions, and keep the country while we are in it, if we give way to them now, it will ever be the case.

This day we start from the battle ground, for the mouth of Otter Creek, where we shall immediately build a fort, which will be done before you can come or send to us. Then we can send ten men to meet you, if you send for them. DANIEL BOONE

Other settlements were made at Boiling Spring and at St. Asaph's in the present Mercer and Lincoln counties. During the same spring, and after completing his treaty with the Indians, Colonel Henderson and his party continued to Fort Boonesborough. Their arrival brought the military strength of the fort up to about sixty men.

Although the Big Sandy Valley was much overrun at this time by small bands of vicious Indians, it was occasionally used of necessity by the leaders of the border militia. On June 12, 1775, Capt. William Russell, stationed at Point Pleasant at the mouth of the Kanawha, dispatched a letter to Col. William Fleming, in which, among other things, he said: "I am this morning preparing to start off our cattle up Sandy, and expect that the command will leave this Wednesday or Thursday at farthest and shall decamp myself with a convoy to the other stores next Monday, and expect to overtake the stock at the Big Painted Lick [near Paintsville] about 60 miles up Sandy."

In the fall of 1775 Col. Robert Patterson and six other young men, together with John McClelland and his family, came to the Royal Spring (now Georgetown) where they made a settlement that became known as McClelland's Fort or Station. Maj. (later General) George Rogers Clark made a prolonged stop at McClelland's upon his first visit to Kentucky. He was there when the fort was attacked on December 29, 1776, by Mingo Indians under Pluggy. On this occasion the entire group from McClelland's took refuge at Harrod's Fort, but only after its militia had been crippled by the killing of John McClelland and Charles White, and the serious wounding of Gen. Robert Todd and Capt. Edward Worthington.

On July 7, 1776, the militia strength of Fort Boonesborough was called upon to pursue the Indians, five in number, who had captured and carried off Betsy and Frances Callaway, daughters of Col. Richard Callaway, and Jemima Boone, a daughter of Daniel Boone. The girls were taken within sight of the fort and were recovered only after a pursuit of about thirty miles. Capt. Billy Bush was in command of the Fort Boonesborough company in this pursuit.[2]

Major Clark was an officer of the Virginia line when he visited the settlements in 1775. Clark's one thought after his visit was to establish in Kentucky an extensive system of public defense. Upon his return to Kentucky, in 1776, he recommended to the settlers the holding of a regular representative assembly from all settlements at Harrodsburg. He urged the right of the region to be taken under the military protection of the mother-state, and, in the event of leaving their petition for protection unheeded, Clark advised the Kentuckians to "employ the lands of the country as a fund to obtain settlers and establish an independent State."

In the early summer of 1776, at a general meeting of the militia, Maj. George Rogers Clark and Gabriel Jones were sent to represent this new community in the General Assembly of Virginia, there to manage affairs for the general good of the western settlements of Fincastle County. Major Clark gives an account of this trip to Williamsburg in which he says that:

> On the third day, Mr. Jones' horse gave out. With very few belongings on my own horse, and in so hilly a country, it was impossible for two to ride at a time. The weather was very rainy.

Our feet wet continuously for three or four days and nights, and not daring to make a fire to dry them, we got what hunters call "scald feet" a most shocking complaint. In this condition, we travelled on, in greater torment than I have ever before or since experienced, hoping to get relief at the station in Powell's Valley.

After presenting a petition to the Virginia Assembly and refusing a personal loan of 500 pounds of powder, Clark accomplished what he regarded as the crowning work of the mission, namely, the securing of 500 pounds of gunpowder for defense of the settlements. The powder was brought down the Ohio River from Fort Pitt (Pittsburgh) to Limestone (Maysville) where it was secreted, Clark and Jones making their way from Limestone on foot to Harrodsburg. Shortly after their arrival Col. John Todd, with his company under the guidance of Jones, went to Limestone to bring the powder to Harrodsburg. On their return they were attacked by Indians at the Blue Licks and Jones was killed, but the powder was brought through safely to Harrodsburg.

In the winter of 1776 Fincastle County's trisection and the establishment of Kentucky County entitled the Kentucky District to separate county officials, including militia officers. During that year a battalion was raised in Fayette County composed of men living on the north side of the Kentucky River. The officers elected by the body were duly commissioned by the state of Virginia.

The establishment and organization of a local militia was most timely, for early in the spring of 1777 the Kentucky District was subjected to several atrocious Indian raids. Furious assaults were made on Logan's Fort, Harrodsburg, and Fort Boonesborough. These assaults were repulsed, and during the summer reinforcements to the extent of forty-five men arrived from North Carolina. In September 100 more men under Col. John Bowman came from Virginia.

Logan's Station, or St. Asaph's, was attacked on May 30 (Boone said July 19), 1777, when it was garrisoned by only fifteen men. The attack was made at milking time in the morning. One of the men was wounded and could not ac-

GOVERNOR PATRICK HENRY

COLONEL BENJAMIN LOGAN
Courtesy, The Filson Club

company the others when they rushed into the fort. At length Colonel Logan saw the wounded, helpless man at a considerable distance from the fort. He opened the gate, rushed out, and under a shower of lead from the Indians succeeded in carrying the man into the fort without harm to himself. Shortly afterward the supply of powder and lead became so low that Colonel Logan determined to go to the Holston to replenish it. He made the trip safely, with two men from the fort, by avoiding the Wilderness Road, then much infested by plundering Indian bands.

Although the Kentucky County records appear to have been lost, a few documents have been preserved that concern the early organization and growth of the Kentucky County Militia. Among these is the record of a commission signed by Patrick Henry, Jr., Governor of Virginia, at Williamsburg, on December 21, 1776. This commission names John Bowman as colonel of the Militia of Kentucky County.

Early in March, 1777, just after Daniel Boone had been regularly appointed to the command of Fort Boonesborough, and before the feeble Kentucky County Militia had been organized a week, a number of Shawnee were lurking unseen about Fort Boonesborough. In a few days Blackfish, with more than forty warriors, besieged Harrodsburg, and during March repeated attacks were made on that fort. Meanwhile, the garrison had been considerably strengthened by arrivals from McClelland's, including Maj. George Rogers Clark, though he did not remain long after the attack. Later in the spring, while some men were working in a turnip-patch near the fort, signs of Indians were seen. Major Clark, with a little detachment, stole out back of the fort and killed an Indian that had been prowling around, and then following the bed of the creek for only a few hundred yards, Clark and his men found a camp that showed evidence of having accommodated probably several hundred Indians.

Before December, 1777, ended, the stock of salt at Harrod's Fort was exhausted and at the other stations the salt supply was depleted. The slim unsalted rations caused sickness. Salt-making within the District of Kentucky was a tedious task on account of the shortage of vessels suitable for evaporating the water. To bring salt in from the eastern settlements was practically impossible. In response to the petitions of the Kentucky settlers and the pleas of Colonel Bowman, Virginia sent several large iron kettles to Kentucky late in 1777. Salt-bearing water was found at various licks, but these points were frequented by Indian hunting parties, because to these licks the buffalo and deer came in large numbers. Thus salt-making could be engaged in at the licks only under a militia guard sufficiently strong to repulse a possible Indian attack. In 1778 Daniel Boone commanded a company of Kentucky County Militia engaged in making salt at the Blue Licks. A militia company from Greenbrier, Virginia, had been detailed to the relief of the Kentuckians, and these men took turns with Boone's men in making salt. The Virginia troops were under command of a Captain Watkins.

Another incident that serves to indicate the diversity of militia duty happened in the winter of 1778. Colonel Bowman had raised a crop of corn on a clearing about midway between Harrodsburg and Danville. With a militia escort Bowman went out to get some corn at the cribs. While there the party was attacked by Indians. This skirmish, known as the Battle of the Corncribs, resulted in the killing of three of Bowman's men. The remainder escaped by taking shelter in the cane.[3]

During the early years powder and salt were two of the most important and usually the most scarce commodities in the western country. Powder was necessary for protection against the Indians, and to kill deer, buffalo, and bear, for food. Maj. Herman Bowmar in a diary mentioned a canoe trip made to New Orleans in 1777 to obtain a supply of powder. This source of supply was sought out only after it was found impossible to bring it through from the eastern settlements.

The year 1778 was rendered memorable in Kentucky because of two great military events in which she was deeply interested. The one was the invasion of the Kentucky District by an army of Indians and Canadians, under the command of Capt. Daigniau DuQuendre, a Canadian officer; the other was the brilliant expedition of Col. George Rogers Clark against the British posts of Vincennes and Kaskaskia.

In February, 1778, Daniel Boone and a company of thirty soldiers were at the lower Blue Licks making salt. A surprise attack was made on the party by about 200 Indians who had commenced their march to attack Fort Boonesborough.[4] Boone and his party surrendered and as prisoners were taken to Detroit. At Detroit all except Boone were delivered over to the British commandant.* Boone was held by the Indians and taken to Old Chillicothe, where he enjoyed a considerable amount of freedom. This victory caused the Indians to postpone their attack on Fort Boonesborough. Some time later, and while still a prisoner at Old Chillicothe, Boone saw about 350 Indians assembled for an expedition against Fort Boonesborough. As soon as an opportunity presented itself, Boone escaped, made his way back to Kentucky and carried an alarm of the impending attack to Fort Boonesborough. At once preparations were made at the fort for the attack, but it was further delayed for nearly a month; evidently on account of the escape of Boone. When the Indians did not appear within a few days as Boone had forecast, it was concluded that he was merely using this story to excuse himself for the capture at the Blue Licks. Sentiment against him became so strong that a court-martial, probably Kentucky's first, was instituted to and did try him. Boone was not only acquitted of the charge against him, but was given the rank of major. Growing impatient because of the delay, Boone, commanding thirty men, set out on an expedition to the Indian towns on Paint Creek. After arriving in the enemy's territory he learned that the Indian forces from Old Chillicothe had passed him on their way to Fort Boonesborough. He beat a hasty retreat and had little more than arrived at the fort when Captain DuQuendre, with between 300 and 400 Canadians and Indians flying the British and French colors, appeared and demanded surrender of the fort. Help could not be obtained from Logan's Fort or at Harrodsburg since these settlements were being besieged by detachments from DuQuendre's force. Though the Fort Boonesborough garrison consisted of only fifty men, it succeeded in withstanding the nine-days attack, after which DuQuendre withdrew having lost thirty men killed and a far greater number wounded. Fort Boonesborough's loss was two killed and four wounded. Immediately before the attack on Fort Boonesborough, Boone had engaged the Indians under pretense of treaty-making while hoping for the arrival of help.[5]

In March, 1778, John Martin took a company from Fort Boonesborough and in bark canoes went up the Kentucky River to hunt buffaloes for food for the station. After that was eaten, or spoiled from want of salt, "Lieutenant Hutchings shot down a large steer of Colonel Callaway's one morning for the use of the soldiers (We were all soldiers, listed [sic] men for three months)." "Col. John Donaldson had come out as an officer but gave up to Col. Dillard." Orders came the first of June to march to the Falls of the Ohio to join some troops from Pittsburgh under Col. George Rogers Clark. "Part of our company mutinied and went in with Col. Donaldson and Mrs. Boone."[6] Daniel Boone had been held captive by the Indians so long that it was generally believed that he had been killed. For this reason his wife, returned to North Carolina.

On October 15, 1778, Capt. James Harrod with sixteen men went to Missouri for a supply of salt. They proceeded from Harrodsburg to the Falls of the Ohio where they obtained a keelboat, went down the Ohio River and up the Mississippi to the salt works on the Spanish side.[7] Here a quantity of salt was purchased and the hazardous return trip begun and completed in December. Those who made the trip with Captain Harrod were Alex Douglass, William Williams, James Pruett, Samuel Douglass, John Phillips, Roswell

Stevens, James Millican, Edward Hammond, Wilson Mattox, John Shelp, Joseph Collins, William Menifee, John Isaacs, Samuel Dennis, and one other man whose name was not recorded.[8]

During 1778 an expedition into the Illinois country was projected by Col. George Rogers Clark as a Revolutionary War move. Upon visiting the western frontier, in 1776, Clark had seen that the British garrisoned posts at Kaskaskia and St. Vincents were the base of Indian raids into Kentucky. Clark had succeeded in obtaining a few troops and some munitions from Virginia to prosecute his campaign against these strongholds. His meager forces were augmented by Kentucky Volunteers, mostly scouts and guides whom Clark enlisted while he sojourned at the Falls of the Ohio, where he established his base. Surprise attacks, first on Kaskaskia and then on St. Vincents, brought victory for Clark and his small force. The prisoners that were taken at both places were sent to Virginia. At the Falls of the Ohio, Clark, in 1782, built Fort Nelson and there established his headquarters.

Among the original papers and vouchers of Col. John Bowman, the first military commander of Kentucky County, are the following documents and lists. Prominent among these is the commission of John Bowman as "Colonel of the Militia in the County of Kentucky," with the signature of Patrick Henry, Jr., "Governor of the Commonwealth of Virginia." The commission was addressed to "John Bowman, Esquire." After reciting his appointment it thus concludes:

> You are therefore, carefully and diligently to discharge the duty of Colonel of the Militia, by doing and performing all Manner of Things thereunto belonging; and you are to pay a ready Obedience to all Orders and Instructions which from Time to Time you may receive from the Convention, Privy Council, or any of your Superior Officers, agreeable to the Rules & Regulations of the Convention, or General Assembly and to require all Officers and Soldiers under your command to be obedient and to aid you in the Execution of this Commission according to the Intent & Purpose thereof. Given under my Hand & Seal,
> Williamsburg this 21st day of December 1776.
>
> P. HENRY, JR.

In 1778, Col. John Bowman was again commissioned county lieutenant of Kentucky County by Thomas Jefferson, then Governor of Virginia. Old records show that for this service Bowman drew a cash salary of £22 and 10s. per month with a subsistence allowance of $50 per month in Virginia script. The following letter from Thomas Jefferson to Colonel Bowman further relates the part taken by Kentucky in the Revolutionary War:

WILLIAMSBURG, *November 6, 1779*

I am to ask the favor of you to give notice to the officer recommended by you for the Western Battalions that as soon as one half of his quota of men is raised and delivered by you, he shall be entitled to his commission. These men are to make part of a battalion which will be commanded by Lieutenant Colonel Knox, and which is to be stationed in Powell's Valley. As this station is so very far from you, your officer is to march his men to the Falls of the Ohio, and there do duty under Major Slaughter this winter; but he is not actually to march till he shall have heard of Major Slaughter's arrival at the Falls; in the meantime, let him employ them in the best manner he can for the public service. Money for their subsistence from the time you deliver them to the officer till he shall have carried them to their rendezvous will be lodged with Major Slaughter. The subsistence account previous to their delivery to the officer, you will settle with the Auditor here.

I am sir, Yr. very h'bl serv't

To the County Lieutenant of Kentucky. TH. JEFFERSON

Records show that Squire Boone, brother of Daniel, was the man recommended by Colonel Bowman to act as officer of the "Western Battalions." In a letter from "Painted Stone" (near Shelbyville), dated June 28, 1780, Boone informs Colonel Bowman that he has proceeded with the enlistment to the extent of twenty-three men, whose names he gives.

In the latter part of May, 1779, 264 volunteers, under the command of Col. John Bowman, left Lexington Blockhouse on an expedition against Shawnee at Old Chillicothe. Benjamin Logan and John Holder were captains under him.[9] Upon encountering the Indians an engagement ensued, and, being greatly outnumbered, Logan's force was compelled to beat a hasty retreat to the main column and the route became general. However, the retreat was covered by the daring bravery of the subordinate officers who courageously charged the enemy during the retreat, thereby forestalling heavy slaughter. Maj. Herman Bowmar stated "that he had an uncle, Elisha Collins, that was in Bowman's Expedition in 1779," and that Elisha Collins repeatedly attributed Bowman's forced retreat to his "lack of foresight, and his inability to maintain discipline and failure to restrain and govern the men," adding that "Bowman had an irascible temper, the only thing unpopular in him.[10] Major Bowmar also stated that "General Logan was a Captain in Bowman's Campaign. He was a brave man and a good officer, but somewhat arbitrary and overbearing."

A letter to Colonel Bowman, written from Fort Boonesborough in the spring of 1780 by Capt. E. Worthington B. Roberts, James Patton, and Ensign Edward Bulger, is as follows:

> Lieut. Abraham Chaplain and * * * Hendricks saith that on the 27th or 28th ultimo, they made their escape from the Indians of the Windot [Wyandot] Nation from off the waters of St. Dusky [Sandusky] and arrived at this place this day; that about 3 or 4 days preceding the said escape they had undoubted intelligence that a large number of different tribes of Indians, in conjunction with the subjects of Great Britain to the amount of 2,000 in the whole, 600 of which are Green Coat Rangers from Cannaday [sic] were preparing to attack this place, with cannon, and after subduing the same their destination was for the Illinois. Capt. Matthew Elliott gave intelligence the Indians were gathering horses to aid the expedition, which is expected to reach this place in 4 weeks * * *. The above information we have just now received and beg you to use the greatest expedition to embody the militia under your command and march them here to repel the Hostile Indians. This is the Humble prayers of the inhabitants of this garrison and of every other son of Liberty, who also beg you would send express to Colonel Crockett to push on his troops to our assistance.

That the information contained in this letter was authentic is borne out by events. Early in March of 1780, Indians made an attack on Ruddle's Station, but were repulsed. A second sudden attack was made the same year in June. The

British commander, Captain Henry Byrd,[11] led a force of 600 British, French-Canadians, and Indians, into Kentucky by way of the Licking River for the avowed "purpose of running the settlers out." Byrd brought six fieldpieces along, the first cannon used in Kentucky. Ruddle's and Martin's stations were destroyed and their garrisons taken, but further advances by Byrd were prevented by the large number of prisoners he had on hand and the impatience of his Indian force. He, therefore, was compelled to turn back to Detroit.

John Conovery came to Kentucky in 1777, lived at Fort Boonesborough one and a half years. In 1779 he settled at Ruddle's Station, and in 1780 was captured by Byrd and carried to Detroit where he was held a prisoner until 1784, then returning to Kentucky. Conovery was probably held in captivity longer than any other prisoner taken by Byrd.

In retaliation for Byrd's invasion, Clark, with his troops from the Falls of the Ohio and a formidable force of volunteers from Kentucky, instituted an expedition against the Ohio Indians. Prompt retaliation for Byrd's invasion was deemed necessary. When Colonel Clark called on the Militia of Kentucky for volunteers to accompany his regiment against the Indian despoilers of Ruddle's and Martin's stations, they flocked to his standard without delay. Clark's call for troops reached Colonel Todd early in July, and he at once sent John Martin and Thornton Farrow with a message to Col. John Bowman, who was then living south of the Kentucky River. Bowman immediately issued a call to the militia of his district, naming the date and point of rendezvous. At Lexington a draft of the militia was made upon receipt of Clark's call, because many in Fayette, disliking Clark, refused to volunteer.[12]

There was a muster going on at that time at Harrodsburg. Between fifty and sixty men attending the muster volunteered to pursue the Indians who had just then killed one Hinton near McGary's Station.

The mouth of the Licking River was the point of redezvous for Kentucky troops to join Clark. When assembled Clark's force, including some 200 Regulars, amounted to nearly a thousand men. From here he marched against the Pickaway towns, and having defeated the Indians in a pitched battle, he destroyed their villages and crops, returned to the Ohio, and discharged his men.

John Taylor, well known in 1780 as a hunter at Fort Boonesborough and on Hinkston Creek of Licking River, was used by military commanders to spy around Millersburg, where there was a crossing on Hinkston Creek, and on Bushy Fork of Hinkston. His scout work in this section compared favorably in effectiveness with that of Simon Kenton at Limestone.

Jacob Stucker, whose deposition was taken at William Theobald's Tavern, Georgetown, 1806, says: "I came to Kentucky in 1779, settling at Bryan's Station. In 1780 I was set to spying along with hunting. My spying territory was the Forks of the Licking down to its mouth and Big Bone Lick. In 1782 I also spyed at Flat Lick and Lower Blue Licks to the Ohio River near Limestone." He said that Barnett Rogers, Thomas Herndon, John Von, and James Twyman spied with him.

The trisection of Kentucky County took place in the fall of 1780, and this division of the territory resulted in a more effective organization of the militia. Kentucky County became obsolete, and in its place Fayette, Jefferson, and Lincoln were erected as new counties in the same territory. Militia officers commissioned in the new counties were, for Fayette, John Todd, colonel, and Daniel Boone, lieutenant colonel; for Lincoln, Benjamin Logan, colonel, and Stephen Trigg, lieutenant colonel; for Jefferson, John Floyd, colonel, and William Pope, lieutenant colonel.

Throughout 1781 Indian raids kept every section of Kentucky in continual alarm. These raids were made by small parties and with great frequency and damage. Indian ravages in Kentucky were worse during the closing years of the Revolutionary War than at any other period. This condition was brought about first, through the hope of the British that, by inciting the Indians to depredations on the frontier, they would be able to weaken the aggressive forces of the Americans in the East. Indian raids for awhile during this year threatened to wipe out the western settlements. In recognition of the dire consequences which were sure to follow the breaking up of her western settlements, Virginia sent troops to the relief of the Kentucky District. The minutes of the court of Montgomery County, Virginia, for April 3, 1782, contain the following entries: "John Cloyd produced to the Court satisfactory proof that he ought to be paid the sum of 24 shillings for a blanket impressed by the Green Bryes [Brier] militia on their way to Caintucky in 1781."

"Peter Wiley produced satisfactory proof that he ought to be paid 35 shillings for a blanket impressed by the Green Bryes militia on their way to Caintucky in 1781."[13]

Indian war bands frequented the two routes of travel of the immigrants coming to Kentucky, the Wilderness Road and the Ohio River. There was almost continuous plundering and murdering by the Indians along these two passageways. At times the onslaught on the Wilderness Road became so severe that travel was made nearly impossible when the traveling party was not under escort by the militia. The militia so detailed not only acted as an escort but a part of the militia escort was detailed as scouts to keep a constant lookout for Indian signs. These scouts ordinarily traveled from several hours to a day in advance of the immigrants under militia escort. If Indian signs were discovered, the scouts reported the fact to the commander of the escort. The escort then engaged in scattering the Indians so that they might not make a concerted attack on the immigrant train.

The party of Lewis Craig, composed of his congregation, came out over the Wilderness Road to Kentucky in a body in 1786. This party rested at Gilbert's Station and sent Robert and Cove Johnson for soldiers to guard them on their way to Bryan Station, requesting the guard, after one Hawkins, not of their party, had been killed on the Wilderness Road while "going in."[14] A Captain McFarlan, cousin to Major McFarlan killed in the Battle of Blue Licks, during the same spring, was bringing a company over the Wilderness Road and met with a defeat at the hands of a mixed band of Indians. All of the company's baggage was taken, three whites were killed and four were taken captive.

The Ohio River was probably the most dangerous route to the West due to the fact that very little protection could be given by the militia. Then, too, the Ohio River was nearer to the hostile Indian tribes of Ohio, who were aware that valuable plunder was brought westward on the river. Many immigrants undertook to man their own boats, and, being unfamiliar with the river, the current would often carry them too close to the northern shore without a moment's warning. Few of these got back on their course without an Indian encounter.

Indian raids rapidly increased in number and atrociousness. Conditions became so bad that the Kentucky Militia was compelled to seek assistance. Accordingly, troops were again sent from Virginia to help in repulsing the Indians. On January 22, 1781, Col. George Rogers Clark was commissioned by Gov. Thomas Jefferson as "brigadier general of the forces to be embodied in an expedition westward of the Ohio."

Clark made this trip westward through the Monongahela country raising troops as he proceeded by enlisting volunteers or drafting men where a fair quota of voluntary enlistments was not readily obtainable. Along with the foot soldiers Clark obtained a troop of some thirty mounted riflemen.[15]

On March 1, 1781, Indians appeared at Francis McConnell's Station and wounded a man James Wiley. Alex McConnell and Josiah Collins were sent express from Lexington to Cross Plains to Col. Boone and returned that night. In their absence the Indians killed John Wymore at the Lexington blockhouse. There was never another white man killed there at the Lexington fort, for Lexington grew very rapidly, as is shown by the fact that in 1779 only twelve men garrisoned that fort.

Soon after Wymore was killed, John Brookey of McConnell's Station was fired on by Indians and wounded. The firing was audible at Lexington, and from that point a company went to McConnell's but arrived after the Indians had left.[16] A few days later a call for help came to Lexington from McClelland's Station where Indians had stolen some horses and had either carried away or killed a Negro. Though a company responded promptly from Lexington, the Indians got away, having ransacked all the cabins and carried off practically everything of value.[17]

In 1781 Colonels Todd and Patterson were going down to Louisville and camped not far from Brown's Station, on Bullskin. They did not venture very near, knowing its neighborhood to be subject to Indian attack. They spent the night, and held their horses in a sinkhole. While there, they repeatedly heard the swivel of the fort. These officers carried an alarm to Louisville and some 300 men were sent to relief of the station.[18]

McAfee Station was attacked on May 4, 1781, two years after the stockaded settlement had been built. This station when attacked had a garrison of thirteen men, but was at an isolated point about seven miles from Harrod's Fort, and its stockade was little better than a barricade. Before the attack, the dogs and stock gave warning, by their uneasiness, of the presence of Indians close by, but this warning, was unheeded. On the morning of the attack the men proceeding to their work in a field were fired on, but succeeded in making their way back to the stockade. A desultory firing lasted then until the Indians retreated, having heard the beat of horse hoofs. Capt. Hugh McGary and his company of forty-five mounted riflemen had responded from Harrod's Fort as soon as the reports of firing were heard there. McGary's men took up pursuit and a running fight resulted.

Two Indians were killed and McGary had one man killed and another wounded.[19]

In the summer of 1781 Capt. James Welch and Frank Campbell, one of Welch's company, engaged in scout duty in the vicinity of Boone's Station. After several days, and when the scout tour had about been completed, Welch became ill and requested Campbell to take his place. As they came to a turn in the lane that led to the fort, Campbell saw some Indians, and thereupon ordered his company to attack them. While alighting from his horse Campbell was shot and scalped by two Indians who had concealed themselves in the brush nearby. The alarm brought the entire strength of the fort, but the Indians successfully avoided an encounter. Josiah Collins related that during 1781 he went from Lexington as one of a guard for John Craig, Faulkner, John Long, and others, and their families, in moving from what was called the Burnt Station to Bryan Station, for they were afraid to remain at Burnt Station on account of their isolation and lack of strength. Burnt Station was known as John Craig's Station until it was burned by the Indians.[20]

A large number of those who served in the Militia of Kentucky between the years 1778 and 1781, are recorded in the pioneer militia company rolls. Some of the names on the original rolls were inaccurately spelled. The rolls were often kept by almost illiterate men. Then, too, names were spelled by their sound, and they were not always pronounced correctly. It is no stretch of imagination to classify these men as soldiers of the Revolutionary War. The expedition of the British Captain Byrd into Kentucky was unquestionably a military move of that war, and many of these men faced Byrd's forces.

The year 1782 was uncommonly prolific in great events. Indian hostility was unusually early and active, leaving no doubt that Kentucky was the dark and bloody ground. Estill's Defeat was the first major militia engagement of the year. In March a party of Wyandots made a raid into the neighborhood of Estill's Station. On the twenty-second of

March, Capt. James Estill and upwards of twenty-five men had started to rout an Indian camp on Lulbegrud, a tributary of Red River. Some men had been left behind to garrison the fort, and others because they were not physically able to go along.[21] The Indians were overtaken on Hinkston's Fork, near Little Mountain (Mount Sterling). An engagement took place, with the creek between the parties, that lasted several hours and resulted in the loss of about one-third on each side. Estill ordered Lieutenant Miller to round the flank and attack the Indians from the rear. The Indian commander at once noticed the separation of Estill's force and quickly ordered his men to cross the creek. This bold and opportune move resulted in the defeat of Estill's force. Captain Estill was among those killed in the engagement.

An equal loss had been inflicted on the enemy. This brilliant fight created a sensation at the time far beyond its real importance. It was followed by stunning blows from the same source, in rapid succession. Details of the Battle of Estill's Defeat are contained in the records of the *Kentucky Court of Appeals* in the case of William Chiles *vs.* Connolly's heirs.

The inventory and appraisal of the estate of Captain Estill is noteworthy because it lists among his property a "Negro fellow named Monk" who was then rated as the best powder-maker in the Kentucky District.

INVENTORY OF CAPTAIN JAMES ESTILL:

One Negro fellow named Monk £80; One do, Nedd £60; do, Peter, £30; 6 head cattle £18; three sheep, £2:8; 24 hogs, £3:15; Kettles and pots, £13:15; three beds, £25; pewter £4; gun, £410; 17 lbs. salt peter and brimstone mixed £3:16; Hat £1:16; Sundry books £5:3; three brids. and pair of harness £1:4; spinning wheel 10:0; three hoes 10:0; four axes and one tomhocke, £1.7; 6; three augers, and one handsaw, £1. Pack of cards, 6:0; old bells, 10:6; chisel and hammer, 6.0; sundry small tools, 15.0; frow 6:0; plow irons, £4; old gun, 15:0; bridle, £1; hatchet, 15:0; plain, 3:0; two bottles, 4:0; two old trunks 12:0; pair of britches and stockings £1:2:6; sundry house vessels, 15:0; table and chairs, £1.2; rasor, 2:6; two old chairs 5:0; 1¼ pounds of lead, 3:6; three cows, £3; horse £25; cash, £1:8:3. Total, £362:12:9.

Kentucky had more of a navy than merely the two naval officers provided by the law of Virginia. During June and July of 1782 a "gunboat" patrolled the Ohio from the mouth of the Kentucky to the mouth of the Licking River. It was manned by Kentucky militiamen and was under command of General Clark. Simultaneously militia parties patrolled the woods where crossings of the river might be made easily by Indians after the boat had passed up or downstream. Even with these guards on duty war bands slipped by. Early in August such a band committed some depredations south of the Kentucky River and inflicted a heavy loss on the small body of militia that pursued. About a fourth of the Kentucky Militia was on active duty at all times during the summer of this year.

In August, 1782, a party of about twenty Wyandots were encountered by Capt. John Holder at the Upper Blue Licks. Holder had seventeen men in his command, but the heavy losses inflicted by the Indian fire on this little band resulted in Holder's defeat. At Holder's defeat John Douglas, George Johnson, and one Clement, were killed, and Captain Fleming and Jim Harper wounded. Jim Harper died several weeks later of wounds received in the battle. That Captain Holder had much experience in matters pertaining to the command of a militia company is shown by the following letter to Col. John Bowman pertaining to military duties. Captain Holder,[22] in furnishing the list of his company to Colonel Bowman, wrote as follows:

HARRODSTOWN, *June 10, 1779*.

SIR: As I can not conveniently call on you at this time, I have sent a list of the men of my company which were on the late Expedition against the Indian towns; and beg you will favor me with the amount of the sale of the Plunder by the Barer, John Martain, to enable me to settle with them.

The supreme test of the Kentucky Militia strength, particularly of Fayette County, started three days later when Bryan Station was attacked by the forces of Caldwell and McKee. Fayette was the least populous of the three Kentucky counties in 1782. It then had only five stockaded hamlets, Lexington, McGee's, McConnell's, Boone's (new) and Bryan stations. The most secure of these was Lexington, and the most populous was Bryan. A force of about 600 composed of Indian bands from the northwestern tribes, together with about 50 whites led by Simon Girty, made a surprise attack on the station. Two men from the station succeeded in getting through the Indian lines to carry an alarm to neighboring settlements. One of them, Tom Bell, volunteered to go to Lexington. Numerous plies of leather and linsey-woolsey were wound around Bell's head to serve as a sort of helmet. They opened the fort gate, and he rode out full speed, leaning flat on his horse. By a ruse the attack was successfully repulsed until help arrived. A party of sixteen mounted men, under command of Daniel Boone, succeeded in forcing their way into the fort through the Indian lines,[23] but another party on foot failed of access to the fort, and by their attempt to get in to render some assistance they sustained a heavy loss.

The Indian siege was repelled chiefy by the garrison staying under cover and by inflicting a fatal fire on any Indian that showed himself. The delay discouraged the attackers, who evidently feared that by prolonging their siege they would subject themselves to the fire of other reinforcements which were certain to arrive. Consequently, they retreated by the trace toward the lower Blue Licks.

When the call for help arrived Col. Levi Todd enlisted the aid of all the men he could obtain from McConnell's Station and Lexington. A company of men from these stations had just previously been called and had gone to Holder's Defeat at the Blue Licks. Few men were left in either of the two forts. An express was hastened to those who had gone to the Blue Licks to return and join Todd's company between Lex-

DANIEL BOONE
From a portrait by
Chester Harding
Courtesy, The Filson Club

SIMON KENTON
Courtesy, The Filson Club

BRITISH CANNON CAPTURED IN BATTLE OF SARATOGA
Museum, Kentucky State Historical Society. (See pp. 99, 112.)

ington and Bryan Station, which was done. The reinforced company then proceeded on to Bryan Station.[24] Bryan Station was further relieved by a company under Major Netherland from Cross Plains. Captain McConnell was among those killed at Bryan Station.

Col. Levi Todd had sent a call to Col. John Todd, who was at Colonel Trigg's on the south side of the Kentucky River. Colonels Trigg and Todd, with Majors McGary and Harlow, raised a number of men and came to Bryan Station on the eighteenth of August.[25]

Among other reinforcements that arrived that day were numerous commissioned officers including those named, Captains Bulger and Gordon, and others. A council of the officers was held at which it was determined to enter into immediate pursuit, though some, among them Major McGary, are said to have advocated waiting twenty-four hours for Colonel Logan who was bringing a strong force from Lincoln County. On the eighteenth of August pursuit was begun, and before noon of the next day they reached the Licking River at the Blue Licks and there discovered the enemy, consisting of about 550 Indians and some 50 white men.[26] Hastily the officers met to decide upon the mode of attack. Boone was well acquainted with the location and offered an opinion as to the position of the Indian force and the best manner of attack, but before a definite course was determined upon the impetuous Capt. Hugh McGary rode to the front and shouted, "Let all who are not cowards follow me." McGary's challenge was electric, and to a man the force plunged in and crossed the river, McGary still at the head. The Kentuckians were suddenly met with a terrific fire, halted, and tried vainly to find cover behind trees. Nearly half of the force was mounted. Both flanks had been covered by the Indians, who appeared determined to cut off retreat. Bulger, Gordon, Harlan, McBride, Todd, and Trigg were among those killed on the battlefield. The rash McGary escaped injury, though deeper in the Indian lines than any other officer. The battle is known to have cost the Kentuckians sixty lives, and seven prisoners were carried off by the Indians. Many thought Boone's estimate of 60 killed was too low and that the number having met death on the field was nearer to 90, or approximately half of the 180 men engaged. In substantiation it is stated that of the ten officers from Bowman's Station who went out, six were killed.[27] From Harrod's Fort sixteen went and only eight returned.[28] Strode's Station sent thirty-five and suffered a corresponding loss.[29]

Some who had been in the battle got back to Bryan Station the day after the encounter. Colonel Logan reached Bryan Station the day after the battle, with 450 men. After all the survivors of the battle had returned to Bryan Station, Logan led his men to the battlefield, gathered and buried the dead, and then assured himself that the Indians had left Kentucky before returning to Bryan Station to disband his troops. In making the call for a force to bury the dead of the Blue Licks battle "orders were for every man who could carry a gun" to report for duty. From several stations, where it was reasonably safe for the women and children to remain alone, every man responded.[30]

After the Battle of Blue Licks it was reported that Col. Levi Todd hastened the departure before Lincoln County troops arrived to guard against his being superseded in command by the popular Logan, who was on the way with his Lincoln regiment. Colonel Trigg also was blamed in part for the defeat, because of his failure to attempt a formation of his command for battle.

In retaliation for Kentucky's loss at the Blue Licks, Col. George Rogers Clark, in November, 1782, led his regiment and the volunteer Kentucky Militia against the Ohio Indian villages along the Miami and Scioto rivers. A thousand mounted Kentucky riflemen rendezvoused at the mouth of the Licking River, where they met Clark and crossed the river to proceed to the Indian towns. Below the mouth of the Licking was a blockhouse where some baggage and a few sick and disabled soldiers were left behind.[31] Years after this expedition Col. William Sudduth related that "In the latter part of August or September, Major Hood and myself were both drafted to go on a campaign under Gen. George R. Clark. We were the frontier fort and but five men strong. We both refused to go. After Clark had started, Colonel Logan raised about three hundred and fifty men to go to the towns on the heads of the Big Miami. I then went as a volunteer. We crossed the river where Maysville now is and proceeded on to the towns."[32] There they joined the other Kentucky Volunteers. No resistance was encountered. The towns were sacked and everything of value was destroyed or carried off as plunder by the troops when they returned. The effect of this expedition was such that no formidable war party of Indians ever invaded Kentucky thereafter.

Upon the close of the Revolutionary War the militia had a brief respite from Indian hostilities. However, the British failed to surrender the posts in the Northwest, and gradually increased their agitation of Indian hostility against the frontier settlements to the extent of again offering bounties for scalps and prisoners. Horse stealing by the Indians continued, but with less loss of human life to the settlements. In 1783 only one major engagement with the Indians took place, this being the bloody battle of Floyd's Defeat. A company of twenty-seven under John Floyd, colonel of the Jefferson Militia, were defeated in August on Bear Grass Creek. In this skirmish seventeen whites were killed or taken captive, and one was wounded. The company rode in three columns with Captain Sturgess in the lead. Though seriously wounded, he broke through the Indian lines and continued until he met a man who was on foot. This man held Sturgess on his horse and brought him in to the fort. The Indians had led Floyd's company into an ambuscade. Those who had been taken prisoner later said there were 470 Indians, and that they could speak English.

It is said that a remote circumstance which preceded Floyd's Defeat, and probably precipitated it was a challenge sent to Colonel Floyd by Colonel Greene who had a station about two miles from Bullitt's Lick. Colonel Floyd's family dissuaded him from acting on the first challenge because of the added peril resulting from the presence of Indians in the neighborhood. A second challenge came, and Floyd determined to accept it to settle the grievance. On the way to Greene's Station the Indians were encountered.[33]

A company went out to bury the dead after Floyd's Defeat, and another party had gone to move Squire Boone's Station down towards Louisville. The latter company was defeated by Indians on Floyd's Fork, a branch of Salt River, with the loss of three men, three or four women, and several children killed. Thomas Ravenscraft commanded this company. Major Clark afterwards sent out some Regulars to bury the dead, and the Indians then left the vicinity.[34]

In the summer of 1784 some depredations were committed along the southern frontier by the Indians, and Col. Benjamin Logan received intelligence that a serious invasion was contemplated. To combat this anticipated attack Logan publicly summoned such citizens as could conveniently attend to meet at Danville on a particular day and consult as to what measures should be taken for the common defense. In the fall of 1784 the first step was taken toward separation of the Kentucky District from Virginia. An assembly, convened by Colonel Logan, had no legal authority, but published a recommendation that each militia company in the district should elect one delegate, and that the delegates thus chosen should assemble in Danville on the twenty-seventh of December, 1784. The recommendation was well received, the elections held, and the delegates assembled. Upon organization Samuel McDowell was elected president, and Thomas Todd, clerk. A great number of spectators were in attendance, who maintained the most commendable order, and the convention, as they styled themselves, debated the question of separation from the parent state with much gravity and decorum, but achieved little other than added impetus to the sentiment in favor of separation, and the subject was referred to a second convention.

Old Jefferson County Court minute books give interesting accounts of the militia in the life of the community. Among these are the following Court orders:

At a Court held April 7th, 1784.

Wm. Pope, Gent, produced a commission from Benj. Harrison, Esq. Governor of the council of this State appointing the said Wm. Pope, a Colonel in the militia of said county, whereupon he took the oath of allegiance and Fidelity and also the oath of office.

Court of November 3rd, 1784.

On motion of R. Chenowith, Gent. its considered by the Court that the petition he intends to prefer to the legislature, concerning the expenses incurred by him in first building the garrison at the Falls of the Ohio, is reasonable, and that the same be certified.

Throughout 1785 small bands of Indians preyed on the more remote and isolated settlements. Several incidents that then occurred are noteworthy because of the speedy and usually effective pursuit given by the militia. Early in the spring of 1785 Indians killed two children of John Constant, near Strode's Station;[35] Constant's leg had been broken by a rifle ball. An alarm was sent to the station, and a company of about thirty pursued in a very short time, but the Indians succeeded in getting into the Knobs and escaped. At about the same time some slaves had been sent out to pick blackberries. After going a short distance they were alarmed at the running of horses in the cane. They related the fact when they got home and the next morning a company of about fifty men under Captain Stucker pursued and overtook the Indians at sundown. They recovered all the horses and killed some half dozen of the Indians.[36]

An incident that transpired in this neighborhood at about the time that the Constant children were killed illustrates the universality of military duty. James Dunlap was drafted for service and approached his captain, asking exemption because he had only one eye. Seeing the captain's hesitancy Col. James McDowell disposed of the request by telling Dunlap that one of the best men who had ever served under him had sight in only one eye. Years later Dunlap related the he had to pay forty shillings to get a man to do his thirty-day tour of duty at that time.[37] Colonel McDowell was then preparing for pursuit of a band of Indians who had stolen some horses and shot a man near Saunders' Station. McDowell, with a command of 93 men, started in pursuit, but soon met Captain Saunders' company that was returning. Saunders reported that they had "killed an Indian down between Elkhorn and the Ohio, and stuck his head on a pole." Thereupon McDowell's men gave up pursuit.[38]

It was in 1785 that Col. William Whitley, then living at Walnut Flat about five miles from the Crab Orchard settlement, led his company of rangers against marauding Indians who had been preying on Wilderness Road travelers. During January the Whitley company trailed an Indian war party, rescued a white prisoner from the Indians, and took one of their number as a captive. In October of the same year a Mrs. McClure and her four infant children were in a party under the leadership of Mr. McClure, westward bound over the Wilderness Road. The party was attacked by Indians, the four children killed, and the mother taken as a captive and carried by the Indian party toward the Ohio River. An alarm was sent to Colonel Whitley, then temporarily absent from home. His wife dispatched news of the attack to him and at the same time issued a call to his company of rangers. As soon as this company of twenty-one riflemen was assembled under Whitley's leadership, it took up the Indian trail, and, at sundown of the second day out, came upon the Indian camp. Most of the Indians escaped through the forest, but Whitley's men killed two, rescued six white prisoners and a large quantity of plunder, as well as sixteen horses. Ten days later a party of immigrants piloted by a man named Moore were attacked on the Wilderness Road. Nine of the immigrants were killed. Colonel Whitley with thirty riflemen followed the Indian band westward over the old War Trace. However, after going some distance, Whitley learned the Indians had not yet passed that point; consequently, he was compelled to turn back. His party had not gone far when they encountered the Indians emerging from a thick canebrake. Whitley's men were spread out in line and the twenty Indians were all mounted on horses and came in single file. When the two opposing parties met, the density of the canebrake prevented them from seeing each other until they were only about ten steps apart. Taken entirely unawares, the Indians at the first fire fled, leaving eight of their number dead. Twenty horses were recovered in this engagement.

During 1783 Simon Kenton had returned to Limestone after a prolonged absence. Soon after his return he erected a blockhouse where Maysville now stands, a point of considerable prominence during the ensuing years, both in the entry of settlers into Kentucky and in Kentucky's struggle to repel the Indian raids. Kenton's determination to build a fort for the defense of northern Kentucky became fixed when his surveying party came upon Joseph Taylor's company, which had shortly landed at Limestone. A band of Indians had attacked and killed all but two of Taylor's party. Thereupon Kenton immediately decided no more time should be lost in erecting a fort. Having completed the survey he was working on, he struck out across country to Salt River and gathered a force of about sixty volunteers to erect a blockhouse at the mouth of Limestone Creek. This fort was built in 1784, the first in Mason County.

In the early summer of 1786 Kenton formed his Mason County Minute Men. He did this after Hezekiah Wood and Lot Masters were killed while on their way to Kenton's Station to hear William Wood's preaching. When these two men did not arrive at the preaching, Kenton immediately organized a party and set out to find them. Their scalped and mutilated bodies were found near the fort. Thereupon Kenton realized the great need of a form of local militia.

Simon Kenton was probably the first spy or scout employed by Lord Dunmore, Crown Governor of Virginia, for duty in the Kentucky District. As such he had rendered inestimable service to the British expeditions against the Miami Indians, and at the same time acquired a wide knowledge that served him well upon his return to Kentucky. His experiences already impressed upon him the absolute need for speedy military pursuit of raiders. He trained spies and scouts, appointed commanders and signal corps, and procured arms and ammunition for his company. This system was quite distinct, a thing apart from the spy system called into service by the county lieutenants and paid for with Virginia funds. These men followed only their leader, Capt. Simon Kenton. For eight years they covered northern Kentucky. They kept no elaborate records, and their method of procedure was simple. When news came of stolen horses or of settlers captured, Kenton merely sent out a speedy call to "his boys." Horses were saddled and the hunt was on. John Masterton was the lieutenant, and Kenton was the captain of the Mason County Volunteer Company. Services extended, usually, from April until November of each year, the months most subject to Indian depredations.[39]

Among the obscure killings by Indians in 1786 was that of Abraham Lincoln's grandfather, with whom at the time was his six-year-old son, Thomas, who was the father of the President. The dead pioneer had three sons, Mordecai, Josiah and Thomas, in the order named. When the father fell, Mordecai sent Josiah to a near-by fort for assistance, then ran into the cabin and, pointing his rifle through a crack between the logs, prepared for defense. Soon an Indian came stealthily up to the dead father's body, beside which sat the little boy, Thomas. Mordecai took deliberate aim at the Indian and brought him to the ground. Josiah returned from the fort with help, and the savages were easily dispersed, leaving behind one dead and one wounded.[40]

In the remote sections where settlements were greatly exposed parties of rangers patrolled the woods. County lieutenants and their subordinates were compelled to be continually on guard. Lincoln County's frontier line was particularly exposed, and, with the Wilderness Road, kept

Colonel Logan almost continually in the public service. Militia under Colonel Logan ranged the Lincoln County vicinity of the Cumberland and Green rivers, where many settlers were killed by Indians, especially in 1786. A similar service was rendered in northern Kentucky by Simon Kenton, who maintained militia companies to escort settlers, arriving at Limestone, as far south as the Blue Licks.[41]

At Hood's Station in March, 1786, Indians stole four valuable horses. Major Hood tried to raise a company to pursue them, but could get only three men. In April three Indians took two more mares belonging to Hood, and by ten o'clock the next morning a company of seventeen men had formed and pursued them, but did not recover the stock. Major Hood was then allowed a guard for the balance of the summer.[42] In May, 1786, a hunting party from Limestone went down to the mouth of Eagle Creek to watch a lick. While sitting at the lick they heard a bell which was shortly silenced. These men at once returned to Limestone, spread an alarm, were reinforced by volunteers, and went back to Eagle Creek by sunrise. They saw but one Indian at the time, but got five horses. These were sold when the company got to Limestone, and the proceeds were divided among the company.[43]

In August, 1786, an expedition against the tribes on the Wabash was projected to discourage their frequent raids into Kentucky. On one of these raids, made by Chief Black Wolf during April, Col. William Christian had been mortally wounded. Some Indians who had been stealing horses were pursued by a company, and two Indians had been wounded so they could not get up. These two shot Isaac Keller and Col. William Christian of the pursuing party. Colonel Christian was rescued and taken to Louisville, but died shortly afterward.[44] In September about one thousand volunteers from Kentucky rendezvoused at Louisville and were attached to the command of Gen. George Rogers Clark. Provisions and ammunition, privately contributed, were loaded on keelboats and the troops began their march overland. A point of rendezvous in the Illinois country was reached by the famished troops fifteen days before the provisions arrived. Waiting for provisions led to unrest among the troops, a condition which was augmented by the increasing intemperance of General Clark, so much so as to cause the men to lose confidence in him. As a result a detachment of 300 men started back to Kentucky, and this, with other prevalent adverse conditions, resulted in a total disorganization of the expedition.

From 1780 to about 1790 piratical acts on the Mississippi River were very common and their victims were usually Kentuckians or Creoles under American protection. While Clark was still at Post St. Vincent's he convened a court of his militia officers to sanction his seizure of a loaded boat belonging to a Creole trader from the Spanish possessions. Clark gave revenge as his reason for the seizure. However, the goods seized served Clark well in paying his irregularly employed troops, and doubtless this was an added incentive to the seizure. Radical Kentuckians acclaimed the wisdom and virtue of the act as a warning to those who molested their shipping on the Mississippi.[45]

Upon returning with his remaining command Clark dispatched Col. Benjamin Logan with instructions to return to Kentucky and raise troops for an expedition against the Shawnee. This Logan proceeded to do, and with about 400 men he crossed the Ohio at Limestone, penetrated the Ohio country to the headwaters of Mad River, sacked eight towns, destroyed crops, killed about 20 Indians, including Chief Blackfish, captured over 70 prisoners, and in all of this sustained a loss of only 10 men killed.

A deposition of Oswald Townsen taken in Madison County in 1803 states that in 1786 he, in company with 100 men, mostly from Madison County, marched to join Col. Benjamin Logan on his campaign against the Shawnee. On this occasion the militia from Madison met at McGee's Station and selected Col. John Snoddy to command until they reached Colonel Logan.

In the spring of 1787 Colonel Todd's expedition against the Ohio Indians was planned. Kenton had gone across the

Ohio River to find out just what the Indians were up to. He discovered a large party, and with his scouting companion, Joshua Baker, hurried back to organize a defense. Scouts were dispatched by Kenton to the Kentucky settlements for horses and men, and in May more than 200 militia were assembled at Limestone. The command consisted of Colonel Todd, Lieutenant Colonel Hinkston, and Maj. William Russell, with Kenton as pilot. As usual the body was referred to as the "Limestone Volunteers," a term applied to any forces recruited by Kenton.

Indian outrages of 1787, in the southeastern part of Lincoln County, induced Colonel Logan, in command of the Lincoln County Militia, to call together his corps of men to range on the waters of the Cumberland and to rendezvous on a branch of Green River at the place where a settler named Luttrell had been killed. Colonel Logan, when within a few miles of the rendezvous, came upon the trail of what he supposed to be the guilty band. Those he followed, and overtook them in Indian territory, killed several, and got possession of property which he identified as belonging to certain white settlers; also some valuable skins and furs, belonging to the hunting party, which he confiscated.

The Indians who escaped availed themselves of the pact of 1785 which Congress had made with the Cherokee, forbidding intrusion on the Indian hunting ground. Thereupon the Governor of Virginia instructed the attorney general of the Kentucky District, Harry Innes, to "institute proper legal inquiries for vindicating the infraction of the treaty." Innes refused to act under such vague instructions. When instructions were given to prosecute Colonel Logan, the people of Kentucky were exasperated, for they considered it an attempt to stigmatize a highly meritorious officer who was doing his duty as he saw it.

The censure of Colonel Logan resulted from the Virginia administration's lack of knowledge of Indian affairs in Kentucky. In the eastern states Indian troubles were now few, and the administration believed conditions in Kentucky to be equally satisfactory. It was even intimated that the Kentuckians were the aggressors in provoking the Indians to attack. The following admonition of the Governor to the State Militia officials had just preceded Colonel Logan's alleged treaty infraction:

Virginia to wit—by his Excellency Edmund Randolph, Esquire, Governor of the Commonwealth.

A PROCLAMATION

WHEREAS, the defence of the Commonwealth is by the laws placed in the militia thereof, and no exertion for the maintenance of discipline ought to be omitted, I do therefore, by and with the advice of the council of State, exhort all officers of the militia, of whatsoever rank, punctually and faithfully to discharge their respective duties. And I do moreover declare, that every person failing herein, shall be prosecuted in the most exemplary manner allowed by law. But from my confidence in the patriotism and character of the officers, I most sanguinely hope, that a resort to the penalties of the law will be unnecessary.

Given under my hand and the seal of the Commonwealth, at Richmond, this 24th day of March, 1787.

EDMUND RANDOLPH
Governor of Virginia

In March or April, 1787, a company from Strode's and other near-by stations pursued some Indians who had been stealing horses in the vicinity. The Indians were encountered, and among those captured was their chief, Bluejacket. Upon capturing Bluejacket his mare and gun were put up at auction for the benefit of the company. Jim Wilson got the gun and mare, and J. Hanks got Bluejacket's arm bands and rings.[46] Many thought that this was the same band that had just shortly before killed Ezekiel Sudduth, brother of William Sudduth, near Hood's Station.[47]

In March, 1788, five men encamped at the Sinkhole Spring on the Wilderness Road. During the night they were fired on by a party of Indians and two were killed on the spot, two made their escape, and the fifth was missing. The Indians took all the horses and baggage. The two who escaped got into a Kentucky settlement, raised a company and went in pursuit of the Indians. With snow on the ground, they were easily followed; the pursuers came on the Indians in the night, fired on them but missed. The Indians ran off leaving their guns and their shot pouches, together with every article they had taken at the Sinkhole Spring. The next day the troops followed them and found where they had encamped and torn pieces of their leggings to cover their feet, and also discovered that they had carried fire from that place. Most of the white men suffered from frozen feet and were compelled to give up pursuit.[48]

In May, 1788, Lt. Nathan McClure, with a part of Col. William Whitley's command, pursued a party of southern Indians who had stolen some horses near Crab Orchard. Lieutenant McClure followed the trail of the Indians to the ridge between Rockcastle River and Buck Creek. Here a party of marauders was encountered and a fierce skirmish ensued. After numerous exchanges of fire, both parties retreated, but not until Lieutenant McClure was mortally wounded. He died the following night in a cave where he had been left. Lieutenant McClure was an active and well-liked officer of the Lincoln County Militia.

During the latter part of May, two young hunters were going to a salt lick, near the Licking River, when they sighted and fired on two Indians riding one horse. The Indians got away, but dropped one of their guns and their baggage. An alarm was given, and the company that pursued overtook and killed both. These two Indians were thought to have been of the party that had stolen a horse on Cane Run of Elkhorn Creek, for the band, when pursued by a company, had fled toward the Ohio River, within ten or twelve miles of which they were overtaken. In the skirmish that ensued one Indian was killed and the stolen horses were retrieved.[49]

About the same time a company pursued some Indians who had stolen horses again at Strode's Station. They overtook them at the Mud Lick, where one Indian was captured, but later escaped.[50] On October 31, 1788, a party of five Indians fired from ambush on several men who, with teams and pack horses, were going to Limestone. They killed a Mr. Latta and took six of the horses. This attack renewed the efforts of the military leaders of the District of Kentucky to guard this section of the frontier, and they ordered General Harmar to act at once and effectively to protect Mason County inhabitants. Thereupon Captain Kearsey with forty-eight soldiers was sent to Limestone for an expedition against the Indians upstream along the Ohio.

Two official notices in the *Kentucky Gazette* of August, 1788, brought a ray of hope to the long-unpaid militia of the district:

> The Commissioners appointed by law to adjust and settle claims for militia service and property or rations furnished or impressed for the use of the militia on duty previous to the commencement of the present year will sit in Lexington on Tuesday the twelfth of August. On which day at twelve o'clock the field officers of Fayette meet at Capt. Thomas Young's Tavern to recommend officers for the troops of horses directed by the late act of Assembly.
>
> The Commissioners appointed for adjusting the claims for militia services done, and forage, provisions and other articles furnished or impressed, in the years 1786 and 1787, will meet for that purpose in Lexington, on the second Tuesday in September next to receive claims of Fayette and Bourbon Counties. At Lincoln Court house the Monday following, to receive those of that and Madison Counties, and at Harrodsburg the Thursday following, to receive those of Mercer and Nelson Counties.
>
> DAVID KNOX, *C. Com.*

In the spring of 1789 there was a large influx of settlers through Limestone. Kenton watched over these new visitors without their knowing it. He procured wagons and pack horses to transport their goods inland, and placed guards near their night camp.

The first permanently organized military company in Kentucky was the Lexington Light Infantry, organized 1789. Its history was one of daring and of blood, through the Indian expeditions of 1789-94, the War of 1812, the Mexican War in 1846-47, and the War between the States, 1861-65. From it came many brave, talented, and brilliant men who left their mark in civil and military life of the Nation.[53] When first organized this company's officers were James

Wilkinson, captain; James Hughes, lieutenant; and Archibald Brown, ensign. The uniform consisted of a blue cloth coat with cuffs, collar, and breast faced in red, white bullet buttons, blue pantaloons, and a wide-brimmed black hat; the brim was turned up on one side and held by a red plume.

Advertisements which appeared in the *Kentucky Gazette* during March, 1789, serve to show the growth and military aggressiveness of Fayette County, and are in vivid contrast to a report made ten years previously when only twelve men garrisoned the fort at Lexington. These advertisements are as follows:

LEXINGTON, *Mar. 5, 1789.*

The Regimental musters for the county of Fayette, are appointed in the following manner; to wit—the first Regiment musters at Col. Levi Todd's on Monday the 30th inst. The 2nd regiment at the Rev. Lewis Craig's Mill on Tuesday the 31st inst. The 3rd Regiment near Col. Marshall's at the place where the Surveyor's Office was formerly kept, on Wednesday the first of April.

The Officers and Soldiers of the Second Fayette Regiment are hereby notified that their Regimental muster is to be held at Mr. Lewis Craig's mill on Tuesday the 31st of this month. They are to take notice that they must appear accoutred as the law directs and also that the Court of Enquiry will meet the second day April next in Lexington at Marshall's Tavern and sit from day to day until the business is finished.

R. PATTERSON, *Col.*

March 5, 1789.

In 1789, with the inception of the U. S. Government, the people of Kentucky were informed that the new Government would speedily organize a Regular Army of sufficient strength to protect the district from further Indian ravages, such outrages having lately increased greatly in frequency and heinousness. The Governor of Virginia wrote the following letter to Henry Lee, the lieutenant of cavalry in the Kentucky District:[54]

RICHMOND, *June 1st, 1789.*

SIR:

The enclosed copy of a letter from the President of the United States rendering it unnecessary that this State should any longer, at her own particular charge, support the troops called into service for the defense of the Western frontier; you will immediately discharge all scouts and rangers employed in your county. In case of any future incursions of the Indians, you will give as early information of them as possible to the office commanding the continental post on the Ohio, nearest point of attack. I have communicated to the President the instructions now sent you and have no doubt but effective measures will be taken to protect all inhabitants of the frontiers.

You will, if possible, furnish me before the meeting of the next assembly, with a statement of the whole expense incurred this year for the pay and support of the scouts and rangers engaged in defense of your country. I am sir,

Your Obedient Servant,

BEVERLY RANDOLPH.

Indian depredations of 1789 include several noteworthy incidents recorded by the press. On February 14 a party of Indians fired on a Mr. Jones and David Stucker, near Emerson's on Dry Run, a branch on North Elkhorn. Stucker was slightly wounded in two places. The next morning Colonel Johnson collected about twenty men to reconnoiter. The Indians were overtaken and surrendered some arms and twenty-one horses. One Indian was killed and several others wounded.

"On March 14th, Indians killed a man and wounded another near May's Lick, on the road from Lexington to Limestone. They were pursued by a company of about forty men." On the fifteenth of March several Indians were seen on Townsend Branch of Licking. "The next evening they stole a number of horses and went off. On the same day a party of Indians stole some horses at Carpenter's Station." Militia pursued in both cases. Shortly afterward "at the Big Crossing of Elkhorn, one Gibson had two negroes taken, and a son killed. Gibson had a militia guard just before this and had dismissed it." One of the men of that guard said he "hadn't gotten out of hearing yet" when he heard the gunshot report. Gibson immediately sent for a new guard. This new guard went to Colonel Johnson's and "drew some to go up and some to go down the creek, and others to stay at Col. Johnson's." [55]

A scouting party of ten or fifteen, raised from the Crossing under Col. Robert Johnson, was defeated above the mouth of Longberry Creek in 1789. There were from forty to fifty Indians in the attack. When they had crossed the stream they were attacked and Johnson gave way, running down to the river. He was first to get into the little flat-bottomed ferryboat. Colonel Johnson was later accused of cowardice for not waiting until all of his men were safely in the boat.[56]

In the summer of 1789, Indians did some mischief near Georgetown. "Some twenty-nine or thirty men under Colonel Johnson went over the Ohio River after them." The Indians were encountered, and a skirmish ensued in which Capt. Sam Grant and Moses Grant, were among those killed. The Grants were brothers and their mother was a sister of Col. Daniel Boone.[57] Some 300 volunteers under Colonels Patterson and Russell, with Jacob Stucker as the pilot,[58] went to bury the dead.

An attack was made on Kenton's Station in March, 1790. Ten persons were killed and the station temporarily broken up, because a letter of March 10, 1790, from Gov. Beverly Randolph to Lt. Henry Lee, forbade Kentucky troops to go out of the state in pursuit of Indians. The order issued upon complaints from the Governor of the Northwest Territory that frequently the Kentucky Militia had pursued Indians into the territory north of the Ohio.

During the early spring of 1790 the Wilderness Road travelers and settlers along Station Camp Creek in Madison County suffered greatly from Indian depredations. Madison County had a boundary line of some forty miles that was constantly harrassed. Col. James Barnett was lieutenant of the county. An official appeal was made by him by letter to Judge Harry Innes, setting out the Indian outrages and the prospect for a continuation of the peril. On the thirteenth of April, Col. Barnett was authorized by President Washington, in cases of imminent danger, to call out scouts for the protection of the county at the expense of the Government of the United States. An act of the Virginia Assembly in 1790 ordered the commanding officers of Mercer, Lincoln, and Madison counties to call out, in their respective counties during October and November of every year, the Indian hunting season, thirty militiamen to guard the Wilderness Road against Indian depredations. The act fixed the pay of officers at six shillings and of guards at four shillings per day, and directed the guards to rendezvous at the east foot of Cumberland Mountains at the Gap. From this point they were to act as escorts to parties westward bound over the Wilderness Road. This act failed to provide against the peril of Indian raids during the spring and summer.

On July 2, 1790, a meeting of residents of Fayette, Jefferson, Lincoln, Mercer, and Nelson counties was held at Danville. At this meeting Benjamin Sebastain was appointed chairman, Christopher Greenup, clerk, and the following resolution was adopted:

Resolved, as the opinion of this meeting that from the frequent depredations of the Indians on the people and property of this district, a meeting of the several field officers within same is highly advisable. And therefore it is requested, that the said officers give their attendance at Danville on Monday the 26th inst. to consider the best mode of defense for the inhabitants of the district.

News of the meeting reached the Capitol, though no appeal for help was made, and was evidently construed as a determination on the part of Kentucky to put an end to Indian troubles regardless of consequences. Without solicitation thereto, on the seventeenth of July, the President, through General Henry Knox, his Secretary of War, sent the following letter to Colonel Barnett and his lieutenants of Lincoln and Mercer counties:

WAR OFFICE, *July 17th, 1790.*

SIR: I had the honor on the 13th day of April last, to address you on the subject of the incursions of small parties of Indians on the western frontier. In that letter I authorized you, in the name of the President of the United States, in certain cases of imminent danger, to call out, for the protection of the county, certain species of patrols, denominated scouts, at the expense of the United States.

I have now the honor, by the direction of the President of the United States, to inform you that the authority contained in said letter relative to said scouts, is to be considered as having ceased and terminated upon your receiving this letter, duplicate of which I have written and transmitted to you.

The President of the United States is anxiously desirous of effectually protecting the frontiers, and he will take all such reasonable measures, as in his judgment, the case may require, and for which he shall be, by the constitution, or by the laws authorized.

He has, therefore, directed me to inform you, that in addition to the measure aforesaid, which have been ordered, he has empowered the Governor of the Western territory and Brigadier General Harmar or either of them, to make the arrangement hereafter described for the internal security of the exposed counties.

The said Governor and commanding officer, or either of them will, under their hands and seals, empower the Lieutenants of such counties lying along the Ohio, as they shall judge necessary, to call forth the number of militia or rangers hereafter mentioned, and under the regulations prescribed.

HENRY KNOX.

The arrangement referred to in the letter of Secretary Knox provided regulations for calling of the Kentucky Militia into the service of the United States. Kentucky troops so called were subject to the following conditions:

1. The said Militia, or rangers, shall, during the time of their actual service in any county, have one subaltern, one sergeant, one corporal, and twelve privates, but such less number may be ordered as the said Governor and commanding officer or county lieutenant may judge requisite.

2. The said militia, or rangers, shall, during the time of their actual service, receive the following rates of pay, which are the same as is by law established for the regular troops of the United States and the militia, viz:

Lieutenants, twenty-two dollars, per month.
Ensigns, eighteen dollars, per month.
Sergeant, five dollars, per month.
Corporal, four dollars, per month.
Privates, three dollars, per month.

3. The said rangers shall be furnished with rations in such manner as the lieutenants of all the counties shall think proper. The United States will allow for such ration six-pence, Virginia currency, or eight and one-third hundreth part of a dollar; the subaltern to have two, and the non-commissioned officers and privates, one ration each.

4. The lieutenants of each county shall be responsible on oath that the said rangers shall be called into service only in cases of imminent danger, and that they may be discharged as soon as the danger shall cease.

That when any service shall have been performed by said rangers, the following evidence therefore will be required:

1. A return of the names, rank, ages, residence and time of service of each of the said rangers.

2. A pay abstract, or account, of the number of said rangers, agreeable to the aforesaid returns.

3. An abstract of the rations agreeable to the aforesaid returns.

4. These papers to be signed and verified upon oath, by the Lieutenants of the county, or commanding officer of the militia, who will transmit the same to Brigadier-General Harmar or the commanding officer of the troops of the United States on the Ohio.

5. Brigadier-General Harmar, or the commanding officer of the troops, will certify on the said return, that the said rangers were ordered into service in pursuance of his authority, or the authority of the Governor of the Western territory.

6. The pay-master of the regiment of regular troops will receive the amount of the said abstracts from the Treasury or pay office of the United States and pay the same to the county lieutenants, and the said county lieutenants will pay each of the rangers, respectively taking triplicate receipts for the payments, two of which he must transmit.

Early in August the county lieutenants received instructions under the order and at once proceeded to organize their troops in compliance. Scouts, or spies as they were called, did much to keep off the Indians. Under Federal order the scout system was later extended towards the Big Sandy, and over towards Greenbrier, Virginia.

The scout served as a sort of link between the frontier soldier and the Regular Army officer. This link was lacking in Kentucky until the scout system was established by the Government. A friction had long existed between the Regular Army and the militia. This attitude was due primarily to training. The frontier militiamen were often uncouth, suspicious and impatient of discipline, holding a feeling of hostility, of sneering envy, for the Regular. The Regular showed a lack or appreciation of the militiaman's virtues and an ever obvious contempt for his shortcomings.

Harmon's first station was built in the Big Sandy Valley below the mouth of John's Creek in 1787. It was a log structure, and was the first outpost in this valley. In the winter of 1789 it was abandoned because of serious Indian raids, and was thereupon burned by the Indians. It was rebuilt in 1790, though farther upstream, at the mouth of John's Creek, and never again surrendered to the Indians.

Bourbon Furnace on Slate Creek, near the present Owingsville, though privately owned was deemed a valuable asset of the Kentucky District. Frequent incursions of Indians into the area endangered the plant, and in 1790 the owners applied to the Board of War of Virginia for a guard. This was granted, and consisted of from twenty to twenty-five men drafted out of the near-by militia companies. These men were required to spend two months per year in the service at the furnace.

On June 29, 1790, one Dickerson and Isaac Baker went to a deer lick, where they were attacked by Indians. Dickerson was killed and Baker was severely wounded in the hand, but recovered. Major Hood and all the men from one furnace guard party went to their relief. John Wade and J. Martin were spies for the furnace, and having seen the tracks of the Indians reported accordingly to the furnace operators. On the next evening a message came from Baker's Station, stating that John Wade and Reuben Coffee were wounded when the militia guard from Bourbon Furnace had an encounter with a party of Indians at Baker's on the morning of June 30, 1790. By ten o'clock that night upwards of 100 men had arrived at Baker's Station from Strode's Station and the neighborhood. These included the company of Major Hood and Captain Smith, who with more men from the furnace guard were at once detailed to Baker's Station. The Indians had not yet molested the station, but upon the arrival of the guard they were in ambush and fired. This furnace guard served not only the furnace but the entire countryside when called upon. It was maintained at Bourbon Furnace from 1790 to 1796.

Among the first acts of the newly organized Federal Government was a military movement to protect the western frontier. To this end Gen. Josiah Harmar was placed in command of a detachment of the U. S. Army detailed for this purpose. On April 18, 1790, General Harmar, with 160 Regulars, and Gen. Charles Scott, with 230 Kentucky Volunteers, marched on an expedition from Limestone toward the upper waters of the Scioto River and then southward to the mouth of that river, now Portsmouth, Ohio. The Kentucky Volunteers on this expedition were mostly from Fayette and Bourbon counties. Officers were not elected until after they had reached the other side of the Ohio River. Fayette troops were the strongest in numbers, and feared, if they elected their men, the Bourbon troops might not go with them. The Bourbon choice was made second in command.[59] The purpose of this expedition was to intercept the hostile Indian bands that frequented this area. However, little was accomplished through the campaign other than the killing of four Indians.

In September, 1790, Harmar's force of 350 Regulars was reinforced by Kentucky and Pennsylvania Militia. Congress had authorized Harmar to call 1,500 men from these two states. These troops rendezvoused at Fort Washington (Cincinnati), and aside from the nucleus of Regulars, consisted of three battalions of Kentucky Militia and one battalion from Pennsylvania. From this point their march was commenced against the Miami towns.

Upon approaching their destination a detachment of Kentucky troops, about 300, under Col. James Trotter, was detailed to reconnoiter, but accomplished nothing except the killing of two Indians. The results angered Harmar and he gave the command to Col. John Hardin.[60] Hardin's men were loyal to him, but questioned the ability of Harmar. In pursuit of the duty assigned, Hardin's command was subjected to a deadly Indian fire, and its defeat took the heart out of the volunteers, and the expedition then left the Miami towns and moved back to Chillicothe, and on October 21, the little army began its march back to Fort Washington.

In the belief that the Indians would return to the Miami towns as soon as the troops left, Harmar detached 400 men to go back to the villages. The Indians had returned with reinforcements and poured a deadly fire on the three widely separated columns of Regulars and militia. The Regulars lost 75 killed and 3 wounded, and the militia suffered a loss of 108 killed and 28 wounded. On the return march Harmar threatened to restore discipline and order among the disgruntled volunteers by firing on them with the artillery. This threat restored order, but at the same time added to the Kentuckians' dislike of being under command of U. S. Army officers.

A sequel to Harmar's Defeat is contained in the following Military Board findings: [61]

> We the Subscribers, have been requested to meet as a board of inquiry into the conduct of Col. John Hardin on the late expedition under the command of Brig. Gen. Harmar against the Maumee Indians. Having met at Capt. Thomas Young's tavern in Lexington for that purpose this 8th day of December, 1790, and having taken an oath, sundry gentlemen officers, who served on the said expedition, testified that Col. Hardin's conduct was that of a brave and active officer, and that we approve his conduct. (signed) Levi Todd, Robt. Johnson, Robt. Todd, John McDowell, Isaac Shelby, Marquis Calmes, James McDowell, Bartlett Colling, William Price.
>
> The witnesses examined on this occasion were Col. Trotter, Col. McMillin, Col. Hall, Maj. Wray, Capt. Bush, Capt. Taylor, Capt. Gaines, Capt. Frazer, Capt. Sanders, Lieut. Hughes and Lieut. McCoy.
>
> Teste—JOHN BRADFORD, *Clk.*

Harmar's Defeat brought about the establishment of Kentucky's Board of War in January, 1791, by the U. S. Congress. This board consisted of Brig. Gen. Charles Scott, Harry Innes, John Brown, Benjamin Logan, and Isaac Shelby, and was authorized to call the Kentucky Militia into the service of the United States whenever deemed necessary.

The establishment of the board was necessary because the Kentucky Militia, more than any other military organization, was protecting the western frontier, and this largely at her own expense. Then, too, the Kentuckians believed that they were more familiar with the Indian problem and could act more quickly if authority for action was established locally. Several times other troops had met with defeat at the hands of the Indians because of being unfamiliar with Indian strategy and tactics. "One Indian to four Regulars, and two Indians to one Kentuckian was the common rating of equal forces" at that day.[62]

Under orders of the Board of War in February, 1791, the following posts on the frontiers were named and ordered occupied by guards for the defense of the district:[63]

Post	No. Men	Post	No. Men
Three Islands	20	Mouth Salt River	10
Locust Creek	18	Hardin's Settlements	12
Iron Works	17	Russell's Creek	15
Forks of Licking	12	Severein's Valley	10
Big Bone Lick	18	Widow Wilson's	5
Tanner's Station	5	Estill's Station	10
Drennon's Lick	10	Stevenson's Station	10
Mouth Ky. River	19	Lackey's Station	8
Patten's Creek	10	Wales Lick	9

A company of sixty Lexington militiamen, under the command of Capt. Joseph McMurtry, was part of the first guard at these posts. The Lexington company was divided into three squads, one at the mouth of the Kentucky River under Captain McMurtry, one at the Big Bone Lick under a Lieutenant Williams, and the other at a point between the Kentucky River and Louisville. Three sets of spies were picked out in each company. They went out at daybreak, camped out overnight, and returned late the second day from a different direction. This first company redezvoused March 1, 1791. The men were drafted for two months, but had to stay a half month longer until relieved by another company.

On April 11, 1791, word came to Walker's Station that some Indians were in the vicinity who had been stealing horses along the frontier. Captain Walker ordered a company to take up pursuit. Seven Indians were encountered about five miles from Walker's Station. All that they had in their possession was taken by the company and included eight horses, seven or eight blankets, several bridles, a brass kettle, "a half bushel of jerk, a bear's gut, a yard and a half or two yards long, full of bear's fat, and seven or eight deerskins."[64] The record makes no mention of any further action taken against the Indians.

In the middle of May, 1791, an expedition, projected by the Kentucky Board of War, was instituted against the Indian towns of the Whitewater country under the leadership of Brig. Gen. Charles Scott. General Scott was authorized to draft 326 privates for 60-day service to which might be attached any volunteers who would enlist. That General Scott was a popular commander is shown by the numbers that rallied to his several calls for volunteers. Nevertheless, he is said by those who disliked him to have been one of the wickedest men in Kentucky in his day. An old record states that Reuben Cove was appointed, by the congregation of the Baptist Church of the neighborhood in which Scott lived, to ask Scott to leave. Before Cove made known his mission, General Scott had entertained him in the best manner of the day. But when the mission was once stated all hospitality ceased and Scott "called his negroes and his dogs to make him leave." It is said that "Old Mr. Shannon" was appointed chaplain by General Scott and served as such on several campaigns, and that "that spoiled him, for he [Shannon] got to tippling too much * * *." [65]

Scott and his men took up their march on the twenty-third of May, and a force of 800 Kentucky troops crossed the Ohio River at Battle Creek, about five miles below the mouth of the Kentucky River, with Gen. James Wilkinson, second in command. The first encounter took place about 155 miles north of the Ohio River. A man on horseback was seen at a distance, but the detachment sent to intercept him was unable to prevent his escape. Near-by two small villages were found. Col. John Hardin, who had enlisted as a private, and Captain McCoy, with 50 mounted infantry and a troop of light-horse, were detached to move on the villages while the main body proceeded toward the town, Kickapoo. A French village on the Wabash was sacked and inhabitants of the Indian villages dispersed, though the Indians continued to hold Kickapoo. Misunderstanding the object of a white flag which appeared on an opposite eminence in the afternoon of July 1, an aged squaw was liberated with a message to the savages that, if they would come in and surrender, their towns would be spared and they should receive good treatment. On the fourth, sixteen of the weakest and most infirm of the prisoners were liberated. On the same day, after having burned the town called Oniatenon and adjacent villages, the troops began their march back to the Falls of the Ohio. The expedition reported thirty-two warriors killed. Forty-one prisoners were delivered to Captain Anderson, 1st U. S. Infantry Regiment, at Fort Steuben.

General Scott's official report of the campaign contains the following statement:

"In the prosecution of the enterprise, I marched four miles from the banks of the Ohio, on the 23rd of May; and on the 24th, I resumed my march and pushed forward with the utmost industry, directing my route to Oniatenon, in the best manner my guides and information enabled me; though I found myself greatly deficient in both. By the 31st, I had marched one hundred and thirty-five miles, over a country cut by four branches of White River, and many smaller streams with steep, muddy banks; during this march, I traversed a country alternately interspersed with the most luxuriant soils, and deep, clayey boggs, from one to five miles in width, rendered almost impervious by brush and briars. Rain fell in torrents every day, with frequent blasts of wind and thunderstorms. These obstacles impeded my progress, wore down my horses, and destroyed my provisions."

This was referred to as the "Blackberry Campaign" of 1791.[66] Because of a scarcity of food, marching was delayed by the soldiers stopping to pick berries. The *Kentucky Gazette* of June 25, 1791, carries a news item much to the point in this respect. "When the famished troops arrived at the Falls of the Ohio they were invited by Col. John Campbell to refresh themselves at his house. A plentiful supply of food and liquor was provided. Tables were kept continually spread."

The following extract from a letter was printed in the *Kentucky Gazette* of July 23, 1791, and refers to the Kentucky troops under General Scott:

I can with much propriety assure you, that during the late War, I have never seen such a respectable and able-bodied Militia taking the field, in defense of their country. They were composed of the first class of citizens, a member of Congress, members of the Senate and Assembly, magistrates, Colonels, Majors, Captains, Lawyers, and others serving as privates in the field—the whole were well mounted and accoutrements were a rifle and a tomahawk; they left the mouth of Kentucky, N. W. of the Ohio on the 24th of May, last.

The following letter to Brig. Gen. Charles Scott indicates that the "Blackberry Campaign" served to incite rather than subdue the Wabash Indians:

SIR: I have lately received a letter from the Secretary of War, informing me that in case a more extensive combination of the Indian nations should be formed than is at present calculated on, the Commanding General of the troops to the Westward is authorized to call for such numbers and species of militia as the nature of the case may require. Should such a demand be made you will consider it as peculiarly your duty to use every exertion in your power to insure the most complete compliance with it.

I am much disappointed at not having been able as yet to procure a complete return of the strength of the militia of your district, let us intreat your attention to this business. If it can be obtained by the next session of the General Assembly, it will be very satisfactory. I am, Sir, etc.

BEVERLY RANDOLPH
Governor of Virginia

Through some unexplained cause the command of this expedition was given to Gen. James Wilkinson. No doubt his popularity at the time, and his aggressiveness, were factors that brought the command of the Eel River campaign to him. The following call for troops appeared in the *Kentucky Gazette* of July 9, 1791:

Volunteers are wanted for an expedition which will start the 20th inst. from the Ohio, under command of General Wilkinson, upon the same principles as of the late one under Gen. Scott.

The appointment of captains of companies will be made at Lexington the 12th inst. I give this information in consequence of intelligence received from the board appointed to conduct military operations in this district. The army will consist of 500 non-commissioned officers and privates, who are to have 30 days provisions at rendezvous. Col. John Hardin of Nelson County and Col. James McDowell of Fayette, are appointed to command as Majors.

LEVI TODD,
Co. Lt. Ky. Co.

Even while expeditions were being projected against the Northwest Indians and a close watch was being kept by scouts and rangers to keep them out of Kentucky, small bands still made their way to the settlements. On June 20, 1791, two Indians appeared at Jacob Stucker's, on North Elkhorn Creek, and stole three horses. The next day a party of about twelve Indians killed a boy three miles from Colonel Johnson's, near Captain Herndon's. Captain Herndon alarmed the neighborhood and raised a company of fifteen men to pursue the band. In the pursuit two Indians were killed, a third wounded, and all the stolen horses recovered.

On July 19, 1791, 300 men were assembled by order of General Scott for an expedition up the Miami River to break up the Indian bands, if possible, which were responsible for the horse stealing in Mason County. This command was given to Col. John Edwards of Bourbon County. Kenton piloted the expedition after having refused to go as captain of a company of spies. Col. William Sudduth raised a company for the expedition and accompanied it as captain. The troops rendezvoused at Limestone and from there proceeded on to the towns that Colonel Logan had destroyed in 1786. These were again plundered and sacked. They then continued to within thirty miles of Sandusky when Colonel Edwards ordered his command to return to Limestone. Many of the men in the expedition looked upon this move as having been prompted by cowardice on the part of Colonel Edwards.[67]

In August, 1791, General Wilkinson started on the expedition against the Eel River towns under authority of the Kentucky Board of War. With his 523 men Wilkinson proceeded to burn several towns and destroy crops. Three weeks after starting, on August 21, Wilkinson had accomplished his mission and brought his prisoners to Louisville where they were delivered to Federal custody.

In 1791, Gen. Arthur St. Clair was made U. S. Military Governor of the Northwest Territory. Another expedition against the Indians of the northwest was commenced by

General St. Clair on November 4, 1791, this against those on the Maumee. The U. S. War Department placed 2,000 Regular troops, consisting of infantry, cavalry, and artillery, at the Governor's disposal. St. Clair was unpopular in Kentucky and no volunteers could be found to serve under him; consequently, 1,000 Kentuckians were drafted. This unpopularity is said to have been due to the attitude that St. Clair assumed toward Kentuckians. On this expedition the supply of powder was known to be in bad condition. A private named Ennis (or Innes) from near Danville offered to condition it, but was prevented from doing so by St. Clair's order. Ennis held a commission in the Kentucky Militia, but the exercise of his command was denied to him by Gen. St. Clair who asserted that Ennis was not sufficiently familiar with military tactics. This incident was widely publicized and had a tendency to augment the Kentuckians' dislike of St. Clair.

St. Clair took up his march to the Wabash where he was engaged and defeated by the Indians. After the retreat had been ordered, the surviving troops returned to Fort Jefferson, twenty-nine miles from the battlefield, and then continued on to Fort Washington. When engaged, St. Clair had 1,400 men and 86 officers, of which he lost 890 men and 16 officers in killed and wounded. The Indian forces, led by Little Turtle and Brant, suffered comparatively slight losses.

In the retreat of St. Clair's troops they were compelled to leave behind some of their baggage and artillery pieces. During the winter General Wilkinson obtained a volunteer force to recover the heavy artillery pieces left on the field in the fall of 1791 by St. Clair.

> By accounts just received from Ft. Washington we are informed that General Wilkinson with 300 men marched from that place on the 24th ult. [January, 1792] with intention to bring in the cannon left on the late expedition.
>
> Lexington Feb. 18th [1792]. It is reported, that Gen. Wilkinson has returned to Ft. Washington, and that he brought in with him one piece of artillery, with all the carriages that were left by the

army, together with a number of muskets. That the snow was between two and three feet deep at the battleground.[68]

The following notice appeared in the *Kentucky Gazette* of March 10, 1792, and contains what appears to be a compromise finding (*ante* p. 49):

> I have the pleasure of informing the public that the general court martial which sat at Madison Court House on the 13th inst. for the trial of James Barnett, Esq., County Lieutenant of Madison, who was arrested under the charge of acquiring profits from his conduct with respect to the furnishing of guards on the frontiers of that county have reported to me that he is not guilty so as to merit censure, and therefore, acquitted him; pursuant to which he is restored to his command.
>
> <div align="right">CHAS. SCOTT, <i>Brig. Gen.</i></div>

With the spring of 1792 came another order forbidding scouting and warring by Kentucky troops beyond the Ohio River. This order left Fort Washington, April 2. The following day a band of Indians, apparently aware of the mandate, swooped down on Mason County, stealing thirty-six horses. An expedition was planned by the county lieutenant despite the orders to the contrary. Captains Kenton and McIntyre led twenty-six men in pursuit, coming up with the Indians about forty miles up the Little Miami. Kenton ordered a night attack which was unsuccessful. Thereupon the Kentuckians made their way back home. Then with a reinforced company they went back and succeeded in routing the Indians and recovering "as many horses as could be ridden and led."

Such was the military condition and history of Kentucky when the district became one of the United States in 1792.

NOTES, REFERENCES, AND SOURCES

1. "Draper MSS," 12CC279.
2. *Ibid.*, 11CC39.
3. *Ibid.*, 13CC172.
4. *Ibid.*, 12CC200.
5. *Ibid.*, 11CC39-41.
6. *Ibid.*, 12CC67.
7. *Ibid.*, 12CC65.
8. *Ibid.*, 12CC105.

MILITARY HISTORY OF KENTUCKY 63

9. *Ibid.*, 12CC65.
10. *Ibid.*, 13CC171.
11. Historical writings vary in spelling of this officer's name, using Byrd, Bird, and Birde. He is frequently referred to as "Colonel Byrd."
12. "Draper MSS," 12CC68.
13. *Annals of Southwest Virginia.*
14. "Draper MSS," 11CC241.
15. *Ibid.*, 11CC264.
16. *Ibid.*, 13CC139.
17. *Ibid.*, 11CC3.
18. *Ibid.*, 13CC87.
19. Roosevelt, *Winning of the West*, Vol. 2, p. 249. Roosevelt's spelling is McGarry.
20. "Draper MSS," 12CC67.
21. *Ibid.*, 11CC43.
22. Capt. John Holder was an ardent Tory when he arrived in Kentucky.
23. "Draper MSS," 12CC190.
24. *Ibid.*, 12CC70—See also *Kentucky Pioneers*, by John Mason Brown in *Harper's Magazine*, June, 1887.
25. *Ibid.*, 12CC190.
26. *Ibid.*, 12CC136.
27. *Ibid.*, 13CC172.
28. *Ibid.*, 11CC224.
29. *Ibid.*, 12CC20.
30. *Ibid.*, 12CC50.
31. *Ibid.*, 12CC136.
32. *Ibid.*, 12CC82.
33. *Ibid.*, 13CC12-13.
34. *Ibid.*, 13CC227-228.
35. *Ibid.*, 11CC173-174. Roosevelt gives date as 1781.
36. *Ibid.*, 11CC123.
37. *Ibid.*, 12CC188.
38. *Ibid.*, 11CC100.
39. Clift, *History of Mason County.*
40. Willis, *History of Shelby County.*
41. "Draper MSS," 11CC122.
42. *Ibid.*, 12CC82-84.
43. *Ibid.*, 12CC141-142.
44. *Ibid.*, 13CC152.
45. Roosevelt, *Winning of the West.*
46. "Draper MSS," 12CC136.
47. *Ibid.*, 12CC142.
48. *Kentucky Gazette*, March 8, 1788.
49. *Ibid.*, May 24 and 31, 1788.
50. "Draper MSS," 11CC79.
51. Issue of August 9, 1788
52. Issue of August 30, 1788.
53. Collin's *History of Kentucky*, Vol. 2, p. 181.
54. *Kentucky Gazette*, August 1, 1789.
55. *Ibid.*, February 22 and March 21, 1789.

56. "Draper MSS," 11CC229-230.
57. *Ibid.*, 12CC85-86.
58. *Ibid.*, 11CC99.
59. *Ibid.*, 12CC197.
60. *Ibid.*, 13CC28.
61. *Kentucky Gazette*, December 17, 1790.
62. "Draper MSS," 11CC124.
63. *Kentucky Gazette*, February 26, 1791.
64. "Draper MSS," 13CC239-240.
65. *Ibid.*, 11CC184.
66. *Ibid.*, 12CC241.
67. *Ibid.*, 11CC103.
68. *Kentucky Gazette*, February 18, 1792.

CHAPTER III

STATEHOOD

Statehood failed to bring to Kentucky all of the benefits which were expected. A free hand in repulsing the northwest Indians was hoped for but forbidden by the Federal Government, and to the further distress of the Kentuckians the President persevered in his determination to use the Regulars against the Indians rather than a force of mounted militia which the Kentuckians contended was necessary to a successful handling of the Indian problem.

However, militia organization and discipline were appreciably enhanced under the new government. The first Constitution of Kentucky provided that, "The freemen of this Commonwealth shall be armed and disciplined for its defense * * *."*1 The legislature speedily enacted a statute designed to make Kentucky's militia structure conform to the then recent Federal act which provided for the arrangement of the militia of the several states into divisions, brigades, regiments, battalions, and companies. It also provided for the exception from the militia of Negroes, Mulattoes, and Indians. The age limits fixed for militia duty, including all able-bodied white males, was from eighteen to forty-five years. None were exempt from militia duty except ministers of the gospel. The geographical divisions established in this act are of importance, and by the text of the statute were fixed as follows:

> Be it enacted by the General Assembly that this State shall be divided into two Divisions, viz, all that part lying South of the Kentucky River to compose the first Division; and the residue of the State lying North of the said River to compose the second Division; and the said Divisions shall be divided into Brigades as follows, the Counties of Jefferson, Shelby, Nelson, Washington and Logan to compose the first Brigade; the counties of Lincoln, Madi-

---

* Notes, references, and sources are indicated by numerals. These refer to corresponding numbers at the end of this chapter. For notes on Chapter III see page 118.

son, and Mercer to compose the second Brigade; the counties of Fayette and Woodford to compose the third Brigade; and the counties of Scott, Bourbon and Mason to compose the fourth Brigade; which Divisions and Brigades shall be officered agreeable to the above recited Act: and shall be divided into Regiments as follows: the Counties of Jefferson and Shelby to form the first Regiment, a Battalion in each County; that part of the County of Nelson lying Northwest of the Beech Fork including Bards Town as far up as the Washington line to form the second Regiment; the residue of the said County including Logan County to form the third Regiment, a Battalion in each County; the County of Washington to form the fourth Regiment; the County of Mercer the fifth; the County of Lincoln the sixth; the County of Madison the seventh; the County of Fayette to be divided into three Regiments; all that part of the County lying between the roads leaving from Lexington to Limestone and Tates Creek to form the eighth Regiment; all lying between the said Tates Creek road and the road leading to General Scott's, including the Town of Lexington to form the ninth Regiment; and the residue of the said County to form the tenth Regiment; the County of Woodford to form the eleventh Regiment; the County of Scott to form the twelfth Regiment; all that part of the County of Bourbon lying between the road leading from Lexington to Paris and from thence to the Blue Licks to compose the thirteenth Regiment, the residue of said County lying above said roads and including the Town of Paris to form the fourteenth Regiment; and the County of Mason to form the fifteenth Regiment.

And each Regiment shall be divided into Battalions and the Battalions into Companies, and the bounds of each Battalion and Company shall be ascertained by the Field Officers of each Regiment.

And as is directed by the Constitution, the officers of Companies shall be chosen by the Persons enrolled in each Company.

Be it enacted that the Militia Companies within the several Counties in the State shall on the twenty-first day of July next meet at some convenient place in the bounds of their respective Companies, and by ballot choose a Captain, Lieutenant and Ensign, balloting for the Captain first, and so on in order until the whole are elected, and if there are more candidates than one for any office, and neither have a majority of votes on the first ballot, the two highest in the vote shall be again balloted for, and if each should have an equal number of votes, they shall continue to ballot for the same until one is elected.

The Commanding Officer of each Battalion shall appoint some fit person in each Company to superintend the election for officers who shall without delay transmit to such Commanding Officer the names of the persons elected and the number of votes that each person so elected shall have, who shall immediately transmit the same to the Colonel, who shall without delay send the same to the Governor; and if any one of the Candidates or any other person supposes that the person returned is not duly elected or that any undue influence hath been made use of to gain his or their election, such Candidate or other person or persons, shall immediately at the close of the election or within three days thereafter give notice thereof to the Superintendent or to the Commanding Officer who shall cause the same to be enquired into and if it shall appear to such Commanding officer, that the person or persons complained of is not fairly elected, he shall order another election and the name of the person or persons so elected shall be transmitted as aforesaid.

And the Officers commanding Battalions shall as soon as possible after the bounds of each Battallion is ascertained appoint an Adjutant to the respective Battalions.[2]

This act became operative at once, and under it and on the same day Governor Isaac Shelby appointed the following staff officers; Benjamin Logan, major general of the 1st Division; Charles Scott, major general of the 2d Division; John Hardin, brigadier general of the 1st Brigade; Thomas Kennedy, brigadier general of the 2d Brigade; Robert Todd, brigadier general of the 3d Brigade; and Benjamin Harrison, brigadier general of the 4th Brigade. At the same time the Governor made field officer appointments.

Pioneer Kentuckians seemed to get a peculiar pleasure out of belonging to a military company. Musters and parades savored as much of a social as a military event. The entire countryside turned out on muster days to see their favorite son, nephew, or grandson march to the martial air rendered by their best drummers and fifers. These latter were nearly always from among the Negroes of the community, slaves or freemen.

The command of Federal troops in the northwest was given to Gen. Anthony Wayne during 1792, in place of General St. Clair. In December an effort was made to conciliate the Indians in northwestern Ohio. Col. John Hardin and Major Truman were sent to negotiate a peace treaty with the hostile tribes. Hardin and Truman were murdered by the Indians, and the peace efforts seemed to incite the Indians to further depredations. Frontier stations were compelled to keep a guard constantly against attack. To relieve this situation the Federal Government provided for an additional appointment of spies or scouts to patrol the frontiers. These appointments were made from among the militia of the state, and were paid by the Federal Government for this service. The original roll of scouts or spies in the service of the United States, under orders of Brig. Gen. Charles Scott, on the frontiers of Madison County, from May 1 to August 22, 1792, embraces six names: Alex. Bayless, William Crawford, David Kincaid, Joseph Logsdon, Jacob Miller, and William Moore, with a total of 648 days of service.

At the same time that efforts were being made by the Federal Government toward peace with the Indians, Kentucky was again forbidden to pursue her Indian invaders beyond the state lines. This edict came as a sequel to the attack on a force of about 100 Kentucky Militia under Maj. John Adair, near Fort St. Clair (now Eaton), in the Ohio territory, by Indians under Little Turtle. In this engagement Adair's troops made a valiant stand, but being greatly outnumbered, were compelled to retreat, sustaining a loss of 6 killed and 5 wounded, together with the loss of their camp equipage and 140 pack horses.

The spring of 1793 brought a renewal of Indian raids, mostly plundering and horse stealing. These engagements were marked with impunity, the Indians being fully aware that the Kentuckians were prohibited from pursuing them beyond the Ohio. On the first of April, Morgan's Station, on Slate Creek, suffered an attack by Indians. The Indians captured and carried off nineteen women and children. The next morning relief arrived from Hanseford's, Troutman's, Anderson's, and Plake's stations, and Montgomery's Fort. By nine oclock these troops were assembled, together with some from Bourbon County, to the number of at least 150. Pursuit was directed by Capt. Enoch Smith. Many of the captives were later killed along the line of retreat when the militia appeared to be gaining in pursuit, and the Indians escaped with the rest into the Knobs country and eluded their pursuers.[3] At about the same time a company from Bourbon County took up pursuit of a band of Indians who had killed the Widow Shanks and one of her children at their cabin about ten miles from Grant's Station toward Paris. The Bourbon Company overtook the Indians some twenty miles to the north and without any loss succeeded in killing nearly all that participated in the Shanks attack.[4]

Sometime in May Captain Stevens raised a company and went in search of Indians who had stolen a number of horses in the vicinity of Strode's Station. They discovered an Indian camp on Red River, where many stolen horses were being held by a large party of Indians. Stevens thought it imprudent to make an attack with his small force and retreated. Upon his return three companies were raised, one from Montgomery, commanded by Captain Downing, one from Bush's settlement, commanded by Capt. Billy Bush, and one commanded by Col. William Sudduth. They rendezvoused along Lulbegrud Creek at Oldfields. The command was given to Col. James McMillen. From the point of rendezvous they proceeded to where Stevens had commenced his retreat. The Indians had evidently been alarmed by Stevens and had gone off with the horses. Thereupon each company returned home by a different route, but discovered no fresh Indian sign.

Another source of anxiety to the new state came during the summer of 1793 through the establishment of Jacobin clubs in central Kentucky by the anti-Federalists. Genet, the Minster of France, sent agents into Kentucky for the purpose of organizing an expedition against New Orleans and the Spanish possessions along the Mississipi. A commission as a "Major General in the Armies of France" was tendered to George Rogers Clark. Upon his acceptance thereof Clark proceeded to issue proposals for aggressive moves against the Spanish posts. Many prominent persons in the state favored the movement because of the economic advantages suggested. The President, during the early fall, had asked Governor Shelby to restrain pro-French sentiment in Kentucky, and a second appeal came from Washington in November, after the Spanish Minister had complained of the armament preparing in Kentucky ostensibly for the use of the French against Spain in the Mississippi country. The President suggested legal prosecution, and in case of necessity the use of the militia to suppress pro-French activities. About the same time General Wayne informed Governor Shelby that the Regular cavalry, wintering in Kentucky, was at the Governor's disposal to suppress any illegal expedition which might be fostered in the state. Governor Shelby made it clear to the President that he would not restrain the Kentuckians in their action in the Mississippi question, and thereupon the President ordered General Wayne to occupy Fort Massac with artillery, to be used to arrest any expedition which might favor a foreign power. This incident closed, without a use of the militia, through the influence of Gen. James Wilkinson of Fayette. The militia of central Kentucky, however, engaged in intensive drilling and other preparations during the interim.

Indian depredations of the spring of 1793 forced the President to urge another campaign, and during the summer Federal troops in the West were concentrated at Fort Washington. Governor Shelby was asked for 1,000 mounted riflemen. A call for volunteers was immediately issued, but the previous experiences of the Kentucky Militia under Federal leadership had been so disappointing that none would volunteer, and a draft had to be instituted. The *Kentucky Gazette* of July 6, 1793, carried the following news item and the subsequent official notice:

> We are informed that 1,000 volunteers are to be raised in this State, and that the General and Field officers, who are to command them, are already appointed.
>
> The Commander in Chief having called on me for a general return of the Militia of this State, I am necessitated again to desire that commanding officers of corps (who have not sent forward their returns) will without delay forward them agreeable to the orders of the 15th of February last.
>
> P. BUTLER, *Adjt. Gen. S. K.*

The *Kentucky Gazette* on September 14, 1793, informed the people that:

> Dispatches from the Commissioners at Niagara were received at Headquarters on Wednesday last, in 18 days from that place, with information that no treaty with the Indians had taken place, and that the Commissioners were on their return; in consequence of which the army are under marching orders, and expresses sent forward to this State for the Volunteers to rendezvous the 20th inst. at Georgetown.

Among the communications of the Governor with State Militia commanders pertaining to the raising of troops is the following letter:

GEORGETOWN, *September 28, 1793.*

SIR: I have just received dispatches from Maj. Gen. Wayne containing a requisition of me, for such a number of militia of the State to be drafted, and marched forward to him as will make up the deficiency of the mounted volunteers that were called for by him heretofore. You will therefore immediately proceed to draft from your regiment of militia under your command, sixty-five men, and to march them to the place on the tenth day of next month; notwithstanding the men may be drafted, I am authorized by General Wayne to say, that all such of them as come forward properly mounted and equipped, shall be considered as mounted volunteers and paid accordingly on condition they join the Legion and the Kentucky Volunteers, at the head of the line at Ft. Jefferson on or before the 15th day of October next.

You are sensible that the honor and interest of the State will so much depend on the success of the present expedition, that I need say little to urge you, to make every exertion to send your quota of men into the field. I am with great respect your most ob. servant

ISAAC SHELBY

To LIEUT. COL. LEVI TODD
Fayette County.

The Kentucky Militia so drafted reached Wayne in October. The season was too far advanced for active operations, and therefore the Kentuckians were discharged. After these troops were home for some time and still unpaid, considerable unrest developed and resulted in a resolution of the House of Representatives being directed to Governor Shelby, as follows:

Resolved, that the Governor be requested to make a statement of the Scouts and guards called into the service of the State and also the number of officers and soldiers ordered into the service of the United States, with the amount of additional pay accruing to the same under his assurance to them.

On December 5, 1793, the Governor replied to this resolution and submitted the data asked. His reply included the following mention of the Wilderness Road Guard:

The garrison stationed on the Wilderness Road, in all 40 non-commissioned privates under the command of two Subaltern Officers, would have been entitled by law to the additional pay allowed by the State to its Militia when called into the Service of the United States if they had been ordered out monthly as militia. The Scouts or spies called into service during the season have been employed at the expense of the United States under powers vested in me by the Sec'y. of War for that purpose.

During the Spring of 1794, Maj. Sam Downey and Colonel Lane, then militia captains, made an appointment, for as many men as were willing to go out on a scout into the mountain country, to meet at Mud Lick. On the first of April, about fifty men assembled; most of them were mounted. They had called by at Morgan's Station for J. Wade to go along as pilot. Because of the objection to the use of horses or shoes which would leave tracks that the Indians would recognize, so many of the volunteers refused to go that the number in the scout party was reduced to thirteen. This small company sighted Indians along Red River, on the night of April 2, and being greatly outnumbered were forced to retreat. Shortly afterward Col. William Sudduth raised a company of men and marched with them up Red River, above the Narrows, then across on the waters of Licking and back home without discovering any Indians.[5]

The following summer 1,500 Kentucky Volunteers, under Gen. Charles Scott, joined the Regulars under General Wayne. After another fruitless effort to make peace with the Ohio Indians, Wayne, on August 20, ordered an attack at Fallen Timbers, the strategy employed resulting in a complete rout of the 2,000 Indians and 70 Canadians in about an hour. The Indians fled toward a near-by British fort, leaving forty dead on the field against thirty-three of Wayne's men killed and forty wounded. News of this victory had a pacifying effect on the Six Nations of the East and the Cherokee in the South. Thereafter only small bands of Indians, usually bent on horse stealing, came into the state, and to these, few killings are attributed.

In August, 1794, Col. William Whitley commanded an expedition against the Southern Indians for the purpose of recovering stolen horses. The following extracts are from a letter of John E. King, who acted as adjutant on the expedition. This letter was written to the editor of the *Kentucky Gazette* on September 25, 1794, and stated in part that: "on the 30th of August Col. Wm. Whitley arrived at Nashville with 100 well equipped volunteers from Kentucky." "At the general rendezvous Colonel Whitley was appointed Colonel Commandant." Whitley's forces "surrounded the town called Nico-Jack." A battle ensued and "the action continued half an hour; our damage was two slightly wounded; we killed 54 and took 19 prisoners; amongst the killed was old Chief Breath." Colonel Whitley proceeded up the river to "Runningwatertown," which he sacked. "About $1,200 worth of spoils were saved and divided among the men." "He burned in all 150 houses." This excursion had barely been completed when the following notice made its appearance in the *Kentucky Gazette:*

October 9th, 1794.
I take this method to inform the public that on the 25th of this instant [sic], I intend to set out from Mr. Samuel Ewing's, who lives in the County of Mercer, on the road leading to Cumberland, intending to be at Nashville in Cumberland on the first day of November next in order to chastise the Indians that are our enemies, and have declared themselves as such to the U. S. The regulations on the success of this business will be decided by the officers whose pleasure it may be to procure companies for the service, Etc.
BENJAMIN LOGAN.

In 1795 the manner of guarding Bourbon Furnace was changed, for fears were entertained that the Indians would be troublesome. Capt. John McIntyre was commissioned by the Board of War to raise the existing guard to thirty men and employ two spies for the furnace for the ensuing six months.[6] McIntyre determined to use his guards for spy duty. The guards were untrained in scout duty and became easy prey for the Indians. Many fatalities of the year are attributed to McIntyre's foolhardy economy. In an interview years later, J. Wade, who had been one of the furnace guard spies, related that early in 1795 the Indians made frequent raids into Bath and adjoining counties. They killed Neely McGuire, one Yeates, and George Barnett. "The 4th was one Ratliffe, a soldier. Wolfe and Ratliffe, two of Mc-

Intyre's soldiers, had been sent out by McIntyre as spies. As they were going up Ratliffe crossed a branch of Beaver." * * * "The Indians shot at Ratliffe and got him and run Wolfe almost to death before he could get in to the Furnace." Consequently the guard was continued another year and discontinued after 1796, when Indian raids ceased.

An advertisement in the *Kentucky Gazette* of June 6, 1795, shows that at that late date Wilderness Road travelers were still protected by a militia guard:

> WILL BE LET to the lowest bidder, at Danville on Tuesday the 30th inst. The contract for supplying the three garrisons posted on the Wilderness road for the next tour of six months duty, which will commence on the 8th of July next.

On November 17, 1797, General James Wilkinson left Fort Wayne with a detachment of light dragoons, two companies of infantry, and a company of artillery and engineers, together with necessary stores and equipment for establishing a post on the Mississippi within the vicinity of Kaskaskia. The post was to be garrisoned by the Kentucky troops which accompanied General Wilkinson. The determination to establish this post was given up in consequence of tranquility being restored in that quarter. General Wilkinson had proceeded but about forty miles from Fort Wayne, down the Wabash, when notified that the post would not be established.[7]

On November 28, 1797, Gov. James Garrard addressed a joint session of the legislature during which he advocated strengthening the military defense of the state. He said in part:

> The deranged state of our militia requires your particular notice. I have never been able to obtain a return of the strength and state of the militia, since I came into office, although it has been an object of continual inquiry. It is not only of consequence that the militia should be properly organized for defense; but the necessary instruments of defense should also be provided; and I am sorry to say, that the State is absolutely destitute both of arms and ammunition.

In 1799 Kentucky's second constitution became operative. It provided that "The freemen of this Commonwealth

(Negroes, Mulattoes, and Indians excepted) shall be armed for its defense * * *."[8] The duty-age limit was eighteen to forty-five years. Clergymen alone continued exempt by statute from military duty of any sort.

On December 23, 1806, the legislature passed an act to prevent unlawful enterprises in the state in order to keep Aaron Burr from further activity in Kentucky against Spain.[9] Under this law measures were immediately taken to order out portions of the militia. Before the militia could be assembled at their posts, all the boats of Burr not intercepted by the authorities of Ohio effected a passage to the mouth of the Cumberland. The two companies of militia which were at this time under the command of Gen Joseph Winlock, of Shelby County, were assembled upon the banks of the Ohio River at Louisville in December, 1806, to intercept Burr's fleet, pursuant to the instructions of Gov. Christopher Greenup. Capt. Johnathan Taylor commanded one company and Capt. Jesse Helmes, the other. The latter company was in actual service from December 25, 1806, to January 26, 1807.

The *Western World* (Frankfort) carried the following news items:

> Orders have been issued from the War Office to the Governors of the Several States, making requisition of 100,000 militia, to be ready to take the field at a moments warning, and authorizing the acceptance of volunteers (Issue of July 30, 1807).
>
> * * * The President of the United States has demanded from this State 5,212 troops, to be held in readiness to march at a moments warning, to be raised either by accepting volunteers or by draft. A volunteer troop of horse is now endeavoring to be raised in Frankfort, consisting chiefly of young gentlemen, who are extremely anxious that a sufficient number may be raised, organized, and kept in readiness for the service (Issue of August 30, 1807).
>
> On Saturday, Aug. 29th, the 42nd regiment under the command of Col. Geo. Trotter, Jr. mustered in Lexington for the purpose of raising its quota of the militia ordered to be held in readiness by the President of the United States. The allotment to this regiment was as follows, viz: 1 Captain, 1 lieutenant, 1 ensign and 87 privates.

The soldiers volunteered as follows, viz:

Under Capt. Vanpelt 103 Infantry)

Under Capt. Tilford 33 Horse) exclusive of officers who were enrolled and notified to hold themselves in readiness to march at a moments warning.

Also the following companies turned out as volunteers and intend offering their services to the governor, viz:

Captain Bodley's men, 25 Light Infantry
Captain Foley's men, 59 Light Riflemen
Captain Hudson's men, 35 Light Riflemen

Making in the whole 255 men exclusive of officers (Issue of September 3, 1807).

In the *Palladium* (Frankfort) on September 3, 1807, the following news item appeared that shows Scott County's military strength in that year:

The Officers of the 12th Regiment of Kentucky Militia, Scott County, composed of 18 companies, assembled in the Courthouse at Georgetown, to make arrangements for the requisition of militia from this regiment—after the accomplishment of which they appointed a committee consisting of Gen. John Payne, Col. J. Thompson, Majors J. V. Webb and David Thompson. James and Richard M. Johnson, Esqs. were to prepare an address declarative of their sentiments [The "sentiments" referred to were those in regard to the attitude of Great Britain toward the United States].

On January 13, 1808, Gov. Charles Scott carried his militia troubles to the legislature in an address, a part of which was as follows:

* * * The aspect of our foreign affairs portends serious consequence to the Union and as calls may be reasonably expected to be made on this State by the General Government for the aid of a portion of our militia, it seems indispensably necessary so to organize our system in that respect as to give the most speedy and prompt effect to such requisitions, and it will be further necessary to consider whether the present militia laws be adequate to the repelling of invasions and suppressing of insurrections. On a well regulated militia we may safely rely for our internal quietude and for our defense in the first moments of a war and to obtain this statutory measure I submit to the wisdom of the Legislature:

1st. Some effective measure for compelling a more speedy compliance with duties required of such officers as may be specially charged to perform them.

2nd. A certain time fixed for making the annual returns to the Adjutant General.

3rd. That no compensations be made to the Brigade Inspectors until they produce the Brigadier General's certificate of their having made a complete Brigade return within limited time.

4th. That the duties of the Adjutant General be more particularly defined.

5th. To provide for removing those officers who may unreasonably absent themselves from their command, or who may be rendered incapable of discharging their duties either through bodily infirmities or mental derangements; and

6th. To define more particularly the mode of making resignations.

Evidently there was little heed paid to this message for on December 13, 1808, Governor Scott returned to the legislature with a word picture which he hoped would give him the appropriation necessary to equip the troops that he then had in training. In part he said:

> It cannot have escaped your attention that on our days of muster and review, many of them are frequently armed with a gun without a lock and some even less than this mere apology for a weapon. Shall it be permitted with such arms for the standing defenders of this Country to parade? I intend not a reflection on my countrymen, for it is but too true, from the scarsity of arms in our state that they are frequently unable to procure better. Permit me Gentlemen, most earnestly to recommend this subject to your consideration. Our parent state has set an example on this occasion well worthy our zealous imitation. It is by establishing the manufacture of arms and warlike accoutrements of every description amongst ourselves, that the evil alone can be remedied. A few cents annually from each citizen devoted to this important object, will produce incalculable advantage and if anyone values his liberty or his independence, he will not murmur at the tribute or the appropriation. It will be a tribute of freedom, and an appropriation for national existence. I am naturally led to these observations from a late requisition made by the President of the United States through the Secretary of War, upon this State, for her quota (being 5005) of the 100,000 Militia directed to be raised upon his orders under the act of congress passed 30th March last, to be detached, organized, armed and equipt, including blankets and knapsacks, and to be ready to march at a moment's warning. I have directed all this to be done but alas! I fear the means are wanting! We have patriotic citizens enough, ready to devote their lives and fortunes to the service of their country; but where are their arms! Where their muskets—bayonets—cartouch boxes—swords, pistols and cannon? The time demands them and yet the difficulty of procuring them is next to an impossibility * * *.

The Governor published the following general order by the direction of the U. S. Secretary of War for the purpose of disbanding the militia, 5,005 of which had been in active training and under orders.

> The Governor and Commander in Chief is happy in having it in his power to announce to the Militia of the State that a late communication of the President of the United States through the Secretary of the Department of War, the detachment of 5,005 Militia, as the quota required to be held in readiness equipt, * * * [to be disbanded]. The officers and men therefore composing said detachment are accordingly discharged * * *.
> Given at Frankfort this 22nd day of May 1809.
>
> CHAS. SCOTT.

The Filson Club, Louisville, has an original inventory of the personnel and equipment of the 2d Division Kentucky State Militia, for 1809. This old document is signed with the flowing signature of "Green Clay, Maj'r Gen'l," eminent Kentucky militarist of his day. It was presented to the club upon its golden anniversary by Miss Mabel C. Weeks, of the New York Public Library. The document is in an excellent state of preservation and the neat handwriting is still legible. Nine brigades of the division were under command of Brig. Gen. Benjamin Letcher and thirteen brigades were led by Brig. Gen. Samuel Letcher. There were 4,372 men and officers in the 2d Division, of which 3,989 were "rank and file" composed entirely of infantry. The listed equipment included 93 swords, 57 espontoons, 1,825 rifles, 315 musquets, 17 scabbards and belts, 3,377 flints, 222½ pounds of powder, 9,608 loose balls, 20 standards, 3 steel rods, 29 drums and 29 fifes. The rods were used in surveying, and "espontoon" is the old spelling of "pontoon." There were seventeen horses, seventeen saddles, four breastplates and four pillons, the latter an old name for saddle blankets.

A note at the bottom of the inventory related that "the above horses, bridles, etc., belong to the generals and field officers."

Besides the major general and his two brigadier generals, there were 2 aides-de-camp, a brigadier quartermaster, 9 lieutenant colonels, 18 majors, 8 adjutants, 7 quartermasters, 3 surgeons, a surgeons's mate, 74 captains, 71 lieutenants, 67 ensigns, 4 sergeants major, 3 fife majors, 3 quartermaster sergeants, and 230 sergeants.

In the fall of 1811 war with Great Britain loomed, and drills became more frequent. In further preparation for such a war Governor Scott again on December 3, 1811, urged the legislature to make provision for arming Kentucky's militia. Excerpts from this message are as follows:

> The Governor of the Indiana Territory having received orders to establish some posts on the lands lately ceded by several Indian Tribes up the Wabash was attacked treacherously on the night of the 6th of November last, by a large party of Indians—When to the honor of our countrymen, though taken under every disadvantage and not superior in number, the enemy was repulsed on a hard fought field, with the loss however which is deeply to be regretted of a number of valuable lives. The hand of British intrigue is not difficult to be perceived in this thing. The movements of the savage in that quarter have indicated it for some time past. The subject of our Militia and arms, however frequently heretofore urged by my former communications to the Legislature, ought not to be overlooked in a season like the present * * *. Our first object should be to obtain arms—If the establishment of an armory, which is so highly desirable, as furnishing a constant supply, is not from its expense and the difficulty of procuring, at present in our power, we should keep it in view—and exert ourselves to raise a competent fund for that object in a way least likely to be oppressive to our citizens. It appears probable to me, however, that we could command a temporary supply from the State of Virginia who is manufacturing them in considerable numbers and perfection. If five thousand stand could be procured, we might be able to pay for them by instalments, which would not be very sensibly felt * * *.

In June, 1812, Congress declared war on England. In anticipation Gen. James Wilkinson had established a recruiting office in Lexington on May 2, 1812. As soon as it became known that a requisition had been made on Kentucky for troops, even before the Governor's orders arrived in Lexington, a company of volunteers was formed and its services tendered. Fayette County speedily raised companies commanded by Captains N. G. Hart, S. W. Megowan, John Hamilton, George Trotter, Jr., John Edmonson, and a Captain Arnold. The latter two were in command of companies of riflemen. Those from Lexington and Fayette County who participated in the war included W. O. Butler (later major general), Maj. Benjamin Graves, on the staff of Colonel Lewis; James Overton, aide to General Winchester;

Charles Carr, paymaster of Dudley's regiment; Charles S. Todd, subsequently Minister to Russia; Thomas Bodley, deputy quartermaster general, and later adjutant general; and Gen. John M. McCalla. Col. John Allen, noted lawyer of Shelbyville, raised a regiment of riflemen and joined General Harrison. He took part in the Battle of Brownstown, January 18, 1813. Colonel Allen's regiment became a part of Gen. John Payne's brigade, and marched with the first troops from Kentucky to reinforce General Hull at Detroit.

Captain Edmonson's company was connected with Colonel Allen's 1st Rifle Regiment, and Captain Trotter's with Col. James Simrall's cavalry command. Another regiment, commanded by Col. William Lewis, and composed of the companies of Captains Hart, Hamilton, and Megowan, from Fayette; Captains Gray, and Price, from Jessamine; Captain Williams, from Montgomery; Captains Martin and Brassfield, from Clark, assembled at Lexington on the fourteenth of August to march to the general rendezvous at Georgetown. Incidentally, Clark County sent eleven companies to the front in this war.

At home the outbreak of the war was accepted as a signal to make taboo every article of British manufacture. Clothing for the militia was made at home and varied widely in pattern, color, quality, and texture. The hunting shirt alone showed a uniformity that betokened Kentucky. Only in official ranks did a uniform appear and that was frequently one worn by an older member of the family in the Revolutionary War. Through the patriotism of her people Kentucky sent her troops into the field without expense to the United States Government for clothing or equipment. Payment to the soldiers was made by the United States on a basis of eight dollars per month, but none were paid until after the close of the war.

Before the Kentucky troops could reach Hull, he had surrendered the Michigan territory, and an attempt to invade Canada from the Niagara frontier failed. The loss of the Michigan territory seemed to liberate the Indian tribes of the northwest and they poured down on the western frontiers in

GOVERNOR ISAAC SHELBY

MAJ. GEN. WILLIAM HENRY HARRISON

great numbers. Kentucky's losses at Tippecanoe and the several threats of Indian invasion produced a belligerent spirit in the state. Seven thousand volunteers offered their services, and 1,500 were already on the march toward Detroit when they received news of Hull's surrender. Hull's surrender seemed to increase Kentucky's military ardor as demonstrated by the fact that when the Governor called for 1,500 volunteers for an expedition against the Indian villages of northern Illinois, more than 2,000 answered the call.[10] These rendezvoused at Louisville under General Hopkins, and from there began their march into the Indian country.

The balance of the Kentucky Volunteers were placed under Gen. W. H. Harrison, the Governor of the Indian Territory. General Harrison had been given the rank of major general of the Kentucky Militia, by Governor Scott. The same rank was later given Harrison in the U. S. Army and he was placed in command of the militia called from Kentucky, Ohio, Pennsylvania, and Virginia, with whatever Regular troops might be available, to proceed against the Indians of the Northwest, retake Detroit, and then march on upper Canada. For this undertaking ample men and provisions were provided, but transportation facilities were inadequate, and consequently the troops suffered greatly from hunger and lack of clothing. So bad were conditions that Colonel Allen's regiment, called Kentucky's best, was restrained with difficulty from returning home.

On January 1, 1813, the Kentucky Volunteers, under General Winchester, were at Fort Defiance. Plans were formulated to attack Detroit, and accordingly the Kentuckians, with Wells' regiment of Regulars, started for the Rapids which they reached on the tenth. Here it was planned that the command of Harrison should be met before proceeding further. Four days later news was received that two companies of Canadians and some 200 Indians were at Frenchtown, on the River Raisin, within striking distance. Frenchtown was thirty-eight miles from the Rapids and about eighteen miles from the British fort, Malden. A detachment of 990 Kentucky Militia was ordered to attack the Canadians at Frenchtown. Colonel Lewis was in command of the Kentuckians, and under him were Colonel Allen and Majors Graves and Madison. On the eighteenth of January the forces met and the British and Indians were compelled to retreat. Intelligence was sent to General Winchester, who dispatched Colonel Wells with 250 Regulars to reinforce Colonel Lewis. Through the carelessness of Colonel Lewis, British reinforcements were overlooked, thus permitting some 2,000 British and Indians to attack and rout the U. S. Regulars who were subjected to heavy slaughter. Kentuckians, regardless of rank, united in an effort to bring the Regulars, under assault, within picket lines, but were unable to do so. Not a Kentuckian who passed the picket line returned. The command of the Kentuckians devolved upon Majors Madison and Graves, who for four hours kept the enemy at bay. The British commander then offered General Winchester terms of surrender, which were accepted, only to be violated later when an adequate guard was not furnished by the British, as stipulated, for the protection of the wounded U. S. soldiers against the drunken and frenzied Indians. As a result all of the wounded were massacred, including Major Graves and Captains Hart and Hickman.

Lt. Col. George Madison was second in command under Col. John Allen. Madison was held as hostage after the massacre of the River Raisin. The British were apprehensive of retaliatory measures for the broken faith of the British commander, Proctor. Madison, at the surrender, had exacted from Proctor a promise of safety for prisoners of war, and since Madison was held in high esteem by his compatriots he was considered an especially desirable hostage.

The following article called *Recollections of The Late War, The River Raisin Battle,* appeared in the *Kentucky Yeoman* (Frankfort) on May 7, 1833:

> Upon the 11th day of January, 1813, the left wing of the Northwestern Army under the direction of Gen. James Winchester, reached the foot of the Rapids of the Maumee of the lakes; the contemplated point of assembling the N. W. Army, under the command of the General-in-chief, William H. Harrison. Winchester encamped his division of the army (about 2,500 men) on the further bank of the Maumee, upon a handsome rising piece of

ground gradually descending in all directions from the center of his camp. His whole command remained in this position until the morning of the 17th of January. Between the 11th and 17th various persons had come to Winchester's camp from the settlements on the Raisin all urging the propriety of a movement upon Frenchtown, a village upon the Raisin 36 miles distant, then in the occupation of the British and Indians. Winchester's latest information was (brought by a confidential agent of Gen. Harrison) that if the American's did not very quickly succor the settlement on the Raisin, that what of property the enemy could not carry away, they would destroy. This determined Winchester to consider the matter. He accordingly, during the night of the 16th, held a consultation with his field officers. The result was that 420 men under the command of Col. William Lewis would set out early on the morning of the 17th to occupy Frenchtown. In conforming with orders Lewis proceeded as far as Presquille, 18 miles, where he arrived at night. An hour afterwards he was joined by Lt. Col. John Allen with 100 men, thus making his whole command 520. Late in the night a person who had made his escape from Frenchtown, of the name of Day, gave information to Lewis of the strength, position, resources, etc. of the enemy. There were two companies of Canadian volunteers, commanded by Elliott and Madison; a fragment of a company of artillerists with 400 Indians, making altogether 500 or 600 belligerents, all under the command of Major Reynolds. Col. Elliott was expected there some time on the 18th with a considerable reinforcement of Indians and Canadians. It then became the indispensable duty of Lewis to anticipate the contemplated junction of Elliott with Major Reynolds. He was bound to do so, as well by the first object he had in view under the orders of Winchester, as by the recent information of Day. Hence before dawn of the morning of the 18th, after consulting with his confidential officers, he had 3 copies of the following order prepared and placed in the hands of the chief of battalions, Allen, Madison and Graves. This order was not read to the detachment until the very eve of the battle:

'SOLDIERS!

Your ancient enemy is before you. The wrongs that he had inflicted upon your country are fresh in your memory. That country calls upon you this day to vindicate her honor and her interests by inflicting upon him condign punishment. In the hour of battle, remember what the Patriot Orator said to you at Georgetown, "You have the double character of the Americans and Kentuckians to sustain." Do so as I feel assured you will and all will be well.

WM. LEWIS'

The army moved before daylight, sometimes on land and a part of the time on the ice of the lake, on which latter place the soldiers threw their blankets, and on them partook of a cold snack about 12 or 1 o'clock. Coming within 3 miles of Frenchtown, where the intermediate country is covered with sedge grass, the commander formed his men in the following order: Col. Allen on the right, Major Graves on the left, and Major Madison in the center. It was at this moment the general order was read. Ballard, acting as major, brought on the attack; as we were forming a piece of artillery was fired at us. The first fire gave to these raw soldiers some alarm, its contents passed 20 feet at least above our heads. A second shot was directed at us, which was answered by the well known voice of Strode, who could, more than any other human being, imitate a cock. That gave us moral confidence for the moment, when Ballard passing the river upon the ice charged upon the town. Battalions of the Graves and Madison regiments followed him and the town was carried in a few minutes. It was at this moment, while the gallant commander was congratulating the successful battalions, that he was alarmed at the noise of firing half a mile to the right. Inquiring of the cause, he found that his second in command, with only 100 men had attacked the entire enemy which he had driven from the town. The enemy had retreated before him a half mile enclosed by houses, fence rails, and a vast deal of fallen timber. Col. Lewis putting his spurs to his horse and approaching Col. Allen, found him at bay with the enemy and peremptorially commanded him to retreat and to throw his soldiers on the ground and sedge grass. This order was reluctantly obeyed. Meanwhile James Garrard acting as the aid of Lewis, brought the battalions of Madison and Graves, by a circuitous route into the roar of the enemy which completed their discomfiture. Twelve men were killed of Lewis' command and 55 wounded—and as far as ascertained that 55 of the enemy were killed; the number of wounded was not known.

When news of the massacre reached Kentucky the legislature authorized Governor Shelby to take active command of reinforcements. Four regiments quickly tendered their services, these under Colonels Dudley, Cox, Boswell, and Caldwell. The brigade thus formed was placed under command of Maj. Gen. Green Clay. A portion of these troops was rushed to reinforce General Harrison below the Rapids of the Maumee where he had established Fort Meigs. The Kentucky Volunteers reached that fort on April 12, and on May 1, Proctor moved against the fort. The British were reinforced by a vast Indian Army under Tecumseh. A heavy fire from the British brought spasmodic fire from Fort Meigs, owing to the limited supply of ammunition on hand.

By May 4, General Clay with the other detachment of Kentuckians had reached Fort Defiance. An attempt was made by Captain Leslie Combs and five men to descend the Maumee to announce Clay's approach to the garrison at

Fort Meigs. Orders given to Colonel Dudley were either misunderstood or ignored, and as a result a large part of his command was slaughtered. The British General Proctor now had a force of about 3,200 men to pit against Harrison and Clay's 2,500 that remained fit for duty.

With news of the attack of Fort Meigs, Shelby authorized Col. Richard M. Johnson to march to the relief of Gen. Harrison, and at the same time authorized Col. Johnson to incorporate in his regiment the cavalry companies organized by Captains Whitaker, Coleman and Payne. During the early spring of 1813, Col. Johnson had raised a regiment of mounted riflemen who were attached to the command of General Harrison

The cavalry force which Col. Johnson originally proposed early in 1812 to throw against the Indians was two regiments of eight companies each, with eighty men to a company, which he deemed a sufficient force to cover the entire frontier from Fort Wayne, along the southern end of Lake Erie, down the Illinois River and across to the Ohio River near Louisville. From within this boundary, it was Col. Johnson's proposal, to drive all Indians. The proposition was submitted to the Governor of Kentucky and to Gen. Harrison by the U. S. Secretary of War in December of 1812. In January, 1813, Gen. Harrison, by letter to the War Department, voiced his disapproval of Col. Johnson's proposal.

On the twenty-sixth of February, 1813, Gen. John Armstrong, as U. S. Secretary of War, wrote Colonel Johnson as follows:

SIR:

You are hereby authorized to organize and hold in readiness, a regiment of the mounted volunteers—the organization as to the number of officers and men to be conformable to the military establishment of the United States. The Governor of the State of Kentucky will be required to commission the officers when selected, to serve four months after being called into actual service; and six months if required by the United States—the pay of the officers and men to commence from the actual service and march of the corps, under the direction of the war department. After marching orders, the contractors' and commissaries' agents in the different districts through which it passes, will supply the regiment with forage for the horses, and provisions for the men, if required so to do. The keepers of military stores will also furnish said corps with ammunition on regular returns of the effective force of the regiment. If any difficulty arises as to rank, the commanding general will settle the same, after the corps shall have reached its place of destination.

Upon his return home from Congress on March 22, Colonel Johnson published this letter. This was followed by an open letter setting out his proposals for organizing a regiment, that appeared in a Lexington paper.[11]

Being authorized by the Secretary of War, to raise, organize, and hold in readiness a regiment of Mounted Volunteers, consisting of 1,000 men rank and file, for the term of four months, you are to associate with yourself four other persons of undoubted capacity, integrity and zeal, except where these persons are designated by a letter accompanying these instructions, and organize a company to consist of not less than 80 rank and file, nor more than 100 with all possible dispatch, and as soon as either number shall be enrolled to transmit without delay a muster roll; containing the name of each individual, according to the form herewith submitted. A captain, a first, second and third lieutenants, and an Ensign compose the commissioned officers of a company, and having selected the officers for the sole consideration of confidence in their ability, influence and merit, the promptitude with which the companies are completed will have its influence in fixing the rank of the officers. The right of approving the platoon officers must be reserved, if required, by one third of the company; they must subject themselves to the votes of the men previous to making the company returns, as the commissions will be filled up according to such return.

It is confidently expected that each company will be completed in less than 20 days from the receipt of this authority. The company to elect the non-commissioned officers, having regard to the merit of candidates. The orderly Sergeant should be a man of business and calculation, as well as a soldier. Each company will be divided into ten messes of ten, and numbered, and each man of each mess to be numbered, the first number to be selected by the mess, who shall be head of the mess, and responsible for its good conduct, its discipline, its strict attention to the regulations of the camp police and to the discharge of all other military duties, in the same respect as the captain is responsible for his company to the Major for his battalion, or the Colonel for his regiment. In exercising the companies in the various evolutions, each mess shall stand together in order of its numbers, and each man according to his number, the head of the mess always in front in the column on the right of the line. Each company may receive 20 supernumeraries to supply deficiencies, detachments of advance guards, reserve corps, supply companies, etc. etc.

It will be the duty of the officers to procure if possible, and immediately study *Colonel Doane's Handbook for Infantry*, the best elementary treatise in the English language is particularly recommended.

The men will receive one dollar per day, as long as they find themselves and horses. In consequence of which, and that the movements of the Regiment may be self existent and not dependent upon any contingency, as the public service may require celerity of movement, each individual will commence the line of march with at least 50 days provisions, viz: 25 lbs. Bacon, without bone, 40 lbs. Bread, 2 lbs. Coffee, 5 lbs. sugar, one quart of salt. But to prevent the possibility of inconvenience, with the order of March, each Captain shall be furnished with authority to call upon the Commissary's and contractors agents of the district, through which they pass, for rations and forage.

The black hunting shirt, or a round about coat, to be the uniform of the respective companies, the men will encumber themselves with as little baggage as possible—one pair of overalls lined with leather, that they will not wear in riding, two shirts, a pair of socks, one good pair of shoes and one pair of Mocasons[sic], and black neck-handkerchief, are recommended, one pair of saddle bags and a bag, a strong hardy horse of value 60 or 70 dollars, 2 blankets, one under the other over the saddle, unless both be necessary to go under the saddle, as the horse must not be injured, and daily reports of the situation of the horses will devolve on heads of messes. The arms, a rifle or musket, a tomahawk and butcher knife—those who do not furnish their own arms will be furnished, and the captains are requested in their return to note the number of those who will not furnish their own arms. Each individual who finds his own arms, is advised to take with him at least two pounds of first rate powder and balls or lead in proportion, for which he shall be allowed 50 cents per pound for powder and 25 cents for lead. In case of marching orders, the Regiment will march by companies to some nearest and most convenient point of safety to the seat of action, as the most expeditious and best for the accommodation of the men.

It is designed to form a corps of reserve out of the supernumeraries of the Regiment to be armed with rifles, swords and Pistols. Those who can procure pistols and swords conveniently, are requested to do it. It is presumed, that this Corps is intended to join Gen. Harrison, whenever he shall open the Spring campaign; or in case of necessity, to unite with the 1,600 Rangers now authorized to carry a campaign against the Indians. Each company must have a Bugle or Trumpet. It is recommended to each mess to take one pack horse to the place of general rendezvous, when one person can take back all the pack horses of a company. Each mess is recommended to procure a small narrow axe and every individual a cap of leather for his gun-lock, to keep it dry in bad weather and also four flints.

These details have been given with a view of making this corps useful, efficient and of small expense to the United States, and to the individuals. A corps which opens to the warrior prospect of glory and honor, and the certainty of maintaining the rights of his country, and of avenging the massacre of his countrymen and friends, by the savages, under British influence.

Mar. 23, 1813.   RICHARD M. JOHNSON

Organization of the regiment was speedily accomplished with James Johnson, a brother, as lieutenant colonel, and Colonels Duval Payne and David Thompson as majors.

Johnson's regiment rendezvoused at Newport on May 22, where it was fully armed. On the twenty-fourth day of May, General Harrison, home on a visit to his family (at North Bend, Ohio) received Johnson's regiment into the service of the United States. Colonel Johnson was thereupon ordered to take command of Fort Wayne and the posts on the Anglaize, and from these bases make incursions against the Indians before the expedition against Malden. At once Johnson determined to raise more men, and three lieutenants were sent back to Kentucky to recruit volunteers.

On May 28 the command arrived at Dayton in the Ohio country. Here organization was completed. The 1st Battalion was under Duval Payne, major; its Captains were Elijah Craig, John Payne, Richard Matson, Jacob Elliston, Benjamin Warfield, and R. B. McAfee. The officers of the 2d Battalion were David Thompson, major, with Jacob Stucker, James Davidson, S. R. Combs, W. M. Price and James Coleman, captains.

In a few days Johnson's regiment proceeded from Dayton to St. Mary's where some intensive training was given the volunteers. Meanwhile, Colonel Johnson obtained some friendly Shawnee from Wopoghconata, to act as guides and spies. On the fifth of June the regiment marched toward Fort Wayne, to protect some boats loaded with provisions. From Fort Wayne an excursion was made toward the southeast end of Lake Michigan, heavy baggage having been left at the fort. The Indian towns called Five Medals and White Pigeon were visited and found unoccupied, after which the troops returned to Fort Wayne, fully convinced that the Indians had concentrated at Malden. During July and

August the British employed every possible means of collecting the warriors into that neighborhood.

From Fort Wayne, Johnson's regiment went to Fort Winchester where Colonel Johnson received a message from General Harrison. General Harrison recommended that attacks be made at Raisin and at Brownstown. To attack Brownstown required that a march of about 100 miles be made, and numerous other handicaps were faced by the fatigued regiment, yet Colonel Johnson determined to make the attack as soon as his troops could be put into condition. The next day General Clay informed Colonel Johnson that the British and Indians had threatened to again invest Fort Meigs, and requested Johnson to march there for its relief, which he did at once.

Colonel Johnson and his command celebrated the Fourth of July at Sandusky. There on the fifth Johnson was apprised of the following order:

WAR DEPARTMENT, *June 9, 1813.*

SIR:

General Howard and Governor Edwards urge the necessity of more troops in the quarter; and there being no other disposable force for that purpose at this time, the President directs that you order Colonel Johnson with his regiment of mounted volunteers directly to Kaskaskias, to report to General Howard.

I have the honor, etc.,
JOHN ARMSTRONG

GENERAL HARRISON

Colonel Johnson remonstrated, pointing out that his horses were unfit to make the journey of 400 miles without conditioning, and that it would require at least 30 days to traverse the distance, that other losses of time would leave but about 20 days until the period of enlistment of his men would expire. Nevertheless, the regiment was ordered to march through Kentucky and rendezvous at Vincennes on the twentieth of August.

Then on the thirtieth of July came General Harrison's call for 1,500 Kentucky troops, while Perry was preparing to carry the war to Lake Erie. At that time it was the custom to enlist an army—perhaps of 3,000 or 4,000 men for the performance of some special duty or specific service. For instance, the army of 4,000 Kentucky Militia raised to invade Canada and destroy Proctor's army (Battle of the Thames) were enlisted for 60 days. They accomplished their mission within their term of enlistment, and were back home in sixty-five days. But the little Kentucky army under Gen. Samuel Hopkins, who were in thirty days' time to subdue the Indians of the Wabash section, had not yet found the Indians when their term of enlistment expired.

Immediately upon receipt of Harrison's request Governor Shelby issued the following circular letter to militia commanders throughout the State:

FRANKFORT, *July 31, 1813.*

DEAR SIR:—

The following address to the militia of Kentucky will inform you of the call that has been made upon the governor of Kentucky for reinforcements to the northwestern army, and of my views as to the mode of complying with it. I forward one to you particularly, sir, under the hope that you will exert your influence to bring into the field all the men in your power. Be so good as to acknowledge the receipt of this letter, and apprise me of the calculation which I may make of the numbers of men that can be raised in your county—whether it will suit your convenience to go with us. I shall at all times take pleasure in acknowledging the public spirit by which you will be actuated—and the obligations you will lay me under.

I have the honor to be, very respectfully, sir, your obedient servant,

ISAAC SHELBY

TO THE MILITIA OF KENTUCKY

FELLOW SOLDIERS—

Your government has taken measures to act effectually against the enemy in Upper Canada. General Harrison, under the authority of the President of the United States, has called upon me for a strong body of troops to assist in effecting the grand objects of the campaign. The enemy in hopes to find us unprepared, has again invested Fort Meigs, but he will again be mistaken, and before you can take the field he will be driven from that post.

To comply with the requisition of General Harrison, a draft might be enforced; but, believing as I do, that the ardor and patriotism of my countrymen has not abated, and that they have waited with impatience a fair opportunity of avenging the blood of their butchered friends, I have appointed the 31st day of August next, at Newport, for a general rendezvous of KENTUCKY VOLUNTEERS. I will meet you there in person. I will lead you to the field of battle, and share with the dangers and honors of the campaign. Our services will not be required for more than sixty days after we reach headquarters.

I invite all officers, and others possessing influence, to come forward with what mounted men they can raise; each shall command the men he may bring into the field. The superior officers will be appointed by myself at the place of general rendezvous, or on arrival at headquarters; and I shall take pleasure in acknowledging to my country the merits and public spirit of those who may be useful in collecting a force for the present emergency. Those who have good rifles, and know how to use them, will bring them along. Those who have not, will be furnished with muskets at Newport.

FELLOW CITIZENS! Now is the time to act, and by one decisive blow, put an end to the contest in that quarter.

ISAAC SHELBY

FRANKFORT, *July 31st, 1813*

It is said that Governor Shelby avoided numbers in making his call, so as to keep from giving intelligence to the enemy of what force he would lead into the field. Four thousand Kentuckians responded to the Governor's appeal and after some delay were accepted by Harrison. Johnson's Cavalry had gone on ahead, and on the twentieth of August arrived at Dayton, Ohio. With Captain Coleman's company Johnson pushed on to the Pickaway towns; the balance, of his command followed after drilling for several days at Dayton. The troops proceeded on to Fort Meigs and encamped to await orders. Orders came to join General Harrison at the River Raisin. Here Johnson's men collected and reburied the bones of those massacred there in June, which had been previously buried by Johnson's men after the massacre, but were now unearthed and scattered over the field again.

In the meantime Colonel Croghan and 150 Kentuckians occupied Fort Stephenson and successfully resisted an attack by 1,500 British and Indians. Early in September, Perry engaged and overcame the British fleet, which gave Harrison command of Lake Erie and with it power to throw a large force against Detroit. Proctor began a retreat as soon as he learned that Harrison with a few Regulars and the reinforcements of Shelby were crossing the lake. This retreat of Proctor deprived him of his Indian support except those under Tecumseh who remained faithful. General Harrison, with about 120 Regulars, the Kentucky Infantry and Johnson's Regiment of mounted riflemen, took up pursuit of Proctor. An engagement took place at Moravian Town, on the banks of the Thames on the fifth of October, where about 500 British and over 1,000 Indians held a strategic position. Harrison formed his line of battle with five brigades of Kentucky Militia, under Generals Allen, Caldwell, Chiles, King, and Trotter. British Regulars had been deployed as skirmishers against these. General Harrison ordered Colonel Johnson's cavalry to make an attack. Johnson saw that his entire command could not be used to best advantage against the British, and thereupon ordered that the British be attacked with one battalion while he engaged the Indians with the other. Johnson's men here made possible what a Canadian cavalry officer, Col. G. T. Denison, depicts as the sole victory of the American forces in an open action during the northwest campaign, adding that Johnson's regiment "fought in two capacities in about as many minutes."

Twenty of Johnson's men led by the 68-year-old Col. William Whitley, who was fighting as a private in the Lincoln County Militia, were picked by Colonel Johnson to move to an exposed position at the Battle of the Thames to draw the fire of Tecumseh's hidden warriors.[12] Colonel Johnson rode with this valiant group, so his device must be considered heroic rather than reckless of human life. These twenty men, fired with a desire to avenge the massacre of the Raisin, in which so many of their relatives and neighbors had fallen, knew that the 1,500 guns in the hands of marksmen, as sure of aim as they themselves, were trained upon them, but they neither wavered nor shrank from the sacrifice. When the smoke of the first fire lifted, fifteen of those heroes were dying. Colonel Whitley, was bleeding from a dozen wounds, but still sat erect and beckoned to the battalion to press forward and make the most of the dearly bought advantages.

After the position of the Indians was ascertained, Johnson's main division could advance to better advantage, being then able to pour a deadly fire on the enemy. Johnson's command was reinforced by detachments of infantry from Trotter's, Donaldson's and Simrall's regiments, after the report of the Indian fire on Johnson's men was heard.

The service of Johnson's regiment as a combat unit is concisely related in Brackett's *History of the United States Cavalry:*

> General Harrison had prepared himself for battle during the night, and early on the morning of October 5th, 1813. Seeing the British infantry in the front and on the right in open order, he gave the order to Colonel Richard M. Johnson to charge with his regiment of Kentucky cavalry. This was promptly executed; and the only movement worthy the name of a cavalry charge which occurred during the second war with Great Britain was gallantly carried out. By it, in fact, Proctor's infantry force was entirely broken up and captured. Johnson then turned to the left, and attempted to charge a large Indian force which was stationed in the edge of a growth of timber, but he found the ground was swampy, and his horses commenced sinking. Seeing this, he ordered his men to dismount, and made the attack on foot. Tecumseh, with his braves, was ready to meet him, and, uttering his Shawnee war cry and discharging his rifle, the Indians and Kentuckians were soon mingled in mortal combat * * *. The fight in the timber was picturesque as well as deadly, the Indians being dressed in their plumes and war paint, and the Kentuckians dressed in hunting shirts of jean fringed with red, wearing round hats with long plumes of white tipped with red. Our victory was complete, and the volunteers soon after returned to Kentucky, where they were discharged.

The charge against the British produced surrender, but that against the Indians under Tecumseh succeeded only after the fall of their leader.[13] This victory closed hostilities in the Northwest. On their return from the Thames the Kentucky troops reached Frenchtown, where they picked up and buried more skeletons of massacred Americans. Then they started homeward and reached Maysville on November 4, 1813, and thereupon were discharged. Notwithstanding General Harrison's successful campaigns against the

British and Indians, he was succeeded by Gen. Duncan MacArthur, once a resident of Mason County. This was in the spring of 1814.

The following excerpts from *A Journal of Kentucky Volunteers Commanded by Gen. Winchester in 1812-1813-1814* portray vividly many of the experiences and hardships of the Kentucky troops in this campaign:

Agreeable to general order, the following regiments rendezvoused at Georgetown, Aug. 14, 1812, to wit:

The first regiment was commanded by Col. John M. Scott, the fifth regiment was commanded by Col. Wm. Lewis, and the first rifle regiment by Col. John Allen, the 17th U. S. regiment by Col. Samuel Wells; the whole under command of Brigadier-General Payne.

16th—The troops paraded early in the morning and were reviewed by Governor Scott. We paraded again at 10 o'clock, and marched to a convenient place in close order where the Rev. Mr. Blythe preached a short sermon, and the Hon. Henry Clay delivered an appropriate address.

17th—The troops were inspected by Major Garrard.

18th—We drew two months pay in advance. There being a general complaint amongst the volunteers respecting sixteen dollars, which were expected to be drawn in lieu of clothing. Major Graves paraded his battalion, and gave them their choice to go on without the sixteen dollars or return home. Six chose to return; these to fix an odium upon them were drummed out of camp and through town.

19th—We commenced our march in high spirits to join Gen. Hull at Detroit, and on in Canada. Each regiment for convenience and speed marched separately to Newport. We arrived at Newport on the 24th; it is 80 miles from Georgetown.

It rained most of the time, which made it disagreeable travelling, and encamping. These hardships tended a little to quench the excessive patriotic flame that had blazed so conspicuously at different musters and barbecues. We drew arms and accoutrements and crossed the Ohio on the 27th. Our destiny was thought to be Ft. Wayne.

Sept. 18th—We arrived at Fort Wayne and met a regiment of 500 mounted riflemen and cavalry from Kentucky.

20th—The Kentucky mounted riflemen started to St. Mary's under command of General Harrison in order to pursue the Indians in some other quarter; their number was about 1500.

Nov. 4th—Four of this army have gone to the silent tomb today never more to visit their friends in Kentucky, the fever is very prevalent in Camp; nearly every day there is one or more buried.

7th—We received information from Kentucky by passengers, of a quantity of clothing sent out for the volunteers.

Dec. 21st—The general has ordered the Commandant of regiments to cause each company to be provided with a sufficient number of sleds to convey their baggage to the Rapids [of St. Mary's River]. It is said these sleds are to be pulled by men, as we have not a horse in camp able to pull an empty sled.

27th—Part of the clothing arrived from Kentucky.

Jan. 10th—Many of the horses gave out and sleds broke down; consequently the plunder had to be pulled or carried by the men. I have seen six Kentuckians substituted instead of a horse, pulling their plunder, drudging along through the snow, and keeping pace with the foremost.

Jan. 25th—Arrived in camp this morning, clothing from Kentucky. A Frenchman who lived in this village [Frenchtown] said when word came the Americans were in sight, there was an old Indian smoking at his fireside; the Indian exclaimed "Ho, de Mericans come. I suppose Ohio men come, we give them another chase": [alluding to the time they chased Gen. Tupper from the Rapids]. He walked to the door smoking, apparently very unconcerned and looked at us until we formed the line of battle, and rushed on them with a mighty shout. He then called out "Kentuck, by God," and picked up his gun and ran to the woods like a wild beast.

1813—Capt. Hart of Lexington was among the wounded in the battle Jan. 22, 1813, at Frenchtown, on the River Raisin. He was one of four prisoners whom the British agreed to send by sleigh to Malden, and instead delivered them to the Indians, by whom they were tomahawked.

The only service of importance performed by the Kentucky Militia in the northwest after the Battle of the Thames was the part they took in what is known as "MacArthur's Raid." Early in August, 1814, the U. S. War Department ordered General MacArthur to organize an expedition against the Pottowatamie Indians on Lake Michigan, who were indulging in a spree of raiding with more vigor than was usual. General MacArthur called upon the Governors of Ohio and Kentucky for 500 mounted men each. They were to rendezvous on September 20, at Urbana, Ohio. The Governor of Kentucky was late in receiving the order, but his quota was encamped at Urbana before the appointed time. On September 20 they were organized into a battalion of seven companies under the command of Col. Peter Dudley of Frankfort, with Elijah Berry as adjutant, Robert Crouch, quartermaster, James I. Pendleton, paymaster, and Dr. John Roberts, surgeon. Kentuckians formed so large a part of the troops participating that it is often spoken of as "Dudley's Raid."

The force was organized and on its way into the Indian country by September 28. They found no Indians, so pushed on to Detroit, where they learned of the critical condition of the American forces at Fort Erie in upper Canada. This explained the absence of the Indians along Lake Michigan. General MacArthur determined to attempt a diversion which would draw the attention of the British forces from Fort Erie where they were sorely pressing the American force. Accordingly, with his 500 Kentucky troops and about 200 from Ohio, MacArthur crossed the St. Clair River, presumably after the Indians, and pushed rapidly into central Canada. At Malcom's Mill the Canadian Militia fled, filling the whole country with alarm. The little band from Kentucky and Ohio, in a strange land that fairly bristled with hostile Canadian Militia, British Regulars, and the warriors of the Six Nations, burned most of the mills upon which the country, as well as the British Army in America, depended for breadstuffs, took many prisoners, and finally were gladdened by the reports of scouts that the American Army had made a get-away from Fort Erie and had reached Buffalo, New York. Then began a retreat of more than 200 miles to Detroit. They reached United States territory and were discharged from duty November 18, 1814, less than two months from the time of rendezvous at Urbana, Ohio. This terminated the war in the Northwest.

The landing of the British force under Sir Edward Packenham at New Orleans on December 22, 1814, brought another call for Kentucky troops. On January 4, 1815, 2,500 Kentucky Militia under Maj. Gen. John Thomas landed at New Orleans to reinforce Gen. Andrew Jackson who, with two regiments of Regulars and about 3,000 Louisiana Militia, poorly armed and untrained, had been unable to prevent the advance of Packenham's troops. When the Kentuckians arrived, arms were available for less than a quarter of the men, the arms having been delayed in transit by boat down from Pittsburgh. Through the illness of General Thomas the

BRIG. GEN. CHARLES SCOTT

FRANKFORT, July 31st, 1813.

DEAR SIR,

THE following address to the militia of Kentucky will inform you of the call that has been made upon the governor of Kentucky for a reinforcement to the North Western Army: and of my views as to the mode of complying with it. I forward one to you particularly, sir, under the hope that you will exert your influence to bring into the field all the men in your power. Be so good as to acknowledge the receipt of this letter, and apprise me of the calculations which I may make of the number of men that can be raised in your county---and whether it will suit your convenience to go with us. I shall at all times take a pleasure in acknowledging the public spirit by which you will be actuated---and the obligations you will lay me under.

I have the honor to be, very respectfully, sir, your obt. serv't.

Brig. General Richard Hickman   *Isaac Shelby*

TO THE
MILITIA OF KENTUCKY.

FELLOW-SOLDIERS,
YOUR government has taken measures to act effectually against the enemy in Upper Canada. Gen. Harrison, under the authority of the President of the United States, has called upon me for a strong body of troops to assist in effecting the grand objects of the campaign. The enemy in hopes to find us unprepared, has again invested Fort Meigs; but he will again be mistaken; and before you can take the field he will be driven from that post.

To comply with the requisition of Gen. Harrison, a draft might be enforced; but believing as I do, that the ardor and patriotism of my countrymen has not abated, and that they have waited with impatience a fair opportunity of avenging the blood of their butchered friends, I have appointed the **31st day of August next, at Newport**, for a general rendezvous of KENTUCKY VOLUNTEERS. I will meet you there in person. I will lead you to the field of battle, and share with you the dangers and honors of the campaign. Our services will not be required more than sixty days after we reach head quarters.

I invite all officers, and others possessing influence, to come forward with what mounted men they can raise: each shall command the men he may bring into the field. The superior officers will be appointed by myself at the place of general rendezvous, or on our arrival at head quarters: and I shall take pleasure in acknowledging to my country the merits and public spirit of those who may be useful in collecting a force for the present emergency.

Those who have good rifles, and know how to use them will bring them along. Those who have not, will be furnished with muskets at Newport.

Fellow Citizens! Now is the time to act; and by one decisive blow, put an end to the contest in that quarter.

ISAAC SHELBY.

Frankfort, July 31st, 1813.

MILITIA CALL
Original owned by Colonel Lucien Beckner
Photostat by Hesse
(See pp. 90-91.)

command of the Kentuckians devolved on Gen. John Adair. Adair's command was reserved to reinforce the assailed points of the line. Carroll's Tennessee Brigade and a detachment of Kentucky Militia formed the center, against which Packenham trained his artillery.

General Morgan had been detached to the opposite bank of the Mississippi with about 1,000 men. Just before dawn of January 8, he was reinforced by 180 Kentucky Militia and a regiment of Louisiana Militia bringing his numbers up to 1,700 men. The position was well fortified with artillery and had it been occupied by trained troops under alert commanders could have easily resisted the British attack.

Commodore Patterson, who had erected this battery for the purpose of annoying the enemy, and General Morgan, were aware of the fact that they had acted in error. Patterson saw that he had waited too long to turn his guns, and Morgan's error was in leaving his right flank weak, uncovered and unsupported, while his main force was uselessly concentrated behind the breastworks. To hide their mistakes they induced General Jackson to report to the War Department that "the Kentucky reinforcements ingloriously fled, drawing after them by their example, the remainder of the forces." Further stigma was heaped upon the Kentuckians by the report of Commander Patterson to the Navy Department. A court of inquiry pronounced the detachment of 180 Kentuckians excusable, after which General Adair pressed General Jackson further and obtained a statement that amounted to retraction of the previous report.[14]

Neither General Jackson nor Commodore Patterson had made any mention in their reports of the 1,100 Kentuckians under General Adair who, with Carroll's Tennessee Brigade, were responsible for victory. In the routed Kentucky detachment was a company of volunteers from Ohio county that had landed on the eve of the battle without arms. This company was among the Kentucky troops hastily armed with old muskets and shotguns and detailed to the command of General Morgan.

The British troop report for the day preceding the battle gave 6,893 men, rank and file. Jackson's report shows that he had 4,695 armed men, rank and file, at his disposal. Over one-fourth of them were Kentuckians. Part of Jackson's force was without arms and could not be employed. On March 17 the Kentucky troops began their homeward march and most of them had arrived by the first of May.

Several times during the ensuing years Kentucky's indignation over the Jackson report was revived and reiterated. The *Argus of Western America* (Frankfort), on October 6, 1824, carried a rather caustic militia news item which, in part, follows:

> It is probably known abroad that a notice was given some time ago calling on the friends of Gen. Jackson in this county to meet in the State House on Saturday last for the purpose of taking measures to promote his election to the Presidency. As that was the day of the Regimental muster in this place, it was thought the most opportune occasion for collecting together the whole strength of the "Hero of New Orleans." It is said that after the defection of the militia on the other side of the river (for the Regiment exercised in South Frankfort) some of the General's friends "ingloriously fled."

Another incident, related to the War of 1812 and Jackson's report, occurred in the Kentucky Senate on January 5, 1840. A resolution was offered requesting the Governor "to have a national salute fired on the public square in the town of Frankfort at sunrise on the morning of the 8th January inst. in honor of the glorious victory obtained by the American Army under the command of General Andrew Jackson over the British Army on the 8th of January, 1815" [Battle of New Orleans]. Many objections were made to this resolution and one member of the senate said: "Read, if you please, the correspondence between General Jackson and General Adair, in relation to this slander, and then tell me whether you can vote to burn gun powder for General Jackson, the man who charged our Kentucky troops with having 'ingloriously fled,' and here, in the Kentucky Senate, we have a proposition to spend money in glorifying the man who slandered our Kentucky troops so grossly on that occasion." However, the resolution was passed with the addition of an ameliorating and qualifying resolution. Thereupon, the Lieutenant Governor, C. A. Wickliffe, issued the following order:

To AMBROSE DUDLEY,
Quartermaster General of Kentucky.

SIR: By a joint resolution of the legislature of the Commonwealth of Kentucky it is requested to order a national salute to be fired on the 8th of January in commemoration of the glorious victory achieved by the brave American officers and soldiers at New Orleans on the 8th day of January, 1815—and the governor has directed that the cannon captured from the British on the 5th of October, 1813, at the battle of the Thames by General William H. Harrison and his brave companions in arms, be alone used in firing the salute.

You are therefore charged with the execution of this order, observing strictly the wishes of the legislature—that the cannon captured from the British on the 5th of October 1813, be alone used in its execution.

Robert Peter in his history of Fayette County relates that:

An amusing incident, too good to be lost, occurred during the War of 1812. An adventurous and exceedingly useful female, born in Fayette County, went out with one of the Lexington companies in the capacity of a washerwoman, shared the captivity at Raisin, and marched with the prisoners to Malden, which was crowded with Indians, among whom were several squaws. The appearance of the washerwoman at once caught their attention, especially as she bore on her back a large basket, well filled with her baggage. One of the squaws came up to her and demanded the bundle, which she very promptly refused to give up. But the squaw seized it, and a struggle for its possession at once drew a crowd of warriors around them who formed a circle to see fair play and enjoy the sport. The pulling operation not being sufficient, the female soldier * * * attacked her with fists, and pulled her hair with vigor until at last her antagonist gave up the attempt and left her in possession of her bundle. With laughter and huzzas for the "Kentucky squaw" the warriors declared she should not be disturbed again, and she marched off in triumph to join her fellow prisoners. The Kentucky squaw remained at Malden about six months * * * and then marched back to Lexington in regular infantry style * * *.

The story of "Kentucky's Militia Pig" was originally printed in *Harper's Weekly:*

The annals of the State of Kentucky set forth an odd incident in connection with the invasion of Canada by the Kentucky troops in 1812. A company of volunteers, destined for Shelby's Army, assembled at Harrodsburg and found a nucleus around which the military recruits of the country gathered in the march to the Ohio. On the outskirts of Harrodsburg, so the story runs, the company saw two pigs fighting, and delayed the march to watch the combat. When the march recommenced it was observed that the victorious pig was following the company, and when the men encamped at night the animal lay down near at hand. Of course the soldiers fed the plump recruit. The next day the pig followed them, and this it did daily on the march to the river. When the men crossed on the ferryboat at Cincinnati, the pig waited awhile, then plunged into the river and swam across, and when the march was resumed the animal took its place on the flank of the moving column.

The pig now became a great pet and was as sure of rations as the men themselves; and, destitute of food as the soldiers sometimes found themselves, no one even hinted at putting the knife to the throat of this follower.

At Lake Erie the pig went on board the boat with the soldiers, but after reaching Bass Island it declined to reembark and remained behind in care of a man who volunteered to look after its wants. When the troops returned to the American side, to the surprise of all, the pig was soon discovered in the right of the line, ready for the return trip to Harrodsburg.

The animal suffered much from cold on this trip, and at Maysville, where the army recrossed the Ohio, it was decided to leave it in the hands of a farmer. Finally the pig was taken to the home of Governor Shelby where it passed the rest of its days in ease and plenty.

The following ballad memorializes the part taken by Kentucky troops in the Battle of New Orleans:

> And Pakenham, he made his brag
>   If he in fight was lucky,
> He'd have their girls and cotton bags
>   In spite of old Kentucky
> But Jackson, he was wide awake
>   And was not scared at trifles,
> For well he knew what aim to take
>   With our Kentucky rifles;
> He led us to the Cypress Swamps,
>   The ground was low and mucky,
> There stood John Bull in martial pomp
>   And there was old Kentucky.
>   —SAMUEL WOODWORTH.

During the War of 1812 a body of New York Militia were encamped on the New York side of the Niagara River, under command of General Stephen van Rensselaer. The troops were ordered across the river to attack the British, but refused to go. Their act, after their previously expressed desire to participate in any move against the British, was ascribed to various causes. However, their action served one admirable end, for through it a new phase of national military law was formulated by the litigation that followed the New York Militia's refusal to go beyond the state line. By reason of this case and resultant legislation future use of the militia of the several states was not made by the United States until after the militia, to be employed, had been mustered into the United States Army.[15]

The Kentucky rifle was named for the backwoodsmen of the pioneer state of the West, who used it with such telling expertness in their defense against Indian and British foes and in their struggle for safety. The American flintlock rifle had been made in Pennsylvania for several decades and had become the only firearm the backwoodsmen would use. It filled the need for a weapon of great efficiency for Indian warfare and big game hunting. Its range was three times that of the smooth-bore musket that preceded it; its trajectory was flatter, its use of ammunition was more economic, and its accuracy incomparably greater. As Kentucky's position as the van of Anglo-Saxon settlement developed, and the fame of her hunters and Indian fighters grew, their favorite weapon, the long rifle, became known as the "Kentucky Rifle," regardless of where the rifle had been made.

Expert riflemakers were in Kentucky from the beginning of its settlement. Squire Boone, brother of Daniel, who had learned the trade in Pennsylvania, had a shop at Fort Boonesborough, and made many rifles in Kentucky during the Revolution and subsequent Indian wars. The troops of Gen. George Rogers Clark, in his conquest of Illinois, used the Kentucky rifle. In the battles of Tippecanoe, the Thames, New Orleans, and in all the battles of the War of 1812 fought in by Kentuckians, the Kentucky rifle was used. By means of the Kentucky rifle the boundary line of the United States was shifted from the Ohio River to the Great Lakes. At the Battle of New Orleans the British, moving in formation and thinking themselves safe because out of musket range, were mowed down by the long Kentucky rifles.

When Napoleon heard of the battle and of the rifle that was so effective in repulsing the English, he decided to use it in his own army, but Waterloo came and his plan was never carried out.

The Kentucky rifle played a prominent part in equipping the early trappers in the Rocky Mountains. Kit Carson, a Kentuckian and famous scout, used the Kentucky rifle. The invention of percussion ignition in 1807 caused the flintlock to disappear from the Kentucky rifle, and the new system was installed on all new guns and the old rifles were altered to use it. Some of the early makers of the rifle in Kentucky were the O'Bryans, at Lexington; the Settles, in Barren and Green counties; the Mills', at Harrodsburg; and Hawken, who made rifles in Louisville when he was young, but later moved to St. Louis where he gained fame as a Kentucky riflemaker. But every neighborhood had its gunsmith and the general average of their output was very high. Some of the feats of the marksmen with the Kentucky rifle, such as driving nails at 100 yards, putting out candles, "barking" squirrels, shooting the heads off of turkeys, and cups of whisky off of the heads of confident friends, have been themes for song and story since the first settlement in Kentucky.

Among the notable Kentucky volunteers of the War of 1812 was Harvey Thacker, a relative of Daniel Boone. He was born in North Carolina in 1743, removed to Kentucky when he was thirty-eight years old, and when sixty-eight years of age he served under General Harrison in the Battle of Tippecanoe; then volunteered and took part in the Battle of New Orleans. At eighty-nine years he saw service in Illinois in the Black Hawk War. He died, at the age of 128 years, on September 15, 1871.[16]

Records of desertion by Kentucky militiamen are few. For many years the law provided that the person apprehending a deserter was entitled to credit for the time the deserter had yet to serve when he deserted. The militia officer to whom the deserter was delivered was commanded by law to issue a receipt for the deserter to the person making the arrest. This receipt was legally assignable. The following is a case selected in illustration of special handling of desertion cases. On the seventh of February, 1815, an act of the legislature was approved for the special benefit of Jeremiah Munsey. The act is as follows:

> WHEREAS, it is represented to the present general assembly, That Jeremiah Munsey did, in the year 1812, apprehend three deserters in the County of Knox, who had deserted from Colonel Jennings' regiment, then at Ft. Jennings; and the same did take back to said Fort, on his own expense, and there delivered up to Captain Garrard, to whose company the said deserters belonged. The said Jeremiah Munsey, did, then and there enrol himself, on the 24th of December, in the said company of Captain Garrard, and faithfully served as a soldier until the ninth of March, the day on which the said regiment was discharged at Cincinnati; for which services he has received no compensation, either from the United States or form this State: Therefore,
>
> Sec. 1. Be it reacted by the General Assembly of the Commonwealth of Kentucky, that said Jeremiah Munsey shall be allowed a credit for six tours of duty, for the time said Munsey served.

The duel engaged in on July 16, 1819, between Francis G. Waring and Jacob H. Holman, near Frankfort, resulted from difficulties growing out of occurrences at a militia muster. Waring attended a muster of the county militia on the fourth of July. The companies drilled on the Peak's Mill Road, about four miles from Frankfort. J. H. Holman was an officer of Waring's company and during the maneuvers a dog which belonged to Waring was killed by a thrust from Holman's saber. This killing brought about a fist fight between Holman and Waring, but the men were separated. The next day Waring sent his challenge to Holman, which resulted in the duel that cost Waring's life. The duel was fought on the Rev. Silas Noel's farm, which was later the home of the warrior-poet, Theodore O'Hara.[17]

Patrollers were guardians of the peace selected from the militia ranks to assist the civil authorities in maintaining order in the community. A tour of patroller duty was usually a total of twenty-four hours, the maximum which any one man could be compelled to serve in one month. By 1820 Kentucky had a large slave population, and it was the chief duty of the patrollers to enforce obedience of the Negroes to the law in the matter of assembling together, traveling from place to place, and other like matters affecting the Negro population. The county courts had jurisdiction in the appointment of patrollers, and such appointments are voluminous in the county court order books from 1815–40. The system of patrollers was a Virginia heritage.

During the fall of 1824 a part of the militia of Mason was ordered out on account of the presence in the county, of a venerable Indian, Mingo Puckshunuble, eighty years of age, and sachem of the Choctaw Nation. He was with a party of distinguished Choctaws on their way to Washington, D. C., when he was killed in Maysville on October 13 by a fall. The aged Indian was buried in Mason County with his native rite, to which the Mason Militia added the white man's tribute of military honors.

During May, 1825, General Lafayette paid a visit to Kentucky, and his approach to any city on his itinerary served as a sort of fuse to touch off a spectacular display of the county militia. He visited Frankfort on May 14, 1825, and was "met by seven military companies and a cavalcade of citizens." The order of procession observed in the escort and reception of Lafayette at Frankfort follows:

(1) An assistant marshal and aides, (2) Division of Cavalry, (3) an assistant marshal and aides, (4) Division of Infantry and Riflemen, (5) Marshal of the day staff, (6) General Lafayette and Committee in barouche, (7) suite of General Lafayette, (8) Governor of Kentucky and suite, (9) Heads of Department of State, (10) Revolutionary officers and soldiers, (11) U. S. Army and Navy officers, (12) Clergy and Court Officials, (13) committees from other places, (14) officers of the Militia in uniform, (15) an assistant marshal and aides, (16) Mounted Military escort, (17) citizens on horseback, (18) assistant marshal and aides, (19) citizens on foot, (20) assistant marshal and aides.

FRANKFORT, *May 7, 1825*

The Marshal of the day announces the following appointments of officers, who will be obeyed and respected accordingly:

Assistant Marshals—Gen. Robt. McHatton, Gen. Jas. Ford, Col. E. H. Taylor, Col. Jas. McConnel, Col. Alex Tilford, Lt. Col. T. H. Bradford, Lt. Col. Samuel Payne, and Maj. John Woods.

Col. O. G. Waggoner, Maj. Chapman Coleman, Capts. C. S. Bidd and Ambrose Dudley, are appointed aides to the Marshal of the day. The assistant Marshals will appoint two aides each. The assistant Marshals and aides will, in addition to the usual military sash, wear a red silk sash thrown over the left shoulder, crossed on the right side, and tied on the left side.

The marshal and his aides will, in addition to the usual military sash, wear a sash of pale blue silk, thrown over the right shoulder crossed on the left side and confined on the right.

A detachment of artillery will be designated to fire a National Salute on the General entering the town limits.

It is understood that the different corps of volunteer companies, from the adjoining counties, have intimated a wish to ride with the division at the seat of government, on the great occasion; the Marshal will feel honored in receiving them into his command. The commandants of such corps shall lose no time in reporting themselves, that their proper positions may be assigned them.

The committee on the part of the State will as soon as intelligence is received of the day of the General's entry, notify me of the same, which will be immediately communicated to the troops, when general orders will issue, assigning to each officer his command, and each corps, whether of artillery, cavalry, infantry or riflemen, their respective stations in line.

PETER DUDLEY, *Col. & Marshall*

The military ardor of the citizen soldier was easily aroused by the rumor of impending war or perpetrated crimes. However, an era of peaceful routine pursuits, lacking the goad of threatened danger, was disastrous to the militia as an organization. The Kentucky Militia personnel waxed militant only under provocation.

In 1825 Governor Desha in an address to the legislature, referred to the militia as being in a disorganized and lifeless condition. He said: "From the deranged state of our militia, neither improvement in discipline nor any other material benefit is to be expected from it. A general revision of the system would seem desirable by which the establishment may be placed on a more respectable footing.

"The scanty attendance on parades arising from a want of discretionary power in the courts for the assessment of fines under proper limits, produces numerous resignations, which not only derange the system, but have become expensive to the government."

Frequent requests were made through the legislature to Congress to set up military schools and armories in Kentucky, and the same desire was expressed by groups of citizens, as in the case in 1825 of the petition of the inhabitants of Pendleton County to Congress to set up an armory on the Licking River.[18]

The following excerpt from *Lonz Powers, or the Regulators*, by James Weir, Sr., portrays, in exaggerated style, incidents that transpired at old-time militia musters. The story is based on events that took place at a militia muster in May of 1845. Here Alonzo Pennington and Simon Davis, militiamen, met. After the muster was concluded these two discussed and entered into a transaction whereby Pennington acquired title to the land and slaves of Davis' deceased wife. That night Pennington (depicted as Powers) murdered Davis for the purpose of recovering the cash and notes given in payment for the land and chattels. During the period of which Weir writes, there were, nevertheless, numerous finely uniformed companies in Kentucky, well drilled and accoutred in the best fashion of the day.

> Every nation has a memorable day—a day of songs and rejoicings. With us the Fourth of July, 22d of February, and Christmas, are all holidays, or days of joy and pleasure. But of all the grand days in this martial old Commonwealth of ours, those set apart for militia training are (at least in the estimation of militia captains) the grandest and most exciting. If you should happen within ten miles of a militia muster on one of these eventful days, every step you took, and every object that met your gaze, would remind you of war, with its glorious and thrilling panoply, its noise and wild tumult. Boys, negroes, and men on foot and on horseback; in cart, wagon, and carriage; single, double, and treble; are crowding from every direction, and hurrying with anxious speed toward the scene where mimic battles are to be fought and won. Old shotguns, rusty rifles, long-untried fowling pieces, cornstalks, and hickory sticks, are in great demand, while the Sunday fineries, drawn from their secret hiding places, adorn the martial forms of their proud-treading owners. Cider wagons, ginger cakes, apples, whisky, and all the other et ceteras of the camp, are rushing pell-mell into the place of rendezvous. Arriving at the parade field, your ears are greeted with every imaginable noise—the squealing

of pigs, neighing of chargers, barking of dogs, braying of asses, laughing of happy negroes, and hoarse commands of military chieftains being mingled together in the most harmonious concord of discord. Jingling spurs, rusty sabers, black cockades, and the fierce little red plume, everywhere meet your wandering eye and fill up the interstices of this moving, animated scene.

Such an exhibition of warlike enthusiasm might have been seen, if you had only been present, dear reader, at Pleasant Grove, on the morning after the night described in our last chapter. Noise and wild confusion were the order of the day. The thrilling fife and a cracked drum were pealing forth their stirring notes, and calling loudly upon the brave sons of old Kentucky to shoulder their arms and sustain the glory of their ancestors. Generals, colonels, majors, captains (we have no lack of titled gentry in Kentucky), and privates were mingled together in a confused mass, talking, laughing, shouting, swearing, drinking, and every now and then taking a pleasant knock-down, merely to vary the bill of entertainment, keep up the excitement, and cultivate a proper military ardor. Candidates were there, too (like all other aspirants for office), shaking hands, treating, speaking, and making known to the warlike assembly the past, present, and future (they were no prophets, merely reasoning from cause to effect) glory and renown of Kentucky and her gallant sons. Horse racing, cock fighting, rifle shooting, wrestling, and boxing, upon this occasion, all had their votaries, and all were busily engaged in their respective amusements. Babel, in her palmiest day, was a mere "tempest in a teapot" compared with a militia muster in the backwoods of Kentucky. The carnival at Rome, or the ancient Saturnalia of the Romans, in the very height of their revelling, would be tame and insipid when placed in juxtaposition with such an occasion. We know of nothing that can be compared for noise and wild confusion, with a regiment of boisterous, merry, reckless militia, along with their chivalrous leaders, adorned with flowing red sash, bullet-button coats, tinfoil epaulets, and stiff, ragged, red plumes, just preceding or succeeding "the training."

But suddenly a great change comes over the moving, tossing mass, gathered on the battlefield at Pleasant Grove. Some order (a devilish little, by-the-by, if it can be called order at all) takes the place of the late disorder, and a comparative calm—in a figurative sense—settles down upon this raging storm. The commanding officer of the day, stripping his saddle of its red girth, belts on his trusty, trenchant blade, dons his swallow tailed blue [coat] adorned with bullet-buttons and red tape, borrows the best charger he can find, scrambles on his back with the assistance of a stump or a kind hand, and, when once safely moored, waves his plumed beaver around his warlike head, and shouts his orders to parade. Now comes a busy, stirring, wild and moving panorama. Men, before ignoble and unknown from the common herd, draw from their bosoms, pockets, and hats, the red plume and sash (that is, if they are so lucky as to have any), and soon become the leaders and chieftains of the day. A fierce struggle now commences as to who shall get their companies first formed into line, or who shall first gain a preemptive right to the shade of a tree under which to marshal and form. Although each company has, or rather has had at some former time, a captain and inferior officers (for they often assemble on parade ground without any), in reality every man in the corps, being fully competent to command, takes the responsibility of giving orders.

It may be thought an easy matter by the inexperienced to form a company of men into a straight line; but, if it is so, our militia captains have never discovered that fact. They commence at one end of the winding line, and with threats, entreaties, and much trouble get a tolerably fair and straight row, especially if there be any corn ridges in the immediate neighborhood, but, unfortunately, before they reach the other extreme, their soldiers having a predisposition for Mahometanism, are generally in a crescent, and then they are compelled to begin afresh. And thus we have seen them go on for hours and hours, and at last end their labors, not being in much better array or condition than at the beginning of their arduous and impossible undertaking. Tall, low, long, short, thin, and fat; old and young, men and boys, clothed with fur and wool hats, caps, and no hats at all; cloth coats and jeans, calico and linsey-woolsey, and no coats at all; boots, shoes, and moccasins, and no shoes at all; new and old pants, white, black, and striped, and no pants at all; shorts ruffled and unruffled, white, black, green, and gray, cotton, linen, and calico, and no shorts at all—are all mingled together in the most beautiful and checkered confusion, giving a motley and ludicrous appearance to the ununiformed, straggling, and crooked corps.

The officers are generally the most silly and ignorant men of the community, for none but such will seek a command in so farcical a concern as a militia company; and most frequently elected, as the saying is, unanimously, for they are considered most "unanimous fools," and no one will vote either for or against them. As for a knowledge of military tactics, they never dream of any such a thing. They are unable (with a few exceptions, of course) to form even a straight line, unless they have the assistance of a ditch or a corn row, and as for giving any other orders save "about face!" (to which they add "right!") "march!" it is a thing not only unknown but unheard of. Those who can read are accustomed to carry *Scott's Tactics* in their pockets, from which they read out the different commands or maneuvers, but as for knowing what is then to be done, after spelling through the various movements, they don't think of such a thing, for it is none of their business. They are placed there to give the orders, and it is the duty of the company to obey; and if they fail to do so, then it is their own fault, for their skillful captains have read out all the necessary instructions as plain as Scott himself could give them.

We know of but one real, genuine, whole-souled, praiseworthy militia captain, and he has now left the country and moved to Arkansas. He was a glorious, jolly fellow, that old captain of ours, and if ever a military leader deserved a monument of brass, he was that one; and we will give a "ten" at any time we are called on towards bestowing that honor to his memory. He was, during his soldiering life, the most popular chieftain of the age—always excepting Old Hickory and his sons, the young Hickories—and we will venture to say his company was the most numerous and well attended of the regiment, so long as he was permitted to drill under his own laws and in his own spirited way. His mode of operating (and we make it known for the benefit of martial spirits) was to form his corps as near into a straight line as possible; but he only attempted this difficult maneuver once a day, and that very early in the morning, for after that, not even with the assistance of a fence or ditch, could he keep them either perpendicular or rectilinear. Then, marching at the head of his brave companions, he opened with a vigorous pursuit of the enemy, and, at a suitable and convenient spot made known to him by his spy (for he always threw out an advance guard), he generally discovered the foe, disguised and changed by the fairies into a half-dozen blue or red (most frequently red) pails, and well filled with mint julep, a ladle in each (a trick of the enemy to induce a charge) and commanded by that old bruiser and man-overthrower, John Barleycorn, always ready and willing (like Wellington at Waterloo) to be attacked. There is no shrinking or giving back in John, and, like Old Zack, the word retreat is unknown in his tactics, let the enemy be ever so fierce and numerous.

Our gallant captain was one of the same sort, a real Murat for daring charges; and, forming his men into platoons of six—for he scorned to take advantage of his superior number—led them manfully to the contest, full upon the battery of the foe, although ready to pour out destruction upon himself and followers. "Make ready!" was his hoarse command, and down went the dippers; "take aim!" and up they came on a level with the mouth; "fire!" and away goes the liquid stream, not of fire, but of firewater, down the thirsty throats of his soldiers. "Next platoon, march!" (there was no pricking of bayonets to urge them on); "make ready, take aim, fire!" and thus each individual of the band had an opportunity to display his nerve and steadiness under a point-blank shot from the stubborn foe. Nor was our noble captain content with battling this little squad of the enemy, for, like the true hero that he was, he allowed the foe to send after fresh ammunition, and bring up the reserve, squad after squad, and still continue the fight, showing no quarter and asking none, until he alone of all that gallant corps is left standing to face the "redcoats." "I see them on their winding way," was the favorite air of this fighting band of heroes, and many a battle have they fought with the "Britishers," as the red pails were called, when spirited on by this good old tune.

The followers of the captain, unlike other militia, were far more steady when going into the fray than when coming out. We remember you well, most jovial son of Mars, and wherever you may now be, and whatever may be your fate, we will never cease to give you honor, although you were a militia captain. We have fought and have been defeated under your banner, but never disgraced, for, like conquerors, we always slept upon the field of battle and close around the battery of the enemy.

The martial farce is now over; the red plumes have vanished, the bullet-buttons are numbered among the things "that were," and bright sabers no longer glitter in the sunbeams. They who but a moment since lorded it over their fellow men, dubbed as generals, colonels, majors, and captains, and as grandly and gloriously as Napoleon and his marshals, or the Grand Turk and his pachas are now but common citizens, without command, and no longer in authority; and (what is still worse for them) liable at any moment to be soundly thrashed by any of the sovereigns they may have been so unfortunate as to insult during the drill!—a privilege not unfrequently enforced, very much to the discomfort of the gallant commanders.

The soul-inspiring drum and fife have ceased, and the old forest no longer echoes back the martial roll. Boys, negroes and stragglers, wanting the excitement of military music, and glutted with warlike pageantry, are now making hasty preparations for departure. Cider barrels and cake baskets are empty; and their happy owners and venders, shaking their swelling purses, go on their way rejoicing. All are now gone, or preparing to leave, save those brave spirits who intend to sleep upon the field and upon their arms, for the very simple reason that they have fallen victims to Bacchus and are unable to leave. And such is a militia muster—a great, grand, sometimes laughable but always silly farce, and not only tolerated, but legalized and even commanded by our laws. Yet do we suffer, and, like good citizens, obey—three times annually leaving our labor and business to undergo this most absurd of all absurdities, a "militia training."

In vivid contrast to this peacetime picture are the contemporary scenes produced by news of a prospect of war. Gen. Zachary Taylor had, in the spring of 1833, asked several southern states for forces to use in Texas in the event of a Mexican invasion. Kentucky troops were hurriedly mustered and held ready for call into the service of the United States. The *Commonwealth* (Frankfort) of May 17, 1833, contains items which reflect the state's military response in emergencies. These are:

THE KENTUCKY VOLUNTEERS: Finer corps of soldiers never mustered afield. We know what stuff Kentucky boys are made of; and if they only get half a chance, they will distinguish themselves and add lustre to the arms of the country. We say this for all the Kentucky forces, without meaning to brag a single bit; and we hope it will not seem invidious if we say the Franklin Volunteers, both Cavalry and Infantry, are not surpassed by any other corps. We feel confident the Volunteers from the Capitol will not be behind any others in maintaining the high renown of Kentucky arms. Brave Volunteers of Franklin, Kentucky expects everyone to do his duty; and we answer for you that every one will do it through field and flood, through fire and blood.

THE MOUNTAIN BOYS OF KENTUCKY: We are informed, as a fact, that as soon as the news of the hostilities reached a certain region of the mountains, 200 noble fellows sprang into their saddles, and armed with their trusty rifles dashed down into the lowlands, inquiring whereabouts was Matamoras, and saying they supposed they must be needed. Those brave fellows cared very little about the forms of requisitions; and no doubt thought there were leaders among themselves quite as fit to head them as any they could get by waiting a month on the President. None but the men of their own rank deserved to lead them, true hearted Kentuckians. In another mountain county, we are advised, the only difficulty in raising volunteers, was the doubt of the people whether they ought to serve under such a Commander-in-Chief as General Polk; but two eloquent Whigs delivering speeches on the subject, showing that it was the country that needed their services, that it was the Government and not Mr. Polk for whom they were to fight, and two companies of brave fellows instantly volunteered, though the population of the county was very small.

There was considerable agitation to abolish the militia as an organization of the state during the decade preceding the war with Mexico. Sentiment in favor of such a discontinuance was widespread, if not general, and was shared alike by the militia and the public. The attitude of the militia is embodied in the following notice which appeared in the *Commonwealth* (Frankfort) November 14, 1835:

At a meeting of the Field Staff, Captains and Subalterns of the 11th Regiment of Kentucky Militia, at the house of Capt. Benj. Wickersham in the town of Mortonsville and County of Woodford on the 7th day of Nov. 1835 it was ordered that Capts. Scearce, Arnet and T. Sullivan be appointed a committee in behalf of this board, to draft a memorial to the Legislature of Kentucky representing the present defective system of the laws for the government of the Militia, and the necessity of its speedy amendment, or the entire abolition so far as practicable, of the whole militia organization, as now regulated by the laws of the State.

It was further ordered that a request be made to the different Regiments of the State to take this matter into consideration and to co-operate with us and the Fayette Committee, for the purpose above mentioned and that in the same manner they present their views through their county representative to the next Legislature.

B. WICKERSHAM,
President

On March 19, 1836, the State Arsenal at Frankfort burned with its entire contents including 4,740 stand of arms, a large quantity of ammunition, and other accessories. This arsenal had been erected in 1834. The brass cannon that had done service in the Revolution and the War of 1812 was among the objects in the arsenal. However, it was not seriously damaged. This piece was captured from Burgoyne at Saratoga, September 19, 1777, then surrendered to the British on August 16, 1812, by Hull; recaptured by Kentucky troops at the Battle of the Thames, and thereupon presented to Governor Shelby by Congress. Shelby in turn presented the cannon to the state of Kentucky.[19]

The war for Texas independence came in 1836, and a sizable number of Kentuckians speedily espoused the cause of Texas. On April 21, 1836, Gen. Sam Houston's 720 Texas troops, embracing many former Kentuckians then residing in Texas, defeated 1,640 Mexicans at San Jacinto, inflicting a loss to the Mexicans of 630 killed, 280 wounded and 730 taken prisoner. During that summer over 600 Kentuckians joined the Texan ranks. These went as volunteers, and were led by Colonel Wilson and Captains Postlethwait, James Allen, and others.

This war between Texas and Mexico brought a new hazard to the southwestern frontier of the United States, and during July, 1836, President Jackson, through Maj. Gen. E. P. Gaines, asked Governor Morehead for troops to protect the border. On July 16, the Governor issued a proclamation calling for 1,000 mounted volunteers of the Kentucky Militia to rendezvous at Frankfort August 17, to proceed to Camp Sabine, Texas. Adjt. Gen. Peter Dudley issued general orders calling attention to the Governor's proclamation and stipulating the term and requirements to which enlistees were to be bound. These orders were as follows:

One regiment of volunteer mounted gunmen to be composed of 10 companies, each company to consist of not more than 100 nor less than 64 rank and file of able bodied efficient men, between the ages of 18 and 45 years. Permission is given to each of the Volunteer companies to elect their own officers, and to prescribe their own uniforms; but the governor and Commander-in-chief reserves the right, and will appoint the commanding officer of the detachment, and will order a detail to be made of the other Field Officers of the Regiment. Each volunteer will provide his own clothing, horse, and trappings; provisions, arms, ammuni-

COLONEL RICHARD M. JOHNSON
From a portrait owned by
The Filson Club
(See pp. 85-88)

COL. JOSEPH HAMILTON DAVIESS
After a portrait owned by
The Filson Club
(See p. 145)

BRIG. GEN. JAMES WILKINSON
From a portrait by John W. Jarvis
Courtesy, The Filson Club

MAJ. GEN. GEORGE ROGERS CLARK
From the Portrait by Matthew Jouett
Courtesy, The Filson Club

tion, camp equipage, etc., for active and efficient service will be furnished by the United States.

The first ten companies organized and reported to me in conformity with the above regulations, will be received and constitute the corps to the exclusion of all subsequent applications; and the first company thus tendered, will have precedence, be entitled to the right of the Regiment and its commanding officer will rank above all others of equal grade.

The troops will rendezvous in Frankfort on Wednesday the 17th of August next; but any company belonging to the Regiment, whose local situation may render it more convenient to join the detachment on its line of march, will be ordered to rendezvous at some point other than the place of general rendezvous in Frankfort. The corps is destined for Camp Sabine, the headquarters of Major General Gaines, of the U. S. Army, commanding on the Southwest Frontier. Reports of the progress made in furnishing the quota required must regularly be made to this office weekly, as on the first intimation of a failure to raise the number of troops required (an event which the Gov. and Commander-in-Chief is not willing to believe, and will not anticipate) immediate resort will be had for supplying such deficiency by draft, or ordering into service, independent corps, en masse to fill the requisition.

P. DUDLEY,
Adjt. General

Prior to August 3, forty-five companies had organized and tendered their services, but only ten of these were accepted. This rush to enlist brought the following comment from the *Commonwealth* (Frankfort) of August 3, 1836:

KENTUCKY VOLUNTEERS

In this state the question is not who must go but who may go. The contest has been for the privilege of forming a part of the regiment destined for the Sabine. The first ten companies with the names of their Captains are:

1. Franklin—Geo. B. Crittenden
2. Henry—Silas W. Hunt
3. Shelby—Henry Crawford
4. Madison—William Jenkins
5. Harrison—F. S. Coleman
6. Oldham—J. A. Walker
7. Gallatin—B. H. May
8. Woodford—Geo. B. Dunlap
9. Jefferson—H. Marshall, Jr.
10. Fayette—Edw. Carter

A second company has been formed in Henry County and 18 other counties have reported but have not been accepted.

Many of the young men who have volunteered to march to the Sabine, are not able to procure horses. Several public spirited farmers have already equipped some of the volunteers, and it is believed that others will do so when the necessity for their aid is known to them. The government is bound to pay for horses lost or injured in the campaign * * *.

Organization of the volunteers proceeded with the appointment of Leslie Combs of Fayette as colonel, Thomas A. Russell of Fayette as lieutenant colonel, and George Boswell of Shelby as major. These troops were profoundly disappointed by the issuance of an order to disband before they had commenced their march.

The next year the militia's hopes for action were again blasted in a like manner when Governor Clark was notified by the U. S. Secretary of War to prepare to muster into service a brigade of Kentucky Volunteers for service against the Seminoles in Florida. This order of August 25 was withdrawn on September 2 because ample troops were found to be available in states nearer to the point of duty.

In November, 1840, General Harrison, then President-elect, visited Kentucky, and while in Frankfort called on Mrs. Solomon P. Sharp. While being entertained in the parlor of her home, Harrison related that in that same room he had been adopted by Kentucky and there given his commission as major general of the Kentucky Militia.

An act of the legislature of 1841 required the compilation of names of all Revolutionary soldiers living in Kentucky. The purpose recited was that ways might be devised "in which a grateful people may do honor to the memory and character of the immortal heroes and patriots, collectively, by whose toil and valor the boon of freedom is inherited."

The summer of 1841 brought the militia into the public eye in a spectacular event. A celebration of the sixty-sixth anniversary of the first settlement of Kentucky took place at Harrodsburg. Participating in this celebration were ten companies of Kentucky Militia, which in their colorful uniforms produced a marked contrast to Kentucky's first militia company that assembled there in hunting shirt, leather breeches and coonskin. The Lieutenant Governor, having been invited to the celebration at Boonesboro, addressed a letter to his staff, the adjutant general, quartermaster general, Colonels Orlando Brown, William B. Kinkead, Nathaniel Hart, Jr., and Thomas W. Riley—requesting them to report themselves either at Frankfort or Lexington, to accompany him to Boonesboro to review the troops that might be in attendance to celebrate the first settlement of Kentucky.

Then from the first to the fourth of July, 1841, an interstate competitive drill encampment took place at "Oaklawn" in Jefferson County. Crack companies of militia from Cincinnati, Dayton, and Columbus, Ohio, and from Kentucky, met, each striving to outrank the other nineteen competitors. A like event took place in Franklin County in July, 1843. At this latter encampment, called Camp Madison, Col. Humphrey Marshall was in command.

Notices contained in several issues of the Louisville Daily *Journal* of February, 1844, relate the organization and some of the activities of the Louisville Legion that year. The following is from among these:

> The Commandants of companies composing the Louisville Legion are hereby ordered to parade their respective companies on Jefferson, between Fourth and Fifth streets, fully equipped and provided with thirteen rounds blank cartridge, on Thursday morning, the 22nd inst., at 10 o'clock, A. M. to celebrate the birthday of the immortal Washington. A gun squad will be detailed from the Louisville Artillery to fire the usual sunrise salute, and a similar detail will be made from the Louisville Guards to fire the midday salute
>
> STEPHEN ORMSBY
> *Colonel Commanding*

The field officers of this regiment were Colonel Stephen Ormsby, Lt. Col. James Metcalfe, Maj. John G. Stein. The companies and their officers were Louisville Guards, 1st Company L.L., Capt. L. Thompson, Lt. Joseph Peterson, Sgt. Charles Miller, Sgt. George Davis; Washington Blues, 2d Company L.L., Capt. William Preston, Lt. R. R. Elliott, Sgt. A. Y. Johnson, Corp. B. F. Steward; Kentucky Riflemen, 3d Company L.L., Capt. George W. Anderson, Lt. Charles W. Bullen, Ensign E. M. Stone, Sgt. John Fuller; Artillery, 4th Company L.L., Capt. A. P. Churchill, Lt. Maury Phillips, Lt. Henry S. Tyler, Ensign Newton Bray; National Guards, 5th Company L.L., Capt. B. Grieshaber, Lt. H. Shone, Ensign C. Knapp, Dr. G. Holland; German National Guards, 6th Company L.L., Capt. Florian Kern, Lt. A. Steinaker, Ensign Jacob Decker, Sgt. R. Bindewalder.

The Kentucky Military Institute was founded in 1845 by Gen. R. T. P. Allen, a graduate of West Point and a veteran of the Seminole War. It was located at Franklin Springs near Frankfort. The Kentucky Military Institute was the third military school to be founded after West Point, Norwich (Vermont) University, and the Virginia Military Institute, antedating it. These three schools have always been "essentially military" institutes. The Kentucky Military Institute was chartered by the state on January 20, 1847, and soon became a leading military school of the country, attaining its position by the indomitable energy of its founder and by the high standard preserved in its faculty personnel, its course of study, and its equipment. Its graduates and ex-cadets are found in every state in the Union, and it furnished many a gallant soldier and officer on both sides in the War between the States.

Legislative changes, pertaining to the militia from 1792 to 1846 were frequent, with nearly every legislature determined to enact a new set of statutes to regulate the state's military affairs. In 1806 a definite effort was made, legislatively, to build up a strong military machine. The Governor was ordered to "raise companies of grenadiers, light infantry, cavalry, riflemen and artillery." Batallion musters were ordered to be held in May, regimental musters in October, and at least four company musters between June and October (inclusive) were mandatory. On all public appearances the general staff and field officers were compelled to be in full uniform with side arms. A general or general staff officer was required to have a blue coat with lapels of buff, gold epaulets and buff "underclothes," boots, spurs, a cocked hat, cockade and a small sword. Field officers wore the same uniform except that their coat collars were turned up and lapels were of red. Field officers were further distinguished by silver epaulets. The regimental staff, captains and subalterns wore the same uniform as field officers, but with no epaulets. This statute[20] also fixed the salary of the adjutant general at $100 per year.

A statute of 1811 changed the uniform by substituting "a

round black hat" for the cocked hat, and prescribed a white waistcoat for all commissioned officers below the rank of general.

The Shakers (Shaking Quakers) were prohibited by their religious tenets from bearing arms. Universal military duty brought many clashes with members of these communities who refused both to serve and to pay the fines imposed for nonperformance of that duty. The following enactment was designed to compel payment: "That when any man belonging to any society who hold community of property, shall be fined by virtue of this act and refuseth, or is not able to pay said fine, it shall be the duty of the sheriff, or other proper officer, to call on the agent or superintendent of the common stock or firm of said society or compact, for said fine or fines; and in case said agent shall refuse to pay or be absent, it shall be the duty of the sheriff or officer aforesaid, to execute and sell so much property belonging to said stock as shall be sufficient to satisfy said fine or fines and costs." [21] Later provision was made that "persons who scruple to bear arms shall furnish a substitute." [22]

In 1815 a further change in uniforms was made. General officers, division, and brigade officers were ordered to wear a "blue coat and pantaloons, made in the fashion of the U. S. Army dress uniform, with yellow buttons, gold epaulettes, boots, spurs, a round black hat, black cockade, white plume and small sword." The regimental field and staff officers wore a like coat and pantaloons with white buttons, silver epaulets, a black cockade, and a white plume tipped with red. Captains and subaltern officers' uniforms were deep blue, red trimmed, and they wore a red plume and one epaulet.

An act of 1818 abolished the regimental drill encampments and three years later company musters were reduced to two per year, in April and June. In 1831 came another reduction in number of company musters, making the muster an annual affair that was held in April. Companies were relieved of attending musters if held at a distance of more than twenty miles from the company's headquarters. This statute of 1831 also repealed the exemption from the service of civil process, while on duty or going to or from musters, that militiamen had held since 1815.[23]

A lack of active duty, an ever-changing militia law, and the boresome routine of musters, culminated in another effort in 1845 to abolish the militia. By action of the regimental officers a movement with this objective was launched through petitions, newspaper articles, and public addresses. Though these efforts seemingly failed, they nevertheless registered an effect on the public mind that was later embodied in the state's new constitution. Doubtless there would have been some legislative abortion of the then existing system had it not been for the outbreak of the war with Mexico.

NOTES, REFERENCES, AND SOURCES

1. Constitution of 1792, Art. VI, Sec. 2.
2. Act of June 24, 1792.
3. "Draper MSS," 12CC24.
4. *Ibid.*, 12CC150.
5. *Ibid.*, 12CC31 and 90.
6. *Ibid.*, 12CC37-38.
7. *Kentucky Gazette*, November 8 and 25, 1797.
8. Constitution of 1799, Art. III, Sec. 28.
9. Burr's Conspiracy. See Collin's *History of Kentucky*, Vol. I, pp. 286-295.
10. Upon the call of Governor Shelby for volunteers the Barren County Militia, was by order, assembled in Glasgow. Here lines of militiamen were formed along Main Street. Patriotic addresses were made, with martial music intended to arouse patriotism, but volunteers were few. Then Jacob Lough and his sons, very proficient with drum and fife, were ordered to play *Yankee Doodle*. The men recruiting the company were marched up the line again. One trip was sufficient, for a full company fell in. Immediate organization took place with John Gorin as captain. Throughout the war John and Thomas, sons of Jacob Lough, were continued in the recruiting services. Then, after many years of separation, these brothers met again at Waveland, Montgomery County, Indiana, and served in the same capacities, drummer and fifer, in the recruiting service of the Union Army.
11. Probably the *Lexington Reporter*.
12. The following are known to have been of the twenty men picked by Col. R. M. Johnson to draw the Indians' fire at the Thames:

Wm. Whitley, private, James Donaldson's Company, Lincoln County.

Ben S. Chambers, quartermaster, Scott County.

Garrett Wall, forage master, Scott County.
Eli Short, assistant forage master, Scott County.
Samuel A. Theobald, judge advocate, Franklin County.
Samuel Logan, second lieutenant, Coleman's Company, Harrison County.
Robert Payne, private, James Donaldson's Company, Lincoln County.
Joseph Taylor, private, J. W. Reading's Company.
Wm. S. Webb, private, Jacob Stucker's Company, Scott County.
Richard Spurr, private, Samuel Comb's Company, Fayette County.
John McGunnigle, private, Samuel Comb's Company, Fayette County.

13. As the lines advanced through the swamp Colonel Johnson saw an Indian Chief, behind a tree, who with commands and praise was urging his warriors on. At the first fire Colonel Johnson's left hand had been wounded and rendered useless, and, when seen by this chief, Johnson received another rifle ball wound. Having fired, the Indian then advanced on Johnson with tomahawk. Johnson dropped his bridle rein for a moment to fire his pistol. The Indian fell dead. Johnson continued in the command of his men, and it was afterwards learned that Tecumseh had been killed in this assault. Whether the chief killed by Johnson was Tecumseh is not positively known.

14. *See* McAfee, *Late War in the Western Country.*
15. *See* van Rensselaer, *The Affair of Queenstown.*
16. Collin's *History of Kentucky*, Vol. I, p. 217.
17. Johnson, *Famous Kentucky Tragedies and Trials.*
18. Connelly and Coulter, *History of Kentucky*, Vol. II, p. 772.
19. Now in the collection of the State Historical Society, Frankfort.
20. *See* Littell, *Statute Law of Kentucky*, Vol. III, Chap. 420.
21. Statute of 1811, Sec. 105.
22. Act of 1818.
23. Hart *et al* vs. Flynn's Executors, 8 Dana, 190.

CHAPTER IV

MEXICAN WAR AND PEACE

On September 6, 1845, Governor Owsley was informed by the U. S. Secretary of War that Gen. Zachary Taylor had been authorized, in case he should need them, to call on Kentucky for auxiliary troops to repel an apprehended Mexican invasion. The number and description of troops, should they be required, were to be stipulated by General Taylor. Governor Owsley replied at once assuring the Secretary of War that Kentucky had lost none of her patriotic zeal which had always led her to be among the foremost in defending the country against foreign aggression. The Governor asserted that he was willing and ready to comply with all constitutional and legal requisitions of the Federal Government, made by the President or his authorized agents; and he assured the Government at Washington that any requisition upon the militia of Kentucky would be accorded prompt and full response.

During mid-September Governor Owsley received intelligence that a strong armed force was being prepared to deliver one Dr. Baker from the Clay County Jail. Baker had been found guilty of the murder of a Mr. Bates, and was awaiting execution. Governor Owsley promptly dispatched Gen. Peter Dudley to Manchester with full discretionary powers so to act as to preserve the public peace and enforce the laws of the state. General Dudley moved to the scene of apprehended insurrection with the utmost celerity, and sent dispatches back to the Governor apprising him of the state of things there, and of his movements. His reports confirmed the Governor in the propriety of his course in taking effective steps to awe the insurgents, preserve the public peace, and enforce the laws. General Dudley, on his way, issued a call for four mounted companies of Colonel Miller's Madison regiment to march forthwith to Manchester. Arriving at the place, however, General Dudley thought the objects of his mission might be accomplished by the aid of only two companies, and accordingly so modified his call upon Colonel Miller's command.

News of the looming war with Mexico was received by the majority of Kentuckians with approbation. The interest of the Kentucky people in Texas affairs had begun as early as the Austin project and had been steadily increased by emigration to Texas, by filibustering expeditions against Mexico, and by participation in the war for Texas independence. There was a "Texas Emigrating Society" formed in Lexington as early as 1825, and that city became the center of the Kentucky emigration to Texas. The Texas settlers were chiefly from the Bluegrass region, and were from all walks of life. Many slaveholders went, taking their slaves with them to their new homes. At the beginning of the Texas Revolution there were few families in Bluegrass Kentucky that did not have relatives or friends in Texas.

That Kentuckians should sympathize with Texas in her revolt from Mexico was inevitable. As a matter fact, recruiting for the Texas Army began as soon as the news reached Kentucky that trouble was brewing, although the United States was officially neutral in the contest. Louisville was the chief recruiting station, but Lexington was the most prominent city in stimulating volunteers and in equipping them for service. There were a dozen Kentuckians among the dead in the Alamo, and Kentuckians fell at Goliad and at San Jacinto. From Bardstown a company of fifty-four men started to Texas in November, 1835, and arrived there in time to be among the 300 men massacred at Goliad, by General Urrea on the twenty-seventh of March, 1836. Four hundred volunteers left Lexington in June, under Col. E. J. Wilson, and in August the 1st Regiment, Kentucky Volunteers, under command of Col. C. L. Harrison, was mustered in at Louisville. In addition to these, practically every county of the Bluegrass and the Purchase contributed both men and money. Stephen F. Austin came to Kentucky in March, 1836, to appeal for help, and his appeal with the news of the Alamo and Goliad was decisive in stirring the emotions of

Kentuckians. The exact number of Kentucky volunteers in the Texas Revolution can, perhaps, never be ascertained, but there were certainly five to six hundred of them. This past friendly association with Texas and antipathy to Mexico played an important role in the speedy recruiting of volunteers when the war with Mexico came a few years later.

No call was made for volunteers under the notice of September 6, 1845, when Governor Owsley was notified by the U. S. Secretary of War that General Taylor was authorized to call on Kentucky for help, but the anticipated requisition for troops came soon after the declaration of war against Mexico on May 13, 1846. The same day Maj. Gen. E. P. Gaines wrote Governor Owsley that a requisition would soon be made and suggested that the Kentucky regiments be put in readiness at once. This letter was opened as it passed through the post office at Louisville and the suggestion it contained increased the already ardent enthusiasm of the Louisville Militia. The local regiment there, the Louisville Legion, promptly began drilling, and on the eighteenth of May its colonel, Stephen Ormsby, went to Frankfort to offer its services to the Governor. Influenced by the evident desires of Gaines, Owsley accepted the Legion and issued an appeal on the same day to the major generals throughout Kentucky to call out the militia and ask for volunteers, who were to organize themselves into companies, and report to him upon having done so.

Funds to arm, equip and move the troops were speedily forthcoming through the efforts of William Preston of Louisville, who obtained a subscription of $50,000 which he deposited in the Bank of Kentucky to the credit of the Governor, for use, if necessary, in getting the troops moved to the Mexican front. The Northern Bank of Kentucky at Lexington made a similar tender in the sum of $250,000. These funds were subscribed for use until the Governor could obtain an appropriation.

In addition to her men and munitions loans Kentucky gave freely of her means for the support of families of volunteers. Typical of this was the action of Covington which subscribed and paid in the sum of $2,000 as a fund to support the families of those who had enrolled as volunteers.* 1

A formal proclamation was issued by Governor Owsley on May 22, 1846, calling for two regiments of infantry and one of cavalry to be attached to the Regular Army for use against Mexico, this being Kentucky's quota of the 43,500 troops requested by the President. The 1st Infantry Regiment, the Louisville Legion, consisting of nine companies, was mustered in before the proclamation was issued. This action was taken because the army of General Taylor was generally believed to be in most imminent danger, and that any delay in reinforcements might prove fatal. Though the Governor was adversely criticised in some quarters, yet the circumstances alone absolved him of any blame, and when the facts became generally known censure gave way to applause. On May 26 the Governor announced that the other two regiments were well filled and that no more volunteers would be received. Over 10,000 men volunteered, of which only 2,500 could be accepted. The companies accepted were almost wholly from central Kentucky, due to the fact that remote counties had been late in receiving the Governor's call. All the volunteers enlisted for a term of one year, and with few exceptions companies were formed by counties. Three of the leading officers who were to take charge of the operations of the war were chosen from Kentucky. Zachary Taylor, major general of the Regular Army; William O. Butler, of Carroll County, major general of volunteers; and Thomas Marshall of Lewis County, brigadier general of volunteers. Many other names that appeared in the company rosters and official lists of the Mexican War appear later in places of prominence both in civil life and in the command of Confederate and Union armies. The training and experience this foreign war provided brought back to Kentucky a military unity which was lacking in 1846, when very few of the volunteers had ever looked upon a line of battle. These volunteers were changed, almost instantly, from citizens to soldiers, for no

---

* Notes, references, and sources are indicated by numerals. These refer to corresponding numbers at the end of this chapter. For notes on Chapter IV see page 148.

effort was made to give them camp training before pressing them into service. The only change was to trade the tools of civil life for implements of warfare.

The Louisville Legion was a well-drilled and well-equipped body of men, and consequently was not long in getting started to the seat of war. It remained in Louisville for about a week after it was mustered in,[2] and meanwhile the ladies of the town made new uniforms for the men. Governor Owsley chartered two steamboats, the *Diana* and *Alex Scott*, and the Legion broke camp at Oakland and went aboard eight days after it had volunteered. It was bound for Taylor's army on the Rio Grande, and, after a short stop at New Orleans, proceeded to its destination.

In the battle and capture of Monterey the Louisville Legion performed a distinguished service in guarding a mortar battery. For twenty-four hours the Legion was exposed to Mexican cannonading without being able to return the fire. In the engagement Gen. W. O. Butler was seriously wounded. The praise earned by the Legion in this instance came through its willingness to submit to fire for so long a time without being able to return it and for displaying no sign of faltering in the duty assigned to it. For its bravery on this occasion the Legion received the thanks of the legislature. The Legion advanced with Taylor into the interior of Mexico, but was not engaged in the Battle of Buena Vista. The discipline of the Legion was good, and it was among the most useful of the Kentucky volunteer regiments.

In all 105 companies tendered their services to Governor Owsley. It was obvious that a force of 15,000 men could easily have been raised by volunteer enlistments. The anxiety and haste to volunteer, which seemed to grip every quarter of Kentucky when the war was heralded, is reflected in the following articles which appeared in the Kentucky press, and in numerous incidents that transpired during the war.

> Kentucky Chivalry is a term not without meaning when the trial comes. The promptness with which the call for troops has been responded to will sustain a little boasting, and which some

may be disposed to laugh at in times of peace. One weeks notice and Kentucky is in the field; and our troops would have been on the way to the scene of action had the orders of the Secretary of War been understood. We can't define the intentions of the War Department at Washington, from official communications. These only become more foggy the more they are attempted to be explained. We understand that Secretary Marcy and General Scott have got their heads together at Washington, and will in time produce something, although we can't undertake to say what it will be. If it is like what has already been issued from that Department, we hope they will first get some one, like Daniel (not Webster) to interpret it, and then a third agent to translate it into English; otherwise we can't be responsible for the result. We must say to the War Department that we have lost all patience with the folly displayed in their management. Do they expect volunteers to be collected and then wait weeks and months on their own expenses? Do they expect the States and individuals to advance the money to repair their blunders? Where are the funds, and where is the paymaster? When shall our volunteers be mustered officially, and have orders to be off? We had rather applaud than censure, but we must say, if the Secretary of War doesn't do better in future and do it quickly, it will cost a good deal more to mend his injured reputation than it would to mend that unlucky pair of breeches which he wore.[3]

To the Editor of the Louisville Journal:

GENTLEMEN: Among the many instances of energy and promptitude displayed by the citizens of Kentucky in answering the requisition of the President for troops one has fallen under our observation we think should be recorded, especially as it is now somewhat uncertain whether the gentlemen engaged in it will have an opporunity to show their patriotism on the battle field, which, of all others, is the way they should prefer.

On last Monday at 11:00 o'clock, A. M., under the summons of General Desha, the 14th and 71st Regiments were paraded at this place [Paris], the proclamation of the Governor read, and in the course of an hour, 100 and upwards of the sons of Old Bourbon enrolled themselves as volunteers. Before the enlisting was completed, they were informed that the requisition for Infantry had been filled, and the company raised must be of dragoons, and it would be necessary for each man to furnish his horse and clothing. The volunteers thus enrolled were marched to the court house, and, understanding that there were two or three married gentlemen among their number, by unanimous vote excluded them —much against their will—announcing that there were young men enough to fill the requisition without taking married men from their families.

The company of "Bachelor Boys" then proceeded to the election of their officers, and while this was in progress, the citizens of the county were subscribing money and horses to equip them, and by 6:00 o'clock the organization of the company was completed, nearly

$1,000 subscribed, the requisite number of horses furnished, and the Captain, W. B. Arnold, Esq., their second lieutenant William M. Garrard, started to Frankfort to report the company as ready for duty.

These gentlemen reached Lexington after dark, ascertained that another company had been formed in Lexington, whose officers had just before started to report it, and it was supposed that that company would fill the requisition. Captain Arnold determined that his company should be reported first. They procured a fresh horse for their buggy, dashed on, and passed in full run the representatives of the Lexington company before they got to Versailles. They proceeded ahead of them, and when they had passed Versailles some three miles, one of the wheels of their buggy broke down and launched them in the road. Nothing daunted by the accident and the bruises, and being determined to beat the Lexington company, as the only chance to get in, Captain Arnold unhitched his horse and without taking time to strip off the harness, he mounted the horse and dashed on to Frankfort, some nine or ten miles distant, leaving Garrard to "bring up the Infantry" on foot.

It is said about midnight there was an awful clatter of horses hoofs down the hill to Frankfort, and Captain Arnold made his appearance on a horse in front of the Governor's Mansion. It was no time for ceremony or etiquette—a few halloes brought the good old Governor to the door, sans coat, sans pantaloons, sans everything but shirt. The company was reported to him, but he informed Captain Arnold that a company had been reported that evening by Captain Milam, of Frankfort, which completed the requisition, but if a new requisition was made the Bourbon troops would go first.

This we think is quick work especially in a country where a large majority of the citizens believed the war might have been avoided. But the Bourbon boys go for their country right or wrong, drunk or sober. To raise the fully equipped 100 dragoons and report them to the Governor at the distance of 40 miles within twelve hours, we believe is almost without parallel, and we sincerely hope the Bourbon troop of Bachelor Boys will yet have the opportunity of displaying their powers in the face of a Mexican regiment. If Arnold and Garrard lead the charge, the devil will certainly have to take the hindmost Mexicans.[4]

There is something, says the Baltimore *Patriot*, in the very air of Kentucky which makes a man a soldier. The news of the war is received there in the same spirit in which the sick Irishman rejoiced, "Oh, doctor, excuse me—there is a fight going on—the first I have seen since I left the Old Country, and I must take a hand in it—it will do me good!" Mr. Clay was right when he called Kentucky "The Ireland of America".[5]

On June 8, 1846, the regiments of McKee and Marshall rendezvoused at Louisville, to which point the volunteers made their way by companies. Those from the interior of the state marched overland, while the counties on the Ohio sent their companies by steamboats. These two regiments were mustered in on the ninth, and at once went into camp at the Oakland racecourse, where Camp Owsley had been established. With the exception of a few companies, these men were undisciplined and unacquainted with the rudiments of military training. Many of them looked upon the war as an adventure and as a welcome break in the monotony of home life, "a chance to see the world." Nothing could cure their disorderliness. In the Cavalry Regiment, Colonel Marshall barely escaped being murdered by his own men. Every visit of the volunteers to Louisville meant a conflict with the peace officers and a trail of outraged citizens. A friendly but exasperated editor of Louisville was finally driven to write: "An order for the speedy embarkation of the volunteers would be hailed with the liveliest satisfaction by the citizens of Louisville." As a matter of fact, the volunteers were not wholly to blame. There was mismanagement resulting in insufficient tents, in irregular rations, and in lack of clothing. McKee's regiment did not receive its arms and equipment until it arrived at Baton Rouge. Finally, June 29, the 2d Infantry Regiment started down the river on the steamboats *Louisville* and *Sultana*. With them went Capt. John S. Williams' independent company of mounted riflemen. This company had been excluded from the cavalry troop quota through error, and thereupon obtained a special acceptance from the U. S. War Department, a gesture of recognition of the service some of the company had previously rendered in the Texas rebellion. Williams's company had joined Scott's army of invasion at Vera Cruz. The stronghold of the enemy was at Cerro Gordo, some miles out on the road to the city of Mexico, and this well fortified position was defended by Santa Anna. The company of Captain Williams was attached to the volunteer regiment of Colonel Haskell of Tennessee. When the brigade of General Pillow assaulted the position of the enemy on the plateau, the advance post of honor was given to Haskell's regiment. In the face of a

MAJ. GEN. ZACHARY TAYLOR, U.S.A.
From a miniature owned by Misses Mary S. and
Willie P. Taylor

MAJ. GEN. SIMON BOLIVAR BUCKNER, C.S.A.
Courtesy, The Filson Club

murderous fire, which twice drove back the assailants, they again rallied and gallantly stormed the enemy's works, and planted the American flag there. Captain Williams led his company in the front, and shared the honors of the victory. For his bravery and daring on the occasion he won the sobriquet "Cerro Gordo" Williams, which long distinguished him in Kentucky. One week after the 2d Infantry left Louisville five steamboats set out with Marshall's Cavalry regiment aboard.

A news item concerning the rendezvous of the regiments at Louisville relates that "Governor Owsley went to Louisville on Tuesday, when he promptly gave orders for the supplies of the troops with everything necessary to their comfort. Although the Volunteers were already mustered into the service of the United States, he told the U. S. Quartermaster that he must furnish them with every requisite, and if Uncle Sam did not foot the bills, he would do it himself. He reviewed the troops on Thursday and returned home on Sunday."[6]

The 2d Regiment of Infantry was under command of Col. William R. McKee, Lt. Col. Henry Clay, Jr., and Maj. C. H. Fry. This regiment was composed of the following companies:

1st, Green County, Capt. William H. Maxey
2d, Franklin County, Capt. Franklin Chambers
3d, Mercer County, Capt. Phil B. Thompson
4th, Boyle County, Capt. S. S. Fry
5th, Kenton County, Capt. George W. Cutter
6th, Jessamine County, Capt. William T. Willis
7th, Lincoln County, Capt. William Dougherty
8th, Kenton County, Capt. William M. Joyner
9th, Montgomery County, Capt. Wilkerson Turpin
10th, Anderson County, Capt. George W. Kavanaugh

The 1st Regiment of Cavalry was commanded by Col. Humphrey Marshall, Lt. Col. E. H. Field, and Maj. John P. Gaines, and consisted of the following companies:

1st, Jefferson County, Capt. W. J. Hardy
2d, Jefferson County, Capt. A. Pennington
3d, Fayette County, Capt. Cassius M. Clay

4th, Woodford County, Capt. T. F. Marshall
5th, Madison County, Capt. J. C. Stone
6th, Garrard County, Capt. J. Price
7th, Fayette County, Capt. G. L. Postlethwait
8th, Gallatin County, Capt. J. S. Lillard
9th, Harrison County, Capt. John Shawhan
10th, Franklin County, Capt. B. C. Millam

Marshall's Cavalry was destined for General Wool's command. Therefore, instead of following the Legion and McKee's regiment to New Orleans, it left the boats at Memphis, Tennessee, under orders to march overland to San Antonio, Texas. It reached Memphis July 7, and encamped opposite the city on the Arkansas side of the Mississippi. Here it remained eleven days. "The encampment presents a wild and picturesque scene," wrote the editor of the Memphis *Enquirer*, and it is said that he might have added with perfect truth that the scene was no more wild and picturesque than the volunteers themselves. The Memphis papers noted that the yelling of the Kentuckians could be plainly heard in Memphis. Finally on, July 18, Marshall's men started west over the military road to Little Rock, Arkansas. With them went 1,200 mounted volunteers from Tennessee, and Capt. J. S. Williams' Company of Cavalry which, like Marshall's men, was destined for Wool's army at San Antonio. It required a week for the cavalry to reach Little Rock, the men suffering considerably from the hot weather, injudicious appetites, and a general inability to take care of themselves. The sick were left along the road at every village, and thirty more were left in improvised hospitals at Little Rock. After a four-days' rest there, they resumed their march again on the twenty-ninth. From Little Rock the route of the little army could be traced by letters written by the volunteers to their friends and published in the home papers, and quite as adequately by the notation in the *Roster* of the places where men of the regiment died. From Little Rock the men went to Washington, in southwest Arkansas. Then they crossed the Red River into Texas, through Douglass to Robin's Ferry, on the Trinity River. Here they took a southerly course across Texas to Washington, and from this point turned west toward San Antonio. But when they reached LaGrange they were met by orders from General Wool to change their march to Port Lavaca, Texas, on the Gulf, and there await further directions. The regiment feared that the order meant it was to be disbanded and remonstrated, but was assured that the purpose was to have it connect with supplies which had been gathered at Port Lavaca. To Port Lavaca it went, since the orders were imperative, the independent company reaching the town August 20, while Marshall's men got in about the middle of September.

On October 4, Capt. T. F. Marshall and Lt. James S. Jackson, of Capt. C. M. Clay's company, took time out to settle an old personal grievance by duel at Port Lavaca. Two shots were exchanged but neither man was touched. Years after, when Jackson was being chided for poor marksmanship in the duel, he said that he had spared Marshall for use by the Mexicans as a target.

At Port Lavaca the commands separated, Williams' company and the Tennessee Volunteers going to Wool's army at San Antonio and Marshall going to Camargo, Texas, to join Taylor. Camargo was reached by the first of November and the weary volunteers went gratefully into camp. They had been on the way for four months and had traveled more than 1,200 miles. Many who had left Memphis as cavalry were reduced to infantry by the time they reached Camargo, having lost their mounts on the way. Some had killed their horses chasing deer, others hunting buffaloes. Their road across Arkansas was marked not only by the sick and dead soldiers they left behind, but also by thousands of scandalized people whose patience and patriotism had been sorely tried by the conduct of the Kentuckians.

It is said that a Kentucky Volunteer, tired of the glories of "masterly inactivity," on reaching a ford near the mouth of the Rio Grande, stopped and looked hesitatingly upon the water. Shaking his head, he remarked: "I shouldn't mind going into that water, for it looks refreshing, but I have made up my mind never to commit another d........d voluntary act as long as I live—you can go on, boys, but I shall wait for special orders."

The following extracts from the letter of an officer of the 1st Kentucky Infantry portrays conditions met with generally by the Kentucky Volunteers:

MONTEREY, MEXICO, *January 15, 1847.*

* * * * * * * * * * * *

Our regiment, as well as other regiments of volunteers, is in an awful condition at present. The men are about half naked. Two-thirds of them have not a blanket to cover their bodies with when they lie down on the ground, for that is their bed. They have over four months pay due, but cannot get it. When any money comes up here, the regular soldiers are paid first, and the ragged volunteer's turn never comes. I think our used-to-be rich Uncle Sam would soon grow sick, if he were out here about a week, with one thin blanket, eight months in use, and the rocky cold ground to lie on, without a coat, and with thin pants with the seats looking as if the dogs had hold of them, and shoes with toes and tops off. Hats and caps look extremely melancholy, and represent every age, description, shape and nation. The sutlers get all of our money, and the volunteers get scarcely anything in return. The clothing that they bring out here is the refuse of every slip-shop, which they buy at a mere trifle, and sell to the soldiers at an enormous price. Pants that cost them about seventy-five cents, they sell for four, five, and six dollars. A suit of clothes, such as it is, costs at the sutler's from fifteen to twenty dollars, about three months' wages. The volunteers cannot help themselves, for cash is not to be had by them. When pay day does come, the first man that goes up is Mr. Sutler. He takes his seat at the head of the table, and is served first. If any money it left the soldier gets it. When our regiment was paid off the first time, after the sutler got his money out of the men, they had nothing left, and a good many of them were in debt to him. The Regulars draw clothing from the Government sutlers and sell to the Volunteers at double what they pay for it. Our men have bought a good many suits of the regulars, and if they could get their money when it becomes due they would not be in want. This they cannot do, but they must have clothing and are forced to go into debt to the sutler, who skins them out of all they can get. Uncle Sam had better see to his dear nephews or they will recollect him hereafter in his troubles.[7]

General Taylor's forces won a decisive victory at Buena Vista after the battle had raged two days, February 22-23. Among the troops here engaged were 330 Kentucky cavalry under Col. Humphrey Marshall, and 571 infantry of the 2d Kentucky Regiment commanded by Col. William R. McKee. It is said that the unruly conduct and wild counter charges of Marshall's cavalry contributed largely to the victory at Buena Vista. The United States forces here engaged consisted of 4,759 men of whom 267 were killed and 456 wounded. Kentucky's loss was disproportionately high, there having been twenty-seven cavalry and forty-four infantry killed, and thirty-four cavalry and fifty-seven infantry wounded. Among the Kentuckians killed were Colonel McKee and Lt. Col. Henry Clay, Jr. Their men made a valiant effort to carry them from the field, but the rescue parties were all killed.

At a very critical point during the Battle of Buena Vista, when it became necessary to sustain one of the columns which was staggering under a charge made by the Mexicans in overwhelming numbers, General Taylor dispatched Lieutenant Colonel Crittenden to order Colonel McKee of the 2d Kentucky Regiment to bring his men into immediate action. Crittenden found the regiment, both men and officers, ready, delivered the order and rode back to the general, by whose side it was his duty to stay. The Kentuckians moved forward in gallant style, led by McKee and Clay, both of whom fell the same day. It so happened that before reaching a position from which they could deliver an effective fire, the regiment had to cross a valley which was broken by ravines and masses of stone. While crossing this valley only the heads of the men could be seen—from the point which General Taylor and Crittenden occupied—and these were bobbing up and down, and crosswise, in such confusion as to impress both Taylor and Crittenden with the idea that the regiment had fallen into disorder. The Mexicans were annoying them at the same moment by a fire, which helped to confirm the opinion of the general that the Kentuckians were thrown into dismay.

General Taylor could only see the heads of the troops, and, misled by their motions in getting across gullies, and going around rocks and other obstructions, into the belief that they were about to give way, turned to Crittenden, a Kentuckian, and with a look indicating deep mortification, exclaimed, "By G......d, Mr. Crittenden, this will not do—this is not the way for Kentuckians to behave themselves when called upon to make good a battle—it will not answer, sir." Crittenden, who was mistaken by the same movements that enraged General Taylor, made little reply other than agree with his superior's comment. In a few moments the Kentuckians had crossed the uneven places and were seen ascending the slope of the valley, shoulder to shoulder, and with the firm and regular step of veterans. On they moved until they reached the crest of the hill where they met the enemy and before the flush of a temporary advantage had subsided, delivered their fire with such regularity and deadly aim that the Mexicans gave way in a precipitious retreat. As the Kentuckians advanced and moved forward under General Taylor's riveted gaze, there could be no mistaking his change of feeling. When they opened fire, the old general's censure changed to admiration. "Hurrah for old Kentuck," he shouted, and rising in his saddle—"That's the way to do it, give them h......ll, d......n them." Then, having expressed his ardent state pride, he went about looking after other parts of the field. The Battle of Buena Vista served the Kentuckians as a gauge of valor. As in the Battle of New Orleans the hopeless prospect faced at Buena Vista was accepted as a test to determine what zealous soldiers could do in the face of superior numbers in a long and hard fight.

The Kentucky Volunteers had enlisted, as previously stated, for twelve months, and when their term expired they had no thought but of going home as quickly as possible.

It was not so much that they were tired of war as that they were homesick for Kentucky. Practically none of them reenlisted at the time. The Legion was the first to get home, reaching Louisville from New Orleans, May 27, 1847. Its first action on disembarking was to march around to the home of Sally Ward and present the colors which she had given it a year before. Captain Williams' company reached Louisville about two weeks later, bringing with it a brass six-pounder captured at Cerro Gordo. McKee's and Marshall's men came in about the middle of July. As each regiment landed it was greeted with a riotous reception, after which the men dispersed to their homes.

After the return of the volunteers, there ensued two months in which Kentucky apparently forgot that there was any such thing as a war in progress. But the war spirit was not dead altogether, as was shown when, on the twenty-sixth of August, the Secretary of War sent the Governor a requisition for two more regiments of infantry. Governor Owsley issued his proclamation on the thirty-first and the men began enlisting again. There was no such excitement, however, as there had been on the occasion of the first call. As a matter of fact, volunteering lagged and the chief reason for it was that a condition of the enlistment was for the "duration of the war." By September 20, the quota was filled. The Governor named October 4 as the date of rendezous and specified Louisville and Smithland as the places, the latter for the companies of Caldwell and Livingston counties.

The counties from which the 3d and 4th Infantry Regiments came were not the same as those which sent the volunteers of the preceding year. Few volunteers now came from the Bluegrass; the mountains and the Pennyrile furnished the mass of the men. Practically none of the volunteers of 1846 reenlisted in 1847. It is probable that most of the companies of 1847 were among those rejected the year before.

The 3d Regiment of Infantry was under command of Col. M. V. Thompson, Lt. Col. T. L. Crittenden, and Maj. John C.

Breckinridge. The regiment was composed of the following companies:

Company	No. of Men.	County	Captain
1	81	Laurel	A. F. Caldwell
2	96	Estill	W. P. Chiles
3	96	Shelby	Thomas Todd
4	91	Bourbon	William E. Sims
5	94	Scott	John R. Smith
6	97	Bath	James Ewing
7	125	Fleming	L. M. Cox
8	101	Nicholas	Leonidas Metcalfe
9	98	Boone	J. A. Prichard
10	97	Fayette	L. B. Robinson

In the 3d Regiment was Captain Cox's company of Fleming Volunteers which contained twenty-five men over six feet tall.

The 4th Regiment was under command of Col. (formerly Captain) John S. Williams, Lt. Col. William Preston, and Maj. W. T. Ward. It consisted of the following companies:

Company	No. of Men	County	Captain
1	70	Caldwell	J. S. Corum
2	94	Livingston	G. B. Cook
3	91	Daviess	D. McCreary
4	92	Hart	P. H. Gardner
5	68	Jefferson	T. Keating
6	94	Adair	J. C. Squires
7	100	Pulaski	J. G. Lair
8	91	Washington	M. R. Hardin
9	114	Nelson	B. R. Hardin
10	92	Henry	A. W. Bartlett

Twelve other companies organized and reported after the two regiments had been formed. The companies that could not be accepted were organized in Mason, Fayette, Montgomery, Bullitt, Madison, Campbell, Hardin, Franklin, and Harrison counties, and three from Louisville. Several others were in process of organizing when word came that no more could be accepted under the requisition. Those accepted embarked at Louisville or Smithland, and proceeded down the river to New Orleans and across the Gulf, where they were attached to the command of General Scott.

Kentucky observed a day of mourning on July 20, 1847,

when her first Mexican War dead were reburied in the state section of the Frankfort Cemetery. Those interred on that day included Col. Wm. R. McKee, Lt. Col. Henry Clay, Jr., Capt. Wm. T. Willis, Capt. Wm. H Maxey, Adjt. E. M. Vaughn, Lt. James Powell, and eleven privates. In the procession to the cemetery were eleven volunteer companies of militia and several hundred of the soldiers recently returned from the Mexican War. It was this occasion that inspired Theodore O'Hara, himself a volunteer of the war, to write as a memorial to Kentucky's war dead:

THE BIVOUAC OF THE DEAD

The muffled drum's sad roll has beat
    The soldier's last tattoo!
No more on life's parade shall meet
    That brave and fallen few;
On Fame's eternal camping ground
    Their silent tents are spread,
And Glory guards, with solemn round,
    The bivouac of the dead.

No rumor of the foe's advance
    Now swells upon the wind;
No troubled thought at midnight haunts
    Of loved ones left behind;
No vision of the morrow's strife
    The warrior's dream alarms;
No braying horn nor screaming fife
    At dawn shall call to arms.

Their shivered swords are red with rust,
    Their plumed heads are bowed,
Their haughty banner, trailed in dust,
    Is now their martial shroud—
And plenteous funeral tears have washed
    The red stains from each brow,
And the proud forms, in battle gashed,
    Are free from anguish now.

The neighing troop, the flashing blade,
    The bugle's stirring blast,
The charge, the dreadful cannonade,
    The din and shout are past—
Nor war's wild note, nor glory's peal,
    Shall thrill with fierce delight
These breasts that never more may feel
    The rapture of the fight.

Like the fierce Northern hurricane
    That sweeps his great plateau,
Flushed with the triumph yet to gain,
    Came down the sorried foe—
Who heard the thunder of the fray
    Break o'er the field beneath,
Knew well the watchword of that day
    Was victory or death.
* * * * * * * * *
Full many a mother's breath has swept
    O'er Angustura's plain,
And long the pitying sky has wept
    Above its moulder'd slain;
The raven's scream or eagle's flight,
    Or shepherd's pensive lay,
Alone now wake each solemn height
    That frowned o'er that dread fray.

Sons of the Dark and Bloody Ground!
    Ye must not slumber there,
Where stranger steps and tongue resound
    Along the heedless air;
Your own proud land's heroic soil
    Should be your fitter grave;
She claims from war its richest spoil—
    The ashes of her brave

Thus, 'neath their parent turf they rest,
    Far from the gory field,
Borne to a Spartan mother's breast
    On many a bloody shield.
The sunshine of their native sky
    Smiles sadly on them here,
And kindred eyes and hearts watch by
    The hero's sepulchre.

Rest on, embalmed and sainted dead!
    Dear as the blood ye gave;
No impious footsteps here shall tread
    The herbage of your grave;
Nor shall your glory be forgot
    While Fame her record keeps,
Or Honor points the hallowed spot
    Where Valor proudly sleeps.

Yon marble minstrel's voiceless stone,
    In deathless song shall tell,
When many a vanished year has flown,
    The story how ye fell;
Nor wreck, nor change, nor winter's blight,
    Nor time's remorseless doom,
Can dim one ray of holy light
    That gilds your glorious tomb.[13]

On September 16, 1847, Kentucky volunteers from Franklin, Montgomery, and Shelby counties, who fell at the Battle of Buena Vista, were accorded military honors upon being interred in the State Cemetery. The following February the legislature appropriated $15,000 to erect a military monument in the State Cemetery "to commemorate the deeds of Kentucky's gallant dead." A year later an act of the legislature directed that "the following names of battles and campaigns be inscribed upon the bands of the military monument: Boonesborough, Blue Licks, Estill's Defeat, St. Clair's Defeat, Harmar's Defeat, Wayne's Campaign, Indian Wars, Tippecanoe, Raisin, Mississiniway, Fort Meigs, Thames, New Orleans, Monterey, Cerro Gordo, Buena Vista, Mexico; that the names of such distinguished citizens of Kentucky as fell in said battles, campaigns and Indian wars, be inscribed on the shaft beneath said bands; and that the dedication on the monument shall show that it is erected by a grateful country in honor of the private soldiers, equally with that of the officers." At the same session resolutions were adopted complimentary to Maj. John P. Gaines, Capt. C. M. Clay, Lt. George Davidson, and thirty privates serving under them, all of whom were taken prisoner by the Mexicans at Encarnacion. Like resolutions paid compliment to Capt. William J. Heady, Lt. T. J. Churchill, and eighteen privates, for valor displayed before being made prisoners by the Mexicans. Still another resolution was addressed in compliment to Maj. John P. Gaines for "honorably withdrawing his parole as a prisoner of war, making his escape to the American Army, and with it gallantly fighting at Cherubusco, Chapultepec, and all the battles fought before the walls and in the city of Mexico—he being the only volunteer from Kentucky who participated in the achievements of General Scott and his army in those memorable victories." Later on it was discovered that Francis M. Lisle, of Clark County, who enlisted in the company of Capt. John S. Williams in 1846, instead of returning with his company remained and went through all of the battles to Mexico City, serving part of the time as volunteer aide to General Twiggs.

The following is a resolution of the Kentucky Legislature of February, 1847, pertaining to the Mexican War:

Resolved, That the conduct of our officers and soldiers at the battles of Palo Alta, Resaca de la Palma, and Monterey is worthy of the highest commendation, and will be borne in lasting remembrance by their grateful country. That the steadiness and gallantry of the volunteers who fought at Monterey, from the highest officer to the humblest soldier, demonstrates the truth of the important principle, that a free Government may safely dispense with large standing armies, and confidently rely on the courage and patriotism of its citizen soldiers for defense.

Resolved, That the private soldier, who abandons the endearments of home and voluntarily dedicates his health, his strength, and his life to the service of the Republic, in a distant region and fatal climate, exhibits chivalry and patriotism which entitle him to the esteem of his fellow citizens and the gratitude of his country.

Resolved, That the Louisville Legion, which, by order of the commanding general, was posted to guard a mortar battery at Monterey, and exposed to the enemy's cannon for about twenty-four hours, without being able to return their fire, displayed obedience, patience, discipline and calm courage, and all the highest qualities which adorn the character of the soldier; thereby giving assurance that they will gallantly sustain the fame of their State whenever it becomes their duty to mingle in the strife of battle.

The Kentucky Legislture on February 23, 1847, adopted resolutions paying compliment to Gen. Zachary Taylor and Gen. W. O. Butler for the services that these men had already rendered in the Mexican War. A further provision was made by the legislature directing that each be given a sword, and that such a sword be likewise presented to the widow of Maj. P. N. Barbour. Major Barbour was among those killed at Monterey. By subsequent legislative action it was directed that Major Barbour's body should be returned to Kentucky for burial in the Frankfort Cemetery.

A state appropriation made it possible to bring home the remains of the Kentuckians who were masacred at the River Raisin, for burial in the State Cemetery. Col. Edward Brooks arrived in Frankfort on September 30, 1848, with those remains which had been found in a common grave, having been unearthed in excavating a street in Monroe, Michigan. An aged Kentuckian, survivor of the massacre, identified them as the bones of his fellow soldiers, having remembered the location of the place of burial. The skulls showed that the tomahawk had been the instrument of death in every case.

In 1850 the Kentucky Legislature extended "the thanks and gratitude of the people of Kentucky, and a sword" to Sgt. William F. Gaines of Georgetown, referring to him as "the boy defender of the 2d Regiment of Kentucky Infantry at the Battle of Buena Vista." The resolution directed that Sergeant Gaines's name be inscribed on a metal plate to be attached to the flagstaff of the regimental colors.

Several incidents of military interest transpired in the fall of 1850. Among them was the Act of Congress of September 29, granting bounty lands, in tracts of 40 to 160 acres, to the privates and non-commissioned officers of the War of 1812, to those of Indian wars waged subsequent to 1790, and to officers of the Mexican War. During this year Capt. B. R. Hardin of Bardstown, who led a Nelson County militia company in the Mexican War, was murdered in the Isthmus of Panama. Another noted figure of the Kentucky Militia, Col. Richard M. Johnson, died on November 19, 1850. The funerals of both of those men were marked by tribute paid them by the militia of their county. Two years later, on July 10, 1852, militia companies, representative of many counties, assembled in Lexington to pay tribute at the funeral of Henry Clay, while distant communities conducted memorial services of a military nature.

The state's first call for militia to do police duty in a feud was made in 1852 when Governor Powell ordered a detachment of forty men to guard the Garrard County Jail. During the latter part of 1849 personal grievances between Dr. H. Evans and John Hill resulted in a deadly enmity. Friends and relatives of both men espoused their causes, and gradually the two factions claimed a large percentage of Garrard County's population. The Hill faction obtained control, in 1850, of the county law enforcement offices, and Dr. Evans soon after sought shelter among kinfolks in Indiana. After a prolonged stay there he returned to his home. During his absence the sheriff with a company of militia under

Colonel Dodd had visited the Evans house to arrest the doctor. Being informed that Dr. Evans' whereabouts were unknown the sheriff and militia remained in the neighborhood for several days awaiting Evans' return.

In 1852 Squire Bruner of Jessamine County called Dr. Evans to see a patient. The doctor arrived safely at the patient's bedside, but his return home was made dangerous by the Hill faction. Bruner had promised an escort of 100 militia for the doctor. This promise was made after the Hills had opened fire upon Dr. Evans when he was attempting to cross the river. However, troops were not then called.

Later, when some members of the Evans faction were in the Garrard County Jail, the jailer, in sympathy with the Hill faction, asked the Governor for a militia guard, alleging that the Evans prisoners were about to escape or be delivered. Upon the request the Governor ordered the forty militia on duty to guard the jail.[7A]

Martial pageantry played a leading role in the laying of the cornerstone of the Henry Clay monument in the Lexington Cemetery on July 4, 1857. The occasion assumed somewhat of a competitive nature by reason of the diverse origin of the militia companies that paraded in review before Governor Morehead, his staff, and visitors. Kentucky companies participating from points outside of Fayette County were: The Falls City Guards from Louisville, the Madison Guards from Richmond, and the Danville Artillery from Danville. From other states came the National Guards from St. Louis, Missouri; the Baltimore City Guards from Baltimore, Maryland; the Cleveland Light Artillery from Cleveland, Ohio; the Columbus Fencibles from Columbus, Ohio; the Indianapolis Guards from Indianapolis, Indiana; the Amoskeag Veterans from New Hampshire; and from Cincinnati, Ohio, came the Guthrie Grays and the Fulton Guards of Liberty in their spectacular "Continental Uniforms."

An act of the legislature of February 23, 1854, directed that a sword be presented to H. E. Read of Larue County, who served as an ensign in Colonel Andrews' regiment of

Voltigeurs (Sharpshooters) in the war with Mexico. The sword was recited by the act as a token of esteem "for gallant services in bearing the flag of his country through all the battles in the valley of Mexico, until he fell covered with wounds under the walls of Chapultepec."

In February, 1858, the authorities at Washington determined to send an armed force to Utah, to bring the rebellious Mormons to terms. Upon intelligence of this situation the legislature of Kentucky, on February 15, authorized the Governor to raise a regiment of volunteers to be offered in aid of the expedition. On the sixth of March Governor Morehead issued a proclamation inviting companies, of 100 privates, 1 captain, 3 lieutenants, and 8 non-commissioned officers, desiring to volunteer for the expedition to Utah, to organize and report to him not later than April 1. Within a month twenty-one companies, more than twice the number needed, were tendered to the state. Among them were three from Louisville, commanded by Captains Rogers, Wales, and Forsythe, being one-seventh of the entire number reported from the state at large. Captains reporting companies were:

Captain Wales, Louisville
Captain Hanks, Anderson
Captain Board, Lexington
Captain Trapnall, Mercer
Captain Pierce, Trimble
Captain McHenry, Daviess
Captain Rogers, Louisville
Captain Moore, Pendleton
Captain Adair, Union
Captain Reese, Kenton
Captain Donan, Hart County
Captain Bacon, Franklin County

Capt. Joseph C. Dear, Shelby County
Captain Landrum, Gallatin County
Captain Miller, Christian County
Captain Gist, Montgomery County
Captain Corman, Boyle County
Captain Holman, Owen County
Captain Daniel, Owsley County
Captain Booker, Washington County
Captain Forsythe, Louisville

The first ten companies above named composed the Kentucky regiment designated for Utah service. These were selected by the Governor by lot on April 9, a week after the volunteer bill had passed both houses of Congress. This bill owed its passage mainly to the efforts of a Kentuckian. In March, 1858, Humphrey Marshall in the House of Representatives delivered a speech on the Army bill. His address was brought about by the fact that some of the friends of the administration insisted that Regulars should be added to the extent of five regiments, complaining that the Army's strength had been neglected. This was a point which Colonel Marshall examined to show that there was more fiction than fact in the assumption. "What," he asked, "has it come to this, that Regulars, mere machines, moved by superior intelligence, must be employed to carry out the purposes of the administration? Men who cannot travel without incumbrances, and who do not get beyond the smell of their pork and beans." Colonel Marshall then showed that volunteers could be procured at once, to march upon being mustered in. He added that if the public exigencies required prompt action, it certainly was not the part of wisdom to await the slow process of recruiting Regulars. He stressed that volunteers, selected "in the west," were equal for any emergency. Marshall's speech resulted in a discontinuation of the attempt to add regiments to the Regular Army.[8]

To complete the regimental organization, Governor Morehead appointed the following field officers: Thomas L. Crittenden, colonel; Thomas L. Hawkins, lieutenant colonel; James S. Jackson, major; Robert Richardson, second major.

Two persons reported companies without a roll of officers or men; one of these by W. M. Fulkerson of Breathitt County, and the other by A. L. Sanders of Carroll County. The Governor would not recognize their reports on account of this deficiency.

The selection by lot of companies for the regiment was made in the following manner: The names of the twenty-one captains were written on slips of paper, also the word "company" on ten other slips. The papers last named, together with eleven blanks, were placed in a hat, and the slips containing the names of the captains were placed in another hat. Two little boys were selected, one of whom drew from one hat a ticket on which was written the name of a captain, the second boy then drew from the other hat a slip, which determined the acceptance or rejection of the company whose captain had been named by the first paper drawn.

That there was a decided antagonism in some quarters to sending Kentucky troops to Utah is borne out by the poison pen of George D. Prentice, yet these caustic comments produced little effect on the ardor of the state's troops. Among these comments are such as the following:

> We beg leave to suggest as a reason why the administration should accept the Utah volunteers from Kentucky, that they are universally admitted to be among the most virtuous young men in the United States.[9]

> If young fellows are a great deal readier to volunteer to go and fight men who have fifty wives apiece than those who have only one apiece, what are we to infer—that they are after the men or the women?[10]

On the seventh of April ex-Governor L. W. Powell of Kentucky and Major General McCulloch of Texas were sent to Utah by the Government as peace envoys. The Volunteer regiment was disbanded when news came that the Mormons had accepted the Government's proposals, borne to them by Powell and McCulloch.

Tribute was paid to the Kentucky Militia on October 14, 1858, by the presentation of a historic sword to the Masonic Grand Lodge of Kentucky by Judge Levi H. Todd, of Indiana, a native of Kentucky. The sword so presented was carried by Col. Joseph Hamilton Daviess when he fell at the Battle of Tippecanoe. The oak case enclosing the sword was made from the tree under which Colonel Daviess died. Admiration for Colonel Daviess had previously been expressed in the literary field. Among the sectarian tracts of the Rev. Stephen T. Badin is a series of open letters on the evidences of Christianity addressed to "A Gentleman of the Bar" (i.e. Col. Joseph Hamilton Daviess). The best known of the Father Badin's fine Latin poems is *Epicedium,* an elegy "on the glorious death of Joseph Hamilton Daviess, Commander of the Horse, who fell a victim to his love of country, in the late battle of the Wabash, the 7th Nov., 1811."[11]

Until 1850 every able-bodied white man from eighteen to forty-five years of age was a potential soldier. In that year militia musters were discontinued throughout the state because the new state constitution provided that "the militia of the Commonwealth shall consist of all free able-bodied male persons (Negroes, mulattoes and Indians excepted) resident in the same, between the ages of eighteen and forty-five years," but made no mention pertaining to their arming or organization as a military force. The law in effect prior to the date when the third constitution became operative was now obsolete.

In 1851 the legislature reestablished a de facto military organization. The acts of this session directed the mustering of such residents as were contemplated by the constitution as the state's enrolled military force. Under the same law company musters were held in April, battalion musters in May, brigade musters in September, and regimental musters in October. A contemporary act directed that the opinion of any court-marital should not be set aside for want of any formality of proceeding or the use of any technical terms, providing it appeared that the accused had a fair and impartial trial. A court-martial could be ordered on charges made by any white person, the charge having been under oath and submitted to the Governor or any militia officer.

Officers or privates failing or refusing to march when ordered into service were subject to trial by court-martial. Guilty officers were fined three months' pay. Non-commissioned officers, musicians, and privates were fined not less the $60, nor more than $100, for a like breach.

An amendment of March 7, 1854, provided for a state-wide regimental muster on the first Saturday in June, 1859, and thereafter in every sixth year, on the first Saturday in June, this to be the only muster.

An act of February 2, 1858, made it an offense and provided a fine of $10 for selling or giving liquor to any Kentucky Military Institute cadet, and also provided that no recovery should be had for goods sold to a cadet under twenty-one years of age.

On March 5, 1860, the legislature made provision for the organization of the Kentucky Militia into a State Guard. The new act divided the entire militia into three classes, namely:

The active or volunteer militia, to be known as the State Guard; the enrolled militia, and the militia of reserve. Under this act provision was made for organizing the State Guard into companies, regiments and brigades. The State Guard was given into the especial charge of a newly created state military official, the inspector general of the State Guard. This act was contested in the Jefferson Circuit Court, and on December 24, 1860, Judge Muir handed down a decision holding that the State Guard law was effective since it did not contravene the constitution or laws either of Kentucky or of the United States.

The passage of the State Guard law and then the belligerency at the time between the Northern and Southern states stimulated the organization of State Guard companies. Several regiments were formed in the state, and active drilling continued until what had once been ridiculed as a "Cornstalk Militia" evolved into a body of men that ranked among the best drilled troops in the West.[12]

The first incumbent of the office of inspector general was Simon Bolivar Buckner, a native Kentuckian, a West Point graduate, and retired officer of the U.S. Army. At the time of his appointment to this office Mr. Buckner was commissioned a major general and at the same time Thomas L. Crittenden was made brigadier general of the State Guard; Lloyd Tilghman and Roger W. Hanson were named colonels.

A report of General Buckner, made in January, 1861, showed the state as owning 11,283 muskets, 3,159 rifles, 2,873 cavalry arms outfits, and 53 fieldpieces. On conditions of the militia the report showed forty-five companies "admirably drilled in rifle tactics, handsomely uniformed and fully armed and equipped." The legislature that received this report made no appropriation for further arming the state. A proclamation of Governor Magoffin reconvened the legislature on May 6, 1861, when the executive urged the necessity for an arms appropriation. This was then made in the sum of $75,000 to be used for the purchase of munitions, none of which was to be used "against either the United States or the Confederate States, except to repel invasion."

NOTES, REFERENCES, AND SOURCES

1. Louisville Daily *Journal*, May 31, 1846.
2. This was the first occasion on which Kentucky troops were mustered into the U.S. Army. Procedure adopted in pursuance of rules established by the van Rensselaer case.
3. The Frankfort *Commonwealth*, May 22, 1846.
4. *Ibid.*, June 2, 1846.
5. Reprinted in the Frankfort *Commonwealth*, June 8, 1846.
6. The Frankfort *Commonwealth*, June 16, 1846.
7. Louisville Daily *Journal*, March 5, 1847.
7A. *See* Thompson, *The Hill and Evans Feud.*
8. Louisville Daily *Journal*, March 22, 1858.
9. *Ibid.*, April 17, 1858.
10. *Ibid.*, May 12, 1858.
11. *See* Townsend, *Kentucky in American Letters, 1792–1912*, Vol. I, pp. 30–34.
12. Organization of Kentucky State Guard.
    Louisville Battalion—organized May 7, 1860.
    Louisville Battalion—organized May 7, 1860.
    Co. 1, Citizens Guards of Louisville.
    Co. 2, National Blues of Louisville.
    Co. 3, Jackson Guards of Louisville.
    Co. 4, Hardin Company of Light Infantry of Elizabethtown.
    Co. 5, Nelson Grays of Bardstown.
    Co. 6, Bitter Water Blues of Shepherdsville.
    Co. 7, Citizen's Artillery of Louisville.
    Lexington Battalion organized June 15, 1860.
    Co. 1, Governor's Guard of Frankfort.
    Co. 2, Lexington Rifles of Lexington.
    Co. 3, Union Greys of Georgetown.
    Co. 4, Lexington Chasseurs of Lexington.
    Co. 5, Woodford Blues of Versailles.
    Co. 6, Jessamine Rifles of Nicholasville.
    Co. 7, The Governor's Red Artillery of Frankfort.
    The Green River Battalion organized June 13, 1860.
    Co. 1, The Warren Voltiguers, Bowling Green.
    Co. 2, The Logan Guards, Russellville.
    The Bourbon Battalion organized June 13, 1860.
    Co. 1, Flat Rock Greys, Flat Rock.
    Co. 2, Kentucky Guards, Leesburg.
    Co. 3, Bourbon Rangers, N. Middletown.
    Co. 4, Harrison Rifles, Cynthiana.
    The Marion Rifle Battalion organized August 11, 1860.
    Company A of Marion.
    Company B of Marion.

    The first encampment of the Kentucky State Guards was held during the week ending August 29, 1860, at Camp Boone, Jefferson County, with Gen. S. B. Buckner commanding.
    The Shelby Battalion, organized September 8, 1860.
    Co. 1, The Shelby Guard.

Co. 2, The Minnie Greys.
Co. 3, The New Castle Guards.
Co. 4, The Trimble Rifles.
The Henderson Battalion organized November 6, 1860.
Co. 1, The Henderson Guard.
Co. 2, The Henderson Cavalry.
Co. 3, The Uniontown Riflemen.
The Kentucky River Battalion organized November 6, 1860.
Co. 1. Governor's Guards, Frankfort.
Co. 2, Woodford Blues.
Co. 3, Woodford Greys.
Co. 4, Owenton Guards.

The first three companies were detached from the Lexington Battalion.

On November 6, 1860, General Buckner directed (Special Order No. 18) that "until the formation of other companies will justify a separate organization the following named companies are assigned to the respective battalions named, viz:

The Mount Vernon Guards to the Lexington Battalion.
The Winchester Company to the Lexington Battalion.
The Beechfork Ranger to the Salt River Battalion.
The Adair Battalion organized November 7, 1860.
Co. 1, Greensburg Guards.
Co. 2, The Adair Guards.
Co. 3, The Pulaski Guards.
Co. 4, The Clinton Guards.

13. For text of *The Bivouac of the Dead*—See Collins *History of Kentucky*, Vol. I, p. 590. *Also* Townsend, *Kentucky in American Letters, 1784-1912*, Vol. I, p. 218-23.

CHAPTER V—PART I

WAR BETWEEN THE STATES

The assertion of states' rights through the secession of the Southern States brought Kentucky face to face with the problem of allegiance to the United States or the Confederate States, though for some time she assumed an outward appearance of neutrality. Numerous public addresses, resolutions of the state legislature, actions by municipalities looking toward a continuation of neutrality or belligerency, and official visits to Kentucky, as well as tempting offers for private gain, were, during this period, determining the factional allegiance of Kentuckians.

On January 21, 1861, George W. Ewing of Logan County introduced resolutions in the legislature indicative of the course many Kentuckians had determined to pursue upon receiving word of the tender of troops and money by New York, Ohio, Maine, and Massachusetts, to the United States; namely, "that it is the opinion of the General Assembly that whenever the authorities of these States shall send armed forces to the South for the purpose indicated in the said resolutions, the people of Kentucky, uniting with their brethren of the South, will resist such invasions of the soil of the South at all hazards and to the last extremity." The resolution embodying this attitude was adopted by the lower house by a vote of eighty-seven to six. Five days later the Kentucky Senate, by a unanimous vote, and the house by a vote of eighty-one to five, sent a peace delegation to Washington upon the invitation of Virginia. On the sixteenth of March the first partisan expression favoring the North came in a public address of James Guthrie at Louisville, in which he lauded the action of Northern States that had tendered men and money to preserve the Union, and indirectly suggested that a force of the Kentucky Militia be likewise tendered. Guthrie had been one of the six Washington peace commissioners. The others recommended the observance of strict neutrality by Kentucky.

The construction of a new state arsenal at Frankfort was provided for by the legislature in an act of April 4, 1861. An appropriation of $19,400 was made for that purpose and for machinery and labor to repair state arms.

A proclamation calling for 75,000 troops was issued by the President of the United States on April 15, 1861, and thereupon the Secretary of War telegraphed the Governor of Kentucky asking for troops, which message and reply is as follows:

WASHINGTON, *April 15, 1861.*

TO HIS EXCELLENCY, HON. BERIAH MAGOFFIN,
Governor of Kentucky,
Frankfort, Kentucky.

Call is made on you by tonight's mail for four regiments of militia for immediate service.

SIMON CAMERON
Secretary of War.

FRANKFORT, *April 15, 1861.*

HON. SIMON CAMERON, *Secretary of War,*
Washington, City.

Your dispatch is reviewed. In answer I say, emphatically, Kentucky will furnish no troops for the wicked purpose of subduing her sister Southern States.

Yours,
B. MAGOFFIN.
Governor of Kentucky.

In a public address at Lexington, on April 17, U. S. Senator John J. Crittenden urged strongly that Kentucky continue her policy of neutrality and her refusal to supply troops to the United States for aggressive moves against the Confederacy. The following day the Union State Central Committee issued an address to the people of Kentucky, saying:

Kentucky, through her Executive, has already responded to this appeal of the President for militia to suppress what he describes as "combinations too powerful to be suppressed in the ordinary way." She has refused to comply with it, and in this refusal she has acted as became her. We approve the response of the Executive. One other appeal now demands a response from Kentucky. The Government of the Union has appealed to her to furnish men to suppress the revolutionary combinations in the Cotton States. She has refused. She has most wisely and justly refused. We would have her arm herself thoroughly at the earliest practicable moment.

Throughout the state, during the spring of 1861, individuals and sometimes groups left, going to Virginia or Tennessee to enlist in the Confederate Army. As early as April 20 Capt. Joe Desha and 100 men left Harrison County to join that army. Others at the same time went into Indiana or Ohio to join the Union forces. The *Courier* (Louisville) on April 27, 1861, said under the head of "Military Movements," "Capt. Anderson's company from Kentucky arrived at New Orleans on Wednesday. They got a handsome reception."

In April the U. S. Secretary of War notified officials of railroads that the transportation of Confederate troops or individuals enroute to join the Confederate Army would be viewed by the United States as an act of treason. Though the railroads of Kentucky openly carried many Confederate recruits, there is no record of any proceedings or even a remonstrance by the U. S. Government against these acts. Obviously the Lincoln administration determined not to offend the Guthrie railroad interests until the state of Kentucky was safely in the Union fold.

During April, Kentucky was compelled to make loans in order to pay for arms already ordered. Loans so made by various banks in the state were upon condition that the money provided be used only "for arming the State for self-defense and protection, to prevent aggression or invasion from either the North or the South, and to protect the present status of Kentucky in the Union."

In a conversation between Lincoln and Garrett Davis, of Kentucky, April 26, 1861, the President stated that it was the duty of Kentucky to have furnished the quota of troops for which he asked, adding that he had "neither power, right, nor disposition to coerce her." Lincoln added there was no intention of making war on any state that did not take up arms against the Union, nor were any campaigns contemplated which would necessitate troop movements across Kentucky.

> Garrett Davis, the "little president of Bourbon County," conferred with the President and some of the members of the cabinet. Mr. Davis is a self-constituted commissioner from Kentucky * * * Probably the mission was to obtain arms for a Union force which he threatens to raise in the Bourbon Nation.*[1]

A sort of a prophesy appeared as a reprint in the *Courier* (Louisville) of May 2, 1861, which was soon fulfilled:

> Capt. John H. Morgan, Senior Captain of the Lexington Battalion, is now by order of the Colonel, acting Major. Capt. Morgan has the Military ability for a much higher command, and if we mistake not, the time will demand his service in a more enlarged sphere.—*Lexington Statesman.*

Governor Magoffin's message of the tenth of May to the legislature relates his efforts to raise money by loans for the purchase of munitions for the state. In this message he reports the number and kinds of arms already obtained and the nature of contracts that he has entered into for further arming. Mention is also made of the fact that the city of Louisville made an effort to purchase arms for defense; that the Confederate States had made no formal requisition on Kentucky for troops, and that there had been no official correspondence with the Confederate Government.

Shortly afterward Governor Magoffin refused to honor a Confederate requisition for a regiment of infantry, but this did not prevent Kentuckians from hearing the call. On the fifteenth of May a Confederate regiment of Kentucky Volunteers was formed at Harper's Ferry, Virginia, under command of Col. Blanton Duncan, the Kentuckians having gone to Confederate recruiting offices in Virginia to enlist.

During the spring of 1861, after large numbers of the

---

* Notes, references, and sources are indicated by numerals. These refer to corresponding numbers at the end of each chapter. Notes on Chapter V, Part 1, are on page 189.

State Guard had resigned and left the state to enter the Confederate service, the legislature ordered the organization of the enrolled militia into companies, to be called Home Guards, for home and local defense exclusively. These were trained, often intensively, in county camps.

In May, 1861, a supply of 5,000 muskets with bayonets and a quantity of ammunition was sent by the U.S. War Department to Cincinnati for distribution to "faithful and reliable Union men" in Kentucky, "requiring that every man to whom a gun was delivered should pay $1.00 for it." County apportionment of the arms for the Home Guards was made upon order of Garrett Davis. Davis ordered 1,500 stand to Fleming and Mason and "the counties backing them," 200 to Boyd, 200 to Greenup, 100 to Montgomery, 100 to Bath, 100 to Clark, 100 to Madison, 200 to Fayette, 200 to Scott, 300 to Bourbon, and 500 to the city of Covington. The arms were distributed, starting May 18. Two days later Governor Magoffin, when apprised of this action, issued an armed neutrality proclamation, and thereby warned both the United States and the Confederate States to refrain from acts of war on Kentucky soil. The Confederacy immediately recalled all recruiting agents from the state. On May 21, the legislature ordered an investigation "as to the arms brought into this State without authority of the laws thereof," and also on inquiry into the pro-Confederate activities of the Knights of the Golden Circle (*see p. 234*). This investigation was referred to the committee on Federal Relations, but adjournment prevented a report from being made.

The legislature, on May 24, provided for the arming of the state under supervision of five commissioners, these being Governor Magoffin, Dr. J. B. Peyton, Gen. Peter Dudley, George T. Wood, and Samuel Gill. An appropriation of $75,000 was made for the purchase of arms and accoutrements, to be distributed equitably between the State Guard and the Home Guards. This Military Board of Commissioners was given power to erect powder mills and was also given control of the state arsenal and arms. The legislature directed that the active militia constituting the State Guard be trained in camps, and reaffirmed that neither the militia nor the state arms were to be used "against the Government of the United States, nor the Confederate States, unless in protecting our soil from unlawful invasion, it being the intention alone that said arms and munitions of war are to be used for the sole defense of the State of Kentucky." In pursuance of this mandate to encamp, the Governor appointed Scott Brown adjutant general, and M. D. West quartermaster general of the State Militia.

The U.S. War Department, on May 28, established the "Military Department of Kentucky" which embraced all of the state within 100 miles of the Ohio River. That the ire of the Kentuckians might not be aroused, the Lincoln administration was careful, during continuation of the states' neutrality, to place native Kentuckians in command. This angle gave the command of the Department of Kentucky to Gen. Robert Anderson who had lately lost his post, Fort Sumter. On the fifteenth of June this department was extended to include all of Kentucky and Tennessee, and its name was changed to "The Department of the Cumberland." However, before this extension was made, Newport was formally occupied and General Anderson's headquarters were established at Louisville.[2] This action followed within a few days after Lincoln had told General Buckner in substance that "as long as there are roads around Kentucky to reach the rebellion, it was his purpose to leave her unmolested, not yielding her right to the position she occupied, but observing it as a matter of policy."[3]

Governor Magoffin still continued to display the courage of his neutrality convictions. On May 28, 1861, he issued the following proclamation:

WHEREAS, numerous applications have been made to me from many good citizens of the Commonwealth, praying for me to issue a proclamation forbidding the march of any forces of this or any other State or States, or to make an apprehended attack upon the Federal forces at Cairo, Illinois, or to disturb any otherwise peaceful attitude of Kentucky, with reference to the deplorable war now waging between the United States and the Confederate states.

* * * * * * * * * * *

Now, therefore I, Beriah Magoffin, Governor of the Commonwealth of Kentucky and Commander in Chief of all her military forces on land or water have issued this my proclamation, hereby notifying and warning all other states whether separate or united, and especially the United States and the Confederate States, that I solemnly forbid any movement upon the soil of Kentucky or the occupation of any port or post whatever within the lawful boundaries and jurisdiction of this state, by any of the forces under the orders of this state aforesaid, for any purpose whatever until authorized by invitation or permission of the legislative and executive authorities of this State previously granted. I also hereby especially and solemnly forbid all good citizens of this Commonwealth whether incorporated in the State Guard or otherwise, making any warlike or hostile demonstrations whatever against any of the authorities aforesaid, earnestly requesting all citizens civil and military to be obedient hereto; To be obedient to the laws and lawful orders of both the civil and military authorities; to remain when off military duty, quietly and peacefully at their homes, and refrain from all words and acts likely to engender hot blood and provoke collision; to pursue such a line of wise conduct as will promote peace and tranquility and a sense of safety and security and thus keep far away from our beloved land and people the deplorable calamities of invasion; but at the same time earnestly counseling my felow citizens of Kehtucky to make prompt and efficient preparation to assume the attitude prescribed by the paramount and supreme law of self-defense—and strictly of self-defense alone; praying Almighty God to have us evermore in His Holy keeping and to preserve us in peace, prosperity and security forever.

Early in June Inspector General Buckner went to Cincinnati for a conference with General McClellan, there in command for the Union. Between them it was agreed that there was to be no Union invasion of Kentucky unless the Confederates should occupy the state. In that event Buckner was to try to preserve the state's neutrality without Union aid; if he could not do this he was to call for Union Army assistance. A similar agreement was reached between General Buckner and Isham G. Harris, Governor of Tennessee. Recruiting for the armies and the arming of the Home Guards was then secondary to the political struggle in Kentucky. With many Confederate volunteers already absent from the state, the Congressional elections in June went for the Union, as did the August elections for the legislature. The June election in Kentucky provoked a Confederate determination to seize strategic river points. As soon as this became known, General Buckner ordered Col. Lloyd Tilghman, with six companies of State Guards to be stationed at Columbus, to preserve the neutrality of that area.

On the twenty-fourth of June, Colonel Tilghman and six companies of the State Guard took up duty at Columbus. Shortly thereafter, through the resignation of Colonel Tilghman, Col. Ben Hardin Helm (brother-in-law of President Lincoln) was placed in command of these troops.

During May and June repeated efforts were made individually and jointly by President Lincoln, the Secretary of War, and the Congressmen from Kentucky (C. A. Wickliffe, G. W. Dunlap, R. Mallory, J. S. Jackson, and H. Grider), to provide for raising Union troops by recruiting within the State,[4] but objection in the form of policy stifled every attempt.[5]

On the first of July William Nelson was ordered to establish himself in the southeastern end of the state for the purpose of enlisting three regiments of infantry from that section. His orders were for like activity in eastern Tennessee directed from his Kentucky headquarters. With his orders came the assurance of 10,000 stand of arms, an ample stock of ammunitions and six pieces of light artillery. These "Lincoln Guns" were intended for the Union Home Guards.

> Company after company of the Home Guards of this city [Louisville] and throughout the State refuse to take the oath to support, not the constitution, which would not be objectionable, but the Lincoln administration which is required of them before distributing among them the arms sent here by the Usurper at Washington for the purpose of inaugurating strife among friends and neighbors on our own soil and around our own doors * * *.
>
> When Major Woodruff's Zonares met to be mustered into the volunteer police army under Maj. Gen. John Dolph, they were required to take this oath before receiving their arms. The objections were so strong that a vote was demanded, resulting in 31 for the oath and 33 against it.[6]

Such acts, especially the bringing of the arms into the state, were viewed with much alarm by Kentuckians. George D. Prentice, editor of the Louisville *Journal*, on August 11, 1861, wrote Senator John J. Crittenden that this action on the part of the Government was "as fearfully equipped for mischief as if it had been contrived by the secessionists themselves or by the Devil himself. It is reckless in the last degree. It is insane." [7]

"The history of no country, or no part or period of the late Civil War, presents a darker chapter than that which records the first six months of the war, and the means by which Kentucky was finally occupied by the Federal Army, and being thus bound, was claimed to be loyal, in the sense of sanctioning such a policy." [8]

During the latter part of June and early July many more members of the Kentucky Militia, including State Guardsmen, left the state to enlist in either the Confederate or Union Army. The Union enlistments were made chiefly at Camp Clay, across the Ohio River from Newport, and at Camp Joe Holt, in Indiana, across from Louisville.

The regiments formed at Camp Boone by the Confederates were made up almost solidly of Kentuckians, while the so-called "Kentucky Regiments," formed for the Union Army at Camps Clay and Holt had on their rosters many who were not from Kentucky; probably as many as one-third were from other states.

Early in July the Confederacy established Camp Boone in Montgomery County, Tennessee, just over the Kentucky line. Here the "Orphan Brigade" [9] and numerous other organizations of Kentuckians were formed and trained. A few days after the camp was opened the commandant requested the Confederate Secretary of War "to receive all Kentucky troops that offer, as we not only get good men, but ultimately secure Kentucky to the South." [10] Fifty companies had made application to be received by the twenty-fifth of July. Kentuckians in so great numbers arrived that Confederate Secretary of War Walker began to question the wisdom of accepting more because of the lack of arms. When this became known, the Kentuckians undertook to solve the problem by obtaining arms before going to the camp. The "Lincoln Guns" of the Home Guards were especially desired by prospective Confederate soldiers, for Confederate military authorities would not accept arms belonging to the state of Kentucky,[11] but directed that all others "shall be retained and used, preserving an inventory and valuation."[12]

Early in July the Governor of Tennessee called Private Nathan Bedford Forrest to Memphis and urged him to undertake to enlist a regiment of volunteer cavalry. General Polk joined in the appeal. Forrest acceded to the joint request and was immediately commissioned colonel and authorized to raise and equip such a regiment. Comprehending his needs, Forrest hastened to Kentucky to procure arms and cavalry equipment and if possible obtain some recruits. His itinerary in Kentucky took him through Paris, Lexington, Mount Sterling, and Frankfort, in all of which he found many of the people in sympathy with the Confederate cause, but reluctant to take up arms in contravention of the state's neutrality.

About the twentieth of July, Colonel (later Lieutenant General) Forrest arrived in Louisville. With his own private funds he purchased 500 Colt's Navy pistols, 100 saddles and a lot of other cavalry equipment. It was with great difficulty that he was able to remove his purchases from Louisville because the Union authorities were apprised of his presence in the city and the object of his visit.

While Colonel Forrest was in Louisville he received information that a company of cavalry was forming for his regiment in Meade County. Thereupon he went to Brandenburg and mustered in the "Boone Rangers," a company of about ninety men under Capt. Frank Overton. This first company was designated "A," and throughout the war its personnel was dominantly Kentuckian. Having given the company orders to prepare to march, Colonel Forrest returned to Louisville where he completed the removal of his purchases from the city. The wagons carrying the arms and equipment, accompanied by Colonel Forrest, proceeded to Brandenburg where the Boone Rangers were found ready to march. The same day he left Brandenburg, with his wagon train under guard of the Boone Rangers, and proceeded toward Bowling Green. Their progress was impeded by the hearty receptions accorded them by the citizenry along the route.

On the evening of the second day out, camp was pitched about twelve miles from Munfordville. Word was there received that two companies of Home Guards were under arms in Munfordville with orders to intercept Forrest's march. Many friends and relatives of the Boone Rangers had accompanied the company. These Colonel Forrest drew up in line with his men, under the Confederate flag, as a railway train was passing their camp. The appearance of the force was further magnified, by the reports of the passengers, to regimental proportions, by the time it reached the Home Guards. On the following morning Forrest pushed on toward Munfordville. A reconnaissance squad found that the Home Guards had retired from the town through which the company and wagon train, still accompanied by their friends, passed unmolested. At Bowling Green the friends of the Rangers turned back, while the troops proceeded through Russellville to Memphis, Tennessee.

After the Battle of Manassas (July 21) the Confederacy began to accept all troops offering from Kentucky. The establishment of Confederate recruiting stations in the state was provided for in an act of the Confederate Congress on the thirtieth of August.[13]

In August, immediately after the Kentucky elections, Camp Dick Robinson was established in Garrard County, by Brig. Gen. William Nelson, in direct violation of Kentucky's neutrality. Companies of enlisted men from throughout the state and from Tennessee were brought here to be formed into regiments. One of the most important considerations in establishing this camp was to expedite Union recruiting in eastern Tennessee. This served as a concentration camp for practically all eastern Tennessee enlistees.[14]

On August 19 Governor Magoffin sent two commissioners to the President to request removal of Camp Dick Robinson from Kentucky. This request was refused for the stated reason that it was established at the ''urgent solicitations of many Kentuckians." The same day that this commission was sent to Lincoln, Governor Magoffin sent George W. Johnson as a commissioner to Richmond to obtain assurance that the Confederacy would continue to respect Kentucky neutrality. President Davis gave Johnson his pledge that the Confederacy would continue to recognize Kentucky neutrality as long as it was maintained by the people of Kentucky themselves, adding that "Neutrality, to be entitled to respect, must be strictly maintained between both parties." Previously, Governor Magoffin had repeatedly urged the legislature that the purpose of the North was to overthrow the Confederacy, while the Southern aim was merely to be let alone. To Magoffin secession from the Union by the Southern States was as much justified as was the revolt of the Colonies against British rule in 1776.

After violations of the state's neutrality, through tolerated Union activities within Kentucky, especially the establishment of Camp Dick Robinson, Confederate troops were moved from Tennessee to Hickman and Columbus to fortify and hold these points for control of Mississippi River navigation. General Fremont put Gen. U. S. Grant in command of forces in southeastern Missouri and let it be known that he intended to occupy Columbus. On the second of September, Union troops occupied Belmont, Missouri, across the river from Columbus. This determined General Polk's action and he ordered General Pillow to Columbus, which he occupied on the fifth of September, Hickman having been occupied by him on the preceding day. This move was opposed strenuously by both President Davis and Secretary of War Walker. However, President Davis became convinced that the action could not be longer avoided, and thus presented the situation to the Confederate Congress and obtained its sanction.

The people of Columbus had, as early as the twenty-second of April, asked the Confederacy to occupy their city. In May, General Pillow, in command of navigation of the Mississippi, asked Governor Magoffin for permission to occupy Columbus and after refusal of his request Pillow decided that such occupation was most imperative and would have moved into Kentucky had he not been dissuaded by General Buckner.

On the seventh of September General Grant occupied Paducah. Union troops were scarcely within the state when the House of Representatives of the Kentucky Legislature, on September 7, by a vote of seventy-seven to twenty, ordered the United States flag hoisted on the State Capitol.

On September 9 the Confederate commander at Columbus, Gen. Leonidas Polk, informed Governor Magoffin that Confederate troops would be withdrawn from Kentucky if Union troops were likewise withdrawn. The subject of neutrality again, and for the last time, occupied the legislature for the four days after receipt of General Polk's message. On September 11 the legislature adopted a resolution demanding removal of Confederate troops. Immediately thereafter it defeated a similar resolution with regard to Union troops. The former was passed over Governor Magoffin's veto on September 13. In Governor Magoffin's veto message he stated his objections to the bill and recited the fact that Federal troops from without the state were allowed to occupy Paducah. The Governor pointed out to the legislature that the driving out of Confederate troops and the retention of Union forces gave the state, which he had tried to keep neutral, unconditionally to the Union.[15] Soon after the Governor's address was published, the *Cincinnati Commercial* carried a news item saying that "It is the intention of the Union companies of Covington to respond to a call from the military authorities in the State, and shoulder their muskets for the defense of the bridges along the Kentucky Central Railroad and preparations are being made for that purpose."[16]

Then on the eighteenth of September, the legislature passed resolutions, which constituted a declaration of war on the Confederacy. The resolutions embodied the report of the committee on Federal relations, and are as follows:

WHEREAS, Kentucky has been invaded by forces of the so-called Confederate States and the commanders of the forces so invading the State have insolently prescribed the conditions upon which they will withdraw, thus insulting the dignity of the State by demanding terms to which Kentucky cannot listen without dishonor; therefore,

1. *Be it resolved* by the General Assembly of the Commonwealth of Kentucky, that the invaders must be expelled, inasmuch as there are now in Kentucky Federal troops assembled for the purpose of preserving the tranquility of the State, and of defending and protecting the people of the State in the peaceful enjoyment of their lives and property. It is further

2. *Resolved*, that Gen. Robert Anderson, a native Kentuckian, who has been appointed to command the department of the Cumberland, be requested to take instant command, with authority and power from this Commonwealth to call out a volunteer force in Kentucky for the purpose of repelling the invaders from our soil.

3. *Resolved*, That in using the means which duty and honor require shall be used to expel the invaders from the soil of Kentucky, no citizen shall be molested on account of his political opinions; that no citizen's property shall be taken or confiscated because of such opinions, nor shall any slave be set free by any military commander, and that all peaceable citizens and their families are entitled to, and shall receive, the fullest protection of the government in the enjoyment of their lives, their liberties and their property.

4. *Resolved*, That his Excellency, the Governor of the Commonwealth of Kentucky, be requested to give all the aid in his power to accomplish the end desired by these resolutions, and that he call out so much of the militia force of the State under his command as may be necessary therefor, and that he place the same under the command of Gen. Thos. L. Crittenden.

5. *Resolved*, That the patriotism of every Kentuckian is invoked, and is confidently relied upon to give active aid in defense of the commonwealth.

After these resolutions had been passed over the veto of Governor Magoffin, he issued a proclamation conforming exactly to their text.

At a meeting of the officers and men of the "Clay Chasseurs" of the Kentucky State Guard, held in Louisville on the fourteenth of September, the following resolutions were adopted: "Resolved that the law under which the Kentucky State Guard was organized, was passed long prior to the inauguration of the existing National difficulties, and was put into operation regardless of all political parties, for the purpose of protecting the honor of the State and defending her liberties." The wrongs and indignities heaped upon the

State (with the consent of the state legislature) are recited, and that section of the Declaration of Independence wherein the Colonies enumerated their grievances against the British Government is quoted verbatim. "Since the Chasseurs object to being under the command of the Lincoln Administration, we decided to dissolve all connection with the military of Kentucky, return our arms and equipage to the proper authorities preferring to exercise, as our own conscience may dictate, our individual right of self protection and self defense." [17]

The outflow of Kentucky State Guardsmen had continued during August and early September to Camp Boone. The regiment of Col. Roger Hanson was followed by a battalion under Col. Lloyd Tilghman, and another force led by William D. Lannom, a state representative. Soon after came Gen. Simon B. Buckner, who had resigned as inspector general of the Kentucky State Guard. Command of these forces in the Confederate service was given to General Buckner with the rank of brigadier general in the Confederate Army. Others that espoused the Confederate cause at this time were Col. William Preston, U. S. Senator John C. Breckinridge, Col. John S. "Cerro Gordo" Williams, George W. Johnson, George B. Hodge, and the secretary of the state of Kentucky, Thomas B. Monroe, Jr., who became a major in the 4th Kentucky Infantry. From the Kentucky Legislature, O. H. Burbridge, L. H. Rosseau, and W. C. Whitaker, went into the the Union Army as commissioned officers.

In mid-September General Buckner led a Confederate brigade, mostly Kentuckians, to occupy Bowling Green.[18] The fortifications which he there erected were named Fort Johnston in honor of Gen. Albert Sydney Johnston of Kentucky, then commander of the Western Department of the Confederate Army. With the commencement of hostilities in Kentucky others of the militia, who had previously been hopeful that neutrality would prevail, now hurried across the line into Tennessee where the Confederates had established two more camps, Burnett and Breckinridge, intended primarily as recruiting and drilling camps for Kentucky volunteers.

In 1857 John Hunt Morgan had organized the Lexington Rifles, a company into which Morgan hoped to take "all of the bloods" of the city. Many did enroll, but about the same time Sanders Bruce, the brother of Morgan's wife, formed a rival company, the Lexington Chasseurs, of an equally select body of men. *The Record Book of the Lexington Rifles* (in the Lexington Public Library) shows that Morgan devoted much time to his company. Drills were held twice weekly, and in addition there were many meetings and social events. This record shows that fines were assessed and collected for tardiness, and that absence without cause was sufficient reason to require the man so offending to resign. These rules were impartially enforced as is shown by fines paid by Captain Morgan. From 1857 to 1861 the uniform of the Lexington Rifles played a conspicuous part in the social life of the Bluegrass and the Pennyrile, and this fact served Morgan in good stead when he sought recruits for the Confederate Army.

It was with about fifty men of this company, who eagerly went South with Morgan early in the war, that the nucleus of Morgan's command was formed. When an order for the disbanding of the State Guards was issued, Captain Morgan determined to save his guns at all hazards. On the night of Friday, September 20, 1861, he had them taken secretly from the armory in Lexington, loaded into wagons, and started south under a small guard. In order to mask his movements and allay any suspicion that might exist as to his design to remove the guns, he caused twelve or fifteen men to parade and tramp heavily about the armory for a time, to create the impression that they were drilling. Next day, when the ruse was discovered, discussions over the affair brought on an affray between the Home Guards and some of the Rifles, which caused a regiment of Union troops, then stationed at the fairgrounds, to be brought into town. Two pieces of artillery were planted to sweep the principal streets, and from that day on Lexington was under military rule.

An order was issued immediately for Morgan's arrest, but he left the city at nightfall with those of his men who were willing to go with him, and they soon rejoined the others who had gone before with the guns. They went into camp in Nelson County for several days, and received a number of recruits. Morgan then resumed his march, and after two days and nights of hard traveling reached Green River, where Col. Roger W. Hanson was in command of a Confederate force. From there they went to Bowling Green, then a Confederate camp, where they were sworn into the service and regularly organized as an independent unit. John H. Morgan was elected captain, Basil W. Duke, first lieutenant, James L. West, second lieutenant, and Van Buren Sellers, third lieutenant. In addition to these the company consisted of sixty-seven enlisted men. This was the beginning of "Morgan's Men" as a Confederate Army organization.

In a short time two other companies—one commanded by Col. Jack Allen, of Shelbyville, and the other by Capt. James B. Bowles, of Louisville, the latter recruited principally in Barren County, were assigned to Morgan's command at the earnest request of their officers and men. Bowles's company was not full, and was consolidated with another partly filled company commanded by Lieutenant Churchill, who became first lieutenant of the new company. These three companies composed what was called "Morgan's Squadron."

On April 3, 1862, the squadron reached Byrnesville, near Corinth, Mississippi, where they found the division of Gen. John C. Breckinridge to which they were attached. On the same day the whole army left its cantonement and began a march to surprise and attack General Grant at Shiloh, in which bloody contest Morgan's Squadron took part.

By this time the squadron had been augmented by a fourth company (D), under Captain Brown. Reinforced also by a few other troops, making his command about 375 strong in all, Morgan went on a raid into eastern Tennessee, before making his first raid into Kentucky (*see p. 178*).

Additional Union Army training camps were established

and maintained within Kentucky. During September, 1861, Gen. George H. Thomas succeeded General Nelson at Camp Dick Robinson. Nelson was detailed to establish Camp Kenton, near the site of Kenton's Fort, in Mason County. Large Union camps were also erected in Pendleton and Nicholas counties, and almost every county had a Union recruiting station. Practically unlimited powers were now conferred on the Military Board by the State Legislature, including the right to order into its own custody the state arms, an act designed to abolish the State Guard.

The State Guard, or active militia, had now been almost entirely absorbed by the Confederate Army, for during the last week in September the remnant of "Buckner's State Guard," about a thousand former guardsmen under Colonels Preston, Hodge, G. W. Johnson, and under Gen. John C. Breckinridge, had passed through Prestonburg bound for Confederate service in Virginia.

By legislative act of September 25 the Governor was ordered to call out a military force of 40,000 for service of from one to three years, and in addition 1,500 sharpshooters and 500 "horsemen and scouts," the latter to "receive $5.00 per month extra pay." This act was vetoed by Governor Magoffin because it deprived him of his constitutional right as commander-in-chief of the militia, but the bill was passed over his veto and thereupon he issued a proclamation making the call for troops as ordered. On September 26 a supplemental act directed these troops to be mustered into the Union Army service.

Even after being so frequently overridden by legislative vote, Governor Magoffin persisted in his policy of neutrality. On the thirtieth of September he issued a proclamation endorsing the resolution passed by the General Assembly entitled, "Resolutions providing for the peace and quiet of the citizens of the Commonwealth," and earnestly enjoined all citizens and residents of the state to be obedient to the requirements thereof. On the same day he signed an act to raise volunteer forces to repel invasion of the state, under the impression that the repulsion of invasion would be made both against Union and Confederate forces. Two days later he vetoed an act requiring information to be given to army officers when he learned that the bill was designed for Union Army advantage.

An act of the legislature, passed October 1, 1861, made it a felony for any Kentuckian, joining the Confederate Army, to invade the state. Punishment was fixed at imprisonment for from one to ten years. Recruiting for and enlistment in the Confederate service were classified as high misdemeanors, punishable by a fine of not more than $1,000 or imprisonment for not more than six months.[19]

During November, 1861, treason indictments were returned in the Federal District Court at Frankfort against thirty-two prominent Kentuckians including John C. Breckinridge, John H. Morgan, Humphrey Marshall, John Mason Brown, and Ben Desha. The next spring hundreds of like indictments were returned by grand juries in Kentucky. Only two trials are recorded as having been held on such indictments. In July, 1862, J. H. Dills was tried for high treason and acquitted. In 1863 a conviction was obtained against Thomas C. Shacklett in the Federal Court at Louisville. The penalty imposed was a fine of $10,000, imprisonment in jail for ten years, and the liberation of his slaves.[20]

Another October act made it unlawful to sell liquor to any officer or soldier within five miles of a military camp. This law came in vivid contrast to an earlier custom of including a specified quantity of whisky in the soldier's ration.

The occupation of Kentucky by hostile forces resulted, in September, in burning of the L.&N.R.R. bridge over Rolling Fork by a Confederate detachment under orders of General Buckner. Union forces destroyed the bridge at Rollin. On the tenth of September Confederate troops engaged the Home Guards in a skirmish at Barbourville, and under orders of General Buckner all the Green River locks were blown up. Other skirmishes took place at Grayson, Lucas Bend, Buffalo Hill, and Smithland.

Two state militia offices became vacant during October by the resignation of Adjt. Gen. Scott Brown and Q.M. Gen.

M. D. West, both of whom joined the Confederate Army. Governor Magoffin, on October 3, appointed William A. Dudley as quartermaster general, and, on the twelfth, John W. Finnell was made adjutant general.

On the sixteenth of October, 1861, Simon Cameron, the U.S. Secretary of War, and Gen. L. Thomas, Adjutant General of the United States, visited Louisville for a conference with General Sherman, General Wood, and James Guthrie. Sherman painted "a gloomy picture of affairs in Kentucky, stating that the young men were generally secessionists and had joined the Confederates, while the Union men, the aged, and conservatives, would not enroll themselves to engage in conflict with their relatives on the other side; but few regiments could be raised." General Sherman informed the Secretary of War that the arms sent to Kentucky had "passed into the hands of the Home Guards and could not be recovered; that many were already in the hands of the rebels."[21] The next day the party visited Lexington where Sherman's opinion concerning Confederate volunteering was confirmed. Guthrie pointed out that the defense of Kentucky would necessarily devolve on the free soil states of the Northwest.

During the last week of October the Union gunboat *Conestoga* was reported as moving upstream on the Cumberland River. Colonel Forrest, in camp at Fort Donelson, was ordered to proceed to the Cumberland and watch for the boat's arrival. General Tilghman was then in charge of the defense of the Cumberland and Tennessee rivers and Forrest was given orders by General Tilghman to report with his command to Hopkinsville. While encamped there Colonel Forrest was detailed to patrol the south bank of the Ohio between the Cumberland and Tennessee rivers. Forrest's regiment proceeded as far as Princeton where Maj. D. C. Kelly was detached with a squadron to intercept a steam transport boat that was due to pass on the Ohio River the next day. Major Kelly captured this boat without resistance, and thereby obtained large quantities of coffee, sugar, blankets, and other army stores for the Confederates.

Meanwhile the *Conestoga* was headed for Canton where the Confederates had a store of army clothing. News of this move was carried to Colonel Forrest who with his entire regiment, Kelly's squadron having returned, took up the thirty-two-mile night march to Canton. The Confederates had just arrived there and been disposed when the *Conestoga* came in sight. Forrest had with him a four-pounder piece of artillery which was placed in position in a thicket that occupied a commanding point above the river. The *Conestoga* anchored at the Canton landing, but after about a half hour there she dropped back a few hundred yards, prepared to make an attack, and opened a heavy fire of grapeshot and canister. Forrest's men, skillful marksmen and well sheltered, fired through the open ports, at close range, with such perfect accuracy and such deadly effect as to compel the vessel to close her ports and get away as fast as possible.

As soon as the *Conestoga* retreated, Colonel Forrest returned to Hopkinsville, where he found two new companies ready to join his regiment. These were Capt. Charles McDonald's company, the McDonald Dragoons, and a company of cavalry from Alabama, bringing his regimental strength up to ten companies.

The Kentucky "Sovereignty Convention" convened at Russellville on the eighteenth of November in a three-day session. Like the pioneer convention at Danville, it was dominantly military in its personnel that embraced over 200 delegates from sixty-five counties. Its acts included the adoption of a "declaration of independence," an "ordinance of secession," and the formation of a provisional government. The executive power of the provisional government was vested in a governor, and Col. Geo. W. Johnson of Scott County was elected to that office. The legislative power was vested in a council of ten.

On the ninth of December, 1861, Kentucky was admitted to the Confederacy by an act of the Confederate Congress. This action gave the Confederacy the right, legally, to draft Kentuckians into the army. Previously jurisdiction over the Kentucky Militia in the Confederate Army was co-existent only with the period of their enlistment. Theoretically the Kentuckian now owed a dual militia duty, and could have been penalized by either government for failure to render such service.

Early in December, 1861, a Union force of some 10,000 infantry and 1,200 cavalry under General Crittenden assembled near Calhoun on the north bank of Green River. Colonel Forrest was sent to make a reconnaissance in the area. When Forrest arrived at Marion he was informed that a few days previously a Union detachment had crossed the Ohio, from Illinois, and had abducted several prominent Kentuckians charged with being Confederate sympathizers. A detachment of Forrest's men sent in pursuit of the murderer of Dr. Van Wick, Forrest's surgeon, met ten Baptist clergymen who were returning from a convention held in Illinois. These were brought to Colonel Forrest who at once determined to use them as a means for recovery of the abducted Kentuckians. Accordingly eight of the preachers were placed under guard as hostages. The other two were liberated on condition that they follow the abductors and obtain the release and return of the Kentuckians within twenty-four hours. Forrest assured the two that he set free that if they failed, he would "hang the remainder all on one pole." Within the appointed time the mission was accomplished by the return of the abducted Kentuckians to Marion. The ten ministers were then permitted to proceed to their homes.

Writing of this expedition, Major Kelly related that "The command found that it was his [Forrest's] single will, impervious to argument, appeal, or threat, which was ever to be the governing impulse in their movements. Everything necessary to supply their wants, to make them comfortable, he was quick to do, save to change his plans, to which everything had to bend * * *." [22]

With this characteristic of Colonel Forrest evidently in mind a private, who overheard Colonel Forrest's threat to hang the hostages, tried to console them by pointing out that they would never be hanged there, adding "for Colonel

Forrest said 'a pole' and there ain't nuthin but trees hereabouts."

The Battle of Rowlett's Station (sometimes called first Battle of Munfordville) took place on December 17, 1861. Union troops engaged were the 32d Indiana Infantry, and on the Confederate side was Colonel Terry's Texas Rangers. Losses in killed and wounded were almost evenly divided. This engagement was followed on the twenty-eighth of December by the Battle of Sacramento between Forrest's Confederate Cavalry[23] and the 3d Kentucky Cavalry with Capt. R. G. Bacon's company of U.S. Regulars. The Confederate loss was two killed and three wounded. The Union forces lost eight killed, nine seriously wounded and sixteen prisoners taken, together with a quantity of munitions left behind when retreating.

A resolution of "thanks to the loyal and brave men who have volunteered to aid and assist the Government of the United States in expelling the invaders from our soil" was tendered by the legislature to the Kentucky Union Volunteers as a Christmas greeting. Sixty-two Union regiments were paid off in Kentucky during this month. To Kentuckians in the Confederate service the same legislature gave notice that an absence from the state for thirty days was good and sufficient cause upon which to issue an attachment.

Placing of the Negro in the Kentucky Militia was first officially suggested by U.S. Secretary of War Simon Cameron, who recommended the arming of the slaves for use as soldiers. To this suggestion the Kentucky Legislature countered with a resolution asking Lincoln to dismiss Cameron from the Cabinet. In order to discourage enlistment in the Confederate service, Senator Garrett H. Davis[24] gave notice on December 25, that he would introduce, in the U.S. Senate, a bill to confiscate the property of any person engaged in the civil, military, or naval service of the Confederacy.

That Kentucky's military prowess was recognized throughout the North is best reflected in the utterance of a Boston clergyman, the Reverend James Conway, who in a sermon on the first of February said that "President Lincoln would like to have God on his side, but he must have Kentucky."

Engagements in Kentucky during January and February, 1862, took a heavy toll in Kentuckians. Both sides lost heavily at the Battle of Mill Springs, and at Forts Henry and Donelson, the latter over the line in Tennessee. The lives of numerous other Kentuckians were lost during the spring in minor engagements.

The Battle of Mill Springs, or Logan's Cross Roads, was fought January 19-20, 1862. Maj. Gen. George B. Crittenden, with the 15th Mississippi, 16th Alabama, 17th, 19th, 20th, 25th, 28th, and 29th Tennessee Infantry regiments and a battery of six guns—about 4,000 Confederate troops—left his camp at Beech Grove, on the north bank of the Cumberland River, at twelve o'clock on Saturday night, to attack the approaching Union regiments. At six o'clock on Sunday morning, while still dark and raining, Crittenden's advance guard reached Logan's Cross Roads, ten miles from camp, and was fired upon by the pickets of the Union forces under Maj. Gen. George H. Thomas. In half an hour the battle was raging furiously, with the Union forces including the 4th Kentucky Union Infantry under Col. Speed Smith Fry, part of the 1st Kentucky Cavalry under Col. Frank S. Wolford, and with the 9th Ohio, 10th Indiana, and 10th Minnesota, altogether about 4,000 in number. For three and one-half hours the battle raged with a determined fire, and the result still remained doubtful.

The Union command was then reinforced by the 12th Kentucky Infantry under Col. W. A. Hoskins, and the 1st and 2d Tennessee Infantry, about 2,500 fresh troops. This made it possible to outflank the Confederates, pour in a deadly fire, and force them to fall back; then the 9th Ohio, by a bayonet charge, broke the Confederate ranks when they were retreating to their camp. Further Union reinforcements included the 10th Kentucky under Col. John M. Harlan, the 14th, 17th, 31st, 35th, and 38th Ohio Infantry regiments, and three batteries of artillery. The Union force now amounted to over 12,000 troops.

General Thomas' report says that by five o'clock in the

afternoon the camp was closely invested, and during the night the Union troops were disposed for an assault of the works at daylight on the twentieth. Meanwhile, two batteries cannonaded the Confederate intrenchments until dark, and the other batteries were directed to fire on the ferry to prevent the Confederates from attempting to cross the river. The Confederates returned the fire with six guns, thus deceiving the Union commanders, while with a steamboat and three barges they crossed their entire force, and, having burned the boats, retreated toward Monticello. The Union assault at daylight revealed an abandoned camp, containing eight six-pounders and two parrot guns, some old flintlock muskets, over 100 four-horse wagons, several hundred horses and mules, and a small quantity of ammunition and commissary stores, all of which could neither be moved nor destroyed by the retreating Confederate Army without discovery by the enemy.

Brig. Gen. Felix K. Zollicoffer was commanding Crittenden's 1st Brigade in the Battle of Mill Springs when he was killed. His death was a disheartening blow to the Confederate troops. General Zollicoffer fell close to the front and was borne off the field by the enemy. Several sources relate that he was killed by a pistol shot by General Fry, yet Fry repeatedly denied having fired the fatal shot. However, General Fry did supervise the removal of General Zollicoffer's muddy, bloodsoaked uniform and had the body redressed in civilian clothing from his own wardrobe. The body was then sent through the lines, under a flag of truce, through Danville to Lebanon and on to Nashville, Tennessee, General Zollicoffer's home.

The fall of Forts Henry and Donelson must receive consideration, though beyond the territorial limits of Kentucky, because of the Kentucky commands there embattled and the fact that the fall of these two forts made Kentucky the theater of war in the West. On the sixth of February, General Tilghman, with a garrison of forty men, surrendered Fort Henry after a terrific bombardment by seven gunboats. About 2,000 Confederate infantry had been sent away before the fort was surrendered after it became obvious that General Grant's charge with 10,000 troops could not be resisted. The Confederate loss was five killed and ten severely wounded.

Fort Donelson, on the Cumberland River a few miles below the Kentucky line, surrendered on the sixteenth of February after a four-day siege. The Confederate commands under Generals S. B. Buckner, G. J. Pillow, and J. B. Floyd, then occupying the fort, consisted of twenty-eight regiments of infantry, of less than half strength, and three battalions of cavalry, a total force of less than 12,000 men. The Union force under General Grant consisted of forty-one regiments of infantry, four regiments of cavalry, ten batteries of artillery and six gunboats, four of which were ironclad. Among these were two Kentucky Infantry regiments, Colonel McHenry's 17th and Colonel Shackelford's 25th. Early on the sixteenth, General Buckner asked for a truce to care for the wounded. This was refused by Grant, though near zero weather prevailed and hundreds on both sides lay wounded or dead on the open field. Shortly afterward General Buckner surrendered. The Confederate loss was 231 killed, 1,007 wounded and 5,079 prisoners taken. The Union loss was 510 killed, 2,152 wounded and 224 captured. These 224 Union prisoners were taken on the fifteenth and had been removed southward before surrender. Before surrender Generals Floyd and Pillow outwitted the Union commanders and escaped with their regiments, going toward Nashville.

Adjt. Gen. John W. Finnell submitted a report on February 18, 1862, which gave the organization and officers of 28 regiments of Kentucky Union Volunteer Infantry as 24,026 men; 6 regiments of cavalry, 4,979 men; and 198 men who composed 2 batteries of artillery. On that date a total of 29,205 men rank and file were in the United States Army service. Though official figures, for that date, of those in the Confederate service are not available, there is little doubt that nearly as many Kentuckians had espoused the Confederate cause.

The Kentucky Legislature went "wild as a March hare"

by enacting legislation, during March, 1862, intended to encourage enlistment in the United States service and discourage further enlistment of Kentuckians in the Confederate Army. Among these enactments was one prohibiting judgment by default from being taken against anyone in the U.S. Army. Another provided that any person indicted or under prosecution for crime might delay his trial by entering the military service of Kentucky or the United States, and that in so doing his bail should not be forfeited until the second term, of the court having jurisdiction, after the accused had left the army service. On the other hand, to discourage Confederate enlistment and other assistance to the Confederacy, it was provided that "any citizen in the Confederate States Army or civil service, or anyone who voluntarily gives aid or assistance to those in arms against the military forces of the United States or of Kentucky, shall be deemed to have expatriated himself, and shall no longer be a citizen of Kentucky, nor shall he again be a citizen except by permission of the legislature."[25] This same session reduced the Military Board of the state to two members, a president and an associate, and increased the board's powers to virtual absolutism.

The hard fought Battle of Shiloh inflicted heavy losses on Kentucky's militia, both Union and Confederate. On the Union side were the 1st, 2d, and 3d Kentucky Cavalry, the 1st, 2d, 3d, 5th, 6th, 9th, 11th, 13th, 17th, 20th, 23d, 24th, and 26th Kentucky Infantry. These suffered a total loss of 500 killed. On the Confederate side were the 3d, 4th, 6th, and 7th Kentucky regiments of infantry, and Cobb's, and Byrne's batteries, which together suffered a loss of 680 killed. The Kentucky troops on both sides were conspicuously gallant and daring. In this battle Kentucky lost her Provisional Governor, George W. Johnson, who was killed while fighting temporarily as a private in the 4th Kentucky Infantry. Maj. Thomas B. Monroe was also among those killed.

The jurisdiction of the Governor and Military Board over the State Militia was virtually annulled, by the appointment, on June 1, 1862, of Brig. Gen. Jerry T. Boyle as U.S.

Military Commandant of Kentucky. By the twentieth of June, Boyle had stationed a provost marshal in every Kentucky county and thereupon instituted a purge of Confederate sympathizers.

The following is part of Governor Magoffin's message of July 13, 1862, delivered to the legislature and then suppressed in the fear that it might jeopardize the freedom of the executive:

> There is another subject to which I respectfully beg leave to call your serious attention: It is the arrest of many of our citizens by military authority. By the constitution and laws of both the State and Nation, the military is subordinate to the civil law in all the loyal States. Where the civil power is too weak to execute the judgment and decree of the courts it is provided by law that the military power may be brought in on requisition. Every citizen is entitled to know the reason of his arrest, and to a speedy trial by his peers or examination before a proper tribunal. A warrant with the oath of the person making the application or complaint must be procured. The warrant is placed in the hands of the proper officer and the person against whom the charge is made is taken into custody to await his trial or examination before the proper tribunal.
>
> The person arrested must be confronted by his accuser, and a fair investigation and a speedy trial must be had. He must have time and process to summon witnesses to testify in his behalf and to meet his accuser. The constitution declares that "No person shall be deprived of life, liberty, or property without due process of the law." And again that no warrant shall be issued but upon probable cause supported by oath or affirmations, and particularly describing the person to be seized. Yet in view of these acknowledged rights and these provisions of the Constitution, numbers of our citizens have been rudely arrested and torn from their families, some of them at midnight, in violation of all laws, justice, and right, by the military power and hurried from the State to loathsome prisons in other States.

An appeal for additional Union troops was made to Lincoln by the Governors of seventeen Northern states on July 1 1862. Governor Magoffin refused to join in this appeal, and thereupon Kentucky became a signatory through the president of her Military Board, John B. Temple. In accordance with the appeal Lincoln issued a proclamation for an additional 300,000 men, Kentucky's quota being 4,000.

Gen. John Hunt Morgan[26] marched into Kentucky on the

eighth of July with 816 men. At Tompkinsville he defeated the 3d Pennsylvania Cavalry. The Union loss was four killed and six wounded, and Major Jordan and eighteen of his men were taken prisoners. General Morgan had several men wounded, one of whom, Colonel Hunt of Georgia, died of his wounds. At Bear Wallow, a Canadian named Ellsworth, one of Morgan's men, tapped the telegraph lines to intercept Union communications and to effectively send decoy messages to Union commanders. On the eleventh of July, Morgan was preparing to destroy the railroad tracks at New Hope when a trainload of Union troops came along and engaged the Confederates in a brief skirmish, after which the train with its load started back toward Louisville. On the twelfth of July, General Morgan captured Lebanon, burned a United States Government warehouse, and took as prisoners Lt. Col. A. Y. Johnson and a part of the 28th Kentucky Infantry. From Lebanon, Morgan marched to Harrodsburg, from there on to Lawrenceburg, and then to Midway. This latter place was the headquarters of the Federal forces in that region, and at that point and at Frankfort were large bodies of Federal troops, much superior in numbers to the forces which Morgan had under his command.

The fear created by General Morgan's success caused General Boyle to issue an order on July 13, "that every able-bodied man take arms and aid in repelling the marauders; every man who does not join will remain in his house 48 hours, and be shot down if he leaves it."

By skillful marches, by scattering his forces and threatening several points at the same time the Federal officers were entirely bewildered, and did not know where to expect a blow. The extreme mobility of his flying column also rendered it difficult to obtain any correct information as to Morgan's force or his intentions. The marching capacity of the squadron may be judged from the fact that at the time it reached Midway it had marched over 300 miles in 8 days, and the men were still fresh and in high spirits.

At Midway extraordinary use of the telegraph was again made by Ellsworth. By "tapping" the wires he interfered with the arrangements of the Union officers and sent their troops in wrong directions under forged orders which he dispatched in place of those he intercepted.

At the first Battle of Cynthiana, on the seventeenth of July, General Morgan defeated the 18th Kentucky Infantry, the Harrison County Home Guards, Captain Arthur's Campbell County Home Guards, and a Cincinnati (Ohio) company with a twelve-pounder under Capt. Billy Glass. These troops were under command of Lt. Col. John J. Landrum. The fighting continued in the streets of the city for about two hours, during which time Colonel Landrum and a few of his men escaped. Upon surrender of the Union command 420 prisoners were taken and paroled, 16 were found to have been killed, and about 40 wounded. Some 300 muskets were surrendered and burned along with the railroad depot. Camp Frazier, Home Guard headquarters, was destroyed as were large U.S. Government stores. The Confederates lost fourteen killed and thirty-three wounded. Morgan then went to Paris, which readily surrendered; then on to Winchester, Richmond, Crab Orchard, Somerset, through Monticello, and back into Tennessee. It is his official report of this expedition that reflects Morgan's popularity with the Kentucky Militia. This report is as follows: "I left Knoxville July 4th, with about nine hundred men and returned to Livingston, Tenn., on the 28th, with nearly twelve hundred men, having been absent just 24 days, during which I traveled over one thousand miles, captured 17 towns, destroyed all Government supplies and arms in them, captured 300 Government horses at Cynthiana, dispersed about fifteen hundred Home Guards, and paroled nearly one thousand Regular troops. I lost in killed, wounded and missing, of the number that I carried into Kentucky, about ninety men."

At Georgetown General Morgan issued the following proclamation to win over any whose affiliation might be uncertain:

KENTUCKIANS

I come to liberate you from a despotism of a tyrannical faction and to rescue my native State from the hands of your oppressors.

Everywhere the cowardly foe has fled from my avenging arms. My brave army is stigmatized as a band of guerillas and marauders. Believe it or not. I point with pride to their deeds as a repudiation of this foul aspersion. We come not to molest peaceful individuals or to destroy private property, but guarantee absolute protection to all who are not in arms against us. We ask only to meet the hireling legions of Lincoln. The eyes of your brethren of the South are upon you. Your gallant fellow-citizens are flocking to our standard. Our armies are rapidly advancing for your protection. Then greet them with the willing hands of fifty thousand of Kentucky's brave. Their advance is already with you.

Then

STRIKE FOR THE GREEN GRAVES OF YOUR SIRES!
STRIKE FOR YOUR ALTARS AND YOUR FIRES!
GOD AND YOUR NATIVE LAND."[27]

General Buell's army was obliged to fall back to Louisville in August, 1862, in consequence of the raid made by Morgan's corps in which he took possession of the Louisville & Nashville Railroad, in Buell's rear, at Gallatin, and so cut off Buell's communications with his base.

At the battle of Hartsville, shortly after the capture of Gallatin, a fight took place between a portion of Morgan's command and some Union cavalry who charged them with sabers; the account of it gives a good idea of Morgan's style of fighting. General Duke describes the attack: "Throwing down the eastern fence of the meadow, some 300 poured into it, formed a long line, and dashed across it with sabres drawn, toward the line of horses which they saw in the road beyond. Companies B, C, E, and F were by this time dismounted, and had dropped on their knees behind a low fence on the roadside, as the enemy came rushing on. They held their fire until the enemy were within thirty yards, when they opened. Then was seen the effect of a volley from that long thin line which looked so easy to break and yet whose fire was so deadly. Every man took dead aim at an individual foe, and, as the blaze left the guns, two-thirds of the riders and horses seemed to go down. The cavalry was at once broken and recoiled. Our men sprang over the fence, and ran close up to them as they endeavoured to retreat rapidly through the gaps in the fence by which they had entered, and poured in such another volley that the rout was completed. However they reformed and came back, but only to be repulsed again.

"They were then pursued by the mounted men, who followed them for some three miles, when Johnson rallied in a strong position on a hill, dismounted his men, and formed them up to check the pursuit. The pursuers followed up swiftly, and seeing the disposition made by the enemy, rapidly formed up, dismounted under cover of a hill, charged and carried the position on foot.

"The Union force on this occasion was carefully picked, and composed of the best cavalry in the Union Army, and placed under General Johnson, who was selected as their best and most dashing cavalry officer, and sent out specially to destroy Morgan's command. It will be seen that Johnson relied on the saber. He was totally defeated, and he himself and a large body of his men captured." General Duke bears testimony to the great gallantry displayed by both officers and men of the Union force, and after referring to their attempt to use their sabers, he says General Johnson "was evidently a fine officer, but seemed not to comprehend 'the new style of cavalry' at all."

These particulars give a good idea of the style of fighting adopted by Morgan, and of the general results of his system. He was the first of the Southern officers to make extensive raids in the enemy's rear, but it was not long before the example was followed by other officers in both armies.

Lincoln's request for 4,000 volunteers from Kentucky was none too well received, and consequently enlistments were speeded up by General Boyle's appointment of Col. Henry Dent of Louisville, as provost marshal of Kentucky with complete control over all county provost marshals. This appointment, with the stringent orders that were thereupon issued, was sufficient to cause Adjt. Gen. Finnell, on August 12, to proclaim that "no more volunteers for one year, but mounted men will be received. The regiments are now full to overflowing." Another report by Adjt. Gen. Finnell on August 16, 1862, made to the legislature, showed 41,703 as the total number of Kentucky Militia who had then entered the U.S. Army as volunteers.

On August 18, 1862, the nominal commander-in-chief of the Kentucky Militia, Governor Magoffin, resigned, and was replaced by James F. Robinson, speaker of the Kentucky Senate, the office of Lieutenant Governor then being vacant through the death of Linn Boyd. The following day George T. Wood, associate member of the Kentucky Military Board, tendered his resignation to become effective August 30. His superior, John B. Temple, had resigned August 16, because of incompatibility with the Union military regime in the state. The Military Board was abolished by the legislature on August 28.

At Big Hill on the twenty-third of August, Col. Leonidas Metcalfe led 400 dismounted Union cavalry, consisting of Houck's Battalion and the 7th Kentucky Union Cavalry against the 1st Louisiana Cavalry which poured such rapid fire that about three-quarters of Metcalfe's men "fled like a pack of cowards," [28] leaving ten killed and forty wounded. Those who took flight were classified as deserters by the adjutant general's report, and in General Orders No. 2 General Nelson instructed county provost marshals to arrest and hold any that might be found.

An order was issued by General Boyle on August 24, to slave owners of central Kentucky directing them to furnish a given number of Negro hands to repair the road from Mount Vernon to Cumberland Gap. The Negroes so furnished constituted the first contingent of slaves impressed into United States military service. Boyle's order brought another legislative effort to prevent the introduction of the Negro in Kentucky military affairs. A legislative act of August 26 provided for a draft of the militia, when necessary, to furnish troops for the use or defense of the state, or to supply any force which might be requisitioned by the United States. This proscription act was followed by a reenactment of the "State Guard" law of 1860.

The Battle of Richmond was precipitated on August 30 by General Manson's acting contrary to the orders of his superior, Gen. Robert Nelson, to avoid a fight and fall back. Instead, Manson marched out to meet the four Confederate brigades under Generals E. Kirby Smith and Patrick Cleburne, bringing on a terrific battle, about five miles from Richmond, that lasted from six to eleven in the morning, when a lull ensued, after which Confederate victory was insured. The Union forces included the 12th, 16th, 55th, 66th, 69th, 71st Indiana, the 95th Ohio, and the 18th Kentucky Infantry. Also the 6th and 7th regiments of Kentucky Union Cavalry and Batteries D and G of the Michigan Artillery.

Upon retreating toward Richmond the Union troops were met by General Nelson who tried vainly to reform them, but a large part fled through woods and fields in utter confusion.

Objective played a prominent part in the efficiency of Kentucky troops, whether Union or Confederate. Official correspondence of August, 1862, portrays the conduct of the contending forces. On August 26 Maj. Gen. Wm. Nelson wrote Governor Robinson complaining of the want of discipline in the Kentucky Union forces, saying: "Robbing, plundering, marauding, are punishable by the articles of war with death; and it is plain why such a punishment is awarded them. They destroy discipline and efficiency, and convert a body of men assembled for the defense of the country into its greatest oppression and worst enemy. The men who rob and steal won't fight. Then again, a regiment without discipline cannot be depended upon, no matter how gallantly led. Metcalfe's mishap on Saturday is a case in point." This "mishap on Saturday" was the Union rout at Big Hill. A Union Army major who had retreated to the Ohio after the Battle of Richmond is quoted as having said: "Don't tell me that these rebel soldiers won't fight. They lived for days on nothing but green corn, giving their horses one ear while they roasted another for themselves, but I tell you they fought like devils."[29]

The following report of Gen. E. Kirby Smith shows it was his intention, after the rout at Richmond, to have attacked Cincinnati if he had not been stopped by General Bragg:

HEADQUARTERS, ARMY OF KENTUCKY

LEXINGTON, KY., *Sept. 3, 1862*

GENERAL: On the 30th Ult. our forces met and repulsed the enemy in three separate engagements. General Cleburne's division which was in the advance about six miles from Richmond, early in the day, drove him from the field before the remainder of my column was brought into action. Falling back about three miles and a half, and receiving reinforcements, the enemy again made a stand, and were again driven from the field in confusion. My cavalry having been sent to the enemy's rear I could not pursue rapidly and he formed his line of battle in the outskirts of Richmond, his force having swelled to the number of 10.000, General Nelson commanding.

Within an hour after our column was deployed for the attack, the enemy was utterly routed and retreated in terrible confusion.

The cavalry came in upon their flank and scattered them in all directions capturing all their artillery, and train. Not a regiment escaped in order. The enemy's loss during the day was about 1,400 killed and wounded. General Miller was killed, General Nelson wounded, and General Manson taken prisoner. The remnant of the Federal force in Kentucky is making its way, utterly demoralized, to the Ohio. General Marshall is in communication with me. Our column is moving upon Cincinnati. The country is rising in arms and all that is needed to accomplish the objects of the campaign is to have our left in communication with our right. If I am supported and can be supplied with arms, 25,000 Kentucky troops in a few days would be added to my command. Breckinridge and Buckner should be here.[30]

I am, General, very respectfully,

Yours obedient servant,

E. KIRBY SMITH, *Major General.*

TO GENERAL BRAXTON BRAGG,
Commanding Army of the West.

Early in September, 1862, the entire manpower of Kenton and Campbell counties was impressed to fortify Covington and Newport against the advance of Confederate forces under General Heth. This order spared none, taking men far past the age limit prescribed by law and those exempted from militia duty by statutory law. Age-enfeebled men fared no better than the clergy in this call.

With the advance of the Confederate Army toward Frankfort, the Kentucky Legislature adjourned to Louisville, and upon convening there on September 3 its first resolution was "that the invasion of the State by rebels, now in progress, must be resisted and repelled by all the power of the State, by all her men, by all her means, and to every extremity of honorable war; and that he who now seeks to save himself by deserting or holding back from the service of the Commonwealth, is unworthy the name of Kentuckian." The power of the Governor to this end was made virtually absolute, "with no other restrictions on his power than what are imposed by the constitution."

On September 3, 1862, Governor Robinson issued a commission to Col. William H. Wadsworth, placing the state troops in Mason County under his command. At the same time Richard Apperson, Jr., was made acting assistant adjutant general with rank of colonel, and T. M. Green and S. W. Owens were made aides-de-camp with rank of captain.

Confederate troops under General Morgan reached Lexington September 4. In a few days Capt. W. C. P. Breckinridge, Lt. S. D. Morgan, and Colonels Cluke and Chenault, obtained nearly a thousand Confederate recruits, and Capt. A. Buford recruited three regiments of cavalry that were placed under command of Colonels Smith, Grigsby, and Butler. News of this advance and recruiting was conveyed to the legislature and resulted in the immediate passage of an act authorizing the formation of additional Home Guard companies of free white males between sixteen and sixty-five years of age. In Louisville these Home Guards together with slaves, impressed by United States military authorities, were used to erect three fortifications at strategic points in the city in anticipation of the advance of the Confederates under Gen. E. Kirby Smith.

On the fifth of September, 1862, the advance forces of General Bragg demanded the surrender of Munfordville which was occupied by General Wilder with 3,100 Union infantry. The following morning General Duncan made an attack, but the Confederates were repulsed after seven hours of fighting. Both armies were reinforced and on the sixteenth another attack was made, and after a stubborn resistance Col. C. L. Dunham, who had assumed command, surrendered. Union forces engaged consisted of the 18th U.S. Infantry, the 28th and 33d Kentucky, the 17th, 50th, 60th, 67th, 68th, 74th, 78th, and 89th Indiana, Conkle's Battery, the 13th Indiana Artillery, and the Louisville Provost Guard. The Confederate forces consisted of General Bragg's army of the Tennessee. Union losses were 50 killed and 3,566 prisoners taken. The Confederates lost 714, killed and wounded.

On September 16, Governor Robinson appointed and commissioned John B. Temple, formerly president of the State Military Board, as paymaster general of the State Militia with the rank of colonel and called him into active service.

On October 4, a month after "Morgan's men were welcomed to Lexington," the Confederate Provisional State Government was inaugurated in Frankfort. This Confederate advance served as a signal for the concentration of both Confederate and Union troops in central Kentucky and precipitated the Battle of Perryville on the eighth of October. The Union troops engaged consisted of Brig. Gen. L. H. Rousseau's Division of 7,000, James S. Jackson's command of 5,500, and Goodnight's Brigade of 1,500, besides which was Maj. Gen. Charles C. Gilbert's 3d Army Corps. Brig. Gen. Robert B. Mitchell's division sent to General McCook about 11,000 men, making 25,000 in all. The Confederates had some 15,000 of General Bragg's best men with three divisions under Generals Cheatham, Buckner, and Anderson, all under the immediate command of Maj. Gen. Leonidas Polk. The two divisions forming the Confederate left wing were under Maj. Gen. Wm. J. Hardee.

Both armies had been preparing for battle since early morning of the eighth of October, skirmishing while getting into position. At half-past twelve in the afternoon the Union commanders were still delaying. The Confederates knew that heavy reinforcements of Maj. Gen. Thomas L. Crittenden's corps were only a few hours away—almost within supporting distance—while nearly half of their own army, Maj. Gen. E. Kirby Smith's forces and Withers' division had been sent toward Frankfort where a battle was anticipated and these could not come up under forty hours. The Confederates began a vigorous attack, and soon brought on a general engagement which General Bragg's official report pronounces "the severest and most desperately contested battle." The fighting continued furiously until dark. General Buell's official report says that this battle is "conspicuous for its severity and deserves to be commemorated for the valor displayed by the armies engaged." Gen. A. M. McCook, commander of the embattled 1st Union Army Corps called the Battle of Perryville "the bloodiest battle of modern times."

The Union loss was 916 killed, 2,943 wounded, and 489 missing. The Confederate loss was placed at 2,500 killed, wounded and missing.

The attitude of many of the Kentucky Militia mustered into the Union Army is contained in an account, written by a member of the 9th Kentucky Cavalry, of the scene after the Battle of Perryville, saying:

> On October 11th, we reached Perryville, and marched over the battlefield. It was a sickening sight. Our dead were all buried; but the blackened corpses of rebel dead, mangled in every way possible, were still scattered over the field. It would be impossible for me to say how many were killed, but the number was enormous in proportion to the number engaged. I saw them lying in pens from eight to ten each. We camped in a wood, about one mile from Perryville, on the Mackville Road, sometime after dark, and discovered a dead body, a rebel, right in our midst; but as we had no spades, nor anything else to dig a hole with, we were compelled to leave him unburied. I have no doubt that many are still unburied, and some have been eaten up by hogs, leaving nothing but the whitened bones to show that a fellow-creature lost his life in a war created by ambitious politicians to lengthen out their time of holding the public purse strings.

At Harrodsburg, on the tenth of October, troops including the 9th Kentucky Cavalry under Lieutenant Colonel Boyle, attacked the Confederate forces retreating from Perryville and took 1,600 prisoners.

It was while briefly encamped at Hopkinsville that "Morgan's Kentucky Brigade" seized a press and printed *The Vidette* on October 28, 1862. The paper was devoted to army news. So far as is known, only one issue was published.[31]

Against the counsel of his closest friends Governor Robinson, on November 25, 1862, adopted the previously established Federal policy of appointing friends and relatives to public office, either to exempt them from military service by placing them in a safe positon far from the battlefront, or to give them a highly lucrative sinecure. Robinson on that date appointed his son, James F. Robinson, Jr., as quartermaster general of the state of Kentucky, in place of William A. Dudley who had resigned. Similar appointments came in rapid succession.

An address to the people of Kentucky was issued in the late fall by James B. Clay, asking men to enlist in Confederate regiments being formed by him in Richmond and at Camp Breckinridge (originally Camp Dick Robinson). Clay's request was accompanied by the admonishment that the Confederacy would soon put in force a conscript law to raise troops. From the headquarters of General Bragg at Nashville an order was issued December 16, 1862, to impress into Confederate Army service all exiled Kentuckians and Tennesseans. Resentment of the order was provocative of the threats of Generals John C. Breckinridge, Simon B. Buckner, and Roger W. Hanson, to resign if its enforcement was attempted.

At Elizabethtown on the twenty-seventh of December, 1862, a teriffic engagement took place between 600 Union troops, including the 91st Illinois Infantry, under Lieutenant Colonel Smith, and General Morgan's cavalry. Five hundred of the Union troops were captured. On the following day Morgan captured two garrisons consisting of about 800 men who were guarding railroad trestles at Muldraugh's Hill, and then destroyed the trestles.

NOTES, REFERENCES, AND SOURCES

1. Louisville *Courier*, May 4, 1861.
2. *Official Records*, Ser. I, vol. 52, part 1, p. 147.
3. McElroy, *History of Kentucky*, p. 536; *also* Lapsley, *Writings of Lincoln*, VI, 325-26.

4. Lapsley, *Writings of Lincoln*, V, 315.
5. "Crittenden MSS," XXVI, 3226-27.
6. Louisville *Courier*, June 1, 1861.
7. "Crittenden MSS," 5353-56.
8. *Memorial History of Louisville*, Vol. I, p. 196.
9. So dubbed because of the large percentage of its officers killed in battle.
10. Official Records, Ser. I, vol. 4, p. 367.
11. *Ibid.*, Ser. I, vol. 4, p. 371.
12. *Ibid.*, Ser. I. vol. 4, p. 378.
13. Official Records, Ser. I, vol. 1, p. 585.
14. *Cincinnati Commercial*, August 25, 1861.
15. Louisville *Courier*, September 14, 1861.
16. Reprinted, *Commonwealth* (Frankfort), September 25, 1861.
17. Louisville *Courier*, September 18, 1861.
18. On September 12, 1861, when General Buckner issued a proclamation denouncing the invasion of the state by the Union Army and calling upon Kentuckians to expel the "usurpers and invaders." Another proclamation, issued when he occupied Bowling Green explained his presence and intention. In it he pointed out that the legislature had "been faithless to the will of the people. They have endeavored to make your gallant State a fortress, in which, under the guise of neutrality, the armed forces of the United States might secretly prepare to subjugate alike the people of Kentucky and the Southern States."—REBELLION RECORD, III, 127-29.
19. *Acts of Kentucky Legislature*, 1861, p. 15.
20. *Tri-Weekly Commonwealth* (Frankfort), July 27, 1863.
21. Collins, *History of Kentucky*, Vol. I, p. 96.
22. "MS Notes of Lt. Col. D. C. Kelly," Huntsville, Alabama.
23. Jordan and Pryor, *Campaigns of Lieut. Gen. N. B. Forrest*.
24. Garrett Davis was, on December 10, 1862, elected U.S. Senator to fill the vacancy occasioned by the expulsion of John C. Breckinridge from that body. Davis was nominated in a caucus of Union members, receiving forty-six votes, to forty-five for James Guthrie, on the final ballot. Upon the seating of Davis, Secretary of War Cameron commented that "Kentucky got the greater of two evils" ("Breckinridge MSS"). This remark was made after Davis had introduced the following resolution in the U.S. Senate on December 15, 1862: "WHEREAS, after it had become manifest that an insurrection against the United States was about to break out in several States, James Buchanan, then President—from sympathy with the conspirators and their treasonable projects—failed to take the necessary and proper steps to prevent it; therefore, he should receive the censure and condemnation of the senate and the American people." The following day by a vote of thirty-nine to three the resolution was tabled (Collins, *History of Kentucky*, Vol. I, p. 117).
25. *Acts of Kentucky Legislature*, March, 1862.
26. Maj. Gen. John H. Morgan, a business man with no professional military training, foresaw the value of a force of mounted

riflemen, and the inadequacy of then existing cavalry tactics and precedents. Therefore he gradually evolved a new system of tactics for his men who were to use the long-range rifle instead of the carbine and saber. Morgan's purpose was to organize a force which could move with rapidity and fight on foot or in the saddle. *See Reminiscences of General Basil W. Duke, C.S.A.*, and Denison, *History of Cavalry.*

    27. Handbill in "Breckinridge MSS," July 15, 1862.
    28. Collins, *History of Kentucky*, Vol. I, p. 110, col. 1.
    29. *Ibid.*, Vol. I, p. 110, col. 2.
    30. *Kentucky Yeoman*, January 30, 1866.
    31. The *Vidette* was published on October 28, 1863, by General John H. Morgan's men during a brief sojourn in Hopkinsville. It was a one-sheet edition of four columns and was devoted to news bearing directly on the war. Mr. Charles M. Meacham, of Hopkinsville, had a copy. A photographic copy is owned by Miss Frances Lander, Hopkinsville.

CHAPTER V—PART II

WAR BETWEEN THE STATES

The flag referred to in the following letter, when first received by the Governor, was used widely in recruiting volunteers for the Union Army:*32

March 4th, 1863

To the Governor of Kentucky:

The 6th Kentucky Regiment sends to you by the bearer, Lieut. Richard T. Whitaker, and entrusts to your care the time worn, battle marked, flag of our country. Since it was given into our keeping it has been treasured, revered, and honored as the proud, beautiful, significant emblem of our country's power and justice.

On the bloodiest battle fields, crimsoned by our blood for our country's honor and safety in the fiercest of fray, it has floated amid the tempest of death. It is almost riddled by the shell and shot of the foe, but has always witnessed the triumph of our arms over treason and rebellion.

'Tis consecrated and hallowed by the blood of many of her brave officers and men. Under it the 6th has fought with honor; under it her soldiers have died with glory. Not a stain rests on it. 'Tis untarnished as honors' brightest emblem.

Kentucky has the right to preserve and cherish it in memoriam of her honored dead and as the sacred evidence of her devotion and loyalty to the constitution and government she has vowed to maintain.

We return it asking for another at your hands, better suited for exposure to rain, wind, and storm, to supply its place.

* * * our past under this old flag shall be our guerdon for the future under the new.

WALTER C. WHITAKER
Col. 6th Kentucky Inf.

Appended is a list of the battles and skirmishes through which it has been borne: Battles—Shiloh, Stone River; Skirmishes—Corinth, Danville, Ky., Pierre Point in Rockcastle, Stewart's Creek, Tenn., Lavergne, Stone River, Woodbury.

On March 21, 1863, Colonel Cluke's Cavalry made an attack on Mount Sterling, then held by the 10th Kentucky Union Cavalry. After about four hours of continuous and

---

*Notes, references, and sources are indicated by numerals. These refer to corresponding numbers at the end of this chapter. Notes on Chapter V, Part II, are on page 236.

desperate fighting the city was surrendered to the Confederates, along with 428 prisoners, 222 wagons loaded with military stores, 500 mules, and nearly 1,000 stand of arms. The Confederate loss was eight killed and thirteen wounded, and Union loss, four killed, and ten wounded. Several buildings, in which the Union troops took shelter, were burned.

On the twenty-fourth of March, General Pegram's Cavalry occupied Danville. Throughout the day their advance had been contested by the 19th and 22d Michigan, the 19th Kentucky, the 2d Tennessee Cavalry, and the 1st Indiana Artillery, but the Confederates succeeded in forcing a Union retreat toward Lexington. Each side lost about twenty-five in killed and wounded, and the Confederates lost thirty men as prisoners.

During the early part of April, 1863, an epidemic of "brain fever," attacked a Confederate regiment encamped in the southern part of the state. The symptoms and mortality rate indicate that the disease was spinal meningitis, though the medical staff made a diagnosis of brain fever at the time.

The Confederacy (Atlanta, Ga.) of March 15, 1863, in an article dealing with Confederate forces then in the field, gives Kentucky credit for "ten regiments of infantry, ten regiments and several battalions of cavalry, and five batteries of artillery." Confederate recruiting in Kentucky became extremely hazardous after issuance of Gen. A. E. Burnside's Order No. 38. Under this order Confederate Captains William F. Corbin and T. G. McGraw were tried by a Union court-martial, found guilty, and were ordered to be shot on May 15, the place of execution being fixed as Johnson's Island, near Sandusky, Ohio. Retaliations for these executions took place in Richmond, Virginia, on July 6, when Union Captains John Flinn and H. W. Sawyer were selected by lot to pay the penalty.

On May 17, the Confederate Congress passed a resolution of thanks to "Gen. John H. Morgan and his officers and men for their varied, heroic and invaluable services in Tennessee and Kentucky on this expedition [starting in January, 1863], services which have conferred upon them fame as enduring as the records of the struggle which they have so brilliantly illuminated."

Several years after the close of the war two letters, said to have been written by General Morgan, appeared among the "unpublished war papers."[33] They deal with events of the spring of 1863 and the latter reflects much of the humor for which its purported author was noted. The cavalry commands of General Morgan and Colonel Jacob had had a series of skirmishes south of the Cumberland River in the early part of May which ended in Colonel Jacob withdrawing to the north side of the river. The first letter is official and was actually sent; information about the second is not authentic though its style and text is said to be characteristic of Morgan:

HDQRS. THIRD CAVALRY DIVISION
NEAR MONTICELLO, KENTUCKY,

COLONEL: *May 12, 1863.*

SIR: I have the honor to acknowledge the receipt of your communication of yesterday which has been just received.

I instructed the officer commanding the detail made to bury my own dead to bestow the same care upon yours, and it has been done.

I cheerfully consent that you take charge of your wounded; while every attention in the power of my surgeon to render them has been, and while they remain within my lines, shall be given them, I desire that they may have the care of their own friends. These men whom I return to you can safely reenter your ranks upon their recovery; knowing that their parole would not be observed, I have not required them to give it. And I may soon have wounded of my own who will need the care I am now bestowing upon these.

I am, Colonel, Your Obed't servant,
JOHN H. MORGAN
Brigadier Gen. Commanding.

HDQR's MORGAN'S CAVALRY
MONTICELLO, *May 12, 1863.*

To the Officer Commanding U.S. Forces,
Somerset, Ky.

SIR: As it has been a custom from time immemorial between belligerent nations, until lately, to ransom prisoners, I have the honor to propose that we revive this time honored usage. I have now in my hands fifteen of your men, including two commissioned officers, as prisoners of war. I propose to exchange them at the following rates: For each private or non-commissioned officer, one barrel of salt; for a second lieutenant, two barrels of salt and a sack of coffee; for a first lieutenant, three barrels of salt and two sacks of coffee; for a captain, four barrels of salt and three sacks of coffee, etc., ascending according to grade.

Believing, from the fighting qualities displayed by your men in the engagement the other day, that they are well "worth their salt," I have the honor to remain,

Your obedient servant

GENERAL COMMANDING

For the defense of the state, as authorized by an act of Congress, Adjt. Gen. Finnell issued a call on May 10, 1863, for the enlistment of 20,000 Kentuckians. All persons enlisting under this act were given a bounty of one month's pay in advance. Payment was made by the United States paymaster general of the state of Kentucky, upon the organization and muster of the company to which the recruit was attached, by a regularly authorized United States mustering officer. A new enrollment of the militia of Kentucky was begun June 15, 1863, under direction of the United States provost marshal, through his deputies in the various counties.

Maj. Gen. Geo. L. Hartsuff, with headquarters at Lexington, was, on June 1, 1863, assigned to the command of the 23d Army Corps, composed of all the United States troops in Kentucky except the 9th Corps and Carter's Division. Scarcely had Hartsuff assumed the duties of his office when he issued "General Order No. 8," as follows:

HEADQUARTERS 23D ARMY CORPS

LEXINGTON, KY., *July 10, 1863*

The persons and property of Union citizens, non-combatants, within the lines of this command are under its especial protection. For every one injured in their person, five rebel sympathizers will be arrested and punished accordingly. For injuries done to the property of Union citizens ample remuneration will be levied upon rebel sympathizers. By command of

MAJ. GEN. HARTSUFF.

In July, 1863, General Morgan made his boldest and most extensive raid through Kentucky, Indiana, and into Ohio, and had it not been for a sudden and totally unexpected swelling of the Ohio River, which rendered all the fords impassable, he might have been entirely successful. After doing great damage in the enemy's rear, he was at last cut off on the banks of the Ohio, and captured with a portion of his command. On this raid Morgan moved with great rapidity. He marched from Summersville, Indiana, to Williamsburg, Ohio, a distance of more than ninety miles, in thirty-five hours. This is said to be the greatest march Morgan ever made.

This bold stroke enshrouded Louisville in new fears of a Confederate attack, and consequently the city council ordered "the enrollment of all males between eighteen and forty-five into companies for service, if required, and all refusing to be enrolled shall be sent to the North [imprisoned]." Nearly five thousand men enrolled and drilled under this order. Recruiting of Negroes had practically ceased because of the urgent protest voiced by the state authorities to the War Department.

Under date of July 28, 1863, a report was made by the adjutant general showing that Kentucky had previously furnished a total of 41,937 men to the United States service. The numbers from each Congressional District are:

First District

Fulton	0
Hickman	9
Ballard	74
McCracken	63
Graves	150
Marshall	216
Calloway	48
Trigg	94
Lyon	70
Caldwell	139
Livingston	21
Crittenden	176
Union	25
Webster	69
Total	1,154

Second District

Christian	545
Hopkins	209
Muhlenberg	539
Henderson	190
Daviess	407
McLean	462
Ohio	1,027
Hancock	188
Breckinridge	537
Grayson	564
Butler	450
Edmonson	110
Total	5,228

Third District

Russell	367
Cumberland	492
Clinton	454
Monroe	613
Metcalfe	415
Barren	328
Allen	387
Simpson	74
Warren	381
Logan	327
Todd	197
Hart	488
Total	4,523

Fourth District

Meade	187
Adair	541
Hardin	386
Bullitt	236
Larue	285
Marion	735
Washington	738
Nelson	239
Spencer	91
Taylor	325
Green	440
Shelby	469
Anderson	261
Total	4,933

Fifth District

Jefferson	5,037
Oldham	248
Henry	352
Owen	82
Total	5,719

Sixth District

Gallatin	136
Harrison	320
Boone	123
Trimble	4
Grant	434
Kenton	600
Campbell	610
Pendleton	578
Bracken	412
Carroll	43
Total	3,260

Seventh District

Nicholas	395
Bourbon	194
Clark	204
Fayette	378
Scott	75
Jessamine	144
Woodford	148
Franklin	488
Mercer	731
Boyle	219
Lincoln	524
Total	3,500

Eighth District

Perry	296
Breathitt	163
Letcher	90
Harlan	116
Knox	408
Clay	465
Owsley	567
Wolfe	84
Whitley	501
Laurel	379
Jackson	250
Estill	703
Madison	477
Rockcastle	371
Garrard	443
Pulaski	1,032
Casey	328
Wayne	448
Total	7,121

Ninth District

Mason	813
Lewis	546
Greenup	625
Boyd	356
Powell	125
Fleming	687
Rowan	154
Carter	591
Lawrence	417
Morgan	162
Johnson	294
Floyd	279
Pike	498
Magoffin	132
Montgomery	252
Bath	568
Total	6,499

Recapitulation

First District	1,154
Second District	5,228
Third District	4,523
Fourth District	4,933
Fifth District	5,719
Sixth District	3,260
Seventh District	3,500
Eighth District	7,121
Ninth District	6,499
Total	41,937

Military interference made the August (1863) elections little more than a formality. All polling places were under patrol of Kentucky troops (in United States Service) and in districts where any doubt existed as to a victory for the Regular Union candidates, the Army authorities were careful to post sufficient non-Kentucky troops so that by intimidation of the voters the desired marking of the ballots would be made. At Bardstown Colonel Butler, of the Indiana Volunteers, struck the name of ex-Governor Wickliffe from the poll book, declaring that no polling place in Kentucky was open to him. Distribution of ballots was made by soldiers, at polls in many counties, and frequently persons voting the Democratic ticket were arrested immediately under charges of disloyalty. This practice, continued throughout the war, made Kentucky "a Union State." In this election Boone, Carroll, and Trimble counties elected "Independent Union" candidates who ran on a "No-men-or-money" platform.[34]

On August 10 General Boyle ordered 6,000 slaves from central Kentucky into the United States military service. Another Negro impressment came on the night of December 13, 1863, when Union soldiers arrested all the men of a Negro congregation in Lexington as they emerged from the church, took them to jail, and on the next day set them to work on military roads. Impressed Negroes were employed as laborers in building the railroad from Lebanon towards Danville, the home of General Boyle. Good faith on the part of Boyle in this act has been questioned by the assertion that there was no military expediency for the act.[35] The dispersal of Negro work crews had a peculiar fascination for so-called guerrilla bands.

When it became increasingly difficult to obtain recruits for the Union Army, a bounty was offered to the Kentuckians to induce enlistment. The draft could not be invoked for the state had already supplied more troops than her allotted quotas.

A detachment of the 14th Kentucky Infantry under Captain Leffingwell was sent out on a raiding expedition, on September 5, by Colonel Gallup, commanding the Eastern Kentucky District. They marched sixty miles, striking Pigeon Creek, Logan County (western) Virginia, where they attacked Major Chapin's Confederate battalion, killing eight, wounding six, and taking eight prisoners. Captain Leffingwell arrived in camp with the prisoners, thirty-seven head of cattle, and forty horses. He marched over 120 miles in less than five days, and without the loss of a man killed or wounded.

On September 25, 1863, Governor Bramlette appointed Dr. I. W. Scott to the office of surgeon general of Kentucky, and named Dr. J. B. Burns to visit, in his professional capacity, Kentucky soldiers hospitalized at Chattanooga. The sick and wounded soldiers of Kentucky in the United States hospitals there were reported to have been denied comforts and necessities made available for the soldiers from some of the Northern states. No report on the subject of Dr. Burns' visit appears to refute the rumor concerning the treatment accorded to the Kentuckians. A similar act of February 27, 1865, authorized the Governor to appoint agents to visit and aid sick and wounded soldiers of Kentucky in

United States hospitals and for the observation of their condition.

Occasional incidents occurred in which the Kentuckians, whether Confederate or Union, rather involuntarily showed that they did not want to be mistaken for other people. The term "butternut" was applied to the walnut-dyed jean which was much worn by most of the Confederate soldiers from Tennessee, and by a natural metonymy the men themselves were "butternuts." One afternoon, soon after the Battle of Stone River (December 31, 1862), a young and rather gasconading Union Army surgeon came into the temporary hospital where Dr. Lytle, also a Union surgeon, was dressing the wound of Lt. Frank Tyron, of the 2d Kentucky Confederate Infantry. The wound was serious, and the surgeon's work made it so painful that the wounded man seemed to be grinding his teeth and his face was almost livid, though not a groan escaped him. The visiting surgeon, standing with his back to the fire, stopped his general chatter long enough to ask: "Doctor, is that a butternut cap'n?" Tyron forgot his pain for the moment and his eyes flashed as he jerked out angrily, "No, sir! I'm none of your butternuts!" Dr. Lytle was quick to apprehend, and he said soothingly "Oh, no! this is a Kentuckian." That was to the point, and the patient became quiescent.

Engagements in northern Georgia (near Chickamauga, Tennessee) on September 19-20, took a heavy toll in Kentuckians from both armies. On the tenth of October, Maj. Gen. Thos. L. Crittenden of the 21st Union Armp Corps was relieved of duty pending an investigation of his conduct in the battles of northern Georgia and at Chickamauga. Another Union Army case was disposed of in October when a court of inquiry exonerated Gen. Don Carlos Buell of all charges then pending against him. Orders of dishonorable dismissal were issued to six Kentucky Union Volunteer officers by the U. S. War Department on December 1, 1863. A major, captain and four lieutenants were found guilty, two of disloyalty, the others for drunkenness, cowardice, or abandoning their post in the face of the enemy.

Col. Leonidas Metcalfe of the 7th Kentucky Union Cavalry on the first of September, 1863, refunded sixty cents on the dollar to residents of Bourbon, Nicholas, and Harrison counties, of funds he had assessed against and collected from them as alleged Confederate sympathizers. This refund was made after pressure was brought to bear upon Colonel Metcalfe by Union authorities, who in turn had been pressed by the Rev. Robert J. Breckinridge,[36] spokesman for several of his coreligionists who had suffered when Metcalfe took up the collection. Many others who were mulcted filed suit to recover money extorted by Metcalfe. In the United States District Court at Covington on December 19, 1863, a continuance was arranged of the extortion cases against Colonel Metcalfe. Continuances were granted by the court from time to time until April, 1867, when settlement was made with all the claimants on a compromise basis.[37]

Metcalfe had many personal enemies and used his military office to obtain revenge. On May 8, 1862, a duel took place at Dover between ex-Mayor William T. Casto, of Maysville, and Colonel Metcalfe. Metcalfe had previously arrested Casto and sent him to prison at Camp Chase, Columbus, Ohio, from which Casto obtained his release. At the first fire, Casto fell dead. It was said that Metcalfe fired before the signal to fire was given.[38] To this incident was added the stigma left by Metcalfe's defeat at Big Hill.

On September 4, 1863, John W. Coffey and Christopher Coffey, of the 27th Kentucky Union Infantry, were executed by a firing squad at Munfordville, having been found guilty by court-martial of the charge of desertion. These men had taken part in the Battle of Big Hill and were apprehended immediately upon arrival at home.

In vivid contrast to these corruption charges and desertions is the record of Monroe County, which, with an enrolled militia of only 704, had up to December 25, 1863, furnished 801 Confederate volunteers. This excess over the enrollment came chiefly from the enlistment of boys under eighteen years.

After the capture of General Morgan, he and his officers

had been confined in the Ohio penitentiary at Columbus and his men were taken to Camp Douglas at Chicago. On the seventeenth of October, twenty-six of the men escaped by digging a tunnel from one of the barracks under the fence that enclosed Camp Douglas. On the twenty-eighth of November, General Morgan and six of his captains made their escape. The manner of escape was long said to have been by tunneling, but recent investigations have tended to detract from this account by showing the impossibility of having constructed a tunnel. Bribery also has been hinted as the means of escape.

The important fact is that the escape was made, and in less than a month Morgan appeared in Richmond, Virginia, having passed through Kentucky, Tennessee, North Carolina, and Virginia, with a side visit to Columbia, South Carolina, and with a reward of $5,000 offered for his apprehension.

On the twenty-sixth of December the legislature empowered Governor Bramlette to raise an additional 5,000 men "for the defense of the State." Thereupon Adjt. Gen. John Boyle issued a statement saying that, without a military organization of its own, the state could not protect itself against guerrillas[39] and bandit robbers. Therefore, companies were commanded to organize at once in each county under the act approved August 31, 1862. As soon as companies were organized, they were armed and subject to be called out to repel invasion or to suppress guerrilla activities. In making his statement, Boyle advised that, unless a sufficient number would soon form themselves into companies, a draft from the enrolled militia would be ordered. The companies were to be, as nearly as possible, filled to the maximum. As soon as a company was organized the commanding officer was obliged by the order to transmit to Boyle's office a complete roster of the officers and men. Officers were thereupon commissioned and orders given.

Hardly had this state defense measure become operative when the President of the United States issued a proclamation ordering a draft of 500,000 men for service of three years, or the duration of the war if less. When news of this proclamation was received, another report was made by the adjutant general showing Kentucky as having sent into Union service the following: 52 regiments of infantry containing 35,760 men, 15 regiments of cavalry containing 15,362 men, and six batteries of artillery containing 823 men, with an additional 2,957 men for 60 days' service, being a total of 54,902. Of that number 39,065 were in the field when the report was made; 3,988 had been discharged, 3,252 had died, 610 had been killed in action, and the remainder were missing, or in hospitals, or had left the service and were counted as deserters.

On January 4, 1864, the Governor issued a proclamation directing the arrest of sundry Confederate sympathizers. In his proclamation he "requests the various military commandants in the State, in every instance where a loyal citizen is taken off by bands of guerrillas, to immediately arrest at least five of the most prominent and active rebel sympathizers in the vicinity of such outrage for every loyal man taken by guerrillas. These sympathizers should be held as hostages for the safe and speedy return of the loyal citizens. Where there are disloyal relatives of guerrillas, they should be the chief sufferers. Let them learn that if they refuse to exert themselves actively for the assistance and protection of the loyal they must expect to reap the just fruits of their complicity with the enemies of our State and people." [40]

Though bands of lawless men were then preying on "loyal citizens" and Confederate sympathizers alike, causing much damage and fear, yet this edict was neither just nor within the legal powers of the Governor. It was this instrument more than any other act or circumstance that brought the detached Confederate command to be treated as a guerrilla band whenever an opportunity presented itself.[41]

By a letter of January 13, 1864, from Governor Bramlette to Gen. J. T. Boyle, remonstrance is made to the recruiting of Kentucky Negroes by a Union Army recruiting officer "for the 1st Michigan Colored regiment." Governor

Bramlette said in part, "No such recruiting will be tolerated here. Summary justice will be inflicted upon any who attempt such unlawful purpose." Previously, on December 14, 1863, the Governor had written Captain Cahill that Kentucky would furnish white men to fill the call upon her for more troops; would not enlist colored men, nor "permit any state which is unwilling to meet the measure of duty, by contributing its quota from its own population, to shelter from duty behind the free negro population of Kentucky."[42]

On January 13, 1864, the subject of expulsion of Senator Garrett Davis was debated in the U. S. Senate, but no action was taken because Senator Henry Wilson (Massachusetts) withdrew his expulsion resolution. Senator Wilson's resolution was based on utterances made by Davis which the Senator from Massachusetts deemed treasonable. These alleged treasonable statements were made in reference to the United States arms shipped into Kentucky in 1861 for the Home Guards, and in opposition to the enrollment of Kentucky Negroes for military service. Then on February 5, Davis, under the sting of the Wilson resolution, made a public statement of his "regret" for having previously introduced an expulsion resolution against his colleague, Lazarus W. Powell.

On the nineteenth of February, Adjutant General Boyle ordered Maj. Thomas Mahoney to muster into one company all the men who refused to go into the 30th Regiment of Kentucky Volunteer Cavalry then being organized as a special guard for the Capitol. These men were marched into Frankfort without arms, where the Governor selected and commissioned their officers. This having been done, they were marched to a point beyond the Tennessee River. In his order Boyle stressed the point that these men were not to be dishonorably dismissed, but that they would be "retained in the State service as infantry soldiers and sent to a distance from the Capitol which they refuse to guard."

The legislature, by a resolution of February 22, continued to protest against the enlistment of Kentucky Negroes for army service, and added a request, directed to the President, to remove camps for United States colored troops beyond the state lines. On the same day recruiting for any service, other than that of the United States, was prohibited under a fine of $500 for each recruit, and by imprisonment of from two to six months. Union authorities, completely ignoring the remonstrances of the legislature against the use of Negro troops, ordered James B. Fry, United States Provost Marshal General, to cause the immediate enrollment of all male Negroes in Kentucky between eighteen and forty-five years of age. This order was issued February 29, and five days later General Burbridge ordered all impressed Negroes released from their work and sent home to their owners so that the enrollment might be accurate.

A meeting of citizens was held in Lexington on the evening of March 10, 1864, as a testimonial of their esteem of Col. (later Adjutant General) Frank Wolford of the 1st Kentucky Union Cavalry. He was presented with a splendid set of cavalry officer accoutrements, and thereupon made a speech of acceptance which gradually transcended into a political address in which he denounced the enrollment of Kentucky Negroes by the U. S. Army, as "unconstitutional, unjust, and another of a series of startling usurpations"; saying, "it is the duty of the people of Kentucky to resist it as a violation of their guaranteed right * * *; the people of Kentucky did not want to keep step to the music of the Union, alongside of negro soldiers—it was an insult and a degradation for which their free and manly spirits were not prepared; while it involved an infraction of the rights of the State, which it was a duty of the governor—under his oath to support the constitution [of the State] and see the laws faithfully executed—to resist with all the constitutional power of the Commonwealth."[48]

The address caused consternation at home, and among the Confederate troops from Kentucky it was heralded as indicating a change in the state's allegiance. However, the speedy arrest of Colonel Wolford put an end to all speculations. In a short time he was released and ordered to report to General Grant at Nashville, but before he could make the trip the charges were dismissed by order of President Lincoln.

Doubtless Wolford's address had a far-reaching effect for on March 21, Governor Bramlette sought the counsel of the Rev. Dr. Robert J. Breckinridge, whom Bramlette later referred to as "a weathercock in politics and an Ishmaelite in religion."[44] Breckinridge was known as an "Unconditional Union man." Though a large slaveholder and with two sons in the Confederate Army, Breckinridge had as early as January 9, 1860, addressed a "very long and very eloquent 'Union' letter" to his nephew, John C. Breckinridge, then Vice President of the United States and Senator-elect from Kentucky. Two days after his conference with Breckinridge, Governor Bramlette, accompanied by Archibald Dixon and A. G. Hodges, went to Washington for an audience with President Lincoln on the subject of the enrollment of Kentucky Negroes. The conference terminated in a compromise whereby the Governor assented to Negro enrollment on condition that no enlistment of them would take place so long as Kentucky continued to furnish her quotas of white men.

A subsequent letter from Governor Bramlette to Col. A. G. Hodges, relates that as a result of their conference at Washington, the state's troop quota was to be based on the reduced militia population. Those who had gone South were no longer counted as a portion of that population. The letter further states that Brig. Gen. Stephen G. Burbridge, commander of the District of Kentucky, was given complete authority over the Kentucky enrollment and draft.[45]

Shortly after his release and prior to the June elections, Colonel Wolford made a number of political speeches opposing the "Unconditional Union" policy and especially Negro enrollment in Kentucky. Charges were again preferred and he was arrested and taken to Washington. On the tenth of July, Wolford returned to Louisville from Washington under parole. Thirteen charges were pending against him as a result of his campaign utterances that were held to have resulted in "discouraging enlistments." His return to Kentucky was for the purpose of standing trial on these charges before a military court. On the eleventh of July, Governor Bramlette wrote Col. R. T. Jacob that "If this arrest was for a political offense * * * we have sufficient material in Kentucky for hostages—among those who favor such arrests. The loyal people of Kentucky cannot be provoked or driven into rebellion against the government; but in self-defense might justly retaliate political arrests—upon those who, among our own citizens, urge or provoke political arrests, and seek to inaugurate political terrorism * * *." Who would have been held as hostages by Governor Bramlette is only conjectural, but it is certain that the Rev. Dr. Robert J. Breckinridge had lost favor with the Governor because "the Kentucky delegation to the Baltimore National Convention which nominated President Lincoln for re-election, went to Washington in a body to call upon the President. Through the Rev. Dr. Robert J. Breckinridge as their spokesman, they entered their protest against the raising of troops in Kentucky for home defense and especially against placing them under command of Gov. Bramlette and Col. Wolford."[46] This antagonism developed from the fact that Colonel Wolford, as a "Union Democrat," had "stumped the State" in the interest of Gen. Geo. B. McClellan as a candidate for President in opposition to Lincoln.

General Forrest made an attack on Paducah on March 25 and demanded the surrender of Fort Anderson, then held by Col. S. G. Hicks with the 122d Illinois Infantry, 16th Kentucky Cavalry, and 1st Kentucky Artillery, together with 220 Negroes. The Confederate fire continued late into the night. Union troops were assisted in the defense of the fort by the United States gunboats *Peosta* and *Paw-Paw*. Union losses were fourteen killed, forty-six wounded and forty prisoners taken. Confederate losses are not known, but were heavy. Much property damage was caused by Forrest's men through the burning of headquarters, quartermaster's and commissary buildings with all stores, the steamboat *Dacotah*, and the railroad depot. Other property damage resulted from the fort's artillery fire.

By voluminous reports and by ardent protest the Kentucky military authorities endeavored to show the U.S. War Department that Kentucky could and would meet her quotas, and that Negro enrollment was resented generally in the state. A report made by Adjutant General Boyle, dated March 1, 1864, shows the enrolled militia strength of the state as 78,202 in the first class, and 34,540 in the second class.

The Governor on April 8, 1864, appointed J. P. Flint commissioner and agent on behalf of Kentucky to visit camps of Negro troops and obtain for their legal owners proper vouchers for such as were from Kentucky. Also to obtain evidences of enlistments of Kentucky Negro troops then in Tennessee and other states to enable Kentucky to obtain proper credits against her quota for troops.[47]

Another Presidential call for troops was made March 14, the number being fixed at 200,000. With this call notice was served that, if the number required was not obtained by April 15, a draft would be resorted to in order to supply any deficiency. "Order No. 34," issued on April 18, directed the enlistment of able-bodied Negroes in Kentucky to be mustered into the U.S. Army in squads and forwarded to training camps outside of Kentucky. Less than a month later, on May 13, a draft of the militia was ordered by the U.S. War Department. Thereupon, Governor Bramlette issued the following appeal:

FRANKFORT, *May 13, 1864.*

KENTUCKIANS TO THE RESCUE! I want 10,000 six-months troops at once. Do not hesitate to come. I will lead you. Let us help to finish this war and save our government.

THOS. E. BRAMLETTE,
Governor of Kentucky.

An order was issued on May 16 by Major Sidell, acting assistant provost marshal for Kentucky, saying that "acceptable negroes will be received as substitutes for white men." [48] In a continued effort to resist the enlistment of Negroes, Governor Bramlette authorized Col. Frank Wolford to raise a regiment of six-months' men. Wolford's commission was

BRIG. GEN. JOHN HUNT MORGAN, C.S.A.
As a Lieutenant, Mexican War

BRIG. GEN. JOHN B. CASTLEMAN

issued June 1, 1864, and, on the sixth of June, Adjt. Gen. D. W. Lindsey issued an order, at the command of Governor Bramlette, postponing the draft ordered for the eleventh of June. The cause for postponement was given as "the prompt response to the call for six-month enlistments."

A large number of enlistments in the Union Army were made by slaves, there having been 110 Negro recruits entered in Lexington alone on the fifth and sixth of June. About 2,000 Negro enlistments were recorded for the District of Kentucky to July 15, 1864. However, these enlistments were made for the United States colored troops and without the consent of the state authorities; in fact, they were made over the state's vehement protest. These 2,000 enlistments included the slaves seized on the seventh of June by Colonel Cunningham, in charge of Negro troops at Paducah, when he made "a raid into Union County" and impressed a steamboat load of Negroes into United States service. The boatload consisted of 158 able-bodied slaves who were being carried by their owners to a point where they would not be enrolled for United States military service.[49]

General Morgan reassembled his command during the early spring of 1864, and on the second of June entered Kentucky from Virginia, through Pound Gap, with approximately 2,400 men. Those second in command were Colonel Giltner, Lieutenant Colonel Alston, and Col. D. H. Smith. At the time General Burbridge, with 6,000 troops, was encamped in Pike County, awaiting an opportunity to enter Virginia and strike at General Morgan, then in command of the department of southwestern Virginia. It was to save that part of Virginia from invasion by Burbridge that Morgan entered Kentucky[50] and commence his far-reaching raids, hoping thereby to compel Burbridge to return westward in the state. Morgan avoided an encounter in the mountain area and passed through Campton to Mount Sterling, then occupied by Capt. E. C. Barlow with about seventy men of the 40th Kentucky Union Infantry. Upon the surrender of Captain Barlow, General Morgan left his dismounted men, about 800, encamped in Mount Sterling, and with the others marched toward Lexington. His movements were made known to General Burbridge who marched on Mount Sterling and defeated the encamped Confederate contingent in a severe battle, taking 250 prisoners, killing 50 and wounding 200. Burbridge lost 35 men killed and 150 wounded.

Among the officers of Morgan's command left encamped at Mount Sterling, was the daredevil Humphrey Marshall, Jr., son of General Morgan's commander in the Mexican War. In the Mount Sterling action, when young Marshall persisted in standing up back of a stone fence, a friend yelled, "Lie down, Humphrey, you'll be killed if you stand there." To which he yelled back, "By God I can't see anything lying down there." At another time some of his brother officers said their stomachs turned at the sight of a spider in the gravy at mess, to which Marshall retorted "One side of my stomach is just as good as the other, let her turn." [51]

On the eighth of June, while Morgan was at Mount Sterling, a detachment of his force under Major Chenoweth was detailed to Harrison County and there cut off communications by burning the highway and railroad bridges and cutting telegraph wires. Simultaneously Morgan detailed Capt. Peter Everett's company to strike at Flemingsburg and Maysville.

The main body of General Morgan's troops entered Lexington on June 9, and forced the Union garrison to fall back, under fire, to Fort Clay. From Lexington, General Morgan's force passed through Georgetown to Cynthiana, where, after a brisk encounter in the early morning of the eleventh of June, he captured the garrison and sacked those houses from which he had been fired upon. News there reached Morgan that General Hobson with 500 Ohio troops was coming northward on the Kentucky Central railroad. Morgan sent a detachment to a point below Kellar's bridge and intercepted the troop train. Hobson's men fought bravely but were captured along with their commander. At dawn the following day General Burbridge arrived in

Cynthiana with 1,200 men and immediately made an attack. Many of Morgan's men were out of ammunition, but his command fought desperately for over an hour before being overpowered and compelled to retreat.

General Morgan had a singular reputation for making provision for his wounded men and burying his dead. In this battle he lost about 300 men, killed and wounded. It is said that after having ridden with his men for a considerable distance, he returned to Cynthiana to assure himself that a body of wounded men who had been overlooked would be cared for by his friends. Among the Confederate wounded of this battle was Jerome Clarke (Sue Mundy, *see Appendix C*).

That the Morgan onslaught of June provoked grave fears in Union quarters is shown by the Kentucky District report of General Ammen[52] dated July 1, 1864. This report deals with military prisons and prisoners in Kentucky and shows that during June, 1864, a total of 2,151 "rebel" prisoners were removed from Louisville prisons to military prisons in the North, to prevent the possibility of their liberation by a successful Confederate attack on the city.

On June 11, another order was issued by Adjutant General Lindsey directing the organization of the entire enrolled militia into regiments for use in emergency. This order was issued after an attack was made on Frankfort by Colonel Pryor's detachment of Morgan's cavalry. To repulse this attack Col. G. W. Monroe used 250 U.S. Regulars and the enrolled militia of Frankfort, including Governor Bramlette.

Gen. E. A. Paine assumed the office of commandant at Paducah on the nineteenth of July and initiated "fifty-one day's reign of violence, terror, rapine, extortion, oppression, bribery and military murders."[53] Nominally, for the benefit of Union soldiers' families living in western Kentucky, General Paine, on August 1, 1864, levied a tax of $100,000 upon residents of his military district. Immediately an order was issued that the collection should be made "from persons known to be or suspected of being Confederate sympathizers." Then, on the tenth of August,

Paine banished to Canada twenty-three prominent residents of Paducah, mostly women and children, sending them under guard of Negro soldiers to Cairo, Illinois. The property of those deported, and of others who fled to avoid deportation, was immediately seized and appropriated.

At the request of Governor Bramlette an investigation of Colonel Paine's conduct was ordered. General Burbridge detailed Gen. S. S. Fry and Col. John Mason Brown to conduct the inquiry, but before they could reach Paducah, Paine had fled. A complete investigation was made which revealed even more than had been charged against him.[54] On the basis of the report Paine was arrested. Before his trial was held, United States Judge Advocate General Joseph Holt struck out a number of the charges made against Paine including those that were "most startling, terrible and easily proved," thereby insuring his acquittal.[55]

Under the guise of enforcement of Burbridge's Order No. 59, General Hovey, occupying Morganfield with Indiana troops, levied $32,000 on citizens of Union County.[56] Extortion was practiced by state military authorities also as is shown by the records that the 48th Kentucky Mounted Infantry, under Col. H. T. Burge, was "thoroughly mounted by pressing horses from disloyal citizens, upon disloyal receipts, payable upon future proof of loyalty."[57]

The formation of additional United States colored troops continued in Kentucky. During July over 12,000 slaves were taken out of the state, some by substitute brokers, others on the promise of their freedom, and still others by the lure of bounty. Two Negro regiments were mustered in at Louisville and six were made ready at Camp Nelson in Jessamine, where the following letter was issued to Kentucky slave holders:

HEADQUARTERS, CAMP NELSON

CIRCULAR: JESSAMINE CO., KY., *July 6, 1864.*

    I. In pursuance with instructions from Brig. Gen. L. Thomas, Adjutant General U.S.A., owners of slaves are hereby notified, that on and after Monday, July 11, 1864, all colored men in Camp unfit for service in the army, and all women and children will be delivered up to their owners upon application to these Headquarters.

II. All officers or other persons, having in their employ negro men fit for service in the army, are hereby directed to report them forthwith to Colonel Thos. D. Sedgwick, commanding U.S. Colored Troops at this post. All men fit for service, as above, who have come into Camp since the issue of War Department Orders, must be reported, no matter at what engaged. A prompt compliance with this circular is expected.

By Command of

BRIG. GEN. S. S. FRY

Evidence of the determination of Union authorities not to distinguish any longer between detachments of Confederate troops and guerrilla bands appears in General Sherman's letter of instructions to General Burbridge, commanding the District of Kentucky. This letter is dated June 21, 1864, and says in part, "Before starting on this campaign [in Georgia], I asked Governor Bramlette to at once organize in each county a small trustworthy band under the sheriffs, and at one dash arrest every man in the community who was dangerous to it * * *; but this sweeping exhibition of power doubtless seemed to the Governor rather arbitrary * * *.

"1st, You may order all post and district Commanders that guerrillas are not soldiers, but wild beasts, unknown to usages of war * * *.

"2nd, * * *.

"3rd, Your military commanders, provost marshals, and other agents, may arrest all males and females who have encouraged or harboured guerrillas and robbers, and you may cause them to be collected in Louisville; and when you have enough—say 300 or 400—I will cause them to be sent down the Mississippi, through their guerrilla gauntlet, and by a sailing ship send them to a land where they may take their negroes and make a colony, with laws and a future of their own * * *." [58]

General Sherman made good his threat, for on the eighteenth of July, twenty-four women and children were sent to the military prison at Louisville and from there by boat to New Orleans, "and thence by sea out of the country" under his order.[59] In a speech at the Democratic National Convention at Chicago, in August, 1864, former Gov. Charles A. Wickliffe said "Many of the best and most loyal citizens of Kentucky—among them 20 or 30 ladies—are now imprisoned by the military in Louisville, in damp and dirty cells, with only straw to lie upon, and the coarsest fare; and the newspapers of Louisville are forbidden to make the slightest allusion to this terrible state of affairs. I proclaim it here and now at the risk of my life." [60]

Another Presidential call for Union troops to the extent of 500,000 came on the eighteenth of July and with it was repeated the admonition that any deficiency would be made up by draft on the fifth of September. On the twenty-fourth of July the U.S. Secretary of War issued Order No. 25 pertaining to the impressment of Negroes for military service. Article I was directed to owners of runaway slaves. They were informed that with their consent such slaves would be be captured and thereupon mustered into the United States colored troops to the credit of the states' quota on the last preceding call for troops. Article II directed that all Kentucky Negroes, who ran away, or were enticed to adjoining states to enlist for bounty, should be seized and returned to be enlisted in Kentucky regiments. In pursuance of this policy all Negro males attending a colored fair in Louisville were seized, on August 16, taken to prison, and the following day were set to work on fortifications.

When Colonel Wolford was relieved of the command of the 1st Kentucky Cavalry, after his Lexington speech, his regiment was placed under command of Col. Silas Adams. The regiment took part in many of the most desperate battles of the spring and summer of 1864 in the vicinity of Chattanooga. On August 26, the regiment arrived at Lexington, destined for service in Kentucky. Upon its arrival it had 618 men with some 200 left behind in Confederate prisons.

An order was issued on the twenty-ninth of August by Brig. Gen. Hugh Ewing, requiring county courts to make a levy of "a sum sufficient to arm, mount and pay" a company of fifty men to be organized in every county and maintained there for its defense. By a proclamation on the fifth of September, Governor Bramlette instructed county officials to refuse obedience to the order or else resign. The proclamation characterized the Ewing edict as "unlawful" and "oppressive," and closed by forbidding the county authorities to obey the order. The order was subsequently revoked by President Lincoln.[61]

Even though Confederate recruiting in Kentucky had been made hazardous, not only by United States military orders but by the state laws, it still continued. Late in the summer of 1864, Col. G. M. Jesse led a force of Confederates into Owen, Henry, Carroll, and Gallatin counties on an expedition to obtain recruits and protect them until they were safely within the Confederate lines. The number of enlistments so obtained is not known, but is said to have been large. No interference was encountered until the recruiting party was intercepted in Oldham County by a detachment of Union cavalry under Colonel Craddock.

To the Confederacy the loss of Gen. John H. Morgan was a severe blow that fell at a most inopportune time. Morgan's successor, Gen. Basil W. Duke, was an able commander, and to General Duke credit is due for a vivid account of General Morgan's tragic death. General Morgan's command was in east Tennessee, and he with some officers of his brigade were being entertained, on September 4, 1864, at the home of a friend in Greenville. The house was surrounded by the Union cavalry, under Gen. A. C. Gillem, one of whom killed Morgan. "His friends have always believed that he was murdered after his surrender; his slayers broke down the paling around the garden in which they killed him, dragged him through and while he was tossing his arms in his dying agonies, threw him across a mule, and paraded his body about the town—shouting and screaming in savage exultation.[62]

" 'It was notorious that his death, if again captured, had been sworn.' The body was dragged from the mule and thrown into a muddy ditch: 'where,' Gen. Gillem said, 'it shall lie and rot like a dog'; but he afterward sent it to the Confederate lines under a flag of truce."[63] After interment in Abingdon, Virginia, and later removed to Richmond, General Morgan's body was subsequently brought to Kentucky and buried in the Lexington cemetery.

During the fall another Union drive against southwestern Virginia was projected under command of General Burbridge with the salt works at Saltville as the objective. Colonel Giltner's cavalry contested the advance of Burbridge into Virginia by a series of sharp skirmishes from Pound Gap to Saltville. There, on the second of October, were assembled under command of General Burbridge 4,000 Union troops consisting of some Michigan volunteers and U.S. colored troops, together with the following Kentucky regiments; Col. Milton Graham's 11th and Col. J. W. Weatherford's 13th Cavalry, Col. C. Maxwell's 26th, Col. F. N. Alexander's 30th, Col. E. A. Starling's 35th, Col. Charles S. Hanson's 37th, Col. D. A. Mim's 39th, Col. C. J. True's 40th, and Lt. Col. L. M. Clark's 45th regiments of mounted infantry, and Maj. C. W. Quiggins' Sandy Valley battalion of 1st Captain Guards. The 2,000 Confederate troops were under command of Brig. Gen. John S. "Cerro Gordo" Williams and included a small brigade under Col. W. C. P. Breckinridge.

The Battle of Saltville, between General Williams' Confederates and 2,500 of Burbridge's troops, continued, desperate at times, throughout the second of October. Confederate reinforcements came up that night and preparations were made for a renewal of the battle on the third, but during the night General Burbridge retreated. The Union loss was placed at 350 killed, wounded and missing. Among the wounded was Col. C. S. Hanson who was left on the field. The Union troops, on their way back to Kentucky, were pursued by the Confederates with much damage to the Union rear guard.[64]

Another expedition against Saltville was conducted December 7-28, 1864, by General Burbridge, with 4,000 men. Kentucky troops included the following: the 11th, 12th, and 13th cavalry, and the 26th, 30th, 53d, 54th, and

55th mounted infantry regiments. The troops suffered much from exposure, the weather being extremely cold. Numerous deaths ensued. General Burbridge's official report said the salt works at Saltville, Virginia, and the lead works at Wytheville, Tennessee, were in ruins and could not be repaired. However, Gen. John C. Breckinridge telegraphed the Confederate War Department that the damage "can soon be repaired; the enemy are being pursued."

On the nineteenth of October a Confederate expedition entered the United States from Canada led by Lt. Bennet H. Young of Nicholasville. Lieutenant Young acted under the orders of the Confederate Secretary of War who authorized the project as a retaliatory measure for the burning of dwellings and the destruction of other non-combatant property, including churches, in the Shenandoah Valley of Virginia, under explicit orders of Gen. Philip Sheridan.

In pursuance of his authorization Lieutenant Young with a company of twenty-two Confederates most of them having escaped from United States military prison, proceeded to make a raid upon the town of St. Albans in Vermont, on the Central railroad, about 15 miles from the frontier; for three quarters of an hour, hold the citizens prisoners of war; seize all the money in their banks, $211,150, and a number of horses; kill one man who resists, and attempt to set fire to the town, but fail in this. Immense alarm along the whole Canadian border, militia enlisted, arms and troops sent from New York, and patrol kept up for some time. The Canadian authorities prove very prompt in arresting the raiders, and securing their money—acting, as the U.S. secretary of state, Wm. H. Seward says, 'in entire conformity with the wishes of the United States.' Under the proceedings in court, for their extradition as burglars and murderers, they are discharged by Judge Coursol on a technical defect in the instrument under which they are tried, released from custody, and the money restored. Their release provokes, Dec. 14, a 'blood and thunder' proclamation from Maj. Gen. John A. Dix, who orders any more such maurauders to be shot down if possible while in the very act, but by all means to be 'followed into Canada' if necessary, and there arrested and brought back. President Lincoln is alarmed at the stupid blunder of Gen. Dix, and, Dec. 17, modifies the order so as to require 'military commanders to report to headquarters at New York for instructions before crossing the boundary line in pursuit of the guilty parties.' The claim was subsequently renewed, under the treaty with Great Britain, for the delivery of Lieut. Young, Wallace, Spurr, Huntly, Tevis, Hutchinson, and their 17 companions [mostly Kentuckians] in the St. Albans raid; but Mr. Justice Smith, at Montreal, held that 'the said attack was a hostile expedition undertaken and carried out under the authority of the so-called Confederate States, by one of the officers of their army, 'and being both a belligerent act of hostility and a political offense, *quoad* the state now demanding extradition,' was not embraced by the Aushburton treaty nor by the statutes of Canada—for neither authorized the extradition of belligerents or political offenders. Therefore the prisoners were discharged.[65]

The following order may have been issued in good faith, but its execution was most ruthless:

HEADQUARTERS MILITARY DIST. OF KY.

LEXINGTON, KY., *Oct. 26, 1864*

The irregular bands of armed men within our lines, disconnected from the rebel army, who prowl through the country, and subsist by depredating upon the property of citizens and of the government are guerillas and will hereafter be treated as such.

They are here without an idea of permanent occupancy or with a reasonable hope of seriously injuring our communication. They form no part of the organized army of the rebellion, and when captured are not entitled to the treatment prescribed for regular soldiers, but by the laws of war they have forfeited their lives.

Frequent robberies and murders committed by these outlaws, demand that the laws of war be stringently meted out to them.

Hereafter no guerrillas will be received as prisoners and any officer who may capture such and extend to them the courtesies due prisoners of war will be held accountable for disobedience of orders.

By command of

BREVET MAJ. GEN. S. G. BURBRIDGE

The following order, aside from reflecting ingratitude for Kentucky's troop contributions to the Union cause, had a detrimental effect on both the Kentucky soldier and farmer!

HEADQUARTERS MILITARY DISTRICT OF KENTUCKY,

LEXINGTON, *Oct. 28, 1864*.

The following information is hereby published: Those owning or feeding hogs in Kentucky are informed that the U.S. government desires to secure the surplus hogs in the State. A fair market value will be paid for all that are for sale.

It is not intended to limit the amounts deemed necessary to be packed for family use; but it is hoped that all will willingly sell to the government any excess of personal wants, and not allow so much to be packed in the country as to invite raids for its capture.

Major H. C. Symonds, Commissary of Subsistence, U.S. army at Louisville, is instructed with the details of this business, and will give all necessary information.

S. G. BURBRIDGE
Major General

Indignation among the farmers at the combination between the United States military authorities and speculators was intense. After the farmers showed their reluctance to sell at a figure considerably lower than that paid by the government in other markets a statement was issued by Major Symonds saying: "My advice to farmers is to sell at once. I make no threats of impressment; but trust that all will realize that they are promoting the interests of their government, while they advance their own interests. I consider that the government has a prior claim to any private parties, and shall take steps to secure such results."

The order was likewise resented by the ranks in the military, for details of soldiers, especially Negro recruits, were set to guard and feed hogs purchased in outlying districts and held there in pens pending shipment to Louisville.

The furore created by Burbridge's hog order caused him to issue a statement saying that he had "nothing whatever to do with the hog business; the whole matter is in the hands of Major Symonds and Colonel Kilburn." [66] Then difficulties arose between Major Symonds and Colonel Kilburn which resulted in the latter's request to be relieved when the United States commissary department at Washington confirmed the action taken on the hog purchasing order.

Scores had been executed by Union military authority and hundreds of unwarranted arrests were made in the state during July and August, 1864, by the same authority. Proscription lists bore the names of the administration's leading political adversaries. Then, in a public address at Lexington on September 24, 1864, the Rev. Dr. Robert J. Breckinridge said: "As to these [illegal arrests and unwarranted military executions], all the fault I have to find is, that more should not have been arrested than were; and many of those that were arrested were set at liberty too soon. * * * When Simon de Montfort was slaughtering the Protestants in the south of France he was appealed to by certain persons —declaring that his men were mistaken, that they were killing many who were good Catholics. To which he replied: 'Kill them all; God knows his own.' And this is the way we should deal with these fellows; treat them all alike; and if there are any among them who are not rebels at heart, God will take care of them and save them at least." [67] This was a prompting which many Kentuckians felt that General Burbridge did not need.

Col. Robert J. Breckinridge, Jr., with Maj. Theophilus Steele, the son and son-in-law, respectively, of the Rev. Dr. Robert J. Breckinridge, led a Confederate force of thirty-two men in an expedition, on the first of November, to Williamstown for the purpose of capturing a large sum of money belonging to the United States Government and reported as being lodged there in the safe of a general store. The money was found to have been removed, but the raiders captured thirty United States muskets. Shortly afterward, Major Steele and several of his men were captured while engaged in recruiting. On November 30, Steele, with other Confederate officers, was transferred from Lexington to Johnson's Island military prison.

On the evening of the second of November, Franklin County was made the scene of four United States military murders. S. Thomas Hunt, a young lawyer of Maysville, was captured while on his way to join the Confederate Army in which he had enlisted. Thornton Lafferty, an aged political prisoner, and two others were taken from the military prison at Lexington to a pasture field near Frankfort where death was inflicted by shooting.[68] None of these men had had a trial of any sort. The bodies were buried where they fell, without coffins and in shallow graves (*see page 250*).

An incident that transpired at this time shows the difficulties experienced by Kentucky Confederate Volunteers in getting to the Confederate lines. On Holly Creek in Breathitt County, on the eleventh of November, a party of Confederate recruits under Lt. J. W. Smith, Jr., encountered Capt. J. A. Stamper's company of Home Guards. In the skirmish that there ensued Lieutenant Smith was seriously wounded and captured; the others escaped and made their way to the Confederate lines.

During November, Paul R. Shipman of the Louisville *Journal* and Richard T. Jacob, Lieutenant Governor of Kentucky, who until his election to that office had held the rank of colonel in the Kentucky Union Volunteers, were arrested for protesting the frequency of military murder in Kentucky. Both men held under arrest were ordered out of the state, Shipman to Washington and Jacob to the South.

On November 14, 1864, Governor Bramlette wrote President Lincoln about the official conduct of General Burbridge[69] pointing out that

His whole course, for weeks past, has been such as was most calculated to inaugurate revolt and produce collisions * * *. I shall need your co-operation to attain that unity and harmony which I desire—and, which, I doubt not you desire—but which he [Burbridge] will try to prevent, in the blunderings of a weak intellect and an overwhelming vanity * * *. He and I cannot hold personal converse after his bad conduct of the last few weeks * * *. The system of arrests inaugurated by Burbridge outrages public judgment and ought to be restricted. His entire want of truthfulness enables him unscrupulously to make false charges to sustain his outrages against public judgment * * *. I beg of you, Mr. President, to assist and give me such aid as you have in your power in preserving peace, order, and unity in Kentucky. Our people are right and true though they have been much bedeviled by the course of subordinate officers * * *.

The fourth arrest of Col. Frank Wolford was made on the twenty-first of November. He was at once forwarded to Covington to be sent to the South. Governor Bramlette thereupon made an appeal to President Lincoln in behalf of these men wherein he referred to "a clique of five persons at Lexington,'' two citizens and three army officers, who controlled the actions of Burbridge.[70] While the Governor was thus engaged, Chief Justice Joshua F. Bullitt and six other prominent Kentuckians arrived in Louisville, having been released from a Union military prison in Memphis. Their release was obtained by Confederate Gen. N. B. Forrest, in exchange for some citizens of Memphis and some Union Army engineers captured in one of his Memphis raids.

By a proclamation of November 23, 1864, Governor Bramlette asked Kentuckians "whose slaves have been taken for army services to devote whatever sum the Government may pay for them to the noble purpose of relieving the wants and supplying the necessities of the wives and children, and widows and orphans," of Kentucky Union soldiers. He related that he would contribute whatever he might receive for the two slaves lost by him, and expressed a hope that a fund of "$500,000 will be dedicated to this patriotic charity." Then on February 7, 1865, he transmitted the thirteenth amendment to the United States Constitution to the legislature for ratification and included statistical data showing the depreciation in assessed valuation of Kentucky slaves due chiefly to loss incurred by their induction into the U.S. Army. In 1860, before the war commenced the state had a slave property asssessed at $107,494,527 which by 1864 had dwindled to $34,179,246.

A trial of more than ordinary consequence was concluded in the Campbell Circuit Court at Newport on the first of December, 1864. Alexander Caldwell, a private in the Confederate Army, had been accused of horse stealing, and was acquitted of the charge though he admitted taking the horse. The defense set up was that Caldwell had taken the amnesty oath. This, the court held, did not absolve him from his offense against the Commonwealth of Kentucky. Under his second plea he showed that he took the horse at the order of his commanding officer, and delivered the horse to that officer. Caldwell's status as a belligerent was recognized, the theft of the horse deemed an act of war, and as such was not a felony; therefore, he was acquitted.

The draft originally set for September 15, in the call for 500,000 troops, was first postponed to September 19. It proved a failure and a supplementary draft was started on the twenty-fifth of November in those counties which had not met their quota and was continued until abeyance orders were issued on the fourth of December. Drafted men disappeared in great numbers, some to join the Confederate Army, others to form guerrilla bands, and some leaving the country. Most of those who were left chose to send substitutes if financially able to do so, and "Negro substitutes could be obtained at a reasonable figure." That the draft failed utterly is borne out by official correspondence and documents, indicating that nearly 7,000 of the men drafted in Kentucky in November and December, 1864, failed to report for duty, and accordingly were listed as Union Army deserters.

Among those known to have been driven into the Confederate service by the draft were 578 men from Breckinridge, Hardin, and Meade counties, who passed through Henderson and Morganfield to join Gen. H. B. Lyon. From Hardin County came a Baptist clergyman, a Mr. Williams, who, when drafted for the Union Army, raised a company and proceeded to join the Confederates. Captain Williams' congregation offered to obtain his relief from military service by purchase of a substitute, but he declined to have another fight for a cause for which he could not conscientiously go to battle for himself.

During December, 1864, the Confederate conscript law was invoked in western Kentucky. Gen. H. B. Lyon, with his regiment of cavalry and a small battery of artillery, initiated a campaign on the ninth of December, when they captured several steamers including the *Thomas E. Tutt* and the *Ben South*. A part of General Lyon's force was left in control of the Cumberland River navigation. The balance of his troops were used as a recruiting party in the western and west central part of the state. Their advance was contested by skirmishes at Ashbridge, Nolin Station, Campbellsville, Elizabethtown, and Burkesville.

The Governor's annual message to the legislature, dated January 6, 1865, contains a complete account of arrests of prominent persons during the previous year, reports on the conduct of Gen. E. A. Paine, and on the "hog purchase order." Five days later, by a special message, Governor Bramlette informed the legislature that the "General commanding" had ordered "immediate steps for the muster out of the State troops, 'in compliance with the orders from the War Department.'" The message adds that "the United States military commander of the Kentucky District has ordered that no organization of Kentucky troops shall take place, either for home defense or otherwise." He reviews the military condition of Kentucky and in part relates that a recent enrollment of those liable for duty showed 133,493. He shows that from the beginning of the war to January 1, 1865, Kentucky furnished 76,335 men to the Union Army, of whom 61,417 were white, and 14,918 Negroes, and that under the call of December, 1864, an additional 7,000 troops were ready to be mustered into the Union service. Other thousands were actively engaged as state forces designated as Capitol Guards, State Guards, Home Guards, and otherwise.

Governor Bramlette had just previously appealed to the U.S. War Department for subsistence and pay for a force of 5,000 troops to be mustered in primarily for intra-state duty against guerrillas. The following letter[71] contains his request and the reasons supporting it:

January 2, 1865

Hon. E. M. Stanton
Secretary of War

The legislature having authorized me to raise 5,000 men for the defense of Kentucky, I have deferred the matter until the condition of affairs demands that we should do something to rid our State of the bands of guerrillas infesting it. The requirements of the Government commanding that the Federal forces be used in other fields has compelled me through the intrusion of good men over the State, to take advantage of the authority granted by the

PERRYVILLE BATTLEFIELD. (See p. 187.)

MUNFORDVILLE BATTLEFIELD. (See p. 186.)

ZOLLICOFFER MONUMENT, ZOLLICOFFER MEMORIAL PARK—Nancy, Ky.
(See pp. 175, 246)

CONFEDERATE MASS-BURIAL MONUMENT—Zollicoffer Memorial Park, Nancy, Ky.

legislature, to raise these men for our protection. The few State forces we now have in the field have and are now rendering material assistance to the Government in keeping open communication with our army at the front and protecting our people. May I have the honor to issue Commissary and all necessary papers. These troops will co-operate with the Federal forces in case of invasion and in ridding our State of guerillas. It will not interfere with enlistments in filling our quotas under any call that may be made.

I am confident that I can restore harmony and by their presence in different localities it will give the citizen confidence to fight for his own home and property against these predatory bands.

THOMAS E. BRAMLETTE
Governor of Kentucky

The request of the Governor was granted, thus paving the way for this new force which was soon after organized. Recruiting of this new body of troops was delegated to Col. S. F. Johnson. Through a misunderstanding the men were enlisted as cavalry though it was the intention of the War Department to enlarge the infantry force for defense of the state. Later events and incidents seem to indicate that the "error" might have been committed intentionally for on the sixth of February, 1865, the U.S. War Department compelled General Burbridge to revoke his own order disbanding Kentucky troops raised for defense against guerrillas. The following letter[72] relates to the error:

March 29, 1865

To HON. E. M. STANTON, SECRETARY OF WAR
WASHINGTON, D. C.

I have the honor to state that, since my communication to you of the 16th relative to authority of Col. S. F. Johnson for recruiting, the Adjutant General of Kentucky has received from Colonel Sidell, muster in rolls of eight full companies recruited by said Johnson as cavalry.

Colonel Sidell informs me that these men were recruited, and mustered in, under authority of your telegram to Maj. Gen. Burbridge dated Aug. 7th, 1864.

They enlisted in good faith as cavalry under orders of Maj. Gen. Burbridge, and as I have already commissioned the officers for the eight companies, as cavalry, by request—I hope that the organization will be allowed to remain as such. I have assurances that the Regiment will be speedily filled to the maximum standard.

The condition of our State is such that Cavalry only is efficient outside of garrisons.

THOMAS E. BRAMLETTE,
Governor of Kentucky.

Kentucky continued to be harassed by bands of outlaws. For a time during the fall and winter of 1864 and 1865 neither property nor life were safe because of the operations of these bands. In desperation the legislature asked the adjutant general to formulate a plan to break up guerrilla plundering, and on January 16, 1865, he submitted a report and recommendations.

An incident that reflected anything but honor on the Home Guards involved occurred January 28, 1865, when eighteen of them busied themselves in plundering the stores of Bloomfield, Nelson County. While so engaged they were attacked by a force of about sixty led by Capt. Jerome Clarke. In the skirmish that ensued seventeen of the Home Guards were killed.[73]

An instance of the determination by Union military authorities to classify individuals or small bodies of Confederates as guerrillas is contained in the execution on January 20, 1865, at Louisville of Nathaniel Marks of Grayson. Marks, a private in Company A, 10th Kentucky Confederate Infantry, had a furlough and was on his way home when arrested. He was tried before a military commission (the same personnel that sat in the case of Jerome Clarke, *see Appendix C*), and was condemned as a guerilla. His protests of innocnence and requests to introduce evidence were ruled out.[74]

Captured Kentuckians of the Confederate Army imprisoned in Camp Douglas, Chicago, Illinois, on February 7, 1865, numbered 1,663. A poll was taken on that day to ascertain which of these prisoners would return to the Confederate Army service. Of this number 1,422 indicated a desire to return to their commands if exchanged.

In order to conserve the militia strength of the state the legislature found it necessary to take action against "substitute brokers" from other states who came into Kentucky offering sums as bounty sufficiently high to induce many to leave the state and enter the Union service elsewhere as substitutes for draftees. This practice was prohibited by an act of February 22, 1865, which made it unlawful to take any male out of the state to be enlisted as the substitute for a resident of another state. The penalty provided was a fine of $1,000 and one year's imprisonment for each offense.

Maj. Gen. S. G. Burbridge was relieved of his command of the Military District of Kentucky on February 22, 1865, and ordered by his successor, General Palmer, to report to General Thomas at Nashville for field duty. News of the change reached the Kentucky public on the tenth of February by the announcement that "Maj. Gen. John M. Palmer, of Illinois, has been appointed to command in Kentucky. Thank God and President Lincoln."[75] Three days after General Palmer took up the duties of his office he issued an order designed to encourage Kentuckians to desert from the Confederate Army. The order directed all Confederate deserters then in Kentucky, or who might come in, to register with the provost marshal of their county, thereby becoming entitled to United States military protection.

On February 22, 1865, Confederate Col. John C. Breckinridge, Jr., was taken prisoner at Versailles. In searching him an order from the Confederate Secretary of War was found directing all persons engaged in Confederate recruiting in Kentucky to obey the orders of Colonel Breckinridge; those failing to do so "will be at once reported to the military authorities in Kentucky as not recognized by the Confederate Government and not entitled, if captured, to be treated as prisoners of war." The following communications deal with the arrest and imprisonment of Colonel Breckinridge:

Feb. 23, 1865

To: MAJOR GENERAL JOHN PALMER
Commanding District of Kentucky

I have the honor to report that a portion of State troops, now stationed at Versailles in Woodford county, did on the 22nd inst., under the guidance of Capt. J. J. Macey the County Provost Marshal, capture, about seven miles east of Versailles, Col. Robert J. Breckinridge of the Confederate army. I telegraphed you this morning in regard to the disposition of the prisoner, but receiving no reply, I deem it advisable to forward him to you, as the arrangements at this point for his secure keeping are inadequate."[76]

      D. W. LINDSEY,
       Insp. and Adj. Gen. of Kentucky.

To: CAPT. THOMAS PRIESTLY   Feb. 23, 1865
Provost Marshal

You will please forward Col. R. J. Breckinridge, the Confederate prisoner now in your charge, to Louisville by morning train securely guarded, and deliver him to Maj. Gen. Palmer commanding the Military District of Kentucky.[77]

      D. W. LINDSEY,
       Insp. and Adj. Gen. of Kentucky.

To: CAPT. THOMAS PRIESTLY   Feb. 27, 1865
Provost Marshal

Citizen H. C. O'Nan has been arrested upon the charge of harboring Rebels. I send him to you with the accompanying papers, and recommend that he be forwarded to Louisville in the morning. Col. R. J. Breckinridge was captured at O'Nan's house."[78]

      D. W. LINDSEY,
       Insp. and Adj. Gen. of Kentucky.

During the years that intervened between the passage of the State Guard Act and the spring of 1865, the Kentucky Legislature had complicated the state's military law by frequent enactments, often in conflict with other unrepealed laws or the constitution. In an effort to overcome this chaotic condition, the Kentucky National Legion Act of March 4, 1865, was passed. A section of this act stipulated "that the militia residing within one mile of the state road leading from London to the Tennessee line, by way of Williamsburg, shall be liable to perform labor thereon, subject to the supervision of the commissioners respectively, provided that no one shall be required to labor more than six days in any one year."

Upon the heels of the National Legion Act, and after receiving reports on United States hospitals, the state determined upon a change of policy in the care of her sick and disabled soldiers. The new arrangement contemplated no further use for the State Military Hospital at Louisville. The disposition of this institution was delegated to the Governor, who by the following letter hoped to effect a sale:

To: MAJ. GEN. JOHN M. PALMER, *April 1, 1865*
Commanding Department of Kentucky
Louisville, Ky.

The State of Kentucky some years back fitted up a hospital at this place for the accommodations of State soldiers, in which United States troops have at times been received, but having now only some six or eight State, and some 40 United States men therein, we desire to discontinue the same by turning it over to the United States authorities. The hospital is well arranged and furnished with all necessary appurtenances, and with room sufficient to accommodate 100 patients. As this has been made a post of United States soldiers, and as troops are constantly passing through, leaving their sick, I think it would be a matter of economy on the part of the War Department to assume control over same.

Mr. Theobold of the Quarter Master General's office who hands you this, can explain in detail all the particulars of the hospital as to supplies on hand. If agreeable to you that the hospital be turned over to the United States, I respectfully request that a Surgeon be assigned to duty in charge of same, with directions to receipt for all stores on hand; and if not please suggest what disposition shall be made of the United States soldiers now in same as patients.[79]

THOMAS E. BRAMLETTE,
Governor of Kentucky.

Soon after came the end of the war with the surrender of General Lee on April 13, 1865, and that of General Johnston on April 26. The latter command contained a large number of troops from Kentucky. During the war the number of Kentuckians under arms far exceeded 100,000. Kentucky furnished seventeen regiments of cavalry, fifty-five regiments of infantry, and other volunteers to the Union Army. After the draft of 1864 was started Senator Garrett Davis discovered that the state had already furnished more than its quota of troops. The draft was therefore voided.

War Department statistics show that Kentucky furnished 51,000 white volunteers and 23,000 Negro volunteers to the Union Army, a total of 74,000 troops. In vivid contrast and in contradiction of these statistics is the following official report:

HDQRS. KENTUCKY VOLUNTEERS
ADJUTANT GENERAL'S OFFICE

S. T. M. MAJOR, ESQ.:   FRANKFORT, *July 5, 1867*

SIR: It appears from the rolls on file in the office that the State of Kentucky furnished the following number of soldiers during the late rebellion, Viz:

Forty-four regiments infantry (white) numbering	43,689
Sixteen regiments cavalry (white) numbering	19,349
Five batteries light artillery (white)	937
Fifteen regiments infantry (colored); two regiments cavalry (colored); four regiments heavy artillery (colored)—numbering in all	25,438
State troops paid by the State of Kentucky, but acting in conjunction with United States troops	13,526
Total number of troops furnished	102,939

Official returns from various counties of this state show that at the commencement of the rebellion, and before our population was disturbed by the war, for the year 1861, the enrolled militia numbered 137,211 and for the year 1865, the enrolled militia 103,401. This diminishment is accounted for by the absence, at the time of taking the lists, of our soldiers in the armies, and by the fact that, according to the best and most reliable estimates, about 15,000 to 20,000 of our population left for the rebel armies.[80]

D. W. LINDSEY,
Adjutant General of Kentucky.

The following table, compiled from records in the office of the adjutant general of Kentucky, shows the state's contribution of men to the Union Army. These figures do not include Negroes, for the constitution of 1850 excluded them from the militia and they continued under such exclusion until the constitution of 1891 became operative. Negroes from Kentucky were mustered directly into the United States service:

CAVALRY

Regiments	No. at Organization	Recruits	Total
1st	900	513	1413
2nd	997	......	997
3rd	1200	......	1200
4th	659	167	826

CAVALRY

Regiments	No. at Organization	Recruits	Total
5th	789	90	879
6th	1007	343	1350
7th	939	203	1142
8th	1235	53	1288
9th	1206	52	1258
10th	1176	59	1235
11th	1001	279	1280
12th	814	876	1690
13th	1198	43	1241
14th	1273	23	1296
15th	503	126	631
17th	1211	55	1266
1st Vet. Cav.	267	......	267
2nd Vet. Cav.	659	......	659
3rd Vet. Cav.	603	......	603
4th Vet. Cav.	594	......	594
6th Vet. Cav.	832	......	832
Patterson's Co. Engineers	43	......	43
Light Artillery	629	656	1285
Detachments unclassified	107	......	107
			23,382

INFANTRY

Regiments	No. at Organization	Recruits	Total
1st	896	209	1105
2nd	876	282	1158
3rd	913	163	1076
4th	803	1055	1858
5th	980	70	1050
6th	890	85	975
7th	1000	169	1169
8th	930	103	1033
9th	930	205	1135
10th	869	100	969
11th	851	128	979
12th	882	112	994
13th	862	120	982
14th	863	462	1325
15th	870	99	969
16th	878	17	895
17th	692	807	1499
18th	779	150	929

INFANTRY

Regiments	No. at Organization	Recruits	Total
19th	835	127	962
20th	873	118	991
21st	874	65	939
22nd	905	108	1013
23rd	942	76	1018
24th	664	400	1064
26th	519	641	1160
27th	627	199	826
28th	677	165	842
30th	826	56	882
32nd	923	......	923
34th	792	102	894
35th	841	121	962
37th	805	71	876
39th	817	541	1358
40th	841	195	1036
45th	874	126	1000
47th	769	177	946
48th	864	18	842
49th	625	321	946
52nd	843	46	889
53rd	918	140	1058
54th	854	......	854
55th	873	169	1042
7th Vet. Inf.	379	......	379
12th Vet. Inf.	639	......	639
14th Vet. Inf.	369	13	382
16th Vet. Inf.	763	......	763
18th Vet. Inf.	646	......	646
21st Vet. Inf.	866	......	866
23rd Vet. Inf.	625	......	625
26th Vet. Inf.	736	......	736
28th Vet. Inf.	394	......	394
			48,893

```
Total Infantry .................................. 48,893
Total Cavalry ...................................  23,382
                                                  ──────
                                                  72,275
State Troops ....................................  12,486
                                                  ──────
                                                  84,761
Deduct veterans re-enlisting ....................   5,407
                                                  ──────
                                                  79,354
```

Kentucky furnished more volunteers to the Union Army than the number of men contributed by any of several larger Northern States, their draftees included. During the war 10,774 Kentucky Union troops were killed in battle, died from diseases, or from wounds received in battle.

The emancipation proclamation of January 1, 1863, applied only to the Negroes in the states in rebellion. Kentucky was considered not in rebellion; consequently, the emancipation proclamation did not free any of her slaves. Soon after the promulgation of that proclamation an act of Congress provided that the enlistment of a slave in the Union Army would automatically free him and every member of his family. Under the stimulus of this inducement thousands of slaves from Kentucky enlisted. They were not all credited to Kentucky, and so their number can only be estimated. Most of the U. S. Army recruiting officers who recruited the Negro troops in Kentucky were from New England states. It has been charged that these officers credited Negro recruits to their own state in order to lighten the draft there.

Kentucky Confederate regiments included the 2d, 3d, 4th, 6th, 8th, and 9th infantry, and the 2d, 3d, and 9th cavalry. In these the personnel was solidly Kentuckian. However, many of the Tennessee and Virginia regiments had Kentucky companies.

In addition to the volunteers furnished by Kentucky to both the Confederacy and the Union, the state raised more than 20,000 troops for intra-state service, nearly all of whom at one time or another performed active service in the field. Three hundred and fourteen Kentuckians served as officers in the United States Volunteer Navy during the war. The number who served as enlisted men is not recorded, but it is fair to assume that there were at least 10 enlisted men for each officer, and that would make a total of more than 3,000 men.

If accurate figures could be obtained, it is believed that the number of Kentuckians who served in the Confederate Army states would not fall far short of 35,000.

Pursuant to an act of the Confederate Congress granting medals and badges of distinction as a reward for courage and good conduct on the field of battle, the following Kentucky soldiers were selected by their comrades in arms because of merit:

The 2d Regiment of Infantry—Pvt. Benjamin F. Parker, Company A; Corp. Mornix Virden, Company B; Pvt. John Conley, Company C; Corp. Frank B. Buckner, Company D; Sgt. William Frazee, Company E; Sgt. Henry Fritz, Company F; Pvt. Louis H. Paradoe, Company G; Pvt. Oscar Hackley, Company I; Pvt. Frank Taylor, Company K.

The 4th Regiment of Infantry—Lt. B T. Smith (killed in action), Company A; Lt. John L. Bell (killed in action), Company K; Sgt. R. H. Lindsey (color bearer), Company D; Corp. Ephraim R. South, Company A; Pvt. John McCreery, Company B; Pvt. John R. Brinkley, Company C; Pvt. Thomas H. Covington (killed in action), Company D; Pvt. William J. Watkins, Company E; Pvt. Fredling Skeggs, Company F; Pvt. Alexander Smith, Company G; Pvt. William N. Blanchard, Company I; Pvt. Mathias Garrett, Company K.

The 5th Regiment of Infantry—Lt. Col. George W. Connor, Adjt. Thomas B. Cook, Capt. T. J. Henry, Company C; Capt. Joseph Desha, Company I; Pvt. Frank H. Hasauk, Company A; Pvt. Samuel South, Company B; Pvt. Richard Yarbrough, Company E; Sgt. F. W. Campbell, Company F; Pvt. Winlock L. Shelton, Company K.

The 6th Regiment of Infantry—Second Lt. James H. Cole, Company G; Pvt. Marcellus S. Mathews, Company D; Pvt. H. Fowler, Company A; Pvt. Henry Haman, Company H; Pvt. John Hinton, Company B; Sgt. F. P. Randle, Company I.

The 9th Regiment of Infantry—Corp. John W. Carrell, Company D; Pvt. Norborn G. Gray, Company B; Corp. Nathan Board, Company G; Pvt. Andrew J. Kirtley, Company C.

The Knights of the Golden Circle was a semi-military secret organization of the Middle West (though not here confined) that flourished from 1861 to 1864. Its chief purpose was said to be the establishment of a Northwestern Confederacy. Upon the outbreak of the War between the States many of the Democrats of the Middle West, who were opposed to the war policy of the Republicans, organized the Knights of the Golden Circle, pledging themselves to bring about peace. In 1863, because of the disclosure of some of its operations, the organization took the name of Order of American Knights. The name was again changed in 1864 when the organization became the Sons of Liberty. The total membership of the order was approximately three hundred thousand, principally in Ohio, Indiana, Illinois, Iowa, Wisconsin, Kentucky and southwestern Pennsylvania.

Fernando Wood of New York seems to have been the chief officer, and in 1864 Clement L. Vallandigham of Ohio was second in authority. The great importance of the Knights of the Golden Circle and its successors was due to their opposition to the war policy of the Republican administration. Their plan was to overthrow the Lincoln government in the elections and give to the Democrats the control of the U.S. Government, which would then make peace and invite the Southern States to come back into the Union on the old footing. The most effective work done by the order was in encouraging desertion from the Union Army, in preventing enlistments, and in resisting the draft. Arrests of leaders and seizures of arms by the United States resulted in a collapse of the order late in 1864. Three of the leaders were sentenced to death by court-martial, but sentence was suspended, and in 1866 they were released under a decision of the United States Supreme Court.

Testimony was offered during the treason trials at Indianapolis to show that this order was responsible for an "organized, formidable conspiracy, military in its character, and created and held in existence for the purpose of aiding any enemies of the Republican organization, and destroying the effectiveness of the Union Army." The number in the states of Ohio, Indiana, and Illinois, was claimed to be 100,000 men able and willing to bear arms. Evidence introduced showed that an avowed purpose of the organization was to release the Confederate prisoners held in the three states, last above named, numbering many veteran soldiers, arm them with guns to be seized from the arsenals of these states, and then move into Kentucky, seizing all the large cities on the way. They were then to take possession of the Louisville & Nashville Railroad. After intrenching at Nashville or Chattanooga, they were to cut General Sherman's communications, thereby placing him between two large armies and separating him from his base of supplies.

One of the witnesses, a person who pretended to rank high in the councils of the order, testified that at a time when the Union authorities were attempting to suppress the rebel sympathizers and guerrillas in Kentucky, he sent instructions of Chief Justice Josiah F. Bullitt (*ante, p. 222*) as grand commander of the state, to select good couriers and runners to aid the Confederates and "to call to arms the members of said secret society or order, and other sympathizers with the existing rebellion, whenever a signal should be given by the authorities of the said secret society or order." This witness added that he took this action "knowing that in Kentucky there were various armed forces in the interest of said rebellion, and that said State was in constant danger of invasion by further rebel forces, did attempt therein to organize and extend a secret society or order, known as the order of American Knights, or Order of the Sons of Liberty, having for its object to aid and assist said rebellion."

The organization doubtless had agents in Kentucky, but it is a fallacy to suppose that any appreciable number of Kentuckians were influenced by them. The allegiance of the Kentuckian was determined by economic, social or political influences, often a combination of these.

NOTES, REFERENCES, AND SOURCES

32. Preserved in collection of Kentucky State Historical Society, Frankfort.
33. *Tri-Weekly Yeoman*, July 9, 1867.
34. Collins, *History of Kentucky*, Vol. I, pp. 127-28.

35. *Ibid.*, Vol. I, p. 128.
36. Sketch of Breckinridge.
37. Collins, *History of Kentucky*, Vol. I, p. 102.
38. The Paris *True Kentuckian*, Apr. 4, 1864.
39. A guerrilla is a member of an independent band engaged in predatory excursions in war times, or one engaged in or assisting in carrying on an irregular warfare in connection with activities of any of the recognized belligerents. Such guerrilla acts, though irregular, may be legitimate.
40. Collins, *History of Kentucky*, Vol. I, p. 130.
41. *Ibid.*, Vol. I, p. 128-29. "Oct. 6—Hays [Hughes], or Hamilton, with 85 Confederates, dash into Glasgow, Barren County, about sunrise, surprising and capturing, and afterwards paroling, 140 Federal soldiers." "Dec. 27—Colonels Hughes, Hamilton, and Dougherty's guerrillas capture Scottsville, Allen County, after defeating and taking prisoners Capt. J. D. Gillum's company of 52d Kentucky * * *." It seems inconsistent that these men should have led "Confederates" on October 26, and guerrillas on the twenty-seventh of December. In this manner detached Confederate commands were frequently misclassified and denied all the rights, sanctioned by civilized usage and prevailing by law between belligerents. (*See Jerome Clarke case, Appendix C.*)

Additional evidence of a determination of U.S. Military authorities to classify Confederate detachments, raiding in Kentucky, as guerrillas is contained in General Burbridge's order of July 3, which required all prisoners paroled by General Morgan or his officer, to report to their regiments for service. The order stated that such paroles had "been given in violation of orders from the U.S. War Department." Suspension of the writ of habeas corpus was ordered by Lincoln when he proclaimed martial law in Kentucky on the fifth of July. Lincoln's stated reason for the proclamation was the prevalence of Confederate and guerrilla raids into the state.

42. Governor's *Letter Book*, Jan., 1864.
43. Collins, *History of Kentucky*, Vol. I, p. 132.
44. *Ibid.*, Vol. I, p. 142. Speech of Governor Bramlette at McClellan ratification meeting in Frankfort.
45. Governor's *Letter Book* of 1864.
46. Collins, *History of Kentucky*, Vol. I, p. 136.
47. Governor's *Letter Book*, 1864.
48. Collins, *History of Kentucky*, Vol. I, p. 133, col. 2.
49. *Ibid.*, Vol. I, p. 134.
50. *Ibid.*, Vol. I, p. 141, quotes Richmond, Virginia *Examiner*.
51. Swiggett, *Rebel Raider*.
52. On Jan. 12, 1864, Brig. Gen. J. T. Boyle was relieved of the command of the U.S. Military District of Kentucky. His successor was Brig. Gen. Jacob Ammen.
53. Collins, *History of Kentucky*, Vol. I, p. 136.
54. Report of Military Commission to investigate conduct of Gen. E. A. Paine, in Kentucky *Senate and House Journal of 1865*.
55. *Journal* (Louisville), Feb. 10, 1865.

56. Collins, *History of Kentucky*, Vol. I, p. 139.
57. Reports of Adjutant General of Kentucky, Vol. II, p. 489.
58. Collins, *History of Kentucky*, Vol. I, p. 135.
59. *Ibid.*, Vol. I, p. 136.
60. *Ibid.*, Vol. I, p. 139.
61. *Ibid.*, Vol. I, p. 140.
62. Duke, *History of Morgan's Brigade*, p. 539.
63. Collins, *History of Kentucky*, Vol. I, p. 140.
64. *Bulletin* (Maysville), Oct. 13, 1864.
65. Collins, *History of Kentucky*, Vol. I, p. 143.
66. *Democrat* (Louisville), Nov. 18, 1864.
67. Collins, *History of Kentucky*, Vol. I, p. 142.
68. *Ibid.*, Vol. I, p. 145-46.
69. *Senate Journal*, 1865, p. 41, and *House Journal*, 1865, p. 49.
70. *Ibid.*, pp. 43–45.
71. Governor's *Letter Book No. 9*, p. 74.
72. *Ibid.*, p. 205.
73. *Commonwealth* (Frankfort), Apr. 4 and May 2, 1865; *also* Adjutant General's *Letter Book No. 10*, pp. 36–40, 130.
74. Collins, *History of Kentucky*, Vol. I, p. 153.
75. *Journal* (Louisville), Feb. 10, 1865.
76. Adjutant General's *Letter Book No. 10*, p. 103.
77. *Ibid.*, p. 134.
78. *Ibid.*, p. 218.
79. Governor's *Letter Book* of 1865, p. 250.
80. *Tri-Weekly Yeoman* (Frankfort), July 6, 1867.

CHAPTER VI

READJUSTMENT AND REORGANIZATION

The close of the war did not bring peace to Kentucky, for the state found itself facing graver problems than that of war; problems in which the disorganized militia played an important part. An organized militia was necessary, yet such a militia could not function properly while the state was continued under Federal military government. No constructive state militia law or organization was forthcoming until after the Confederates were restored to power in the state. The chaos of the first few years after the war was augmented by the plundering of guerrilla bands and activities of the Freedman's Bureau.

The thirteenth amendment became operative December 18, 1865, and freed all Kentucky slaves who had not previously enlisted in the Army. Kentucky had refused to ratify the amendment, and to accomplish the freeing of the slaves there had been a year of wholesale enlistment of Kentucky Negroes in the U.S. Army under the urging of John M. Palmer, Military Governor of Kentucky. In all, Palmer enlisted over 29,000 Negroes against the protests of the Kentucky Legislature and general public.

Lexington and Louisville became the two favorite centers of the freed slaves. Louisville was the state headquarters of the U.S. Army, and to it slaves were drawn in large numbers in quest of liberation. Many slaves had been freed under the Act of Congress of July 17, 1862, that liberated all slaves of secessionists, which slaves were then, or might afterwards be, enrolled in labor battalions. Wives, mothers, and children of such slaves thereupon became free, unless these or any of them were the property of loyal owners.*[1] This method of emancipation was strengthened by the Act

---

* Notes, references, and sources are indicated by numerals. These refer to corresponding numbers at the end of this chapter. Notes on Chapter VI are on page 277.

of Congress of March 3, 1865, which made the families of slave soldiers free regardless of ownership. In a New Year's greeting to Negroes at Louisville[2] General Palmer said that it was his purpose to accomplish emancipation as quickly as possible. Squads of Negro soldiers were sent over the state by Palmer to bring in slave "recruits" for the U.S. Army and thereby "coin Freedom,"[3] which the state legislature had refused to grant by ratifying the thirteenth amendment. In this way from 70 to 100 slaves were enlisted daily, thereby freeing an estimated 500 persons per day.[4] The state resented the procedure and by a heavy vote of the legislature resolved to ask the U.S. Secretary of War for the cause of the continued recruiting of Negroes. A subsequent resolution requested the removal of Negro troops from the state, and recited the plundering of public buildings as a part of the Negro's "many outrages upon the lives and property of the citizens."[5]

Opposition to the retention of Federal troops in Kentucky did much to eradicate animosities between Confederate and Union veterans of Kentucky, and speed up the restoration of the Confederates to civil and political rights and ultimate control of the state. The hearty reception of the Confederate veteran upon his return both by civilians and Union veterans was due to his honorable conduct as a soldier and to his generally high position in the social and economic life of the state. The late Nathaniel S. Shaler, a man of international reputation, a graduate of Yale University, and a Union soldier, said, "The Kentucky troops in the Confederate Army, being fewer in number and from the richer and more educated part of the state, were as a whole a finer body of men than the Federal troops of the Commonwealth." Between the Confederate veterans, as against all others, a bond of fellowship existed that gradually grew stronger as their numbers decrease through the years. The Union Army veteran was handicapped by being a living reminder of the cause that had brought untold anguish to the state, and the Home Guard was disliked both by the Cenfederate and Union veterans.[6]

Nullification of the state expatriation law in 1865, and the efforts of the legislature to obtain the pardon of prominent Confederate officers, brought an avalanche of radical resentment, not only within the state but from the states to the North.[7] Throughout the war the conservative element had been in the minority, but, with the restoration of the elective franchise to Confederate veterans, the radicals found themselves hopelessly beaten at every election.

In the eastern Kentucky mountains paroles and amnesties meant little. Here the Confederates were few in number and very often were most unwelcome upon their return. This hatred was augmented by the marked propaganda of radical politicians. In numerous cases hatred so conceived soon aligned family against family and gave rise to some of the state's bloodiest feuds, several of which necessitated calls of the militia, mentioned hereafter.

A report by Adjt. Gen. D. W. Lindsey was made to the legislature on May 22, 1865, showing the action taken under the act of January 26, 1864, which empowered the Governor "to raise a force for the defense of the State." Under this act 2,225 men had been placed under arms. Col. P. B. Hawkins' 1st Kentucky Capital Guards were composed of the Frankfort, Paducah, and Big Sandy Infantry Battalions, 1,313 men rank and file, together with the Mercer County State Guards consisting of 98 men. When these were mustered out, after six months' duty, they were replaced by eight battalions and one company still in service when the report was made, consisting of Captain Perin's Casey County State Guards, Col. Silas Adams' regiment, and the companies from Green River, Middle Green River, North Cumberland, South Cumberland, Three Forks, Hall's Gap, and Frankfort. The legislature on June 3 repealed the act under which these troops were raised, providing in the repealer that the force under arms should not be mustered out until the safety of the state would permit.

An editorial from a newspaper, widely circulated after the war, relates the Federal Government's unwillingness to recognize the state military department as able to preserve order within the state. This article said in part: "During the absence of General Palmer at Washington City the troops in the State—negroes chiefly—will be under command of Gen. Jeff. C. Davis, of Indiana, who will be remembered as the slayer of Gen. William Nelson."[8] A similar usurpation of the state's police power came in General Brisbin's "Order No. 15" that "any returned Confederate soldier found armed, or dressed in any part of the Confederate uniform, shall be arrested and sent beyond the limits of this division, not to return. Returned Confederates are notified that they must at once discontinue the dangerous and obnoxious practice of carrying arms and wearing the Confederate uniform." This order resulted from the attitude assumed by Thomas Speed of Kentucky, then Attorney General of the United States. Confederate veterans and exiled civilians, even though paroled, were held by him to have no right to return to the state. He foresaw that upon their return they would be welded, politically, to the conservatives, and thereby outnumber the radical element in the state.

Peculiar situations developed in the state's readjustment endeavors. Many Union men were forced into the conservative party because of their attitude toward the adoption of the thirteenth amendment. Among these was John M. Harlan, a veteran Union volunteer army officer and later an associate justice of the U.S. Supreme Court. Harlan maintained that ratification should not be made because the amendment was an invasion of state's rights, and that on this principle he would oppose it regardless of the number of slaves in the state.[9]

The August elections of 1865, though conducted with United States military interference (under the guise of supervision) on every hand,[10] gave the state back into the hands of the conservatives. This military interference, directly chargeable to orders of General Palmer, was in violation of an Act of Congress of February 25, 1865, which forbade military interference with elections. At the close of the war 21,000 United States soldiers were stationed in Kentucky "to maintain peace and order." On August 15,

1865, the U.S. Secretary of War ordered 5,000 of these mustered out. Further reductions during the fall brought the number on duty down to 6,000. These were employed, to the exclusion of the Kentucky Militia, for police duty within the state. The state was freed from martial law, imposed by Lincoln, by the proclamation of President Johnson on October 12, 1865, and United States troops were then withdrawn.

The following letter of the state military department is typical of a myriad of like pieces, dealing with the disbanding of the Volunteer Army:

To: COL. W. D. B. MORRILL   *Oct. 23, 1865*
Military Agent of Kentucky
Louisville, Kentucky

I am in receipt of your letter of this date, and as requested I enclose your financial statement with accompanying vouchers for Sept. 1865. You can include this in your report for September and October.

The following is a list for Kentucky organizations still in the service and their locations per last advice, viz:

7th Ky. Vol. Inf. Clinton, La.
21st Ky. Vol. Inf. Camp Stanley, Texas, 2nd Brig., 2nd Div., 4th A. C.
23rd Ky. Vol. Inf. Camp Stanley, Texas, 2nd Brig., 2nd Div., 4th A. C.
28th Ky. Vol. Inf. Camp Stanley, Texas, 2nd Brig., 2nd Div., 4th A. C.
Battery A, 1st Ky. Light Artilery, Victoria, Texas.[11]

                     D. W. LINDSEY
                     Adjutant General of Kentucky.

The abrogation of martial law tended to popularize the President with the Confederate veterans. Gen. Basil Duke in a letter, dated April 8, 1865, to W. C. P. Breckinridge had said that "If anybody should want to impose on Andy Johnson it would be a good thing to be able to help him." In the celebrations on February 22, 1866, martial salutes and airs rendered in tribute to Johnson eclipsed those ascribed to Washington.[12]

Legislative changes of the fall of 1865 had swept away most of the wartime acts that embodied the hatred of the radicals for all that savored of Confederate sympathy. In 1864 the Court of Appeals held[13] that the orders of a superior officer excused the acts of his subordinate when done in pursuance of orders. In the case of the Louisville & Nashville Railroad vs. Simon Bolivar Buckner damages were assessed against the defendant by default in his absence during the war. The decision held Gen. Buckner personally liable for the destruction of railroad property ordered by him as an act of war. In contravention of this court decision the legislature enacted a law prohibiting the dismissal of any civil action brought for damages for personal injury, or property damage under plea of martial law, or because of the suspension of the writ of habeas corpus. The act opened the courts to Confederate soldiers and sympathizers to prosecute claims against Union men for personal injury or property loss. Within a year thereafter some 500 suits had been filed under the act. Confederates were urged to avail themselves of the opportunity to redress the wrongs that had been perpetrated upon them.[14]

In 1866 Kentucky organized an Agricultural and Mechanical College, under the Federal Land Grant Act of 1865, as a department of the school that was then called Kentucky University. The act of Congress donating the land script required any agricultural and mechanical college receiving the benefit of the act to give instruction in military tactics. In accordance with the provisions of this act, regular instruction in infantry drill was given to the students of Kentucky Agricultural and Mechanical College at stated times. The exercises were made attractive and valuable as a means of physical development, as well as of collegiate discipline.

Students of the School of Tactics were organized into a military corps known as "The Corps of Cadets of the Agricultural and Mechanical College of Kentucky University," and were placed under the immediate government of the professor of military tactics as commandant of cadets. Officers and non-commissioned officers were appointed by the faculty from among those cadets who, beside the necessary qualifications, were distinguished for general good conduct and academic attainments. Cadets were organized into companies, and the several companies constituted a battalion.

Between March 1 and December 1 there was an infantry or artillery drill and dress parade every school day. During the balance of the year there was the usual drill on such days as might be named in orders. There was a weekly inspection of cadets, under arms, every Friday. The rules of military police and military discipline were exemplified as far as possible. To this end, and that good order might be maintained among cadets, they were made subject to the orders of the commandant, and to such military regulations as might be prescribed, except when in actual attendance upon some lecture, at labor, or at meals.

The uniform of cadets, then worn on duty and at such other times as might be ordered, were of grey cloth, cut and trimmed as that worn by the cadets of the United States Military Academy, except the buttons, which were the Kentucky state button.

Military training continues as a part of the curriculum of the University of Kentucky. The band of the Cadet Corps has won numerous trophies in band contests. Many officers came from these student ranks during the World War, and the Cadet Corps has won numerous other distinctions throughout its history.

Immediately after the war strenuous efforts were made by the legislature to reduce military expenditures. In 1867 all acts authorizing the state government to borrow money for military purposes were repealed. This having been done, a strong opposition to any military appropriation developed, and would probably have succeeded had it not been for the appointment of Frank Wolford as adjutant general, a most opportune appointment because of Wolford's popularity, not only with the Confederate and Union veterans, but with the people of the state as a whole. This same legislature on January 24, 1867, directed the Governor to purchase gold medals for James Artus, Dr. William T. Taliaferro, John Tucker, and John Norris, "as survivors of the Kentucky volunteers who at the request of Commodore Perry—with such ready alacrity and heroism, repaired on board his fleet and assisted in achieving the glorious victory of September 10, 1813, over the British fleet on Lake Erie." Later a like medal was given to Ezra Younglove, also a survivor of the same battle. An apropriation of $6,000 was also made for expenses incident to the compilation of a "Report of Kentucky Officers and Soldiers during the late War."

Extensive burials of soldiers were made during the War between the States at Perryville, Mill Springs, and New London, in Laurel County; near Lebanon, in Marion County; and at Camp Nelson, in Jessamine County. Later, by reason of burials including men from various states, jurisdiction over these cemeteries was ceded to the United States by an act of the Kentucky Legislature, of March 8, 1867. Data collected to May 20, 1868, on military cemeteries in Kentucky, shows the following numbers of interments of Union soldiers as having been made during the war:

Louisville	3,871	Covington	441
Camp Nelson	1,611	Lebanon	368
Perryville	1,430	Danville	355
Bowling Green	1,090	Richmond	241
Lexington	822	London	219
Logan's Cross Roads	701	Frankfort	111

In 1867 a resolution was introduced in the legislature calling for an appropriation of $10,000 to defray the costs of bringing home, for reinterment, Kentucky's Confederate dead who were buried beyond the state lines.[15]

The death of Theodore O'Hara, veteran of four wars, occurred in Alabama on June 10, 1867. O'Hara, a resident of Franklin County, had served with conspicuous bravery in the Mexican War, with Walker in Nicaragua, with Lopez in the Cuban expedition, and in the Confederate Army. His valiant military record is, however, eclipsed in fame by his literary services to Kentucky (*ante, p. 137*).

Upon the death of Gov. John L. Helm on September 8, 1867, five days after his inauguration, Lt. Gov. John W.

Stephenson succeeded to the governorship. Immediately after Stephenson's inauguration, on September 13, he appointed Col. Frank Wolford adjutant general. The appointment of Wolford was received by the Federal Government as an ultimatum of the Governor, and was construed as a determination on the part of Kentucky to manage, without Federal intervention, her internal military affairs.

A report of the efforts of the state military department to procure peace and order was made by the Governor in his message to the legislature. This legislature also received a report of the state's military equipment from Quartermaster General Hewitt. Among items listed were 8 pieces of artillery and 18,077 stand of small arms on hand in the state arsenal.

In 1868 an attempt was made to rewrite the state militia law to meet changed conditions. Immediately the radicals charged that such a change would imperil the state because the legislature was almost solidly composed of Confederate veterans.[16]

In the firing of the salute on the anniversary of the Battle of New Orleans in 1868 thirty-seven shots were fired instead of thirty-six, the number of states at that date. The officer that ordered the firing was sought out and asked if he had intended to recognize the separation of West Virginia from the mother state. In reply he gave assurance of no such intention, but rather that the extra round was for "the glorious State of Old Virginia—God bless her."[17] A subsequent act of the legislature directed "one gun extra for Old Virginia, the Mother of states and presidents."

In the realignment of partisans a meeting of the conservative Union men was held in Louisville on January 8, 1868, looking to a union with the Democratic element in the state. It was on this occasion that Col. Frank Wolford, a Union veteran, paid high compliment to the state's Confederate veterans.[18]

The first assemblage of Confederate veterans in Kentucky after the war took place in Lexington on April 17, 1868, upon the occasion of the reinterment of Gen. John H. Morgan in the Lexington Cemetary (*ante, p. 216*). Many of those who served under him were present. The following year, on May 20, the graves of Confederate soldiers in the Louisville Cemetery were, for the first time, decorated with flowers and Confederate emblems. On the twenty-ninth of May, 1868, the first monument to the memory of Confederate dead in Kentucky was dedicated at Cynthiana, with Col. W. C. P. Breckinridge presiding.

In his *Courier-Journal* (Louisville) Christmas editorial of 1868, Henry Watterson, a Confederate veteran, stressed the non-partisan character of the state militia, now under control of Frank Wolford as adjutant general.

The policy of General Lindsey in regard to the militia organization of the state had been substantially as follows: To list all males, liable under the law for military duty, into an Enrolled Militia to form the 112 regiments that the law prescribed for the counties, then of like number.[19] From Enrolled Militia in each regimental district one company of Active Militia was organized. These companies were organized into regiments and called the Kentucky National Legion, which was thoroughly disciplined. The Enrolled Militia was relieved from military duty in time of peace, and in lieu of military service the tax collector was authorized to collect a tax of $1 per capita from these. Under this system every 100,000 Enrolled Militia would produce 10,000 Active Militia, and $90,000 per annum to cover expenses of every kind while on a peace footing. If this amount was found insufficient, the tax per capita was to be increased on the Enrolled Militia.

The legislature defeated the object of General Lindsey's plan by repealing the tax on the enrolled personnel. The Kentucky National Legion existed in fair condition in the cities, but in the country there was little or no discipline.

A new strife followed the war, leaving the state dotted with crimes and defaced with speedy non-judicial punishments that frequently brought on a type of private warfare. The Regulators and Skaggs Men were of these years.

These were organized bands of men who instituted a reign of terror by acts of lawlessness perpetrated in the guise of punishment of their victim for some offense, actual or fancied. To bring about the displeasure of these self-constituted guardians of the law was to invite them to mete out their own version of justice. The seizure of prisoners by them was frequent. These bands were especially active in the counties south of the Kentucky River. They were not of the Ku Klux Klan organization, but were local groups that were nurtured in community animosities.

Legislative measures were taken in 1867 to stop this organized lawlessness. The Governor was authorized to offer a reward of $500 for the arrest of members of bands accused of a particular act of lawlessness.[20]

In 1868 Governor Stevenson commissioned Adjt. Gen. Frank Wolford to organize three companies of militia for police duty in the turbulent regions. This was done and Wolford's troops had a pacifying effect on the countryside so long as they were on duty in a particular community, but their withdrawal was frequently followed by the resumption of outlaw activities. More than 100 cases of violence are recorded for the four years succeeding 1867.[21]

During the summer of 1869 considerable disorder occurred in Marion County through the activities of Regulators and other lawless bands. The atrocious acts continued until mid-August when Circuit Judge George W. Kavanaugh asked for troops to assist civil authorities in restoring order in Marion and adjacent counties. The principal official military correspondence in this case serves to relate the duties delegated to the troops, and the zeal with which these duties were performed. On August 21, 1869, Governor Stevenson sent a letter to the quartermaster general saying that he had received information from George W. Kavanaugh, judge of the Seventh Judicial District, that Clem Crowdus was hanged by a band of lawless persons in Marion County. Judge Kavanaugh asked that soldiers be sent to Marion County to aid authorities in bringing offenders to justice and in protection of human life and against further violations of the law.

Col. F. M. Hewitt, the quartermaster general, was ordered to proceed. Colonel Hewitt was authorized to offer secret rewards if deemed necessary for the detection, arrest and conviction of the murderers of Crowdus. He was also given power to call out additional troops if necessary from Louisville. None were to be called from Marion, Boyle, Washington, Anderson, or any other contiguous counties.[22]

On September 9, 1869, Governor Stevenson received a report on the situation in Marion County for Adjutant General Wolford. This was followed on the tenth of September by the Governor's letter of thanks to the Helm Guards, Waddell Grays, and Thomas Zouaves, for their services during the Crowdus case disorder.[23]

The detail of soldiers was continued on duty. On the second of October, Capt. S. T. Leary, in charge of the Marion County force, informed the Governor that Pvt. Allie Cooper had been killed by a citizen named Rollins. The attack on Cooper was made under aggravated circumstances and without any provocation.[24] In reply the Governor communicated with Captain Leary, condoling the death of Private Cooper and recommending the strictest discipline of the troops to prevent any possible demonstration.[25] The trial of Rollins was held at the next regular term of court, and a conviction for the murder of Cooper was obtained.

In 1870 elaborate ceremonies in Frankfort marked the reburial of Thornton Lafferty and his fellow victims of the Burbridge retaliatory orders (*ante, p. 220*). The occasion was proclaimed a day of mourning by the Governor. The bodies, exhumed from their shallow pasture-field graves, were borne through the city to the Frankfort Cemetery. A parting volley was fired by a squad of cadets from the Kentucky Military Institute. Numerous Confederate dead had been brought home during 1869-70, but few if any reburials aroused public sympathy as did this occasion, which *The Yeoman* characterized as a "simple act of justice."[26]

Elections, after the Negro was enfranchised, presented a knotty problem to the Democrats for there was always the overhanging peril of clashes between the races. The use of the militia for police duty would have brought criticism and the charge of intimidation. Rival candidates in Lexington met before the autumn elections of 1870 and agreed as a precautionary measure, that the militia should not be paraded on election day, either armed or unarmed.[27]

Governor Stevenson appointed J. Stoddard Johnston of Louisville, adjutant general, on March 8, 1870, to succeed Frank Wolford, resigned. The speedy confirmation of this appointment by the senate indicates that no prejudice existed against Johnston because of his Confederate Army service.

In November, 1870, Harrison County Confederate dead, numbering forty-seven, were brought home and reinterred in Battle Grove Cemetery, Cynthiana.

By further excavations made in Monroe, Michigan, thirty additional skulls and numerous bones were unearthed on February 25, 1871, skeletons of Kentuckians who were massacred by the Indians after the Battle of the River Raisin. These, too, were brought to Kentucky for burial in the Frankfort Cemetery (*ante, p. 140*). Another incident recalling a part taken by the Kentucky Militia in national affairs was the granting of a Federal pension of $8 per month to Capt. Thos. A. Theobald of Frankfort, a veteran of the War of 1812. This grant, the first to a Kentuckian, was made on June 21, 1871. Captain Theobald had served as a first lieutenant in Merrill's Company of Mounted Rifles.

Upon his inauguration, September 5, 1871, Gov. P. H. Leslie appointed Col. James A. Dawson adjutant general, and Gen. Lafayette Hewitt quartermaster general. One of Governor Leslie's first official acts was the delivery of an address to eighty-three veterans of the War of 1812 who assembled at Lexington on October 5, 1871.

On April 11, 1872, Governor Leslie was notified by W. T. Boone, judge of Hickman County, that bands of lawless men had made an attempt to break into the jail of Hickman County. Judge Boone related that he did not know whether the object of the mob was to lynch or liberate prisoners, and that when this attack had been repulsed the mob threatened to return in greater force. The Governor was asked, by Boone, for 100 stand of arms for a like number of Hickman County Militia to be called out by the Governor for special duty in the case. In compliance with the request Governor Leslie appointed a special mustering officer and ordered him to "muster in a company of Militia in Hickman county pursuant to militia law in Myer's supplement." The order further stated that "Papers will be forwarded by mail. One hundred stands of arms and twenty rounds of ammunition were shipped you yesterday, and will arrive at Columbus on tonight's train. You will make arrangements to receive them."

The revision of the militia law in 1867 re-established the Kentucky State Guard, but a complete reorganization was not then made. This statute made commissioned company officers personally responsible for the safekeeping of the state property in their charge, yet failed to provide for any armory or other place in which to keep such property. A statute of 1873 made it the duty of the county judge to provide a safe place to keep public arms and other military property.

This act of 1873 also provided that the militia of reserve should be called only in cases of extreme danger to the state, and after the State Guard was found unable to handle a situation.[28]

Early in September, 1874, a press notice appeared calling attention to the annual meeting of the Kentucky Association of Veterans of the War with Mexico. Members were urged to visit Frankfort on the fifteenth to take part in the funeral ceremonies for Major Cary H. Fry, Capt. Theodore O'Hara, and Adjutant Cardwell.[29]

Activities of Skaggs Men in Hardin County during September compelled the Governor to call out sixty men on September 24 for duty in Elizabethtown. Fox Hewitt was appointed special mustering officer.[30]

During March, 1875, the Regulators caused considerable disturbance in the western part of the state. Company A of the 1st Regiment was detailed for duty in Todd County, and continued there from March 16 to April 6.[31]

In the Thirteenth Judicial District a heavy criminal docket and threats of violence brought a call from Judge Robert Riddell for a military guard during the April session of this court at Beattyville. Under orders of the Governor, Adjutant General Dawson detailed Capt. Joseph Blackwell with ten men of his company for duty so long as required by Judge Riddell. The guard successfully preserved order and was dismissed when disposition of the criminal docket had been made.[32] Captain Blackwell, with twenty men, was ordered on June 23 to report to Judge W. H. Randall of the Fifteenth Judicial District, on July 5, for police duty during the session of this court while occupied with the criminal docket.[33]

During the fall of 1876 the Goss-Allen prize fight was billed for Cincinnati, Ohio, but strong protest was made to the fight being held there. As a result arrangements were hurriedly made to move across the Ohio River where both Covington and Newport afforded desirable accommodations. When this plan became known, the civil authorities of both these Kentucky cities asked the Governor for military assistance to prevent the fight from being staged in their cities. In compliance with the request, Capt. Frank Wood, commanding the Covington Light Guard, was directed to assemble his company at his armory in Covington and hold it in readiness to move to any point where it might be necessary to aid the civil authorities in preventing the prize fight.

During the summer of 1877 five men accused of the murder of Carrie Anderson of Worthville were held in jail at Carrollton. Among them was the then incumbent sheriff, a deputy sheriff, and a former sheriff. Public opinion was pitched high against the accused and a lynching was feared. Upon request of civil authorities the Governor ordered Adjt. Gen. J. M. Wright to call out troops. The Covington Light Guards, under Capt. Frank Wood, were detailed to guard the prisoners during their trial and remained on duty at

Carrollton from the seventh to the fifteenth of July. Subsequent developments again indicated possible violence and on July 24 the Van Voast Light Guards of Newport under Capt. Christopher Hak, and the Covington Light Guards under Captain Wood, were instructed to report for duty at their respective armories on July 25. In the meantime the prisoners were removed to safety and orders of dismissal were entered for the military units called.[34]

Louisville was subjected to a series of acts of violence, during mid-summer of 1877, which culminated in a riot involving life and large property interests. On July 24, Mayor Charles D. Jacob asked Governor McCreary to send by a train supplied by the city 500 guns with 40 rounds of ammunition with which to arm and equip 500 special policemen. The mayor asked that the shipment be sent under a guard of at least ten militiamen.

On Tuesday afternoon 500 guns were shipped by special train. They were received at LaGrange by a body of 200 citizens acting as special policemen for the city of Louisville. Later, upon requisition, 200 additional guns were sent.

After quiet was restored, a troop review and parade was held at the armory. The Louisville Legion and Light Artillery, combined under the command of Major Overstreet W. Harris, were reviewed and inspected by Mayor Jacob before a large assemblage that completely filled the armory. "The turn-out of the military far exceeded expectations," and the uniforms are said to have "looked as bright as ever, notwithstanding their recent rough usage." The colors of the Light Artillery were draped with black in memory of Lieutenant Bly, killed during the riot, but otherwise the scene was one of great brilliancy. A news item relates that "after the inspection and review the orchestra rendered the liveliest of dance music until 11:00 o'clock, and the floor was filled with dancers to the last minute."

The Kennedy trial at Lancaster, was based on the following facts: In Lancaster on the twentieth day of February, 1877, Grove C. Kennedy shot and killed Elbert D. Kennedy of Lancaster, his cousin by blood and his uncle by marriage.

When he fired the fatal shot Grove Kennedy was standing behind one of the columns of the courthouse portico, and holding his pistol with both hands, took steady aim, the bullet hitting his uncle in the cheek, under his right eye which was blind.

It came out in testimony that there had been a disagreement, and perhaps bad feeling between Elbert D. Kennedy and Grove, on account of a suit which the latter brought against his uncle for the settlement of an estate. Elbert D. Kennedy in his answer made certain allegations which Grove pronounced lies, and stated that if Elbert swore to the pleading he would kill him. Elbert failed to swear to his answer until compelled to do so by a rule of court obtained by Grove's counsel. Elbert was sent for, tried to compromise with his nephew in the courtroom, and failing in that, swore to his pleading. The contingency having arisen, Grove drew a pistol on the old man, but was then disarmed. He then menaced the store where both were standing. Elbert was unarmed, and had so declared to the court. The sheriff led him away. Grove followed in hot haste. Captain Singleton, the town marshal, called to him saying: "Don't follow that old man, he is not armed. I had as soon shoot an old granny woman as shoot him." Grove went, however, and in a minute more had executed his threat and slain Elbert D. Kennedy.

The following order was issued by the Governor on September 29, 1877:

> Captain W. S. Miller, Jr. commanding State Guard in Garrard County. You are ordered to report with 20 men of your company, armed and ready for active service, to W. M. Kerby, Sheriff of Garrard County at such a time as he may need your aid in arresting G. C. Kennedy or Samuel Holmes who are represented to be fugitives from justice.

Public sentiment crystallized against Grove Kennedy to such an extent, after his arrest, that his life became endangered. Thereupon he was taken to the Jefferson County Jail to await trial. The date of trial being set, the Governor ordered Kennedy's return to Lancaster under military guard. A detachment of the McCreary Guards escorted the prisoner from Louisville to Lancaster, and remained there during the trial.

Louisville papers ridiculed the Governor for sending a military guard with Kennedy and sneered at the young men who composed it. The following is from the *Interior Journal* (Stanford):

> We commend the wisdom of Governor McCreary in sending the squad of militia to guard Grove Kennedy at Lancaster. A guard without bias could not have been gotten in Garrard, and it was a precautionary measure in sending men who have had no feelings in the matter that will be valuable alike to the Commonwealth and to the prisoner himself. We do not believe that, with Mr. Kennedy's present belief in his ability to clear himself on the charge of wilful murder, that he would attempt his escape; neither would his friends assist him in it; but if matters should not turn out as well as he and they expect, the tug of war might come, and then the well-drilled soldiers would come in mighty handy. They don't look like boys that would be scared.

The guard was continued until the close of the trial, during which no incident of lawlessness transpired.

Kentucky militia law was rewritten in 1878. Under the revised act able-bodied male citizens from eighteen to forty-five years old, with specified exceptions, were made to constitute the state militia, which was divided into two classes. The first class embraced all organized volunteers and was designated as the State Guard. The second class contained all others liable for military duty and was called the Militia of Reserve. Under the act the Governor was empowered to direct the organization of a State Guard company in any county where he might deem such a company necessary to preserve the peace of the county. Companies so organized were limited to a minimum of forty and a maximum of eighty men. These companies were then organized into regiments of from eight to twelve companies. The act further provided that there should be no military companies in the state other than those forming the Kentucky State Guard. At the discretion of the Governor, companies of cadets could be organized among youths under eighteen years to be attached to regiments. However, these cadet companies

LOUISVILLE FLOOD OF 1937. (See p. 355)

PADUCAH, FLOOD OF 1937

STATE REFORMATORY CAMP—Flood of 1937. (See p. 360)

REFORMATORY CAMP MESS LINE

could not be designated for active duty beyond the limits of their own county.

Early in 1878 Maj. John B. Castleman was requested by some citizens of Louisville to form a regiment for the protection of the city in emergencies like the riot of 1877. This Major Castleman agreed to do upon receiving the assurance that $20,000 would be raised in the city to defray immediate expenses of such organization. The funds were subscribed and the Louisville Legion was revived and mustered into service. Major Castleman and four of the captains in this regiment had earned distinction in the Confederate Army, and one captain in the Union Army. During the next twenty years this organization, designated as the 1st Regiment, Kentucky State Guard, and more familiarly known as the Louisville Legion, was most frequently subjected to calls for detachments for police duty.

In October of 1878 a detachment from the Louisville Legion was ordered on duty for several days to guard a prisoner in the Jefferson County Jail against the apprehended attack of a mob. In December of the same year Breathitt County was the scene of grave disorders. The adherents of the two desperadoes named Little and Strong conducted a kind of guerrilla warfare, which terrorized the mountain community and set at defiance the lawful authorities, affairs culminating in the murder of a judge. A detachment of the Legion, including a platoon of Battery A, mounted as cavalry, was sent to aid the civil authorities.

The troops detailed, after many hardships, succeeded in arresting and imprisoning the principal offenders, and in restoring quiet and order. Because of a lack of transportation facilities the troops were forced to march seventy miles over the mountains and carry their equipment on this five-day trek through mud and snow. The quartermaster's train of two wagons followed, one drawn by horses and the other by oxen. These detachments remained on duty in Breathitt until late in February, 1879. More than twenty of those arrested were confined in the Jefferson County Jail until trial the following summer, for which they were taken back to Breathitt County by an escorting detachment of the 1st Regiment that remained on duty three weeks until completion of the trial.

On these expeditions the men cut and hauled the wood, and usually did their own cooking. Having at the time no fatigue clothes they wore dress uniforms. "They had no overcoats until they reached Mount Sterling, and those there issued by the State are credibly averred to have had only one recommendation, inasmuch as they had done duty through the War of 1861, and had served as food for moths ever since—they instantly transformed, in appearance, the bright, fresh recruits into the oldest of veterans."[35]

In October, 1879, considerable disorder ocurred in Carter County. Six deaths resulted in a short interval from a renewal of the Holbrook-Underwood feud. The miners and furnace men of the Eastern Kentucky Railroad Company were then on a strike, and had ordered the railroad company not to run trains. At Hunnewell, a station in Greenup County, some 300 men had congregated. When Governor Blackburn received a request for troops he had only unofficial reports of the conditions in Carter County. To determine definitely what course should be pursued the Governor detailed Col. J. W. Bryan to make a complete investigation of the situation. Upon receipt of Colonel Bryan's report troops were immediately ordered to the scene. A press item of that time makes the following comment:

> The troops in Carter have no political significance, as all the parties are Republicans, as indeed are a majority of the people in that region. Governor Blackburn acted properly in refusing to send troops until he was properly advised of the necessity. The Civil officers are able to execute the law if they will try * * *. It will be seen that the Governor pursued the proper course in declining to send troops upon the mere statement that the feud between the Holbrooks and Underwoods was in progress and should be suppressed. The Governor does not deem it proper to employ the military arm until he is assured that the civil power is incompetent to enforce the laws, and he will maintain that position in all cases that may hereafter arise.[26]

In 1880 Governor Blackburn appointed a committee of three to design a flag for the Kentucky State Guard, to serve as the official military banner of Kentucky. Such a flag was designed and adopted, and served until the Kentucky National Guard emblem displaced it. A specimen of the old banner is preserved among the state military relics.

During this year internal industrial disturbances occurred in all of the state's larger cities, yet in only three instances were the local police unable to restore order. In these cases State Guard detachments were detailed to the scene under the following orders:

To MAJOR JOHN B. CASTLEMAN, *Commanding 1st Battalion, Kentucky State Guard, known as the Louisville Legion—*

S. S. Hamilton, Sheriff of Jefferson County, having formally applied to the Executive for a military force, for the preservation of the public peace in said county on the 2nd day of April, proximo: You are therefore ordered to assemble such portion of your command as may be necessary for the purpose indicated, at your armory, on the day named, and hold it in readiness to aid the civil power if necessary to do so. You will report to such civil officers—present—as provided in sections 8 and 36, of an act, approved April 8, 1878, in relation to the Militia of this Commonwealth.[37]

Captain Frank Wood, Commanding Covington Light Guard with 30 men of his command is assigned to active duty. He will report immediately on receipt of this order to the County Judge or Sheriff of Kenton County and aid in maintaining the civil law.[38]

At a competitive drill held at Nashville, Tennessee, on March 25 and 26, 1881, wherein troops from several states participated, a detachment of the Louisville Light Artillery, was awarded the first prize of $500 as the best drilled unit of artillery, and the same unit won another first prize, a gold medal, for target practice, an achievement by a portion of the State Guard that reflected success and honor for the entire organization.

On June 1, 1881, Governor Blackburn ordered Adjutant General J. P. Nuckols to proceed to Washington, District of Columbia, and urge upon the proper authorities, a settlement of Kentucky's war claims that then remained open.[39]

Another competitive drill encampment was held in Louisville on June 23 and 24. The order of Knights Templar, and other Louisville societies, made preparations for the encampment to be held in connection with a benefit for the Widows' and Orphans' Home of Louisville. The order pertaining to this encampment recites that "organized troops of other states will be permitted to enter upon the Domains of this Commonwealth for participation therein, with arms and equipment, as military bodies." [40]

Because of disorder in Frankfort during September, the Governor ordered Adjutant General Nuckols to give Sheriff E. O. Hawkins such military assistance as might be necessary. Under this order Capt. J. Lampton Price with thirty members of the McCreary Guards of Franklin County was assigned to duty which continued for five days.

The Yorktown (Virginia) Centennial was held in October, 1881. Official military representation of Kentucky was delegated by the Governor to the Lexington Guards, Capt. J. R. Morton, forty men; Bowling Green Guards, Capt. M. H. Crump, forty-five men; Monarch Rifles, Owensboro, Capt. S. H. Ford, forty men; Mason County Guards, Capt. A. C. Respass, thirty men; and the 1st Platoon Louisville Light Artillery, Lt. A. C. Bly, twenty-five men. The whole was under Maj. John R. Allen of Lexington.[41]

The Neal-Craft case of 1882-83 was punctuated with State Guard activity. William Neal and Ellis Craft were accused, with George Ellis, of a most heinous crime. Ellis, tried first, was hanged by a mob after conviction. On January 4, 1882, the adjutant general ordered Capt. A. C. Respass, with the Mason County Guards, to Catlettsburg, and two days later issued a like order to the McCreary Guards of Frankfort and the Lexington Guards, placing the whole under command of Maj. John R. Allen. In two hours after the order was issued the Mason Guards left Maysville for Catlettsburg. Speedy and effective service by the Guardsmen and their delivery of the prisoners in the Fayette jail brought the Governor's commendation.[42]

In October the prisoners were returned to Catlettsburg for trial. Troops detailed as a guard included the Blackburn Guards, McCreary Guards, Lexington Guards, Emmett Rifles, Nuckols Guards, one company of the 1st Regiment detailed by Col. J. B. Castleman, and a detachment of the Louisville Light Artillery, all under command of Maj. John R. Allen.

On October 31 excitement gripped Catlettsburg; its streets were filled with guardsmen who mingled with crowds of civilians, among whom were many rough looking persons. The courthouse was crowded to overflowing as the prisoners, Neal and Craft, were marched in, surrounded by bayonets. Then a change of venue was asked by counsel for the prisoners. Feeling against the prisoners was evident in a whispered public opposition to a change of venue, which malevolence was intensified when the court granted the request of the prisoner's attorneys, and designated Carter County as the place of trial.

That night the prisoners were returned to their cell in an upper room of the courthouse to remain there until the next day when the steamboat, *Granite State,* would carry them to Maysville, a stage in the trip back to the Fayette County Jail, where they were to be held until the next term of the Carter Circuit Court. During the night a strict guard was maintained, for grave fears of mob violence existed in all quarters. No demonstration was made though until after the prisoners had been escorted to the wharf, preparatory to boarding the boat at noon on the first of November. Then a furious mob gathered, and after the prisoners and soldiers had boarded the *Granite State* the mob followed on a ferryboat. From the ferryboat an intermittent fire was opened on the troops, but was not returned until it became evident that further delay would prove fatal to the safety of the prisoners and their guard. Major Allen ordered his men to fire, and almost instantly the ferryboat was disabled, thus making it possible for the *Granite State* to proceed unmolested. In the battle several of the soldiers were injured and the mob had numerous members wounded and several killed.

Upon arrival in Lexington a squad of soldiers conveyed the prisoners to the jail, and the balance of the battalion proceeded to the armory. Major Allen made a brief speech, thanking the officers and men for their coolness and good conduct during the whole time, and especially while under fire of the mob. After dinner at the Phoenix Hotel the soldiers left for their homes. Later a commendatory order from the Governor was published saying in part: "The conduct of the Commanding Officer is fully approved and that of the entire force is equally deserving of praise."[43]

In Boyd County condemnation of Governor Blackburn and the State Guard was widespread. Newspapers had erroneously attributed to the Governor a statement, made prior to the clash between the troops and the mob, that sufficient troops would be sent to protect the prisoners if every man, woman, and child in Boyd County were killed in the attempt. The citizens of Ashland did not entertain any idea that the shots that carried death and suffering to men, women, and children on the streets and in houses were random shots, but that "Allen and his vandals" were deliberate in their intention to inflict terrible punishment upon Ashland for presuming to want to stop the lynching of the two prisoners. Later, an old soldier expressing the opinion of many in the Ashland district said: "Yesterday's work showed Major Allen absolutely unfit to command a body of troops, as his soldiers displayed an utter want of discipline in firing a single shot after the volley that disabled the ferryboat. Allen and his men knew well enough that their first volley silenced the shots from the ferryboat, and still they continued to fire volley after volley into the ferry and into the people on the banks. They are condemned as murderers in the sight of God and decent men." The soldiers claimed that at least 200 shots were fired at them before they returned the fire.

The coroner's jury in the cases of Col. L. W. Rupert, George Keener, Alex Harris, and Willie Searcy, who were killed by the State Militia at this place on Saturday, November 1, convened again this afternoon and heard the testimony of Captain Vandyke of Greenup, who was an eye witness to the awful tragedy, and whose testimony was clear and to the purpose as that already given, and also the testimony of Sheriff Kounz of Boyd County. The jury met tonight and brought in verdicts in each case as follows: With the exception of name, we do find that the killing of

George Keener aforesaid was directly, under command as stated, and that the said firing by the troops resulted in the death aforesaid was not in the line of their duty, but was wanton and reckless, and we find Major John R. Allen, in command, responsible and culpable, in directing and permitting the fire aforesaid. Given under our hands this 18th day of November, 1882.

JOHN RUSSELL	JULIUS C. MILLER	R. C. POAGE
L. E. VESSEY	JOHN J. PARRILL	GEORGE CASP

Neal and Craft were convicted on February 7, 1883, and were executed in Catlettsburg.

On May 28, 1883, Adjutant General Nuckols ordered Company F, 2d Regiment (Cerro Gordo Guards) to report to Judge Robert Riddell at Mount Sterling to preserve peace during the trial of a criminal case, the court having been apprehensive of the probability of disorder.

In July, 1883, the 4th Battalion, 2d Regiment, with the Proctor Knott Guards, and the Bullitt Light Infantry, were ordered to encamp at Grayson Springs for military instruction, Maj. M. H. Crump commanding.

An order of July 26, 1883, directed Captain Veach's Light Artillery to fire a salute of twenty-one guns upon the arrival of the President of the United States in Frankfort, enroute to attend the opening of the Louisville Exposition. During the same month Company C, 2d Regiment, under Capt. E. W. Fitzgerald, was ordered to report to A. E. Cole, judge of the Fourteenth Judicial District, for police duty during a session of that court.

From the first to the fifth of September the entire State Guard was assembled at Frankfort for military instruction. Camp Blackburn was established for the use of the troops. During this interval the entire State Guard participated in the inauguration of Gov. Proctor Knott.

Governor Knott named Col. John B. Castleman, of the 1st Regiment, as acting adjutant general. Under command of the Governor the whole State Guard was ordered to encamp at Louisville on August 18, 1884, for military instruction. At the same time Colonel Castleman issued an order for the modification of the tactics employed, as follows:

1. The length of the direct step in Command Quick time will be thirty inches measured from heel to heel; the cadence will be at the rate of ninety steps per minute for common time, and one hundred and twenty steps per minute for quick time. A natural swinging motion of the arms will be permitted when marching.
2. The length of the short step and back step in common and in quick time will be fifteen inches.
3. The length of the double step will be thirty-five inches and the cadence will be at the rate of one hundred and eighty steps per minute.
4. When the Manual of Arms is executed while marching each motion will correspond with the Cadence of the step.
5. Paragraphs of Tactics affected by this order are modified accordingly.[44]

The following are typical of replies to letters that were received by the adjutant generals asking for information pertaining to matters of the War between the States:

To: T. C. LINCOLN, ESQ.   Nov. 15, 1884.
Livermore, Iowa.

Replying to your favor of the 8th inst. I have the honor to inform you that the number of white troops in the Federal Army was 72,275. This was the number mustered into U.S. service. A large number of State troops did U.S. service that were never mustered in, and in consequence were not credited to Kentucky's quota.

There were also a number of Regiments of colored troops from Kentucky in U.S. service.[45]

                                           JOHN B. CASTLEMAN

To: THE ADJT. GEN. OF THE STATE OF OHIO   Feb. 20, 1885

Referring to your favor of the 11th inst. regarding the payment of bonus to soldiers of late war by the State of Kentucky, I have the honor to inform you that this State paid no bounty, nor made any provision therefore for the soldiers in the war of 1861-65.

As to the colored troops from the State, they were U.S. soldiers, officered by the Government and never mustered into the State Service. Their pay account was of course kept by the authorities at Washington.[46]

                                           JOHN B. CASTLEMAN

In April, 1885, Governor Knott ordered troops sent to Rowan County to quell disorders there. The guard so established was discontinued August 19, when Companies D, F, and H of the 2d Regiment were relieved.

During March, 1886, the Governor ordered six companies of the State Guard to Greenwood. Trouble had broken out there because some residents resented the introduction of convicts into the vicinity as miners. The employment of convicts in this work was bitterly protested by the native miners, and early in the afternoon of March 6, 1886, a force of about 350 armed people appeared at the prison stockade and demanded of the contractors that the convicts be returned to Frankfort at once, and their employment discontinued. The contractors were informed that unless directions were obeyed, they themselves would be "disposed of," the stockade burned, and the convicts released. After a parley the contractors were given until noon the following day to comply. Taking advantage of the respite the contractors communicated with the state authorities at Frankfort, whence an order was issued that a detail of the State Guard proceed to Greenwood. The order was received in Louisville at 6:00 p. m. and by 7:30 the same evening the Legion was, by special train, on its way to the scene of trouble. Detachments from the 2d and 3d Regiments were also sent, but later.

At daybreak the following morning, when the first contingent of troops debarked at Greenwood, camp equipage and a Gatling gun were carried or hauled by the men up the mountain on which the stockade was situated, and here, in a blinding rain, guard was mounted, tents pitched, and preparations completed. Beyond a few shots at sentries no demonstration was ever made. It was, however, deemed necessary to keep a detachment at Greenwood for over two months until grievances were adjusted.[47]

The Kentucky National Guard held a camp of instruction at Crab Orchard from August 7-16, 1886, known as Camp Hindman, which was under command of Col. M. H. Crump.

Albert Turner, a Negro, was arrested in Louisville in April, 1887, charged with the offense of assaulting Jennie

Bowman. He was committed to jail, and said that William Patterson, another Negro, was with him, and that they jointly committed the offense.

Turner, when arrested, said he had never seen Patterson until the day of the murder when, in passing Jennie Bowman's home, he was asked by Patterson if he was not hungry. Turner answered he had plenty to eat. Then Patterson said that they could get some money by going through "that house," as the ladies had all gone away in a carriage. Turner consented to go in, and they went around to the back door, found it ajar, and entered. Patterson went upstairs and Turner remained downstairs near the pantry. Soon the girl appeared, coming from the outside, and a struggle ensued between them; then Turner knocked her down and she was lying on the floor, insensible and groaning, when Patterson came downstairs and kicked her several times. After this she was carried up the stairs and placed upon the bed. Patterson picked up an iron poker and struck her over the head several times. Turner said that he went downstairs after this and did not see Patterson any more until Sunday night last.

The assault upon Jennie Bowman by two men in broad daylight incensed the populace and with the sensational articles published in the press of Louisville, culminated in the organization of a mob, composed of some 5,000 persons, who marched to the jail to obtain Turner and Patterson to hang them. The police acted with great caution, arrested the leaders, and required them to give bond or go to jail. The city was filled with excitement, and the authorities feared that trouble would result. The Governor ordered out the 1st Regiment, and placed it in charge of Judge W. L. Jackson. The appearance of the militia on the scene had a tendency to quiet the mob spirit.[48]

The Tolliver-Martin feud had its origin in a partisan warfare that commenced in August, 1884, in a race for the office of "high sheriff" of Rowan County. From the first Monday in August, 1884, to the twenty-second of July, 1887, twenty-three men had been killed. The trouble in the beginning was political, but afterward assumed the form of organized brigandage.

On the afternoon of election day in 1884, a riot occurred and John Bradley was killed and several others wounded. Soon afterwards John Martin killed Floyd Tolliver, and Martin was arrested and removed to the Clark County Jail for security. Craig Tolliver, accompanied by several friends, later presented to the Clark County jailer a forged paper purporting to be an order for the delivery of Martin, who was to be taken to Morehead for trial. Possession of Martin was thus obtained and the parties started by train, apparently for Morehead. At Farmer's Station one of the "custodians" of the prisoner leveled a pistol at the engineer and stopped the train, while the others shot Martin to death. No one was indicted for the murder. The trouble had lost all political significance and plain diablerie now became the ruling principle.

Craig Tolliver and his faction became the autocrats of Morehead, dealing imprisonment or death as they chose. The faction terrified the community, prohibited criticism, and defied authority.

Two young men, thought to be witnesses against some members of the Tolliver faction, were decoyed from their home and deliberately murdered. Their cousin, Boone Logan, a young lawyer, having criticized the killing, was banished. Later he organized a party, and on the twenty-second of June, 1887, surrounded Morehead, and engaged the Tolliver cohorts in a pitched battle. Craig Tolliver and three of his followers were killed. Afterwards an armed band took possession and held the town. The Circuit Court was to convene the first of August. A detachment from the Louisville Legion was ordered to Morehead and remained five weeks. It was an exciting court session, the last attended by troops in that county. All factions were dispossessed of their arms, even those who professed a solicitude to assist the troops. No serious disturbances occurred, the presence of the soldiers having restored confidence and quiet. It was thought good policy, upon the adjournment of the court, that guns and ammunition taken from individuals at Morehead should be brought to Frankfort. For obeying this order the commander of the troops was indicted, but was pardoned by the Governor without a trial. There were those who criticised the conduct of the military as extremely insubordinate to the civil authority, but such censure was overshadowed by the fact that the soldiers preserved the peace.

A legislative investigation followed the report of the proceedings at Morehead, and official changes were made for Rowan County. Those indicted for the killing on the twenty-second day of June were pardoned, and the community has since earned favorable mention for law and order, and is now a prominent educational center.

Upon the arrival of the Kentucky National Guard in Frankfort for the inauguration of Gov. Simon B. Buckner in September, 1887, they were called out on dress parade in the presence of Governor Knott, his staff, Governor-elect Buckner, and a mass of citizens. Schneider's Band headed the parade. The companies were formed at right angles, and the officers brought forward to the presence of Governor Knott, Adjutant General Castleman, and other distinguished guests. Governor Knott then presented General Castleman with a beautiful sword, in recognition of his service and as a token of gratitude for the honor that his official conduct reflected upon the closing administration.[49]

The guardsmen were summoned to the inauguration by Adjutant General Castleman under the following general orders (No. 12, of August 23, 1887):

1. General Simon Bolivar Buckner, as Adjutant and Inspector General, organized the Kentucky State Guard in 1860.

2. In order to enable companies of the present organization to witness the inauguration of Governor Buckner on the 30th inst. the State will furnish the transportation to a voluntary encampment at Frankfort, which will commence on the 29th and continue two days. The discipline will be strict. Rations must be furnished by the companies attending. Cooking will not be allowed on the grounds. Company Commanders are directed to telegraph the Adjutant General on Friday morning next exactly the number that will attend from his Company, and transportation will be accordingly furnished.

Early in 1888, at Nashville, the Louisville Light Infantry won a competitive drill, and thereby a first prize of $2,500, against many crack companies. The Louisville Light Infantry was then an independent organization subject only to duty in Louisville and Jefferson County. It was organized in 1886 by authority of the state legislature, the charter being obtained by Hon. Wm. L. Jackson, Jr., Gen. Basil Duke, and Maj. W. Saunders. It was sworn into service by Wm. L. Jackson, Sr., judge of the Jefferson Circuit Court.[50]

An outbreak of the French-Eversole feud in the Perry County district resulted in a call for the State Guard. Troops were accordingly ordered out by Governor Buckner on October 29, 1888, for duty in Hazard. Under date of November 14, 1888, Adjutant General Hill made a report to Governor Buckner that upon his (Hill's) arrival in Hazard he had called out forty-four of the Reserve Militia, all that he had arms for, and that he had authorized Captain Sohan to muster them in and had given him instructions. These forty-four men were mustered in to reinforce the detail of sixty-three men and four commissioned officers of the 1st Regiment, brought from Louisville to Hazard by Captain Sohan.

Captain Sohan's report of November 27, 1889, gives a detailed account of the services rendered by the detachment, and of the hardships experienced by his command. The trip from Louisville was by train to London, then by wagon for the remaining seventy-five miles to Hazard. Along this line of march the troops were joined at various points by Judge Lilly, court officials, and refugee citizens of Hazard, all of whom were awaiting the troops as an escort back to town. The troops reported officially to Judge Lilly on November 5, whereupon he indicated that he would not need a guard until court convened on the seventh. In part Captain Sohan's report related that:

> Perhaps no part of the State Guard has ever passed through a more severe test of discipline and endurance. Certainly none have ever responded more gallantly and faithfully to the demands made upon them. The march from Louisville to Hazard and back was particularly trying, the camp each night being but temporary, the men could not make themselves comfortable, and suffered severely

from the cold. The road is simply indescribable, being so rough that most of the command preferred walking to riding in the wagons provided. We frequently marched for hours in the water, the natural bed of the creeks being the only available way through the hills, and this was generally the best part of the road; at other times it took all hands to help the teams up the hills, or to keep them from falling over precipices. Through it all the men were cheerful and uncomplaining, and though allowed every possible liberty, there was not a single serious breach of discipline, and but few of even a trivial sort. This, I think, speaks well for the training and reliability of the command from which the detail was taken.

At the Washington Centennial celebration in 1889 in New York some fifty thousand troops were assembled as guests of the city. Kentucky was represented by her 1st Regiment of State Guards, and five companies of the 2d Regiment. The parade of the soldiers from the various states drew the following comment from the *Army and Navy Journal:*

A cordial welcome was given to Governor Buckner of Kentucky. A fine band led the famous Louisville Legion. Splendidly uniformed in dark blue coats with white cross belts, light blue trousers, white helmets with white plume, no organization attracted more attention. They passed with twelve companies in single rank—the formation of the future—marching perfectly.

On September 5, 1889, Governor Buckner commanded Adjutant General Hill to hold in readiness a force not exceeding sixty guardsmen, rank and file, for duty in Harlan County. The Judge of the Fifteenth Judicial District had expressed anxiety as to the ability of county officers to maintain peace and order during the fall term of that court.[51]

On March 27, 1890, a great cyclone cut a wide swath through Louisville. Many persons were killed and property damage ran high. When the local police became powerless to protect the devasted areas, the 1st Regiment was detailed to assist in police duty in the stricken section, and continued on duty there for seven days.[52]

A renewal of disorder in the southwestern mountain counties was made the subject of a special communication to the legislature by Governor Buckner. The following letter outlines conditions then existing and the proposed remedies:

I respectfully transmit to you a communication from the judge of the 19th Judicial District enclosing a petition from a number of citizens of Perry County requesting that troops be sent from some other section of this state for the purpose of protecting the circuit court during its sittings in the counties of Perry and Knott. The communication should command your serious consideration.

At the beginning of your session your attention was invited to the disturbed condition of some of the counties in the State, in the hope and expectation that your wisdom would frame enactments which would remedy the evils which were then indicated; but as yet no legislation tending to the solutions of these difficulties has reached the executive office. It is deemed appropriate to present these matters, in their present phase, for such legislative action as may be deemed advisable. The facts leading to the present condition of affairs may be briefly summarized. In the autumn of 1888, on the representation of the Circuit Judge, a detachment of the State Guard was ordered to Perry County for the protection of the court. During the stay of the detachment a military company was organized in Perry County and mustered into the State Guard.

As the county seat was remote from any line of transportation, and as the cost to the State for transporting troops from a distance was very great, it was deemed a matter of economy to organize, arm and equip a company on the spot, where they were needed. It was deemed proper in other respects, as there would be constantly present an organized force of citizen soldiery, subject to the call of local civil authorities whenever their assistance might be needed. This force is still present and subject to the call of the Circuit Judge or other proper officers in case of necessity. If summoned by these officials to aid them in enforcing the law, the cost must be defrayed, as it ought to be, by those to whose assistance they are called, and who are under obligation to vindicate their claim to the right of local self-government.

If summoned by the Executive from a distance the expense will be many times greater and must be paid out of the State treasury. In either case the troops will alike be subject to the orders of the local civil authorities without interference on the part of the Executive. As far as the present emergency is concerned the Executive will endeavor fully to discharge his duties; but whatever may be his actions under existing laws the situation has attained such gravity that legislative action is absolutely essential to a proper solution of the question involved.

The presence of troops, whether local or from distant counties, will be sufficient to protect the court but not to obtain justice. They cannot and ought not influence the findings of grand juries or the verdict of petit juries, or the testimony of a single witness. They can render peaceful the sitting of the court; they can relieve the community from the sense of immediate danger from lawless men, but they cannot remove the apprehension of danger to be encountered after the withdrawal of the troops. On the departure of the troops, if from a distance, the lawless elements though but a small part of any community resume their aggressions, and the more numerous law-abiding element of society which, if resolute to the enforcement of laws, relapses into a condition of chronic timidity, due alone to the absence of organized effort under the direction of efficient officers of law. It is this condition of things that confronts us in a number of counties in the State, and to which we have no right to close our eyes. It is a difficult problem to solve, requiring the application of wisdom and true statesmanship on the part of the General Assembly; but difficult as it may be, it cannot be concealed and is not impossible of legislative solution, unless republican government is to be considered a failure.

I will not venture to renew any of the suggestions which failed at the beginning of your session, to awaken the attention of the General Assembly to what impressed me as one of the most important questions which could command their attention. If I could have done this, I feel assured that your study of the question would have found expression before this time in salutary legislation. In the same time, the difficulties attending the administration of justice are increasing, the sphere of local disturbances in enlarging and the necessity of legislative action becomes daily more urgent. Your cheerful consideration is already asked.[53]

On July 9, the Governor ordered a guard composed of one captain, two lieutenants, a surgeon, the quartermaster and commissary of subsistence, four non-commissioned officers and sixteen privates to move to Jackson to arrive on the twenty-fourth, and from that point escort the judge of the Nineteenth Judicial District to Hazard. The guard was ordered to remain there during the special term of the Perry Circuit Court for the purpose of protecting the court.[54]

From July 20 to 28, 1890, the 1st Regiment encamped near Middlesboro for instruction purposes. This point was selected because the Governor felt that the presence of the troops there would have a salutary effect on the lawless element in nearby counties.

A report was made to the Governor, on May 5, 1892, by Col. M. H. Crump, inspector general, covering the state troop inspection which Colonel Crump had completed shortly before. This report shows the condition and efficiency of the Kentucky State Guard, and makes several com-

123d CAVALRY
KENTUCKY
NATIONAL
GUARD
Passing in
Review, 1936
(See pp. 395-401)

138th FIELD
ARTILLERY
Maneuvers,
Ft. Knox, 1938
Courtesy
Capt. Walter R.
Calvert, Jr.
(See pp. 378-384)

REPRESENTA-
TIVE GROUP,
149th
INFANTRY
Fort Knox,
Kentucky,
August, 1935
(See pp. 384-395)

GUARD OF HONOR FOR NATIONAL COMMANDER, PAUL V. McNUTT
The American Legion National Convention at Louisville, Sept. 30–Oct. 3, 1929

parisons of status. A brief abstract from the report shows the standing of the regiments as follows:

Quarterly Inspection, March 31, 1892—(Maximum 100).
Order of merit is based on attendance, condition of property and soldierly qualifications.
1st Regiment, headquarters, Louisville. Colonel John B. Castleman, commanding, Efficiency 57.
2d Regiment, headquarters Bowling Green, Colonel T. J. Smith, commanding, Efficiency 55.
3d Regiment, headquarters, Harrodsburg, Colonel E. H. Gaither, commanding, Efficiency 53.
Attendance: 1st Regiment, present 285; absent 210; total 495; percentage present 57.
2d Regiment, present 177; absent 129; total 306; percentage 54.
3d Regiment, present 241; absent 168; total 409; percentage present 58.

By the act of March 13, 1893, the militia laws of Kentucky were completely revised and an organization was provided for in conformity to the regulations of the United States Army.

On May 26, 1893, Governor Brown gave Colonel Castleman permission to take the 1st Regiment "from July 10 to July 20, to visit the World's Fair, at Chicago, Ill., and there hold an encampment," with the understanding that the state should not be responsible for any expense incurred on the trip.[55] At the ensuing election of regimental officers Colonel Castleman was re-elected, with Morris B. Belknap as lieutenant colonel and David W. Gray and John Mansir as majors of its two battalions, each consisting of four companies. The entire regimental staff was reappointed, including Lieutenants James B. Smith and Roy McDonald as adjutant and quartermaster respectively. Newspaper accounts of the trip, and of approbation voiced by the Legion for Colonel Castleman's making the trip possible, are profuse.

The State Guard held its annual camp of instruction, for 1893, at Bowling Green from the first to the thirtieth of August.

During the fall of 1893 violence was threatened in Nelson County when a Negro was arrested for a statutory offence. The accused had subsequently been removed to the Louisville

Jail for safety. It was discovered that the prisoner would probably be lynched upon his return to Bardstown for trial at the November term of the Circuit Court unless military force was employed to aid the civil authorities. To preserve the peace the Governor ordered that a detail not exceeding thirty men rank and file, with requisite officers, be made from the 1st Regiment, and ordered into active service to report for duty on Wednesday morning, November 8, at six o'clock, under command of Maj. J. H. Mansir, to A. D. Pence, sheriff of Nelson County, who was then in the city of Louisville.[56] This detail accompanied the sheriff and his prisoner to Bardstown where the trial was held and the accused convicted. The verdict was satisfactory to the people and the law was therefore permitted to take its course. Prior to the verdict repeated attempts were made to take the Negro from the troops and serious mishaps were avoided only by the coolness and good judgment of officers and men. The detail was on duty from the eighth to the thirteenth of November.

Governor Brown, on May 1, 1894, appointed Andrew J. Gross adjutant general and chief of staff, with the rank of brigadier general.

During this year the annual camp of instruction was held in Paducah from July 25 to August 23.

In the spring of 1894, on the eve of adjournment of the legislature, its session having been marked by much excitement and bitterness of feeling engendered by a protracted struggle over the senatorial election, the Frankfort companies of the State Guard, by direction of the Governor, took possession of the Capitol Building. The Governor also sent a telegram to Louisville directing the Legion to report at Frankfort on the following morning. The order was promptly obeyed, and the regiment remained at Frankfort for two days, until the legislature had adjourned. The executive order declared the cause of this call for troops to be the "danger, actual or threatened, to the lives of certain members of the legislature, and to disturbances of the public peace which the civil authorities were unable or unwilling to preserve." Neither house of the assembly requested executive interference, and the employment of the military force on this occasion was resented or approved, according to the partisan feelings of the critics of the Governor. The Louisville Legion had no share in this censure, and their conduct was complimented on all sides.

The annual camp of instruction for 1895 was held at Henderson from July 20 to August 25.

Daniel R. Collier was appointed adjutant general by the Governor on September 10, 1895. Two days later, Walter S. Forrester was made assistant adjutant general.

The 1st and 2d Regiments were summoned to Frankfort to participate in the inauguration of Gov. W. O. Bradley. Various reasons were ascribed for the omission of the 3d Regiment, chief of which was the belief that partisanship of the regiment's personnel was the determining factor in making the call.

On the twenty-ninth of December, Governor Bradley ordered Lt. H. S. Whipple, instructor of the State Guard, to go to Barbourville and investigate a disorder in which certain members of the Bradley Guards were alleged to have participated.[57]

During the closing days of its session in 1896, the State Legislature was frequently interrupted by disputes and quarrels that originated from partisanship. Conditions became so grave that troops were called for duty in the Capitol.[58]

An instruction camp was established at Mammoth Cave in 1896. It was opened to the 1st Regiment on July 11, this regiment remaining until July 20; the 2d Regiment from July 22 to August 1, with the 3d Regiment following from the third to the thirteenth of August.[59]

On October 31, Governor Bradley telegraphed Colonel Castleman as follows: "Am informed great excitement in Louisville, Ky. Take possession of Armory and see that guns are not seized by anybody. I will be in Lancaster on Monday and Tuesday."[60]

Governor Bradley received a telegram on January 5, 1897, from F. P. James of Mercer County, stating that turnpike raiders in his county were preparing to destroy tollgates. A similar communication was received from B. F. Beach, judge of Mercer County. Both officials asked for troops, alleging the inadequacy of the county law enforcement agencies to protect the threatened property and arrest the raiders. In compliance with the request the Governor ordered Col. E. H. Gaither of the 2d Regiment to report immediately to Sheriff F. P. James, with fifteen men from Company G and thirty-five men from Company E of the 2d Regiment. The presence of this force in the county prevented the raiders from carrying out their threats.[61]

Upon receipt of Lieutenant Whipple's report on the implication of the Bradley Guards of Barbourville in local disorders (*ante, p. 275*) the Governor commanded this company to be mustered out.[62]

Colonel Castleman and a detachment of the 1st Regiment were ordered on duty February 6, 1897, to assist R. E. Young, sheriff of Marion County, to escort William Black from the Jefferson County Jail to Lebanon for trial, to protect Black against mob violence during the trial, and to guard him after the trial until he was safely out of Marion, whether convicted or acquitted.[63]

The Pearl Bryant murder case of 1896-97 was tried in Campbell County, and resulted in the conviction of two students, one of whom (Jackson) became a "public idol" after the conviction, because of a conclusion by the public that he was innocent and could have been spared if the other convicted man had confessed the crime, which the public concluded he had committed from the evidence adduced. Jackson's sojourn in the Newport Jail was marked by a continuous stream of callers, gifts of food and flowers, letters of sympathy, and with all this was the rumor that Jackson's sympathizers would never permit him to be hanged, certainly not in Newport or Campbell County. March 20, 1897, was the date set for the execution. On the sixteenth, Governor Bradley, at the request of the sheriff of Campbell County, ordered Capt. Noel Gaines and fifty men of Company B, 2d Regiment, to report to the sheriff on the nineteenth and assist him in preserving order until after the execution had taken place.⁶⁴

During the summer of 1897 several calls were made for troops to assist local law enforcement officials to discharge their duties. In May, Maj. John R. Allen was ordered to take forty men of his battalion into Bath County to sustain the sheriff in maintaining order. During June, Col. E. H. Gaither, with thirty men from Company A, and forty men from Company B, of the 2d Regiment, were ordered to escort a prisoner, George Dimming, from the Jefferson County Jail to Frankfort for trial and protect the accused during the trial. A like service was rendered by Col. T. J. Smith with thirty men from Company A and thirty men from Company B of the 3d Regiment during the trial of Tol Stone at Bowling Green. In the same month, Capt. Noel Gaines, with Company B, 2d Regiment, was ordered to protect one Taylor held in the Franklin County Jail.

Company D, 3d Regiment, attended the Centennial Exposition at Nashville, Tennessee, on June 22-23 as the official military representatives of Kentucky.

The State Guard annual camp of instruction for 1897 was held from July 6 to 30, at Fountain Ferry Park, Louisville.

On October 22, 1897, Governor Bradley ordered Colonel Castleman to place a sufficient number of the men of the 1st Regiment "on duty at the Armory at Louisville, to protect same on the day of the approaching election."⁶⁵

NOTES, REFERENCES, AND SOURCES

1. McPherson, *History of the Rebellion*, p. 274.
2. *Observer and Reporter* (Lexington), Jan. 10, 1866.
3. *Official Records*, Sec. 3, Vol. III, p. 564.
4. Collins, *History of Kentucky*, Vol. I, p. 159.
5. *Acts of Kentucky, 1865*, p. 166, Resolution of June 3.
6. Thompson, *History of the First Brigade*, chap. 2-3.
7. *Commonwealth* (Frankfort), Dec. 15, 1865.
8. *Maysville Eagle*, Sept. 28, 1865.
9. Coulter, *Civil War and Readjustment in Kentucky*.

10. *New York Herald* quoted in *Observer and Reporter* (Lexington), Aug. 23, 1863.
11. *Adjutant General's Letter Book No. 17*, p. 360.
12. Collins, *History of Kentucky*, Vol. I, p. 170.
13. L. & N. R. R. vs. Simon B. Buckner.
14. *Commonwealth* (Frankfort), Oct. 27, 1865.
15. Session of Jan. 3, to Mar. 11.
16. *Observer and Reporter* (Lexington), Mar. 18. 1868.
17. *The Yeomen* (Frankfort), Jan. 11, 1868.
18. Collins, *History of Kentucky*, Vol. I, p. 185.
19. *Adjutant General's Letter Book No. 25*, p. 616.
20. *Acts of Kentucky, 1867*, p. 102.
21. *Commonwealth* (Frankfort), Mar. 31, 1871.
22. *Executive Journal, 1868–1870*, p. 172.
23. *Ibid.*, p. 196.
24. *Executive Journal, 1868–1870*, p. 233.
25. *Ibid.*, p. 234.
26. Quoted by Collins, *History of Kentucky*, Vol. I, p. 207.
27. *Observer and Reporter* (Lexington), July 23, 1870.
28. *Acts of 1873*, Art. I, Sec. 1.
29. *The Yeomen* (Frankfort), Sept. 10, 1874.
30. *Adjutant General's Order Book, 1874*, No. 22.
31. *Ibid.*, No. 27, of 1874.
32. *Ibid.*, No. 28, of 1875.
33. *Ibid.*, No. 32, of 1875.
34. *Adjutant General's Order Book of 1877*, Nos. 7–10 inclusive.
35. Johnston, *Memorial History of Louisville*, p. 223.
36. *The Yeomen* (Frankfort), Oct. 25, 1879.
37. *Executive Order Book of 1880*, Order of Mar. 30.
38. *Ibid.*, Order of Dec. 18.
39. *Executive Order Book of 1881*, Order No. 1.
40. *Adjutant General's Order Book, 1881*, Order No. 6.
41. *Courier-Journal* (Louisville), Oct. 13, 1881.
42. *Adjutant General's Order Book, 1882*, Special Orders Nos. 1, 2, and 3.
43. *Ibid.*, General Order No. 3, of 1882.
44. *Adjutant General's Order Book, 1884*, General Order No. 5.
45. *Adjutant General's Letter Book No. 37*, p. 542.
46. *Ibid.*, p. 806.
47. *Ibid.*, Special Order No. 67, Nov. 6, 1886.
48. *The Western Argus* (Frankfort), Apr. 28, 1886.
49. *The Western Argus* (Frankfort), Sept. 1, 1887.
50. *The Herald-Post* (Louisville), June 17, 1928.
51. *Executive Journal No. 1 of 1887–1889*, p. 473.
52. Johnston, *Memorial History of Louisville*, p. 228.
53. *Executive Journal*, No. 2 of 1890-91, p. 180.
54. *Ibid.*, p. 258.
55. *Adjutant General Order Book of 1893*, Special Order No. 19.

56. *Ibid,.* of 1893, Special Order No. 52.
57. *Ibid.,* of 1895, Special Order No. 21.
58. *Executive Journal No. 1, 1895–97,* p. 162.
59. *Ibid.,* p. 248.
60. *Ibid.,* p. 382.
61. *Executive Journal No. 1, 1895–1897,* p. 425.
62. *Adjutant General's Letter Book of 1897,* Special Order No. 2.
63. *Executive Journal No. 1, 1895–1897,* p. 354.
64. *Ibid.,* p. 431.
65. *Executive Journal No. 2, 1895–1897,* p. 63.

CHAPTER VII

THE WAR WITH SPAIN

The sinking of the *Maine* crystallized public opinion in Kentucky, and war was thereupon seen as inevitable. The lethargy and quietude of the spring disappeared, the guns of the feudists at the headwaters of the Kentucky River were silenced, and the silver tongue of the opposition to the Goebel election law gave way to the steel fang of the militarist.

When word of this naval disaster came, the Kentucky State Guard speedily offered its services to the Governor. The Louisville Legion was the first to volunteer its service to the U.S. Government. This was done under the following resolution:

Resolved, That the Louisville Legion, First Regiment Kentucky State Guard, requests the Governor of Kentucky to tender the National Government its services in this or any foreign country where it may be needed.

The members ask to be assigned to duty amongst the first called for, should the emergency arise.

The Regiment of seven hundred, rank, file, and officers—two battalions—is sufficiently equipped for active service. They are armed with Springfield, Model '73, 45-70 rifles. The men are instructed in rifle practice. Each company is also instructed in drill of 83 Model Gatlings, of which the regiment has four. One company is drilled in the use of three-inch rifles, model '64, Muzzle loaders, of which the Regiment has four as part of its equipment.

JOHN B. CASTLEMAN, *Colonel*.

The Kentucky State Guard in 1898 consisted of the three regiments of infantry, existing by mandate of the law. The colonel having seniority was John B. Castleman of the 1st Regiment, the Louisville Legion. The 2d Regiment was commanded by Col. E. H. Gaither. This regiment was made up chiefly of companies from the Bluegrass area, and was looked upon as "Lexington's Regiment." From the Pennyrile and Purchase*[1] came the 3d Regiment under command of Col. T. J. Smith. By an order of April 23, 1898, Governor Bradley directed that, by recruiting, the regimental strength should be brought to 12 companies of 103 men each. This order dissipated hopes of speedy departure for the seat of war. The recruiting continued until the full strength specified by Governor Bradley was obtained. Shortly thereafter the Governor ordered the company strength reduced to eighty-four men. Even with this drastic reduction there was still an insufficient supply of arms and equipment. The 1st Regiment fared better than the other two, for its regular arms were better at the time, and deficiencies were remedied by the fund subscribed for that purpose through the efforts of the Citizen's Central Relief Commission of Louisville. Many Louisville business men subscribed $100, and thereupon became honorary members of the Louisville Legion

Governor Bradley called a conference of regimental commanders on April 23, at which time it was decided that, when the call for troops came, the State Guard companies would be mustered in as volunteers until the quota was filled. On the same day the call was received, specifying three regiments of infantry and two troops of cavalry. In response to the call the Governor stated that he would have Kentucky's quota ready in ten days.

On the thirtieth of April, Governor Bradley issued an order to Adjutant General Collier to assemble the State Guard at Lexington and muster out the entire Guard so that the men might volunteer in the U.S. Army.[2]

Mobilization of the Guard presented the chief problem, and after three days Lexington was accepted as the point best suited for troop concentration. Adjutant General Collier immediately began to mobilize the Guard, and Captain Ballance of the U.S. Army conducted the muster. The 2d Regiment was called first, and by companies, arrived in Lexington on May 6. During the next two days the companies of the

---

* Notes, references, and sources are indicated by numerals. These refer to corresponding numbers at the end of this chapter. Notes on Chapter VII are on page 292.

3d Regiment trekked in from the Purchase and Pennyrile. The 1st Regiment did not arrive until May 13, due to a lack of men and equipment, and possibly to an animosity between Colonel Castleman and Governor Bradley. Even after the three regiments were assembled, they were not encamped together. The 2d and 3d Regiments went to Camp Collier, established in the south end of Lexington at Tattersall's, the horse barns being used as barracks because no tents were available. The 1st Regiment went into camp on the Chautauqua grounds near "Ashland," and named their camp for Governor Bradley. Then came the following orders:

FRANKFORT, *May 20, 1898.*

1. All members of the Second Regiment of the Kentucky State Guard, officers and men who have enlisted in the U.S. Volunteer service, are hereby honorably discharged from the Kentucky State Guard service.

2. The officers and men belonging to the said regiment, who failed to enlist on account of physical disability, or from any other cause, are likewise honorably discharged from the State Guard Service.

3. The second paragraph of this order is not made as a reflection upon any officer or man, who failed to enlist in the United States Volunteer Service, but because the remnant left in each company is so small, it is deemed for the best interest of the Kentucky State Guard, that the entire organization be mustered out of the service, without prejudice to any one. This order is to take effect from this date.[3]

By Command of Gov. W. O. Bradley

D. R. COLLIER
Adjt. Gen. Ky.

HEADQUARTERS KENTUCKY STATE GUARD

FRANKFORT, *June 6, 1898*

SPECIAL ORDERS No. 69. The First and Third Regiments of the Kentucky State Guard are hereby mustered out of the organized militia service of the State of Kentucky, for the reason that the interest of the State Guard requires such action.

By command of Gov. W. O. Bradley

WALTER FORRESTER,
Asst. and Act. Adjt. Gen.

The sojourn in Lexington was distasteful to the troops who believed all their troubles at an end when they arrived there. No thought had been given to routine, that soon became "red tape" to the soldiers who saw no need for organization other than that under which they had seen duty, within the state. The rigorous physical examinations and other exacting qualifications required of them made it seem for awhile that the Spaniards would see very few of the Guards at all. The Governor and regimental commanders were loud in a protest that was intermingled with expletives from the perturbed troops. Requirements were relaxed by the War Department but the rejections were still so high that depletions of ranks delayed action through recruiting and mustering in of other enlistees.

Another source of delay was the "three cornered animosity" between the Governor, the Guard, and Captain Ballance. While their altercations were being carried on the Guard was drilling; drilling as they had never drilled before, and often on an empty stomach or one that would have been better off if emptied, for food was none too good and was usually cooked in the manner of its quality.

Delays brought desertions, desertions brought delays, and delays prolonged the mustering in, for no company could now be accepted with less than 106, the full strength set by a new order from the War Department. Recruiting officers for each of the regiments were kept out in the state to secure new men to replace deserters and those rejected.

Mustering in consumed considerable time, having been completed in the 2d Regiment on May 20, and in the 3d on May 28, but the Louisville Legion mustering was delayed until the first week in June. Until the last man was mustered in, no intimation was made of the destination of the Kentucky contingent. Orders then came to move to Chickamauga. Here the 2d Regiment was attached to the 3d U.S. Army Corps, and the 1st and 3d Regiments to the 1st U.S. Army Corps. At Chickamauga there were some compensations such as new arms and uniforms that bulged through "Washington's red tape," horses and spurs for the cavalry units. Camp life was enlivened by the long distance verbal feud between Governor Bradley and Colonel Castleman that furnished extensive reading when the hometown papers came through. Finally, on July 27, the 1st and 3d Regiments moved to Newport News with Puerto Rico as a final destination. On August 4, half of the 1st Regiment embarked, and six days later the remaining six companies with Colonel Castleman followed. The 1st Regiment was the first Kentucky organization to reach the seat of the war. The 3d Regiment was left behind on account of an epidemic of measles and mumps, and the 2d Regiment was still sweltering at Chickamauga where typhoid fever raged and had taken a heavy toll from the Kentucky troops.

Upon arriving in Ponce, Puerto Rico, the Kentuckians proceeded to Mayaguez, but the battle that loomed there failed to materialize. This contingent of six companies then proceeded to Arroyo to join the balance of the regiment under Colonel Castleman, and was thereupon assigned to garrison duty at Guayama. Colonel Castleman was ordered to assume command of all troops in Ponce, detail necessary guards to preserve discipline, and report or correct any unsanitary conditions in surroundings, among troops or elsewhere. In execution of his orders, Colonel Castleman detailed his son, Maj. David Castleman, to duty as provost marshal because of the prevalence of yellow fever, rather than detail any other officer to face this extreme danger.

Governor Bradley was directed by the War Department, on June 21, to enroll a fourth regiment of infantry. In pursuance of the order, D. G. Colson was named colonel, and Lexington was again designated as the point of mobilization. This regiment was recruited in the mountain area of the state where Guard companies were few. Consequently, the personnel of the regiment was almost entirely of raw material. The recruits commenced arriving in Lexington during the last week of June. A camp was established in Loudoun Park and named Camp Hobson, but this name was soon changed to Camp H. C. Corbin because of the preference of the men. Until they were mustered in, it was impossible to maintain discipline. A large percentage had never been in a city before, and the urge for sightseeing was far stronger than that for drilling. "French leave" became so general that it was found necessary to enclose the camp with a high fence. Not a few lamented the lack of "jowl and greens," which they preferred to the roast beef of the army kitchen.

On July 4, the 4th Regiment was mustered in, and for the next six weeks was drilled and prepared for active duty. Then, on August 12, came the peace protocol. With it came news that the War Department had determined to establish a large camp at Lexington to supplant the one at Chickamauga. The camp was erected and troops began to arrive. Among them came the 3d Regiment, still nursing mumps and measles, and a grudge against Colonel Smith because he did not get them to Puerto Rico. Their arrival, in such a frame of body and mind, in an unfinished camp, only added to their discontent. Soon petitions were circulated asking to be mustered out; but this was not accomplished until May 16, 1899, and only after the regiment had been sent to Jacksonville, Florida. The 2d Regiment was left at Chickamauga, and also petitioned to be mustered out. Instead of being mustered out, it was sent to Anniston, Alabama.

The Governor borrowed from the State National Bank, Frankfort, $3,000, subject to action of the General Assembly to equip hospitals, trains, and bring home sick Kentucky soldiers from Fortress Monroe and Camp Thomas, Chickamauga Park. He ordered Adjutant General Collier to take a hospital train, with twelve persons, to Chickamauga Park, and bring away seventy-five sick soldiers, taking to their homes all who could reach there promptly, and bringing to the hospital at Frankfort those who could not. Col. Walter S. Forrester, assistant adjutant general, took another hospital train to Fortress Monroe, with eighteen persons, and brought away 100 sick soldiers, bringing to the hospital at Frankfort those who were not able to go home.[4]

On the seventh of September, 1898, Governor Bradley accepted the resignation of Adjutant General Collier, and thereupon appointed as successor to that office, Wilbur R. Smith of Lexington.

The 2d Regiment remained in service until October 31, 1898. Until the new camp was ready, the two troops of cavalry were held at Chickamauga; then they were sent back to Lexington, and shortly thereafter were mustered out. The 1st Regiment was held on duty in Puerto Rico until December. On December 4, it embarked and arrived in Louisville December 12, and was mustered out on February 24, 1899.

Soon after the peace protocol was signed, home folks had petitioned the War Department to have the 1st Regiment returned to the state and mustered out. On hearing of this, the following letter was addressed to the U.S. Adjutant General by Colonel Castleman:

HEADQUARTERS COMMANDING OFFICER
TROOPS AT PONCE

PONCE, *October 18, 1898.*

BRIGADIER GENERAL H. C. CORBIN, *Adjutant General*
Washington

Friends in Kentucky have no authority for asking that the First Kentucky be relieved from duty. These men are soldiers. The government will determine when the regiment is no longer needed.

COLONEL CASTLEMAN

The success of Colonel Castleman in military affairs aroused jealousy and an effort to belittle his work. Among the rumors spread at that time is one still occasionally heard, to the effect that, after embarkation orders had been issued by the U.S. War Department, there was a substitution of Castleman's Regiment for that of the 3d Regiment. To verify or disprove such claims the subject was laid before the War Department by letter and excerpts from the reply of that department are as follows:

It appears from the records on file in this office that the 1st and 3rd Regiments Kentucky Volunteer Infantry, War with Spain, arrived in Newport News, Virginia, July 28 and 29, 1898, respectively, for transportation to Puerto Rico.

The 1st Regiment Kentucky Volunteer Infantry, War with Spain, left Newport News, Virginia, August 3, 1898, and arrived in Puerto Rico, August 10, 1898, but no record has been found to show that the order directing this regiment to proceed to Puerto Rico was originally issued to the 3rd Regiment Kentucky Volunteer Infantry, War with Spain.

The records also show that the above mentioned 3rd Regiment left Savannah, Georgia, January 18, 1899, and arrived in Cuba January 21, 1899.

The several organizations in the United States Volunteer Army that served in Cuba during the period of the War with Spain left the United States at various times between June 14, 1898, and February 17, 1899, and proceeded to Cuba in compliance with specific orders directed to each organization, and no record has been found of an order containing a complete list of all the organizations designated for transportation to Cuba.[5]

The four regiments that were mustered into the Federal service as Kentucky Volunteer Infantry, War with Spain, and the two troops of cavalry volunteers were augmented by a number of Kentucky Negro recruits, who were mustered into the United States service and assigned to the 10th U.S. Cavalry, one of the two colored U.S. Regiments.

A report of Kentucky troops mustered into United States service shows that many of the volunteers were discharged because of illness, and eighty-two deaths resulted from accident or disease while in the service. A survey of this report shows a large number of desertions, and would seem to place a stigma on Kentuckians. However, this report is little different from that of any other state. It is a notorious fact that the men deserted through the urge of self preservation. They were willing, even anxious, to wage war, but refused to eat the rations which were furnished. "Rotten Bully Beef" caused most of the desertions.[6]

Colors carried by the four Kentucky State Guard Regiments during the War with Spain were as follows:

The 1st Regiment carried, for regimental and headquarter's use, the usual United States flag and the blue and white regimental flag. The latter was of silk on which was embroidered the Kentucky coat of arms and other devices. This was presented to the regiment by mothers and sweethearts of the regiment. Both of these banners became tattered during the Puerto Rican campaign. They now constitute part of the flag collection in the rooms of the Kentucky State Historical Society, Frankfort.

The 2d Regiment carried the regulation United States flag furnished by the War Department, and a blue silk flag, regulation size, on which was embroidered the Kentucky coat of arms, with the motto, *United We Stand, Divided We Fall,* and the inscription, "Second Kentucky United States Volunteer Infantry." This flag was presented to the regiment by the Daughters of the American Revolution of Lexington, and was given into the keeping of the commander, Col. E. H. Gaither, Harrodsburg.

The 3d Regiment had the United States flag and a silk flag, regulation size, presented by patriotic ladies. The latter flag had embroidered on one side the Kentucky coat of arms, on the other the American eagle in the attitude of swooping down upon an enemy. Both of these banners reposed in the care of Col. Thomas J. Smith, Bowling Green, who commanded the volunteer regiment in 1898 and later was in command of the 3d Regiment, State Guard.

The 4th Regiment had a United States flag and a regimental flag, the latter also presented by patriotic ladies. The latter was of silk, regulation size, on one side of which was embroidered the Kentucky coat of arms, on the other an American eagle in attack pose. Both of these banners were for a time in the possession of the commander, Col. David G. Colson, of Middlesboro. Subsequently, they were turned over to David R. Murray, adjutant general of Kentucky, who was the lieutenant colonel of the 4th Regiment. With Colonel Colson's consent they were given for preservation, as relics of the War with Spain, to the Kentucky Society of Colonial Dames, to be kept in the rooms of the Kentucky State Historical Society, Frankfort, where they are now displayed.

Troop A, Kentucky Volunteer Cavalry, commanded by Capt. U. S. G. Perkins of Middlesboro, carried only a small guidon, four by six and one-half feet and the U.S. flag presented by Governor Bradley. This is now in the possession of Union College, Barbourville.

Troop B, Kentucky Volunteer Cavalry, commanded by Capt. Jefferson Prater of Salyersville, had a guidon similar to that Troop A, but the whereabouts of Troop B's guidon is unknown.

That the state profited, by her experience in collecting previous war claims against the U.S. Government, is shown by the action of Governor Bradley. The following orders, selected from a large file of those pertaining to this subject, are indicative of the Governor's determination to make a speedy settlement if possible:

DANIEL COLLIER FRANKFORT, *Feb. 8th, 1899*
Adjutant General of Kentucky

You are hereby ordered to proceed to Washington and confer with the officers of the War Department, with the view of having proper steps taken to procure proper settlement concerning the property furnished to the State by the various regiments which entered the service in the late war with Spain, and procuring the return of an equal amount of property of similar character to this State, for the purpose of reorganizing the Kentucky State Guard, and all other matters connected with the furnishing of property to this State by the Government and the disposition thereof. You will also collect all the orders of the Department connected with the service of the four Kentucky Regiments in the late war, a roster of the same with accounts of all soldiers and officers mustered in and out, the deaths, resignations, removals, desertions and discharges of soldiers and officers, and the date thereof, and all other historical matter on file in the department.[7]

GOV. WILLIAM O. BRADLEY

HEADQUARTERS, ADJUTANT GENERAL OF KENTUCKY

SPECIAL ORDERS NO. 27 FRANKFORT, *May 19, 1899*

Asst. Adj. Gen. Walter S. Forrester is hereby directed to proceed to Washington, D. C. and on behalf of the State of Kentucky, to secure for the use of the militia of the State such ordnance as may be due the State under the law and to secure from the War Department a settlement of the property accounts of the State with the United States: He will also take such steps as may be necessary to secure tentage in place of that turned over by the State to the United States Volunteers: and he will also secure from the Adjutant General's Office, such information as will complete the military history of the Kentucky troops in the Spanish War.

D. R. COLLIER, *Adj. Gen.*

Upon the mustering out of the State Guard in May, 1898, new companies were formed for intra-state duty. These were ordered by Governor Bradley on the twelfth of August, 1898, "to go into camps of instruction and upon practice marches." By the Governor's order the period of instruction was fixed at a maximum of fourteen days during which the expenses of any one company should not exceed $400. The companies that encamped under this order, from August 17 to October 21, were those from Bowling Green, Lexington, Peewee Valley, and Frankfort.

The Governor, on June 8, 1898, ordered Assistant Adjutant General Walter S. Forrester to take with him the "Forrester Guards" from their home station at Peewee Valley to Manchester in Clay County, there to report to Judge Wm. L. Brown and act under his directions for the purpose of "securing the arrest and trial of all violators of the law, and upholding the peace and dignity of the Commonwealth of Kentucky." [8]

Governor Bradley issued the following order to Adjutant General D. R. Collier on June 29, 1898:

> You will on the 3rd of July next go to the city of Louisville, Ky., and under order of Graves Circuit Court convey Bob Blanks, from the jail of Jefferson County, on the 4th day of July to Graves county for trial. You will take Captain Calhoun's Company K.S.G. from Lexington including fifty men and officers for whom transportation has been arranged on its arrival in Louisville and proceed with them to Mayfield. You will afford protection to Blanks and if convicted and sentenced to the penitentiary you will give him conduct to the Eddyville Penitentiary unless judgment should be suspended, in which case you will return him to the jail aforesaid. In the event he should be convicted and death penalty adjudged you will convey him to said jail for safe keeping until further ordered. If acquitted, you will bring him back to a safe point and turn him loose.
>
> You are not to interfere with the civil power in any way. Your whole duty is to see at all hazards that the defendant Blanks is protected from all unlawful violence and that the law is in every way enforced and the decency and honor of the Commonwealth protected.
>
> If he should be placed in jail at Mayfield you will see that the jail is securely guarded. Upon the happening of contingencies, I rely on your coolness and good sense to do all for the accomplishment of the purpose set forth in this order.[9]

During the summer Governor Bradley "ordered Colonel Forrester to go to Barbourville and consult with the County Judge and other county authorities looking to the enforcement of the laws at the approaching term of Circuit Court."[10] Colonel Forrester was also commanded to investigate civil conditions in Clay County, especially to determine whether officials were making a reasonable effort to preserve the peace of the county. The report of Colonel Forrester was made on the twenty-fifth of July, showing that the turbulent condition in Clay County resulted entirely from the Howard-Baker feud and concerned only members of the embattled factions. Colonel Forrester opined that troops would be necessary and should be sent upon request. The situation at Barbourville was portrayed by the report as being within the power of control of local authorities.[11]

In accordance with the request of H. C. Eversole, judge of the Clay Circuit Court, the Governor issued the following order to Col. Roger D. Williams to lead a detachment of troops into Clay County in June, 1899:

> You will take one hundred good and reliable men with necessary cooks, surgeons, and tentage, and Gatling guns if you think best, and go with them to Manchester in Clay County, Kentucky, so as to reach that point on Sunday next. You will report to H. C. Eversole, Judge of the Clay Circuit Court and act under his direction for the preservation of the peace and the enforcement of law and order.[12]

NOTES, REFERENCES, AND SOURCES

1. "Purchase," all of Kentucky west of the Tennessee River. "Pennyrile," the Pennyroyal region that embraces that section of the State between the western coal fields and the Tennessee Line, and between the Cumberland River and approximately the parallel of longitude through Burkesville.

2. *Executive Journal No. 2 of 1897–1899*, p. 334.

3. *Adjutant General's Order Book for 1898.* Special order of May 20.

4. *Executive Journal No. 2, 1897–1899*, p. 394.

5. Letter of U.S. Adjt. Gen. E. S. Adams to U. R. Bell, Director Federal Writers' Project in Kentucky, dated August 8, 1938, now in files of Federal Writers' Project in Kentucky.

6. *Report of the Adjutant General of the State of Kentucky. Kentucky Volunteers, War with Spain, 1898-99.*
7. *Executive Journal No. 2 of 1897-1899.* Order No. 7 of 1899.
8. *Ibid.*, p. 356.
9. *Ibid.*, p. 365.
10. *Ibid.*, p. 377.
11. *Ibid.*, p. 379.
12. *Ibid.*, p. 491.

CHAPTER VIII

POLITICAL TURMOIL AND THE STATE GUARD

The post-war reorganization of the State Guard was fraught with numerous obstacles. Late in the summer of 1899 the Louisville Legion was reorganized as a State Guard Regiment, and shortly afterward the 2d and 3d Regiments were likewise revived. Old quarters of the regiments were now unfit, public sentiment in favor of reorganization was lethargic, and military appropriations were difficult to obtain because of the state's tempestuous political condition. Then, too, the military equipment that the state owned at the outbreak of the late war had been used during the war, or had become so obsolete as to be unfit for troop use. Claims had been filed with the U.S. War Department for the war materials and equipment used, but settlement was delayed.

Early in 1900, Milton, Charles, and William Kendall were accused of murdering Eugene Cassell at his home near the line of Fayette, in Jessamine County. They were hucksters with bad reputations, were stealing Cassell's chickens, and when Cassell came out to investigate the disturbance at his barn they shot him. Feeling was bitter in Jessamine after the murder and the prisoners were taken to the Fayette County jail for safe-keeping when arrested.

A petition to the Governor requesting troops for the protection of the Kendalls, when being brought back for trial, was signed by every magistrate of the county and by the county judge. The jailer of Jessamine County gave notice that he would not be responsible for the prisoners unless a military guard accompanied them. Governor Taylor issued an order on January 22, 1900, for troops as a guard for the prisoners from Lexington to Nicholasville. The order was forwarded at once to Capt. C. W. Longmire, instructing him to take eighty men of the Lexington State Guard Company, proceed with the prisoners to Jassamine County, and report to the jailer.

Political strife and events leading up from the gubernatorial election of 1899 resulted in much turmoil. After the Goebel-Taylor-Brown campaign and election, W. S. Taylor was inaugurated as Governor in December, 1899. William Goebel served notice on Mr. Taylor of a contest of the election, setting out among other causes that: "The election in Louisville was void because the Governor, William O. Bradley, called out the militia on the day before the election, and the said militia was in charge of the polling places in said city on said election day in command of W. O. Bradley, Governor * * *."

While this contest was in progress several military events transpired. During the early part of January upwards of a thousand armed men from eastern Kentucky assembled in Frankfort. On January 4, 1900, Governor Taylor issued the following order to Adjutant General Collier in order to insure control of the State Militia:

> In view of the fact that rumors, threats, and warnings are continually coming to this office, that the State property now in the Arsenal is in danger of seizure or destruction and that said property is of great value to the state and should be protected, therefore you are hereby ordered to detail Capt. D. B. Walcutt, Co. B, 2d Infantry, Kentucky State Guard, to guard and protect said property at the Arsenal, and in the event of trouble to preserve the peace.*[1]

William Goebel, State Senator from Kenton County, and contestant for the office of Governor of Kentucky, was mortally wounded on the morning of January 30, 1900, on the statehouse grounds. He was shot by a man who was hiding in the Capitol Building. Senator Goebel had just passed the fountain and was within 100 feet of the steps of the Capitol Building when a shot, which was apparently fired from a rifle, rang out and Goebel dropped to the ground. Col. Jack Chinn, who was with him, bent forward to render assistance and three more shots were then fired in rapid succession. These were evidently intended for Colonel Chinn. Eph Lillard, who had accompanied Senator Goebel

---

* Notes, references, and sources are indicated by numerals. These refer to corresponding numbers at the end of this chapter. Notes on Chapter VIII are on page 325.

and Colonel Chinn from the Capital Hotel, was entering the Capitol when the shots were fired, and hastened to where the wounded man lay. Senator Goebel was borne by friends to Dr. Hume's office in the Capital Hotel, and shortly after to his room in the hotel.

The shooting of Senator Goebel was generally deplored. Republicans and Democrats were equally eager to learn the condition of the wounded man from time to time. Immediately after the shooting, the Governor dispatched Captain Davis, policeman of the Executive Building, to General Collier with instructions to order out such troops as were necessary to keep the peace. Those of the 2d Regiment who lived in Frankfort and others who were in the arsenal were immediately summoned to the scene, and within twenty minutes after Senator Goebel fell the statehouse grounds and the Executive Mansion were under military guard. Telegrams were sent immediately to Colonel Williams at Lexington, and Colonel Mengel at Louisville, to hasten to Frankfort with what guardsmen they could assemble. Colonel Williams arrived at four o'clock with some 150 men, making the total number on guard duty about 200. The military authorities consulted with the civil authorities, who offered to assist in keeping the peace. Harlan Whitaker, of Butler County, was arrested as he emerged from the Capitol Building shortly after the shooting of Mr. Goebel. Several pistols and a large knife were found on his person when searched. Whitaker declared that he was innocent, and naturally had fears as to his safety in the Franklin County Jail. He was removed to Louisville for safe-keeping.

Governor Taylor's next military moves are set out, in part, in the following order of January 30, 1900, to Adjutant General Collier:

> You will immediately assemble the entire available force of State Guards at your command and have them report to you at the Capitol. You will assume personal command of all forces so assembled, and establish as perfect a police system as you possibly can, assuming all responsibility under this order for the maintenance of the public peace. You will immediately put yourself in communication with the County Judge of Franklin County, with

Mayor of the City of Frankfort and the Sheriff of Franklin County, and act as far as in your judgment the public peace will permit you in harmony with those officers. You are instructed that the purpose of this order, under the deplorable event which has just occurred and the excitement consequent therefrom, is to maintain the public peace and secure protection to every citizen.[2]

Under another order of the Governor the Frankfort militia at once took over the police duty of the Capitol Square. That night (January 30) the 1st Regiment arrived from Louisville with Col. C. C. Mengel in command. As soon as the regiment was announced as having arrived, Governor Taylor adjourned the legislature by the proclamation which is here given:

TO THE GENERAL ASSEMBLY OF THE COMMONWEALTH OF KENTUCKY

WHEREAS, a state of insurrection now prevails in the State of Kentucky and especially in Frankfort, the Capitol thereof, by virtue of the authority vested in me by the Constitution of Kentucky, I do by this proclamation adjourn at once the General Assembly of the State of Kentucky to meet at London, Laurel County, Kentucky, Tuesday, the 6th day of February, 1900, at 12 o'clock. Given under my hand at Frankfort, Kentucky, this 30th day of January, 1900, at 9 o'clock, P. M.[3]

The following is the constitutional authority under which the Governor issued his adjournment proclamation:

The first General Assembly, the members of which shall be elected under this constitution, shall meet on the first Tuesday after the first Monday in January, 1894, and thereafter the General Assembly shall meet on the same day every second year, and its sessions shall be held at the seat of government, except in cases of war, insurrection and pestilence, when it may, by proclamation of the Governor, assemble for the time being elsewhere.[4]

Some 500 armed soldiers were quartered in the state buildings and on Capitol Square. Sentinels were stationed at every corner around the square. Gatling guns were strung out around the building, facing the streets on every side. Col. Roger D. Williams arrived in the city during the afternoon with two companies of the 2d Regiment. He was placed in active command of all troops, being the senior colonel of the state. The Louisville Legion, in command of

Col. C. C. Mengel, arrived on a special train composed of a flatcar with the two Gatling guns of the regiment; a baggage coach, in which was stored the ammunition, and nine coaches. Eight companies constituted the regiment, but there were less than 400 soldiers in the regiment. The other officers were Lt. Col. D. W. Gray, Quartermaster I. E. Barnett and Majors Gifford and Colston. Orders were at once issued by Colonel Williams that the Legion should be quartered in the third and fourth stories of the Capitol Building. Colonel Williams' two companies were in the rear of the adjutant general's office. There were eighteen companies from central and eastern Kentucky in the 2d Regiment and these were also brought to Frankfort on a special train. Lt. Col. Sam Morrow, of Somerset, was in command of the 2d Regiment. The other officers in the regiment were Quartermaster William Burkley and Majors J. Embry Allen and Nelson Edwards.

That night the Governor and his secretary, Mack Todd, decided that it would not be safe for them to venture to their homes, and they spent the remainder of the night in the Capitol Building. The doors of the building were guarded by soldiers, and every man who entered was called on to show a pass. These were signed by Adjutant General Collier, and only those persons having business in the Capitol Building were able to get one. The Executive Mansion, with Governor Taylor's family, was guarded by about thirty soldiers. It was deemed best to take no chances.

For several hours after the troops had been stationed at all the entrances to Capitol Square and at all the doors of the statehouse, the snow fell thick and fast. The uniforms of the soldiers, beaten by snow and wind, made a desolate picture for those who passed by or stopped to meditate on the graveness of the situation. Many would walk up to the entrance of the grounds, as if they intended to go in, but in a flash crossed bayonets were presented and the journey ended. Often the person would say he had business in the statehouse, but if he could not describe his business and name his man he was refused. If the guard concluded to pass an individual in, a soldier escorted him to his destination. Great crowds of men, women and children hung around Capitol Square all day, discussing the situation and watching the maneuvers of the troops. They were kept from the sidewalks at the entrances in order that ingress and egress might not be blockaded.

The soldiers shivered in the cold and pulled their capes over their heads for protection against the blinding snow. They would pass to and fro, and stamp on the ground to keep up the blood circulation in their feet. Capt. D. B. Walcutt, who succeeded Colonel Dixon in command, had a soldierly bearing and was seen about the Capitol Building at all times. He would frequently go to Adjutant General Collier's office but would be gone only a few minutes.[5]

The fact that it was publicly announced that a state of insurrection prevailed seemed to enrage the populace which was vehement in announcing that their rights had been infringed upon. They complained of the squads of soldiers stationed in various places and that the usurpation of the civil authority by the military was an outrage.

The members of the Contest Board proceeded to the Capitol Building at two-thirty o'clock in the afternoon of January 30, to resume their session. They passed the guards at the gate all right, but when they went to ascend the steps in the Capitol Building they found crossed bayonets with the command that they could proceed no further. The guards announced that Capt. D. E. Walcutt had left orders to let no one pass up. Chairman Hickman remarked that they could not go against bayonets. After a few minutes Committeeman Renick moved that the board adjourn to meet at the City Hall at five o'clock. Presently former Governor Bradley and other attorneys appeared, and agreed that there must be some mistake as to the orders. Captain Walcutt then came up and said there was no intention to exclude members of the committee, or anyone else who had business in the building.

Before the Contest Board met in the afternoon the following letters were filed with the chairman from the attorneys of the contestees:

GENTLEMEN:—We feel ourselves compelled to decline to appear before your Board this afternoon at 5:00 o'clock at the City Hall.

Information which we consider reliable, has reached us that some of the counsel for the contestees are in danger of assassination, if opportunity be given. The room in the City Hall in which you propose to meet is a small one, and admission to it is controlled entirely by an officer, whose sympathy is wholly against the contestees. The hour at which you meet renders it certain that it will be dark when the board adjourns.

While we are ready to perform any duty at any risk, we do not feel it incumbent upon us, under the great excitement which exists today, and under the circumstances which now environ us, and with the information which has been received heretofore and reported today, to appear before you. We feel confident that the existing excitement will measurably subside by tomorrow. We are informed that the civil authorities of the city of Frankfort and County of Franklin and the Adjutant General of the State are in harmonious communication for the purpose of taking steps to preserve the public peace and to prevent crime. We believe, therefore, that the sittings of the board can be safely resumed tomorrow in the Statehouse.

That no postponement may be had in the making of your report we now express our willingness to have the time allotted to us for argument. We make this communication with the utmost respect to the board and submit the subject contained therein to the board and to its causes.

The Contest Board assembled in the afternoon at five o'clock in the City Hall. Only Attorneys Breckinridge and Edelen appeared for the contestees. At this juncture the board adjourned to meet in executive session at seven o'clock and decide the matter. By a vote that evening at eight o'clock, the Contest Board voted to seat William Goebel, Governor, and J. C. W. Beckman, Lieutenant Governor, of Kentucky.

The House and Senate were to meet the next morning at ten o'clock and adopt the majority report of the Contest Board, thereby declaring Messrs. Goebel and Beckham, Governor and Lieutenant Governor respectively. It was presumed that Taylor and Marshall would be asked to vacate at once. With Taylor and Marshall under protection of the militia, the only recourse left to the Democrats was an application to the courts to compel Governor Taylor to vacate.

By January 31 there were about 1,250 soldiers on duty in Frankfort, which included all of the 1st Regiment and sixteen companies of the 2d Regiment, under command of Col. Roger D. Williams. They messed in the rear of the Capitol Square, where campfires were kept burning night and day after their arrival. Long trenches had been dug, and the aroma of the food cooking could be detected several squares away.

Three hundred men, in reliefs of 100, were stationed on guard at the Capitol, 150 at the county jail in similar reliefs, 120 at the penitentiary in reliefs of 40 each, and 30 at the Governor's Mansion in reliefs of 10 each. These details, owing to the extreme cold weather, were relieved every two hours. The relief corps, marching in or out of the Capitol grounds, with shouldered arms, presented a warlike scene. The soldiers were at all times orderly and had nothing to say to the crowds that are gathered along the route of march.

The Governor's proclamation was read from the Capitol stairway by Adjutant General Collier at ten o'clock on the morning of January 31, to the members of the legislature as they came into the crowded hallway. A large number of the representatives and senators, mostly Democrats, had come in a body from the Capital Hotel. They were passed in at the front gate by the guards, and were then escorted by a platoon.

Adjutant General Collier announced to the legislators that they would be permitted to pass into the legislative chambers singly, get their belongings, and must then pass out again. As soon as the proclamation was read, Speaker Trimble, of the house, mounted the stairway and declared the House of Representatives adjourned to the City Opera House, there to meet at once. Thereupon, Adjutant General Collier reiterated that the Governor had adjourned the legislature until February 6, to meet in London, and that if any attempt was made to hold a session anywhere else, at any other time, it would be treated as an unlawful assembly, and he would see that it was dispersed. Mr. Trimble then left the hall, followed by a dozen or more of his party members. They went to the Opera House, where they found a company of soldiers on duty with fixed bayonets. Mr. Trimble and others held a hasty conference in the middle of the street, and decided that he, with one or two others would formally demand admittance to the Opera House. This admittance was refused by the commander of the squad on guard. Speaker Trimble then turned to Clerk Ed. Leigh and the other followers and declared the legislature adjourned to meet at the courthouse immediately.

When the Democratic members left the Capitol Building for the Opera House, Adjutant General Collier immediately ordered fifty picked men under Lieutenant Gray to march some distance behind the legislators. These soldiers met the crowd returning to go to the courthouse. Collier gave the command to wheel, and there a race began for the courthouse, about a block away. When the soldiers and the crowd reached the corner, the order was given by Colonel Gray to double-quick; this they did and were drawn up in line in front of the courthouse by the time Speaker Trimble had reached the entrance to the building.

By this time several persons in the crowd had become furious, and were making loud demonstrations. They were admonished by Speaker Trimble to remain quiet and orderly. Again Speaker Trimble declared the house adjourned, subject to his call at any time, and at any place, the members to be notified by the pages. He then returned to the Capital Hotel followed by the legislators and the crowd that had gathered, attracted by the peculiar proceedings of the soldiers marching and counter-marching through the principal thoroughfares of the city. Colonel Gray followed after with his detail of soldiers, and took his stand in front of the hotel, with another platoon that had previously been stationed there.

Most of the Republican members of the legislature went to the Senate Chamber or the House of Representatives and took all their possessions preparatory to obeying the proclamation of Governor Taylor to convene at London. The Democrats declared they did not care to run up against bayonets, and they would leave what they had in the halls in the care of the soldiers. After the militia had refused to allow the Democratic members of the legislature to meet, Senator Goebel's physicians were asked if he could be consulted in regard to what should be done. Permission was given, and several of the leaders were allowed to see the wounded man. He expressed no surprise when informed of the situation, and urged his friends to proceed in a lawful manner.

After a quorum of the legislature was obtained the report of the contest committee was adopted, thereby unseating Governor Taylor and declaring William Goebel and J. C. W. Beckham duly elected Governor and Lieutenant Governor, respectively. Though mortally wounded, Mr. Goebel at once took the oath of office. He immediately ordered the troops on duty in Frankfort to return home. However, circumstances caused the commanding officers to ignore Governor Goebel's order. On the contrary, they obeyed the Taylor orders and formed a heavier guard around the Governor's Mansion, then occupied by Taylor. Taylor's adjutant general continued to prevent a meeting of the legislature in their chambers.

On February 3 Governor Goebel died, and within an hour Mr. Beckham was sworn in as Governor. He at once appointed Gen. John B. Castleman, adjutant general. A week later Governor Taylor's orders were still recognized by the Kentucky State Guard then on duty. These, with the exception of about 200 men, were relieved of duty by order of Taylor on February 10. In the meantime the Democratic faction of the legislature had been meeting in the Jefferson County Courthouse. Authority continued to be disputed, and on March 22 Governor Beckham called for duty in Frankfort that part of the State Guard that was known to recognize the authority of General Castleman.

Governor Beckham issued the following proclamation which contains his reason for calling out the State Guard:

TO THE PEOPLE OF KENTUCKY:

In the present crisis which exists in our State I feel it my duty to explain to you my position and to outline the policy which I intend to pursue in the effort to restore peace, quiet and order to our Commonwealth. It was the policy of my distinguished and lamented predecessor to conduct this contest, which has so much agitated our people, in a way to commend his course to all law-abiding and conservative people of the State. That policy I have, to the best of my ability, also pursued, and intend to continue in the same line.

In calling out the military force to protect the courts in Frankfort, I wish to say that no one is more averse to military rule than I am.

I believe that it should be the last resort that any official should use, and I lament the necessity that requires it at this time.

As your Chief Executive, it is my desire and intention always to rely more upon the law than the bayonet, and I prefer to be supported more by the strong common sense and by the patriotism of our law-abiding people than by any military power whatever. Every honest citizen should submit without hesitation to the control of the constituted authorities and to the courts—the great safeguard of our liberties.

According to law, the civil authorities of the county of Franklin have presented to me a statement of facts which shows that a condition of lawlessness is threatened here with which they are unable to deal, and they have called upon me for assistance. I have in compliance with their call ordered here certain State troops to place themselves completely under the authority of the Sheriff of the county with instructions that they shall assist him in protecting the court of this county from threatened intimidation as well as to protect the prisoners who are to be tried by that court on tomorrow. These troops shall be strictly under the control of the civil authorities in preserving order and protecting the dignity of the court, that justice may be done to all parties. I regret exceedingly the necessity that requires such action and that there should be any who would seek to interfere with the action of the judicial tribunals in our State, but the condition exists and I must meet it. When the situation is such in your Capitol City that the Judges in your courts and other officials need personal protection from bodily harm and threatened interferences with their action, then I deem it my duty, as Governor of the Commonwealth, to give them such protection as they may need. Such is the situation here now, and I intend, that so far as I have the power, to protect the courts. In my earnest effort to uphold the law and to protect the constituted tribunals, I call upon the good and law-abiding people of our Commonwealth to aid and assist me, not by physical force, but by moral support. We have placed our case in the hands of the law and we must continue to rely upon the law. Let no action of violence or lawlessness be committed anywhere, and let our people who have shown such patience and conservatism heretofore continue to show it.

My great trust and reliance is in the strong common sense and integrity of the people of our State, and trusting in that I believe that out of our present difficulties there will soon come peace, order and restoration of the law.

Senator Crenshaw on February 13, 1900, offered the following resolution, which was adopted and sent to the House, where, under the rules, it had to lay over a day:

WHEREAS, The General Assembly of the Commonwealth of Kentucky, duly organized according to law on the 2d day of January, 1900, were holding their sessions, as required by law, in the city of Frankfort, the seat of government of this State, and in the halls of the State house, set apart to them for said purpose, when, on the 30th day of January, 1900, without the authority of law, the Hon. William S. Taylor, then acting as governor of Kentucky, when peace and good order had reigned in the city of Frankfort, the capitol of the State, and as well known to every man, woman and child in said city, no disorder of any kind had been created except that which was fomented and introduced by the said Hon. W. S. Taylor and his assistants in bringing to the city of Frankfort, armed partisans, numbering nearly 1,000, and the unfortunate and ever-to-be regretted assassination of the Hon. William Goebel on the said day of January, 1900, when he was peacefully walking along the streets of Frankfort to attend to his official duties as Senator of Kentucky, by a shot fired by an assassin from the Executive building, occupied at the said time by the said Hon. William S. Taylor and his assistants; and whereas, fifteen minutes after said shot was fired the said Hon. William S. Taylor surrounded the said State House and Capitol grounds with armed militia, and from thenceforth has refused, by threats of violence, to permit the General Assembly of Kentucky to assemble at its halls in said city of Frankfort, in the Capitol building, and has the same with armed soldiers, who, with fixed bayonets pointed at the members of this General Assembly, refused to permit them to enter said Capitol building, and refused to allow them to hold their sessions at other places in the city of Frankfort, and finally compelled the General Assembly, by a joint resolution, to adjourn to the city of Louisville for the transaction of its business; and, whereas, this General Assembly, in accordance with the law, adjudged not legal from under the solemnities of their oath of office that the said Hon. William S. Taylor has not been elected Governor of Kentucky, and that, therefore, he is now usurping the functions of said position, and that the Hon. William Goebel has been elected Governor of Kentucky, and the Hon. J. C. W. Beckham, Lieutenant Governor of Kentucky, and, whereas, by the death of the said Hon. William Goebel the said J. C. W. Beckham became and is now the lawful Governor of the State of Kentucky, and as such has been recognized by this General Assembly and every department of government and is entitled to all the rights and provisions appertaining to said office, and the said William S.

Taylor, notwithstanding said fact, is still in possession of the State House and the Executive chambers thereof and surrounded by military force under his orders and directions and refuses to remove the troops surrounding the said buildings and to allow the General Assembly of Kentucky, the representative of the people of the State, elected by them and who are desirous of discharging their duties under their oath of office, as prescribed by law; and, whereas, it has been held by the courts throughout this land that the political departments of government have the sole jurisdiction to determine the legality of the government, and that the government recognized by the political departments must be accepted as such; and, whereas, the Hon. J. C. W. Beckham has been and now is recognized by the General Assembly of Kentucky and all the other departments of government as the Governor de jure and de facto of the State of Kentucky, shall, according to the decisions of the various courts, fix and establish his title beyond question, as held by the Supreme Court of the United States in the case of Luther vs. Border *(7 Howard, page 1)*, more than half a century ago, which decision has been approved in numerous cases since said time and has never been overruled, and that, therefore, the people are entitled to have the services and the judgment of their representatives without molestation; and, whereas, great costs and expenses have been incurred and our treasury depleted by the defiance upon the part of said Taylor to the law of the land and his attempt to create insurrection and to cause bloodshed in this fair name, and, in order to restore peace and harmony in our State and have the law of the land enforced in all departments of government;

Now, THEREFORE, BE IT RESOLVED by the General Assembly of the Commonwealth of Kentucky, That we, as the General Assembly of the State, demand that the said W. S. Taylor immediately withdraw his military troops from and around the Capitol and the State House of Kentucky, and that he permit without molestation and hindrances, this General Assembly to meet according to law, in the State House, in the rooms assigned by law for the purpose to them, and transact the lawful business of the State, and that he vacate the Executive building, which he now occupies without right and contrary to law, and that the Hon. J. C. W. Beckham, being the Governor of Kentucky be allowed to enter said State House and take possession of the archives and records of the State departments and transact the business of the people of Kentucky who are law-abiding citizens and do not desire the shedding of more human blood, and that the rights of the people, as adjudged by the legal tribunals, shall be, and we demand that they be, respected by the said W. S. Taylor and his coadjutors; and

BE IT RESOLVED FURTHER, That by reason of the conduct of the said Hon. W. S. Taylor, the Court of Appeals of Kentucky, the highest tribunal of this State, has been denied access to the court room in said Capitol and, at the point of bayonets, have been refused admission thereto, and have been compelled not to hold court, by reason of the acts of usurpation and force and violence on the part of said Taylor, as aforesaid.

BE IT RESOLVED by the General Assembly, that we demand that the said Taylor immediately cause said troops to be removed and permit said Court of Appeals to discharge the duties of their office, as required by law, without molestation or hindrances.

Adjutant General Collier continued to act under Governor Taylor's orders. Consequently, units of the State Guard found themselves under opposing commands, from February 3, to May 22, 1900, virtually two small and distinct armies representative of the two major political parties of the state. Though coming in contact daily, no disorders took place between the men.

Alonzo Walker, a Louisville stenographer, was arrested and placed under guard, charged with inciting mutiny among the troops. Mr. Walker was confined in one of the cloak rooms in the Capitol Building, under a heavy guard. In the main hall of the building guns were stacked on both sides and a squad of soldiers stood in front of them. Hundreds of people came in from the country and surrounding counties to view the situation, and crowded around the square all day, gazing on the warlike scenes within. According to orders the soldiers were compelled to ignore the many jeers and sneers aimed at them, under penalty of being arrested.

Toward the end of February a rumor was widely circulated that smallpox had broken out among the troops. This was denied by Dr. U. V. Williams, president of the Franklin County Board of Health. He said he had received a letter from Dr. McCormick, secretary of the State Board of Health, to the effect that two soldiers of the Covington company, supposed to be suffering from malaria had been sent home and were later stricken with smallpox, and that a member of the Morgantown company, who had also been sent home, was suffering from the same disease. Dr. Williams called on Governor Taylor and suggested the fumigation of quarters previously occupied by the diseased men. After these officials were unable to agree as to whether the cost of such fumigation should be borne by the county or the state, the matter was postponed and ultimately forgotten.

Early in February there were grave fears that influence

would be brought to bear at Washington which would result in martial law for Frankfort, if not all of Kentucky. These were generally dispelled by arrangements for a military display on the occasion of the funeral of Major General Lawton in Washington. The only Federal troops then stationed in Kentucky were four companies of the 2d U.S. Infantry, at Fort Thomas. All of these companies were under orders to proceed to Washington. Although their stay in the National Capital would be brief, the removal indicated that United States troops would not be used in this purely internal disturbance.

Seventy-five men, under the command of Major J. Embry Allen, arrived in Frankfort on the twenty-second of March. They came under orders from General Castleman, who had been appointed adjutant general by Governor Beckham. Twenty of the men were from Winchester, under command of Captain Gnadinger. They were provided with arms and amunition from the armory at Lexington.

Governor Taylor, on March 25, officially notified President McKinley and Secretary of War Root that there were two armed forces in Frankfort, and a conflict was liable to occur at any time. He telegraphed the President that a reign of terror existed and that the troops of both factions were using arms supplied to Kentucky by the U.S. War Department. The telegram was signed by W. S. Taylor as Governor of Kentucky. The reply received from Washington related that the matter had been laid before the Secretary of War, and that the latter would take immediate steps to have the arms belonging to the United States returned to their proper custodian.

There was a long discussion of the Kentucky situation in the President's Cabinet meeting on March 27. Shortly before eleven o'clock, the hour of meeting, Senator Deboe and Representative Pugh of Kentucky went to the President and had a conference that continued for some time after the members of the Cabinet arrived. It was known in a general way what the Taylor faction leaders would have the National

Administration leaders do in their behalf. They asked the Administration to recognize Governor Taylor as the Chief Executive of the state by such methods as the President might deem best, the only stipulation being that the people of the country be left in no doubt regarding the National Administraton's position.

It was suggested by Deboe and Pugh that use of Federal arms by two factions of the State Militia provided an opportunity for the National Administration to recognize Taylor. The representation was that one or the other of these military factions was using Federal arms improperly, and that President McKinley should decide which side should be deprived of its arms.

As soon as the Kentuckians had left the White House the Cabinet continued the discussion. The stand was taken at once that the Federal Government had no function in the Kentucky dispute, and it would be unwise as well as unjust for the Administration to interfere. President McKinley held that the use of Federal arms by the State Militia afforded no excuse for Federal interference; that arms were loaned to the state, and that the state alone was responsible for their safekeeping. It was unanimously held by the Cabinet that the Kentucky courts should be allowed to settle the troubles in the state without molestation or interference.

Two drunken soldiers, two police officers, and two opposing military forces, figured in a stormy scene on the night of April 7. About ten o'clock Patrolmen Hagan and Onan, of the Frankfort city police, heard pistol shots in the lower part of Frankfort. They found two privates (Taylor faction) in an intoxicated condition, discharging their revolvers in the air. The policemen arrested the soldiers and started with them for the jail. On the way they were overtaken by a squad of about eighteen other State Guardsmen, who overpowered the officers and liberated their captured comrades. All of the soldiers then hurried to Capitol Square. The report spread that two policemen had been killed. Chief of Police Williams heard it, ran to the Capital Hotel to summon all the deputies in sight and started for the Statehouse. His squad numbered about twenty-five men. En route he was reinforced by a patrol of (Beckham) soldiers from Lexington and regular policemen. Evidently the troops at the Statehouse had heard of the coming of Chief Williams' party, for a detail with weapons ready was hurriedly drawn up in the Capitol grounds, as if to repel an attack. Captain Longmire sent his men back to their barracks and succeeded in dissuading the others from attempting to enter the Statehouse enclosure. The city officers sided with Captain Longmire, and a clash was avoided. That night the Beckham troops were kept under arms, but none of them were allowed to leave their quarters in the courthouse. Later, Adjutant General Collier held a conference with city and county local authorities with a view to finding out who was responsible for the trouble, which so nearly resulted in a riot. The Taylor troops insisted that members of the Beckham Guards fired the shots that started the uproar, while the two policemen were positive that the disturbers were Taylor militiamen. The city judge proposed that Adjutant General Collier line up his forces and allow the policemen to pick out the alleged offenders and then turn the parties so indicated over to the city for trial. The row increased the friction existing between the police department and the State Guardsmen on duty at the Statehouse. One reckless act or any harsh word from either side might easily have provoked a clash.

Such were conditions until the U.S. Supreme Court rendered a decision in May in favor of Governor Beckham. Upon receipt of intelligence of the decision Governor Taylor instructed his adjutant general that:

> The Supreme Court of the U.S. having decided in favor of Mr. Beckham, nothing now remains to be done except to dismiss the militia and surrender your office to your successor appointed by Mr. Beckham. You are therefore directed to dismiss the militia at once and to surrender your office to your successor as soon as the mandate of the U.S. Supreme Court is filed, or if you wish, you may do so at once. Tender to the members of the militia my kindest regards and sincerest thanks for their manly, true and patriotic services.[6]

On the same day Adjutant General Collier relinquished his command by the following letter:

GEN. JOHN B. CASTLEMAN FRANKFORT, *May 22, 1900*
Frankfort, Ky.

SIR: In view of the decision of the Supreme Court of the United States, in the contest of Taylor vs. Beckham, I have the honor to turn over to you as Adjutant General of Kentucky the command of the Kentucky State Guard and all the property and buildings belonging to same, without awaiting the mandate of the Court. Allow me to thank you for your universal kindness and courtesy and to suggest that in my opinion it is due to you more than any one else in Kentucky that trouble is averted. Wishing you a successful and peaceful administration, I am, dear sir,

Very truly yours,

D. R. COLLIER.

After political calm had been restored, Governor Beckham ordered the 1st and 2d Regiments mustered out. This was completed on December 15, 1900. During the election contest the legislature appropriated $10,000 for the purchase of 1,000 Winchester rifles and other military supplies.

On January 17, 1901, Judge T. L. Morrow of the Whitley Circuit Court requested troops to suppress a riot at Corbin. Accordingly, Governor Beckham ordered Col. R. D. Williams to take a detail of 100 men from the 2d Regiment, including a Gatling gun detail, and report to the Whitley Sheriff.[7] The appearance of troops on the scene immediately had a pacifying effect, and two days later it was agreed that the soldiers had accomplished their purpose and were accordingly relieved.

During the latter part of the summer disturbances occurred in the "Black Patch" tobacco growing area. Bands of men, later called "Night-riders" because most of their acts of violence were nocturnal, undertook to dominate the dark leaf tobacco industry of the state. Their activities were primarily intended to produce a sales policy, but very often the methods they employed fell into the class of lawless acts.

Early in September, Adjt. Gen. D. R. Murray made an investigation of conditions in dark leaf tobacco-marketing centers.[8] He advised that troops be held in readiness for active duty there. Accordingly, an order was issued to Capt. Hal Griffith of Battery A, Louisville Light Artillery, to hold thirty of his men with a Hotchkiss and a Gatling gun in readiness at his armory to move upon notice to Hopkins County. A like order was issued to Maj. E. H. Watt, 3d Infantry. Neither detachments were moved, and both were relieved on the twentieth of September.

Orders of September 25, placed troops on duty at Madisonville under personal command of Adjutant General Murray.[9] The units detailed were companies of the 3d Regiment from Owensboro and Bowling Green, under immediate command of Major Watt, and were continued on duty there until the middle of November.[10]

Battery A was organized in Louisville early in 1901, and with Battery B of Lexington was formed into a battalion under Capt. J. H. Mansir. The Lexington Battery B was mustered out in December, 1901, and a new Battery B was organized in Louisville and placed under command of Capt. Jesse McComb. At the same time a Drum and Trumpet Corps was organized at Louisville. Then, in February, 1903, Battery C was organized at Louisville.

Fleming County experienced considerable disorder during January, 1902, as an outgrowth of political strife. On the seventeenth of January, Circuit Judge J. P. Harbeson and Sheriff O. Collins jointly asked that a detachment of the Guard be detailed to Flemingsburg to assist civil officers. Accordingly the adjutant general detailed Capt. F. L. Gordon with forty men of Company A, 2d Infantry, and Lt. J. A. Dodd with ten men from Battery B.[11]

One other call for police duty was made during the year. A detail of seven men was sent to Mammoth Cave in July for the purpose of guarding stores forwarded there preparatory to the encampment of the Guard.[12]

On the twelfth of June, 1903, Judge James Harbeson of the Mason Circuit Court, and Sheriff J. R. Robertson, notified the Governor that three Negroes were to be tried, charged with the crime of robbery committed under such circumstances that the mob spirit was incited in the county. Adjutant General Murray personally directed the police activities of a detachment of the 2d Regiment during the trial, which was held without any attempt of violence.[13]

For the purpose of holding maneuvers, Camp Young was established at West Point in 1903. All units of the Guard, except those on active duty in the state, were called to participate in the maneuvers from the first to the tenth of October.[14]

Governor Beckham, on December 17, appointed Capt. C. W. Longmire of the 2d Infantry to act as provost marshal during the inauguration ceremonies, a gesture of gratitude for Captain Longmire's loyalty during the early days of the Beckham administration.[15]

The Hargis-Cockrell feud of Breathitt originated in the election of 1899. James Hargis was the Democratic candidate for county judge and Ed Callahan was the Democratic candidate for sheriff. The election went to the Democrats and the Republicans filed a contest. After the election the prominent old law partnership of J. B. Marcum and O. H. Pollard dissolved because of party alignments. In the contest suit Pollard represented the Democrats and Marcum the Republicans.

While depositions in the contest case were being taken in Marcum's office, an argument arose, and both Hargis and Callahan drew pistols. They, with their attorney, were thereupon ordered out of Marcum's office. Warrants were issued for Marcum, Callahan, and Hargis. Marcum paid a fine, but Hargis refused to be tried by Police Judge Cardwell. Tom Cockrell, the town marshal, and his brother, Jim Cockrell, undertook to arrest James Hargis. Later the case in police court was dismissed at the suggestion of Attorney Marcum.

In July, 1902, Ben, brother of Judge James Hargis, met Tom Cockrell in a "speakeasy." A fight ensued in which Ben Hargis was killed. Prosecution of Tom Cockrell by the Hargis family produced a deadly enmity, and shortly afterward a son of John "Tige" Hargis (nephew of James Hargis) was killed by a member of the Cockrell faction. Wide ramifications of the case linked it up later to the Strong-Callahan feud.

Though the Hargis-Cockrell strife had existed for several years, it had not received much notice from the outside world until Attorney James B. Marcum was killed on May 5, 1903. During the preceding years some thirty men had met death in this inter-family struggle. Upon the killing of Marcum a special term of circuit court was called by Judge D. B. Redwine for the purpose of a grand jury investigation of the circumstances leading to the death of Dr. B. D. Cox, Jim Cockrell, and Marcum. The situation had been discussed by Governor Beckham and Judge Redwine in a conference at Frankfort, and a decision was reached to send troops to Jackson to preserve order during the special session of court. An order was issued under which Col. Roger D. Williams, with 100 men, and Major Mansir's Battery, with a Gatling gun, went on duty in the courthouse yard and in the courthouse. A squad under Capt. Hal Griffiths was sent to the hills to arrest Tom White. During the first ten days almost continuous duty was required. After the arrest of White, rumors indicated that a jail delivery would be attempted. This resulted in a doubling of the military guard. The Jett-White trial was held and ended with a hung jury. By order of Judge Redwine the case was then transferred to the Harrison Circuit Court, where a conviction of both was obtained. On August 21 all of the troops were withdrawn from Jackson except a provost guard of twenty-five men which remained on duty there until December 3, bringing to an end active duty of six months and ten days.[16]

In 1903 Congress enacted a militia law that embraced all males from eighteen to forty-five years of age, and divided them into two classes: First—the organized militia of the state; Second—the entire remainder. This (Dick) law gave the state five years (to 1908) to adopt laws to make its organized militia conform to prescribed Federal regulations. The states participated in the annual appropriation of $1,000,000, upon compliance with these Federal regulations.

The limit of such state troops was 100 men for each Congressional representative, and the President was given power to call out the State Guard. The benefits of the new act provided a stimulus for this Kentucky State Guard. The primary purpose of the law was to bring about uniformity in the militias of the several states, and to relieve the states of a portion of the burden incident to maintaining their militia. Federal funds received by any state under the act were to be used for arming and training the State Guard. Consequently state appropriations could thereafter be devoted to providing armories and for other intra-state military purposes. To obtain the Federal benefit it was further necessary for the State Guard to pass inspection by the U.S. War Department. This Kentucky failed to do in 1908 and 1909. However, conditions were sufficiently improved by 1910 to entitle the state to a share of the Federal grant.

By order of Governor Beckham a salute was fired on February 3, 1903, to commemorate the death of Governor Goebel.[17]

In August a detail of fifty, including officers and men, was sent to Maysville to protect Thomas D. Maybrier, on trial in the Mason Circuit Court. Maybrier was charged with murder, committed under aggravated circumstances. Public feeling was pitched high against the accused, and it was feared that he would be seized by a mob when returned from the Fayette Jail unless strongly guarded. The Guard being on duty, the trial proceeded without any serious disturbances.[18]

The Kentucky State Guard entered into active competition with the Guards of other states at the Louisiana Purchase Exposition at St. Louis in 1904. On August 24, Governor Beckham ordered the State Guard to encamp on the fairgrounds at St. Louis, Missouri. The 3d Regiment under Col. Jouett Henry was ordered to be encamped there from September 2 to 9. The 2d Regiment under Col. R. D. Williams was allotted the week from September 12 to 19. Finally came Col. Briscoe Hindman, with the 1st Regiment, during the week from September 22 to 29. In the competitive drills and in band contests Kentucky won numerous trophies and much favorable mention.

Until the state legislature, in 1904, ordered the Jefferson County Fiscal Court to erect an armory in Louisville, repeated efforts to obtain such a building had failed. Under this act the county appropriated $450,000 for the building. Upon the resignation of Briscoe Hindman as colonel, a petition was sent by the regiment to Gen. William B. Haldeman to act as commander. Haldeman accepted the colonelcy and through his popularity and military ability was able to build up a worthy combat organization. A cadet company was organized in Bardstown on March 15, 1905, under the act of 1893. On April 27, this company was attached to the 1st Regiment.[19]

By an executive order of July 12, Paducah was designated as the point at which the State Guard should be assembled for drills and target practice in 1905. Camp Yeiser was here established and continued from the seventh of August to the second of September. While on duty here orders came for Col. R. D. Williams to assume command of Companies C and E, 2d Regiment, and to report to the sheriff of Logan County for the purpose of protecting the court and prisoners during the W. R. Fletcher and Guy Lyons trials.[20] A subsequent order relieved Colonel Williams and gave the command of this detail to Maj. E. B. Bassett.

The protection of courts and prisoners in 1906 necessitated several calls for the Guard. In January Company K, 2d Infantry, under Capt. Geo. E. Albrecht, was sent to Middlesboro.[21] Then in July the Graves Circuit Court requested a guard during the trial of Allen Mathis on a statutory charge. The heinousness of the attack charged to Mathis was such that the mob spirit of the county had been thoroughly excited. Companies D, E, and I, 3d Infantry, under Maj. E. B. Bassett, were detailed to this duty.[22] Again in August a detail was ordered to Barbourville during the summer term of the Knox Circuit Court. Companies A and B, 2d Infantry, under Col. J. Embry Allen, comprised this detachment.[23]

On the twenty-ninth of May, Governor Beckham granted permission for a squad of four men and one officer to act as an escort for the Lincoln cabin from New York to Louisville.[24]

Night-rider troubles kept the State Guard in active service much of the time during 1906 and 1907 when the entire western tobacco-growing section of the state was terrorized by lawless bands through raids and other depredations. County officers were powerless or unwilling to deal with the situation. Troops were called out when this condition became impressed upon the state officials and the public.

The night-rider raids originated from the failure of attempts of the farmers of the "Black Patch" to pool their tobacco crops in an effort to boost prices. When the pool did not function to suit some of the growers they deserted the pool, hauled out their tobacco, often at night, and sold independently. Then an organization of poolers was formed, and frequently resorted to desperate measures in order to hold the pool intact. Those who refused to join the band suffered penalties of various sorts such as having their tobacco beds scraped, their crops destroyed, or their barns burned. In some cases men were taken out at night by bands of masked men and severely whipped.

A night-rider raid was made in the summer of 1907 in Princeton, Caldwell County. The trouble that caused that raid finally culminated in December by a raid on Hopkinsville in Christian County. The telephone exchange was shot up, a warehouse burned, and the community terrorized. Capt. Edward Clark, commanding Company D of the 3d Regiment, with an organized posse pursued the raiders for some twenty miles. The Governor then ordered out more troops. Among these was Company G, 3d Regiment, under Capt. P. P. Price. Capt. Dan Carrell, commanding Company H of the 1st Regiment, left Louisville with his men early in the morning of December 17, and Colonel Haldeman was ordered to proceed with the command to Hopkinsville to confer with the civil and military officers and instruct Company H as to its duties.[25] This company was on duty at

Hopkinsville until January 13, 1908. It was stationed at the courthouse and patrolled the surrounding country. The men were fired on several times and returned the fire, but there were no casualties. This was during the early part of their service, for later the lawless element seemed to realize that the troops could and would maintain order, and ceased their attempts at intimidation. Upon the departure of the 1st Regiment detachments from Hopkinsville, Company D of the 3d Infantry was ordered into service there, and assumed charge of all duties previously assigned to Company H.

A warehouse in Lebanon was attacked in January, 1908, and at once Capt. E. T. Meriwether was sent with a detail of ten enlisted men from Company G, 1st Regiment, to Lebanon, where the detachment remained on duty without incident for twelve days.

On February 10, Colonel Haldeman was ordered to "select two trusted officers and eighteen men, who will proceed at once to Marion, in civilian clothes, carrying ammunition and revolvers in their handbags. The detachment will not proceed in a body, but one officer and two or three men will take the first train out of Louisville. The remaining men, going by separate trains, will follow during the day reporting on arrival to the County Judge of Crittenden County, William Blackburn, for such instructions as he may deem necessary."[26] These troops were relieved in five days, but in April trouble again arose and Capt. Robert N. Krieger was detailed to Lebanon with a company of fifty picked men of the 1st Regiment, and remained over a month. Some of the men were mounted, and these were sent into surrounding country to preserve the peace. However, there was no serious trouble while they were there.

The night-rider organization, although begun by tobacco planters in self-defense, had its ramifications. The members proceeded to mete out punishment on whomsoever they thought deserved it, conducting a sort of guerrilla warfare.

The next trouble for which the 1st Regiment was called was the activities of night-riders in Logan County. In July,

1908, a Negro named Russell Browder was arrested for shooting a man who was commonly reputed to be a leader of the night-rider organization in Logan County. A mob was formed to punish the Negro, but the sheriff of Logan County spirited him away to the Jefferson County Jail for safe-keeping. Then four other Negroes were arrested on misdemeanor charges. The night-riders, believing these Negroes to be inimical to their cause, removed them from the jail and lynched them. Anticipating trouble when Browder would be returned to Logan County to stand trial, the Governor ordered troops sent to Russellville.

Adjt. Gen. P. P. Johnston in his special order of August 11, 1908, said:

> As many troops in Western Kentucky as may be needed to preserve the rights and protect the lives and property of the citizens will be concentrated in the County of Logan to aid the civil authorities, especially to protect the prisoner, Browder, if he is ordered back there for trial.
>
> The failure to protect the four men in jail there recently, and the failure to arrest and prosecute a single one of the mob, [which] took them at will, without hindrance or outcry from the civil officers, and lynched them, induced the apprehension that the lawless element so far dominates the good people and officers of that locality, that they are helpless to protect the rights and lives of the citizens, and are deterred from calling aid that at least fails to condemn lawless methods.
>
> The commanding officer will, therefore, see that a sufficient number of soldiers under the command of prudent, careful and brave officers, are in striking distance of the civil officers in charge of Browder, to protect them and their prisoner from insult and violence, from the time said prisoner is taken from the Louisville jail until they receive further orders. The commanding officer will respond to every lawful call for aid from civil officers, and after being called on will use his best judgment and all the power at his command to give the relief called for. But if from intimidation, sympathy with friends among the lawless, or any other cause, a felony that is threatened, or about to be committed, is not promptly stopped by the civil officers, the commanding officer will not wait, when delay would be acquiescence to an unlawful purpose, but will interpose at once to prevent the commission of a felony, and arrest every man who threatens or is about to commit such a crime.
>
> If any attack is made on the troops, or any of them by which life is endangered, they may defend themselves by discharging their firearms, and when the attack is general, the commanding officer may order his troops to fire.

Capt. Dan Carrell of the 1st Regiment was sent to Russellville under secret orders from the Governor, and with him went twenty men. Five enlisted men accompanied Browder to Logan County. Later the sheriff spirited Browder out of jail again, to take him back to Louisville, and subsequently he attempted to bring Browder back to Russellville secretly. Fearing violence, Captain Carrell detailed ten men to meet the train at Bowling Green, and fifteen others to prevent any demonstration at the Russellville station, where a great crowd had formed. There was no trouble, and the prisoner was tried and sentenced to be hanged. He was later pardoned by the Governor. The troops under Captain Carrell were ordered home August 14.

State Guard detachments during this year saw duty because of night-rider violence, in Bath, Bracken, Caldwell, Calloway, Christian, Clark, Crittenden, Fayette, Fleming, Fulton, Harrison, Logan, Lyon, McCracken, Marion, Marshall, Mason, Muhlenberg, Montgomery, Todd, Trigg, Shelby, and Woodford counties. In some of these mounted infantry patrols were established.[27] Brig. Gen. Roger D. Williams was in charge of all troop duty in the "Dark Leaf" area.[28]

Twenty picked men of the 1st Regiment were sent to Fort Benjamin Harrison, Indiana, in September, 1908, to participate in a camp of instructions and maneuvers that was conducted there starting September 21, under orders of the U.S. War Department.

On the occasion of the Lincoln Centennial ceremonies on February 12, 1909, Capt. W. R. Caperton was ordered to take a detail of "at least forty men and two commissioned officers to Hodgenville to act as an escort to the President of the United States."[29] When President Taft again visited Hickman on the twenty-sixth of October, Capt. C. G. Henderson, with a squad of eighteen men from Company K, 3d Regiment, was detailed there on police duty.[30] Other police duty during the year was rendered at the Benson Station Quarry, where convict labor was being used,[31] and night-rider activities in Grant and Mason were suppressed by the Guard during the fall.[32]

Several orders entered during 1909 portend the eventual transformation of the State Guard from a comparatively isolated state organization into a unit of the Federal system contemplated in the act of 1903. These orders show Kentucky bringing her troops up to the U.S. Army requirements by a sort of a precipitation process. Originally, a detail from the 1st Regiment was sent to Fort Benjamin Harrison for instruction; this detail was then used in the tutelage of the 1st Regiment, the officers of which eventually served as instructors of the 2d and 3d Regiments.

In 1910 schooling of the Guard was carried on intensively under the instructorship of Captain Charles D. Clay, U.S.A., retired, and Capt. W. N. Hughes, U.S.A., retired, assisted by Sergeants J. C. Barnes and Louis Dieckman of the U.S. Army. Through the combined efforts of these men and the state military department officials, the Kentucky troops were enabled to pass the United States inspection of 1910 and thereupon Kentucky became entitled to participate in the Federal grant established by the act of Congress in 1903.

On the night of the twenty-fifth of May an attempt was made at Hopkinsville to assassinate Milton Oliver, a witness for the commonwealth in prosecutions growing out of night-rider activities. Col. E. B. Bassett and a squad of six men of Company H, 3d Infantry, were detailed to guard Oliver and other state witnesses against violence. Later, Col. Bassett was ordered to escort Oliver to the state line when he might desire to leave the state. In September, when Oliver returned to Hopkinsville to testify a guard was reestablished under Col Bassett and was shortly afterward increased to protect both Oliver and his home.[33]

Police duty during court sessions and in guarding Government property at Somerset afforded active duty to relieve the monotony of intensive instruction during 1911.[34] In May, Captains J. H. Evans of the Medical Corps, Sidney Smith of the 1st Regiment, and C. R. Smith of the 3d Regiment, were ordered to San Antonio, Texas, to participate in a joint encampment of the Regular Army and the militia for maneuvers and field instruction.[35] At home an "Inter-State Rifle Competition" was held September 30 and October 1 at the Orell Rifle Range, Valley Station. The Kentucky team competed with others from Indiana and West Virginia State Guards.[36]

In calling detachments to Frankfort for the inauguration of Governor McCreary on December 12, 1911, the adjutant general was careful to specify that the guardsmen should come clad in "olive drab field service uniform, with cap, and overcoat." Units so called included Companies A and D, 2d Regiment, Companies I and L, 3d Regiment, and Company B, 1st Regiment. The Cadet companies of the State University (now the University of Kentucky) and Kentucky Military Institute, were included in the order.

In February, 1912, Gen. Roger D. Williams was sent to Salyersville to investigate a disturbance. In July, Capt. J. S. Cisco, with three officers and thirty-three men, was ordered to Magoffin County, after Lee Patrick, member of a prominent family, had been killed. Augustus Arnett, of another influential family, was accused of the murder of Patrick. Ramifications of the case involved a considerable number of persons in the county.[37]

Kentucky participated in a State Guard encampment at Anniston, Alabama, during July, 1912, in which troops from several of the southeastern states took part. Governor McCreary, on July 24 ordered Col. J. Tandy Ellis to attend the encampment for the purpose of observing and inspecting the Kentucky Brigade. These annual encampments differed widely from the old regimental musters, yet, with their strict discipline, they were still looked upon as a holiday by the guardsmen. However, the Federal control and discipline exercised over the State Guard, and the instruction received by it prepared the way for the more strict discipline that came when the Kentucky troops were mustered into Federal service a few years later.

Col. J. Tandy Ellis was ordered to Pineville in December, 1914, to investigate the necessity for sending troops to capture John Hendrickson and others charged with murder.

Upon receipt of Colonel Ellis' report, Capt. G. C. Bailey, with Company I, 1st Infantry, was ordered to Bell County to assist civil authorities in the apprehension of the accused men.[38]

All officers of the Medical Corps of the State Guard were ordered to attend a camp of instruction from June 7 to 12, 1915, held at Fort Oglethorpe, Georgia. A similar order sent the Medical Corps and the 1st Field Hospital Company to McClay Station, Sparta, Wisconsin, for instruction from the second to the tenth of August.[39]

In 1916, an act of Congress defined the Army of the United States as the Regular Army, the Volunteer Army, the Officers Reserve Corps, the Enlisted Reserve Corps, the National Guard of the several states, while in the service of the United States, and any other land forces that might be organized.

The Hay-Chamberlain Army Reorganization Bill provided for a maximum of 800 enlisted men in the National Guard for each Congressional representative. Under this law, organizations of the State Guard could not disband without the consent of the President. Reorganization under the latter law was begun shortly before Kentucky troops were ordered out for Mexican border duty.

Raids by Mexicans into Texas during the spring of 1916 brought a Federal call for troops for police duty along the border. The Kentucky Brigade was mobilized at Fort Thomas, on June 25, 1916, under orders of Adjt. Gen. J. Tandy Ellis, after a call for the services of the Kentucky troops had been received from the U.S. Secretary of War by Gov. A. O. Stanley. The brigade was under command of Gen. Roger D. Williams, and consisted of the 1st Regiment under Col. William A. Colston; the 2d Regiment under Col. J. Embry Allen, and the 3d Regiment under Col. Jouett Henry. Shortly after the concentration at Fort Thomas, Governor Stanley commissioned Capt. Allen Gullion lieutenant colonel of the 2d Regiment and, upon the resignation (soon after) of Colonel Allen, he was succeeded by Lieutenant Colonel Gullion *(see p. 337)*.

The Kentucky Brigade trained at Fort Thomas until August and then moved to Fort Bliss, near El Paso, Texas. A camp for the Kentucky contingent was established about two miles from Fort Bliss and named Camp Owen Bierne. The name of the camp was fixed as a tribute to Sgt. Owen Bierne of the U.S. Army who had been killed by a Texas Ranger. The Kentucky Regiments were attached to the 10th U.S. Provisional Division under Brig. Gen. Charles G. Morton. Kentucky troops were used to patrol a sixty-mile stretch of the border along the Rio Grande to Fort Hancock. In February, 1917, the Kentucky Brigade was ordered back to Fort Thomas and was mustered out of the United States service and returned to home stations.

NOTES, REFERENCES, AND SOURCES

1. Adjutant General's Special Order of 1900, No. 10.
2. *Ibid.*, of 1900, No. 13.
3. *Ibid.*, No. 14.
4. Constitution of 1891, Sec. 36.
5. *Louisville Dispatch*, January 30, 1900.
6. *Executive Journal, 1899-1901*, Letter of May 21, 1900.
7. Adjutant General's Special Orders of 1901, No. 7 (Beckham Administration).
8. *Ibid.*, No. 75.
9. *Ibid.*, No. 79-80.
10. *Ibid.*, No. 84.
11. Adjutant General's Special Orders of 1902, No. 3.
12. *Ibid.*, No. 47.
13. *Ibid.*, No. 34.
14. *Ibid.*, Nos. 65, 72.
15. *Ibid.*, No. 83.
16. *Ibid.*, Nos. 29, 53, 70, 76, 77, 80, 81, 83.
17. Adjutant General's Orders of 1903, No. 7.
18. Executive Order of August 22, 1904.
19. Adjutant General's Orders of 1905, Nos. 23, 29.
20. *Ibid.*, No. 60.
21. Adjutant General's Special Orders of 1906, No. 2.
22. Executive Order of July 29, 1906.
23. Adjutant General's Special Orders of 1906, No. 43.
24. *Ibid.*, No. 47.
25. Adjutant General's Special Orders of 1907, Nos. 39½, 41, 42.
26. Adjutant General's Special Orders of 1908, No. 11.
27. *Ibid.*, No. 46.
28. *Ibid.*, No. 44.
29. Adjutant General's Special Orders of 1909, No. 14.

30. *Ibid.*, No. 126.
31. *Ibid.*, No. 45.
32. *Ibid.*, Nos. 124, 135.
33. Adjutant General's Special Orders of 1910, Nos. 70, 73, 125, 132.
34. Adjutant General's Special Orders of 1911, Nos. 32, 37, 77, 80, 155, 177.
35. *Ibid.*, No. 70.
36. *Ibid.*, No. 159.
37. Adjutant General's Special Orders of 1912, No. 125.
38. Adjutant General's Special Orders of 1914, No. 152.
39. *Ibid.*, Nos. 77, 89.

CHAPTER IX

WORLD WAR

The approaching entrance of the United States as a belligerent in the World War brought about much military activity in Kentucky during the early part of April, 1917. Adjt. Gen. J. Tandy Ellis came home from New York and reported that at a meeting of the National Guard Association the delegates had heartily favored federalization of all State Guards. Recruiting was rapidly bringing the Kentucky State Guard up to its maximum peacetime strength, and by the tenth of April permission had been obtained for further recruiting to war strength. On the twelfth of April, Federal military officials were engaged in selecting two mobilization camp sites for the Kentucky Guard. At the same time the state military authorities were puzzling over a Federal order. The Government had instructed all states to bring their Guard units up to full strength, in Kentucky's case 10,000 men. Kentucky had less than 3,000 guardsmen, and a special session of the legislature, called by Governor Stanley, would have been necessary to secure funds to pay the additional men. The U.S. Government did not assume the obligation of paying these additional guardsmen, although Federal officers were preparing to mobilize 10,000 Kentucky troops.

While these problems occupied the Kentucky military staff officers, field officers and men were detailed to guard duty within the state. Under Special Order No. 36 of March 31, 1917, Companies C, F, K, and L, of the 2d Regiment, were detailed to active duty. Captain Staples, with Company C, was sent to Covington to report to the county judges of Kenton and Campbell counties, to guard the property of the Chesapeake and Ohio Railroad Company there, including the shops at Covington, where five sentry posts were established and maintained. At the bridge spanning the Licking River, three sentry posts were maintained and other posts were established when deemed necessary.

Captain Short, with Company F, was sent to Lexington to report to the county judge of Fayette County, and to At the Netherland shops, one mile east of Lexington, three guard the interests of the C. & O. R.R. Company there. sentry posts were established and maintained; at Sinking Creek Tunnel, one mile east of Fultz, two sentry posts were set up; at the Needle's Eye Tunnel, near Aden, thirty-three miles west of Ashland, were two sentry posts; at the Triplett Tunnel, one mile west of Soldier and fifty miles west of Ashland, two sentry posts were established.

Major Poage, with Company K, was sent to Ashland to report to the county judge of Boyd County. Company K was detailed to guard the C.&O.R.R. Bridge, one mile east of Catlettsburg, where four sentry posts were established. Other sentry posts were maintained at Ashland Tunnel, one mile west of Ashland; at Easthaus Tunnel, one mile east of Princess; and at Williams Creek Tunnel, nineteen miles west of Ashland.

Captain Lusse with his company was ordered to report to the county judge of Franklin County. After a conference with the county judge and state military officers, boundaries were prescribed within which no person could enter without a pass signed by a designated authority. Sentry posts were established and maintained within the restricted zone.

On the third of April companies A, B, D, E, F, G, H, I, and M, 2d Infantry, and Companies B, C, E, H, I, and K, of the 3d Infantry, were ordered out for guard duty in the state. Captain Dillion with Company A, 2d Infantry, was stationed at Falmouth and placed under orders of the Pendleton County judge. Captain Dillion's guard sector included all points on the Louisville & Nashville Railroad lines in Pendleton County, beginning with the Bank Lick Bridge, the city of Falmouth, the two Grant Tunnels, the Cruiser Creek Bridge, and the Licking River Bridge at Falmouth.

Sentry posts at these points were immediately established and maintained.

Capt. James V. Gross, with Company B, 2d Infantry, was stationed at Livingston and established outposts at the L.&N. Railroad bridges and tunnels in the vicinity. These included the bridges over Round Stone Creek, the Kentucky River Bridge at Ford, the Evans Branch Viaduct, the Houston Creek Bridge at Paris, the Townsend Creek Bridge, the Licking River bridges near Cynthiana, and the tunnel near Berry.

Company D, 2d Infantry, under Capt. George W. Jenkins, established headquarters at Corbin from which point outposts were established for this company at the Rockcastle River Bridge, Laurel River Viaduct, Lynn Camp Creek Bridge, Watts Creek Bridge, Cumberland River Bridge, and Clear Creek bridges, Nos. 1, 2, and 3.

Capt. William M. Phipps with Company E, 2d Infantry, was ordered to proceed to Jackson to establish sentry posts at Dumont Tunnel near Quicksand, at the bridges over the North Fork, and at the Line and Campbell tunnels. Headquarters were established at Dumont Tunnel.

At Irvine, Capt. W. S. Taylor established headquarters for Company G, 2d Infantry, which was detailed to guard the L.&N. Railroad interests between Winchester and Irvine. Outposts were established at the Calloway Creek Viaduct, the Woodards Creek Viaduct, at the Red River Bridge, and at the viaducts over Howard Creek and Dry Fork.

Company H, 2d Infantry, under command of First Lt. Ashby D. Debusk, was ordered to report to the judge of Bell County and to establish guard posts in the vicinity of Middlesboro. Sentry posts were maintained by this company at Cumberland Gap, Patterson Creek, and Bradford Gap tunnels; at other tunnels in the vicinity and also at the bridges over the Cumberland River and Richland Creek.

Hazard was made the headquarters of Company I, 2d Infantry, under Capt. Isaac Wilder, who established outposts in Perry County at the bridges over the North Fork of the Kentucky River, and at the Hazard Tunnel.

In Lee County the bridges at Maloney and over the Middle Fork near Tallega, together with the Tyler, Mud, and Chenowee tunnels, were guarded by Company M, 2d Infantry, under First Lt. H. B. Jones.

Capt. Charles F. Thomasson, with Company C, 3d Infantry, was detailed to guard duty in McCracken County. Headquarters were established at Paducah and sentry and cossack posts were maintained at the Paducah shops of the Nashville, Chattanooga and St. Louis Railroad Company, and at the Illinois Central Railroad Company shops. Other outposts were maintained by this company at the Clark's River and Island Creek bridges.

Guard duty in Carlisle and Hickman counties was assigned to Company F, 3d Infantry, under Capt. Arthur L. Donan. Headquarters were established at Wickliffe, and cossack and sentry posts were maintained at all of the Mobile and Ohio Railroad Company bridges and trestles in these two counties.

Company E, 3d Infantry, under Capt. James D. Sory, Jr., was sent to Lyon County where headquarters were established at Madisonville. This company established and maintained guard posts at the Tennessee River Bridge near Gilbertsville and at the Cumberland River Bridge near Grand Rivers.

The Illinois Central Railroad Company property in Ohio County was placed under the guardianship of Company K, 3d Infantry, commanded by Capt. Ben M. King, with headquarters established at Rockport. Outposts were ordered to be established at the Green River Bridge at Rockport, and at the Echols Tunnel. Further duty was assigned from time to time by the regimental commander.

Under command of Capt. Terry A. Humble, Company I, 3d Infantry, was detailed to Grayson County to establish guard outposts for the protection of the Illinois Central Railroad Company property in that county. These posts were maintained at Rosine Tunnel, at Keyser Tunnel near

Leitchfield, and at the Big Clifty Viaduct north of Grayson Springs.

The bridge over Salt River at West Point, the two viaducts at Tioga, and the Muldraugh Tunnel, south of West Point, were placed under guard of Company H, 3d Infantry, commanded by Capt. Clarence B. Shown. Other transitory guard duties were assigned to this unit at various times by the Bullitt County judge after conference with Illinois Central Railroad Company officials.

Railroad property in Todd and Christian counties was likewise protected by the establishment of sentry and cossack posts at vulnerable points. Company B, 3d Infantry, under Capt. Harley Higginson, established headquarters at Kelly, and outposts at the Elkhorn Viaduct near Allensville, and at the Green Lick Viaduct north of Kelly.

At the same time the following named officers and enlisted men of the 2d Regiment were ordered into active service: Lt. Col. Frank L. Ripy was stationed at Paris, Maj. Charles W. Longmire at Winchester, First Lt. John B. Terry at Paris, First Lt. John W. Rodman at Winchester, Regimental Sgt. Maj. R. E. Adams at Lexington, Band Leader John P. Edwards at Hazard, and First Sgt. Charles R. George at Hazard. The men so detailed were given instructions as to their duties by their regimental commanders upon reporting at designated stations.*[1]

On April 5, 1917, several assignments to active duty were made from the 3d Infantry. Maj. Talbott Berry was sent to Leitchfield, Maj. H. W. Rogers to Paducah, and Regimental Sgt. W. T. Radford to Hopkinsville. These assignments were made for the purpose of completing the cordon of sentry posts in the western section of the state

In accordance with the call of the President of the United States transmitted through the Secretary of War to the Governor of Kentucky, dated April 12, 1917, all units of the

---

* Notes, references, and sources are indicated by numerals. These refer to corresponding numbers at the end of this chapter. Notes on Chapter IX are on page 343.

Kentucky National Guard were placed in the service of the United States, effective on and after April 13, 1917.

These troops were called into the Federal service in view of the necessity of affording a more perfect protection against possible interference with commercial and military channels and instrumentalities of the United States in the state of Kentucky. Units then on guard duty, pursuant to state military orders, remained thereon. The initial muster by Federal authorities was made at field stations. Those units that were not in the field under state orders assembled in their armories at their respective home stations, pending orders from the District Commander.[2]

The Kentucky Guard was ordered, on April 17, 1917, to begin mobilization at Camp Stanley, about three miles out of Lexington, on the Versailles Pike. At the same time Gen. Roger D. Williams ordered squads of guardsmen to engage in a state-wide campaign to obtain recruits.

On April 20, 1917, the War Department ordered married men and those who had dependents, to be mustered out of the State Guard. Mustering out of these men took place at Camp Stanley. Vacancies so caused were speedily filled by recruiting.

On April 20, Col. Jouett Henry, commander of the 3d Regiment, with the machine gun company of the regiment, from Henderson, arrived at the mobilization camp site near Lexington. Seven other companies of same regiment arrived the next day. Formal muster-in began on the morning of the twenty-first, and 125 men of the 2d Regiment, were discharged because of dependent families. On May 8, seventy-two men were mustered out of the 1st Regiment for the same reason.[3]

The headquarters and camp of the 2d Regiment were moved from Lexington to Winchester, Sunday, April 29, due to redistricting of state by the War Department.[4]

On May 19 telegraphic orders from Major General Barry, commander of the Central Department of the U.S. Army, ordered Col. Wm. A. Colston, 1st Regiment, to bring up his regiment to full war strength of 2,002 men. This was accomplished on the seventh of June.[5] Other regiments of the state received like orders and on June 19, information was received that a fourth regiment would be formed.

On the seventh of July, Companies A, B, C, and D, the 1st Battalion of the 1st Regiment, were suddenly ordered to a camp under construction on Preston Street Road, near Louisville, for guard duty, and by six o'clock that evening they were established there with full equipment. On July 9 word came of a Presidential proclamation drafting state troops of all states into service to be effective on the fifth of August. Word came on the thirteenth of July that the Kentucky troops would receive final preparation for service in France at Camp Shelby, Hattiesburg, Mississippi, and were to proceed to that camp on the fifth of August.

In a ceremony witnessed by 2,000 people on Sunday, July 23, the old Louisville Legion presented the drum and trumpet, used by it in the War with Spain, to the 1st Regiment. The next day the Belgian War Mission, in Louisville to inspect the building of Camp Taylor, reviewed the 1st Regiment. During the week of the twenty-fourth of July an extensive drive by 1st and 2d Regiments was begun to recruit to full war strength. The 1st Regiment was short 74 men, and the 2d was short 203, due to transfers and discharges. On July 27 all Kentucky National Guard Reservists were called into service with orders to report on the fifth of August.

On July 23, the adjutant general had issued the following general order:

1. All reservists of the National Guard of Kentucky will be drafted into the Federal service in accordance with the Proclamation of the President of the United States, dated July 3, 1917. When the men were furloughed to the Reserve their status as members of the units of the National Guard ceased, and they will report as privates, unassigned, located at the place shown on the transportation request as the destination of the reservists.

2. They will not be assigned to units until mustered by an Officer of the Regular Army and will then be assigned under orders from the Department Commander.

3. Each man will report with his uniform and all government property of every description which may be in his possession, and

will so arrange his departure from his home station as to arrive at the Camp on the morning of August 5, 1917.

4. The transportation request consists of 2 parts, original and memorandum. Both copies will be completed by the reservist, showing place, date and signature of reservist; original (blue) copy will be given to the railroad ticket agent in exchange for a railroad ticket; memorandum (white) copy will be mailed immediately to the Property and Disbursing Officer at Frankfort, Kentucky, in the return envelope inclosed for that purpose.

5. The receipt of this order and transportation will be acknowledged immediately by the reservist, by letter, to the Adjutant General of Kentucky, Frankfort, Kentucky.

6. The descriptive cards of the men will be sent to the Commanding Officer of the Camp by the Adjutant General of the State.

7. The travel directed is necessary in the military service.[6]

Brig. Gen. Roger D. Williams, commander of the Kentucky Brigade, was ordered on August 20, to assume command of the 63d Brigade, 28th Division, U.S. Army, and to report for duty at Camp Shelby, on August 25. Jouett Henry, senior colonel of the brigade, was placed in command of the Kentucky Brigade temporarily, pending the appointment of Gen. Williams' successor. Gen. Williams with Company C of the 2d Regiment, and Company A of the 3d Regiment, arrived at Camp Shelby, on August 22. A farewell parade by the 1st Regiment, redesignated as the 159th Infantry, was held the afternoon of Friday, August 24, 1917. On the ninth of August a vote was taken among officers of the 159th Infantry and resulted in changing the regiment from infantry to artillery. It was then assigned, as an artillery regiment, to the 63d Field Artillery Brigade of the 38th Division, and became officially known as the 138th Field Artillery.

Col. Jouett Henry, commanding officer of the Kentucky troops at Camp Stanley, Lexington, received orders directing the movement of 4,000 soldiers, the 2d and 3d Regiments, to Camp Shelby, as soon after September 24, as possible, and four days later the 3d Regiment arrived at that camp. By October 9 the entire Kentucky contingent had arrived there. The 2d Regiment (now the 149th Infantry) was isolated from the rest of the camp because of epidemics of meningitis, mumps, and measles.[7]

The 1st Regiment of Infantry became the 138th U.S.

Field Artillery. The 2d Regiment of Infantry became the 149th U.S. Infantry. The 3d Regiment of Infantry was transferred partly to the 149th Infantry and partly to the 137th and 138th U.S. Machine Gun Battalions.

The 38th U.S. Division was organized in August, 1917, at Camp Shelby, Mississippi, from National Guard troops of Kentucky, West Virginia, and Indiana. This division, commanded by Maj. Gen. R. L. Houze, was designated for replacements, and in May, 1918, only the official skelton of the division continued at Camp Shelby. The men of the ranks were sent overseas and were replaced by draftees from Illinois and Arkansas. In June another replacement contingent was sent overseas from Camp Shelby, and later, still others; each time they were replaced by draftees. In September, 1918, the 38th Division went overseas as a unit. Upon arrival in France the division was sent to the LeMans area, where it was continued as a replacement division. The personnel of most of the units had been withdrawn and sent to other organizations, leaving the division skeletonized. This division remained in the LeMans area until its return to the United States in December, 1918.

Under the provision of General Order No. 95, U.S. War Department, of July 15, 1917, cantonments in the various states were designated for troops. The cantonment at Louisville was named Camp Taylor in honor of Maj. Gen. (President) Zachary Taylor and was placed under command of Maj. Gen. H. C. Hale. Here at Camp Taylor the 84th U.S. Division was organized in August, 1917, from drafted men of Kentucky, Indiana, and southern Illinois. The division was depleted to fill up other organizations. When it changed station to Camp Sherman, Ohio, in June, 1918, it was again raised to authorized strength, the greater part of the recruits coming from Ohio.

The first element of the 84th U.S. Division arrived in France September 21, 1918; the last October 25, 1918. The division (less artillery) was sent to the West Perigeux area near Bordeaux with headquarters established at Nenoic on September 28, 1918. The artillery brigade was sent to

Camp de Souge. In October the 139th U.S. Engineers was transferred to St. Nazaire for construction work. The remainder of the division was broken up to provide replacements for combat units at the front, and early in November headquarters and the permanent cadre of organization was transferred to LeMans. The division returned to the United States in January, 1919.

Kentucky troops soon lost their state organization identity, having been merged with other troops in various divisions, chief of which were the 1st, 2d, 3d, 4th, and 42d U.S. Divisions. This latter unit, known as the Rainbow Division, was composed of the Guardsmen from Kentucky and twenty-five other states.

Activities of the Kentucky troops are contained in brief in General Pershing's report to the Secretary of War. At Marshal Foch's request the 1st U.S. Division was transferred from the Toul sector to Chaumont on Vexin and shortly after, on April 26, 1918, this division went into the line on the Picardy battlefront. The 2d Division, having been held in reserve near Montdidier, was sent to check the progress of the Germans toward Paris. The Rainbow Division, in part, was in the line east of Rheims, where they held their position unflinchingly. The 3d Division held the bank of the Marne opposite Chateau Thierry. A single regiment of the 3d Division, the 38th Infantry, prevented the advance of the Germans. The Germans had gained a position which compelled this regiment to open fire in three directions, thereby repulsing the German troops, 600 of whom were taken prisoners. During July the 3d Division made its way into Roncheres Wood and was relieved. The Rainbow Division then captured Sergy, whereupon it was relieved. Kentucky soldiers fought in the front ranks in all of these engagements which terminated in the reduction of the Marne salient.

In August the American Army under General Pershing took over the battlefront from St. Mihiel to Verdun. On September 12 an attack was begun by the seven American divisions which terminated in repulsing the salient commanded by the German Crown Prince. Thereupon the Americans turned toward Metz and Sedan. In the Battle of St. Mihiel the 2d, 3d, and 42d divisions, played a leading part, the 1st division having been held in reserve. At the time of the armistice, Kentucky soldiers, as always, were in the advance of the American Army toward the Sedan.

During the war, Student Army Training Corps in Kentucky were established and maintained in the following schools: Berea, Bethel, Centre, Georgetown, Kentucky Wesleyan, Ogden, and Transylvania colleges; corps. were also maintained at the Universities of Louisville and of Kentucky and at the Eastern and Western Kentucky State Normal Schools (now designated as Teacher's colleges).

Among the Kentuckians who attained distinction in France were five who attained the rank of major general. These included Maj. Gen. Henry T. Allen of Bath County who commanded the 80th Division. He was the general commanding the Army of Occupation in Germany. General Allen took over command when General Pershing returned to the United States. Maj. Gen. Hugh L. Scott, a native of Danville, was chief of staff (1914–17), and commander of the 78th Division. Maj. Gen. William L. Sibert of Bowling Green, was director of America's Chemical Warfare. From Winchester came Maj. Gen. Frank Long Winn, and Maj. Gen. George B. Duncan of Lexington was in command of the 82d Division.[8]

Those Kentuckians who attained the rank of brigadier general were Preston Brown, Logan Feland, Adrian S. Fleming, W. O. Johnson, N. P. McClure, Cyrus Radford, J. T. Thompson, Roger D. Williams, John S. Winn, and George C. Saffarans. Twenty-three Kentuckians attained the rank of colonel; they were E. B. Bassett, D. Y. Beckham, John Chambers, W. A. Colston, Joseph Garrard, J. T. Geary, Allen Gullion (now Major General and Judge Advocate General of the U.S. Army), H. L. Hawthorne, Jouett Henry, Woodson Hocker, F. C. Kelland, George Liberoff, J. P. McAdams, John Montgomery, V. L. Peterson, Charles H. Morror, J. R. Proctor, Evan Shelby, H. K. Taylor, Francis McUsher,

Charles D. Winn, H. S. Wygant, Scott Dudley, and Charles Young.

In aviation distinguished services were performed by Maj. Victor Strohm and Lt. J. O. Creech. Howard Kinne, who received a commission as an artillery officer at Fort Benjamin Harrison, was assigned to aviation. He served in France with the 99th U.S. Aerial Squadron, and was one of the first American aviators killed in the war. Richard C. Saufley, naval aviation officer, was killed near Pensacola, Florida, while on duty during the war. Lt. Keeling Pulliam of Lexington was killed accidentally while an aviation student in California.

More than 300 Kentuckians won special honors in the World War, and two of them were awarded the Congressional Medal of Honor. This decoration is awarded only by Congress, on recommendation of the Commanding General. It is the highest honor an American soldier can receive for personal bravery, and is bestowed only in cases of outstanding gallantry and bravery above and beyond the line of duty. Out of the few Medals of Honor awarded by Congress during the World War, two were bestowed on Kentuckians, Capt. Samuel Woodfill and Sgt. Willie Sandlin. When General Pershing was requested, in the summer of 1919, to name 100 men of the U.S. Army whose acts of gallantry were typical of the fighting spirit of the American forces, he selected Capt. Samuel Woodfill, Fort Thomas, Kentucky, as one of that number. Woodfill's ancestors were Revolutionary soldiers and members of the Lewis and Clark expedition. Captain Woodfill spent all of his adult life in the army, serving in the Far West, Alaska and the Philippines, on the Mexican border, and in Europe.

The character of the service rendered in France by Captain Woodfill was extraordinary in its nature. During the Meuse-Argonne offensive he captured several machine guns and killed nineteen Germans while commanding his company. It was while he was first lieutenant of Company M, 60th Infantry, 5th Division, and in the Meuse-Argonne offensive, on October 12, 1918, that Lieutenant Woodfill so singly distinguished himself.

The story of the splendid fight for which he was awarded the Medal of Honor is told in the official citation as follows:

> By direction of the President under the provision of the Act of Congress approved July 9, 1918, the Medal of Honor has been awarded, in the name of Congress, to the following named officer for the act of gallantry set after his name. Following is General Pershing's cabled recommendation, which has been approved. First Lieutenant Samuel Woodfill, 60th Infantry. For conspicuous gallantry and intrepidity above and beyond the call of duty in action with the enemy at Cunel, France, October 12, 1918. While Lieutenant Woodfill was leading his company against the enemy his line came under heavy machine gun fire, which threatened to hold up the advance. Followed by two soldiers at twenty-five yards this officer went out ahead of his first line toward a machine gun nest and worked his way around its flank, leaving the two soldiers in front.
>
> When he got within ten yards of the gun it ceased firing and four of the enemy appeared, three of whom were shot by Lieutenant Woodfill. The fourth, an officer, rushed at Lieutenant Woodfill, who attempted to club the officer with his rifle. After a hand-to-hand struggle Lieutenant Woodfill killed the officer with his pistol. His company thereupon continued to advance until shortly afterwards another machine gun nest was encountered. Calling on his men to follow, Lieutenant Woodfill rushed ahead of his line in the face of heavy fire from the nest, and when several of the enemy appeared above the nest he shot them, capturing three other members of the crew and silencing the guns. A few minutes later this officer, for the third time, demonstrated conspicuous daring by charging another machine gun position, killing five men in one machine gun pit with his rifle. He then drew his revolver and started to jump into the pit when two other gunners only a few yards away turned their guns on him. Failing to kill them with his revolver, he grabbed a pick lying nearby and killed both of them. Inspired by the exceptional courage displayed by this officer, his men pressed on to their objective under severe shell and machine gun fire.

Captain Woodfill came through this thrilling experience unharmed, except that he suffered a slight shrapnel wound and was gassed.

For his services during the World War Captain Woodfill was awarded, besides the Congressional Medal of Honor, the Cross of the Legion of Honor, the Crois de Guerre, and other decorations from Belgium, Italy, and Montenegro.

In addition to these evidences of his intrepidity in action, he has many citations from his superior regimental officers.

Sgt. Willie Sandlin was another of the conspicuous heroes of the World War. Born near Buckhorn on January 1, 1891, he had the misfortune to lose his mother while he was a very small boy. He grew to manhood with few advantages. At an early age he enlisted in the Regular Army. The hardships of youth had taught him the lesson of taking care of himself. Straight as an arrow, with keen, alert, but steady black eyes, black hair, powerfully muscular, but not of heavy build, he was a splendid type of the sturdy men who come from the Kentucky mountain counties. He was not assertive, but almost timid.

During the summer of 1918, Sergeant Sandlin passed through several engagements, but it was at Bois des Forges, France, on September 26, 1918, that the supreme test came and was met with a splendid showing of courage and self-reliance seldom equalled in the annals of warfare. He was at that time with Company A, 132d Infantry. His line was ordered to advance to a certain objective. The advance was vitally important. Just as the line started it was held up by a withering fire from carefully placed German machine gun nests, two guns to each nest.

Sandlin noticed that there was a narrow lane between the zone of fire of the two guns in the nest in front of his part of the line. Securing a full supply of hand grenades, he charged the nests single-handed. Advancing within seventy-five yards of the guns, he threw his first grenade, which fell short and exploded without effect. He ran about thirty yards nearer the nest and threw the second grenade, which struck the nest. After throwing two more grenades, he charged the nest. Finding two of the gunners unhurt, he bayoneted them. In this charge the two Germans emptied their automatic revolvers at him. He accounted for a total of eight Germans in that nest.

Thereupon, his part of the line advanced, and the other German machine gun nests were quickly flanked. The second line German machine guns were hurriedly reached and again Sergeant Sandlin did almost the same thing in the same way, killing the men in that nest with grenade and bayonet. He at once advanced on a third machine gun nest with grenade, automatic and bayonet. The American line then went through to its objective. It is known that Sandlin accounted for twenty-four Germans that day. He was in the thick of the fighting throughout with grenade, rifle, and automatic.

Sergeant Sandlin's remarkable feats of arms were of exceptional military importance, since they were the means of letting this line through to the day's objective. Sergeant Sandlin voluntarily and deliberately ran into the jaws of death, into dangers so great that he could hardly hope to come out with his life. His quickness, his coolness, his unerring aim, enabled him to accomplish what he set out to do.

General Pershing's official recommendation of Sergeant Sandlin is as follows:

Sgt. Willie Sandlin, Company A, 132d Infantry (A.S. No. 278103). For conspicuous galantry and intrepidity above and beyond the call of duty with the enemy at Bois de Forges, France, September 26, 1918. Sergeant Sandlin showed conspicuous gallantry in action at Bois des Forges, France, on September 26, 1918, by advancing alone directly on a machine gun nest which was holding up his line with its fire. He killed the crew with a grenade and enabled the line to advance. Later in the day Sergeant Sandlin attacked alone and put out of action two other machine gun nests, setting a splendid example of bravery and coolness to his men.

By direction of the President, under the provisions of an Act of Congress, approved July 9, 1918, Sergeant Sandlin was awarded the Congressional Medal of Honor.

Kentucky claims Breathitt as the only county in the Nation that did not draft a single man. The first American soldier killed in action in France after America went into the war was Corp. James B. Gresham of McLean County. The most wounded American is said to have been Sgt. Samuel Joseph, of Hazard, who received 102 injuries.

During the war the ranking United States naval officer from Kentucky was Rear Admiral Hugh Rodman, of Frankfort, who was in command of the American fleet when the German naval command in the North Sea surrendered.

Kentucky's participation in the World War is best shown by the records of the U.S. War Department. A total of 84,172 persons, officers and men from Kentucky, served in the U.S. Army, of whom 12,584 were Negroes. This total includes 80,000 enlisted men, 3,747 commissioned officers, 241 nurses, 153 army field clerks and 22 U.S. Military Cadets. A breakdown of these figures shows 12,759 men in the Regular Army, 7,518 Kentucky Guardsmen, 2,526 from the Reserve Corps, 2,734 volunteers, and 58,635 drafted men. Of these 41,655 were on overseas duty. While in the service 2,418 deaths occurred among Kentucky troops, of which 890 were killed in battle.

To the end that Kentucky's World War history would be recorded accurately, the Kentucky Council of Defense inaugurated a state-wide movement in 1918, while war was still raging, to preserve military service records and the activities of the civilians in all branches of war work. A local war historian was appointed in each of the counties of the state, and a state war historian was appointed to supervise the work. The plan adopted contemplated a record for each county of purely local activities, and the collection, in the central state office, of material of state-wide interest.

In many of the counties the local war historians completed this work, had the material bound in substantial form, and placed in the office of the clerk of the county court. These surveys contain a complete statement of the service of each soldier, sailor, marine, and nurse, from the county, and a report of the work done by the civilians, including the County Council of Defense, Local Draft Board, Red Cross, Liberty Loan Committees, and all other organizations which helped win the war. Many records contain photographs and letters of the service men, especially those who died in service.

In March, 1920, the Kentucky Legislature continued the existence of the Council of Defense until March, 1922, for the sole purpose of completing the war history work. The

Governor appointed as members of the new council, Edward H. Hines, of Louisville, as chairman, and Young E. Allison, of Louisville, as state historian. The collection of World War records of Kentucky soldiers has been completed and is available to the public in the office of the Adjutant General of Kentucky at Frankfort, where records of Kentucky soldiers in all the wars of the Nation, in which Kentucky participated, are preserved.

NOTES, REFERENCES, AND SOURCES

1. Adjutant General's Special Orders of 1917, No. 38.
2. Adjutant General's General Orders of 1917, No. 4.
3. *Courier-Journal* (Louisville), April 21 and May 8, 1917.
4. *Ibid.*, April 27, 1917.
5. *Ibid.*, June 5, 1917.
6. Adjutant General's General Orders of 1917, No. 7.
7. *Courier-Journal* (Louisville), September 24 and October 9, 1917.
8. *Kentucky Progress Magazine*, November, 1930.
9. *Loc. cit.*

CHAPTER X

KENTUCKY NATIONAL GUARD ORGANIZATION

From the close of the World War until the summer of 1920 military activity in the state was confined mostly to police duties; the protection of prisoners and the preservation of peace was the extent of this activity.

Kentucky military history, since the War with Spain, has gradually become more closely merged with that of the U.S. Army, and especially so since the World War with its heavy casualties to American troops that were attributed to insufficient training and organization. In consequence of this obvious defect in the American Army a revision of the United States military law was made in 1920 through the passage of the National Defense Act which states that: "The army of the United States shall consist of the Regular Army, the National Guard of the United States, the National Guard while in the service of the United States, the Officers' Reserve Corps * * * and the Enlisted Reserve Corps." *[1] Under this act it became the duty of the War Department General Staff to prepare plans for the national defense, and the use of the military forces for that purpose. Initial organization and territorial distribution was made under plans and supervision of the General Staff of the War Department by a committee composed of equal numbers of U.S. Army General Staff and National Guard officers. Policies and regulations affecting the organization and distribution of the National Guard of the United States and all policies and regulations affecting the training of the National Guard were, under the act, to be prepared by committees from appropriate divisions of the War Department. When any subject to be studied or dealt with affects the National

---

*Notes, references, and sources are indicated by numerals. These refer to corresponding numbers at the end of this chapter. Notes on Chapter X are on page 369.

Guard the committee involved consists of equal numbers from the Regular Army and the National Guard.[1A]

Under this act the National Guard of the several states and the Organized Reserves, along with the Regular Army, are trained for immediate participation in the event of a national emergency. In case of an emergency, participation would now be on the basis of approximately 40 per cent Regular Army and 60 per cent National Guard Troops. In 1938 the strength of the Regular Army was 12,838 officers and 165,000 enlisted men; of the National Guard, 14,236 officers, 207 warrant officers, and 182,745 enlisted men. In the Organized Reserves were approximately 2,000 men who receive a limited amount of instruction to keep them prepared for emergency service.[2] The law places the responsibility of training the National Guard and Organized Reserves upon the General Staff of the Regular Army.

The governing body of the National Guard of the United States is the National Guard Bureau. In 1938 this bureau was composed of thirty commissioned officers, five of whom were National Guard officers. A National Guard officer serves as chief of this bureau. His appointment is made by the President, subject to confirmation by the Senate. The 1938 incumbent of this office was Maj. Gen. Albert H. Blanding of Florida.

After the National Defense Act had been in operation a few years, its provisions were deemed inadequate to provide for the certainty of calling National Guard organizations into service. An amendment to the National Defense Act in 1923 created the National Guard of the United States, composed of the identical personnel of the National Guard of the several states, but with a Federal status. The amendment provides that the officers of the National Guard shall be commissioned and that General officers shall be appointed by the President and confirmed by the United States Senate. The National Guard of Kentucky occupies a dual status—one of Federal and one of state. It is subject to call under the provisions of both, the Federal and state laws and may be called either by the President of the United States or by the Governor of the state.

Under the National Defense Act and its amendment of June 15, 1923, "the states and territories have the right to determine and fix the location of the units and headquarters of the National Guard within their respective borders: Provided, that no organization of the National Guard, members of which shall be entitled to and shall have received compensation under the provisions of this Act, shall be disbanded without the consent of the President, nor, without such consent shall the commissioned or enlisted strength of any such organization be reduced below the minimum that shall be prescribed therefore by the President.[3] The Secretary of War is hereby authorized to procure * * * and to issue from time to time to the National Guard, upon requisition of the Governors of the several states and territories or the Commanding General of the National Guard of the District of Columbia, such number of United States service arms, with all accessories, Field Artillery material, Engineer, Coast Artillery, Signal and Sanitary material, accoutrements, field service, the National Guard in the several states, territories, and the District of Columbia: Provided, That as a condition precedent to the issue of any property as provided for by this Act, the State, Territory, or the District of Columbia desiring such issue 'shall make adequate provisions,' to the satisfaction of the Secretary of War, for the protection and care of such property."[4]

The responsibility for maintaining the National Guard rests on both Federal and state governments. The Federal Government must provide necessary arms, uniforms and equipment required by the National Guard and funds necessary for its training. The state is bound to carry out the training schedule set up by the Federal Government. The state must also provide "suitable shelter for personnel and suitable storage facilities for Federal property" issued by the War Department for the use of the National Guard. All funds and property must be accounted for in the manner prescribed by the Federal Government. "Whenever any State shall, within a limit of time to be fixed by the President, have failed or refused to comply with or enforce any requirement of this Act, or any regulation promulgated thereunder and in aid thereof by the President or the Secretary of War, the National Guard of such State shall be debarred, wholly or in part, as the President may direct, from receiving from the United States any pecuniary or other aid, benefit, or privilege authorized or provided by this Act or any other.''[5]

The National Guard of the United States, embracing the Guards of the several states, consists of eighteen infantry and four cavalry divisions. The strength and personnel of the Kentucky National Guard is given in *Appendix G*. The National Defense Act of 1920 and its amendment of 1923, together with the Kentucky military enactments of 1932, 1936, and 1938, established a positive and rigid military policy for the state.

In the organizational set-up of the Kentucky National Guard, several features of the World War military organization were retained. Kentucky continues to constitute a part of the 38th Division commanded by Maj. Gen. Robert Tyndall, Indiana. The 5th Corps Area of the U.S. Army is comprised of Kentucky, Indiana, Ohio, and West Virginia.

The Kentucky allotment of the 38th Division is the 138th Field Artillery Regiment, commanded by Col. Sidney Smith; the 149th Infantry Regiment, comanded by Col. Roy Easley, parts of the 113th Medical Regiment, parts of the 113th Quartermaster Regiment, and certain special Division troops, such as an Ordinance Company, Tank Company, and Military Police Company. Brig. Gen. Ellerbe W. Carter commands (1938) the 63d Field Artillery Brigade of which the 138th Field Artillery is a part. The Kentucky Allotment of the 75th Infantry Brigade (command vacant 1938) is the 149th Infantry Regiment.

The 22d Cavalry Division of the U.S. Army embraces Kentucky, Ohio, and Pennsylvania. The 123d Cavalry Regiment, Col. Henry J. Stites commanding (1938), constitutes the Kentucky allotment.

After the World War there was a brief interim of comparative internal peace and order during which few calls for troops were made. Among the early post-war calls was one from the State Penitentiary. On February 12, 1920, Capt. W. S. Taylor was ordered to take a detail of eight men to Eddyville to prevent any demonstration before or during the electrocution of Will Lockett, a Negro, who was convicted of murder committed under aggravated circumstances. In April, 1920, Captain Taylor, with eight men, was assigned to investigate the burning of a tobacco chute in Graves County. Company D, 2d Regiment, under command of its captain was ordered to Bracken County in May to preserve order during the Marksberry murder trial. A similar duty was performed in Washington County during July. In the same month the Governor ordered a detail of officers and fifty men to Pike County to quell a disturbance in the Tug River section. Cavalry Troop A and part of Troop B were ordered on active duty December 20, to escort Lee Elliston from the Jefferson County Jail to Madisonville where he was docketed on a murder charge.[6]

With the advent of spring in 1921, violence again visited the Tug River section of Pike County. Several details of troops were made and speedily restored peace. In June the Governor ordered troops to Barbourville after the sheriff and his deputies had resigned. Thirty men, under the adjutant general, were ordered to Mount Vernon, on August 20, to preserve the peace during the trial of one Bailey on a murder charge. In December violence in Knox County again required the presence of troops, and early in the same month twenty-five officers and men were sent to guard the Breathitt County Jail.

During the late fall of 1921 labor trouble at the Newport Rolling Mills resulted in a strike. Rioting and other forms of violence became so widespread that a request was made for a military guard. On December 23 the adjutant general was ordered by the Governor to send an adequate force to the scene.[7] The strike continued into 1922 with considerable resentment among the strikers, to the presence of the troops in Newport. On February 2 the Governor ordered an additional force on duty in Campbell County, the entire number not to exceed 500 men. Other strikes during the year necessitated military duty in both the eastern and western coal fields of the state.

At the Fort Knox encampment of the Kentucky National Guard in August, 1922, Col. F. W. Shaw, inspector of the 5th U.S. Corps Area, pronounced Kentucky's Cavalry as "the best looking unit in this National Guard area." Cavalry horses were equipped with white saddlecloths, yellow brow bands, and white halter ropes, all of which were made at the State Reformatory. With 20 out of every 100 men qualifying as marksmen and sharpshooters, Regular Army officers declared that the Kentucky Infantry could outshoot all other National Guard Infantry in the United States. Colonel Holbrook, of the Whitesburg Company, and Capt. Wiley Morris, of the Ordnance Department, carried off honors as Kentucky's best marksmen and thereby became entitled to participate in the national rifle match at Camp Perry, Ohio.

In the decade after 1922 the routine of drills, encampments, and police duty of various types, was broken by the detailing, February 4, 1925, of Capt. J. L. Topmiller with three officers and seven men of the Service Company, 149th Infantry, to Sand Cave to assist in the attempt to rescue Floyd Collins who was known to be imprisoned in the cavern. The rescue work continued until Collins was found dead at a considerable distance from the surface where he had been trapped by the fall of loose rock.

Governor Morrow, on October 3, 1923, ordered Capt. B. A. Radford to take three officers and twenty-five men of Troop C, 123d Cavalry, to Eddyville to assist Warden John Chilton of the State Penitentiary in restoring order in that prison. During the morning of that day three convicts, Monte Walters, Lawrence Griffith, and Harry Ferland, made a desperate effort to escape. Several persons were killed and the prison was in chaotic condition. The prisoners involved in the attempted break had barricaded themselves in the mess hall. Various plans were formulated to induce them to come out and surrender, but this they refused to do.

A detachment of Company L, 149th Infantry, ordered to reinforce the detail already on duty, arrived on Friday morning. That night the Board of Charities and Corrections met in the prison to consult with Warden Chilton. On Saturday efforts were renewed to dislodge the three men. In the afternoon five picked men entered the building and found the bodies of Ferland and Griffith. Ferland, lying on his back with a newspaper over his face, had two bullet holes through his heart. The body of Griffith lay nearby with a bullet hole also through the heart and his gun still clutched in his right hand. Evidently, Griffith had killed Ferland and then himself in a suicide pact. The body of Walters was found in another part of the building. Since no further disorder seemed imminent, the guardsmen were ordered off duty.

On March 3, 1924, the legislature appropriated $60,000 to provide armories in all counties of the state where National Guard home stations were maintained. Other funds subsequently became available.

Floods in Fulton and Perry counties during 1927 further varied the experience of the Guard and in a manner that served as valuable training for duty that was to come a few years later.

Disorder in the coal fields of Harlan County, during the spring of 1931, resulted in a call for military assistance. This assistance was ordered on May 6, 1931, Special Order No. 51, under which units from all of the Kentucky National Guard regiments were detailed to the scene together with detachments from the hospital and police companies. These troops quickly succeeded in restoring order and were thereupon returned to their home stations.

The spring of 1934 brought disturbances in Frankfort which portended danger to the Governor and his family as well as a wholesale delivery of State Reformatory prisoners. As a precautionary measure an order was issued on the thirtieth of May under which Maj. Carey Graham, Capt.

F. C. Gayle, and twenty-nine enlisted men of Troop A, 123d Cavalry, went on duty in Frankfort to guard Governor Laffoon and his family, to assist in preventing an unlawful delivery of prisoners at the State Reformatory, and in protection of Frankfort peace generally.[8]

In December, 1934, a breach of the peace occurred in the eastern coal field through the existence of combinations, involving county peace officers, designed to prevent unionization of workers in certain mines. On the eighth of December, 1934, the following order was issued by Adjt. Gen. H. H. Denhardt:

> Capt. Diamond E. Perkins, two officers and 42 men of Co. "A", 149th Infantry, are ordered on active duty for the purpose of maintaining law and order in Harlan County, and specifically for the purpose of protecting the lives of William Turnblazer and other members of the United Mine Workers of America, who are now held prisoners in the Lewallen Hotel by the Sheriff of Harlan County.[9]

During the latter part of May, 1935, the home of the superintendent of the Black Mountain Coal Corporation was dynamited, and on the first of June troops went on duty in Harlan County under Adjutant General Denhardt. These were withdrawn shortly. Early in July another detail was sent into Harlan to guard the property of the mining company. These troops were removed from the county by proceedings instituted in the Harlan Circuit Court. Judge James Gilbert granted a writ of eviction and an injunction to restrain Adjutant General Denhardt from again sending guardsmen into the county unless requested by county authorities. The removal of troops under the court order was made at once, but two enlisted men were retained on police duty at the Black Mountain mines to guard company property.

Troops under command of Adjutant General Denhardt went on duty in Harlan County again early in August and continued there during the Democratic primary under the following order of Governor Laffoon:

> WHEREAS, it has been repeatedly represented to me, the undersigned as Governor of Kentucky, that a condition of unrest now

exists in Harlan County and has so existed for a long period of time, that numerous men have been beaten, bruised, knocked down and seriously wounded by men acting as Deputy Sheriffs of the County. That the right of free speech is denied citizens of the Commonwealth and others; that the right of peaceful assemblage is not permitted unless the assemblage is to the liking of Theodore Middleton, the Sheriff of the County; that houses have been dynamited, homes shot into and that, in fact, a reign of terror now exists in said county, and has so existed for some months.

It further appearing that the Sheriff of said County in collusion with other officials and by the use of numerous deputies in intimidating, brow beating and terrorizing the citizens of the county and seeking by force to impress his will upon the people in defiance of law, right and justice; and it appearing that the partisans of the said Sheriff's political faction are contemplating committing wholesale election frauds in Harlan County in the forthcoming primary election to be held Saturday, August 3, 1935, some 15,400 Democratic ballots having been printed for said primary when never but once in the history of primary elections in said county were there ever more than one or two thousand ballots used in a Democratic primary.

It having been further represented to me by officials of the county and other good citizens that already a large number of said ballots have been stolen from the Courthouse for unlawful purposes; that by reason of threats of violence and other acts of intimidation many of the voters of the County are afraid and do not feel free to cast their votes on election day.

It further appearing from reports received from officials and other good citizens of Harlan Co. that Theodore Middleton is very partisan in his attitude and has had appointed as election officers many of his own deputies and members of his family who are his partisans and who belong to his political faction, and has also had appointed as election officers many others, in fact a great majority of the election officers who are his partisans and who will do his bidding while acting as election officers, that none but the partisans of his faction have any real representation at the polls.

It further appearing from absolutely reliable authority that conditions of lawlessness exist in Harlan County under the protection of some of the officials, that citizens of the county and visitors therein are bodily assaulted, beaten and wounded whether by Deputy Sheriffs or under their protection, and people visiting the County on legal business have been and are being forced to leave the County by reason of threats made by those in authority, and it having been made to appear to me that these outrageous conditions will continue to exist and the lives and property of the people of the County have been and are in a constant state of peril and that the officials of said County are either unwilling or unable to properly enforce the laws of the Commonwealth, and that conditions are such that especially on election day irreparable harm may be done to citizens and others and that property rights will be endangered unless outside protection be given.

Now, therefore, in order that the lives, constitutional rights and property of the people of Harlan County may be properly safeguarded and protected and that the right of free speech and peaceful assemblage may be maintained and that a fair, honest and peaceful election may be held on Saturday, August 3rd., and that the votes cast in said election may be legally and honestly counted as cast the Adjutant General of Kentucky, Henry H. Denhardt, and all of the National Guard of Kentucky or so much thereof as the said Adjutant General may by military order or orders direct, are hereby ordered on active duty.

The said Denhardt will cause all or such part of the National Guard, as he may deem necessary, to be assembled and they will proceed into Harlan County for the purpose of preserving peace and order in said county, for the further purpose of guaranteeing to the people of said county the right of free speech and of peaceful lawful assemblage, and for the further purpose of guaranteeing to the people of said County the right to have a fair, honest, free, and legal election. He is further ordered and authorized to use such force as may, to him, seem reasonably necessary to attain these ends.

The said Adjutant General is further ordered and directed to keep a sufficient number of the National Guard on duty in Harlan County as he may deem necessary so long as the conditions hereinbefore described may continue, and until the withdrawal of said troops shall be ordered by the Governor.

Witness my signature, as Governor of Kentucky, this August 1, 1935.

RUBY LAFFOON
Governor of Kentucky

Subsequently an indictment was returned against Adjutant General Denhardt in the Harlan Circuit Court, charging a violation of the election laws.

Malfeasance had openly been charged against several of the county officials who were said to be allied with anti-union interests, and for other corrupt practices. County Attorney Elmon Middleton had been active in criminal prosecutions and had otherwise incurred the displeasure of the lawless element. Middleton's removal was desired after he repeatedly refused to betray the trust of his office. Death alone could remove him and this was brought about by planting a charge of dynamite in his automobile on September 6. Immediately after the killing of County Attorney Middleton, orders were issued for detachments of the 123d Cavalry and 149th Infantry to go on duty at Harlan.[10]

Disorders recurred in Harlan County in 1936 and in 1937 before a Congressional investigation was instituted. In Federal Court true bills were returned against fifty-five persons. The U.S. Department of Justice collected evidence which was presented in Federal Court at London in 1937. The case of the fifty-five defendants required fifty-two days for hearing and terminated in a mistrial as a result of an expression, by one of the jurors, when a poll of the jury was being taken after its disagreement, of prejudice against labor organizations.

The supreme test of the Kentucky National Guard's efficiency came during the latter part of January and in February, 1937, when all of the lowlands of the state, on the Ohio River and far upstream along its Kentucky tributaries, were inundated. The Ohio was already high, because of unseasonal thaws at its headwaters, when heavy and almost continuous rains brought new high water marks at nearly every point. With the high water came peril for life and property, far more dreadful than was at first anticipated. Entire communities became engulfed with no means of escape under their own control. Others stayed in their homes, hoping and believing that they were safe, until it became too late to leave without assistance from the outside.

On January 21, 1937, Lt. Gov. Keene Johnson, during the absence of Governor Chandler in Washington, telegraphed the U.S. Secretary of War as follows: "Disaster impending from floods various places in the state. Absolutely necessary to use National Guard equipment. Please grant authority by wire." This message was followed on the twenty-fifth of January by a telegram by Adjutant General McClain to Gen. Malin Craig, chief of staff, U.S. War Department, as follows: [11]

Conditions in Kentucky of which you are cognizant provoke this unusual request. The safety, peace, happiness, and health of several hundred thousand of our citizens in the Ohio Valley prompts this Department in breaking precedent. Particularly does this condition apply to the centers of population of Kentucky and on the Ohio River. Every resource of the National Guard in this State has been utilized to the fullest extent compatible with the safety of our people. We are at a standstill. Such centers of population as Louisville, our largest city, Paducah, Covington, Dayton, Newport, Hickman, Henderson and others will suffer an untold loss; and several hundred thousands of our population will feel the effects in the utmost degree. Consequently, I do not feel embarrassed, acting in the capacity that I do, in making the following request to alleviate the conditions that exist in different localities. In my opinion, and that of our closest observers and advisors, the use of Federal troops is absolutely necessary. Regardless of regulations and recognizing the fact that every resource has been utilized for the protection of our people, we request that two regiments of Infantry, two companies of engineers, medical officers with medical supplies, be ordered to report for duty to Louisville immediately. There is a possibility that conditions will necessitate help other than this. You may be assured that this request will not be made unless positively necessary.

By radio, on January 24, Captain Blackwell notified Adjutant General McClain that: "County Judge Claude A. Walker, Hickman, Kentucky, asked Governor Chandler to send the Kentucky National Guard to guard the Reel Foot Lake Levee, some threats have been made to blow it up. Very urgent. 1,000 families will be made homeless and inundated. Troops will have to be brought out of Louisville by boat." Three days later Judge Walker informed Governor Chandler that:

We have four thousand refugees, and impossible to feed and take care of them without assistance. What we need is army kitchen, blankets, cots, and provisions. Hickman being a town of only two thousand cannot take care of this many people as much as they would like to do so. People being fed once a day and sometimes not this often. There are more refugees coming all the time and if possible we would like to have you assist us in procuring some army kitchen and other material referred to above. It is absolutely necessary that we have some assistance. We also need badly forty additional troops for guard duty. Have just been informed that you have equipped army kitchen at Bowling Green and additional troops there. Troops can move to Hickman via Nashville. Road is open.

The distress message from Hickman brought many offers of assistance from out of the state. Among these are one made by the Chicago *Herald and Examiner*, for which the adjutant general expressed the state's gratitude by the following reply:

Appreciate your offer by phone for a plane to carry a doctor and nurses and supplies to the flood stricken area at Hickman. You have permission of this office to report to the Director, Emergency Relief and the Director of the Red Cross at Hickman as soon as you possibly can make it. We are grateful to you for the assistance which you offer to give.

Other emergencies that state troops had met in bygone days were different. The Indian raids of earlier days struck at a particular point, never threatened any great number of lives, and their duration was usually very short. Then too, if the siege was prolonged, as in the case of Boonesboro or Bryan Station, help could usually be summoned. In the several wars there was always more or less opportunity for preparation to meet a given situation. Even during internal disorders, quelled by troops, there was never any great area involved, and the number of lives and value of property jeopardized by such incidents was comparatively small, even in the night-rider disorders. True enough the wartime raiders and guerrillas struck quickly and often without warning, but never in the history of the state was jeopardy so far-flung as during the flood of 1937.

The flood distress extended from the Big Sandy to Mills Point, and far into the state. Persons living in cities as far inland as Frankfort were brought face to face with an entirely new and desperate situation. Potential disaster loomed wherever the flow of a stream slackened. No one denied that an emergency existed. From the inundated area came call after call for troops to perform those duties which the particular situation required to be done. Proclamations of martial law by Governor Chandler were issued as the troops responded to these calls and after the civil authorities of the particular community had affirmed their inability to cope with the situation that confronted them.

The ensuing messages and proclamation are representative of many like pieces on file pertaining to conditions resulting from the flood. On the twenty-fifth of January, Mayor Neville Miller of Louisville informed Governor Chandler that:

Have just sent the following telegram to Senators Alben W. Barkley, M. M. Logan and wish you to follow to assist us in getting immediate action: 'Flood situation here desperate. Imperative need for at least two Regiments of Infantry, two companies of engineers fully supplied with pontoon equipment and ample number of medical officers with supplies of vaccine, medicine, etc. Martial law being declared now by Governor for entire State of Kentucky. Our Health Department, Police Department, and Public Works and Engineering Departments have broken down physically and need every assistance at once. Any delay can have only the most serious consequences. Get to President Roosevelt and all other necessary officials at once. Eliminate all formality and give us action. Please follow through to see that action is given and people and supplies are dispatched here immediately. Have already lost twenty hours in trying to get action at Washington and do not know how many deaths have resulted. About two hundred thousand people in flood area in Louisville alone out of population of three hundred twenty thousand. All electrical service out of commission and darkness will continue at least a week or two weeks. Water being rationed. Serious shortage of coal. Transportation facilities impaired almost beyond use. What little telephone service remains is seriously threatened.'

In compliance with Mayor Miller's request, troops were ordered on duty in Louisville and Governor Chandler issued the following proclamation with Mayor Miller as provost marshal:

WHEREAS, the Honorable Neville Miller is the duly elected, qualified and acting Mayor of the City of Louisville, Jefferson County, Kentucky, and the chief executive of said city; and,

WHEREAS, approximately two-thirds of the area of said city is now submerged in the greatest flood in the history of said city and approximately two hundred thousand residents of said city reside in the flooded area; and,

WHEREAS, the said Neville Miller, Mayor of the city of Louisville has advised the Government of the Commonwealth of Kentucky that the civil officers and agencies of the city of Louisville are unable to protect the health, lives, and property of the inhabitants and residents of said city during the emergency and that the aid of the military forces is necessary and imperative, and has requested the Governor of the Commonwealth of Kentucky to declare martial law and request that Federal troops be sent to the city of Louisville to aid and assist in protecting the health, lives and property of the residents and citizens of said city; and,

WHEREAS, the Governor of the Commonwealth of Kentucky is fully informed and knows of the imperative need of centralized direction of all forces, civil and military, to aid in rescuing the citizens and residents of the city of Louisville in the flooded area and in protecting the health, lives, and property of said citizens and residents:

Now THEREFORE, the premises all considered, it is ordered and directed by the Governor of the Commonwealth of Kentucky that martial law be and the same hereby is proclaimed for the entire city of Louisville, and the Honorable Neville Miller, mayor of the city of Louisville, hereby is designated as Provost Marshal to be in supreme charge and direction of all civil and military authorities and agencies in the city of Louisville, and he is hereby vested with full power to command and direct said forces and all of them in rescuing people from the flood area and moving them to places of safety, in preserving peace, and in protecting the health, lives and property of the citizens and residents of the city of Louisville, and to issue and enforce such orders, commands, rules and regulations as may be proper, expedient and necessary to accomplish the ends aforesaid.

It is further ordered and directed by the Governor of the Commonwealth of Kentucky that Colonel Sidney R. Smith be the commanding officer of all companies and divisions of the National Guard and the military forces which are or may be assigned to duty in the city of Louisville, and said Colonel Sidney R. Smith will work in coordination with and under the orders and directions of the said Neville Miller as provost marshal in directing all of said military forces.

This order and proclamation shall be and remain in full force and effect until modified or terminated by further executive order and proclamation of the Governor of the Commonwealth of Kentucky.

Given under my hand as Governor of the Commonwealth of Kentucky at Frankfort, Kentucky, this January 25, 1937.

The following letter from Mayor Neville Miller to Adjutant General McClain, dated February 19, is in commendation of the service rendered by the Guard in Louisville:

It was certainly a great relief during the flood to know that you were standing ready to help us at all times and I want to thank you for your cooperation and for the splendid way in which you, and all the members of your organization, came to our assistance.

The people of Louisville realize now, as never before, what the Adjutant General's department means to the State of Kentucky and I want to congratulate you on the splendid service rendered and to thank you personally and on behalf of the citizens of Louisville for all which you have done for us.

In detailing troops an effort was made to send those stationed nearest to the point of duty. However, it was frequently necessary for a detail to make a lengthy detour because of inundated roads.

Protection of the sufferers was the chief duty of the soldiers. This protection assumed various forms, all equally important, requiring discretion, alertness, and fortitude in degrees never before exacted. Police duty was required to prevent brigandage and enforce sanitary, fire prevention, and other emergency rules and regulations that became effective upon the advent of martial law. Evacuation of many communities and areas became necessary as the river rose. Such evacuation could not be accomplished speedily, and with limited facilities, except by some centralized authority, and this was delegated to the Kentucky National Guard by Governor Chandler. This authority, coupled with manpower, enabled the State Military Department to accomplish a stupendous task. Illustrative of this particular phase of the task was the speed and effectiveness of the Guard in evacuating the State Reformatory. Here were 2,906 men and women, confined in a century-old building on an uncertain foundation surroundsd by an ever-rising tide. For days they had been without heat, light, or food. Among them were desperate characters, one sentenced to death. Occupants of lower tier cells had been moved up as the river rose, and a rumor began to circulate that the Dix River Dam had broken. A prison break seemed imminent when Governor Chandler, called home from the National Capital on January 21, entered the prison in a skiff and promised these wards of the state that they would be removed to safety. To fulfill that promise was no small task.

Evacuation of the Reformatory was begun while a fifteen-acre prison camp was being built at Frankfort, beyond reach of the floodwaters. Guardsmen took the most hardened group of prisoners to Lexington where they were confined in the Fayette County Jail. Women prisoners were transferred to the old prison school building. Still others were moved to the Federal Narcotic Farm at Lexington, to the jails at Winchester, Mount Sterling, Georgetown, Owenton, Lawrenceburg, Lebanon, Harrodsburg, Danville, Williamstown, and Richmond. About 800 male prisoners were confined in the Frankfort Armory until the prison camp was ready.

The erection of the Frankfort Reformatory prison camp

was speedily accomplished under the direction of Governor Chandler, and by the joint efforts of the National Guard, under the direction of the office of the adjutant general, and other state agencies including a part of the personnel of the Highway Department. This camp, with full lighting, heating, and sanitary facilities, was completed in less than one week, and in another week all prisoners were brought back from various jails and institutions in which they were temporarily confined during the flood. After the prisoners were installed in their new quarters, under the supervision of Warden James Hammond, the camp was placed under the patrol of some 300 officers and enlisted men of the Kentucky National Guard. Administrative details pertaining to the work of the National Guard at the prison camp had been assigned to Maj. Joseph M. Kelly, assistant adjutant general, with Supt. E. O. Huey, of the State Police, assisting. Several units of the National Guard continued on guard duty at the prison camp until June, 1937.

Medical aid and sanitary measures were secondary only to the removal of sufferers from flood-imperiled zones. To assist in this work, the Kentucky National Guard units, trained for this duty, were assigned, and medical and hospital facilities were provided. Among the orders and messages relating to this work is a communication of January 23, 1937, to Col. Sidney Smith at Louisville saying: "Dr. McCormack requests that two motorboats and four sailors from Great Lakes be detailed to him at the Brown Hotel for continuous duty in carrying his doctors and nurses and medical supply."

In a report from Madisonville, dated January 27, Lt. James K. Ramsey, 149th Infantry, states in part that: "In conference with county authorities and American Red Cross it was thought supplies were sufficient for the present except serums and vaccines which have been promised by the State Department of Health for delivery tonight. North and East end of the county almost entirely submerged. Almost all of the inhabitants have been evacuated to high points and are being removed to Madisonville, Kentucky, where there are ample accommodations and facilities."

Evacuated persons were transported to refugee camps at various points beyond danger. Subsistence then became a weighty problem, for these evacuated persons needed food and shelter. Churches, schools, armories, and other public and private buildings were generously made available. Food was contributed by the Red Cross, by firms, organizations of various types, and by individuals, but the Red Cross required help from the troops to guard and distribute provisions and in several cases required the army kitchen outfits of the Guard. A sheaf of brief messages to the War Department and to several U. S. Army posts portray the efforts of Governor Chandler and Adjutant General McClain to obtain an adequate supply of cots, blankets, camp outfits, medical supplies, boats and various other supplies necessary to enable the Guard to perform its service under the ever increasing demands made upon it. While these requisitions were being made, communities and states, near and remote, were tendering every manner of assistance. Typical of these messages is one received from the adjutant general of Wisconsin as follows:

> Wisconsin contemplates sending into Kentucky food and other supplies. In order to function intelligently and effectively I have been directed by higher authority to determine the cities to which such supplies should be consigned. Or the Rail Head to which consigned. Whether truck facilities are available at Rail Head to convey supplies to destination. Whether medical personnel or supplies are needed and if so their nature. Wire by Western Union collect.

Generally, the Guard was charged with the performance of any and all tasks that others could not do or left undone. The effectiveness of their work is best related by the fact the Guard was able to and did control every situation with which it was confronted, thereby preventing lawlessness and alleviating distress.

Approbation of the work done by the Kentucky National Guard is set out in many press items and editorials of the day. To these must be added the large file of messages expressing praise and gratitude for the work done by the

Kentucky National Guard. Representative of this file of messages are the following:

ADJUTANT GENERAL G. LEE MCCLAIN   *March 8, 1937*
Frankfort, Kentucky

DEAR GENERAL MCCLAIN: I wish to express the appreciation of the people of Maysville and Mason County for the gallant and heroic services of the State Guards during the recent flood here.

They started doing rescue work—moving people and their belongings from their homes—and made many risky trips through the swift currents in boats that leaked, using sticks as oars. They accomplished jobs that looked impossible to accomplish.

They enforced all orders of the Health Department, transported all provisions to four thousand people in East Maysville, and also transported provisions, with the assistance of the Highway Department, to Vanceburg, Springdale, South Ripley, and Dover, kept telephone lines in operation, running new wires when necessary, and even went to Blue Licks and ran wires for the main long distance lines so we could have outside communication.

The Guards kept guard over all boats and prevented looting and thievery, and thanks to the commanding officers, we did not lose a life, and there was no sickness or looting and, considering what we went through, the work accomplished was marvelous.

Lieut. Kehoe was of great assistance to me as Provost Marshal; in fact I owe all military credit to him.

Thanking you again for the assistance of the National Guards, I am,
         Very truly yours,

         GEORGE H. FITZGERALD
         Sheriff of Mason County

GENERAL G. L. MCCLAIN   PADUCAH, KY., *Mar. 8, 1937*
Frankfort, Kentucky

MY DEAR GENERAL MCCLAIN: We have notified Captain Johnson that we are agreeing to release the National Guards when they change shifts at five o'clock tomorrow morning, Tuesday, March 9th. I wish to take this means of expressing my sincere appreciation and gratitude to you for the assistance these boys have given us in preserving law and order in our city. The guardsmen have conducted themselves in a manner that reflects credit to the organization and the state. I wish also to take this opportunity to commend to you Major Orin Coin and Captain Johnson. They have been most cooperative and have made excellent officers.

Please, General, accept on behalf of the citizens of Paducah our sincerest appreciation for the services performed.

         Most sincerely yours,

         L. V. BEAN
         City Manager

The flood emergency relief duty reports received from the commanders of the various details are also expressive of Kentucky's gratitude for services rendered by the National Guard. Among these and representative of them is the following excerpt from the report of Capt. Boone Pelfrey, 149th Infantry, reporting from Greenup:

> I desire to especially commend the services and the spirit of cooperation manifested by all and especially the acting mayor, Chief of Police, and his staff of Deputies, Messrs. Curry, Callahan, Rice and Stanley Craft for their services and boats: Attorney Nickle and wife and Mr. W. C. Nickle, Mr. Sturgill, Mr. Bachelor and Glenn. Mr. Morton, Mr. Herald, and Weeks and last but not least the Colored boys who did the cooking.

In his report from Russell, Sgt. E. R. Kaiser, Company E, 149th Infantry, says in part: "Members of my detail were treated with every consideration and extended every courtesy while on duty in Russell, and were given every cooperation by the Mayor, Chief of Police and the Sheriff."

HEADQUARTERS SEVENTH CAVALRY BRIGADE
FORT KNOX, KENTUCKY

Subject: Commendation   *February 12, 1937*

To: HIS EXCELLENCY, THE GOVERNOR OF KENTUCKY

1. I desire officially to commend the commissioned and enlisted personnel of the 138th Field Artillery, Kentucky National Guard, and other units attached thereto, commanded by Colonel Sidney Smith, for the splendid service rendered by them in Louisville during the recent flood disaster.

2. The arduous duties performed by them, including guarding private as well as public property, safeguarding life, actual rescuing of endangered persons during the flood period, and enforcing the quarantine, all combine to justify the confidence of the American people in their military forces and to merit my particular admiration.

3. The good judgment displayed by all ranks under most difficult conditions, the fine cooperation with other units and untiring effort through long hours of exposure to render assistance to the distressed people of Louisville reflect great credit to this fine regiment.

DANIEL VAN VOORHIS
Brigadier General, U. S. A., Commanding

Troops called during the flood first engaged in active duty on January 21. The last element so employed was relieved on June 8, 1937. During this period 172 officers and 2,022 enlisted men were called into service. All of the units participated except Company C, 149th Infantry, which was held in reserve to quell an anticipated disturbance in Harlan County. The following tables relate the scope of duty performed by the officers and men of the Kentucky National Guard during the disasterous flood period:

KENTUCKY NATIONAL GUARD ON FLOOD DUTY—1937

Name of Unit	Location	Where Sent	Officers	Men	Days Duty
38th M. P. Co.	Jackson	Frankfort, Ky.	1	30	56
38th Tank Co.	Harrodsburg	Frankfort	3	45	69
113th Ordnance Co.	Bardstown	Frankfort	2	21	66
Hdq. Co. 75th Brig.	Bowling Green	Paducah	2	32	32
Med. Dept. Det. 149th Inf.	Bowling Green	Paducah	1	11	24
Hdq. Co. 149th Inf.	St. Matthews	Frankfort—Louisville— St. Matthews	1	31	17
			1	7	25
Service Co. 149th Inf.	Bowling Green	Bowling Green—Hawesville— Bardstown	3	54	29
Howitzer Co. 149th Inf.	Carlisle	Maysville—Augusta	3	54	14
Hdq. Co. 1st Btn. 149th Inf.	Lexington	Lexington	2	35	25
		Frankfort	1	0	97
Co. A, 149th Inf.	Harlan	Paducah	3	60	30
Co. B, 149th Inf.	Somerset	Frankfort—Shepherdsville	1	45	69
Co. D, 149th Inf.	Williamsburg	Paducah—Williamsburg	3	52	30
Hdq. Co. 2d Btn. 149th Inf.	Maysville	Maysville	2	34	21
Co. E, 149th Inf.	Olive Hill	Ashland—Vanceburg— Greenup—Russell— Winchester	3	56	24
Co. F, 149th Inf.	Booneville	Frankfort—Shelbyville	2	42	39
Co. G, 149th Inf.	Ashland	Ashland—Catlettsburg— Greenup	3	46	13
Co. H, 149th Inf.	Ravenna	Frankfort	3	46	69
		Lexington	1	0	55
Hdq. Co. 3d Btn. 149th Inf.	Madisonville	Madisonville	2	30	40
Co. I, 149th Inf.	Marion	Paducah	3	37	47

KENTUCKY NATIONAL GUARD ON FLOOD DUTY—1937

Name of Unit	Location	Where Sent	Officers	Men	Days Duty
Co. K, 149th Inf.	Livermore	Livermore—Barlow	3	47	39
Co. L, 149th Inf.	Mayfield	Paducah—Barlow	3	46	47
Co. M, 149th Inf.	Russellville	Hickman—Russellville	3	46	45
Hdq. and Hdq. Bty. 63d F. A. Brig. and 138th F. A. Brig.	Louisville	Louisville—Jefferson Co.	60	600	24
Hdq. Bty. 63d F. A. Brig.	Louisville	Louisville—Jefferson Co.	2	15	19
Bty. F, 138th F. A.	Louisville	Louisville—Jefferson Co.	1	20	27
Co. G, 113th Med. Regt.	Richmond	Lexington—Frankfort	2	10	65
Co. H, 113th Med. Regt.	Richmond	Lexington—Frankfort	3	11	55
125th Wagon Co.	Hopkinsville	Paducah—Eddyville	3	43	14
125th Wagon Co.	Pikeville	Catlettsburg	3	25	31
Med. Dept. Det. 123d Cav.	Hopkinsville	Paducah	1	15	38
Hdq. Troop and Band, 123d Cav.	Glasgow	Louisville—Carrollton—Glasgow	4	60	47
Machine Gun Troop 123d Cav.	Hopkinsville	Paducah—Eddyville—Frankfort	3	49	39
Troop A, 123d Cav.	Frankfort	Frankfort	3	50	121
Troop B, 123d Cav.	Lexington	Frankfort	2	50	69
Troop E, 123d Cav.	London	Frankfort	2	30	9
Troop F, 123d Cav.	Covington	Covington	3	59	17
Troop I, 123d Cav.	Springfield	Frankfort	2	45	69
Troop K, 123d Cav.	Monticello	Frankfort—Lexington—Peewee Valley	3	40	31
Hdq. Det., Q. M. Train	Frankfort	Frankfort	1	13	10
		Frankfort	2	10	70
			1	0	67
State Staff Detachment	Henderson	Henderson	1	23	37

INDIVIDUAL OFFICERS

Name of Officer and Unit	Location	Where Sent	Days Duty
Brig. Gen. G. L. McClain Adjt. Gen. Ky. N. G.	Frankfort	State-at-Large, and Adjutant General's Office	99
Lt. Col. W. S. Taylor Hdq. 149th Inf.	Louisville	St. Matthews	14
Col. Henry J. Stites Hdq. 123d Cav.	Louisville	Western Half of Ky.	4
Col. Roy W. Easley Hdq. 149th Inf.	Louisville	Eastern Half of Ky.	4
Maj. Joseph M. Kelly 123d Cav.	Frankfort	Frankfort Prison Camp	115
Maj. Oren Coin Hdq. 3d Btn. 149th Inf.	Livermore	Paducah—Livermore	40
Maj. Frank S. Lebkuecher State Staff	Frankfort	Frankfort Prison Camp	100
Capt. Robert C. Riggs Med. Dept. Det. 123d Cav.	Lexington	Frankfort	71
1st Lt. Jackson A. Smith 123d Cav.	Frankfort	Frankfort and Prison Camp	114

In addition to the above service, on April 1, 1937, a composite unit was organized with picked men from various National Guard Units on duty at the Prison Camp, Frankfort, Ky., and detailed to duty at that station. The number of men and dates of active duty were as follows:

From	To	Officers	Men	Days Duty
April 1	April 30	12	109	30
May 1	May 31	12	99	31
June 1	June 6	2	6	6

INDIVIDUAL OFFICERS

Name of Officer and Unit	Location	Where Sent	Days Duty
Brig. Gen. Ellerbe W. Carter Hdq. 63d F. A. Brig.	Louisville	Frankfort—Lexington Jefferson County	19
Lt. Col. John A. Polin Hdq. 123d Cav.	Springfield	Frankfort (Prison Camp)	28
Maj. Walter F. Wright Hdq. 63d F. A. Brig.	Louisville	Louisville	19

INDIVIDUAL OFFICERS

Name of Officer and Unit	Location	Where Sent	Days Duty
Maj. George E. Nelson Hdq. 2d Squad. 123d Cav.	Covington	Covington	17
Maj. John R. Settle 38th Div. Staff	Louisville	Frankfort (Prison Camp)	18
Maj. Robert C. Graham Hdq. 1st Squad. 123d Cav.	Frankfort	Frankfort	136
Capt. Edw. F. Seiller Hdq. 149th Inf.	Louisville	Louisville—Aide to Director State Board of Health	17
Capt. Hugh B. Gregory Hdq. 123d Cav.	Springfield	Frankfort	26
Capt. Gaylord S. Gilbert Hdq. 123d Cav.	Louisville	Louisville—Frankfort	37
Capt. Edw. B. Blackwell 38th Div. Staff	Bowling Green	Bowling Green	13
Lt. Franklin L. Ullrich 38th Div. Staff	Louisville	Bowman Field—Louisville	16
Lt. Mortimer M. Benton Hdq. 2d Btn. 123d Cav.	Louisville	Louisville	14
Lt. James R. Dorman Hdq. 123d Cav.	Louisville	Louisville	2
Lt. Thos. J. Hieatt Hdq. 63d F. A. Brig.	Louisville	Louisville	13

NOTES, REFERENCES, AND SOURCES

1. *Code of the Laws of the United States of America of 1935.* Title 10, chap. 1, sec. 2.
   1A. Numerical Strength as of 1938.
2. *Ibid.*, Title 10, chap. 2, secs. 34, 37.
3. *Ibid.*, Title 10, chap. 2, sec. 68.
4. *Ibid.*, Title 10, chap. 2, sec. 83.
5. *Ibid.*, Title 10, chap. 2, sec. 116.
6. Adjutant General's Special Orders of 1920, Nos. 14, 18, 26, 97.
7. Adjutant General's Special Orders of 1921, Nos. 49, 50, 51, 64, 99, 103, 149, 152.
8. Adjutant General's Special Orders of 1934, No. 70.
9. *Ibid.*, No. 170.

10. Adjutant General's Special Orders of 1935, Nos. 137, 138.

11. Papers, Letters, and Messages referred to in matter pertaining to the flood of 1937 are carried in separate file in the office of the adjutant general, State Capitol, Frankfort. These may be inspected upon request. Orders of the adjutant general are carried in the file with other orders for 1937.

CHAPTER XI

LINEAGE OF THE REGIMENTS KENTUCKY NATIONAL GUARD

The three regiments of the Kentucky National Guard trace their lineage to the Virginia Colonial line. They and their predecessor militia organizations participated in all of the wars of the Nation. After 1860, until her troops were mustered into the Federal service in 1917, Kentucky maintained, in times of peace, three regiments of infantry. Upon organization of the Kentucky National Guard the U.S. War Department ruled that Kentucky should maintain the 138th Field Artillery, successor to the 1st Infantry Regiment, and the 149th Infantry which replaced the 2d Infantry Regiment. In addition Kentucky was ordered to maintain the the 53d and 54th Machine Gun Squadrons in place of the 3d Regiment. Certain auxiliary troops were also designated. On April 1, 1929, the 53d and 54th Machine Gun Squadrons were reassigned as the 123d Cavalry, thus perpetuating the state's historic three regiments as lineal successors of the Jefferson, Fayette, and Lincoln regiments.

Auxiliary troops designated to be maintained in Kentucky are those complemental to the State regimental organization, to perfect its divisional and brigade set-up.

Staff and Headquarters Detachment, 63d Field Artillery Brigade, was Federally recognized on February 14, 1923. The brigade commander was then Ellerbe W. Carter, at present (1938) still commanding the brigade. Headquarters Battery at that time was commanded by the first lieutenant or a member of the staff. The battery was separated from the staff in 1928, and on July 31, 1935, was converted to a motor-drawn battery. Headquarters Battery is now commanded by a captain, assisted by a second lieutenant. The captain serves as communications officer for the Brigade, with the second lieutenant serving as assistant communications officer.

The State Detachment Quartermasters Corps, Henderson, is an outgrowth of several former National Guard units that have been stationed in Henderson. One of the earliest of these, Company B, 3d Kentucky National Guard, was located at Morganfield under the command of Maj. Talbott Berry. After the War with Spain this company was disbanded and later reorganized at Henderson by Captain E. C. Walker. In 1916 Company B was commanded by Capt. Harley Higginson; its first lieutenant was Robert C. Soaper. A Machine Gun Company was organized during the training period on the Mexican Border and Lieutenant Soaper became its captain. After nine months training, both Company B and the Machine Gun Company were called home. At the entrance of the United States into the World War, the two companies went to Camp Stanley, Lexington, Kentucky, later going to camp Shelby, Mississippi, and became part of the 38th Division.

There were no military organizations of any kind in Henderson after the World War, until March 30, 1926, when the State Detachment of the Quartermaster Corps was organized by Capt. Wesley N. Royster. This detachment has (1938) one officer and twenty-six enlisted men. Its personnel consists largely of the higher grades of noncommissioned officers, as its purpose is to serve the Administrative, Supply, and Transportation needs of the Kentucky National Guard. In the organization are two World War veterans, Capt. Wesley N. Royster, who served as first sergeant in the 149th Infantry during the war, and Master Sergeant Charles A. Brown, who was with Company B and the Machine Gun Company during the war.

The 38th Military Police Company, commanded by First Lieut. Arch Cope and Second Lieut. P. Watt Howard, was accorded Federal recognition on July 10, 1922. It is commanded at the present time (1938) by Capt. Arch Cope, who has continued in command of the company since its organization with the exception of a period of about one year. This company's home station is at Jackson.

The organization has attended fifteen annual field encampments at Fort Knox, Kentucky. During these encampments the Company has been in complete charge of all police duties for the entire 38th Division. The Company has also been in charge of traffic and information posts at different points in the Divisional Camp and has handled troops and traffic in connection with the annual review of the 38th Division, second Army maneuvers, and Divisional and smaller unit maneuvers. The unit competed in riot and squad drill in 1933 and 1934, winning first place in 1933 and second place in 1934.

The 38th Tank Company is the successor of Company D, Kentucky State Guard, which was organized at Covington for state duty in the absence of the regular unit on Federal service in France during the World War. In March, 1921, this unit was converted to the new 38th Tank Company and was extended Federal recognition under date of March 29, 1921, under the command of Capt. Louis V. Crockett. The 38th Tank Company disbanded in March, 1932, and a new company under the same designation was organized at Harrodsburg, in June 1932, and was extended Federal recognition under date of July 5, 1932. Its officers were Capt. Bacon R. Moore, First Lt. George W. Biggerstaff, First Lt. Truman Mayes, Second Lt. Charles D. Clarkson, and Second Lt. Davis H. Gritton, all of whom were in service in the World War.

Each year the Company has passed Federal Inspection with a satisfactory rating and has attended field training at Fort Knox. In 1936 it was engaged in the Second Army Maneuvers. The Tank Company has two "M-2-T-2" tanks. Captain Moore completed the Tank School course at Fort Benning, Georgia, on June 17, 1933, and Staff Sergeant Parsons completed the Tank Course at the same school in the fall of 1936.

In May, 1938, Lieutenant Biggerstaff was promoted to

Captain and assigned to duty on the State Staff. Second Lieutenant Gritton was promoted to First Lieutenant and Pvt. George A. Van Arsdall was promoted to second lieutenant.

The 113th Ordnance Company was organized on June 19, 1936, and received Federal recognition June 22, 1936. Capt. Alvan W. Wells, Commanding Officer, a graduate of the College of St. Thomas, was a member of the Officer's Reserve Corps and was on duty with the Civilian Conservation Corps in the Ninth Corps Area. He accepted a commission in the Kentucky National Guard and was Federally recognized June 22, 1936, at the time of the Company's recognition. Second Lt. Benjamin W. Poor, is a graduate of Staunton Military Academy and a senior in the Reserve Officers Training Corps at Lehigh University. The company's home station is at Bardstown.

The company consists of twenty-eight enlisted men divided as follows: two sergeants grade II, four sergeants grade IV, two corporals grade V, six privates first class grade VI and fourteen privates grade VII. All privates receive specialists rating with the exception of three.

The 113th Ordnance Company participated in the Second Army maneuvers at Fort Knox in 1936, and since that time has continued to serve in its training periods at Fort Knox.

Headquarters Company of the 75th Infantry Brigade was organized at Bowling Green, and received Federal recognition on January 30, 1924, under the command of Capt. Alex M. Chaney. Captain Chaney served from that date until April 26, 1926, when he resigned to accept a position on the staff of Brig. Gen. Henry H. Denhardt. The Communications Officer of the newly organized Company was second Lt. George P. Allen, who also served until April 26, 1926. The Company has always been made up of Warren County men. Many members of the Company have gone into responsible positions since their service in the Kentucky National Guard.

Officers who have served this Company since its institution

at Bowling Green, are Capts. Alex M. Chaney, Jesse S. Taylor, Joseph S. Garman, Joseph W. Seemes, and Maurice D. Burton, and Second Lieutenants George P. Allen, Henry Clay Anderson, Kelly Sloss, Macon Newman, and W. Weldon Peete.

Company G, 113th Medical Regiment, was originally organized as Field Hospital Company No. 1, on June 3, 1916. The unit was mustered in for Mexican Border service and served from August 30, 1916, to March 9, 1917.

The Company was drafted and reorganized as the 113th Sanitary Train August 5, 1917, and was later demobilized and reorganized as the 137th Hospital Company, June 13, 1921, at Winchester. Maj. Benjamin Cockrell, M. D., was company commander. On February 13, 1923, the 113th Medical Regiment was organized in Indiana and Kentucky, and the 137th Hospital Company was absorbed by the regiment.

The Hospital Company was disbanded February 3, 1927, but was reorganized in Richmond, February 16, 1927, with the following commissioned personnel: Captains J. B. Floyd, company commander, M. M. Robinson, J. W. Hill, J. W. Scudder, T. J. Turley, and C. W. Hembree. On January 1, 1937, the Company was redesignated Company G, 113th Medical Regiment.

The present commissioned personnel consists of Capt. J. H. Rutledge, company commander, Capt. Thomas Clouse, Capt. B. L. Pope, Capt. R. W. Sandlin, Capt. G. N. Hembree, and Capt. H. H. Rutledge.

When the unit was reorganized in Richmond, it was made up of equal numbers of local men and students from Eastern Kentucky Teachers College, and the same ratio has been maintained. Several of the students have been able to continue educations with the money received as drill pay in the National Guard.

Company H, 113th Medical Regiment, oldest unit in date of Federal recognition and station, was first recognized as Field Hospital Company No. 2, on June 3, 1916. Only a few units of the 149th Infantry and the 138th Field Artillery date their Federal recognition prior to that of Company H.

The Company was re-recognized as the 138th Hospital Company, July 1, 1922, with its station at Richmond. The company was commanded by Maj. Omer F. Hume from the date of its recognition until Major Hume's resignation, June 29, 1928. Capt. Robert M. Phelps has commanded the organization since June 30, 1928. The 138th Hospital Company became part of the 113th Medical Regiment when that organization was formed and Federally recognized February 16, 1923.

The Medical Department Detachment, 38th Division, Quartermaster Train, was organized in Barbourville. Assisting with the organization of the Detachment were Capt. Joseph J. Canalla, Instructor of the 149 Infantry; Capt. Ben Herndon, Commanding Officer of Company C, 149th Infantry; Sgt. Albert B. Strickland, sergeant instructor of the 149th Infantry; and Capt. James E. Parker, who later became commanding officer of the detachment. Official recognition was accorded the new organization on the night of its founding.

During the first years of the Medical Detachment's existence Maj. Thomas W. Woodyard and Sergeant Strickland rendered much service that insured the success of the organization.

Capt. Benjamin F. Pigg, V. C., was transferred to the Detachment and took command of the Veterinary Section on July 2, 1930, remaining until his resignation on August 21, 1933. Captain Pigg's place was taken by Capt. Boyd Jeffers on April 3, 1934.

The organization was redesignated July 1, 1937, as Medical Department Detachment, 113th Quartermaster Regiment, and under the new table of organization the Detachment was allowed one Major, one Captain, and eleven enlisted men. Captain Parker was promoted to Major on July 1, 1937. Of those who entered the outfit on May 1, 1929, only three remained until 1938. These men are Major Parker, First Sgt. Jack R. Ketcham, and Pvt. Harry M. Faulkner.

Headquarters Company, 113th Quartermaster Regiment, came into existence during the World War through the organization of the 113th Supply Train in October, 1917. The unit served with the 38th Division in France and was mustered out of Federal service July 6, 1919.

At a conference of military authorities at Fort Benjamin Harrison, Indiana, in March, 1921, the state of Kentucky was alloted a portion of the 38th Division Quartermaster Train, the new designation for the 113th Supply Train.

The 125th Wagon Company, stationed at Hopkinsville, was the first unit of the train organized in Kentucky. Federal recognition was extended the company on October 1, 1922.

Headquarters Detachment, 38th Division Train, was organized at Frankfort in June, 1924, and was Federally recognized July 7, 1924. The detachment, consisting of two officers and eleven enlisted men, attended thirteen annual field training periods at Fort Knox as a part of the train. On July 1, 1937, the unit was Federally recognized as Headquarters Company, 113th Quartermaster Regiment, and attended the 1937 field camp with the new regiment.

Company C, 113th Quartermaster Regiment was organized by Capt. Vego E. Barnes, as the 125th Wagon Company, 38th Division Quartermaster Train, and the company was extended Federal recognition October 1, 1922. It continued under that designation until July 1, 1937, at which time the 38th Division Quartermaster Train was converted to the 113th Quartermaster Regiment and this company was designated as Company C, of the new Regiment.

Captain Barnes served as commanding officer of the company from October 1, 1922, to April 1, 1937, when he was appointed major of the Quartermaster Corps on the state staff, and upon organization of the 113th Quartermaster Regiment in July, 1938, he was made commander of the 2d Battalion.

Captain Barnes was assisted in organizing the company by Graham B. Cowherd, who enlisted in the company July 3, 1922, as a private, and was advanced through the ranks until he became company commander on April 1, 1937. Captain Cowherd enlisted in the U. S. Marine Corps in April, 1918, at the age of seventeen, and served with the 6th Regiment overseas. He was wounded in action on November 10, 1918, and was awarded a Purple Heart by the War Department.

Company D, 113th Quartermaster Regiment, was organized on May 24, 1924, as Regimental Headquarters Company, 148th Infantry, by Col. Charles Morrow. The unit was commanded by Capt. Robert B. Doak and for four years functioned as headquarters company before being converted to Company C, 149th Infantry. In May, 1928, the unit came under the command of Capt. K. D. Kaessee, who was succeeded by Capt. Ross Rutherford. The company was given a new designation, when Company C became the 126th Wagon Company, 38th Division Quartermaster Train, under command of Capt. Chas. Thornbury. In July, 1937, the company underwent another change in designation and became known as Company D, 113th Quartermaster Regiment. It now functions as a motor-drawn company.

Capt. Vernon Sanders, present commanding officer, is a veteran of the organization, having worked himself up from the rank of private in the Regimental Headquarters Company. Captain Sanders is assisted by First Lt. John M. Sword and Second Lt. Grant Phillips, Jr.

The 138th Field Artillery is the successor organization and entitled to historical continuity with the following predecessor units:*[1]

A. Since World War—138th Field Artillery;

B. During World War—138th Field Artillery;

C. Up to World War and during Mexican Border trouble —1st Kentucky Infantry;

D. Prior to Mexican Border trouble to the War with Spain—1st Kentucky Infantry;

E. During the War with Spain—1st Regiment Infantry, Kentucky Volunteers, U. S. Army;

---

* Notes, references, and sources are indicated by numerals. These refer to corresponding numbers at the end of this chapter. Notes on Chapter XI are on page 401.

F. Prior to the War with Spain to War between the States—1st Kentucky Infantry (Louisville Legion);

G. War between the States—5th Kentucky Infantry (Louisville Legion);

H. Kentucky neutrality—Louisville Legion;

I. Prior to War between the States to Mexican War—Louisville Legion;

J. Mexican War—First Regiment Foot, Kentucky Volunteers;

K. Prior to Mexican War to 1839—Louisville Legion;

L. Prior to 1839 to War of 1812—First Rifle Regiment, Kentucky Militia;

M. Prior to War of 1812 to and including Revolution—Jefferson County Militia Regiment;

N. Prior to 1780, a part of the Kentucky County Militia of Virginia.

The 138th Field Artillery embraces the Medical Detachment, Headquarters and Service batteries. The 1st Battalion consists of Batteries A, B, and C. The 2d Battalion is composed of Headquarters Battery and Combat Train, and Batteries D, E, and F.

The Medical Detachment, 138th Field Artillery, its home station in Louisville, was Federally recognized on June 30, 1922, and immediately attached to the 138th Field Artillery. The commanding officer at that time was Maj. Benjamin D. Choate, who still (1938) serves. His staff is (1938) composed of Capt. Franklin Walker, Medical Corps, and Capt. Herman R. Moore, Dental Corps. Major Choate and Captain Moore, are veterans of the World War. The detachment has been on active duty at Fort Knox, for field training with the 138th Field Artillery, two weeks each year since 1922.

Officers who have served with the Medical Detachment other than those mentioned above are Capt. Thomas Craig, Medical Corps; Capt. Edward P. Whistler, Medical Corps; Capt. Gordon S. Buttorff, Medical Corps; Capt. Byron Bizot, Medical Corps; Capt. Floyd M. Kearns, Veterinary Corps; Capt. Vincent D. Bohannon, Veterinary Corps; and Capt. Charles E. Palmer, Veterinary Corps.

Headquarters Battery, 138th Field Artillery, was Federally recognized June 2, 1923, and since that time has attended each annual summer training encampment at Fort Knox.

The battery commander, Capt. Howard R. Norman, has a medal awarded by the State of Kentucky for his twenty-one years of faithful service. First Lt. Beckham Garrett has served for fifteen years. There are seven enlisted men in the battery who hold medals for prolonged service.

The total service of Captain Norman, First Lieutenant Garrett, Master Sergeant Stier, First Sergeant Wirth, Staff Sergeants Fahringer and Ohlson, Sergeants Maddox and Schanks, and Privates Cunningham and Fleck, is 137 service years. Headquarters Battery has numerous members who are ex-service men of the U.S. Army, Navy, and Marine Corps. Its home station is at Louisville.

The Service Battery, 138th Field Artillery, was recognized on February 8, 1922, under the command of Capt. Isadore L. Shulhafer, supply officer of the old 1st Infantry and the 138th Field Artillery during the World War. Other officers on the staff were First Lt. Courtney J. Kamman and Second Lt. Herman Kaiser. In July, 1922, Lieutenant Kamman was transferred and replaced by First Lt. George R. Evans, and Ester D. Barnett was recognized as second lieutenant in the same month. The home station of this battery is at Louisville.

The band section was gradually brought into existence through the efforts of Master Sgt. Harry M. Currie, who was later commissioned. At his resignation, in October of 1923, the band was taken over by Lt. Joseph H. Hillebrand. In April, 1925, Lieutenant Hillebrand resigned and C. E. Norman was appointed warrant officer.

On August 30, 1932, Captain Shulhafer was retired with the rank of major, and Lieutenant Barnett was promoted to captain. In July, 1935, former Lt. J. P. Hesse was recommissioned and reassigned. Captain Barnett commanded the battery until his resignation, April 15, 1937, at which time Samson K. Bridgers, former commander of Battery B, 138th Field Artillery, was recommissioned and reassigned to command. In November, 1937, Lynn Thayer was appointed warrant officer band leader.

Headquarters Battery, 1st Battalion, was organized after the World War as Troop A, 1st Cavalry, and Federal recognition of the unit was obtained as Troop A, 54th Machine Gun Squadron, Cavalry, June 2, 1920. The troop was commanded by Capt. John R. C. Norman.

The unit was redesignated the Headquarters Detachment and Combat Train, 1st Battalion, 138th Field Artillery, on October 1, 1921, under command of Capt. R. N. Holmes. On September 9, 1925, it was again designated Headquarters Battery and Combat Train, 1st Battalion, 138th Field Artillery. The battery was commanded by Capt. James R. Gilman from September 30, 1922, to July 2, 1933. It was then commanded by First Lt. John R. Settle, who was promoted to the rank of captain on July 28, 1933. Captain Settle was given the rank of major on June 8, 1936, at which time First Lt. Bernard W. Cunningham took command. Lieutenant Cunningham received his commission as captain on June 22, 1936. First Lt. Leslie W. Boyer commanded the battery from November 14, 1937, until June 1, 1938, when Capt. Clarence L. Jones was designated battery commander.

Battery A, 138th Field Artillery, was organized as Company A of the Louisville Legion on June 30, 1878, under Capt. J. B. Castleman, who later commanded the 1st Infantry during the War with Spain. During this war the battery was commanded by Clarence L. Grinstead, and was known as Company A, 1st Kentucky Infantry, U.S. Volunteers. The company was mustered out on February 24, 1899.

Company A was reorganized and mustered into Federal service once more, April 9, 1904, under command of Capt. Neville S. Bullitt. In 1915, Company A was commanded by Capt. John R. C. Norman, and went to the Mexican border under the leadership of Capt. Preston A. Vance. In 1917, the unit became Battery A, 138th Field Artillery under the command of Capt. Pinkney Varble. Battery A, 138th Field Artillery, went overseas under the command of Capt. Robert Cain, who was succeeded by Capt. Frederick Kornfield, who in turn was succeeded by Capt. Ewing G. Wells in 1922. In the fall of 1923, C. Claude Watkins took command of the battery. On January 14, 1934, Captain Watkins was promoted to major in command of the 1st Battalion, and Lee F. Tinsley became battery commander.

Battery B, 138th Field Artillery, served on the Mexican Border in 1916 as Company B, 1st Kentucky Infantry, under the command of Capt. Leo Medley. In the spring of 1917, the organization was converted to Battery B, 138th Field Artillery. Later in the same year Captain Medley was replaced by Capt. Ralph M. Strother, who commanded the battery through the World War and until it was mustered out in January of 1919. The battery was reorganized in 1921 under command of Captain Briggs and was given Federal recognition on August 3, 1921. Following Captain Briggs, Captain Cloud commanded the company. He was succeeded by Capt. Frank B. McAuliffe. Capt. Samson K. Bridgers became battery commander on May 14, 1929, and continued in command until April 30, 1935, when Capt. Walter R. Calvert, Jr., was assigned to the organization.

Battery C, 138th Field Artillery, was reorganized and Federally recognized August 17, 1921, under the command of Capt. Woodford Delaney, with Lt. Edward Hardy, who became battery commander in 1922, as executive officer. On November 1, 1924, command of the battery was assumed by Capt. Alexander G. Kirby until his transfer to Regimental Headquarters, May 31, 1938. Capt. Philip R. Ross, was appointed commander June 1, 1938.

Headquarters Battery and Combat Train, 2d Battalion, 138th Field Artillery, was Federally recognized on May 10, 1922, with Capt. Edwin B. Kirk, First Lt. George R. Evans, and Second Lt. Raymond A. Schwab.

Captain Kirk resigned his commission on October 1, 1922, and was succeeded by Capt. Courtney J. Kamman, who commanded the organization until May 15, 1935, when he resigned to accept a captain's commission in the Reserve. Capt. Leo E. Dentinger, formerly battery executive of Battery F, 138th Field Artillery, took command of the organization on May 23, 1935. Other officers on the staff include First Lt. Ralph D. Denham, who was transferred to the battery October 2, 1927, and Second Lt. George H. James, commissioned from the ranks July 12, 1934.

Battery D, 138th Field Artillery, was Federally recognized on October 21, 1921, under the command of Capt. William F. Reeser. Junior officers at the time of organization were First Lt. John G. Heyburn and First Lt. Alexander Heyburn. On January 21, 1922, Herman Erhart was appointed second lieutenant and assigned.

On February 10, 1922, Lieutenant Erhart was appointed captain and assigned to the command of Battery E, 138th Field Artillery. On March 5, 1923, Lt. John G. Heyburn was appointed captain and assigned to headquarters, 138th Field Artillery, as plans and training officer. Captain Reeser resigned on June 30, 1923, and was succeeded by Captain Erhart, who was transferred back to Battery D.

In November, 1924, Captain Erhart was transferred to headquarters, 2d Battalion, and First Lt. Alexander Heyburn was appointed captain and assigned command of the battery. Captain Heyburn commanded the unit from 1924 to July 20, 1933, at which time he was transferred to headquarters, 2d Battalion, as battalion adjutant.

On the transfer of Captain Heyburn, First Lt. E. R. Gregg, of the 2d Battalion Staff, was appointd captain and has been in command from July 21, 1933, to date. The battery officers at present are First Lt. Edward B. Schnell, Second Lt. Cecil McMasters and Second Lt. Ralph M. Decker.

Battery E, 138th Field Artillery (.75 mm. horse drawn), was Federally recognized December 1, 1921. It was converted to Battery E, 138th Field Artillery (.75 mm. motor drawn) January 1, 1935. Men who have commanded the battery from the time of its organization are Captains E. S. Pitke, W. S. Ball, Donald Ross, Jesse Lindsay, and C. J. Cronan.

Battery F, 138th Field Artillery, was originally organized in October, 1917, when the old 1st Infantry was converted to the 138th Field Artillery. The battery was made up of the enlisted personnels of Companies G and H, and the Machine Gun Company of the old 1st Infantry Regiment. Its first commanding officer was Capt. George M. Chescheir, who formerly commanded the Machine Gun Company of the 1st Kentucky Infantry and who is now (1938) the Regimental Executive Officer of the 138th Field Artillery, with the rank of lieutenant colonel. Among the original enlisted men of Battery F, were C. Claude Watkins, present commander of 1st Battalion, 138th Field Artillery, and Capt. Stephen C. Boldt, commanding officer of Battery F. Corp. George Moore, still an active member of Battery F, was among the original enlisted personnel and has served continuously except for the two years before the Regiment was reorganized after the World War. Leaving Camp Taylor, in October, 1917, Battery F saw service at Camp Shelby, Mississippi, as a part of the 38th Division, and supplied over one hundred replacements for oversea service during the early part of 1918. The unit went to Europe in September, 1918, and returned to the United States during Christmas week of the same year.

In December, 1921, the unit was reorganized and received Federal recognition on December 21. Since its reorganization the unit has trained annually at Fort Knox, and took an active part in the Army maneuvers at Fort Knox in 1936.

The 149th Infantry is the successor organization and entitled to historical continuity with the following predecessor units, viz.:[1]

A. Since World War—149th Infantry;
B. During World War—149th Infantry;
C. Up to World War and during Mexican border trouble —2d Kentucky Infantry;
D. Prior to Mexican border trouble to the War with Spain—2d Kentucky Infantry;
E. During the War with Spain—2d Regiment Infantry, Kentucky Volunteers, U.S. Army;
F. Prior to the War with Spain to War between the States—2d Kentucky Infantry having been reorganized after War between the States as 2d Regiment Infantry, Kentucky

BRIG. GEN. ELLERBE W. CARTER
63d F. A. Brigade,
38th Division

LT. COL. JOSEPH T. O'NEAL
Staff, 38th Division

State Guard. Mustered out Federal Service June, 1864. Eastern and western theaters of operations;

G. War between the States—2d Infantry, Kentucky Volunteers having been mustered into Federal service, 1861, as 2d Infantry Kentucky Volunteers;

H. Kentucky neutrality, 2d Regiment, Kentucky State Guard;

I. Prior to War between the States to the Mexican War— Reorganized in 1850 as 2d Infantry Regiment Kentucky Militia after being mustered out of Federal service in 1847;

J. Mexican War—2d Regiment, Kentucky Volunteers; organized in 1846 and became part of Taylor's army at the Battle of Buena Vista;

K. Prior to Mexican War to War of 1812—2d Regiment, Kentucky Militia;

L. War of 1812—2d Regiment, Kentucky Militia;

M. Prior to War of 1812 to and including Revolution— Lincoln County Militia Regiment;

N. Prior to 1780, a part of the Kentucky County Militia of Virginia.

Under the National Guard organization of 1938, the 149th Infantry consists of a Medical Detachment, Service Company, Howitzer Company, a Regimental Headquarters Company, three Battalion Headquarters companies, and twelve Letter companies, A through M.

The Medical Department Detachment, 149th Infantry Regiment, was Federally recognized August 19, 1921, and attended its first encampment that year, under the command of Capt. E. W. Stone and First Lt. Elwood Sanders, with an enlisted strength of thirty-one men. In 1922, Maj. Morton W. Moss, who commanded the unit until 1929, and Capt. Charles E. Francis, now Major in command, were recognized and assigned to the unit.

The Headquarters Company, 149th Infantry, was first organized as a part of the 149th Infantry at Camp Owen Bierne, El Paso, Texas, on September 15, 1916, during the Mexican Border campaign. The unit was made up of men transferred from rifle units of the Kentucky regiments.

The company was mustered out of service on February 12, 1917, but was recalled on April 12, 1917, for World War duty. Overseas the company furnished men for replacements in the trenches.

Under the new National Defense Act of 1921, the company was recognized on July 6, 1921, at Bowling Green, under Capt. Clinton H. Hinton; on May 26, 1924, at Pikeville, under Capt. Robert B. Doak; on June 1, 1926, at Anchorage, under Capt. Marcus J. Clarke; on June 1, 1927, at Anchorage, under Capt. Robert D. Powell; on February 4, 1931, at St. Matthews, under Capt. Earle B. Williams; and on April 22, 1937, at St. Matthews, under Capt. Jasper L. Cummings.

First Lt. Clarke organized the Headquarters Company, 1st Battalion, 149th Infantry, at Anchorage, March 27, 1925. With the redesignation of Lieutenant Clarke's unit he was appointed captain. Each commanding officer of Headquarters Company, after Captain Clarke, served as second lieutenant and communications officer of the 149th Infantry, prior to being commissioned captain.

The Service Company, 149th Infantry, originated with the formation of an infantry company in Bowling Green on November 26, 1879, when a group of citizens petitioned the Governor for permission to organize.

Company A, 3d Kentucky Infantry, left Bowling Green for service on the Mexican Border in 1916 under the command of Capt. Cooper R. Smith, First Lt. Malcolm H. Crump, Jr., and Second Lt. William T. Runner. After intensive training on the border and service at Canutillo, Texas, the company was mustered out of Federal service at Louisville on March 9, 1917. During the World War the members of Company A served with other units of combat, and the company lost its identity.

Upon reorganization of the National Guard of Kentucky it was decided by interested persons to organize a Service Company in Bowling Green. On April 6, 1921, the company was mustered in by Lt. Col. Charles H. Morrow, the officers being Capt. Alex Chaney, First Lt. Hamilton

Graham, First Lt. E. B. Blackwell, and Second Lt. Henry J. Potter. A few weeks later Julius T. Topmiller was sworn in as warrant officer and band leader.

The Howitzer Company, 149th Infantry, was organized and Federally recognized on April 12, 1924, with Capt. E. B. Blackwell of the state staff as mustering officer. Alger Hanks, sergeant instructor on duty with the National Guard, assisted Captain Blackwell in the organization of the company. Clarence B. Pumphrey was the first commanding officer of the organization, and Fisher B. Henry was first lieutenant. Henry resigned after a few weeks and Everett J. Beers of Carlisle, was appointed first lieutenant to fill the vacancy. The company's home station is at Carlisle.

In 1927 Pumphrey resigned as commanding officer and Everett J. Beers was promoted to the place, George C. Caywood being promoted to first lieutenant, June 6, 1927. Beers resigned in May, 1929, and Robert L. Norton was assigned to the post. Upon the resignation of Captain Norton, on May 15, 1933, First Lieutenant Caywood was appointed commanding officer. Teddy Poe was appointed first lieutenant on May 19, 1933, and Robert O. Henry was appointed second lieutenant on June 6, 1933. These officers have served in the capacities named since their promotions, and with four of the enlisted men, have been members of the company since its organization. The other original members of the unit are Sgt. Stanley Hardin, Corp. Cecil Scott, Pvt. Homer Frederick, and Pvt. Jesse Purcell. Nine-year medals have been issued to twelve members of the organization.

Headquarters Company, 1st Battalion, 149th Infantry, was organized at Harlan, on July 6, 1921, where it remained until 1925, when it was moved to Anchorage. In 1926 this organization was moved to Cynthiana and from there to Olive Hill in 1927. In 1928 the unit was located in Salt Lick, from which point it was moved to Lexington on May 16, 1930. It has remained in Lexington since that time.

The unit operates a short wave radio station (W9HDY) which has supplied several commercial operators to stations in Louisville and Lexington. The signals of this station have been heard in every section of the United States and by many stations in South America and Mexico.

Company A, 149th Infantry, was moved from Beattyville, and reorganized at Harlan in 1928, Federal recognition having been extended on March 16, 1929. Capt. Doc L. Nolan was the first commanding officer. Captain Nolan remained in command until March, 1933, when he was relieved because of ill health, and Capt. D. E. Perkins assumed command of the company, serving until the present.

Company B, 149th Infantry, was organized and Federally recognized on December 8, 1923, but the lineage of the company can be traced to a detachment of soldiers who served with Gen. Zachary Taylor in the Mexican War.

During the War with Spain another organization of Company B's forebears came to the defense of the country as Company I, 1st Kentucky Volunteers. Its officers were Capt. Viola Trimble, Lt. Will Campbell, and Lt. Charles Morrow. This unit is credited with service in Cuba and Puerto Rico. Following the War with Spain, Company I was mustered out of service with the regiment. A State Guard company was organized in Somerset and designated Company G, 2d Kentucky Infantry. In 1908, Capt. Henry Waddell commanded Company G, the unit which was the remote parent of Company B. The unit was mobilized at Fort Thomas in June, 1916, and served on the Mexican Border with the 2d Infantry, Kentucky National Guard, until February, 1917. At the entrance of the United States into the World War, the company served in France as a part of the 149th Infantry Regiment.

After the war, the 38th Division was reorganized and Company B, 149th Infantry, was allotted to Somerset. Capt. William S. Taylor was the first commanding officer of the new unit. During the summer encampment at Fort Knox in 1924, this unit, the youngest company in the regiment, won the Gen. Roger D. Williams cup for the best all-round company.

Captain Taylor has had as his successors Captains Louis

Tartar, Brinkley R. Gooch, and Harold W. Cain, the latter commanding officer in 1938.

Company C, 149th Infantry, is an outgrowth of the several militia companies that have been formed in Knox County since the Revolutionary War. During the War between the States, Knox County furnished the entire 49th Regiment, commanded by Col. John G. Eve. The 7th and 11th Regiments were made up of Kentucky mountain men, including many from Knox County. Over 60 per cent of the members of Company C are descendants of these veterans. Company C has its home station at Barbourville.

During the War with Spain, Knox County again furnished her quota of men, having organized Troop A, under the command of Capt. U. S. G. Perkins. In the interval between the War with Spain and the World War, the local company was designated Company B, 2d Kentucky Infantry. In 1916 a Knox County company saw service on the Mexican Border under the designation of Company M, 1st Kentucky Infantry. During the World War this unit was designated Company C, 113th Ammunition Train, 38th Division, and saw service in France.

After the World War, and the reorganization of the National Guard under the National Defense Act, the local unit was reorganized by the present company commander, as Company G, 2d Battalion, 149th Infantry, and was Federally recognized as such May 4, 1921. In 1928, the organization was redesignated Company C, 1st Battalion, 149th Infantry.

Since the World War this organization has contributed more than fifty men to the ranks of the Regular Army. The unit has had considerable active duty assigned to it within the State, including duty during the steel strike disturbances at Newport, in which service Pvt. Robert Deaton lost his life in the performance of his duties.

Company D, 149th Infantry, was Federally recognized on April 14, 1921, with Capt. (now Colonel) Roy W. Easley, First Lt. E. A. Woods and Second Lt. Fred W. Kerr. Colonel Easley is now regimental commander, Lieutenant Woods is dead, and Lieutenant Kerr is with the company as ranking lieutenant of the regiment. Colonel Easley was promoted in October, 1924, and Captain Mackey was placed in command of the company and has served to the present.

In 1933 an explosion in the armory building caused all records and equipment of the company to be destroyed by fire. The company has made astonishing progress in face of hardships, and has received a high rating on the yearly Federal inspection reports. Its home station is in Williamsburg.

Headquarters Company, 2d Battalion, 149th Infantry, was transferred to Maysville from Beattyville, on June 1, 1934. The original members still in the company are Sergeants Alfred P. Parker, Marion Bess, Robert F. Miller, Ernest A. Mefford, Corporals James J. Kinsler, and S. A. Miller and Pvt. Robert B. Huff.

Company E, 149th Infantry was so designated on July 1, 1921. The company was stationed at Whitesburg, under the command of Capt. Henry M. Holbrook. Company E was reorganized at Salt Lick, March 25, 1927, and was then commanded by Capt. Corbet L. Gullet.

The company was reorganized at Olive Hill on February 16, 1928, and was then commanded by Capt. Walter E. Miller. Capt. Boone Pelfrey, Lieutenant Foster, and Lieutenant McDowell, were appointed officers in the organization on September 16, 1931.

The company is at present commanded by First Lt. William D. Foster, who saw service during the World War and who is a graduate of the Infantry School, Fort Benning, Georgia. Lt. Clifford McDowell, the junior officer, enlisted February 16, 1928, and was graduated from the Citizens Military Training Corps in 1931. He was commissioned September 16, 1931, along with the commanding officer, and has served continuously since enlistment. The non-commissioned officers have gained their efficiency by long continuous service and through the aid of army extension courses.

Company F, 149th Infantry, was first organized as Company I, 2d Kentucky Infantry, at Booneville, April 16, 1910.

Isaac Wilder was elected captain; Daniel W. Barrett, first lieutenant; and Edward Combs, second lieutenant.

In the first six years of the company's existence it attended encampments at Fort Benjamin Harrison, Indiana; Anniston, Alabama; at Orell, near Louisville; Middlesboro, Blue Grass Park, Lexington, and Owensboro, Kentucky. The company saw service on the Mexican Border in 1916, being mustered out at Fort Thomas on February 15, 1917. On April 1, 1917, the company was called out by Governor Stanley for guard duty in the Eastern Kentucky coal fields. In preparation for World War duty, the company arrived at Camp Shelby, Mississippi, on September 29. There the designation of the company was changed to Company F, 149th Infantry, and the roster was increased to 238 men.

After the war the company was reorganized at Booneville, May 14, 1921, with Capt. Charles L. Seale, First Lt. Daniel W. Barrett, and Second Lt. Henry B. Moore. James H. Harvey was appointed captain on May 1, 1923, to succeed Captain Seale, who had been appointed major. Captain Harvey resigned March 13, 1925, and on March 18, 1925, Captain Barrett took command.

Company G, 149th Infantry, at Ashland was recruited in the fall of 1927. The company was mustered into service on December 6, 1927, as the 126th Wagon Company, 38th Division, Quartermaster Corps. The officers of the company at that time were Capt. Gustavus H. May, First Lt. Robert T. Barrett, and Second Lt. Thomas E. McCracken, who have continued with the organization.

The new company attended field training at Camp Knox for the first time in August of 1928. In July, 1929, the organization was redesignated Company G, 149th Infantry, and attended camp under Col. Jackson Morris, commanding the 149th Infantry. In the fall of 1929 one officer and eight men were selected to form part of the composite rifle company to represent the 149th Infantry in the parade of the American Legion during the national convention in Louisville.

At the 1930 encampment at Camp Knox, Company G was awarded the Henry H. Denhardt trophy for efficiency, competition being among the units of the 75th Brigade. The Regimental baseball trophy was also won by the company that year. Later in the fall of 1930, Company G had a football team which won the city championship in the semi-pro league at Ashland.

There are three members of the organization, in addition to the officers, who attended the first field encampment of the unit in 1927. The men are First Sgt. Thomas W. Jones, Supply Sgt. Cecil D. Butler, and Sgt. Frank R. Johnson. These men were awarded a medal at the last field encampment for nine years of faithful service in the Kentucky National Guard.

Company H, 149th Infantry, was organized at Ravenna, under the command of Capt. Monroe T. Bach, a veteran of the World War. The company received Federal recognition on March 18, 1932, with an authorized strength of three officers and sixty-three enlisted men. When organized, the company was quartered in a leased building which later proved too small for a machine gun company. Through the efforts of Captain Bach an armory was built for the company. Construction of the armory was completed in August, 1934, and occupied on arrival of Company H at its home station after its third encampment at Fort Knox. The armory was named Bach Hall in memory of the company's first commander. Captain Bach died at Jackson, in August, 1933, while the company was on its annual field encampment, and Capt. Walter L. McPherson, being a commissioned first lieutenant, second in command to Captain Bach, took command of the unit. Captain McPherson received a commission as captain Company H, on December 30, 1933.

Headquarters Company, 3d Battalion, 149th Infantry, has for its background the many notable military organizations formed in Hopkins County since the county's organization in 1807. The earliest militia of the county was organized during the Indian wars preceding the War of 1812. In the War of 1812, Capt. Michael Wolf recruited his company, which was a part of the 1st Kentucky Mounted Infantry commanded by Lt. Col. Samuel Caldwell. The unit was called into service under Gen. Samuel Hopkins by Gov. Isaac Shelby, September 8, 1812, and proceeded to Vincennes in a campaign against the Kickapoos.

In the following years, the organized militia was carried on as a unit of the 76th Infantry Regiment and was commanded by Col. Alexander M. Henry and his successors.

Headquarters Company, 3d Battalion, was mustered at Madisonville on May 24, 1926, by Capt. Gershom Cronader and received Federal recognition June 1 of the same year. For two consecutive years, 1930-31, Headquarters Company won the National Defense Trophy for having a highter percentage of its members qualifying with the rifle than any other organization in the state. A five-man team won the 3d Battalion Rifle Match at Madisonville in 1931, and won the same match held the next year at Livermore.

Company I, 149th Infantry, was transferred from Pikeville to Marion, and was mustered into Federal service by Col. Charles Morrow, on March 9, 1925, with the designation Company C, 149th Infantry, Kentucky National Guard. The designation of the company was changed to Company I, 149th Infantry, on June 12, 1926.

Company K, 149th Infantry, was originally organized on April 25, 1921. Charles F. Thomasson and forty-nine other men secured permission to organize a rifle company of infantry at Livermore. Maj. Thomas W. Woodyard was ordered to muster the company into service. At its muster on April 30, 1921, it was designated Company K, 1st Infantry. On June 11, 1921, Federal recognition was extended the company, and it was designated as Company K, 149th Infantry. Its officers were Capt. Charles F. Thomasson, First Lt. Oren Coin, and Second Lt. Cammeron A. Brown. On June 14, 1922, Captain Thomasson was promoted to the rank of major and assigned to the command of the 3d Battalion, 149th Infantry; First Lieutenant Coin was promoted to captain; Second Lieutenant Brown was promoted to first lieutenant; and Sgt. Ernest E. Price was made a second lieutenant.

On June 14, 1929, Captain Coin was promoted to major to succeed Major Thomasson; First Lieutenant Brown was made captain, and First Sgt. Brodie L. Payne was made First Lieutenant.

Company K has one man, Sgt. Otis P. Whitaker, who has been with the company since its organization. He has served as mess sergeant since March 1, 1924.

Company L, 149th Infantry, was organized by Capt. John T. Roach and was recognized Federally on February 22, 1922. At the death of Captain Roach, one month later, First Lt. Fred A. Crawford was promoted to captain and served as company commander until his resignation July 7, 1928. First Lt. Joseph Leech was then promoted to captain and has since served in that capacity. Company L has its home station at Mayfield.

Company M, 149th Infantry, is the successor of Company M, 3d Kentucky Infantry, organized in Russellville, April, 1902, with Capt. Marmaduke B. Bowden, First Lt. Caldwell Browder and Second Lt. C. J. O'Connell as officers. The company was demobilized in 1905. Company M was revived in Russellville on May 7, 1916, by Capt. A. M. Stevenson, First Lt. E. J. Felts, and Second Lt. John F. Logan, and entered the Federal service for duty on the Mexican Border in July, 1916. Captain Stevenson, commanding officer, failed to pass the physical examination and Lieutenant Felts became captain, Lieutenant Logan, first lieutenant, and Sgt. Dorris Hanes became second lieutenant. The company did guard duty at Camp Owen Bierne and other points along the Mexican border until February 2, 1917, when it was ordered home.

Company M went into Federal service at the entrance of the United States into the World War and served under the the designation of Company B, 113th Engineers. Following the war, the company was demobilized June 26, 1919.

On June 14, 1922, Company M, 149th Infantry, was Federally recognized in Russellville. Its officers, all of whom were

World War veterans, were Capt. O. P. M. Squires, First Lt. S. H. Brown, and Second Lt. B. C. Griffith. Company M used an old one-story concrete building for an armory until 1933, when a new armory was put under construction and completed in 1934. The building is of brick and stone with hardwood floors.

Since 1922 Company M has been commanded by the following captains: O. P. M. Squires, June 22, 1922–August 1, 1922; S. H. Brown, August 1, 1922–April 3, 1924; B. C. Griffith, April 4, 1924–September 5, 1925; O. P. M. Squires, September 6, 1925–February 1, 1926; E. W. Flowers, February 2, 1926–January 5, 1927; Joe M. Brown, January 6, 1927–October 10, 1928; John F. Flowers, October 11, 1928–December, 1929; Henry O. Price, December 20, 1929, incumbent, 1938.

The 123d Cavalry, Kentucky National Guard, is the successor organization and entitled to historical continuity with the following predecessor units:[1]

A. Since April, 1929—123d Cavalry;

B. Prior thereto and since World War—53d and 54th Machine Gun Squadrons;

C. During World War—138th Machine Gun Battalion;

D. Up to World War and during Mexican border trouble—3d Kentucky Infantry;

E. Prior to Mexican border trouble to the War with Spain—3d Kentucky Infantry;

F. During the War with Spain—3d Kentucky Infantry; Kentucky; Volunteers, U.S. Army;

G. Prior to the War with Spain, to the War between the States—3d Kentucky Infantry;

H. War between the States—2d Kentucky Cavalry;

I. Kentucky neutrality, 3d Regiment, Kentucky State Guard;

J. Prior to War between the States to Mexican War—3d Regiment, Kentucky Militia;

K. Mexican War—1st Regiment, Kentucky Volunteer Cavalry;

L. Prior to Mexican War to War of 1812—3d Regiment, Kentucky Militia;

M. War of 1812—3d Regiment, Mounted Riflemen;

N. Prior to War of 1812 to and including Revolution—Fayette County Militia Regiment;

O. Prior to 1780, a part of the Kentucky County Militia of Virginia.

Units constituting the 123d Cavalry are Headquarters Troop and Band, Machine Gun Troop, Medical Detachment and three squadrons. The 1st Squadron is composed of Troops A and B; Troops E and F compose the 2d Squadron, and the 3d Squadron consists of Troops I and K.

Headquarters Troop and Band Section, 123 Cavalry, Glasgow, was Federally recognized April 1, 1929. Its officers at the time of recognition were Capt. Albert E. Ely, First Lt. Sam Sears, Second Lt. Walter E. Nunn, and Warrant Officer Edward S. Pedigo.

Edward Pedigo was promoted to first lieutenant and assigned to the Regimental Staff. Sgt. Clayton Simmons was promoted to warrant officer and directed the band for about three years. When Simmons resigned he was replaced by Sgt. Wayne E. Tyree, who is the present warrant officer and band director. Richard L. Garnett served as second lieutenant for a time, but resigned following an automobile accident. William H. Jones, Jr., was appointed captain at the expiration of his term as commanding officer of Headquarters Troop, 123d Cavalry. Captain Jones was adjutant general of Kentucky at the time of the Headquarters Troop and band section's Federal recognition.

Captain Ely was assigned to the regimental staff as supply officer. Upon the resignation of Captain Jones, who served only a short time as commanding officer of Headquarters Troop and band section, Captain Ely was transferred back to the troop and served as commanding officer until his resignation in 1934. At this time First Lt. Sam Sears was promoted to captain and assigned to Headquarters Troop as commanding officer.

All officers and about ten of the enlisted men have been members of the troop since 1929. The officers of the troop at present are: Capt. Samuel Sears, commanding; First Lt. Jesse A. Cassady, communications officer; Second Lt. Robert Abner, staff platoon; Second Lt. Fred R. Ganther, scout car section; and Warrant Officer Wayne E. Tyree, band.

The Medical Department Detachment, 123d Cavalry, with its home station in Hopkinsville, was organized and Federally recognized April 15, 1922. Capt. Philip E. Haynes was instrumental in the organization of this unit and still commands the detachment in the capacity of major. The five other officers on the staff are Capt. Robert C. Riggs, M.C.; Capt. Omar S. Meredith, D.C.; Capt. George W. Pedigo, V.C.; Capt. John R. Stifler, V.C.; and Lt. Delmus M. Clardy, M.C. Three of these officers are veterans of the World War and have seen continuous military service since that period.

The Medical Detachment has had the honor of supplying the primary military background of several West Pointers, one of these, Lt. Littleton W. Pardue, entered the academy after serving one enlistment period in the detachment.

Troop A, 123d Cavalry, located in Frankfort, was formed and Federally recognized November 30, 1921 as Troop A, 54th Machine Gun Squadron under command of Capt. Carl D. Norman. On its conversion into cavalry in 1929, the unit was redesignated Troop A, 123d Cavalry.

The troop has been at the head of the inaugural parade of every Governor since its organization. In addition the the troop has served President Franklin D. Roosevelt on two occasions, once on his visit to Fort Harrod, and again upon his visit to the Lincoln Memorial, Hodgenville.

The present officers of the troop are Capt. F. Coburn Gayle, only charter member of the troop; First Lt. Louis P. Smith, and Second Lt. Albert C. Smith.

The stables of the troop, built in 1932 and modernized in 1937, are a show place. Concrete aisles and stands, overhead hay racks, central watering fountain, and electrically lighted stalls make the stables the best of their kind.

Troop B, 123d Cavalry, was originally organized at Louisa, as Troop C, 53d Machine Gun Squadron. On July 27, 1920, Capt. David L. Thompson and Second Lt. Garland Webb assembled the organization at Louisa, where it was inspected by Capt. William O. Reed, Cavalry, U.S.A., and both officers and the unit received Federal recognition as of that date.

On June 28, 1924, Troop C, 53d Machine Gun Squadron, was transferred from Louisa to Lexington and placed under the command of Captain Maurey. Captain Maurey was succeeded by Capt. Eugene Payne Wilkerson shortly afterward, and on January 1, 1925, Capt. Frank S. Wright took command of the organization. Capt. Cabel Breckinridge took command in January, 1926, and was succeeded by Capt. Dewey S. Congleton, the present commander, on October 18 1927.

In 1929, this organization was redesignated Troop B, 123d Cavalry, being one of the six letter troops forming the nucleus of the regiment. The troop holds its annual field training at Fort Knox, under the leadership of Captain Congleton, assisted by First Lt. James D. Foster and Second Lt. Vernon N. Chandler. The unit has many trophies won at Fort Knox in competition for platoon efficiency, mess management, stable management, and other features consistent with army life.

Troop E, 123d Cavalry, is a successor of the old Company A, 2d Kentucky Infantry, organized at London 1910 with James G. Eversole as captain, James K. Dillon, first lieutenant and Russell Dyche, second lieutenant. Until 1916 the activities of the unit were confined chiefly to summer encampments.

In 1916, with Capt. James K. Dillon in command, it participated in the Federal mobilization of the National Guard on the Mexican Border. During the World War, the unit was given the designation of Company A, 149th Infantry and as such saw service in France after training at Camp Shelby, Mississippi. Although serving principally as a training unit, supplying men to combat units in France, a segment of the original company was kept intact and eventually was mustered out of service at the close of hostilities.

With the reorganization of the National Guard after the war, Capt. Dillon again took command at London, and through his efforts in 1920, Troop B, 53d Machine Gun Squadron became the first Federally recognized National Guard unit in Kentucky. Shortly after Captain Dillon relinquished command to become squadron commander with the rank of major, and later became lieutenant colonel of the 123d Cavalry. He was succeeded in command of the troop by Capt. Guy Tuggle, who was subsequently succeeded by Capt. Charles B. Dillon. Under his command in 1929 the troop was converted into Cavalry Rifle Troop E, 123d Cavalry. Capt. Walter B. Rawlings assumed command in 1932, and the following year Capt. Willis G. Hackney, then supply officer, 149th Infantry, was transferred to Troop E as commanding officer.

Shortly after the War Department had authorized the formation of the 123d Cavalry, Maj. George E. Nelson was commissioned to organize a troop of cavalry in Covington. In February of that year, Major Nelson held the first meeting of those interested in the project, and by May the required fifty men had been enlisted. On June 10, 1929, Captain (now major) Cronander, Cavalry, U.S.A., inducted the troop into service, and the unit was designated Troop F, 123d Cavalry, and was extended Federal recognition from that date. The original officers of the troop were Capt. George E. Nelson, First Lt. Harry E. Rauch and Second Lt. Fred M. Warren.

Although the unit was recognized and accepted on June 10, 1929, it was not until March 15, 1930, that the troop actually was equipped as a cavalry unit, when the first shipment of sixteen horses was received. In April of 1932, Captain Nelson was promoted to major of cavalry and assigned command of the 2d Squadron, and First Lieutenant Warren was thereupon promoted to captain and made the troop's second commanding officer. Troop F acted as the Governor's Horse Guards and Guard of Honor for Governor Chandler in Washington, D.C., during the Presidential inauguration in January, 1937.

The present officers of the troop, two of whom are graduates of Fort Riley Cavalry School, are Capt. Fred M. Warren (Riley, 1931), First Lt. R. Ray Gorrell, and Second Lt. Steve J. Meade (Riley, 1938).

Troop I, 123d Cavalry, was originally Federally recognized on June 2, 1921, as Troop A of the 53d Machine Gun Squadron. The troop was organized by Lt. Col. William O. Reed, U.S.A., and the following officers were appointed by the Governor of Kentucky: Capt. John A. Polin, First Lt. Hugh B. Gregory, Second Lt. Charles J. Haydon, and Second Lt. Joseph L. Montgomery. Louis A. Barber was first sergeant.

On April 1, 1929, when the 123d Cavalry Regiment was organized the officers and enlisted men of Troop A, 53d Machine Gun Squadron, were transferred to Troop I. 123d Cavalry. Captain Polin was promoted to the rank of major on May 1, 1930, and assigned the command of the 2d Squadron, 123d Cavalry. First Lieutenant Gregory was promoted to captain of Troop I to fill the vacancy left by Captain Polin. At the same time Second Lt. George W. Gardiner was promoted to first lieutenant.

On December 18, 1933, Captain Gregory was transferred to the Regimental Staff and First Lieutenant Barber of the Division Staff was promoted to the rank of captain of Troop I. On May 16, 1935, Henry W. Merritt was promoted to the rank of captain of the troop, which rank he now holds.

Of the original troop, the following men are still members: Capt. Henry W. Merritt, First Sgt. George W. Moore, and Stable Sgt. James L. Overall. First Sergeant Moore has the record of never having missed a drill since he became a member of the troop. The three officers now commanding the troop are Captain Merrit, First Lt. William C. Mudd, and Second Lt. Joseph E. Polin.

Troop K, 123d Cavalry, was organized as Troop B, 54th Machine Gun Squadron, mustered in and Federally recognized December 29, 1921. In 1929 Troop B became Troop

COLONEL SIDNEY SMITH
138th Infantry, Ky. N. G.

COLONEL HENRY J. STITES
123d Cavalry, Ky. N. G.

COLONEL ROY W. EASLEY
149th Field Artillery, Ky. N. G.

K in this regiment. Since 1924, thirty-eight trophies have been won by this troop during the summer encampments. The trophies have been awarded for the most efficient troop, troop morale, mess management, stable management, platoon efficiency, officer's jump, officer's charger, manual of arms, best mounted trooper, mounted potato race, best mounted non-commissioned officer, best drilled enlisted man, best drilled recruit, best pistol shot, best rifle shot, mounted wrestling, and mounted tug of war. The troop has also been active in the state fairs, county fairs, and fox hunts, winning many prizes and trophies. The armory of the troop was built and dedicated in 1928. The officers of the troop are Capt. Joel L. Stokes, First Lt. Raymond O. Cook, and Second Lt. Edward B. Allred.

The Machine Gun Troop, 123d Cavalry, is located at Hopkinsville, Christian County. When Company D, of the old 3d Kentucky Regiment, stationed at Hopkinsville, was mustered out of service following the World War, a group of citizens of the city organized a troop of cavalry. On February 10, 1922, the troop was Federally recognized and mustered in as Troop C, 54th Machine Gun Squadron. The first troop commander was Capt. Allen Radford. Capt. Radford was succeeded by Capt. J. C. Hanberry, who in turn was succeeded by Capt. (now Major) Joseph M. Kelly. On May 1, 1930, the 123d Cavalry Regiment having been organized, Troop C became a component of the regiment and was redesignated as the Machine Gun Troop. Capt. Alvin H. Schutz was placed in command succeeding Major Kelly, who was given command of the 3d Squadron. First Sgt. James S. Gourley has served in this troop continuously since its organization on February 10, 1922. Six of its seven sergeants and one corporal have served for more than nine years.

NOTES, REFERENCES, AND SOURCES

1. For the purpose of summarizing the history of the three Regiments of the Kentucky National Guard, namely, 149th Infantry, 138th Field Artillery, and 123rd Cavalry, and to permanently establish the lineal connection between these organizations, and

their predecessor units through the several wars and campaigns in which such Kentucky troops participated; the World War; the Mexican Border trouble; the War with Spain; the War between the States; Kentucky's neutrality immediately prior to and during the first four months of the War between the States; the Mexican War; the War of 1812; and the American Revolution; a chain of succession was published by Adjutant General's General Orders No. 1 of February 8, 1933.

See also *Historical Annual, National Guard of the Commonwealth of Kentucky, 1938.*

APPENDIX A

GOVERNORS OF VIRGINIA 1776–92

Last Royal Governor, John Murray, Earl of Dunmore, 1772–June 29, 1776.
Gov. Patrick Henry, June 29, 1776.
Gov. Thos. Jefferson, June 1, 1779.
Gov. Thomas Nelson, June 12, 1781.
Gov. Benjamin Harrison, November, 1781.
Gov. Patrick Henry, December, 1784.
Gov. Edmund Randolph, December, 1786.
Gov. Beverly Randolph, December, 1788.
Gov. Henry Lee, December, 1791.

John Bowman was commissioned colonel of the Kentucky County Militia by Gov. Patrick Henry on December 21, 1776, and again commissioned by Gov. Thomas Jefferson in 1778, under which commission he served as the chief militia officer of Kentucky County until its trisection in 1780.

GOVERNORS AND ADJUTANT GENERALS OF KENTUCKY

Gov. Isaac Shelby, June 4, 1792–June 1, 1796.
    Adjt. Gen. Percival Butler (exact date of first appointment not in *Executive Journal*, but known to have served through whole of Governor Shelby's administration; see Collins *History of Kentucky*, Vol. II, p. 121).
Gov. James Garrard, June 1, 1796–September 5, 1804.
    Adjt. Gen. Percival Butler.
Gov. Christopher Greenup, September 5, 1804–1808.
    Adjt. Gen. Percival Butler.
Gov. Charles Scott, September, 1808–12.
    Adjt. Gen. Percival Butler.
Gov. Isaac Shelby, September, 1812–16.
    Adjt. Gen. Percival Butler, to 1814.
    Adjt. Gen. John Adair, 1814–17.
Gov. George Madison, September 5, 1816 (died October 14, 1816).
    Adjt. Gen. John Adair, 1816–17.
Gov. Gabriel Slaughter, October 19, 1816–20.
    Adjt. Gen. Oliver G. Waggoner (commissioned September 18, 1817).
Gov. John Adair, September, 1820–24.
    Adjt. Gen. Oliver G. Waggoner.
Gov. Joseph Desha, September, 1824–28.
    Adj. Gen. Oliver G. Waggoner (resigned January 29, 1828).
    Adjt. Gen. Preston S. Loughborough (commissioned January 29, 1828).

Gov. Thomas Metcalf, September, 1828–32.
  Adjt. Gen. Peter Dudley (commissioned December 10, 1829).
Gov. John Breathitt, September, 1832 (died February, 1834).
  Adjt. Gen. Peter Dudley.
Gov. James T. Morehead, February 25, 1834–August 30, 1836.
  Adjt. Gen. Peter Dudley.
Gov. James Clark, August 30, 1836 (died August 27, 1839).
  Adjt. Gen. Peter Dudley.
Gov. Charles A. Wickliffe, August 27, 1839–September, 1840.
  Adjt. Gen. Peter Dudley.
Gov. Robert P. Letcher, September, 1840–44.
  Adjt. Gen. Peter Dudley.
Gov. William Owsley, September, 1844–48.
  Adjt. Gen. Peter Dudley.
Gov. John J. Crittenden, September, 1848 (resigned July 30, 1850).
  Adjt. Gen. Peter Dudley.
Gov. John L. Helm, July 30, 1850–September 1, 1851.
  Adjt. Gen. Peter Dudley (resigned April 15, 1851).
  Adjt. Gen. John M. Harlan (commissioned April 16, 1851).
Gov. Lazarus W. Powell, September 1, 1851–55.
  Adjt. Gen. John M. Harlan.
Gov. Charles S. Morehead, September, 1855–59.
  Adjt. Gen. John M. Harlan (commissioned September 17, 1855).
Gov. Beriah Magoffin, September, 1859 (resigned August 18, 1862).
  Adjt. Gen. Scott Brown (commissioned September 12, 1859).
Gov. James F. Robinson, August 18, 1862–September 1, 1863.
  Adjt. Gen. John W. Finnell (commissioned August 19, 1862; resigned September 1, 1863)
Gov. Thomas E. Bramlette, September 1, 1863–67.
  Adjt. Gen. John Boyle (commissioned September 1, 1863; resigned August 1, 1864).
  Adjt. Gen. D. W. Lindsey (commissioned August 1, 1864).
Gov. John L. Helm, September 3, 1867—served one day and died September 4, 1867.
Gov. John W. Stevenson, September 4, 1867 (resigned February 13, 1871).
  Adjt. Gen. Frank L. Wolford (commissioned October 2, 1867; resigned March 8, 1870).
  Adjt. Gen. J. Stoddard Johnston (commissioned March 9, 1870).
Gov. Preston H. Leslie (Acting) February 13, 1871–September 1, 1871.
  Adjt. Gen. J. Stoddard Johnston.
Gov. Preston H. Leslie, September 1, 1871–September 1, 1875.
  Adjt. Gen. James A. Dawson, September, 1873–75.
Gov. James B. McCreary, September, 1875–79.
  Adjt. Gen. J. M. Wright, 1875–79.
Gov. Luke P. Blackburn, September, 1879–83.
  Adjt. Gen. Joseph P. Nuckols, September, 1879–83.
Gov. J. Proctor Knott, September, 1883–87.
  Adjt. Gen. John B. Castleman, September, 1883–September 30, 1887.

MILITARY HISTORY OF KENTUCKY 405

Gov. Simon Bolivar Buckner, September 1, 1887–91.
Adjt. Gen. Sam E. Hill, September 30, 1887–91.
Gov. John Young Brown, September, 1891–December, 1895.
Adjt. Gen. A. J. Gross, September, 1891–December 10, 1895.
Gov. William O. Bradley, December 10, 1895–99.
Adjt. Gen. D. R. Collier, December 10, 1895 (resigned September 8, 1898).
Adjt. Gen. Wilbur R. Smith, September 8, 1898.
Gov. William S. Taylor, December, 1899–January 31, 1900 (removed by court order).
Adjt. Gen. D. R. Collier, appointed December 13, 1899.
Gov. William Goebel, January 30, 1900 (died February 3, 1900).
Adjt. Gen. not named (John B. Castleman, acting).
Gov. J. C. W. Beckham, February 3, 1900–December, 1903.
Adjt. Gen. John B. Castleman (commissioned February 3, 1900–November, 1900).
Adjt. Gen. David R. Murray (commissioned November 30, 1900).
Gov. J. C. W. Beckham, December, 1903–December, 1907.
Adjt. Gen. W. P. D. Haley (commissioned December 10, 1903; resigned April 19, 1906).
Adj. Gen. Henry R. Lawrence (commissioned April 19, 1906).
Gov. Augustus E. Wilson, December 10, 1907–11.
Adjt. Gen. P. P. Johnston (commissioned December 13, 1907–11).
Gov. James B. McCreary, December 12, 1911–15.
Adjt. Gen. W. B. Haldeman (commissioned January 5, 1912).
Gov. Augustus O. Stanley, December 7, 1915–19.
Adjt. Gen. James Tandy Ellis (commissioned December 20, 1915).
Gov. James B. Black, May 19, 1919–December 9, 1919.
Adjt. Gen. James Tandy Ellis (continued in office).
Gov. Edwin P. Morrow, December 9, 1919–23.
Adjt. Gen. James W. Deweese (commissioned December 20, 1919; resigned November 1, 1920).
Adjt. Gen. Jackson Morris (commissioned November 1, 1920).
Gov. William J. Fields, December 11, 1923–27.
Adjt. Gen. Jouett Henry (commissioned December 11, 1923; resigned March 19, 1924).
Adjt. Gen. James Arthur Kehoe (commissioned March 19, 1924).
Gov. Flem D. Sampson, December, 1927–31.
Adjt. Gen. William H. Jones, Jr. (commissioned December 13, 1927).
Gov. Ruby Laffoon, December, 1931–35.
Adjt. Gen. Henry Denhardt, December, 1931–35.
Gov. Albert Benjamin Chandler, December, 1935 (Incumbent).
Adjt. Gen. G. Lee McClain, December, 1935 (Incumbent).

APPENDIX B

Confederate Pensions

Kentucky approved a Confederate Home act on March 27, 1902. A subsequent act of February 26, 1904, provided an appropriation for such a home to take care of dependent and infirm Confederate veterans. A Confederate Home at Peewee Valley was opened in 1905 with a capacity of about 400. During the first decade of the Home's operation its population varied between 350 and 400. About 1915 numbers began to dwindle, and few new applicants appeared. A gradual decrease continued until 1932 when the institution was discontinued. Quarters were thereupon provided, for the few survivors, in the Peewee Valley Sanitorium. In 1938 a single survivor was maintained by the state at the Sanitorium.

A Confederate pension law was enacted March 11, 1912. Records are not available of the total amount paid to the pensioners. However, the following Confederate Pension Department allowance in the state budget is of relative importance:

1928–29 was $225,000	1934–35 was $195,000
1930–31 was 215,000	1936–37 was 170,000
1932–33 was 210,000	1938–39 was 160,000

In 1938 a total of twenty-five Confederate veterans drew state pensions, the amount being $50 per month each. There are 408 widows of veterans on the pension rolls (1938). These are divided into three classes drawing $50, $40, or $30 per month.

APPENDIX C

JEROME CLARKE TRIAL

(Abstract of U. S. War Department's record).

Jerome Clarke, whose alias, Sue Mundy, is said to have been given him because a girl bearing that name had stolen a horse and then had maintained that Clarke was really the culprit, was tried by a military commission at Louisville, in March, 1865. The charge was that of "being a guerrilla," the specifications including the claim that, although the accused was a citizen of Kentucky and the United States and "owing allegiance thereto," he had taken up arms as a guerrilla, "not acting with any lawfully authorized or organized military force at war with the United States," and that he "did fire upon a detachment of the 30th Regiment, Wisconsin Volunteer Infantry, commanded by Captain Lewis O. Marshall . . . did wound privates John G. White, John Robbins and W. A. Wadsworth." Clarke, who alleged that he fired in self-defense, when they were about to capture him, was found guilty and was sentenced to be hanged in Louisville, March 15, 1865.

The detail for the court of trial was as follows: Brig. Gen. Walter C. Whitaker, Bvt. Brig. Gen. J. H. Hammond, Colonel Graham of the 11th Kentucky Volunteer Cavalry, Col. T. H. Bringhurst, and Lt. Col. A. M. Flory of the 46th Indiana V.V.I., Col. S. A. Porter, Lt. Col. E. M. Bartlett of the 30th Wisconsin Volunteer Infantry, Maj. J. L. Wharton of the 5th Kentucky Volunteer Cavalry, Maj. U. H. Foster, and Lt. Col. William H. Coyl of the 9th Iowa Infantry who served as Acting Judge Advocate for the Department of Kentucky.

The first witness was Major Cyrus T. Wilson of the 21st Kentucky Volunteer Infantry, who had been ordered to proceed with fifty men to a point ten miles beyond Brandenburg, and to catch Mundy and his companion, Magruder, if possible. Going to the home of Dr. Lewis, who had been "tending on Magruder," Wilson compelled him to guide the force to a tobacco barn in Meade County, owned by one Cox. When there was no answer to the demand to open the door, the men were directed to break it down with a rock, whereupon shots were fired from within. After an exhange of shots, Dr. Lewis was sent in with a flag of truce to demand surrender. A man named Medkiff was with Mundy and Magruder. Mundy demanded a parley with Major Wilson, who was later joined by Captain Marshall, whose testimony at the trial was substantially the same as that of Wilson. Mundy was advised that they had orders to take him, dead or alive, and that while he would probably meet death in Louisville, his life would be prolonged for a few days. Wilson further argued that there would be one chance in a thousand or ten thousand for him to escape. This appeal helped to influence Mundy, who was being urged by Magruder to give himself up and, after a "smoke together," the surrender was made. Captain Marshall, three of whose men had been seriously wounded in the exchange of hostilities, declared on the witness stand: "If the flag of truce had not been sent up, I should have set the building on fire."

According to Wilson, Mundy said that there was "enough published against him to kill" him at Louisville. He seemed to resent being called Mundy, for, he asserted, "the publication made concerning him fooling Morgan . . . was all damn stuff and there was nothing of it about his having an introduction to Morgan as Sue Mundy and asking him and receiving from him a Lieutenancy." Marshall swore that Mundy had said "he knew damned well he had got to die when he got to Louisville, that he knew there were charges enough to swing him up."

William M. Bradley, of Company A, 14th Illinois Infantry, testified that when he was in a party of four, near New Castle, they were taken by a group of about fifteen, over which, he thought, Mundy was in command. Bradley was shot because he could not double-quick "faster on account of a sore" on his leg. Another man died from wounds inflicted.

Hiram Meadows, private in Company G, 1st Wisconsin Infantry, with his brother and a few other men, on Christmas Day, 1864, were out on their "own hook foraging," but went a little too far and were captured by Sue Mundy and ten of his men, and were marched all that afternoon and the following night. The brother gave out and was threatened with being shot. This, Meadows testified, was done "right before my eyes." The remaining prisoners managed to escape at night while the guard was being changed.

Private Alfred Hill was on board a train near St. Mary's that was fired on by the Mundy band. He also saw Mundy in New Haven, robbing the citizens. Hill and a small posse pursued Mundy and his followers, according to Hill's testimony.

John Brant, a railroad brakeman, residing at Bardstown, described his having seen Mundy on several occasions. Near Bardstown, Mundy had thrown a train off the track and had burned one car. Mundy and about twenty-five or thirty of his men had later engaged in "a little fight" at Bardstown with Companies A and B of the 54th Kentucky.

The accused, after the evidence against him had been presented, requested time to prove he had been a regular Confederate soldier. The court, however, after deliberation, decided that "such evidence would not be material in the present case, as the accused was charged with certain crimes that would cause even a detached Confederate soldier to be punished."

According to the statement presented by Clarke (Mundy), he had entered the Confederate Army from Henderson, had been at Bowling Green for a time, and was captured at the Battle of Fort Donelson. After imprisonment at Louisville for six months, with General Buckner, he was exchanged and was sent to Vicksburg. He was, he declared, also in the Battles of Chattanooga and Ringold, and later saw service in several states. On his return to

Kentucky, he fought at Mount Sterling. At Cynthiana, he and his comrades "had a fight and captured Hobson," but were whipped the next day by General Burbridge, and scattered. After various skirmishes, he withdrew to Nelson County, where he threw off the Confederate uniform and dressed as a citizen. It was when he was accused by the townspeople of being a rebel soldier that he joined Magruder. He admitted capturing the train on the Lebanon Railroad, and also said he met Sam Beard at Pound Gap and was present at the death of Beard. Having been ordered to go to Paris, he got as far as Brandenburg, where he was joined by Medkiff. They were "bushwhacked and Magruder was wounded." Clarke (Mundy) took Magruder to Meade County and there they were captured.

APPENDIX D

Military Memorials

PARKS

Blue and Gray State Park is three miles northeast of Elkton on State 181. It is located between Fairview, the birthplace of Jefferson Davis, and Hodgenville, the birthplace of Abraham Lincoln, and in location and name it commemorates the divided sentiment of Kentucky and the symbolical coincidence of supplying the Commanders-in-Chief of both the Union and Confederate armies. The park was established in 1925, when citizens of Todd County donated the eighty-six–acre tract to the State Park Commission.

Blue Licks Battlefield State Park, on the east side of Licking River along U.S. 68, is the site of the battle by that name (*ante, p. 33*). A granite shaft, bearing the names of those who fell in the battle, stands near the main park entrance. Many of the participants of this battle are buried in a stone walled enclosure near-by. The park, established in 1926, comprises thirty-seven acres. In it is a museum containing the Curtis-Hunter collection of prehistoric bones and relics.

Butler Memorial State Park, near Carrollton on U.S. 227, was named for Gen. William Orlando Butler, outstanding member of a family which distinguished itself in military affairs. In the little cemetery near the old Butler mansion are the graves of Percival Butler, Kentucky's first adjutant general, and Gen. William Orlando Butler, two of the five sons of Thomas Butler who, together with their lineal descendants, engaged in military service in all the wars of this country. General Lafayette is said to have remarked of this family of soldiers, "When I wanted a thing done well, I ordered a Butler to do it."

The park consists of 350 acres, largely the gift of citizens of Carroll County. In the last decade numerous improvements have been made.

Columbus-Belmont Memorial State Park, just outside of Columbus on State 123, overlooks the Mississippi River and occupies the site of Confederate fortifications. During the War between the States, when the Confederates seized and fortified the bluff at this point (*ante, p. 162*), Columbus attained national prominence as "the Gibraltar of the West." The fortifications and great trenches have been restored and landscaped, and the remains of the water battery are still discernible. A great anchor with the links of its huge chain is one of the show pieces of the park. Many of the smaller relics gathered from the trenches have been assembled in a museum, and the Confederate dispensary has been restored.

The park, embracing around 330 acres, also commemorates the blockhouse which, according to local tradition, was established here in 1780 by George Rogers Clark. However, the first authentic record of a military post at this point begins about 1804. At the time of the Burr Conspiracy, United States troops were rushed to Columbus. From this time on Columbus, as a strategic military point, assumed an importance comparable to the great forces that were moving for control, not only of the Mississippi River but of the entire mid-continental region.

Levi Jackson Wilderness Road State Park, near London on U.S. 25, was named for a Revolutionary soldier who received land here for his military services. It is also the site of the Defeated Camp Massacre where forty pioneers, traveling over Boone Trail, stopped one night in October, 1786, and were attacked by Indians. All but three of the company were either slain or taken captive. Two of the survivors escaped by hiding in a hollow tree. McNitt's Defeat Monument, bearing the name of the company's leader, marks the traditional place of the massacre.

Nearly all of the land, 375 acres, was donated by Levi Jackson's grandchildren as a tribute to the pioneers slain here. Numerous improvements add to the attractiveness of the park.

Perryville Battlefield State Park, two miles north of Perryville on the Mackville Road, is the site of the battle of that name (*ante, p. 187*). The battlefield embraces seventeen acres in which a Confederate monument was erected in 1902, and another for the Union dead in 1931.

Pioneer Memorial State Park, in Harrodsburg, on the site of old Fort Harrod and its immediate environs, is rich in historical interest. A reproduction of the old fort, 64 feet shorter than the original which was 264 feet square, portrays some of the military aspects of pioneer life in the Kentucky wilderness. The stockade of logs twelve feet high, the two blockhouses with portholes in the floor of the overhanging second story and in the outer walls, as well as other precautions taken by the pioneers against Indian attacks, suggest the semi-military conditions under which the pioneers lived. The Pioneer Cemetery, the oldest in the West, contains the graves of over 500 settlers, inhabitants of the fort, soldiers of the Clark expedition, the Blue Licks battle and other frontier Revolutionary engagements.

The George Rogers Clark Memorial, erected with funds provided by Congress in commemoration of "The First Permanent Settlement of the West," is a heroic granite bas-relief. The central section depicts Clark as a statesman and military leader. To his right is a group symbolizing Youth and Old Age, and to the left is a portrayal of a Frontier Soldier's farewell. Prostrate in front of the bas-relief is a granite reproduction of the map showing the territory involved in the early settlement and defense of this area (Northwest Territory, Kentucky, portions of Virginia and Pennsylvania).

The Mansion Museum, in the park, in addition to numerous other collections, has a Confederate room containing paintings and prints of many leaders of the South and relics of battlefields; a George Rogers Clark room containing prints and papers pertaining to Clark and his conquest, and a gun room containing an interesting collection of firearms.

The twenty-eight–acre park, was developed through the efforts of the citizens of Harrodsburg and Kentucky.

Zollicoffer Memorial Park, on State 235, one mile south of Nancy, was established by the United Daughters of the Confederacy in memory of Felix K. Zollicoffer who fell at the Battle of Mill Springs (*ante, p. 175*). A granite shaft erected to the memory of General Zollicoffer and bearing an epigraph stands near the entrance to the small wooded park. Near-by is a low granite monument marking the mass burial place of 120 Confederate soldiers who fell in this same battle.

THE STATE CEMETERY

The Frankfort Cemetery was incorporated by an act of the legislature, February 27, 1844. The State Cemetery was originally confined to a mound in the center of the Frankfort Cemetery. It was taken over by the state in 1847, and named "State Mound" by a "legislative committee appointed to select the location for a public burying ground, and the most fitting place for a monument to its soldiers of all wars." The mound was acquired by gift of the trustees of the Frankfort Cemetery to the state.

The cemetery is located on the brow of a hill overlooking the Kentucky River and the city of Frankfort. In 1848, $15,000 was appropriated "to erect a monument to those who have fallen in defense of the country." Robert W. Launitz of New York was employed to do the sculptural work. Most of the carving was done by him in Italy. The material for the monument was imported from the noted quarry of C. Fabricotti, Carrara, Italy, and it was then considered the best monumental marble ever brought to America. At the time it was received it was free from all blemishes and was uniform in color. Some of the blocks now show the effects of exposure, and some have become discolored in places.

The monument rests on a base of Connecticut granite, twenty feet square, which is supported by a foundation of stone. Many of the blocks in the monument weigh 5 tons each, the weight of the whole being more than 150 tons; the height of the monument is 65 feet. It is enclosed by an iron fence.

The statue of *Victory*, which crowns the work, and the four eagles at the corners were sculptured in Italy from models prepared by Mr. Launitz. Other relief figures on the panels, the coat of arms, and the rest of the marble work, were carved in New York City.

On the western face of the upper base is the inscription, "The principal battles and campaigns in which her sons devoted their lives to their country are inscribed on the bands and beneath the same are the names of her officers who fell. The names of her soldiers who died for their country are too numerous to be inscribed on any column."

On the northern face of the upper base is inscribed: "Military Monument, erected by Kentucky, A. D. 1850."

On the east side is the legend, "Kentucky has erected this column in gratitude equally to her officers and soldiers."

On the south face is the coat of arms of Kentucky, with the motto of the state: "United we stand; divided we fall." The names of twenty-two battles and campaigns are inscribed on the bands, and beneath these bands are the names of eighty-four officers who fell in battles.

Of the four cannons near the monument, two were captured from the enemy at the Battle of Buena Vista, both of which were spiked before they were surrendered; the other two belonged to the state.

MEMORIAL BUILDINGS

Louisville Memorial Auditorium, northwest corner South Fourth and West Kentucky streets, is a massive Bedford stone, neo-Classic building, erected as a memorial to the soldiers, sailors and marines of Jefferson County, who died in the World War. Ten fluted Doric columns support the pediment of the broad, shallow portico; behind them four huge doorways pierce the front wall of the building. Beneath the skylighted dome is the auditorium, seating 3,151. The interior is decorated in soft shades of blue and gray. Spanish marble surfaces the lower halls. On the second floor is the trophy room where flags of the allied and associated nations are displayed.

Memorial Hall on the Campus of the University of Kentucky, Lexington, costing $135.000, was dedicated in 1929 to the memory of Kentucky's World War dead. Funds for the building were obtained by public subscription in the state. The building is of red brick in the Georgian style with a tower, 123 feet high. The pediment of the portico is supported by large white columns.

Entry to the auditorium is through a marble vestibule, in which are four large illuminated glass enclosed tablets displaying by counties the names of the Kentuckians who lost their lives in the World War. A bronze plaque carries the names of the twenty-one University of Kentucky students who died in this conflict.

The auditorium of Memorial Hall seats 776 on the first floor and 283 in the balcony. Portraits of former presidents and prominent faculty members of the university adorn the walls. Antique tinted glass is used in the windows throughout the building.

Memorial Hall of Union College, Barbourville, now used as a gymnasium, is a tribute of the community and the college alumni to their World War dead. Funds for its erection were obtained by public subscription, chiefly in Barbourville.

MONUMENTS, STATUES, AND TABLETS

Adair County, monument, memorializes Battle of Green River.

Athens (near) iron tablet, site of Boone's New Station, by Historical Marker's Society.

Cadiz (courthouse yard), fountain to Confederate dead, Alex. Posten Chapter, U.D.C.

Cynthiana, marble monument, Confederate dead, 1869, by Cynthiana Confederate Memorial Association.

Cynthiana, marble monument, "Harrison County Volunteers who fell at Buena Vista."

Graves County, monument on site of Camp Beauregard.

Harrodsburg, gate to Abraham and John Bowman.

Harrodsburg (Spring Hill Cemetery), Granite statute atop shaft, rank and file (Confederate), by Wm. Preston Camp No. 96, U.D.C.

Hickman (cemetery gate), arch, Confederate dead.

Hopkinsville, fountain, to Colonel Woodward by Christian County Chapter, U.D.C.

Lexington (Courthouse Square), bronze tablet, World War dead of Fayette County.

Lexington (Mill and Main streets), bronze tablet, site of Lexington Blockhouse, 1916, by Lexington Chapter, D.A.R.

Lexington (Richmond Road), iron tablet, Maj. Gen. Levi Todd Home, by Historical Marker Society.

Lexington (Versailles Pike), iron tablet, Fort Clay site, by Historical Marker Society.

Lexington (Bryan Station Pike), stone wall, Bryan Station, 1896, by Lexington Chapter, D.A.R.

Lexington (cemetery), granite monument, Fayette County Confederate dead, 1874, by surviving Confederate veterans.

Lexington (Iron Works Road), iron tablet memorializes hauling of cannon ball for battle of New Orleans; by Historical Marker Society.

Lexington, statue, John C. Breckinridge, by state.

Lexington, bronze equestrian statute, John Hunt Morgan, by Coppini, 1911, by Kentucky Division, U.D.C.

Lawrenceburg, monument to Confederate dead, by Capt. Gus Dedman Chapter, U.D.C.

Louisville (Cave Hill), marble monument to Gen. Geo. Rogers Clark.

Louisville, monument to the rank and file of the Confederacy, by Kentucky Division, U.D.C.

Louisville (St. Boniface Church), bronze tablet to Confederate poet-priest, Father A. J. Ryan, by Father Ryan Memorial Association.

Louisville, bronze equestrian statue, to John B. Castleman, by R. Hinton Perry, 1913, by public subscription.

Louisville (South Fourth Street), auditorium, World War dead.

Louisville (Seventh and Main Streets), bronze tablet on granite monument, Fort Nelson.

Louisville (near), monument to Zachary Taylor; U.S. Government.
Mayfield (Courthouse Square), monument to Confederate dead by public subscription.
Mt. Sterling (near), monument, marks site of Estill's Defeat.
Monticello (Public Square), bronze ("Doughboy") monument, World War dead.
Morgantown (near), marble monument, at site of first blood shed in War 1861-65, Granville Allen, Company D, 17th Kentucky Infantry.
Paducah, statue of Gen. Lloyd Tilghman, 1909, by Paducah Chapter, U.D.C.
Peewee Valley (cemetery), marble monument to Confederate Home dead.
Princeton (Courthouse Square), monument to Confederate dead, by Tom Johnson Chapter, U.D.C.
Russellville (Public Square), arch to Confederate dead.
Scott County, monument on site of McClelland's Fort, by Big Spring Chapter, D.A.R.
Washington (old courthouse yard), bronze marker to Albert Sidney Johnston, by Kentucky Division, U.D.C.

APPENDIX E

BIOGRAPHICAL SKETCHES

GOVERNORS, 1775–1938

The Last of the Royal Governors

DUNMORE, John Murray, Fourth Earl of (Royal gov. of Colonial Va., 1771–76); *b. Scotland, 1732; d. Ramsgate, England, 1809; s. William Murray, Third Earl of Dunmore, and Catherine (Nairn) M.; ed. that of the country nobleman of that day; elected one of the sixteen Scottish peers sitting in Parliament, 1761 and 1768; appt. by the Crown Royal gov., Colony of New York, 1770; advanced to post of Royal gov. of Va., 1772; had two counties, Dunmore and Fincastle (the latter divided, in 1776, into the counties of Montgomery, Washington, and Kentucky), named in his honor, 1772; quarreled with and dissolved Va. ho. burgesses over question of submitting petition for redress of grievances to British Crown, 1773; repeated action because of legislative opposition to Boston Port Bill, 1774, and that year led part of Va.'s military forces in "Lord Dunmore's War" against the Indians north of the Ohio from Ft. Dunmore (Pittsburgh) to the Scioto Valley (Ohio); meanwhile Col. Andrew Lewis, commanding the second army, had fought and won, Oct. 10, 1774, the battle of Point Pleasant; throughout tenure of office pursued an arbitrary course which alienated the Colony, and, threatened with hanging, took refuge on Brit. warship *Fowey*, June, 1775; spent the following year attempting, by repressive measures which included the burning of Norfolk, to re-establish the authority of the Crown, but, not successful in his attempt, sailed for England, July, 1776; returned, as Scottish peer, to Parliament; became, subsequently, Royal gov. of the Bahamas. In 1759 he m. Lady Charlotte Stewart, dau. Earl of Galloway; one of their children, Virginia, was adopted by the Province.†

---

* KEY TO ABBREVIATIONS USED IN THIS APPENDIX—(a) *Referring to persons:* b.—born at; d.—died at; dau.—daughter of; ed.—went to school; grad.—graduated from college; m.—married; s.—son of. (b) *Referring to positions held:* adjt. gen.—adjutant general; brig. gen.—brigadier general; capt.—captain; col.—colonel; comm.—committee; Cont.—Continental; dep.—deputy; gov.—governor; ho. rep.—house of representatives; lt.—lieutenant; maj.—major; mem.—member; M.C.—member of U.S. Congress; sen.—senator. (c) *Referring to political parties:* A.—American or "Know Nothing"; Anti-F.—Anti-Federalist; D.—modern Democrat; D.R.—Democrat-Republican (prior to 1825); F.—Federalist; N.R.—National Republican (prior to 1825); R.—Republican party, 1856 and after; U.—Union party of 1864; W.—Whig. (d) *Other abbreviations:* c—time uncertain, but about; (q.v.)—for further information look under the name mentioned.

† NOTE.—John Murray, Fourth Earl of Dunmore, Viscount Fincastle, Baron of Blair, etc., etc., last Royal Governor of the Province of Virginia, is so intimately connected with the events immediately leading up to the Revolution that some account of his life properly precedes the biographical sketches of the Governors of Virginia and Kentucky.

Governors of Virginia

HARRISON, Benjamin (fourth gov. Va.-Ky., 1782-84); b. c 1726, "Berkley," Charles City Co., Va.; d. "Berkley" 1791; ed. William and Mary College; mem. ho. burgesses, 1749-75; opposed Stamp Act, 1764; mem. Cont. Congress of 1774-77; mem. Va. ho. of del. 1777-81, and speaker 1778-81; elected gov. Va. 1781; mem. ho. of del. 1784-91; known in history as "the Signer" (i.e. of the Dec. of Independence) appended his signature to the act whereby Va. ceded to the Federal government the Northwest Territory. Married, c. 1745-50, Elizabeth Bassett; their third son, William, b. 1773, became ninth Pres. of the United States; their great grandson, Benjamin, became the twenty-third president.

HENRY, Patrick (first and fifth gov. Va.-Ky.)—1776-79; 1784-86. (Anti-F.) b. Hanover Co., Va., 1736; d. "Red Hill," Va., 1799; s. of John and Sarah (Winston) H.; ed. at home; failed in business and studied law; obtained license to practice, 1760; brilliant legal career; Va. ho. burgesses 1765; oratory won leadership; appt. leader of Va. delegation to first Cont. Cong., 1774; sat in second Cont. Cong., 1775; led in drafting the first constitution of Va. and elected first (Revolutionary) gov. of the state, 1776, serving three terms; authorized the George Rogers Clark expedition; again in 1784, elected gov. (two terms); in later life retired to "Red Hill" on the Staunton river; offered U.S. Sec. State post by Washington, also that of Chief Justice, U.S. Supreme Court, but declined both positions. Twice married: first wife Sarah Shelton, who d. during the Revolution; the second, Dorothea Dandridge, whom he m. shortly after becoming gov.; father of a large family.

JEFFERSON, Thomas (second gov. Va.-Ky., 1779-81. Anti-Federalist); b. "Shadwell," present Albermarle Co., Va., 1743; d. Monticello, Va., 1826; s. Peter and Jane (Randolph) J.; grad. William and Mary College, 1762; studied law under George Wythe of Williamsburg, later a signer of the Declaration of Independence; intimate with Patrick Henry during early life; mem. Va. ho. of burgesses, 1769-75; mem. Cont. Congress of 1775; mem. of committee for drafting Declaration of Independence, 1776; elected gov. of Va., 1779; appt., 1784, member of American Mission to France, remaining at that post until 1789; U.S. Sec. of State 1789-93; author of the Ky. Resolutions of 1798 (State's Rights basic theory); pres. U.S., 1800-1808; purchased La., 1803; principal founder of the University of Va., 1819; spent his later years at "Monticello." In 1772 Jefferson m. Martha (Wayles) Skelton of Charles City Co., Va.; six children born to this union; two grew to maturity.

LEE, Henry (eighth gov. Va.-Ky., 1791-95 last of the Virginia govs. of Ky., Federalist); b. "Leesvania" near Dumfries, Va.; d. Cumberland Island, Ga., 1818; s. Henry and Lucy (Grymes) L.; grad. College of New Jersey, 1771; capt. of cavalry, 1777; intimate friend of Washington; brilliant cavalry leader, known to history as "Lighthorse Harry"; led independent force known as "Lee's Legion" in battle of Paulus Hook and other engagements; including Eutaw Springs, 1781; mem. Va. ho. delegates, 1785; Cont. Cong.

1785–88; gov. Va.; led army that quelled Whisky Insurrection (Pa.) without loss of life, 1794; M.C. 1799; as spokesman of Congress, delivered oration in which Washington was referred to as *"first in war, first in peace, and first in the hearts of his countrymen";* later years clouded by financial difficulties; twice married; first in 1782, to his cousin Matilda Lee; second, 1793, to Anne Hall Carter; both marriages were fruitful; by Anne, he had a son, Robert E., leader of the armies of the Confederacy. His body lies in the Lee chapel at Washington and Lee U., Lexington, Va.

NELSON, Thomas (third gov. Va.-Ky., 1781, Anti-Federalist); b. Hanover Co., Va., 1738; d. Hanover Co., 1789; s. William and Elizabeth (Burwell) N.; grad. Cambridge Univ., England, 1761; served in Va. ho. burgesses, 1761, 1774, 1775; mem. Va. state const. convention and advocated separation from Gr. Britain, signer Declaration of Independence, 1776; mem. Continental Congress, 1777 and 1779; brig. gen. and commander-in-chief of Va. militia 1777–80; gov. Va.-Ky. 1781, and led, as commander-in-chief, 3,000 Va. militia at siege of Yorktown, after which, on acct. of ill health, he resigned as gov. (Nov. 1781); a conservative, he opposed, successfully, extreme measures against the Tories, and together with Patrick Henry (q.v.) largely directed Va.'s course of action throughout the Revolution; wealthy, he backed with his personal credit Va.'s expenditures for military purposes, and lost his entire fortune; retired, in 1781, to "Offley" in Hanover Co., a remnant of his once great estate, where he died; is buried in an unknown grave at Yorktown. In 1762 he m. Lucy Grymes of Middlesex Co., Va.; eleven children, among them Hugh N. (1768–1836) of "Belvoir," Albemarle Co., Va.

RANDOLPH, Beverly (seventh gov. of Va.-Ky. 1788–91); b. Chatworth, Henrico Co., Va., 1754; d. Cumberland Co., Va., 1787; s. Peter and Lucy (Bolling) R.; grad. William and Mary College, 1771; mem. gen. assembly Va. during Rev. War; pres. executive council Va., 1787; elected gov. Va., 1781, serving three years.

RANDOLPH, Edmund Jenings (sixth gov. Va.-Ky., 1786–88); b. "Tazewell Hall," near Williamsburg, Va., 1753; d. in retirement, 1813; s. John and Araina (Jenings) R.; ed. William and Mary College and in law with his father; aide to Washington, 1775; served in Va. ho. burgesses and as atty. gen.; mem. Cont. Cong. 1799; elected gov. Va., 1786; delegate Constitutional Convention, 1787; first U.S. atty. gen.; U.S. Sec. State, 1794–95; resigned and devoted later years to law and to historical writings preserved by Va. Hist. Soc. In 1776 he m. Elizabeth Nicolas of his native state; four children.

Governors of Kentucky

ADAIR, John (gov. 1820–24, D.R.); b. Chester Co., S.C., 1759; d. "Whitehall" Mercer Co., Ky., 1840; s. William and Mary (Moore) A.; left school to join Col. Sumpter's command in War of Am. Rev.; migrated to Ky. 1786, and later farmed in Mercer Co.; member 1792, of Ky.'s first constitutional convention; U.S. sen., 1805–1806; served War of 1812, as aide to Gov. Shelby during the Ohio campaign, and later as adjt. gen. with rank of brig. gen.; in this capacity commanded Ky. troops at Battle of New Orleans (1815); elected gov., 1820; M.C., 1831-33; body lies in Frankfort Cem. In 1782 Adair m. Catherine Palmer, native of N.C.; nine children.

BECKHAM, J. Crepps Wickliffe (gov. 1900-1907, D.); b. "Wickland," near Bardstown, Ky., 1869——; s. W. N. and Julia (Wickliffe) Beckham; ed. U. of Ky., 1884-86; LL.D. 1902; began practice of law 1889; lt. gov. 1899; filled unexpired term of William Goebel (q.v.), Feb. 8, 1900-Dec., 1903; elected gov. full term 1903-1907; U.S. sen. 1915-21; chm. public service comm., Frank, 1939. In 1900 Beckham m. Jean Raphael Fuqua of Owensboro; two children living; res. "Castlewood," Louisville.

BLACK, James Dixon (gov. 1919, D.); b. 9 mi. e. Barbourville, Knox Co., Ky., 1849; d. Barbourville, 1938; s. John G. and Clarissa (Jones) Black; grad. Tusculum College (Tenn.) 1872; served as state rep. 1876-77; pres. Union Col., Barbourville, Ky., 1911-12; lt. gov. 1915-19, assuming the Governorship and filling out the unexpired term (May to Dec., 1919) of Gov. A. O. Stanley (q.v.); engaged in farming, law, banking and business. In 1875 Black m. Jeanette Pitzer, of Barbourville; three children.

BLACKBURN, Luke P. (gov. 1879-83, D.); b. Woodford Co., Ky., 1816; d. 1887; s. of Edward M. Blackburn, farmer; grad. medicine, Transylvania U. 1834; hero of the cholera epidemic, Versailles, 1835; removed to Natchez, Miss., 1846, where, in 1854, by rigid quarantine, he prevented an outbreak of yellow fever; during 1850 visited Europe, studying hospital methods; during 1861-65 served as surgeon under Gen. Sterling Price, C.S.A.; to Ky. and elected gov. 1879. Blackburn was twice married; first to Ella Boswell of Lexington, who d. 1855; second, to Julia M. Churchill; one child, Dr. Cary Blackburn, by first wife.

BRADLEY, William O'Connell (gov. Dec., 1895, to Dec. 1899, R.); b. near Lancaster, Ky., 1847; d. Washington, D.C., 1914; s. of Robert McAfee and Nancy (Totfen) Bradley; ed. public schools, Somerset, Ky.; studied law with his father; admitted to bar in 1865; co. atty. Garrard Co., 1870; elected gov. 1895; U.S. Sen. 1908; died in office. He married, in 1867, Margaret R. Duncan.

BRAMLETTE, Thomas E. (gov. 1863-67, U.); b. Cumberland Co., Ky., 1817; d., Louisville, 1875; began practice of law, 1837; served in Ky. legislature; state's atty., 1848; in 1850 resumed practice of law; elected judge of Sixth Judicial District 1856; resigned to lead (Col.) the Third Ky. Inf. (U.S. Army); appt. U.S. dist. atty., but resigned to head coalition ticket under Union party designation; after retiring from Governorship, 1867, practiced law in Louisville. Bramlette was twice married; first, in 1837, to Sallie Travis; subsequently, shortly before his death, to Mary Adams of La.

BREATHITT, John (gov. 1832-34, D.); b. near New London, Va., 1786; d. Governor's Mansion, Frankfort, Ky., 1834; s. William Breathitt, farmer, who removed to Logan Co., Ky., in 1800; poor educational opportunities; became school teacher and surveyor; acquired extensive land holdings and studied law, practiced throughout later years; admitted to bar, 1810, elected gov. 1832; d. while in office; married twice; first wife Miss Whitaker of Logan Co.; second, Susan M. Harris of Va.; three children.

BROWN, John Young (gov. 1891-1895, D.); b. Claysville, Hardin Co., Ky. 1835; d. Henderson Co., Ky., 1904; s. of Thomas Dudley and Eliza (Young) Brown; grad. Centre College, 1855; adopted the profession of law; elected M.C. 1859 but was refused seat on account of age; again elected, 1868, but seat was refused him because of Confederate service; disability later removed. M.C. 1873-77; practiced law in Henderson; elec. gov. 1891. In 1860 Brown m. Rebecca, dau. of U.S. Sen. Archibald Dixon.

BUCKNER, Simon B. (gov. 1887-91, D.); b. near Munfordville, Hart Co., Ky. 1823; d. "Glen Lily," Hart Co., 1924; s. Aylett Hartswell and Elizabeth Ann (Morehead) Buckner; grad. West Point, 1844; prof. of ethics, West Point, 1845; served under Gen. Taylor in Mexican War; asst. instructor, infantry tactics, West Point, 1848-55; Indian campaigns, 1855-60; in command Ky. State Guards, rank maj. gen., 1861; resigned to join Confederacy; surrendered Fort Donelson to Gen. Grant, 1862; exchanged and in command (maj. gen.) of Confederate troops, Ky. campaign of 1862; later given rank of lt. gen. in command of the dept. of the southwest; elect. gov. in 1887; v. pres. candidate (Palmer and Buckner) on Gold Dem. ticket, 1896; later, farmer at "Glen Lily" near Munfordville. Twice married; Buckner's first wife was Mary Kingsbury, who d. shortly after War bet. States; his second, Delia H. Claiborne of Va.

CHANDLER, Albert Benjamin (gov. 1935-39, D.); b. Henderson, Ky., 1898; grad. Transylvania College, 1921; member R.O.T.C. 1918; Harvard, 1922; LL.D., U. of Ky., 1924; engaged in practice of law in Versailles; lt. gov., 1931-35; gov. 1935-incumbent. In 1925 Chandler m. Mildred Watkins of Keysville, Va.; four children. Residence, Governor's Mansion, Frankfort, Ky.

CLARK, James (gov. 1836-39, W.); b. Bedford Co., 1779; d. Frankfort, Ky., 1839; s. Robert and Susan Clark, who early migrated to Clark Co., Ky.; studied under Dr. Blythe, later of Transylvania U.; went to Virginia to study law with his brother, Christian; located in Winchester, Ky., 1797; served in state legis., 1807-08; judge of Court of Appeals, 1810-12; M.C., 1813; resigned in 1816; judge circuit ct., 1817-24; M.C. 1825; elected gov. 1836; d. in office Sept., 1839. Clark m. Mrs. Thornton (*nee* Buckner); several children.

CRITTENDEN, John Jordan (gov. 1848-50, W.); b. Woodford Co., Ky., 1786; d. Louisville, Ky., 1865; s. John Crittenden, col. in Continental Army and pioneer in Woodford Co.; ed. common schools, Washington Acad., and William and Mary College; studied law under George Bibb; practiced in Russellville, Ky.; served in War of 1812; speaker of Ky. ho. rep., 1817; U.S. Sen. 1817; resigned in 1819 to practice law in Frankfort; served in state leg. during late 1820's; U.S. sen. 1835-1841; resigned to accept post of U.S. Attorney Gen.; on death of Pres. Harrison (1841) resigned and chosen to fill out sen. term of Henry Clay; re-elected for full term, 1843; elected gov. for term 1848-52; resigned 1850 to become atty.

gen. under Pres. Filmore; U.S. Sen. 1855-61; M.C. 1861 until death, which occurred in Louisville, July 25, 1863. Crittenden married three times: first, in 1815, Ally O. Lee of Woodford Co.; second, Mrs. Marie (Innes) Todd; third, Mrs. Elizabeth Ashley, who survived him.

DESHA, Joseph (gov. 1824-28, D.R.); b. Monroe Co., Pa., 1768; d. Georgetown, Ky., 1842; migrated to Ky. 1781; ed. limited; farmer, Harrison Co.; took part in Indian wars of the period, serving under Gen. Wayne; maj. gen. of volunteers, War of 1812; Battle of the Thames; M.C. 1816-19; upon expiration of gov. retired to farm. In 1789 m. Peggy, dau. of Col. James Bledsoe, early U.S. Sen. from Kentucky.

FIELDS, William Jason (gov. 1923-27, D.); b. Carter Co., 1874; s. Christopher and Alice (Rucker) Fields; ed. U. of Ky.; engaged in farming, law, and real estate, Olive Hill, Ky.; M. C. 1911-25; resigned to assume Governorship, 1923; member of Ky. compensation bd., 1939. In 1893 Fields m. Dora McDavid of Rosedale. Ky.; six children. Residence, Olive Hill.

GARRARD, James (gov. 1796-1804, D.R.); b. Stafford Co., Va., 1749; d. Bourbon Co., Ky., 1822; s. William and Mary (Lewis) Garrard; served as col. of militia in Rev. War; migrated to Ky. in 1783, settling on Coopers Run in Bourbon Co.; farmer and minister of the gospel (Baptist); member of Va. Legislature, 1779; second gov. of Ky., twice elected. In 1769 Garrard m. Elizabeth Mountjoy of Stafford Co., Va.; twelve children.

GOEBEL, William (gov. 1900, D.); b. Carbondale, Pa., 1845; d. Frankfort, Ky., Feb. 3, 1900; s. William and Augusta (Greenclay) Goebel of Germany; ed. Ganbier College (Ohio) and Cincinnati Law School; attorney with John M. Carlisle, Covington, Ky.; contested, in 1900, election of William S. Taylor (R.); shot on Old Capitol grounds Jan. 30, 1900; seated gov. by Ky. Legislature, Jan. 31, 1900; d. three days later. Bachelor.

GREENUP, Christoper (gov. 1804-1808, D.R.); b. Va. (probably Loudoun Co.); c. 1750; d. Blue Lick Springs, Ky., 1818; migrated to Frankfort, Ky., prior to close of Rev. War; lawyer; clerk of court for the District of Ky., 1785; M.C. (one of two first from state of Ky.) 1792-97; after serving as gov. 1804-1808, served in Ky. Legislature from Franklin Co., also as justice of peace. In 1787 Greenup m. Mary Catherine Pope; he engaged in banking, general business, and promotion of various industries.

HELM, John Larue (gov. 1850-51, also Sept., 1867, D.); b. near Elizabethtown, Hardin Co.. Ky., 1802; d. Elizabethtown, 1867; s. George and Rebecca (Larue) H.; studied law with Ben Tobin of Elizabethtown; admitted to bar, 1823; and made co. atty. Hardin Co.; ho. rep. eleven years, between 1826, 1843; seven years in the state senate during two following decades; lt. gov. 1848; in 1850, upon Gov. Crittenden's resignation (q.v.) became gov. for remainder of term; during 1850's became president Louisville & Nashville R.R., completing the original construction project; el. gov. 1867; died at his home, Elizabethtown, five days after assuming office, Sept. 8, 1867. Helm m. Lucinda, dau. of Ben

Hardin. Twelve children; one son, Gen. Ben Hardin Helm, was killed at Chickamauga.

JOHNSON, George W. (C.S.A., Provisional Gov., 1861–62); b. near Georgetown, Ky., 1811; d. Pittsburgh Landing, Tenn. (Battle of Shiloh) Apr. 9, 1862; s. of William and ——— Johnson of Scott Co., Ky.; grad. Transylvania U.; studied law and engaged in law and farming in Scott Co.; mem. Ky. Legislature 1838–39; on outbreak of War between the States took active part in devising and setting up provisional C.S.A. constitutional state government, effected at Russellville, Ky., Nov., 1861; under the set-up Johnson was chosen gov. and Ky. admitted to the Southern Confederacy; as civilian head of the state, cooperated in every way with the C.S.A. under command of Gen. Albert Sidney Johnston, to whose army he attached himself; during the first day of the Battle of Shiloh, Apr. 6, 1862, served as a volunteer on the staff of Gen. John C. Breckinridge; was that night enrolled as a private in Company E., 4th Ky. Inf., C.S.A.; the following day wounded, and d. April 11, 1862.

KNOTT, James Proctor (gov. 1883–87, D.); b. Marion County, Ky., 1830; d. Lebanon, Ky., 1911; s. Joseph Percy and Maria (McElroy) K.; ed. common schools, Marion and Shelby Co.'s, Ky., and in law; admitted to bar (Missouri) 1851; atty. gen. (Mo.) 1860; lawyer, Lebanon, Ky., 1863; M.C. 1867 to 1871; 1875–83; elected gov. 1883; in 1887 resumed law practice in Frankfort; prof. of civics and economics, Centre College, 1892; dean Dept. of Law (Centre College) 1894; retired to Lebanon, 1901. Twice married; second wife Sarah R. McElroy, Bowling Green, Ky.

LAFFOON, Ruby, b. Madisonville, Ky., 1869; s. John Bledsoe and Martha (Earle) Laffoon; ed. pub. sch. and Washington and Lee U.; practiced law in Madisonville; co. atty. Hopkins Co.; judge fourth judicial district, 1921; re-elected in 1927 for six-year term; elected gov. of Ky., Nov., 1931; in 1935 resumed the practice of law in Madisonville. Married Mary Nisbit of Waco, Texas; three children.

LESLIE, Preston H. (gov. 1871–75, D.); b. present Clinton Co., Ky., 1819; d. Helena, Mont., 1907; s. Vachel and Sally (Hopkins) L.; orphaned at early age; secured common school and legal education; lawyer and farmer, Glasgow and in Jackson Co.; served two terms, Ky. senate; lt. gov. 1871; succeeded John W. Stevenson as gov. upon election of latter to U.S. sen. (Feb., 1871); elected gov. to succeed himself 1871; retired to practice of law 1875; died while Territorial Governor of Montana, 1907. In 1841 L. married Louisa Black, Monroe Co., Ky.; Louisa d. 1858; the following year he married Mary Kuykendall of Boone Co., Mo., by this marriage he had three children.

LETCHER, Robert Perkins (gov. 1840–44, W.); b. Goochland Co., Va., 1778; d. Frankfort, Ky., 1861; removed to Ky. 1805; ed. in private school, and in law, under Humphrey Marshall; M.C. 1822–35, practiced law in Garrard Co. in 1837, speaker of the lower house of the legislature; upon retirement from governorship, 1844, resumed law at Frankfort, where he resided. Twice married, first to Mary Epps, then to Charlotte Robertson. No children.

MADISON, George (gov. Sept.-Oct., 1816, D.R.); b. Augusta Co., Va., c. 1873; d. Paris, Ky., 1816; s. John and Agatha (Strother) Madison; migrated to Ky. 1780; ed. common school; state auditor more than 20 years, (1796 et seq.; maj. in War of 1812; gov. June 1-Oct. 14, 1816, died in office.

MAGOFFIN, Beriah (gov. 1859-62, D.); b. Harrodsburg, Ky., 1815; d. Harrodsburg, 1885; s. Beriah M.; m. Jane McAfee; grad. Centre College, 1835; grad. (law), Transylvania U., 1838; after brief legal experience in Jackson, Miss., returned to Harrodsburg where he enjoyed a valuable law practice; served in Ky. sen., 1850; gov. 1859; resigned Aug. 18, 1862. In 1840 he m. Anna M. Shelby, dau. of Gov. Isaac Shelby; five sons and two daughters.

McCREARY, James Bennett (gov. 1875-79, U.D.); b. Madison Co., Ky., July 8, 1838; d. Richmond, Ky., Oct. 8, 1918; ed. Centre College, (Danville) and Cumberland University (U. of Tennessee) LL.B., 1859; practiced law, Richmond, Ky., served as maj. in 11th Ky. Cavalry (C.S.A.) 1862-65; lt. col., 1863; Ky. Legislature (House) 1869-75; gov. first term, 1875-79; M.C. 1884-96; U.S. sen. 1902-1911; again elected gov. for term 1911-15; upon expiration of term retired to home in Richmond. In 1867 McCreary m. Catherine Hughes of Lexington.

METCALFE, Thomas (gov. 1828-32, N. R.); b. Fauquier Co., Va., 1770; d. Nicholas Co., Ky., 1855; s. Capt. and Sally Metcalfe, who migrated to Ky. in 1785, settling finally in Nicholas Co.; meager schooling; by trade a stone mason; nicknamed "Old Stone Hammer" in allusion to his trade and to his forthright way of dealing; Ky. ho. rep., 1812-17; served under Gen. W. H. Harrison, War of 1812; M.C. 1818-28; elected gov. 1828, on N.R. (John Quincy Adams') ticket; subsequently served in Ky. sen. and on state board of internal improvements; appt., 1848, to fill out two years unexpired term of U.S. Sen. J. J. Crittenden. In 1820 built "Forest Retreat," his home, 1820-50.

MOREHEAD, Charles Slaughter (gov. 1855-59, A.); b. Nelson Co., Ky., July 7, 1802; d. near Greenville, Miss., Dec. 22, 1868; s. Charles and Margaret (Slaughter) Morehead; ed. Transylvania University; lawyer, Christian Co., and later Louisville; atty. gen. 1832-37; elected gov. on A. ticket, 1855; in 1861 imprisoned in Boston without trial as a sympathizer with the South; released later on parole, and fearing arrest went to Canada, 1862; subsequently to Mississippi where, in 1868, he died.

MOREHEAD, James T. (gov. 1834-35, D.); b. Bullitt Co., Ky., 1797; d. Covington, Ky., Dec. 28, 1854; s. Armstead Morehead of Fauquier Co., Va.; ed. Transylvania U., 1813-15, and studied law, Bowling Green, 1818-30; lt. gov. 1832, succeeding Gov. John Breathitt (q.v.) in 1834; resumed practice of law, Frankfort, 1836; U.S. sen. 1841-47; retired from sen. to Covington, Ky., where he resumed practice of law. Married Susan Roberts of Logan Co., Ky.

MORROW, Edwin P. (gov. 1919-23, R.); b. Somerset, Ky., 1878; d. Frankfort, 1935; s. Thomas Z. and Catherine (Boadley) Morrow; ed. St. Mary's College and (1900) Cincinnati Law School; practiced law Lexington and Somerset; city atty., Somerset 1903-1907; U.S.

dist. atty. 1910; elected gov. 1919; member U.S. railroad labor board 1923-26; board of mediation, Washington, D.C., 1926-34. In 1905 Morrow m. Katherine Hall Waddell, Somerset; two children.

OWSLEY, William (gov. 1844-48, W.); b. Va., 1782; d. near Danville, Ky., 1862; s. of William and Catherine (Bolin) Owsley, who migrated to Lincoln Co., and located near Crab Orchard in 1783; ed. sufficient to teach school; became dep. sheriff; while so employed; studied law under John Boyle who later was chief justice of Ky.; appt., 1812, at the age of 31, to Ky. Court of Appeals; resigned in 1828, and retired to his farm in Garrard Co.; later resumed practice of law in Frankfort, lived there until 1843; resumed farming in Boyle Co.; elected gov. in 1844; at expiration of term retired to his farm near Danville. In 1803 Owsley married Elizabeth Gill, one of his school pupils; five children.

POWELL, Lazarus Whitehead (gov. 1851-55, D.); b. Henderson Co., Ky., 1812; d. Henderson, 1867; s. Lazarus and (McMahon) Powell; ed. St. Joseph's College and (law) Transylvania U.; also studied law with John Rowan; admitted to bar, 1835; engaged in farming in Henderson Co.; law partnership with Archibald Dixon of Henderson; elected gov. 1851; served as U.S commissioner to Utah, 1858; U.S. sen. 1859-65; resumed practice of law, Henderson, 1865; Powell Co., Ky., named in his honor. In 1837, Powell m. Harriett Ann Jennings (d. 1846); three sons.

ROBINSON, James Fisher (gov. 1862-63, D.); b. Scott Co., Ky., 1800, at "Cardome," outskirts of Georgetown, Ky., 1892; s. of Jonathan and ———— (Black) Robinson, both of Pa.; grad. Transylvania U., 1818; engaged in law in Georgetown and farming at "Cardome" throughout life; member of Ky. sen. during the late 1850's; succeeded to the Governorship upon resignation of Beriah Magoffin (q.v.), 1862, and served until successor was elected, 1863; was three times married; eight children.

SAMPSON, Flem D. (gov. 1927-31, R.); b. London, Ky., 1875; ————; s. Joseph and Emoline (Kellums) S.; grad. Valparaiso, LL.B., 1894. Lawyer, Barbourville, Ky., 1906-10; judge Thirty-fourth Judicial Dist. of Ky., 1911-16; justice Kentucky Court of Appeals, 1916; chief justice 1923-28; elected gov. 1928. Since 1932, practicing law, Barbourville and Louisville; circuit judge. He married, in 1897, Susie Steele, Barbourville; two children. Res. Barbourville, Ky.

SCOTT, Charles (gov. 1808-12, D.R.); b. Cumberland Co., Va., 1739; d. "Canewood," Clark Co., 1813; very little formal education; served with distinction under Washington in French and Indian War; col. in Rev. Army; settled on farm in Woodford Co., 1785; Scott Co. named in his honor; served as maj. gen. under St. Clair and Wilkinson in Indian wars; gov. 1808. In 1762 Scott m. Frances Sweeney of Cumberland Co., Va., who d. 1804; in 1807 he m. Judith Cary Bell Gist, widow of Col. Nathaniel Gist; thereafter resided at "Canewood," Clark Co.; in 1854 body reinterred in State Cemetery, Frankfort, Ky.

SHELBY, Isaac (gov. 1792-96 and 1812-16, D.R.; b. present Washington Co., Md., 1750; d. "Traveller's Rest," near Danville; s. of Evan and Letitia (Cox) Shelby; common school education, learned surveying; lt., Va. Colonial troops 1774, in "Lord Dunmore's War," Battle of Point Pleasant; in charge of (western) Va. commissary, 1777-78; member Va. House of Burgesses from Washington Co., Va.; col. 1779; led his reg. of western riflemen at the decisive Continental victory of King's Mountain, N.C., 1780; located in Ky. 1780; for several years high sheriff of Lincoln Co. and (1792) member Ky. constitutional convention; chosen first gov., seated June 4, 1792, and served four years; elected to second term 1812; by authority of Ky. Legislature personally led Ky. troops at Battle of the Thames; retired, 1816, to "Traveller's Rest," Lincoln Co., his estate 5 m. s. of Danville. In 1784 Shelby m. Susanna Hart, dau. of Capt. Nathaniel Hart, of Boonesborough, to them were born eleven children. Shelby's activities included, beside surveying and farming, service as trustee of Transylvania U., also, of Centre College, and as first pres. Ky. Agricultural Society.

SLAUGHTER, Gabriel (gov. 1816-20, D.R.); b. Va. 1767; d. at "Traveller's Rest," Mercer Co., 1830; s. Robert and Susan (Harrison) S., pioneer settlers in Ky.; little formal education; successful Mercer Co. farmer; col. Ky. troops, Battle of New Orleans; lt. gov. 1808-12; again elected lt. gov. and on death of Gov. George Madison, Oct., 1816, succeeded to the governorship; in 1820 retired to his Mercer Co. farm.

STANLEY, Augustus Owsley (gov. 1915-19, D.); b. Shelbyville, Ky. 1867; s. (Rev.) William and Amanda (Owsley) Stanley; grad. Centre College, 1889; began practice of law 1894; M.C., 1903-15; gov. 1915-19; resigned Governorship, May, 1919, to become U.S. sen., 1919-25; appt. to joint international (U.S.-Can. boundary) commission, 1925. Present address: Washington, D.C. In 1903 Stanley married Sue Soaper of Henderson.

STEPHENSON, John White (gov. 1867-71, D.); b. Richmond, Va., 1812; d. Covington, Ky., 1886; s. Andrew and Mary (White) Stephenson; grad. Virginia U., 1832; read law in Vicksburg, Miss.; removed to Covington, Ky., 1841; M.C. 1857-61; lt. gov. 1867; succeeded John L. Helm who died immediately after inauguration; elected to succeed himself in 1868; U.S. sen. 1871-77; pres. Am. Bar Assn., 1884-85; prof. Cincinnati Law School. In 1842 Stephenson m. Sibella Winston of Newport, Ky.; five children.

TAYLOR, William Sylvester (gov. Dec. 1899-Jan. 31, 1900, R.); b. Butler Co., Ky., 1853; d. Indianapolis, Indiana; ed. common schools and in law; county judge Butler Co., 1886-94; atty. gen. Ky., 1895-99; el. gov. 1900, but in contested election was removed from office, Jan. 31, 1900, by action of Ky. Legislature upheld by U.S. Supreme Court; later went to Indiana and died there.

WICKLIFFE, Charles Anderson (gov. 1839-40, W.); b. on Sulphur Run, near Springfield, Ky., 1738; d. Harvard Co., Md., 1869; s. Charles and Lydia (Hardin) W.; ed. in law; practiced, Bardstown; served as aide to Gen. Winlock, also to Gen. Caldwell War of 1812; M.C. 1823-33; lt. gov. 1836-39 succeeding Gov. Clark (q.v.) Oct. 5, 1839, to June 1, 1840; U.S. Postmaster General, 1841-45. Married.

WILSON, Augustus Everett (gov. 1907-11, R.); b. Maysville, Ky., 1846; d. Louisville, 1931; s. Hiram and Ann (Ennis) Wilson; grad. Harvard, 1869; studied law, Harvard (1870), and with John M. Harlan of Louisville; junior partner with Harlan, 1874-79; elected gov. 1907; board of overseers, Harvard U., 1910-18; continued practice of law in Louisville until death.

Adjutant Generals, 1792-1938

ADAIR, John (adjt. gen. 1814-17). For biographical sketch see Governors of Kentucky—Adair, John.

BOYLE, John (adjt. gen. 1863-64); resided Danville, Boyle Co., prior to War between the States; commissioned lt. col. 9th Ky. Cav., Aug. 22, 1862; hon. mustered out Sept. 11, 1863; appt. adjt. gen. by Gov. Thos. E. Bramlette, Sept. 1, 1863; resigned Aug. 1, 1864; succeeded by Daniel Weisiger Lindsay (q.v.).

BROWN, Scott (adjt. gen. 1859-61); b. Va.; d. Franklin Co., Ky.; early settled on farm s. of Frankfort; appt. adjt. gen. by Gov. Magoffin; served in Ky. Sen., 1873-77; m. Miss Munday of Va.; one son, Judge Reuben B., mentioned.

BUTLER, Percival (adjt. gen. c. 1793-1814); b. Carlisle Co., Pa., 1760; d. Carrollton, Ky., 1921; s. Thomas and Eleanor Butler, Irish immigrants; served as capt. in Continental Army; came to Jessamine Co., Ky., in 1785; removed to Carroll Co., at confluence of Kentucky River with the Ohio, in 1796; extensive farmer; appt. first adjt. gen. of state by Gov. Shelby, c. 1793, continuing in office until c. 1814 *(see Gov. Adair)*; as adjt. gen. took part in expeditions led by Gen. Samuel Hopkins against the Indians along the Wabash; when law was passed requiring adjt. gen. to live in Frankfort resigned and passed remainder of life developing his plantation. He m. Mildred Hawkins of Ky., by whom he had a large family, including Gen. William O., Maj. Thomas L., and Pierce, a leading attorney of that time.

CASTLEMAN, John Breckinridge (adjt. gen., 1883-87; 1900-1903); b. "Castleton," Fayette Co., Ky., 1841; d. Louisville, 1918; s. David and Virginia (Harrison) Castleman; ed. Fort Hill Acad. and Transylvania U.; joined Gen. John H. Morgan's command, C.S.A., 1861; returned to Ky. 1866; grad. in law U. of L., 1868; entered the insurance field; active in state political life; twice adjt. gen.—from 1883-87, and again during the troublous period of 1900-1901 *(see Collier);* served as brig. gen. during the War with Spain, 1898; organized Am. Saddle Horse Breeders' Association, 1892, and long its president. In 1868 he m. Alice Barbee of Louisville; five children.

COLLIER, David R. (adjt. gen. Dec. 12, 1895—resigned Sept. 8, 1898); second appt. Nov. 1, 1898-99; third appt. by Gov. William S. Taylor, Dec. 13, 1899; succeeded by John B. Castleman (q.v.), May 22, 1900; *also see Wilbur R. Smith;* b. Garrard Co., Ky., 1840; d. ———; s. Alexander Collier; common school education; served in War between the States with 3d Ky. Inf., as second lt., capt., major, and colonel; resigned because of wounds received in service; returned to Garrard Co. and engaged in farming, stock raising and mercantile business; active in state politics (Republican party); appt. survey of customs and custodian of public property, 1889, served throughout Harrison's administration; appt. adjt. gen. by Gov. Wm. O. Bradley; resigned; reappointed; and again appt. by Bradley's successor, William S. Taylor, who was unseated by the legislature in favor of Wm. Goebel (q.v.); Collier served as Taylor's adjt. gen. until May 22, 1900, when a decision of the U.S. sup. court divested Gov. Taylor and his appointees of office. Collier m., 1865, Mary E. Hoskins of Danville; three children.

DAWSON, James A. (adjt. gen. 1873-75); b. Hart Co., 1834; d. Hart Co., Ky.; s. Ransom, A. D., Hart Co. farmer; ed. common schools, and studied law; admitted to bar 1859; served with Union Army, 1861-63; appt. in charge Kentucky regional land office (U.S.) 1863-71; manager and ed. Louisville *Ledger*, 1871-75; appt. adjt. gen. by Gov. Leslie, 1873, serving two years; resumed practice of law, Hart Co. In 1870, he m. Margaret Connelly of Des Moines, Ia.; three children.

DEWEESE, James M. (adj. gen. 1919-20); b., Ky., 1878; grad. Valparaiso Univ., 1901; served in Ky. Nat. Guard 1908-16; capt. inf., U.S.A., 1917-19; capt. field artillery, U.S.A. 1919; adjt. gen. Ky., 1919; U.S. Army, 1920-39. Forwarding address, c/o War Dept., Washington, D.C.

DENHARDT, Henry H. (adjt. gen., Mar., 1932-35); b. Bowling Green, Ky., 1876; d. Shelbyville, Ky., 1937; grad. Cumberland College (Tenn.) 1899; practiced law, Bowling Green; city atty., Bowling Green, 1900; co. judge, Warren Co., 1910-20; during World War with 319th Field Artillery; overseas, battles of Argonne and St. Mihiel, promoted lt. col. Field Artillery; active in National Guard; brig. gen. commanding 75th Brigade; adjt. gen., 1932-35. In 1905 Denhardt m. Elizabeth Glass from whom he was divorced in 1933.

DUDLEY, Peter (adjt. gen. 1829-50) b. c. 1789; d. Frankfort, 1868; business man, Frankfort; served as lt. and capt., War of 1812; on building committee of Old Capitol, 1829; appt. adjt. gen. 1829, and successively reappointed; serving until 1850.

ELLIS, J. Tandy (adjt. gen. 1915-19); b. Carroll Co., Ky. 1868; s. Dr. P. C. and Drusilla (Tandy) Ellis; ed. A. and M. College (now Univ. of Ky.); grad. Conservatory of Music, Cincinnati, O.; maj. 3d Ky. Inf.; journalist, radio columnist, and free lance writer; appt. adjt. gen. by Gov. Stanley, 1915; given rank of brig. gen. In 1898 he m. Harriet B. Richardson of Lexington; lives Ghent, Ky.

FINNELL, John William (adjt. gen. 1861-63); b. Clark Co., Ky., 1821; d. Covington; s. N. L. Finnell, Lexington and Covington editor and publisher who d. 1850. The son grad. Transylvania U., 1837; studied law under Richard Menifee; grad. in law Transylvania, 1840; practiced law in Carlisle and, later, Covington; mem. of legislature, 1845; editor Frankfort *Commonwealth*, 1849; sec. of state under Gov. Helm; appt. adjt. gen. by Gov. Magoffin and served under Gov. Robinson; returned to Covington and the practice of law; managing editor Louisville *Commercial*, 1870-72;

returned to Covington. He m., in 1854, Elizabeth Tureman of Carlisle; six children.

GROSS, A. J. (adjt. gen. 1891–95); appt. adjt. gen. by Gov. John Young Brown, Sept., 1891, and served throughout that administration; also as Ky. state senator.

HALDEMAN, William Birch (adjt. gen. 1912–15); b. Louisville, Ky., 1846; d. Louisville, 1937; s. Walter Newman and Elizabeth (Metcalfe) Haldeman; ed. public schools of Louisville and (later) grad. Ky. Mil. Inst., also studied law, Gonzales, Tex.; served with Gen. Morgan's command (C.S.A.), 1862; later with "Orphan Brigade" and as midshipman (C.S. Navy); returned to Louisville, 1871; gen. mgr. and editor of *Louisville Times;* appt. adjt. gen. 1911. In 1876 he m. Lizzie Robards Offutt of Shelbyville; two children.

HALEY, W. Percy (adjt. gen. 1903–1906); b. 1875; d. Louisville, Feb. 16, 1937; s. Dennis and Purcell H., Frankfort, Ky.; ed. public schools of Frankfort; served as page in Ky. sen., 1887; sergeant-at-arms, Ky. ho. rep., 1898; appt. by Gov. Beckham to post of adjt. gen. after death of Gov. Goebel; served as member, later president, state board of control; assisted materially in the development of the eastern Kentucky coal fields; named by Pres. Wilson collector of internal revenue for the seventh collection district; resigned, and made deputy com. of internal revenue under U.S. Secretary of the Interior, Roper; later connected with the development of the Tobacco Pool of the early 1920's. Bachelor.

HARLAN, John Marshall (adjt. gen. 1851–59); b. Boyle Co., Ky., 1833; d. Washington, D.C., 1911; s. James and Elizabeth Shannon Harlan; grad. Centre College, 1850; studied law, Transylvania U.; admitted to bar, 1853; practiced law in Frankfort and Louisville; appt. adjt. gen., 1851; serving until 1859; elected judge Franklin Co., 1858; defeated for Congress, 1859; opposed Lincoln in 1860, preferring the Const. Union Party platform; col. 10th Ky. Vol. Inf. (U.S.A.), serving under Gen. Thomas; resigned in 1863; elected (U. ticket) atty. gen. Ky., 1864; supported, as conservative Republican, the R. ticket of 1868; mem., in 1877, of comm. to bring about political harmony in La.; appt. assoc. jus. U.S. Supreme Court, 1877, serving approx. 34 yrs.; termed "the great dissenter" because of adherence to states' rights interpretation of Constitution. He m., in 1856, Malvina F. Shanklin of Evansville, Ind., six children.

HENRY, Jouett (adjt. gen. Dec., 1923–Mar., 1924); b. Hopkinsville, Ky., 1861; ed. common and private schools; major, Hopkinsville, 1902–1906; insurance and underwriting; entered Kentucky Nat. Guard 1882; col'., 1904; served in War with Spain, and on Mexican border; World War service overseas; discharged with rank of col., 1919; appt. adjt. gen., 1920. In 1903 he m. Lizzie E. Evans of Houston, Tex., who d. 1925.

HILL, Samuel E. (adjt. gen., 1887–91); b. 1844, Morgantown, Ky.; d. c. 1900; s. Daniel S. and Malinda (Ewing) Hill; in 1850 removed with parents to Ohio Co., Ky.; reared in Hartford; educated at Hartford Seminary; enlisted, 1862, in 12th Ky. Cav. (U.S.A.); later elected capt.; still later breveted major; capt.

before he was 19 years old; twice recognized for bravery in action; after war studied law; grad., 1867, Louisville Law School; practiced law in Hartford; in 1877 elected to Ky. Sen.; appt. adjt. gen. by Gov. Buckner; upon conclusion of term removed to Lexington, where he practiced law; served as U.S. Court Commissioner for the Seventh Judicial District of Ky. In 1869, Hill m. Naomi Baird; three daughters.

JOHNSTON, Phillip Preston (adjt. gen. 1907-11); b. King George Co., Va., 1840; d. ———; Scotch-Irish descent; in early life became marble cutter, Baltimore, Md.; served in C.S.A. during 1861-65, receiving comm. as maj.; grad. in law Ky. Univ., 1868; practiced law in Lexington and elected city atty. 1870; served in state sen. 1877; appt. adjt. gen. by Gov. Willson, 1907, served four years. In 1870 he m. Miss Chiles, of Fayette Co.; three children.

JOHNSTON, Josiah Stoddard (adjt. gen. 1870-71); b. New Orleans, 1833; d. ———; s. J. Stoddard and Eliza (Woolfolk) Johnston; ed. West. Mil. Inst. and grad. Yale U., 1853; grad. Louisville School of Law, 1854; planter, Ark., 1859-62; major, C.S.A.; journalist and historian, Frankfort, 1867; appt. adjt. gen. 1870; elected sec. state, 1875; younger brother of Gen. Albert Sidney Johnston, C.S.A.

JONES, William Henry (adjt. gen. 1827-31); b. Glasgow, Ky., 1895; s. Henry and Mollie (Bell) Jones; overseas World War service 1917-18; appt. adjt. gen. by Gov. Flem D. Sampson, 1927; printer and publisher; res. Glasgow. In 1922 m. Nina Beaty of Burnside; elected to Ky. Sen. from 19th sen. district, 1935.

KEHOE, James Arthur (adjt. gen. 1924-27); b. Maysville, 1895; s. of ex-congressman James and Hannah (Kane) Kehoe; ed. pub. sch. Maysville, Emerson Institute and Columbia Preparatory Academy, Washington, D.C.; grad. U.S. Military Acad. 1918; served with 63d Inf. and in China; hon. disc., Oct., 1920; engaged in private tobacco business; field service director eastern Kentucky and south Ohio district of Burley Tobacco Pool; sec. treas. eastern warehousing corporation of the pool; appt. adjt. gen. by Gov. William J. Fields, Apr., 1924. He m. dau. Richard Morris of Frankfort, Ky.; resides in Maysville; no children.

LAWRENCE, Henry R. (adjt. gen. 1906-1907); b. Trigg Co. Ky., 1873; s. George H. and Terece Olive (Sumner) Lawrence; ed. pub. school Trigg Co., ed. and pub. *Cadiz Record;* appt. adjt. gen. by Gov. Beckham, 1906, serving until Dec., 1907; Ky. ho. rep. 1921. In 1915, he m. Mary Louise Terry; no children.

LINDSEY, Daniel Weisiger (adjt. gen. 1864-67); b. Frankfort, Ky., 1835; d. 1917; s. Thomas N. and Lucy (Weisiger) Lindsey; grad. Ky. Mil. Inst., 1854; grad. Louisville School of Law, 1857; lawyer in Frankfort; Ky. ho. rep. from Franklin Co., 1857-59; Col. 22d Ky. Vol. Inf. (U.S.A.) 1861; brig. gen. 1863; resigned army commission upon request of Gov. Bramlette to accept the office of inspector general of Ky., Oct. 31, 1863; held this position until resignation of John Boyle (q.v.) Aug. 1, 1864, upon which he assumed the joint office of inspector general and adjt. gen.; at close of war continued in office as adjt. gen. until Oct. 2, 1867, during which time he edited a two-vol. special report of the Ky. adjt.

gen.'s office covering all Ky. military enlistments and commissions during 1861–66 inclusive; practiced law in Frankfort, 1867–1917; also active in industrial and civic affairs. In 1864 Lindsey m. Catherine McIlvaine Fitch of Daviess Co.; four children.

LOUGHBOROUGH, Preston S. (adjt. gen. 1828–29); upon resignation of Oliver G. Waggoner (q.v.), Jan., 1828, Loughborough succeeded, by appt. of Gov. Joseph Desha, to adjt. generalship, being in turn succeeded, Dec. 10, 1829, by Peter Dudley (q.v.).

McCLAIN, George Lee (adjt. gen. 1935–   ); b. Bardstown, Ky., 1895; s. William and Nina (Cochrane) McClain; grad. Univ. of Ky., 1919; officer's training school, 1918 until end of World War; educator and journalist; adjt. gen., 1935 to date. He m., in 1923, Catherine Spalding, Bardstown; resides, Bardstown.

MORRIS, Jackson (adjt. gen. 1920–23); b. Crockettsville, Ky., 1875; ———; s. Nacy W. and Louisa (Spicer) Morris; grad. in law George Washington U., Georgetown, D.C., 1907; law div., U.S. Internal Rev. Bur., 1907–1908; asst. sec. state Ky.; private sec. Gov. Wilson; law practice and city atty., Pineville, Ky.; served as maj. overseas, World War; retired to practice law in Somerset and, later, in Louisville; served as col. 149th Inf., Ky. Nat. Guard 1922–23, also as col. on U.S.A. general staff, Washington, D.C., 1927–29. In 1908 Morris m. Mona Christian of Newark, N.J.; two children; residence, Louisville, Ky.

MURRAY, David R. (adjt. gen. 1901–1903); b. Cloverport, Breckinridge Co., Ky., 1847; d. Cloverport, Sept. 21, 1919; s. Col. David R. and Anna Maria (Crittenden) Murray; ed. Cloverport public schools and, in law, at Univ. of Michigan; served in War between the States as adjt. 17th Ky. Vol. Cav. (U.S.A.), and as lt. col. 4th Ky. Vol. Inf. during War with Spain; upon graduation in law began practice in Cloverport, where he maintained his home until death; served as state sen., 1877–81; appt. adjt. gen. by Gov. J. C. W. Beckham. In 1867 Murray m. Anna Fisher of Cloverport; three children reached maturity.

NUCKOLS, Joseph Preyer (adjt. gen. 1879–83); b. Barren Co., Ky., 1828; d. Scott Co.; farmer, Barren Co.; organized a company of State Guards prior to 1861, which, on outbreak of War between the States, retained organization as C.S.A. troop; he remained in Barren Co. until after election, 1861; with troop he joined Col. Trabue's regt.; was wounded at Battle of Shiloh; col. succeeding Trabue; disabled at Chickamauga; financially ruined by war; appt. adjt. gen. by Gov. Blackburn, 1879.

SMITH, Wilbur R. (adj. gen. Sept.–Oct. 1898); b. Oct. 23, 1853, in Ohio; d. ———; s. E. W. and Margaret (Lane) Smith; was appt. adjt. gen. by Gov. Bradley, Sept. 8, 1898, and resigned October 31.

WAGGONER, Oliver G. (adjt. gen. 1817–28), was Ky. sec. state under Gov. George Madison, succeeding John Pope in that office, 1816; the following year Gov. Madison appointed him adjt. gen., which office he held until Jan., 1828.

WOLFORD, Frank Lane (adjt. gen. 1867–70); b. Adair Co., Ky., 1817; d. Columbia, Ky., 1895; s. John and Mahalie Wolford; admitted to bar of Casey Co., Ky., served in War with Mexico, Battle of Buena Vista; became a leading criminal lawyer of the Green

River region; col. 1st Ky. Vol. Inf. (U.S.A.), 1861-64; dismissed from service for criticising Pres. Lincoln; on ticket with McClellan as V. Pres. candidate, 1864; appt. adjt. gen. by Gov. Stevenson, 1867; retired to practice of law at Liberty, later at Columbia; M.C. 1882, and reelected, serving until death. Wolford was twice married; first wife d. prior to 1861; second wife, Betsy ———; eleven children.

WRIGHT, J. M. (adjt. gen. 1875-79); was appt. by and served as adjt. gen. during the term of Gov. James B. McCreary.

APPENDIX F

KENTUCKY NATIONAL GUARD OFFICERS, WORLD WAR

The following list of officers was published by the Adjutant General in General Orders No. 6 of June 1, 1917:

Commander-in-Chief

Stanley, A. O., Governor, December 7, 1915; Frankfort.

General Officer

Williams, Roger D., Brigadier General, 1st Brigade, July 9, 1906; Lexington.

Adjutant General's Department

Ellis, J. Tandy, Brigadier General, The Adjutant General, September 2, 1914; Frankfort.
Gordon, Maurice K., Major, 1st Brigade, December 5, 1916; Madisonville.

Inspector General's Department

Breckinridge, Henry S., Major, March 19, 1912; San Mateo, California.

Judge Advocate General's Department

Rock, Logan N., Major, March 19, 1917; Frankfort.

Quartermasters Corps

Woodyard, Thomas W., Major, Quartermaster, September 1, 1908; Frankfort.
Morris, Jackson, Major, March 30, 1911; Pineville.
Fitschen, Fred W., Captain, July 3, 1915; Carrollton.
Johnson, William S., Captain, June 19, 1916; Frankfort.
————, Captain (vacant).

MEDICAL DEPARTMENT

Field Hospital No. 1

Hibbitt, Charles W., Major (Acting Chief Surgeon), August 14, 1909; Louisville.
Percefull, A. C. Larkin, Captain, July 6, 1916; Louisville.
Parsons, Albro L., First Lieutenant, May 11, 1916; Louisville.
Grant, Owsley, First Lieutenant, July 1, 1916; Louisville.

Walker, Allen Huddleston, First Lieutenant, May 25, 1917; Wilsonville.
Bedinger, John Van Doren, First Lieutenant, May 25, 1917; Louisville.

Ambulance Company No. 1

Wilson, Dunning S., Captain, February 5, 1912; Louisville.
Hill, David L., First Lieutenant, May 11, 1916; Louisville.
Lanahan, Charles R., First Lieutenant, April 27, 1917; Louisville.
Harris, Desha H., First Lieutenant, April 27, 1917; Louisville.
————— (vacant First Lieutenancy).

Detachment of Sanitary Troops—1st Infantry

Duncan, Ellis, Major, January 29, 1912; Louisville.
Bruce, James W., First Lieutenant, May 11, 1916; Louisville.
Byrne, Walter, Jr., First Lieutenant, July 7, 1916; Russellville.
Kavanaugh, Charles N., First Lieutenant, May 5, 1917; Louisville.

Detachment of Sanitary Troops—2d Infantry

Evans, John H., Major, June 26, 1911; Beattyville.
Adams, Roscoe C., Captain, June 26, 1914; Salyersville.
Trabue, Eugene McDowell, First Lieutenant, December 4, 1916; Louisville.
Walker, Eva Walter, First Lieutenant, April 21, 1917; Louisville.

Detachment of Sanitary Troops—3d Infantry

Nisbet, William K., Major, July 15, 1916; Earlington.
Sory, James D., Sr., Captain, June 1, 1917; Madisonville.
Wright, Burnett W., First Lieutenant, June 29, 1916; Bowling Green.
Harl, Virgil A., First Lieutenant, September 13, 1916; Owensboro.

DENTAL CORPS

Bryant, Ura M., First Lieutenant, 2d Infantry, August 5, 1916.
Meredith, Omar S., First Lieutenant, 3d Infantry, August 14, 1916; Leitchfield.
Royalty, Hubert S., First Lieutenant, 1st Infantry, August 19, 1916; Hardinsburg.

MEDICAL SECTION

National Guard Reserve

Simpson, Virgil E., Captain, May 1, 1917; Louisville.
Marcum, Carlo B., First Lieutenant, May 16, 1917; Big Creek.
Brock, Oscar D., First Lieutenant, May 16, 1917; London.
Claypool, Don Palin, First Lieutenant, May 16, 1917; Louisville.

Military History of Kentucky

Ordnance Department

————, Major, Chief of Ordnance (vacancy).

Signal Corps

Company B

Holstein, Otto, Captain, September 1, 1915; Lexington.
Pulliam, Keeling G., First Lieutenant, March 13, 1916; Lexington.
Welsh, Thomas A., First Lieutenant, May 10, 1917; Lexington.

Inspector-Instructor

Gibson, Easton R., Captain, 19th U.S. Infantry; Lexington.

1st Regiment Infantry

Colston, William A., Colonel, July 1, 1912; Louisville.
McBryde, Robert J., Jr., Lieutenant Colonel, July 11, 1912; Louisville.
Mallinckrodt, Harris, First Lieutenant, Chaplain, July 14, 1915; Louisville.

Headquarters Company

Baird, David M., Captain (Regimental Adjutant), May 17, 1917; Louisville.

Supply Company

Shulhafer, Isidore L., Captain, July 2, 1912; Louisville.
Shea, Charles E., Second Lieutenant, November 15, 1916; Louisville.

Machine Gun Company

Chescheir, George M., Captain, July 4, 1916; Louisville.
Wells, Ewing G., First Lieutenant, June 25, 1916; Louisville.
White, John, Second Lieutenant, June 24, 1916; Louisville.
Esch, Wilhelm, Second Lieutenant, November 10, 1916; Louisville.

1st Battalion

Carrell, Daniel M., Major, July 1, 1912; Louisville.
Norman, John R. C., First Lieutenant, Adjutant, May 17, 1917; Louisville.

Company A

Vance, Preston C., Captain, July 20, 1916; Louisville.
White, James M., First Lieutenant, April 18, 1917; Louisville.
Varble, Pinkney, Jr., Second Lieutenant, April 18, 1917; Louisville.

Company B

Medley, Leo, Captain, October 9, 1916; Louisville.
Gilman, James R., First Lieutenant, October 6, 1916; Louisville.
Strother, Ralph G., Second Lieutenant, October 16, 1916; Louisville.

Company C

Carter, Ellerbe W., Captain, January 8, 1913; Louisville.
Gray, Joseph R., First Lieutenant, July 20, 1916; Louisville.
Barnes, Lyman E., Second Lieutenant, July 18, 1918; Louisville.

Company D

Wickliffe, Charles A., Captain, May 19, 1905; Louisville.
Ewing, Benjamin F., First Lieutenant, November 15, 1916; Louisville.
Young, Bentley, Second Lieutenant, October 16, 1916; Louisville.

2D BATTALION

Smith, Sidney, Major, May 17, 1917; Louisville.
Caye, Woolsey M., First Lieutenant, Adjutant, July 4, 1916; Louisville.

Company E

Colston, Curtis M., Captain, June 5, 1913; Louisville.
Stone, Henry H., First Lieutenant, August 21, 1913; Louisville.
——————, Second Lieutenant (vacancy).

Company F

Cain, Robert, Captain, January 29, 1912; Louisville.
Williams, Clifford V., First Lieutenant, November 10, 1916; Louisville.
Laird, Harry R., Second Lieutenant, July 10, 1916; Louisville.

Company G

Offutt, Benjamin F., Captain, March 22, 1916; Louisville.
Willings, Harold, First Lieutenant, June 17, 1916; Louisville.
Beam, Rosenham, Second Lieutenant, June 23, 1916; Louisville.

Company H

Kinsolving, Herbert B., Jr., Captain, June 1, 1916; Louisville.
Otte, W. Clarke, First Lieutenant, May 23, 1917; Louisville.
Frederick, Lewis, Second Lieutenant, November 6, 1916; Shelbyville.

3D BATTALION

Short, Thompson B., Major, July 10, 1914; Lexington.
Norman, Stone W., First Lieutenant, Adjutant, January 30, 1914; Richmond.

Company I

Morrison, Bain, Captain, August 3, 1916; Lexington.
Mahoney, Ben, First Lieutenant, August 4, 1916; Lexington.
Young, David H., Second Lieutenant, June 20, 1916; Lexington.

Company K

Rives, Howard P., Captain, September 22, 1916; Shelbyville.
Wright, Frank S., First Lieutenant, April 18, 1917; Shelbyville.
O'Sullivan, Daniel M. J., Second Lieutenant, April 18, 1917; Shelbyville.

Company L

Barnes, James C., Captain, July 4, 1916; Louisville.
Hardesty, Frank J., First Lieutenant, June 15, 1916; Eminence.
Williams, Roger, Jr., Second Lieutenant, July 20, 1916; Lexington.

Company M

Dishman, Edward B., Captain, July 30, 1916; Barbourville.
Kennedy, David W., First Lieutenant, November 6, 1916; Richmond.
Briggs, George W., Second Lieutenant, August 17, 1916; Lexington.

2D REGIMENT INFANTRY

Smith, George T., Colonel, March 20, 1917; Beattyville.
Ripy, Frank L., Lieutenant Colonel, March 20, 1917; Lawrenceburg.
DeMoss, Harry M., First Lieutenant, Chaplain, August 10, 1916; Lexington.

Headquarters Company

Terry, John H., Captain (Regimental Adjutant), April 4, 1917; Cynthiana.

Supply Company

Lusse, Frank H., Captain, June 2, 1915; Frankfort.
Darnell, Jefferson L., Second Lieutenant, April 12, 1917; Frankfort.

Machine Gun Company

Back, Monroe T., Captain, August 5, 1916; Jackson.
Harris, Howell, First Lieutenant, April 12, 1917; Jackson.
Combs, Shade H., Second Lieutenant, April 12, 1917; Quicksand.
Miller, John C., Second Lieutenant, April 12, 1917; Quicksand.

1st Battalion

Jones, Roger W., Major, April 4, 1917; Lexington.
Stamper, Carter D., First Lieutenant, Adjutant, April 9, 1917; Beattyville.

Company A

Dillion, James K., Captain, January 1, 1916; London.
Harper, Joseph M., First Lieutenant, May 18, 1916; London.
Lewis, Henry R., Second Lieutenant, April 12, 1917; London.

Company B

Groos, James V., Captain, November 15, 1910; Harlan.
Blair, John H., First Lieutenant, November 27, 1914; Harlan.
Howard, Freeman H., Second Lieutenant, July 18, 1917; London.

Company C

Staples, Frederick W., Captain, July 26, 1916; Lexington.
Spurr, Richard J. H., First Lieutenant, October 27, 1916; Lexington.
Walcutt, Hardin, Second Lieutenant, April 11, 1917; Lexington.

Company D

Jenkins, George W., Captain, August 25, 1916; Whitesburg.
Adams, Townsel C., First Lieutenant, April 4, 1917; Whitesburg.
Fugate, George, Second Lieutenant, April 14, 1917; Lexington.

2d Battalion

Longmire, Charles W., Major, June 25, 1907; Frankfort.
Rodman, John W., First Lieutenant, Adjutant, April 3, 1917; Frankfort.

Company E

Phipps, William M., Captain, February 16, 1917; Salyersville.
Carpenter, Alexander, First Lieutenant, April 4, 1917; Salyersville.
Arnett, Arba, Second Lieutenant, April 11, 1917; Salyersville.

Company F

Short, Blaine, Captain, November 29, 1911; Jackson.
Cope, Arch, First Lieutenant, January 5, 1917; Jackson.
Lawson, Clarence J., Second Lieutenant, January 12, 1917; Jackson.

Company G

Taylor, William S., Captain, June 24, 1914; Somerset.
Waddle, Stanley A., First Lieutenant, April 4, 1917; Somerset.
Bethurum, John J., Second Lieutenant, August 29, 1916; Somerset.

Company H

DeBusk, Ashby B., Captain, April 4, 1917; Middlesboro.
Ford, Toulmin G., First Lieutenant, April 11, 1917; London.
Blevins, Samuel, Second Lieutenant, April 11, 1917; Colmar.

3D BATTALION

Poage, Robert O., Major, March 5, 1917; Ashland.
Showalter, Daniel E., First Lieutenant, Adjutant, April 11, 1917; Frankfort.

Company I

Wilder, Isaac, Captain, April 16, 1910; Booneville.
Hogg, Hiram, Jr., First Lieutenant, April 4, 1917; Booneville.
Seale, Charles L., Second Lieutenant, April 11, 1917; Booneville.

Company K

Wise, Keith B., Captain, April 9, 1917; Ashland.
Barrett, Robert, First Lieutenant, April 11, 1917; Ashland.
Layman, Carl K., Second Lieutenant, April 11, 1917; Ashland.

Company L

Wright, Walter, Captain, April 11, 1917; Manchester.
Pulliam, James M., First Lieutenant, July 25, 1911; Frankfort.
Wilhelm, John, Second Lieutenant, June 29, 1915; Frankfort.

Company M

Cornelius, William, Jr., Captain, December 23, 1913; Beattyville.
Jones, H. Bascom, First Lieutenant, May 24, 1913; Beattyville.
Treadway, Carl R., Second Lieutenant, July 20, 1915; Beattyville.

3D REGIMENT INFANTRY

Henry, Jouett, Colonel, May 27, 1904; Hopkinsville.
Bassett, Erskine B., Lieutenant Colonel, December 17, 1908; Hopkinsville.
Hawkins, John S., First Lieutenant, Chaplain, July 28, 1916; Earlington.

Headquarters Company

Winfree, Ben S., Captain (Regimental Adjutant), September 18, 1913; Hopkinsville.

Supply Company

Evans, William S., Captain, May 25, 1917; Russellville.
Nisbet, Benjamin L., Second Lieutenant, May 25, 1917; Madisonville.

Machine Gun Company

Soaper, Robert C., Jr., Captain, September 28, 1916; Henderson.
Collett, Frank A., First Lieutenant, September 28, 1916; Bowling Green.
Flack, Lawson B., Second Lieutenant, July 25, 1916; Hopkinsville.
Eastin, Robert McB., Second Lieutenant, April 5, 1917; Henderson.

1st Battalion

Denhardt, Henry H., Major, April 28, 1909; Bowling Green.
Cherry, William H., First Lieutenant, Adjutant, February 20, 1911; Bowling Green.

Company A

Smith, Cooper R., Captain, January 12, 1913; Bowling Green.
Crump, Malcolm H., Jr., First Lieutenant, May 25, 1914; Bowling Green.

Company B

Higginson, Harley, Captain, February 9, 1915; Henderson.
Linton, Bennie, First Lieutenant, October 13, 1916; Henderson.
Fowler, Robert W., Second Lieutenant, February 28, 1916; Henderson.

Company C

Thomasson, Charles F., Captain, September 15, 1911; Livermore.
Coin, Oren, First Lieutenant, September 15, 1911; Livermore.
Atherton, Alney, Second Lieutenant, July 14, 1913; Livermore.

Company D

Stites, Henry J., Captain, March 30, 1915; Hopkinsville.
Clark, Alvan H., First Lieutenant, June 22, 1915; Hopkinsville.
Armstrong, Cecil P., Second Lieutenant, July 25, 1916.

2d Battalion

Rogers, Henry W., Major, June 14, 1913; Earlington.
Hill, Thomas M., First Lieutenant, Adjutant, December 28, 1916; Providence.

Company E

Sory, James D., Jr., Captain, January 22, 1917; Madisonville.
Bourland, Charles R., First Lieutenant, January 22, 1917; Madisonville.
Gordon, Randolph, Second Lieutenant, January 22, 1917; Madisonville.

Company F

Donan, Arthur L., Captain, December 13, 1915; Providence.
——————, First Lieutenant (vacancy).
Foxwell, John B., Second Lieutenant, December 28, 1916; Providence.

Company G

Wilson, Ben W., Captain, July 1, 1913; Earlington.
Peyton, Thomas, First Lieutenant, January 30, 1917; Earlington.
Hayes, Robert T., Second Lieutenant, October 13, 1916; Hopkinsville.

Company H

Barnett, Allison J., Captain, April 26, 1917; Hartford.
Barnett, Estil L., First Lieutenant, September 6, 1916; Hartford.
Speck, Roy B., Second Lieutenant, April 5, 1917, Bowling Green.

3D BATTALION

Berry, Talbot, Major, July 8, 1914; Morganfield.
Jenkins, Allen, First Lieutenant, Adjutant, August 1, 1902; Bowling Green.

Company I

Humble, Terry A., Captain, November 7, 1914; Leitchfield.
Taylor, William W., First Lieutenant, June 5, 1915; Leitchfield.
Thurman, William H., Second Lieutenant, July 19, 1915; Leitchfield.

Company K

King, Ben M., Captain, October 24, 1916; Owensboro.
Sibert, William O., First Lieutenant, October 24, 1916; Bowling Green.
Grady, William T., Second Lieutenant, October 24, 1916; Owensboro.

Company L

Clark, Edward W., Captain, June 23, 1916; Hopkinsville.
Walker, Harry F., First Lieutenant, May 19, 1917; Murray.
Meloan, John Hendrick, Second Lieutenant, May 9, 1917; Murray.

Company M

Felts, Ernest J., Captain, July 17, 1916; Russellville.
Logan, John F., First Lieutenant, July 17, 1916; Russellville.
Hanes, Doris, Second Lieutenant, July 17, 1916; Russellville.

APPENDIX G

Roster Kentucky National Guard

As of December 31, 1938

COMMANDER-IN-CHIEF

Governor Albert B. Chandler, Frankfort, Kentucky

MILITARY DEPARTMENT—Frankfort, Kentucky

Brig. Gen. G. L. McClain	The Adjutant General
Maj. Joseph M. Kelly	Asst. Adjt. General
Maj. F. S. Lebkuecher	Arsenal Keeper
Col. Thomas W. Woodyard	Survey Officer
Corp. John Gilligan	Clerical
Lt. Jackson A. Smith	Clerical
Gordon H. Sympson	Clerical
J. V. Patterson	Clerical
Mrs. Hume Sory	Secretary
Mrs. Dan Sweeney	Stenographer
Mrs. Bertha Patterson	Stenographer

STATE STAFF

Brig. Gen. G. L. McClain	Frankfort, Kentucky
Maj. William H. Hansen, Cav.	Lexington, Kentucky
Maj. Carl D. Norman, Cav.	Frankfort, Kentucky
Capt. Wesley N. Royster, Q.M.C.	Henderson, Kentucky
Capt. Earle B. Williams, Inf.	Bardstown, Kentucky
Capt. Boyd Jeffers, V.C.	Lexington, Kentucky
Capt. Raymond O. Cook, Cav.	Monticello, Kentucky
Capt. George W. Biggerstaff, Inf.	Harrodsburg, Kentucky

QUARTERMASTER CORPS

State Detachment

Capt. Wesley N. Royster

Sergeants		
Brown, Charles A.	Hicks, Sam E., Jr.	Funston, Howard J.
Field, Maurice E.	Powless, Charles R.	Griffin, Hubert P.
Watson, Jack B.	Schutz, William F.	Moats, Otis R.
	Critser, Gordon C.	

MILITARY HISTORY OF KENTUCKY 443

Corporals
Alexander, Hubert N.
Critser, Elmas E.
Lienenbach, Joseph E
Wilke, Willis W.

Privates
Combest, Herbert S.
Danhieser,
  Norman E.
Nickens, Alton E.
Patmore, William H.
Durbin, Willie
Guill, Hudson W.

Lienenbach,
  Raymond F.
Polley, John D.
Sanderfur, Harold M.
Schutz, John H.
Smith, Louis A.
Wilson, Charles R.

2D ARMY TROOP, 38TH DIVISION

DIVISION STAFF *(Kentucky Allotment)*

LT. COL. JOSEPH T. O'NEAL ....Louisville, Kentucky
LT. COL. COOPER R. SMITH ....Bowling Green, Kentucky
MAJ. JOHN S. HAWKINS, Chaplain................Elizabethtown, Kentucky
MAJ. JOHN R. SETTLE ....Louisville, Kentucky
CAPT. EDWARD B. BLACKWELL ....Bowling Green, Kentucky
CAPT. JOE S. GARMAN ....Bowling Green, Kentucky
FIRST LT. FRANKLYN ULLRICH ....Louisville, Kentucky

63D FIELD ARTILLERY BRIGADE (Louisville, Kentucky)

BRIG. GEN. ELLERBE W. CARTER
MAJ. WALTER F. WRIGHT
CAPT. WILBUR S. BALL
CAPT. ALEXANDER G. SAND
FIRST LT. THEODORE J. HIEATT
FIRST LT. GEORGE C. LONG
FIRST LT. ROLLIN F. RISEN
SECOND LT. GUY D. ATTKISSON, JR.

HEADQUARTERS BATTERY

CAPT. HARLAN B. MONROE   SECOND LT. LOUIS H. COTTON

Sergeants
Bohon, Elbert M.
Kiefer, Paul T.
Horlander,
  Charles D.
Seng, Rudolph A.
Bodine, Preston B.
Raffety, Carl H.
Scott, Chas. E.

Corporals
Saddler, Olaf S.

Shiveley, Harry T.
Polley, James L.
Schmidt, Harry A.
Wettig, George W.

Privates
Bolus, Paul G.
Denkler, Edward
  G., Jr.
Howard, Elbert B.
Knoop, Harry J.
Page, Chester A.

Borgal, Charles E.
Church, John S.
Denkler, Roy T.
Heims, James E.
Hoyt, Robert F.
McBride, Bernard J.
Mondun, Arthur
  B., Jr.
Rieger, John A.
Stamer, John P.
Bonn, Robert C.
Gibson, Robert E.

Kittrell, James D.
Knoop, Virgil W.
Popham, Joseph M.
Briney, William C.
Church, William E.
Heim, Cyril F.
Howard, Russell J.
Keown, Alvin
McGee, Theodore A.
Nay, Benjamin F.
Schmidt, Edward E.
Toombs, William A., Jr.

138TH FIELD ARTILLERY

HEADQUARTERS

(Louisville, Kentucky)

COL. SIDNEY SMITH
LT. COL. GEORGE CHESCHEIR
CAPT. ALEXANDER G. KIRBY
CAPT. FRANK B. MCAULIFFE
FIRST LT. LELAND NILES

MEDICAL DEPARTMENT DETACHMENT—138TH FIELD ARTILLERY

(Louisville, Kentucky)

MAJ. BENJAMIN D. CHOATE
CAPT. BYRON BIZOT
CAPT. GORDON S. BUTTORFF
CAPT. HERMAN R. MOORE

Sergeants
Helm, Stanley A.
Edelhauser, Edwin G.
Choate, Benjamin D., Jr.
Owen, Louis

Corporal
Rhodes, Charles

Privates
Ball, Charles T.
Morehead, E. C.
Cunningham, James
Fort, Prather
Helm, Jack
Leffert, John J.
Owen, Floyd H.
Watkins, Carl

Atkins, Frank
Ernst, Robt. E.
Swift, Timothy
Cunningham, Thos.
Hale, Herman
Kiefer, Rudolph H.
Moore, Henry
Switzer, Thomas C.
Watkins, Wallace R.

HEADQUARTERS BATTERY—138TH FIELD ARTILLERY

(Louisville, Kentucky)

CAPT. HOWARD R. NORMAN   FIRST LT. BECKHAM GARRETT

Sergeants
Stier, Frank H.
Dodson, Eugene S.
Ohlson, William R.
Sames, Richard H.
Scheen, Samuel R.
Wirth, Walter H.
Fahringer, Archibald A.
Maddox, Loyd E.
Schanks, Kenton L.
Young, John P.

Corporals
Bailey, Albert B.
Harmon, Grover C.
Metcalfe, John J.
Schneider, Jerome E.
Bryan, Ambrose L.
Helming, Victor P.
Moore, Raymond E.

Privates
Cunningham, William T.

Gerber, Bernard J.
Ludlow, James H.
Baird, Norman J.
Bower, William J.
Coats, George J.
Coyle, James G.
Dunham, William H.
Furkin, Walter W.
Gibson, William R.
Gwinner, John K.
Higdon, James B.

Marshall, Albert B.
Bishop, Charles E.
Fleck, Stephen G.
Korfhage, Owen L.
Mackin, James E.
Bates, James L.
Brown, Robert L.
Cook, Perry L.
Cushing, John A.

Frilingsdorf,
  William H.
Gerber, Charles E.
Hettinger, John E.
Keevil, Thomas L.
Miller, Craig S.
Miller, Harold S.
Perkins, Russell A.
Price, Thomas R.

Greenwell, Thomas A.
Sames, Paul S.
Young, Kenneth F.
Neeb, Walter P.
Popham, Alfred L.
Russell, William M.
Slaughter, Thomas L.

SERVICE BATTERY—138TH FIELD ARTILLERY

(Louisville, Kentucky)

CAPT. SAMSON K. BRIDGERS
SECOND LT. (Vacancy)

FIRST LT. HENRY L. HEITZ
SECOND LT. JOSEPH P. HESSE

Sergeants

Haywood, James G.
Finck, Perry W.
Finck, Edward C.
Maas, Frank M.
Worley, Earley B.
Marker, Edward J.
Waterfill, Bernie B.
Hibbs, Melvin S.
Uebelhor, Lee J.

Corporals

Evans, Charles F.
O'Keefe, William
Clark, Thomas J.
O'Connell, Charles R.
Walsh, Charles D.

Privates

Berry, Herman
Cundiff, Charles W.
Harris, Arthur L.
McCoy, James J.
Chancey, James D.
Hanners, Elmer P.
Jones, Everett H.
Pollard, Ralph G.
Taylor, Orel T.
Allen, Woodrow W.
Black, Dawson D.
Dunford, Charles H.
Faulkner, Robert E.
Gerrard, Charles D.
Hatcher, Thomas J.
Jones, William L.

Lesley, John E.
Moffett, James S.
Nally, Joseph R.
Tunget, James W.
Walsh, William C.
Avis, Claude J.
Dickerson, Walter W.
Evans, Millard D.
Foley, Ray
Gruneisen, William C.
Houglin, William L.
Leezer, Raymond G.
Meyers, Clyde L.
Murphy, Wade E.
Schoenman, Carl J.
Vance, Charles E.

BAND SECTION—SERVICE BATTERY—138TH FIELD ARTILLERY

WARRANT OFFICER LYNN W. THAYER.................Louisville, Kentucky

Sergeants

Galati, Joseph
Hoon, Delbert F.
Schwiermann,
  Bernard J.
Griffith, Robert B.
Reinacker, Ralph J.

Corporals

Vonnahme, Sumner A.
Hanley, James R.

Privates

Echols, Minor
McAllister,
  Kenneth L.
French, Norman H.
Maddox, Kenneth J.
Montgomery,
  George M.
Pickering, Charles A.
Roberts, Bobby H.
Crowder, Samuel W.

Ellis, Gene
Wittenauer,
  Edward A.
Keith, James
Martin, Edward A.
Nord, Edward J.
Ringo, Elmer A.
Roberts, William R.
Shaw, Gordon

HEADQUARTERS—1ST BATTALION—138TH FIELD ARTILLERY
(Louisville, Kentucky)

MAJ. CLARENCE C. WATKINS
CAPT. BRUCE VANCE   FIRST LT. HUGH J. RAY

HEADQUARTERS BATTERY AND COMBAT TRAIN—1ST BATTALION—138TH FIELD ARTILLERY

CAPT. CLARENCE L. JONES
FIRST LT. LESLIE W. BOYER   SECOND LT. NORMAN T. BIERBAUM

Sergeants
Staib, Norbert J.
Jenkins, Howard K.
McKinney, Norbert J.
Barfield, Emmett M.
Conrad, Overton L.
Wheeler, William E.

Corporals
Bush, Richard H.
Staib, Elmer R.
Fowler, John L.

Privates
Atherton, Hulen T.
Keown, Eldridge H.
Schneider, John W.
Batsis, Thomas
Cheatham, Dorchester C.
Crouch, Thomas O.
Fulner, Simon L.
Holzknecht, Theodore J.
McNabb, John J.
Mosby, Frank K.
Angel, Thomas
Barfield, George R.
Mattingly, Louis G.
Wheeler, William L.
Blakeman, William L.
Cox, Herbert A.
Elder, Walter S.
Girard, Robert J.
Lilly, George D.
Mercer, John O.
Mullins, Bruce D.
Troxle, Clarence A.
Wheeler, Lowell K.
Watters, Dawson E.
Barfield, George R.

BATTERY A—138TH FIELD ARTILLERY
(Louisville, Kentucky)

CAPT. LEE F. TINSLEY   SECOND LT. JACK T. KEELING
FIRST LT. ELMER N. CARRELL   SECOND LT. LARRY C. DAWSON

Sergeants
Wilson, Frederick A.
Benfield, George H.
Guynn, Fred W.
Renfro, Henry E.
Arthur, Everett G.
Comstock, Lloyd H.
Howlett, Earl E.
Williams, Edgar W.

Corporals
Benfield, John J.
Geoghegan, Roy E.
Sailor, Freeman W.
Terry, Jesse J.
Cook, Arthur D.

Howlett, Jesse E.
Scott, Witherspoon

Privates
Davis, Ralph E.
Garrett, Sidney W., Jr.
Hagan, Louie T.
Hughes, James A.
Mathews, Joe B.
Schroerlucke, Orville H.
Thompson, Chas. D.
Barr, John J.
Brown, Raymond J.
Crady, Kenneth L.

Chaney, George H.
Fahringer, Louis G.
Gary, William S.
Howlett, Charles E.
Jones, Elbert C.
Stucker, Jos. J.
Williams, James H.
Bolton, Robert E.
Craddock, Jesse L.
Crompton, Leslie S.
Crutcher, Paul M.
Embry, Wendell T.
Hardin, James A.
Howlett, James R.
McCawley, Robert L.
Dickerson, William O.

MILITARY HISTORY OF KENTUCKY 447

Hughes, Leonard L.
Langford, Claude
McCulloch, Arden O.
Mulrooney, George H.
Powell, John S.
Schichinger, Wilmer W.

Stevenson, William L.
Taylor, Lowell A.
Davis, Herbert M.
Dobbs, Dewaine W.
Friess, Raymond J.
Hicks, Curle M.
Hughes, James B.

Jones, Edward W.
McCormick, Earl W.
Miller, Lee W.
Phillips, Harold S.
Riedling, Carl W.
Scott, John J.
Stucker, Harold L.

BATTERY B—138TH FIELD ARTILLERY

(Louisville, Kentucky)

CAPT. WALTER R. CALVERT, JR.   SECOND LT. ERMAN N. DIETZ
FIRST LT. RICHARD A. WHITTY   SECOND LT. CLARENCE L. GEOGHEGAN

Sergeants
Hall, Morris
Carr, Hershall M.
Heady, Clarence R.
Monroe, Duke W.
Bryant, William O.
Draut, Woodson E.
Leister, George K.
Monroe, Wilbur H.

Corporals
Dawson, Eugene T.
Morrisey, Charles M.
Vickers, Carl B.
Greenwell, Bernard J.
Underwood, Thomas C.
Wilson, Marion O.

Privates
Ballard, Belvie
Ford, Joseph R.
Garrett, Ray W.

Herron, Howard
Korb, Frank
Oakes, James R.
Tingle, Albert L.
White, Roy C.
Bennett, Bruce M.
Brown, John C.
Cook, Walter M.
Dawson, Robert P.
England, Clifton R.
Finley, Perry W.
Gilland, Melvin L.
Hill, William A.
Keith, Avery C.
Leonard, Harry J.
McKinstry, Henry L.
Neal, Prentice C.
Pieplow, William F.
Pitts, Herbert L.
Sharp, Gene G.
Stocking, William G.
Wolf, Otmar G.
Bibb, Wililam R.
Gabbert, John W.

Guess, John E.
Hooks, Herschel
Moran, James H.
Parker, Emmett E.
Welsh, Herbert B.
Baker, John L.
Bradley, Moreman E.
Clark, William S.
Daniel, Dewitt O.
Ellis, Carl W.
Epley, Prentice M.
Garrett, Henry C.
Hibbs, John E.
Jull, Richard K.
Kirn, George A.
McDonald, George R.
Moore, James A.
Oakes, Archie W.
Parker, Joseph J.
Schott, Leo F.
Stevens, William L.
Wagner, William F.
Yeager, Robert V.

BATTERY C—138TH FIELD ARTILLERY

(Louisville, Kentucky)

CAPT. PHILIP R. ROSS   SECOND LT. LEE J. DUVALL
FIRST LT. LEO J. SCHULTHEIS   SECOND LT. JOSEPH P. MATTINGLY

Sergeants
Bertholf, Henry R.
Hargrove, Percy L.
Martin, Edward C.
Smith, James N.

Wilson, Woodrow H.
Gill, William J.
Kennedy, Fredolph A.
Morris, James H.
Wilson, Eugene A.

Corporals
Bertholf, Frank M.
Link, Edgar W.
Strange, Maurice U.
Bell, Hugh W.

Booth, Carl W.
Shea, Thomas H.

Privates

Belke, James W.
Bertholf, Irvin L.
Bryant, Harvey C.
Fahringer, Paul H.
Johnson, Elmo W.
Stinson, Russell S.
Wilson, Kenneth L.
Berry, Fred W.
Brown, Morgan R.
Corley, Chester R.
Dues, William E.
Ewing, John M.
Bell, Arvin
Berghaus, Raymond

Bodenbender, Edward S.
Downs, William W.
Hargrove, Louis E.
McGoff, Vincent
Peters, William E.
Swiggum, Thomas D.
Baird, William C.
Boes, Oscar
Brunson, Joseph R.
Corley, Oscar B.
Erwin, James E.
Freeman, Murray
Games, Clifton W.
Perkins, Raymond C.
Gnau, John T.
Kaelin, Raymond F.
Lowe, Leonard
Neighbors, Jack C.

Patterson, Everet E.
Samuels, Kenneth D.
Shain, Charles T.
Schultz, Wm. B.
Sloan, George I.
Williams, Robert J.
Wirth, John L.
Givens, Kenneth L.
Harris, Jas. D.
Kuerzi, Albert F.
Morgan, William B.
Ofcacek, Frank R.
Rosells, Lloyd L.
Schroerlucke, Chas. D.
Shreve, Robert W.
Sindelar, Emil
Webb, William T.
Wilson, John S.

HEADQUARTERS—2D BATTALION—138TH FIELD ARTILLERY

(Louisville, Kentucky)

MAJ. JAMES E. HARDY
CAPT. ALEXANDER HEYBURN
FIRST LT. EUGENE T. LINDSAY
FIRST LT. ARCHIE WATERS

HEADQUARTERS BATTERY AND COMBAT TRAIN—2D BATTALION—138TH FIELD ARTILLERY

(Louisville, Kentucky)

CAPT. LEO E. DENTINGER
FIRST LT. RALPH D. DENHAM   SECOND LT. GEORGE H. JAMES

Sergeants

Stoltz, Edward
McConnell, Charles G.
Owen, Milton L.
Smyser, John H.
Bunch, James E.
Cheatham, William L.
Rothfuss, Frank L.

Corporals

Burgraff, Clarence H.
Nortoff, Thomas J.
Boyle, Walter O.

Gribbons, Carl E.
Owen, Nelson R.

Privates

Bell, John E.
Fowler, James W.
Miller, Estell W.
Stoltz, Raymond
Bazzell, Basil V.
Fecht, John
Gribbons, Charles J.
Knoop, Albert H.
Moore, Melvin M.
Wallace, Harold P.

DeWeese, Norman C.
Zur Schmiede, John C.
Cheatham, James D.
Frank, Robert L.
Pierce, Raymond E.
Barrow, Richard D., Jr.
Demaree, Lois B.
English, Marshall A.
George, Norris M.
Hertog, William, Jr.
Kurtz, Jacob J.
Stone, Thomas A.
Wheatley, Delbert K.

BATTERY D—138TH FIELD ARTILLERY

(Louisville, Kentucky)

CAPT. EDD R. GREGG
FIRST LT. EDWARD B. SCHNELL
SECOND LT. CECIL C. MCMASTERS
SECOND LT. RALPH M. DECKER

Sergeants
Reeser, Meade D.
Alvey, Eugene H.
Ashby, Lawrence A.
Cowles, Ralph A.
Shelburne, Augustine D.
Smith, Percy R.
Thurman, Rozel G.
Vittitow, Joseph M.
Wettereau, William

Corporals
Allen, Clay R.
Delph, Edward A.
Hash, Russell T.
Nalley, Sidney M.
Stahl, Raphael R.
Wagner, Phillip C.

Privates
Fowler, William L.
Gardner, Griffin A.
Gordon, John E.
Hall, Charles J.
Hickerson, Alvan W.
Marmillot, William E.
Nilest, Ray G.
Reeves, George D.
Simpson, Joseph H.
Stratton, Daniel J.
Vowels, Freeman N.
Wirth, George D.
Alvey, James W.
Barrickman, Ira G.
Bennett, Robert L.
Biddle, Marvin L.
Bonney, William O.
Brock, Albert L.
Brown, Virgil S.
Caskey, Joseph K.
Crady, Robert L.
Davis, Joseph A.
De Monbrun, Harold A.
De Monbrun, Raymond W.
Fowler, Robert L.
Drysdale, William T.
Hagmann, Willard J.
Hill, George A.
Key, Carl S.
Kuchenbrod, Raymond E.
Pratt, Edward C.
Reeves, Ernest T.
Schalk, Ivan E.
Spillman, John W.
Strange, George W.
Wells, Howard C.
Wurfel, Paul G.
Goettel, Harry C.
Higdon, Glennial
Humbert, Frank W.
Koehler, Robert L.
Maybery, Calvin C.
Quill, Benjamin V.
Risinger, Melvin B.
Sims, William R.
Stein, Samuel J.
Vollenhals, John K.
Wurfel, Lloyd C.
Young, Arnold D.

BATTERY E—138TH FIELD ARTILLERY

(Louisville, Kentucky)

CAPT. J. CHARLES CRONAN
FIRST LT. CARL V. WILSON
SECOND LT. JOHN O. DUVALL
SECOND LT. THOMAS V. ROSE

Sergeants
Owens, Raymond C.
Cook, Arthur B.
Miller, Earle C.
Price, Jesse M.
Wheeler, Mogan C.
Cable, Clyde L.
Goldsmith, Darwin E.
Pirrman, William J.
Smith, Jos. E.

Corporals
Frankel, Nathan C.
Schaffer, James W.
Zettwoch, Walker L.
Barlow, Bowman O.
Miller, Robert R.
Settle, Byron
Barnes, William T.

Privates
Greer, James R.
Fuhs, Raymond E.
Holly, Edward F.
Kehler, George A.
Owens, James P.
Smith, Eddie F.
Bennet, Melvin J.
Berry, William H.
Chinn, Paul A.
Cline, James W.
Evans, Raymond A.
Griley, Thomas A.
Heichelbech, Albert
Ivy, Frank H.
Nally, Thomas E.
Shewmaker, William R.
Bell, James D.

Berry, John R.
Brill, John A.
Clark, Fred
Epperson, George B.
Epperson, Robert L.
Hagan, Louis B.
Horn, Sylvester M.
Horsley, Ernest C.
Lancaster, James T.
Lowry, John J.
Lewis, George R.

Lucas, Earl H.
McGrew, Wilbur H.
Price, James O.
Rayner, William N.
Roland, William C.
Trinkle, Charles E.
Ulmer, William T.
Watson, Joseph S.
Wilson, Ernest J.
Ivy, John
Leibrock, Pete

Hargrave, William B.
Maze, Victor J.
Mattingly, Thos. S.
Miller, Henry W.
Quinn, Patrick
Rymer, George W.
Stein, Raymond C.
Turner, William H.
Waggoner, Sterling P.
Whitehead,
  Raymond A.

BATTERY F—138TH FIELD ARTILLERY

(Louisville, Kentucky)

CAPT. STEPHEN C. BOLDT   SECOND LT. CHARLES W. BRISCOE
FIRST LT. ALLEN K. CARRELL   SECOND LT. WILLIAM D. GNAU

Sergeants

Oberle, Joseph J.
Lott, John W.
Rogers, Bernard M.
Young, Jerome E.
Higgins, William E.
MacDonald, Robert L.
Weir, Frank H.
Young, John E.

Corporals

DeHart, John T.
Hall, Walter F.
Gnau, Raymond J.
Huff, Henry T.
Moore, George H.
Tuchscherer,
  Benjamin T.
Sheffield, Patrick

Privates

Batts, Lamar
Brunner, Marvin
Deutsch, Edward E.

Meyer, Sam
Warren, George E.
Anthony, Robert E.
Baldwin, Anthony
Betz, James H.
Boyd, Carl
Carver, Norville B.
Cunningham,
  Clifford T.
Hawkins, Albert W.
Himbaugh, Thomas
Lee, Edward B.
Miles, John E.
Mitchell, Courtney L.
Montgomery,
  George C., Jr.
Ogdon, William S.
O'Neal, Charles G.
Perkins, John D.
Rudd, Charles H.
Smith, Emmett W.
Strickler, William R.
Warren, Charles M.
Anthony, Coleman L.
Blandford, James

Caswell, Clyde C.
Eastin, Robert E.
Risk, Robert N.
Weir, Franklin H.
Baete, William L.
Ball,
  Wilbur Scott, Jr.
Blandford, Charles W.
Cardwell, Kendall S.
Chandler, Clifford F.
Hattemer, Joseph C.
Henry, Herbert B.
Johnson, Louis M.
Miles, Chester B.
Mitchell, Charles C.
Mitchell, James H.
Myers, Leon H.
Oglesby, Wm. B., Jr.
Paris, William R.
Purdum, Herbert J.
Seitz, Charles E.
Spencer, James D.
Thompson, Hurley J.
Wilson, John D.

75TH INFANTRY BRIGADE

BRIG. GEN. (vacancy)
MAJ. JULIUS L. TOPMILLER .... Bowling Green, Kentucky
FIRST LT. FRANK W. STARKS, JR. .... Louisville, Kentucky

HEADQUARTERS COMPANY—75TH INFANTRY BRIGADE

(Bowling Green, Kentucky)

CAPT. MAURICE D. BURTON   SECOND LT. WILLIAM W. PEETE, JR.

Sergeants
Garrison, Edw. W.
Newman, James A.
Carpenter, Sidney C.
Pace, Larry B.
Pearson, Chester L.
Perkins, John C.

Corporals
Blackburn, Tilman O.
Clarkson, Nat H.
Ewan, Avory L.
Garrison, Lucien N.
Graham, John D.

Hills, Henry E.
McElroy, Herschel A.

Privates
Bailey, Henry V.
Bradshaw, Byron N.
Craft, Lionel B.
Downing, Robert G.
Gardner, William R.
Gott, George B.
Will, Joe O., Jr.
Hammond, James C.
Lyle, Theodore J.
Newman, John W.
Noel, Phillip J., Jr.
Rabold, Stanley J.

Robinson, Billy G.
Richardson, Ralph H., Jr.
Speans, Ralph T.
Stiles, William A.
Taylor, Chas. L., Jr.
White, Charles F.
Arterburn, Haskel E.
Fields, Glenn R.
Hanks, Jack A.
Harris, Wm. H.
McElroy, Jack R.
Roemer, William A.
Sale, Homer G.
Stiles, Garland H.
Smith, Harry, Jr.

149TH INFANTRY

HEADQUARTERS—149TH INFANTRY

(Louisville, Kentucky)

COL. ROY W. EASLEY

LT. COL. WILLIAM S. TAYLOR   CAPT. ARTHUR C. BONNYCASTLE
MAJ. JESSE S. LINDSAY   CAPT. CARROLL C. HART
CAPT. ERWIN L. AVERITT   CAPT. EDWARD F. SEILLER

MEDICAL DEPARTMENT DETACHMENT—149TH INFANTRY

MAJ. CHARLES E. FRANCIS .... Bowling Green, Kentucky
CAPT. LOGAN FELTS .... Russellville, Kentucky
CAPT. GEORGE M. MAHAN .... Louisville, Kentucky
CAPT. GEORGE M. WELLS .... Bowling Green, Kentucky
CAPT. CHARLES A. WOOD .... Auburn, Kentucky

Sergeants
Alvis, Zach H.
Francis, James D.
Holland, Floyd H.
Holland, Lively R.

Corporal
Francis, Charles

Privates
Bailey, Walter
Clark, Lullus E.

Dunn, Chester
Gregory, Wallace
Cullin, Kemp
Holtzclaw, LeRoy
Lewis, Harry L.
McCluskey, Cleon
McKellar, Fred B.
Surratt, Maurice D.
Thomas, Roger W.
Becker, Robert T.
Bowman, William C.
Brown, William C.

Bryant, Lester A.
Cameron, Joe D.
Duncan, Herschel C.
Hoofnel, Edwin T.
Mitchell, Raymond H.
Perkins, James I.
Roundtree, Maurice
Stahl, Layton H.
White, Ted
Potter, Roy
Sikes, Joe
Steen, Paul T.

MILITARY HISTORY OF KENTUCKY

HEADQUARTERS COMPANY—149TH INFANTRY

(St. Matthews, Kentucky)

CAPT. JASPER L. CUMMINGS   SECOND LT. JAMES C. TOMLINSON

Sergeants
Peege, Robert E.
Schneider, Otto B.
Mackey, William B.
Chandler, Urey E.
Dishon, Raymond E.
Lishen, Ross E.
McKee, George R.
O'Leary, Thomas W.

Corporals
Chamberlain,
 Russell E.
Corbett, Frederick J.
Dawson, Percy L., Jr.
Hurst, Edwin J.
Langford, Louis Y.
Scott, Curtis A.
Sonne, John J.
Wood, George D.

Privates
Baringer, Charles F.
Boston, Joffre H.
Brumleve, David J.
Byrum, Raymond C.
Ellis, Robert B.
Fiegel,
 Phillip R., Jr.
Haas, Linus L.
Hager, Marion J.
Horne, Everett C.
Johanboeke,
 Milton F.
Kehrer, Merlin R.
May, Rex II
McDonnell,
 Patrick J.
Moss, Harry E.
O'Nan, Willard C.
Seiller, Joe A.
Barker, Joseph L.
Bearup,
 Floyd H., Jr.
Black, William H.
Clark, Joseph S.
Deering, William R.
Figg, Norman H.
Garner, Carl V.
Hampton, Roy A.

Hubbard, Hubert R.
Lambertus, Willard L.
Maloney, David E.
Owen, Robert T.
Hubsch, George W.
Shields, Gayle
Taber, James H.
Weyler,
 Edward H., Jr.
Williams, Marion F.
Deforrester, Grover C.
Fort, Chas. W.
Geoghegan,
 William F.
Hodge, James B.
Karlen, Albert H.
Langford, William M.
Miller, Robert B.
Rommel, George I.
Schwab, Roy J., Jr.
Smith, Lewis C.
Walters, Jordan T.
Willett, Thomas L.
Wright, John F.

SERVICE COMPANY—149TH INFANTRY

(Bowling Green, Kentucky)

CAPT. HENRY J. POTTER   FIRST LT. EDWIN B. TOPMILLER
FIRST LT. WILMER H. MEREDITH   SECOND LT. SAMUEL P. MARTIN

Sergeants
Daugherty, Eldred T.
Keller, William J.
Vale, Fred G.
Campbell, Henry G.
Brizendine, Henry A.
Givens, James C.
Cossey, Charles R.
Givens, John M.
Meredith, Nelson A.
Mercer, James D.

Corporals
Mitchell, Edwin O.
Sowders, Howard T.
Wilson, Delbert

Privates
Jackson, John A.
Ashby, Harry D.
Cossey, Ray N.
Houchens, Hubert H.
Lowe, Forest W.
Mitchell, Albert W.
Runner, George P.

McKenzie, Malcolm L.
Reynolds, Charles W.
Young, Mota E.
Hodges, Horace E.
Lowe, Henry W.
Young, James H.
Causey, Harold W.
Harman, Charlie D.
Lindsey, Howard P.
Manning, Earl R.
Newton, Guthrie B.
Richardson, **Finis**
Webb, Benjamin I.

SERVICE COMPANY, BAND SECTION—149TH INFANTRY

(Bowling Green, Kentucky)

WARRANT OFFICER JOE H. RUST

Sergeants
Ashby, Walter N.
Burton, Robert H.
Daugherty, Troy L.
Moore, Haskel
Winkenhofer, Gus

Corporals
Denham, Elmer G.
Young, James B.

Privates
Ashby, Thomas W.
Burton, Edwin D.
Martin, Jimmie A.
McNair, Henry J.
Butler, Farley P.
Capshew, Fred D.
Coleman, James V.
Daniels, Esco R.
Derrington, James M.

Graham, Nelson V.
Hildreth, Hugh W.
Jones, Thomas E.
Lincoln, Joy I.
Wagner, Henry F.
Wilson, Richard C.

HOWITZER COMPANY—149TH INFANTRY

(Carlisle, Kentucky)

CAPT. GEORGE G. CAYWOOD

FIRST LT. TEDDY POE SECOND LT. ROBERT O. HENRY

Sergeants
Snelling, Taylor
Barnett, David
Boaz, James
Green, Julian
Taylor, Matthew

Corporals
Butler, James
Cartmill, John
Caswell, Ray
Reinsmith, Sanford
Scott, Cecil
Vaughn, William

Privates
Armstrong, Charles
Barton, Charles
Brothers, Maurice
Brothers, William
Burden, Samuel
Frederick, Homer

Hamm, Clyde
Lowe, George
Morris, Sam W.
Purcell, Jesse
Snapp, Quentin
Stone, Allen K.
Storey, Stanley
Woodall, Frank
Blake, Charlie
Burden, Maxwell
Crawford, Stanley
Dayton, Willie C.
Feeback, Orville
Gaunce, Garnett
Gaunce, Preston E.
George, Lloyd
George, Marion
Gillespie, Gill
Guthrie, Paul J.
Hardin, Stanley
Hill, Chester K.
Honaker, James
Johnson, Ulysses

McClanahan, Thomas
Kendall, William G.
Kerns, Alton
Laughlin, William
Lawrence, James
Moss, Clarence
Rawlings, Edgar
Rice, Howard
Selby, Thaddeus
Shields, Julian B.
Smart, John C.
Vise, Albert
Wagoner, William
McClary, Frank T.
McIntosh, Frank
Reinsmith, Otis
Ritchie, Robert
Shannon, Everett S.
Stanfield, Gilbert
Taylor, Wesley
Wade, Owings
Woodall, Berry C.

HEADQUARTERS—1ST BATTALION—149TH INFANTRY

(Bowling Green, Kentucky)

MAJ. JOSEPH W. SEEMES

HEADQUARTERS COMPANY—1ST BATTALION—149TH INFANTRY

(Lexington, Kentucky)

FIRST LT. GEORGE W. ADAMS SECOND LT. CHARLES S. POTTER

Sergeants
Logdon, Frank T.
Anderson, William M.
Baker, Herbert E.
Colvin, Achel B.
Sullivan, Clemont A.

Corporals
Ellis, Hubert H.
Huffman, Edgar T.
Jeter, William T.
McFadden, Robert M.
Underwood, Henry A.

Privates
Daily, Lewis P.
Doyle, Edwin D.
Erd, Claude G.
Jacobs, Edward
Kuntz, Teddy P.
Underwood, Robert
Wright, Kyle
Bealert, James L.
Bell, William E.
Casey, Herman
Conn, Omar H.
Haley, Harry V.
Mitchell, Henry O.
Schumacher, Robert T.
Tackett, Walter L.
Warner, Merritt
Clay, Evan I.
McClanehan, Ray A.
Redding, William H.
Scruggs, George P.
Thomas, James B.

COMPANY A—149TH INFANTRY

(Harlan, Kentucky)

CAPT. DIAMOND E. PERKINS

FIRST LT. DALLAS C. KELLER SECOND LT. FLETCHER W. VOWELL

Sergeants
Jarvis, Colonel A.
Ball, Hager
Hensley, Roy
Kidd, Cecil
Lewis, Edwin R.
Pyles, Leo H.

Corporals
Lawson, George M.
Short, Denham
Stewart, Emery O.
Pyles, Richard A.
Thomas, Lawrence

Privates
Allen, Alex
Bailey, James
Clem, Hemp
Clem, Willis
Cross, Lewis M.
Delph, Raymond
Fields, Zetler
Hodge, George W.
Holmes, Rufus
Laws, Harold F.
Lewis, Elmer
Owens, Earl
Smith, James H.
Anderson, James T.
Baker, Virgil L.
Blanton, Charles K.
Brackett, Ulyses
Brooks, John E.
Caldwell, Walter
Cloud, Robert F.
Evans, Billie C.
Hansel, Raymond
Hibbard, Earl
Howard, Clarence B.
Howard, Willis
Large, Bonham D.
Long, Eugene H.
McCreary, Pearl
Owens, Edward
Parton, Clarence R.
Rose, James
Siler, Carl R.
Walker, Lewis C.
Caldwell, George
Caudill, Joseph D.
Cooper, Levi
Fields, Charley
Hibbard, Claud
Honey, John F.
Howard, Marion R.
Kirkland, Iria
Lloyd, Roy C.
Miracle, Otis V.
Mullins, Alvin, Jr.
Owens, Tommie
Pyles, Jess F.
Shoemaker, Loyd
Stephens, Woodrow W.
Wilson, Lon

COMPANY B—149TH INFANTRY

(Somerset, Kentucky)

CAPT. HAROLD W. CAIN

FIRST LT. WILLIAM J. BARNES   SECOND LT. LUTHER H. GARRISON

Sergeants
Slessinger, Sam
Bugg, Guy
Hammonds, Alfred
Jones, James E.
Barnes, Teddy
Davis, Herold
Humble, Robert V.
Wilson, Gale

Corporals
Coomer, Carl
Hall, Oliver
Hudson, Charles
Phillips, Larry
Edwards, Clestal
Higgins, Ray E.
Leigh, Alford
Roysdon, Homer

Privates
Compton, Eliza
Hall, Charlie
Owen, Robert D.
Petrey, Chester
Trimble, Othel
Bingham, Eugene
Denney, Walter
Floyd, Ray
Godsey, Roy C.
Herrin, Carl
Hughes, Raymond
Isaacs, Sam
Jones, Kenneth H.
Lester, Vestal
Lovins, Edward
Mounce, Elbert L.
Ping, Lindsay
Randolph, Silas
Roy, William K.
Stigall, Ralph H.
Sullivan, Willie
Dailey, William
Muse, Melvin
Petrey, Roscoe
Petrey, Marshal
Turpin, Jack
Brown, Earl
Denney, Wallace
Garner, John
Hall, Albert D.
Hubble, Paul
Hutcherson, James
James, John W.
Keith, Hardin
Logan, William N.
Mounce, James M.
Phillips, Russell
Prows, Lucien L.
Richards, Bill S.
Shadoan, Lester
Stout, Leroy
Sutton, Estle
Tarter, Paul
Thompson,
  Hubert E.
Wilson, Mirkle
Tipton, James E.
White, Alonzo H.

COMPANY C—149TH INFANTRY

(Barbourville, Kentucky)

CAPT. BEN C. HERNDON

FIRST LT. SILAS B. DISHMAN   SECOND LT. OLLIE J. WILSON

Sergeants
Hauser, Gus E.
Faulkner, William C.
Fuller, Tod
Hale, Jefferson E.
Hawn, Louis B.
McDonald, Edward
Turner, Howard T.
Woolum, Marion T.

Corporals
Corey, John T.
Hammons,
  William E.
Hemphill,
  William H.
Hammons, Arnold B.
Jackson, Carson
Mays, Everett D.
Mitchell, Ralph L.
Smith,
  Charles H., Jr.

Privates
Fox, Otis E.
Fox, Stevie F.
Hammons,
  Lawrence R.
Jackson, Roy H.
Martin, Lavoy
Mays, Reese A.
Martin, Ersel
Moore, Lloyd
Pickard, Caleb P.
Roberts, Charles F.
Smith, Paul F.
Shupe, Richard L.
Turner, Frank
Willis, Elbert J.
Alley, Willie
Bailey, Virgil J.
Coone, Eugene R.
Davis, Edgar
Davis, Homer

MILITARY HISTORY OF KENTUCKY

Ely, Charles L.
Hammons, Glen D.
Jones, Joseph D., Jr.
Martin, Elmer L.
Pridemore, James L.
Miller, Joe N.
Miller, Haskell H.
Neal, James E.
Osborne, William
Payne, James E., Jr.

Rice, Homer
Stewart, James R.
Woollum, Henry L.
Wilson,
  William F., Jr.
Davis, William E.
Downey, Arthur C.
Hammons, Joe
Hammons, Rufus M.
Hubbard, Chester

Miles, Howard
Miller, Jess
Miracle, Lowell
Osborne, John G.
Pickard, John S.
Pope, Justice
Roberts, Elvy B.
Valentine, Robert G.
Woollum, Paul J.

COMPANY D—149TH INFANTRY

(Williamsburg, Kentucky)

CAPT. ELBERT T. MACKEY

FIRST LT. FRED KERR   SECOND LT. LEE LeFORCE

Sergeants

Sharpe, Clifford M.
Brown, James A.
Isaac, Malcolm
Kerr, Luther C.
Longsworth, Everett
Sharp, Ellis H.
Walker, Ward W.
Warren, George W.

Corporals

Ball, Floyd G.
Cox, Walter H.
Holt, Spurgeon
Jones, John L.
Sharp, Glenn W.
Ingram, Robert C.
Meadors, Hobart W.
Smith, Henry

Privates

Brown, Hubert R.
Bryant, Clyde

Eastin,
  Christopher C.
Longsworth,
  Wilbert L.
Robinson, Paul E.
Sharp, Floyd A.
Walker, Arnold P.
Wilder, Vernon M.
White, Joseph C.
Ballard, Roy B.
Bishop, Levy
Brummett, Roy L.
Chappell, Kenneth K.
Douglas, Arthur R.
Heatwale, Forest J.
Longsworth,
  James L.
Miller, Jack
Petry, Clarence L.
Powers, Edward E.
Rains, Marion E.
Sharpe, Elbert T.
Taylor, Wilbert J.
Warren, Carrol H.

Witherspoon, Cecil
Brummett,
  William F.
Cooper, Ernest N.
Lawson, Roscoe
Perkins, Joseph H.
Rollins, Charles N.
Toliver, Charles V.
Wilder, Baylor W.
Barnhill, Earl I.
Bays, Clement A.
Brown, Joe L.
Bryant, John
Davis, William C.
Ellison, Ted R.
Hill, Lee A.
Meadors, Joe W.
Oliver, Jesse V.
Petry, Henry H.
Price, Albert E.
Reynolds, William H.
Skeen, Eugene H.
Toliver, Floyd A.
White, Ralph W.
Bennett, Earl P.

HEADQUARTERS—2D BATTALION—149TH INFANTRY

(Lexington, Kentucky)

MAJ. FREDERICK W. STAPLES

MILITARY HISTORY OF KENTUCKY 457

HEADQUARTERS COMPANY—2D BATTALION—149TH INFANTRY

(Maysville, Kentucky)

FIRST LT. JAMES A. KEHOE   SECOND LT. JOHN D. KEITH

Sergeants
Miller, Robert F.
Austin, Percy L., Jr.
Cobb, Forrest R.
Huff, Bailey P.
Parker, Alfred O.

Corporals
Cobb, Lewis P.
Kinsler, James J.
Mefford, Ernest A.
Spence, Berry W.
Slattery, William H.

Privates
Chain, John T.
Gullen, Milan W.
Harney, Willett M.
Manion, Charles A.
Newell, Harry S.
Racel, James M.
Bess, Marion
Cooper, Omar W.
Cooper, Roy T.
Dickson, Winn E.
Dickson, William P.
Fox, Charles J.

Hickey, James L.
Lundergan, Eugene F.
Parker, Frank F.
Ravencraft, Jos. W.
Stambough, Warren G.
Tincher, Landreth A.
Wilson, Marvin
Woodward, Given M.
VanCamp, Marion S.

COMPANY E—149TH INFANTRY

(Olive Hill, Kentucky)

CAPTAIN (vacancy)

FIRST LT. WILLIAM D. FOSTER   SECOND LT. CLIFFORD MCDOWELL

Sergeants
Jaynes, Frank L.
Carter, Roy L.
Collins, Rubin
Green, Bert
Parsons, Bert
Pelfrey, Everett E.
Phillips, Clarence E.
Phillips, Everett T.

Corporals
Burton, James D.
Carter, Grant R.
Edison, Jack W.
Fisher, Clyde F.
Gee, Hurst A.
McGlothin, Jessie E.
Tackette, Van D.
Wilson, Ralph L.

Privates
Blankenbeckley, Fair V.

Callihan, Curry L.
Carroll, Earnest
Clay, Charles L.
Collins, Edward L.
Gee, Edward G.
Hensley, Clayton T.
McDowell, William
Mobley, Hurston M.
Moreland, Edward L.
Mundy, Edwin F.
Perkins, Boone C.
Rice, Fred A.
Stephens, Erwin G.
Walker, Clatis P.
Bishop, Homer
Bowling, Reece M.
Bradley, Everett F.
Carpenter, Jake
Carter, Gussie, Jr.
Caudill, Greely
Coleman, Guy, Jr.
Dehart, Jack J.
Duncan, Arvill
Duncan, Willie

Foster, Ruric W.
Fouch, Glenn M.
Gearhart, Arvel P.
Jarvis, William E.
McDowell, Clarence T.
McDowell, Wayne W.
Mobley, John W.
Nichols, Earnest
Raybourn, Russell J.
Rose, Uhlan
Sparks, Lisses
Wilburn, Haskel B.
Wilcox, Roy L.
Lawhorn, Hayze
McDowell, Johnie E.
McDowell, Wade E.
Mundy, James A.
Parsons, Johnnie E.
Rice, Richard M.
Smith, Ralph L.
Swanigan, John G.
Wilcox, Clarence J.

COMPANY F—149TH INFANTRY

(Booneville, Kentucky)

CAPT. DANIEL W. BARRETT

FIRST LT. TINSLEY BOWMAN SECOND LT. ARCH TURNER

Sergeants
Barrett, Moffatt
Baker, Edward D.
Barrett, Raplh
Bowman, Ernest
Rice, Chester
Seale, Willie
Sebastain, Kelley
Wilder, Isaac H., Jr.

Corporals
Abshear, Herman
Abshear, Rosevelt
Bowman, Jim
Halcomb, Hurston
Moore, Brown
Seale, Willard
Taylor, Elwood

Privates
Addison, Conley
Baker, Robert
Barrett, Monroe

Bowman, Sim
Dean, Ezekiel
Lynch, Wheeler
Moore, Clyde
Moore, Harlan
Riley, John
Seale, Luther
Wilson, Walker D.
Barker, Fred
Barrett, Vernon
Brandenburg, Arco
Brewer, Posey
Campbell, Hargis
Chandler, John
Dean, Thomas
Gabbard, Jake
Isaacs, Charley
Martin, Ernest
Meyers, Bennie
Newman, Robert L.
Rice, Robert
Smith, James T.
Wilson, Clifton

Mays, Sam
Moore, George
Riley, Edward
Rowlett, Swift
Terry, Ed
Barker, Carl
Barrett, Sam
Bowles, Gilbert
Brandenburg,
  Thomas
Campbell, Arch
Campbell, Luchen
Cooper, John G.
Dean, Woodrow
Gabbard, Orville
Marshall, David
Moore, Ray
Neeley, John
Noble, Edd
Riley, Wilson
Turner, Arch
Wilson, Marshall

COMPANY G—149TH INFANTRY

(Ashland, Kentucky)

CAPT. GUSTAVUS H. MAY

FIRST LT. ROBERT T. BARRETT SECOND LT. THOMAS E. MCCRACKEN

Sergeants
Jones, Thomas E.
Allen, Arbie W.
Blankenship,
  Joseph R.
Dailey, Jouett T.
Johnson, Frank R.
Layman, Gilbert
Lowman,
  Theodore B.
Tier, Martin F.

Corporals
Anson, George E.

Bushong, Herbert H.
Cunningham,
  Charles F.
Delaney, Carl N.
Frazier, William N.
May, John C.
McNeal, John M.
Pennington,
  Albert L.

Privates
Borders, James W.
Cox, Wendell T.
Dodson, Walter A.
Fannin, Kenneth V.

Hall, Manuel
Hamilton, Calhoun
McNeal, Morris L.
Scaggs, Marcel
Slone, Henry T.
Sturgill, Clabe B.
Thomas, Grover
Vanhoose, Carl
Walters, Fred H.
Woods, John F.
Bishop, Clifford
Brown, Freeman C.
Bunch, Edward
Butler, Cecil D.
Dennis, Joe

Edwards, Eugene B.
Greene, Henry H.
Hall, George D.
Hayes, Kenneth J.
Gesling, Raymond G.
Blankenship, John O.
Holmes, John V.
Johnson, Orville E.
Olivieri, Pietro
Roberts, LeeRoy

Smith, Thomas D.
Stanley, William D.
Twinam, Frank L.
Waller, Clifton E.
Weis, Hassell V.
Wheatley, William L.
Hern, Russell
Howell, Clarence E.
Litteral, Lonzie
Patrick, Herschell

Shingleton,
  Donald M.
Sparks, Charles S.
Tier, George J.
Versey, Tony P.
Waller, Lloyd E.
Weis, Leo
Williams, Charles A.

COMPANY H—149TH INFANTRY

(Ravenna, Kentucky)

CAPT. WALTER L. MCPHERSON

FIRST LT. BRUTUS C. MCGUIRE   SECOND LT. (vacancy)

Sergeants
Lewis, Ferrell J.
Arvin, Edward B.
Benton, Edward
Dalton, Earnest R.
Freeman, Manual
Hawkins, Lee B.
Preston,
  William D., Jr.
Richardson,
  Arnold O.

Corporals
Bybee, Roy
Durham, Owen R.
Farley, Elmo J.
Howard, Langley
Johnstone,
  Kenneth E.
Mays, George L., Jr.
McKinney, Clifton
Wise, William E.

Privates
Benton, Tommy B.

Burns, Raymond M.
Henderson, Otis
Kidwell, Thomas B.
Nicholson, James F.
Slone, Harrison
Baker, Orville
Benton, John R.
Christopher,
  Wayne S.
Durham, James A.
Green, Charles W.
Henderson,
  Raymond W.
Hunt, James E.
Lannin,
  Nicholas D., Jr.
Mays, Edward
Noland, Joseph
Roberts, Robert C.
Sams, Raymond
Spurlock, Roy T.
Stevens, James C.
Terrell, Ralph A.
Turpin, Charles E.
Witt, Gordon

Williams, Clarence E.
Drake, Elmo J.
Holbrook, Clyde
Murrell,
  Charles T., Jr.
Patrick, Harold M.
Wright, Charles W.
Benton,
  Raymond W.
Bragg, Wallace C.
Dunaway, Harlan
Edwards, Charles M.
Green, Harold W.
Hughes, Barney B.
Jackson, Charles P.
Masters, Halmire B.
McKinney, Omar
Richardson, Leighton
Rogers, Herbert J.
Spurlock, Gene P.
Stigall, Thomas G.
Street, Marion S.
Thomas, Raymond R.
Webb, Jessie R.
Wiseman, Roy J.

HEADQUARTERS—3D BATTALION—149TH INFANTRY

(Livermore, Kentucky)

MAJOR OREN COIN

HEADQUARTERS COMPANY—3D BATTALION—149TH INFANTRY

(Madisonville, Kentucky)

FIRST LT. JAMES K. RAMSEY   SECOND LT. JAMES L. MOORE

Sergeants
Offutt, Clifton R.
Hall, Robert V.
McLemore, James W.
Moore, Norvell H.
Ramsey, David F.

Corporals
Beeny, James D.
Brown, Arthur O.
Collins, Gregory P.
Ligon, Herbert A.
Melton, Clifton J.

Privates
Dann, Bennie
Darnell, Dennis M.
Henry, Ashiel B.
Melton, William S.
Rector, Elmo W.
Rice, John K.
Stone, Clifton W.
Babb, John B.
Bone, George A.
Brown, Harry W.
Bruce, John F.
Day, Bertram E.

Frederick,
  Thomas B.
Nisbet, Louis Y.
Oldham, David L.
Oldham, William M.
Ramsey,
  James K., III
Utley, Thomas E.
Vinson, Thomas L.
Walker, Marion T.

COMPANY I—149TH INFANTRY

(Marion, Kentucky)

CAPT. JAMES R. JOHNSON
FIRST LT. CALVERT P. SMALL   SECOND LT. RANDALL W. WOODALL

Sergeants
Minner, Oris M.
Bracey, Wilford R.
Hillyard, Burnie H.
Hinchee, Teddy
Hinchee, Harvey B.
Holloman,
  Thomas H.
McDowell, Ernest R.
Woodall, Paul A.

Corporals
Buckalew, Lonnie W.
Elder, Robert A.
Gipson, Virgil H.
Hunt, Elvis R.
Jeffreys, Charley A.
Shaver, Aubrey M.
Sisco, Henry
Travis, Elvis L.

Privates
Asbridge, Eugene

Asbridge, Robert G.
Butler, Raymond N.
Eskew, James K.
Howerton,
  Newcom F.
James, Earl F.
McNeely, Barney C.
Railey, Sam L.
Sutton, Vernon A.
Wigginton, Joseph K.
Woodall, Allen A.
Woodall, Virgil P.
Armstrong, John H.
Boyd, James A.
Brantley, Wilbur O.
Brantley, Floyd R.
Clark, John R.
Clark, Willis N.
Curnel, Zelma L.
Harper, James A.
Hughes, Marvin W.
Hunt, Willard C.
Haynes, William D.

James, Eldon R.
Johnson, Douglas F.
Johnson, Harold D.
Kirk, Wynyard M.
Long, Earl R.
Marvel, Denver L.
McMican, Robert E.
Riley, Raymond G.
Stallions, Hubert
Truitt, Chester E.
Whitt, George W.
Woodall, James C.
Wyatt, Willie A.
Kimsey, Ovid H.
Lynn, Corbett E.
Lucas, Sammie M.
McConnell, Marion C.
Patmor, James M.
Sisco, Ernest
Travis, Olvie A.
Waters, Frank L.
Whitsell, James W.
Woodall, Carl R.

COMPANY K—149TH INFANTRY

(Livermore, Kentucky)

CAPT. CAMERON A. BROWN

FIRST LT. BRODIE L. PAYNE   SECOND LT. ERNEST E. PRICE

Sergeants
Frizzell, Raymond M.
Beller, William N.
Carman, Roy C.
Eubank, Ewel R.
Girvin, Gilbert E.
Whitaker, Norman R.
Whitaker, Eddie R.
Whitaker, Otis P.

Corporals
Cobb, Clifton
Cook, William O.
Gray, Calvin E.
Logsdon, James A.
Moseley, Harold J.
Robertson, Lawrence D.
Whitaker, Leo
Youngston, John

Privates
Boyken, John J.
Caudle, Carl C.
Conrad, Louis
Davis, John W.
Frizzell, Wesley M.
Gonterman, Marvin
Niceley, Edgar T.
Thompson, William W.
Williams, Gilbert L.
Baird, Grover C.
Daugherty, Hayden
Boyken, Calvin L.
Daugherty, William E.
Frizzell, Tom
Girvin, Fred
Isaacs, Winford C.
Porter, Luther H.
Stogner, Junior D.
Whitaker, James W.
Willis, Harvy
Gray, James E.
Colburn, William R.
Fulkerson, Elmer L.
Eastwood, Robert B.
Kassinger, David A.
Thornberry, Irvin F.
English, Fitzhugh N.
Howley, Lucian H.
Snyder, James E.
Tucker, Cecil J.
Ashby, Jay P.
Boyken, William G.
Burden, William T.
Daugherty, James W.
Downs, Louis E.
Fielden, Edgar M.
Fortner, Abe
Gholson, Wayne B.
Girvin, Raymond O.
Kassinger, Darrell
McReynolds, James C.
Stienogle, Elvin O.
Roark, Roger
Vertrees, James F.
Willis, Elbert
Young, George L.

COMPANY L—149TH INFANTRY

(Mayfield, Kentucky)

CAPT. JOE LEECH

FIRST LT. WILLIAM P. BOWDEN   SECOND LT. WILLIAM W. ROBERTS

Sergeants
Holder, John L.
Covington, Icam G.
Earp, Ruffie R.
Hancock, Hunter M.
Henderson, Dillon J.
Hicks, Amos
Stanley, Allen D.

Corporals
Anderson, Cecil
Bowden, Marion D.
Guthrie, Raymond C.
Harrell, William H.
Hughes, Elton C.
McAdoo, Joe A.
Mills, William A.
Taylor, James T.

Privates
Adams, James K.
Allen, Dorris C.
Allen, James W.
Allred, William C.
Brooks, Maxwell E.
Collier, James F.
Forester, Cletus W.
Galloway, Raymond C.
Hall, Roger H.
Holmes, Delmer L.
Kinsey, Roy L.
Martin, Harold D.
Puckett, Carl
Shockley, Joe L.
Smith, Larry J.

Adams, Ford B.
Allen, Carl E.
Allen, George E.
Allred, Thomas E.
Bell, Raymond L.
Brady, Harold E.
Cash, Wm. S.
Faulkner, William
Garland, John M.
Haneline, Thelma
Beasley, Marshall W.
Hicks, Clarence F.
Hughes, Kelly V.
Jordan, Jullian C.
McClure, R. C.
Mills, Rex V.
Payne, William H.
Pullen, Gipson H.
Sanderson, Harold K.
Stevens, Quelton
Tucker, Terrell A.
Willis, James A.
Huie, Robert
Malone, Victor E.
Melton, Carl L.
Morris, James A.
Porter, Dempsey W.
Rule, Delmas
Skinner, Harold G.
Stevens, Raymond C.
Waggoner,
  William S.
Wilson, Lester E.

COMPANY M—149TH INFANTRY

CAPT. HENRY O. PRICE ....Russellville, Kentucky
FIRST LT. KENNETH HOUSE ....Adairville, Kentucky
SECOND LT. OTIS R. OGLES ....Russellville, Kentucky

Sergeants
Brodie, Martin L.
Benninson,
  Clarence E.
Cornelius, Cecil R.
Cornelius, Charles H.
Davis, Earl V.
Greer, Luther M.
Penick, Orville K.
Walton, Warren W.

Corporals
Brown, Claud A.
Brown, Clifford A.
Fuqua, Felix M.
Greer, Roy F.
Higgins, Francis L.
McCormick, Will L.
Smith, Robert L.
Tandy, Herbert L.

Privates
Allen, Clarence E.
Bailey, Letcher O.
Benninson, Jessie E.
Hinton, Lawrence
Page, Thomas D.
Strange, Joe G.
Thomas, Marion
Boisseau, Otis
Davis, John P.
Frye, Jonnie
Herndon, Harry C.
Keith, Euing M.
Law, Robert E.
McCormick,
  George T.
Moore, Carl D.
Price, Rhoads
Russell, Elwood M.
Sanford, David B.
Walton, William O.
Penick, Malcolm I.
Shoulders, Edward
Baggett, Lemore M.
Campbell, Cecil V.
Flowers, John F.
Graham, Brodie D.
Johnson, Claypool B.
Robinson, Kermit T.
Browder, Charles L.
Cornelius, Warren L.
Simmons, Marion K.
Wilkins, Wendell M.
Cornelius, Donald W.
Humphrey, Willie F.
Robinson, Curtis E.
Sanford, Lucian E.
Addison, Mortimer C.
Burchett, James W.
Hanley, Walter L.
Keith, Kid K.
Lyons, Clifford B.
McLaughlin,
  George B.
Price, William H.
Rogers, Clyde D.
Sales, Pershing
Simmons, Adrian A.
Shelton, Richard
Wilkins, Buis M.

113TH QUARTERMASTER REGIMENT

38TH DIVISION

HEADQUARTERS

(Frankfort, Kentucky)

LT. COL. VEGO E. BARNES ....Frankfort, Kentucky
CAPT. DILLMAN A. RASH ....Louisville, Kentucky

MILITARY HISTORY OF KENTUCKY 463

MEDICAL DEPARTMENT DETACHMENT
(Barbourville, Kentucky)

MAJ. JAMES E. PARKER   CAPT. (vacancy)

Sergeants
Ketchem, Jack R.
Carroll, Thomas C.
Hammons, Orvel J.

Privates
Disney, Edison
Turner, Green B.
Faulkner, Harry M.
Jackson, Homer A.

Faulkner, Arnold D.
McNeil, Oscar M.
Partin, Russell D.
Pritchard, Evy C.

HEADQUARTERS COMPANY—113TH QUARTERMASTER REGIMENT
(Frankfort, Kentucky)

CAPT. ERNEST SHEETINGER   FIRST LT. MARION A. LONGMIRE

Sergeants
Oerther, Joseph J.
Oerther, Clarence V.
Bacon, Alex H.
Patterson, John V.
Williams, Theodore W.

Corporals
Gilligan, John W.
Morrison, John W.

Privates
Austin, Kaylor E.
Bacon, James B.
Oerther, George F.
Stagg, Grosjean M.
English, Frank B.
Gordon, Carl E.
Gordon, James A.
Glenn, John H.
Hale, Robert A.
Lynch, Edward P.

Hanrahan, Dennis A.
Thompson, George B.
Bowman, Francis W.
Crittenden, Cecil W.
Hanrahan, George B.
Johnson, Morrow B.
Nord, James E.
Oliver, Lawrence H.
Thurman, James R.

HEADQUARTERS, 2D BATTALION, 113TH QUARTERMASTER REGIMENT

MAJ. FRANK S. LEBKUECHER ....Frankfort, Kentucky
FIRST LT. JOHN L. HANBERY ....Hopkinsville, Kentucky

COMPANY C—113TH QUARTERMASTER REGIMENT
(Hopkinsville, Kentucky)

CAPT. GRAHAM B. COWHERD   SECOND LT. JOSEPH E. BLANDFORD

Sergeants
Pritchett, Sidney E.
Chambers, Elmer R.
Chewning, Elmus
Dowdy, Carl E.
Hester, McGraw
Wash, Creighton O.
White, John L.

Corporals
Crabtree, Jasper
Fleming, John H.

Jenkins, William R.
Thomas, Floyd C.
Thomas, Noble E.

Privates
Cayce, John W.
Curtis, Walter E.
Duncan, Claude H.
Fletcher, Hayden H.
Gillard, Herbert R.
Mason, William T.
Renshaw, Estel H.

Aldridge, Joel E.
Aldridge, Woodrow W.
Brummett, Jimmie
Clark, John W.
Harris, Emory W.
Johns, Victor A.
Jones, Miller
Ladd, Jewell J.
Latham, Virna L.
Lyle, Ennis B.
Martin, Coleman A.

Mays, Jack H.
McCorkle, Joseph T.
Miller, James D.
Oliver, Otho L.
Petty, George D.
Renshaw, Walter E.

Rives, John E.
Rogers, William C.
Smith, Carl W.
Woosley, Hugh E.
Hancock, Charles G.
Whitaker, Claude W.

Whitaker, Hubert E.
Whitaker, Robert A.
Coffman, Howard B.
Jackson, Hubert, Jr.

COMPANY D—113TH QUARTERMASTER REGIMENT
(Pikeville, Kentucky)

CAPT. VERNON SANDERS   SECOND LT. (vacancy)

Sergeants
Robinson, Campbell
Easterling, Celcis
Huffman, Charles
Kinney, Willie
Mathews, Joe
Reynolds, John F.
Wright, Stallard H.

Corporals
Anderson, Woodrow W.
Jenkins, Walter
Ratliff, Curtis
Ratliff, Lon
Tackett, Jerdon

Privates
Adams, Edward
Bartley, Albert
Branham, Richard
Dye, Jack
Helvey, Hugh
Huffman, Bart
Mullins, John
Mullins, Samuel
Johnson, Buster
Tackett, Dave
Wright, Joseph
Allen, Homer
Bailey, Howard
Baldridge, Orville
Ballard, William
Banks, James

Belcher, William
Chaffin, Richard
Coleman, Don
Gillispie, Robert
Harper, Herbert
Huffman, Elster
Lumpkins, Dennis
Lowe, Odis
Maynard, Elde
McKinney, Robert
Murray, John
Parsons, Press
Parsons, Johnnie
Prather, Everett
Rasnick, Arthur
Thompson, Earl L.

HEADQUARTERS DETACHMENT 3D BATTALION—113TH QUARTERMASTER REGIMENT
(Pikeville, Kentucky)

FIRST LT. JOHN M. SWORD

Sergeants
Blair, Troy
Sanders, Jesse H.

Corporal
Duty, Hetzel

Privates
Coleman, Paul E.
Owens, Paul W.
Roberts, Wm. R.

COMPANY F—113TH QUARTERMASTER REGIMENT
(Campbellsville, Kentucky)

CAPT. JAMES W. SMITH   SECOND LT. ROBERT B. HAYES

Sergeants
Bryant, James G.
Hayes, John A.
Pike, Abner

Corporal
Shively, Eugene B.

Privates
Netherland, Clarence
Newton, William T.

Seaborne, Roy
Wade, George H.
Cave, Manuel A.
Cole, David V.
Darnell, James H.
Garrison, Paul W.
Mardis, John T.
Miller, John R.
Netherland, Wm. E.
Pike, William G.
Spurling, Charles E.
Daugherty, James H.
Shipp, Lester A.
Smith, Lester H.
Stark, Russell K.
Watson, Earl T.
Weatherford, Edwin L.
Willson, George H.
Young, John R.

COMPANY G—113TH MEDICAL REGIMENT

(Richmond, Kentucky)

CAPT. JOHN H. RUTLEDGE
CAPT. GEORGE N. HEMBREE
CAPT. ROBERT W. SANDLIN
CAPT. THOMAS CLOUSE, JR.
CAPT. RUSSELL L. POPE
FIRST LT. HAROLD H. RUTLEDGE

Sergeants
Wilcox, Eugene
Grace, Winford W.
Hamblen, William T.
Reeves, Walter W.
Rogers, James T.
Evans, George W.
Forbes, Wallace G.
Norris, Walter B.
Terrill, William W.
Todd, Vernon
West, John D.

Corporals
Baker, R. E.
Eades, Charles G.
McWhorter, Charles B.

Privates
Anderson, Thomas J.
Brown, Richard L.
Cornelison, Owen P.
Edwards, Frank W.
Fife, John C.
Floyd, Charles N.
Howell, Atlas B.
Hughes, Elmo K.
Jones, John L.
Kerrick, Cecil C.
McCarthy, Albert L.
Rayburn, Henry D.
Short, James H.
Taylor, Ray
Boucher, Edgar F.
Broaddus, Edgar W.
Broomfield, Wm. L.
Combs, Orlie C.
Davis, Earl A.
Dyehouse, Wm. J.
Fife, Paul E.
Foster, Alvin C.
Guy, Woodrow Q.
Hendren, Drexel J.
Hickey, Elmer J.
Johnson, Harold J.
Downing, Edward P.
Jones, Christopher W.
McWhorter, Harry
Miller, Richard
Mullikin, Josiah W., Jr.
Muncy, El H.
Pittman, Robert E.
Powell, Russell W.
Prater, James H.
Robinson, Ben
Robinson, Paul A.
Shetler, Vernon
Stewart, Raymond H.
Teater, Oakley M.
Tollner, John D.
Turpin, Ruben L.
Tussey, Raymond G.
Tyler, Herman H.
Yelton, Edwin A.
Zaring, Allen

COMPANY H—113TH MEDICAL REGIMENT

CAPT. ROBERT M. PHELPS ....Richmond, Kentucky
CAPT. OSCAR D. BROCK ....London, Kentucky
CAPT. RUSSELL I. TODD ....Richmond, Kentucky
FIRST LT. MASON G. POPE ....Richmond, Kentucky
FIRST LT. JAMES R. ALLMAN ....Richmond, Kentucky
FIRST LT. CHARLES B. BILLINGTON ....Richmond, Kentucky

Sergeants
Hamblen, James B.
Agee, Coy
Bowles, Arthur M.
Fielder, Frederick T.
Manuel, Alvin
Fletcher, Rufus
Manuel, Earl F.
Moberly, Robert J., Jr.
Moores, Edgar S.
Moores, Elkin W.
Stewart, John F.

Corporals
House, Harvey D.
Lear, Everett C.
Stewart, Harold S.

Privates
Allen, Howard U.
Baber, Woodrow W.
Black, Frank B.
Brookshire, Hollie H.
Cobb, Jake W.
Green, Franklin C.
Hackett, Max R.
Hamilton, Earl B.
Mason, Daniel
Moore, James F.
Noland, Tom F.
Oliver, John W.
Parks, Robert E.
Sharp, Arbor, Jr.
Walters, Burton
Wells, Fred R.
Adams, William C.
Baker, Edward M.
Benton, Burgin L.
Benton, Cleophas
Brookshire, Nevel J.
Bush, Earl R.
Cain, Phillip L.
Cunliffe, Chas. C.
Curry, W. T.
Dickerson, William E.
Fritz, James E.
Hensley, Henry C.
Johnson, Neville
Kelly, Alexander Z.
Kennedy, Joe H.
McCoy, Woodrow
McQueen, James P.
Marcum, Clarence
Matthews, Thomas J.
Metcalf, David G.
Metcalfe, Joe W.
Moores, Eugene D.
Moores, Jesse T.
Powell, Aaron F.
Powell, Ormond E.
Powell, Wesley A.
Richardson, Virgil
Roark, James R.
Todd, Harvey B.
Wood, Russell
Young, Carlos

SPECIAL TROOPS (Kentucky allotment)

38TH MILITARY POLICE COMPANY

(Jackson, Kentucky)

CAPT. ARCH COPE   SECOND LT. (vacancy)

Sergeants
Frasure, John
Carpenter, Marcus
Williams, Carl
Young, Clyde

Corporals
Barnett, Clyde
Fugate, Walter
McIntosh, Daniel
Pugh, Benjamin
Walk, Herbert

Privates
Collier, Charles
Combs, Woodrow
Cope, Price
Dykes, Nathan
Dunn, Lucas
Frazier, Harlan
Goff, Bert
Hensley, Mize
Lovens, Elbert
McIntosh, Billie
Roark, Price
Russell, Alfred
Russel, Charles
Smith, John
Spencer, Luther
Stidham, Fred
Stidham, Bryan
Tharp, Jerry
Thomson, Robert
Williams, Carl, Jr.
Williams, Leonard
Williams, Robert
Winburn, Johnnie
Bach, Rollin
Barnett, Roy
Collins, Sidney
Burnett, Ray
Combs, Ed
Combs, Price
Coomer, Hillard
Criswell, James
Hadden, Robert
Hester, Robert
Lynch, Olen
Spencer, Leonard
Taulbee, Patrick
Terry, Seldon
Terry, Woodrow
Watking, Gordon
Williams, Dorsey
Young, Connor

38TH TANK COMPANY

(Harrodsburg, Kentucky)

CAPT. BACON R. MOORE
FIRST LT. DAVIS H. GRITTON SECOND LT. EDWIN RUE
FIRST LT. TRUMAN MAYES SECOND LT. GEORGE A. VAN ARSDALL

Sergeants
Rowland, Sam
Parsons, James B.
Darland, Owen
Gentry, Richard
Gritton, Claude S.
Terhune, William G.
Wilson, Maurice E.

Corporals
Annss, Joe
Conley, Archie H.
Curd, John
Elliott, Edwin
Fuqua, John
Gentry, Wm.
Hourigan, Kenneth
Lawson, William J.
Preston, Everett
Steel, Henry
Terhune, James

Privates
Carter, Elmer
Dean, Robert
Denny, Wallace
French, Morgan
Hourigan, Horace
Hourigan, Stanley
Leonard, Fred
Leonard, Hugh
McAnly, Carl
Osborne, Howard L.
Pearson, John W.
Blacketer, Wm. E.
Bottoms, Johnnie
Elliott, Virgil T.
Fowler, Harold B.
French, Edward
Freeman, Raymond
Gillespie, Elmo
Gibson, James A.
Harlow, Dudley
Huff, Lawrence

Huffman, Arthur
Huffman, Joe
Keller, LeRoy
Matherly, Leslie G.
Mills, Cecil G.
Noel, Donald
Pearson, Leslie
Pinkston, James E.
Rogers, Major
Reed, Roy J.
Rue, Insco
Steel, Willard
VanDivier, Allen T.
Payne, Dillard
Pearson, Randell
Rodgers, Carrol
Ryan, Ernest
Rue, Arch B.
Sparrow, Eugene
Tatum, Cecil G.
Votaw, Lawrence

113TH ORDNANCE COMPANY

(Bardstown, Kentucky)

CAPT. ALVAN W. WELLS   SECOND LT. BENJAMIN W. POOR

Sergeants
Hart, Charles W.
Metcalfe, Charles N.
Cecil, Francis L.
Cox, David L.
Keene, Paul
Simms, Francis M.

Corporals
Cecil, Samuel K.
Riley, William E.

Privates
Clark, James P.
Hayden, James E.
Keene, William L.
Metcalfe, Julian
Noel, Fred V.
Edelen, Henry C.
Edelen, Rod N.
Greenwell, Rodney K.
Hurst, Billie
Ice, Alvin E.

Johnson, Albert I.
Linder, Jack H.
McDowell, Luther E.
Morley, Stanley L.
Morton, Leonard J.
Roby, Felix P.
Roby, Marion C.
Welch, Thomas J.

G.H.Q. RESERVE, 22D CAV. DIV., 54TH CAVALRY BRIGADE
123RD CAVALRY

HEADQUARTERS
(Louisville, Kentucky)

COL. HENRY J. STITES	Louisville, Kentucky
LT. COL. JOHN A. POLIN	Springfield, Kentucky
CAPT. THOMAS E. BATES	Owensboro, Kentucky
CAPT. GAYLORD S. GILBERT	Louisville, Kentucky
CAPT. HUGH B. GREGORY	Springfield, Kentucky
FIRST LT. JAMES R. DORMAN, JR.	Louisville, Kentucky
FIRST LT. HENRY M. JOHNSON	Louisville, Kentucky

MEDICAL DEPARTMENT DETACHMENT
(Hopkinsville, Kentucky)

MAJOR PHILIP E. HAYNES	Hopkinsville, Kentucky
CAPT. OMAR S. MEREDITH	Leitchfield, Kentucky
CAPT. GEORGE W. PEDIGO	Glasgow, Kentucky
CAPT. ROBERT C. RIGGS	Lexington, Kentucky
CAPT. JOHN R. STIFLER	Lebanon, Kentucky
FIRST LT. DELMUS M. CLARDY	Hopkinsville, Kentucky

Sergeants
Butler, Leslie T.
Wade, William E.
Chambers, Walter T.
Thompson, William F.

Privates
Clark, Billy W.

Peden, Warren G.
Pelham, Gentry
Simmons, Harry P.
Alder, Cecil D.
Anderson, Charles T.
Fields, Illey G.
Fort, Lee J.

Hammonds, William H.
Keller, Joseph G.
Keller, Richard W.
Means, Forest A.
Mulrenin, Paul E.
Wade, Major H.
Wade, Will E.

HEADQUARTERS TROOP
(Glasgow, Kentucky)

CAPT. SAMUEL SEARS
FIRST LT. JESSE CASSADY

SECOND LT. ROBERT ABNER
SECOND LT. FRED R. GANTER

Sergeants
Hazelip, Warner S., Master
Palmore, Aaron O., Master
Peden, Charles H., First
Bowles, Guy W., Tech.

McQuown, Geo. W., Tech.
Reynolds, Garl'd B., Tech.
Chambers, Sam'l R., Staff
Chapman, Henry B., Staff
Church, Clyde, Staff

Dickinson, William, Staff
Taylor, Fred B., Staff
Compton, Elton
Emberton, Emmett A.
Froedge, Robert Y.
Harpst, Robert E.
Houck, Herman H.

Jones, Ellis D.
Potts, William C.
Sharp, Millard T.
Speck, Malcolm C.
Steen, Henry B.
Taylor, Frank
Trabue, William H.

Corporals

Delk, John L.
Froedge, William T.
Reynolds, Joseph C.
Dougherty, Russell E.

Privates

Ard, Lawrence W.
Brooks, Gordeon B.
Gooden, Paul
Landrum, James R.
Morgan, Robert L.
Shaw, Julius J.
Shipley, James E.
Shirley, James H.
Bradley, George P.
Colman, James C.
Compton, Reid
Curd, Oscar F.
Daniels, Orval D.
Durham, Kelly
Deering, Stanley E.
Ferrell, William D.
Forrest, Hobert H.
Froedge, Charles O.
Grisson, William H.
Holmes, Alfred R.
Jump, Forrest B.
Parker, Frank R.
Parrett, Edward L.
Parrett, Paul D.
Pedigo, Garnett V.
Reece, Morris A.
Reynolds, James E.
Samson, William L.
Sater, Windell L.
Smith, Herbert C.
Smith, Schuylor E.
Stovall, Shelby H.
Trabue, Gordon A.
Washburn, Lewis C.
Woodward,
  Stanley W.
Young, Russell

HEADQUARTERS TROOP—BAND SECTION

(Glasgow, Kentucky)

WARRANT OFFICER WAYNE E. TYREE

Sergeants

Walden, William C., Tech.
Moss, Otis, Staff
Dickinson, Jack T.
Gabbard, Wm. D.
Morris, Walter S.
Page, Edwin

Corporals

Doyle, Raymond E.
Neville, Charles B.

Privates

Biggers,
  Harold C., Jr.
Boone, Buford
Neville, Leland H.
Potts, Hall B.
Underwood, Rollin D.
Biggers, Gilbert M.
Bush, Bill
Chism, James
Goodman, Roy M., Jr.
Harlow, Garland

Pedigo, Durwood, Jr.
Page, Leon
Pedigo, James A.
Speck, Morris
Vaughn, Richard S.
Wheeler, Oscar L.
Witty, Gordon

MACHINE GUN TROOP

(Hopkinsville, Kentucky)

CAPT. ALVIN H. SCHUTZ
FIRST LT. JOHN C. FLEMING
SECOND LT. WILLIAM E. KEITH
SECOND LT. EDWIN GARNER, JR.

Sergeants

Gourley, James S.
Gary, Melbourne S.
Carter, Paul V.
Garland, Edgar
Grubbs, John B.
Hays, Walter L.

McShane, Thomas P.
Williams, George E.

Corporals

Adams, James P.
Atwood, Wm. F.
Cansler, James E.

Cowherd, Paul K.
Ladd, Robert E.
Miles, Elliott R.
Minton, John J.
Saturley, Gaither D.

Privates

Belk, Raymond W.
Cornette, Charles N.
Davis, Wallis E.
DeHart, James L.
Gary, Jerome
Hayes, Taft
Hammond, Hugh R.
Jackson, Thomas W.
Moseley, Joe D.
Putty, Elmer H.
Riggins, Leslie G.
Stewart, Jesse R.
Anderson, Henry
Campbell, Livingston L.
Boyd, Willard
Cannon, James P.
Cranor, Charles H.
Fields, Ernest C.
Gee, Phil S.
Gamble, Paul W.
Fletcher, George T.
Fletcher, Samuel T.
Gafford, Woodson
Hamby, Leslie W.
Holmes, Kester J.
Henson, Jesse E.
Johnson, Archie B.
Lacy, Howell B.
Lewis, Reams P.
Lohorn, Roland B.
Marquess, Jas. W.
Meyers, Alva G.
Mitchell, Daniel S.
Mitchell, Leonard R.
Morgan, John W.
Myers, James R.
Nelson, Wharton
O'Daniel, Raymond W.
Pugh, William H.
P'Pool, Amos O.
P'Pool, John A.
Profit, James W.
Seay, Thomas T.
Shelton, Arch P.
Shepherd, James W.
Winfree, Ben S.

HEADQUARTERS, 1ST SQUADRON
(Frankfort, Kentucky)

MAJOR ROBERT C. GRAHAM   FIRST LT. JACKSON A. SMITH

TROOP A
(Frankfort, Kentucky)

CAPT. F. COBURN GAYLE

FIRST LT. LOUIS P. SMITH   SECOND LT. ALBERT C. SMITH

Sergeants

Snow, Cecil L.
Alexander, Clay W.
Atchison, Charles M.
Gordon, Grover A.
Gravitt, Alex
McDonald, John H.
Pardi, John H.

Corporals

Daniels, Kirthwood
Hale, Clarence
Jones, Ray C.
Mitchell, Harlan I.
Tucker, Howard J.
Tucker, William S.

Privates

Brown, Edward A.
Crane, Eugene
Dean, Irvine
Greenwell, Holt J.
Hamilton, John C.
Haydon, Raymond
Martin, Marion
Meccia, Joseph A.
Newton, Murry N.
Pointer, Hanley S.
Skinner, Wm. C.
Smith, Robert L.
Snow, Herbert E.
Young, Clarence
Alexander, Chas. E.
Baker, Thomas A.
Barnett, Jos. H.
Beaucham, Joseph
Cleri, Frank L.
Conway, Albert J.
Courtney, Garret
Courtney, Joe
Crane, Arbie C.
Crane, Floyd T.
Downey, Vernon
Finnell, Donald O.
Florian, Joseph H.
Gale, Albert C.
Games, Tom E.
Games, William D.
Goins, Dewey J.
Goins, Joseph B.
Gordon, Edward T.
Hulker, Selbert B.
Lawrence, George L.
Kong, Basil
Martin, Robert H.
McKinney, Wallace M.
Payne, Spencer C.
Quire, Forrest
Shearer, William N.
Smith, Robert E.
Spalding, Arthur P.
True, Lee E.
Williamson, Frank P.
Woolums, Everett E.
Young, Charles F.

TROOP B

(Lexington, Kentucky)

CAPT. DEWEY S. CONGLETON

FIRST LT. JAMES D. FOSTER   SECOND LT. VERNON N. CHANDLER

Sergeants
Waller, Iloff H.
Adams, Presley S., Sr.
Bailey, Elmer T.
Dargavell, William T.
Johnson, Robert S.
Sallee, Coleman T.
Smith, Chester

Corporals
Hammond, William B.
Johnson, Mason B.
O'Lee, Benjamin W.
Powell, Lewis F.
Robinson, Herschell B., Jr.

Privates
Beamis, Bruce B.
Campbell, Wm. F., Jr.
Curd, Marion O.
Fox, Harold D.
Newberger, Morton B., Jr.
Sayre, Frank J.
Shotwell, Edwin C.
Stringfellow, Marvin B.
White, John F.
Wilson, James M.
Anderson, William J.
Bittenbender, Edward H.
Caywood, Bronston
Chambers, Elwood N.
Courtney, William, Jr.
Crisp, Dennis
Day, Claude D.
Dickstein, Richard S.
Fleming, Raymond G.
Griffin, Adron F.
Hamersley, Gordon R.
Jones, Jerry W.
Lambert, Elmer A.
Hamilton, Howard B., Jr.
Dimock, Shubael E.
Gamboe, Vernon C.
Chauncey, Leslie W.
Smith, Woodrow W.
Litsey, Raleigh B., Jr.
Littrell, Obie V.
Mathews, Herman H.
McMullin, Clifton C.
Meier, Joe E.
Mitchell, Albert R.
Robinson, William T.
Sayre, Fabius J.
Sayre, Robert L.
Sizemore, Louis
Snapp, Rayburn F.
Spears, Lyn W.
Stone, Thomas F.
Stringfellow Herbert M.
Stull, Lyn R.
Walls, Robert N.
Walton, Riley C.
White, Rankin
Wilson, John T.

HEADQUARTERS, 2D SQUADRON

(Covington, Kentucky)

MAJ. GEORGE E. NELSON   FIRST LT. RANKIN RAY GORRELL

TROOP E

(London, Kentucky)

CAPT. WILLIS G. HACKNEY

FIRST LT. ARMON E. RUSSELL   SECOND LT. JOSEPH R. MATHEWS

Sergeants
Weaver, Carl H.
Blankenship, Stanley
Hendrix, Corsie
Jones, Calvin
Kirby, Clyde M.
Lewis, Alford L.
Stamper, Charles C.

Corporals
Benge, Chester G.
Benge, Eugene
Brewer, William J.
Bryant, William E.

Parman, David C.
Powers, Ralph M.

Privates

Couch, Marion
Hubbard, Robert
Miller, Roy C.
Morgan, James T.
Rush, Charles
Rush, Tillman
Simpson, Arthur
Williams, Jas. T.
Weaver, Gordon J.
Bacelieri, Chas.
Bolton, Thos. J.
Brown, Clyde C.
Burnette, Leo
Burnette, Alton O.
Cornett, Everett L.
Cornett, John H.
Cornn, Jas. L.
Ellison, Q. C.
Frasier, Delmore
Hacker, Marion A.
Hall, John W.
Hendrix, Felix C.
Hibbitts, Arthur
Johnson, Earl M.
Jones, Clement H.
Karr, Glenn A.
Kelley, Brady O.
Mize, Earl M.
Morgan, George W.
Morgan, Sam K.
Reams, Charles
Reams, William
Reams, Oscar C.
Rush, Sam J.
Setser, Charles P.
Shelley, Aubrey E.
Sherman, Elmer G.
Slusher,
 Raymond E.
Stanifer, Harry I.
Sweet, Birchel H.
Vires, Banford
Wagner, Damon B.
Watkins, Mark A.
Wyatt, Fred A.
Young, Luther M.

TROOP F

(Covington, Kentucky)

CAPT. FRED M. WARREN ....Southgate, Kentucky
FIRST LT. STEVE J. MEADE ....Covington, Kentucky
SECOND LT. HERMAN H. REED ....Newport, Kentucky

Sergeants

Courtney, Edward J.
Carran, Karl L.
Carson, Wellman W.
Procter,
 Harry L., Jr.
Schworer, Phillip G.
Stulhbarg, Milton W.

Corporals

Fisher, Albert P.
Marqua, Ronald E.
Signom, James D.
Vess, Samuel P.
Voorhees, Charles F.
Wagenlander,
 Albert E.

Privates

Beyersdoerfer,
 Gilmore E.
Blakely, John R.
Crowe, John W.
Cummings, James H.
Dilts, Cecil H.
Dolsey, Herbert S.
Foltz, Ambrose J.
Hartz, Harry P.
Henderson,
 James Ward
Holaday, John R.
Holt, William G.
Signom, Robert E.
Southgate,
 Henry H., Jr.
Spare, Albert J.
Abernathy,
 Carroll E.
Agee, Robert L.
Black, Massie W.
Campbell,
 Douglas H.
Clayton, Sam
Dailey, Gilbert L.
Dickerson,
 William N.
Fenton, Kermit D.
Fogle, Ralph E.
Frisch, Homer L.
Haney, William
Holt, Robert R.
Holthaus, Arnold J.
Newman, Robert A.
Campbell, Joseph F.
Cottengim, Clyde W.
Crusie, Lawrence J.
Goodman, Albert C.
Hehman, Thomas L.
Johnson, Elbert R.
Johnson, James T.
Jones, Richard P.
Marqua, Victor V.
Martin, Jack T.
Mason, Joe W.
Moore, Robert A.
Moore, William I.
Mozea, Blaine
Pfirman, Edward J.
Pryne, Clarence E.
Sanders, Charles C.
Vitali, Gene C.
Wehry, George E.
Wiglesworth,
 Ward T.
Works, Lawrence E.
Zieverink, Joseph W.

MILITARY HISTORY OF KENTUCKY 473

HEADQUARTERS, 3D SQUADRON
(Frankfort, Kentucky)

MAJ. JOSEPH M. KELLY .... Frankfort, Kentucky
FIRST LT. MORTIMER M. BENTON .... Louisville, Kentucky

TROOP I
(Springfield, Kentucky)
CAPT. HENRY W. MERRITT
FIRST LT. WILLIAM C. MUDD   SECOND LT. JOSEPH E. POLIN

Sergeants
Moore, George W.
Dowling, Thomas W.
Keene, Joseph B.
Keene, Richard P.
Overall, James L.
Reddon, Roy C.
Wheatley, Charles J.

Corporals
Carrico, Chas. M.
Carrico, John L.
Clements, James R.
Colvin, Irvine T.
Mudd, Joseph S.
Settle, Charles P.

Privates
Allen, Kilburn N.
Bugg, Bennie G.
Burns, Robert H.
Clements, Joseph C.
Clements, William A.

Cornish, Clifton C.
Elliott, Frank
Harmon, Wesley O.
Hays, Joseph W.
Kays, Paul
Litsey, Alfred L.
Logsdon, John W.
Mackin, James F.
Mudd, Maurice A.
Spalding, Ivo
Allen, William L.
Briscoe, James
Boone, Thomas H.
Boswell, Ralph
Carney, Charles
Carney, Clyde
Chandler, Robert
Cheatham, John T.
Cheser, James L.
Cornish, Ruel V.
Fauth, James
Grisby, Gladys
Grisby, William P.

Spalding, Patrick B.
Hardin, Roscoe
Hyde, Richard
Hale, Joe
McMichael, Manzony
Miller, Aaron F.
Mullins, John F.
Neikirk, Charles E.
Paris, Charles
Pinkston, John R.
Porter, Marion E.
Porter, Melvin
Russell, James
Settle, Marlin
Smock, Samuel L.
Spalding, James
Spalding, Lester
Taylor, George N.
Wayne, Robert
Wiggington,
  William T.

TROOP K
(Monticello, Kentucky)
CAPT. JOEL L. STOKES
FIRST LT. EDWARD B. ALLRED   SECOND LT. JACK C. PHILLIPS

Sergeants
Caylor, Ed. L.
Barrier, Ray G.
Bertram,
  Herschel B.
Duncan, Clarence D.
Gregory,
  Herschel L.

Lair, Ike B.
Shearer, Wm. D.

Corporals
Bertram, Randall
Denney, Walter H.
Garner, Roy
Lester, Leon D.

Pruitt, Odie E.
West, Henry T.

Privates
Bell, Milton
Boles, Elmer B.
Barrier, Bob
Carrender, Lee B.

Castle, Pat
Caylor, Jim
Davidson, Dellas
Green, Jack
Hill, Goldman B.
Kennedy, Porter G.
Morris, Edgar R.
Pyle, Glanton I.
Pyle, Gleason O.
Sumpter, George
Sumpter, Willie
Thomas, Ira D.
Abbott, Earnest
Atwood, William C.
Barrier, Cedric
Bow, Preston P.

Brown, Cecil R.
Brown, Edward G.
Buck, Richard M.
Castle, Joe
Crabtree, Roscoe A.
Correll, Carter
Correll, Ed.
Crawford, John B.
Dobbs, Leonard R.
Davis, Ira H.
Gregory, John M.
Gregory, Robert E.
Guffey, Chester R.
Higginbotham, Harold A.
Hicks, Robert

Abbott, Thurman T.
Holstein, Coy E.
Jenkins, Wm. R.
Kennedy, Harry R.
Lair, Charlie R.
Lair, Logan W.
Lester, Arlin
Lester, Ray
Lester, Grady E.
Lester, Willie H.
Rigney, Lester L.
Thornton, Roy
Troxel, Earnest M.
Troxel, Joe L.
Walcutt, Hulen D.
Woody, Al

BIBLIOGRAPHY

BOOKS AND PAMPHLETS

Battle, J. H., and W. H. Perrin. *Counties of Todd and Christian, Kentucky.* 2 vols. Chicago: F. A. Battey Pub. Co., 1884.

———. *Also see* Perrin, W. H.

Bodley, Temple. *George Rogers Clark.* Boston: Houghton Mifflin Co., 1925.

———. *History of Kentucky.* Chicago: S. J. Clarke Pub. Co., 1928.

Bogart, W. H. *Daniel Boone and the Hunters of Kentucky.* Boston: Lee & Shephard, 1874.

Brackett, A. G. *History of the United States Cavalry.* New York: Harper & Bros., 1865.

Butler, Mann. *A History of the Commonwealth of Kentucky.* Louisville: Wilcox, Dickinson & Co., 1834 (Louisville: J. A. James & Co., 1836).

The Centenary of Kentucky. Proceedings at the Celebration of the Filson Club. Louisville: J. P. Morton & Co., 1892.

Clark, George Rogers. *Sketch of His Campaign in the Illinois.* Cincinnati: Robert Clarke & Co., 1907.

Clift, G. Glenn. *History of Maysville and Mason County, Kentucky.* 2 vols. Lexington: Transylvania Ptg. Co., 1936.

Collins, Richard H. *History of Kentucky.* Covington: Richard H. Collins & Co., 1874.

Connelly, W. E., and E. M. Coulter. *History of Kentucky.* 5 vols. Chicago: American Historical Society, 1922.

Cook, J. F. *Old Kentucky.* New York: Male Pub. Co., 1908.

Cottrell, Robert Spencer. *History of Pioneer Kentucky.* Cincinnati: Johnson & Hardin, 1917.

Coulter, E. M. *The Civil War and Readjustment in Kentucky.* Chapel Hill: University of North Carolina Press, 1926.

———. *Also see* Connelly, W. E.

Darnell, Elias. *Journal of Kentucky Volunteers Commanded by General Winchester in 1812–1813.* Philadelphia: Lippincott, Grambo & Co., 1854.

Daveiss, Joseph H. *The sketch of a bill for an uniform militia of the United States with reflection on the state of the nation, addressed to the Secretary of War.* Frankfort: Henry Gore, printer, 1810.

Denison, George T. *A History of Cavalry.* London: Macmillan & Co., 1913.

Discourse of Robert J. Breckinridge. (Speech delivered at Lexington, Jan. 4th, 1861.) Cincinnati: Faran & McLean, 1861.

Duke, Basil W. *Reminiscences of General Basil W. Duke, C.S.A.* Garden City: Doubleday, Page & Co., 1911.

Elliston, R. H. *History of Grant County, Kentucky.* Williamstown, Ky.: E. H. Eyer, 1878.

Evans, Clement A., editor. *Confederate Military History.* Atlanta: Confederate Pub. Co., 1899.
Flint, Timothy. *The Life and Exploits of Colonel Daniel Boone.* Cincinnati: Queen City Pub. Co.
Freeman, L. L., and E. C. Olds. *History of Marshall County, Kentucky.* Benton: Tribune-Democrat, 1933.
George, Henry. *History of the 3d, 7th, 8th and 12th Kentucky, C.S.A.* Louisville: 1911.
Gorin, Franklin. *Times of Long Ago.* Louisville: J. P. Morton & Co., 1929.
Green, Thomas Marshall. *Historic Families of Kentucky.* Cincinnati: Robert Clarke & Co., 1889.
Hay, John. *See* Nicolay, J. G.
Henderson, Archibald. *The Transylvania Company and the Founding of Henderson, Kentucky.* 1929.
Historical Annual, National Guard of the Commonwealth of Kentucky, 1938. Baton Rouge, La.: Army and Navy Pub. Co., 1938.
History of the Ohio Falls Cities and Their Counties. 2 vols. Cleveland: L. A. Williams & Co., 1881.
Hulbert, Archer Butler. *Boone's Wilderness Road.* (In the series, *Historic Highways of America.*) Cleveland: A. H. Clark Co., 1903.
James, James Alton. *Life of George Rogers Clark.* Chicago: University of Chicago Press, 1928.
Jillson, Willard Rouse. *The Big Sandy Valley.* Louisville: J. P. Morton & Co., 1923.
———. *Filson's Kentucke.* Facsimile reproduction of 1784 ed. Louisville: J. P. Morton & Co., 1929.
———. *Tales of the Dark and Bloody Ground.* Louisville: C. T. Dearing Ptg. Co., 1930.
Johnson, L. F. *Famous Kentucky Tragedies and Trials.* Louisville: Baldwin Law Book Co., 1916.
Jordon, Thomas, and J. P. Pryor. *The Campaigns of Lt. Gen. N. B. Forrest.* Cincinnati: J. P. Miller & Co., 1868.
Kennan, George. *Campaigning in Cuba.* New York: Century Co., 1899.
Kenton, Edna. *Simon Kenton.* New York: Doubleday, Doran & Co., 1930.
Kniffin, G. C. *Also see* Perrin, W. H.
Lester, W. W. *The Transylvania Colony.* Spencer, Ind.: Samuel R. Guard Co., 1935.
McAfee, Robert B. *History of the Late War in the Western Country.* Lexington: Wordley & Smith, 1816.
Marshall, Humphrey. *The History of Kentucky.* 2 vols. Frankfort: George S. Robinson, 1824.
Meecham, C. M. *History of Christian County, Kentucky.* Nashville: Marshall & Bruce, 1930.
Morton, M. B. *Kentuckians are Different.* Louisville: Standard Press, 1938.

Nicolay, J. G., and John Hay, editors. *Complete Works of Abraham Lincoln.* Vol. VI. New York: F. D. Tandy Co.
Olds, E. C. *See* Freeman, L. L.
O'Malley, Charles J. *History of Union County, Kentucky.* Evansville, Ind.: Courier Co., 1886.
Perkins, James H. *Annals of the West.* Cincinnati: James R. Alnack, 1846.
Perrin, W. H. *History of Bourbon, Scott, Harrison and Nicholas Counties, Kentucky.* Chicago: O. L. Baskin & Co., 1882.
——————. *History of Fayette County, Kentucky.* Chicago: O. L. Baskin & Co., 1882.
——————. J. H. Battle, and G. C. Kniffen. *Kentucky: A History of the State.* Louisville: F. A. Battey & Co., 1888.
——————. *Also see* Battle, J. H.
Peter, Robert. *History of Fayette County, Kentucky.* Chicago: O. L. Baskin, 1882.
Pryor, J. P. *See* Jordon, L. F.
Pusey, William Allen. *The Wilderness Road to Kentucky.* New York: George H. Doran Co., 1921.
Quisenberry, Andrew C. *Lopez's Expedition to Cuba.* Louisville: J. P. Morton & Co., 1906.
Ranck, George Washington. *Boonesborough.* Louisville: J. P. Morton & Co., 1901. Filson Club publication, No. 16.
Ridenour, George L. *Early Times in Meade County, Kentucky.* Louisville: Western Recorder, 1929.
Roosevelt, Theodore. *The Winning of the West.* 6 vols. New York: G. P. Putnam's Sons, 1889–96.
Rothert, Otto S. *History of Muhlenberg County, Kentucky.* Louisville: J. P. Morton & Co., 1913.
Sargent, Herbert H. *The Campaign of Santiago de Cuba.* 3 vols. Chicago: A. C. McClurg & Co., 1907.
Shaler, N. S. *Kentucky, A Pioneer Commonwealth.* 1st and 4th eds. Boston: Houghton, Mifflin & Co., 1884, 1888.
Smith, E. C. *The Borderland in the Civil War.* New York: Macmillan Co., 1927.
Smith, S. K. *Army Life, and Public Services of D. Howard Smith.* Louisville: Bradley & Gilbert Co., 1890.
Smith, Z. F. *History of Kentucky.* Louisville: Courier-Journal Job Ptg. Co., 1886.
Spalding, M. J. *Sketches of the Early Catholic Missions in Kentucky.* Louisville: B. J. Webb & Bros., 1844.
Speed, Thomas. *The Union Cause in Kentucky.* New York: G. P. Putnam's Sons, 1907.
——————. *The Wilderness Road.* Louisville: J. P. Morton & Co., 1886. The Filson Club publication, No. 2.
Starling, Edmund L. *History of Henderson and Henderson County, Kentucky.* Henderson: 1887.
Summers, Lewis Preston. *Annals of Southwest Virginia, 1769–1800.* Abingdon, Va.: 1929.
Taylor, Harrison D. *Ohio County, Kentucky, in the Olden Days.* Louisville: J. P. Morton & Co., 1913.

Thompson, E. P. *History of the Orphan Brigade.* Louisville: L. N. Thompson, 1898.

Thompson, J. J. *The Hill and Evans Feud.* Cincinnati: W. P. James, 1854.

Thwaites, Reuben Gold. *Daniel Boone.* New York: D. Appleton & Co., 1902

Townsend, John Wilson. *Kentucky in American Letters, 1784–1912.* 2 vols. Cedar Rapids, Iowa: Torch Press, 1913.

Van Rensselaer, Solomon. *A Narrative of the Affair of Queenstown.* New York: Leavett, Lord & Co., 1836.

Volwiler, Albert Tangeman. *George Croghan and the Westward Movement.* Cleveland: A. H. Clark Co., 1926.

Willis, Geo. L., Sr. *History of Shelby County, Kentucky.* Louisville: J. P. Morton & Co., 1929.

Winsor, Justin. *The Westward Movement.* Boston: Houghton, Mifflin & Co., 1899.

Government Documents, Manuscripts and Other Official Sources

An Act Authorizing a Detachment from the Militia of the U.S. Approved June 24, 1797. (Printed Copy.) Also contains extracts from an act entitled: "An Act more effectually to provide for the National Defence by establishing an uniform militia throughout the U.S." (Passed May 8, 1792.) Archives Room, Kentucky State Historical Society, Kentucky Militia Folder in filing case.

Acts of the General Assembly of the Commonwealth of Kentucky, 1792–1938.

Annual Reports of the Adjutant General, 1860–65. In Kentucky Documents, Kentucky State Historical Society, Old Capitol Building, Frankfort.

Annual Report of the Inspector General: 1861. In Kentucky Documents (see above).

Annual Report of the Quartermaster General: 1861. In Kentucky Documents (see above).

Barbour, J., and John D. Carroll. *The Kentucky Statutes.* Louisville: Courier Journal Job Ptg. Co., 1894.

Bullitt, J. F., and John Feland. *General Statutes of Kentucky.* Frankfort: Major, Johnson & Barrett, 1877, 1879, 1881 eds. Louisville: Bradley and Gilbert, 1887, 1888, 1890 eds.

Bullock, E. I., and William Johnson. *General Statutes of the Commonwealth of Kentucky.* Frankfort: Yeoman Office, 1873.

Carroll, John D. *Kentucky Statutes.* Louisville: Courier-Journal Job Ptg. Co., 1903, 1909 eds. Louisville: Baldwin Law Book Co., 1915, 1919, 1922 eds.

The Code of the Laws of the United States of America in Force, January 3, 1935. Washington: Government Ptg. Office, 1935.

Commager, H. S. *Documents of American History.* New York: F. S. Crafts & Co., 1934.

Drafts in Kentucky during Civil War. No. 142 in Senate Documents; 61st Congress, 1st Session.

Fayette County Circuit Court Records. Office of the Circuit Court Clerk's Office, Lexington.

Fleming, Walter Lynwood, editor. *Documentary History of Reconstruction.* Cleveland: A. H. Clark Co., 1906-1907.

Hening, William Waller. *The Statutes at Large of Virginia.* 12 vols. Richmond, Va.: R. & W. & G. Barton, 1810-23.

Journal of the House of Representatives of the General Assembly of the Commonwealth of Kentucky, 1792 to date.

Journal of the Senate of the General Assembly of the Commonwealth of Kentucky, 1792 to date.

Kentucky General Assembly. *Enrolled Bills: 1792.* In Archives Room, State Historical Society, Old State Capitol Building, Frankfort.

——————. *Minute Book for 1839-40.* MS in Library of Kentucky Legislature, Frankfort.

Kentucky *Executive Journals.* The journals of the governors of Kentucky. 1792-1938. In Archives Room, State Historical Society *(see above).* Kentucky Volunteers, War with Spain, 1898-99. (Report of the adjutant general of the state of Kentucky.) Frankfort: Louisville Globe Ptg. Co., 1908.

Letter Book of Governors Adair, Desha, and Metcalfe, 1820-32. In Archives Room, State Historical Society *(see above).*

Letter Book of Governor James Clark: 1836-39. In Archives Room, State Historical Society *(see above).*

Letters of Isaac Shelby to the House of Representatives: 1793. File Box 1, Archives Room, State Historical Society *(see above).*

Littell, William. *Statutes of Kentucky.*

Littell, William and Jacob Swigert. *Digest of the Statute Law of Kentucky.* 2 vols. Frankfort: Kendall & Russell, 1822.

Loughborough, P. S. *Digest of the Statute Law of Kentucky.* Frankfort: A. G. Hodges, 1842.

Manuscripts of the 1937 Flood. Unassembled MSS on file in the office of the Adjutant General, Frankfort. Official letters, messages and reports of the Kentucky Military Department.

Militia Laws. (In the series, *Kentucky Laws, Statutes, Etc.*). Frankfort: Johnston & Bohanan, 1815.

Morehead, C. S., and Mason Brown. *Digest of the Statute Law of Kentucky.* 2 vols. Frankfort: A. G. Hodges, 1834.

Myers, H. *Digest of the General Law of Kentucky.* Cincinnati: Robert Clarke & Co., 1866.

Papers, Acts, and Resolutions of the Kentucky Legislature Relating to the War between the States of 1861. Report of the Military Board. In Kentucky Documents *(see above).*

Pirtle, Henry. *Carroll's Kentucky Statutes.* Louisville: Standard Ptg. Co., 1930.

Poore, B. P., compiler. *Federal and State Constitutions, Colonial Charters and Other Organic Laws of the United States.* Part II, 2d ed. Washington: Government Ptg. Office, 1878.

Sawyer, George P., editor. *Treaties and Proclamation of the United States of America.* Vol. XII. Boston: Little, Brown & Co., 1863.

Stanton, R. H. *Revised Statutes of Kentucky.* 2 vols. Cincinnati: Robert Clarke & Co., 1860, 1867 eds.

Statutes at Large of the United States. 1861–65, 1903, 1908, 1918–22.

The War of the Rebellion: A compilation of the Official Records of the Union and Confederate Armies. 129 vols. Washington: Government Ptg. Office, 1900.

Wickliffe, C. S., S. Turner, and S. S. Nicholas. *Revised Statutes of Kentucky.* Frankfort: A. G. Hodges, 1852.

Periodicals

Brown, John Mason. "The Kentucky Pioneers," *Harper's Magazine,* LXXV, June, 1887.

Filson Club History Quarterly. Oct., 1926 to date (13 vols., 49 nos.—Jan., 1939).

Kentucky State Historical Society Register. January, 1903–38. A quarterly.

Kentucky National Guard Journal, Vol. I, No. 1. Only this one issue published.

Newspapers

Barr, T. I. *Scrapiana,* No. 1. (Newspaper clippings in a scrapbook, 1823–45.) In the Filson Club, Louisville.

The Cincinnati Commercial.
The Commercial [Louisville].
The Commonwealth [Frankfort].
The Courier [Louisville].
Courier-Journal [Louisville].
The Kentucky Gazette [Lexington].
The Louisville Journal.
The Observer and Reporter [Lexington].
The Yeoman [Frankfort].
The Western World [Frankfort].

Manuscripts

Calk Manuscripts. Archives, University of Kentucky Library, Lexington.

Draper Manuscripts. Archives, Wisconsin State Historical Society, Madison, Wis. Photostats in Filson Club, Louisville.

CORRIGENDA*

Page 85, line 14, read—Col. Johnson originally proposed *in Congress*
Page 141, line 36, read—among *kinsfolk* in Indiana
Page 248, line 2, read—the Lexington *Cemetery*
Page 268, line 14, read—the Kentucky *State* Guard
Page 277, line 22, read—at *Fontaine* Ferry Park
Page 300, line 27, read—Capt. D. *B.* Walcutt
Page 301, line 1, read—*letter was* filed
Page 301, line 35, read—J. C. W. *Beckham*
Page 302, line 23, read—120 at the *Reformatory*
Page 303, line 14, read—under Lieutenant *Colonel* Gray
Page 311, line 14-15, read—with city and *county authorities*
Page 337, line 36, read—Charles H. *Morrow*
Page 347, line 21, read—field *uniforms, clothing, equipage, publications, and military stores of all kinds, including public animals, as are necessary to arm, uniform, and equip for field* service the National Guard.
Page 369, note 3, read—Title *32.* Chap. *1,* secs. *6, 16*
        note 4, read—Title *32,* Chap. *3,* sec. *33*
        note 5, read—Title *32,* Chap. *3.*

---

* In the preparation of this work every precaution was exercised to avoid mistakes, both in substance and in form. The above errors were found after printing and are hereby corrected.

INDEX

Act of 1790 (Va.), established Wilderness Road Guard, 50.
Active Duty in 1782, 31.
Acts (Military), of 1851, 146.
Adair, Gen. John, at New Orleans, 97.
Adjutant General, salary of, in 1806, 116.
Agriculture and Mechanical College of Ky., 244.
Alamo, The, fall of, 122.
Allen, Maj. J. Embry, 299, 309, 324.
Allen, Maj. Gen. H. T., 337.
Allen, Col. John, regiment of Volunteers, 80.
Allen, Maj. John R., 260-63, 277, 324.
Allison, Young E., state war historian, 343.
American Knights, 235-36.
Ammen military report, 211.
Anderson, Carrie, murder trial, 253.
Anderson, Gen. Robert, 156.
Anniston, Ala., encampment at, 323.
Anti-Federalists in Ky., 69.
Aerial Squadron, 99th U.S., 338.
Armories, appropriation for, in 1924, 351.
Armory at Louisville occupied during election of 1897, 277.
Arms on hand, 1867, 247.
Arms Report of 1861, 147.
Arrests and executions, unwarranted, by U.S. Govt., 219-20.
Artillery first used in Ky., 24.
Ashbridge, skirmish at, 224.
Ashland, 262; troops on duty at, 328.
Attempt to abolish militia organization, 111, 118.
Austin, Stephen F., asks aid for Texas, 122.
Aviation service, World War, 338.
Artillery Brigade, 63d Field, 371.
Artillery 138th Field, 371; lineage of, 378; 1st Battalion, 381; 2d Battalion, 382.
Bach Hall, 392.
"Bachelor Boys" of Bourbon County, 126.
Bailey murder trial, 349.
Baker, Dr., trial, 121.
Band, 138th Field Artillery, 380.
Barbour, P. N., 140.
Barbourville: disorder, 275; troops ordered on duty at, 292, 317, 349, 376.
Bardstown Company, massacred at Goliad, 122.
Bardstown: disorder, 273; cadet company organized 317; N.G. company at, 374.
Barnett, Col. James, 49; court-martial findings in case of, 62.

Baseball trophy, regimental, 392.
Bassett, Col. E. B., 317, 322.
Bath County disorder, 277.
Batteries: 138th F.A., A, 381; B, 382; C, 382; D, 383; E, 383; F, 383.
Battles of: Big Hill 183, 201; Blue Licks, 33-34; Buena Vista, 125, 133, 139; Chapultepec, 143; the Corncribs, 18; Cynthiana, first 180, second, 211; Estill's Defeat, 29-30; Fallen Timbers, 72; Grove Cemetery, 251; Hartsville, 181; Logan's Cross Roads, 174; Manassas, 161; Mill Springs, 174; Monterey, 125; Munfordville, 186-87; New Orleans, 96-100; anniversary, 247; Nico-Jack, 73; Perryville, 187-88; Richmond, 183; River Raisin, 81, 251; Rowlett's Station, 173; Sacramento, 173; St. Mihiel, 337; Saltville, Va., 216-17; San Jacinto, 112; Shiloh, 177; Thames, 90, 92, 99, 112; Tippecanoe, 81, 145.
Bean, City Mgr. L. V., of Paducah, 363.
Beattyville, 253.
Beckham, Gov. J. C. W., declared elected Lt. Gov., 301; sworn in as Gov., 304; proclamation calling out Guard, 304-306, 309; orders 1st and 2d Regts. mustered out, 312; 314, 315-16, 318.
Belgian War Mission inspects Camp Taylor, 333.
Belknap, Col. Morris B., 273.
Benson Station Quarry, disorder at, 321.
Berry, Maj. Talbott, 372.
Big Hill deserters executed, 201.
Big Painted Lick, 14.
Big Sandy Valley, 14.
Bivouac of the Dead, The, 137-38.
Black, William, trial at Lebanon, 276.
"Blackberry Campaign," 58-59.
Blackburn, Gov. Luke, 258-59.
Blackburn Guards, 260.
Blackfish, Chief, killing of, 42.
Blanding, Maj. Gen. Albert H., 346.
Bloomfield, Nelson County, stores plundered, 226.
Blue Jacket, captured, 44.
Blue Licks, 18-19, 32-34.
Bluegrass area, 281.
Board of War, Kentucky's, 55-57, 60, 73.
Boiling Spring Station, 3, 14.
Boone, Daniel, 13, 15, 17-18; captured, 19; 20, 25, 32, 33, 34-49.
Boone Rangers, 160.
Boone, Squire, 22, 36, 101.
Boonesborough, Fort *(see Fort Boonesborough).*

Bounty offered, 199.
Bourbon Furnace, 53, 73-74.
Bourbon's Company of "Bachelor Boys," 126.
Bowling Green Guards, 260.
Bowling Green: occupied by Confederate Army, 165; soldier burials at, 246; State Guard encampment of 1893, 273-74.
Bowman, Jennie, murder, 265-66.
Bowman, Col. John, 21, 23.
Boyle, Brig. Gen. Jerry T., appointed commandant of Ky., 177-78; 183.
Boyd County, 262.
Bradley, Gov. W. O., inauguration, 275-77, 282-83, 285-86, 290-92, 296, 300.
Bradley Guards, 275-76.
Bragg, Gen. Braxton, 184-88.
Bramlette, Gov. Thos. E., 199; against recruiting Negroes, 204; 206, 207-208, 209, 211-12, 221-22; annual message, 1865, 224-25; on State Military Hospital at Louisville, 229.
Breathitt County: disorders, 257-58; skirmish, 221; 341; troops guard jail, 349.
Breckinridge, Maj. Gen. John C., 135, 165, 167-69; 189, 217.
Breckinridge, Col. J. C., Jr., taken prisoner, 227-28.
Breckinridge, Rev. Dr. Robert J., 201, 206-207; advocates slaughter of all Confederate sympathizers, 219-20.
Breckinridge, Col. Robert J., Jr., 220.
Breckinridge, Col. W. C. P., 186, 216, 243, 248.
Brisbin, General, Order No. 15, 242.
Brooks, Col. Edw., 140.
Browder, Russell, trial, 319-21.
Brown, Gov. John Young, 273-74.
Brown, Col. Orlando, 114.
Brown, Brig. Gen. Preston, 337.
Bruce, Capt. Sanders, 166.
Bryan, Col. J. W., 258.
Bryant, Pearl, murder trial, 276-77.
Buckner, Gov. Simon B., 147, 165, 169, 176, 189, 244; inaugurated, 268; 269-72.
Buell, Gen. Don Carlos, 181, 188; exonerated, 200.
Bullitt, Chief Justice Joshua F., released, 222.
Bullitt Light Infantry, 263.
Burbridge, Brig. Gen. S. G., 216-17; order against guerrillas, 218; hog purchase order, 219; 220; official conduct of, 221; 225, 227.
Burkesville, skirmish at, 224.
Burr Incident, The Aaron, 75.
Bush, Capt. Billy, 15.
Bush's Settlement, 69.
Butler, Maj. Gen. W. O., 124, 140.
"Butternut" Captain, 200.
Byrd, Col. John, 1.
Byrd's Invasion, 24, 29.

Cadet Company organized in Bardstown, 317.
Cadet Corps, Ky. University, 244-45; 323.
Caldwell, Alexander, trial, 222-23.
Caldwell, Lt. Col. Samuel, 393.
Call in 1837 for troops against Seminoles in Florida, 114.
Calloway, Col. Richard, 15-20.
Cameron, Simon, U.S. Secy. of War, dismissal asked by Ky., 173.
Campaign against Pickaway towns, 25.
Campaign of 1793 against the Wabash Indians, 70.
Campbellsville, skirmish at, 224.
Camps: Owen Bierne, established, 325; 385; Blackburn, 263; Boone, 159, 165; Bradley, near Ashland, 283; Breckinridge, 165, 189; Burnett, 165; Clay, 159; Collier, Lexington, 283; Corbin, H. C., 285; Douglas, 226; Souge, 138th F.A. Brig. sent to, 336; Douglas, 226; Hindman, 265; Hobson, 285; Holt, Joe, 159; Kenton, 168; Madison, Franklin County, 115; Nelson, 212; soldier burials at, 246; Owsley, Oakland Racecourse, 128; Perry, Ohio, 350; Dick Robinson, 161; 168, 189; Shelby, Hattiesburg, Miss., 333, 335, 372, 391; Sherman (Ohio) troops trained at, 335; Stanley, A. O., 332, 372; Yieser, Paducah, 317; Young, West Point, 314; Zachary Taylor, built 333, 335.
Cannon captured from Burgoyne at Saratoga, 112.
Carrell, Capt. Dan, 318-19, 321.
Carrollton, 253-54.
Carter County, disorders, 258.
Carter, Brig. Gen. Ellerbe W,. 348, 371.
Castleman, Maj. David, 285.
Castleman, Col. John B., 257-61; named acting Adjt. Gen., 263; tactics modified by, 263-64; presented with sword, 268; visits World's Fair at Chicago with his regiment, 273; 275-77; 281, 283, 285, 287; appointed Adjt. Gen. by Gov. Beckham, 304, 309, 312.
Casto-Metcalfe duel at Dover, 201.
Catlettsburg, Neal-Craft trial, 260-61.
Cavalry: 123d, 371; lineage of 123d, 395; 2d Regt., 395; 123d Headquarters Troop and Band, 396; 123d Machine Gun Troop, 396; 123d Medical Detachment, 397; 123d Troop A, 397; 123d Troop B, 398; 123d Troop C, 398; 123d Troop E, 398; 123d Troop F, 399; 123d Troop I, 400; 123d Troop K, 400; 123d, 1st Squadron, 396-97; 123d, 2d Squadron, 396-98; 123d, 3d Squadron, 396-400.

MILITARY HISTORY OF KENTUCKY 485

Cerro Gordo, 128; artillery piece captured at, 135.
"Cerro Gordo" Williams, 129-30, 135, 165, 216.
Chandler, Gov. A. B., 355, 357; flood proclamation, 358-59; 360, 361-62, 399-400.
Chateau Thierry, 3d Div. at, 336.
Chescheir, Lt. Col. George M., 384.
Chickamauga, troops at, in 1898, 284-85, 287.
Chiles (Wm.) vs. Connelly's Heirs, 30.
Chinn, Col. Jack, 296-97.
Christian, Col. Wm., killed, 41.
Citizens Central Relief Commission of Louisville, 282.
Citizens Military Training Corps, 390.
Clark County Volunteers, War of 1812, 80.
Clark, Maj. Gen. George Rogers, 14-17, 19-21, 25, 27, 31, 34-36; 41-42; seizure of Creole boat, 42; commissioned by France, 69; 101.
Clarke, Jerome (Sue Mundy), wounded at Cynthiana, 211; 226; trial, 407.
Clay Chasseurs dissolve, 164-65.
Clay, Maj. Gen. Green, 84.
Clay, Henry, 94, 127; funeral, 141; dedication of monument, 142.
Clay, Lt. Col. Henry, Jr., 129; killed in Battle of Buena Vista, 129, 133; 137.
Cleburne, Gen. Patrick, 184-85.
"Clique of five persons at Lexington," 221-22.
Cloyd, Capt. Joseph, 1.
Cockrell, Maj. Benjamin, 375.
Collier, Adjt. Gen., Daniel L., 275, 282-83; resigns, 286-87, 290-91, 296-97, 299, 300, 302-303, 308, 311; relinquishes adjutant generalship, 312.
Collins, Floyd, efforts to rescue, 350.
Colors carried in War with Spain, 288-89.
Colson, Col. D. G., 285.
Colston, Col. William A., 324, 332.
Columbus and Hickman occupied, 162.
Combs, Col. Leslie, 114.
Commanders of Fayette, Jefferson, and Lincoln regiments, 25.
Competitive drills: Nashville, Tenn., 259; Louisville, 259-60; Nashville, 269; St. Louis, Mo., 317; Valley Station, Orell Rifle Range, 323.
Competitive Drill at "Oaklawn," Jefferson County, 115; Camp Madison, Franklin County, 115.
Conestoga, U.S. gunboat, 170-71.
Confederate: Volunteers, 153; Secretary of War Walker, 159; Recruiting prohibited, 169; conscription resisted, 189; sympathizers arrested, 203; recruiting by Col. G. M. Jesse, 215; conscript law invoked, 223; Army prisoners at Camp Douglas, 226; regiments serving during war, 233; Confederate Congressional honors to Ky. soldiers, 234; first assemblage of veterans, 247; first monument erected at Cynthiana, 248; dead brought home, 250; State Government, inaugurated, 187; Ky. forces, 1863, 194.
Constitution: first, 65; second, 74; third, 145-46; fourth, 230.
Cooper, Pvt. Allie, killing of, 250.
Corbin: riot, 312; troops on duty at, 329.
Coroner's verdict against State Guard, 262-63.
Council of Defense work, 342.
Covington: fortified, 185; soldier burials at, 246; Light Guards, 253, 254; troops on duty at, 327.
Crab Orchard encampment, 265.
Craig, Gen. Malin, 355.
Creech, Lt. J. O., 338.
Crenshaw resolutions, 306-308.
Crittenden, Maj. Gen. J. J., 152.
Crittenden, Maj. Gen. Thos. L., 133, 135, 144, 200.
Crois de Guerre, Cross of the Legion of Honor, awarded to Capt. Samuel Woodfill, 339.
Crowdus, Clem, killing of, 249-50.
Crump, Col. M. H., 265; report of 1892, 272-73.
Cumberland River navigation under Confederate control, 223.
Cumberland and Tennessee rivers patrolled, 170.
Cyclone of 1890 at Louisville, 270.
Cynthiana: first battle, 180; second battle, 211; first monument in memory of Confederate dead erected, May 29, 1868, 248; Confederate dead reinterred, 251; troops on duty at, 329.
Danville: occupied by General Pegram's Cavalry, 194; soldier burials at, 246.
Davis, Garrett, 153-55, 190; expulsion resolution in U.S. Senate, 204.
Davis, Gen. Jeff. C., 242.
Daviess, Col. Joseph Hamilton, 145.
Denhardt, Brig. Gen. H. H., 352-54; 374; trophy for efficiency, 392.
Denison, Col. G. T., 92.
Department of the Cumberland, 156, 164.
Department of Ky., established, 156.
Desertion case, 102-103.
Dick law enacted, 315-16.
Dimming, George, trial at Frankfort, 277.
Dishonorable dismissals, 200.
District of Ky., 1.
Donaldson's Regiment, 93.
Draft Act of 1777, 6.
"Drummed out," 11.
Dudley, Gen. Peter, 95, 121.
Dudley's Raid, 96.

486   MILITARY HISTORY OF KENTUCKY

Dudley, William A., 189.
Duels: Casto-Metcalfe, 201; Marshall-Jackson, 131; Waring-Holman, 103.
Duke, Gen. Basil W., 181; succeeds Brig. Gen. John Hunt Morgan, 215; 243, 269.
Duncan, Col. Blanton, 154.
Duncan, Maj. Gen. George B., 337.
DuQuendre's Ky., expedition, 19.
Easley, Col. Roy, 348, 389-90.
Eastern Kentucky R. R. strike, 258.
Eddyville, troops on duty at, 350-51.
Edwards, Col. John, of Bourbon, 60.
Edwards, Maj. Nelson, 299.
Eel River campaign, 59.
Election Contest Board report, 300.
Elections under U.S. Military supervision, 242.
Elizabethtown — Engagement at, 189; skirmish at, 224, 252.
Ellis, Adjt. Gen. J. Tandy, 323-24, 327.
Elliston, Lee, trial, 349.
Emancipation Proclamation, 233.
Emmett Rifles, 260.
Encampments: at Fontaine Ferry Park, Louisville, 263, 277; Henderson, 275; Fort Knox, 273, 350, 373-74; Grayson Springs, 263; Oglethorpe, 324; Paducah, 317; San Antonio, Tex., 322.
Enrolled Militia, 248.
Epicedium, 145.
Estill's Defeat, 29-30.
Estill, Capt. James, Inventory, 30.
Evans-Hill fued, 141-42.
Eve, Col. John G., 389.
Everett, Capt. Peter, 210.
Ewing, Brig. Gen. Hugh, order, 214-15.
Executions and Arrests, unwarranted by U.S. Govt., 219-20; Nathan Marks executed, 226.
Expatriation law nullified, 241.
Extortion, by state military authorities, 212.
Falls of the Ohio, 8, 20-21, 22, 24.
Falmouth, troops on duty at, 328.
Farmers Station, 267.
Fayette County Militia Regt., 396.
Federal interference feared, 308, 309.
Federal Land Grant Act of 1865, 244.
Feland, Brig. Gen. Logan, 337.
Feuds: Evans-Hill, 141-42; Hargis-Cockrell, 314-15; Holbrook-Underwood, 258; Howard-Baker, 292; Tolliver-Martin, 266-68; Strong-Callahan, 315.
Field, Lt. Col. E. H., 129.
Fifth Corps Area of U.S. Army, 348.
Fincastle County, Va., 1, 16.
Finnell, Adjt. Gen. John W., report of, 176; 182; enlistment call, 196; reports, 197-98, 203.
First Fort in Mason County, 39.
First Meeting of Kentuckians, 50.
First permanent military company in Ky., 46, 114.
First Regt. Cavalry, officers and companies (Mexican War), 129-30.
First Regt. Ky. Vol. Cav., 214.
First Settlement in Kentucky, sixty-sixth anniversary of, 114.
Fitzgerald, Sheriff George H., of Mason County, 363.
Flag designed for Ky. State Guard, 258-59.
Flags and Guidons of Ky. Regts., 288-89.
Fleming, Brig. Gen. Adrian S., 337.
Fleming, Col. Wm., 14.
Flemingsburg, attack on, 210; troops on duty in, 313.
Fletcher, W. R., trial, 317.
Flood duty, tabular, 366-69.
Flood of 1937, 351, 355-56; scope of, 357, 358-69.
Floyd, Gen. J. B., 176.
Floyd's Defeat, 35-36.
Forrest, Col. Nathan Bedford, 160; at Marion, 172.
Forrester, Col. Walter S., Asst. and Acting Adjt. Gen., 283, 286, 291-92.
Fort: Anderson, 207; Benjamin Harrison, troops sent to, 321-22, 391; Benning, Ga., 373, 390; Bliss, troops at, 325; Boonesborough, 13-20, 23-24; Donelson, 170, 174-76; Harrod, 17, 28, 34; Henry, 174-75; Jefferson, 61, 71; Johnston, 165; Kenton's 168; Knox, encampment of 1922, 350; 373-74, 379-84, 391; Logan's (St. Asaph's), 16, 20; McClelland's, 14; Mason County, 39; Massac, 70; Meig's Hostilities at, 84-85, 90, 91; Nelson, built, 21; Oglesthrope, Ga., encampment at, 324; Pitt (Pittsburgh), 16; Riley Cavalry School, 400; Stephenson, 91; Thomas, troop mobilization, 324; 391; Washington, 61; Wayne, 74, 88-89.
Fontaine Ferry Park, Louisville, encampment at, 277.
Fourth Regt. Infantry, officers and companies (Mexican War), 136.
Frankfort: attack on, 211; soldier burials, 246, 250; disorder at, 260; visit of U.S. President, 263; State Guard assembled for military instruction, 263; inauguration of Governor Buckner, 268; disorders of 1894, 274; Dimming trial, 277; State Guardsmen on duty in, 298; legislature adjourned to London, 298; inauguration of Gov. James McCreary, 323; troops on duty at, 328, 351-52; Reformatory prison camp, 360-61.
Frankfort Cemetery, 251.
Freedman's Bureau, 239.
French-Eversole feud, 269.
Frenchtown, attack on, ordered, 81.

Military History of Kentucky 487

Frontier Guard posts, 50, 56.
Fry, Maj. C. H., 129.
Fry, Col. Speed Smith, 174.
Gaines, Maj. Gen. E. P., U.S.A., 112.
Gaines, Maj. John P., 129, 139.
Gaines, Sgt. William F., 141.
Gaither, Col. E. H., 281.
Gallatin, Cavalry skirmish at, 181.
Garrard, Gov. James, 74.
General Order No. 8, 196.
Georgetown (Royal Spring), 14, 25.
Girty, Simon, at Bryan Station, 32.
Goebel-Brown-Taylor campaign, 296.
Goebel, William, State Senator, mortally wounded, 296-98; contest committee votes to seat Goebel as Gov., 301; declared elected, 304; death of, 304.
Gordon, Capt. F. L., 313.
Goss-Allen prize fight, 253.
Grant, Capt. Samuel, killed, 49.
Gray, Lt. Col. D. W., 299, 303.
Grayson Springs encampment, 263.
Green Coat Rangers (Canadian), 23.
Green River locks blown up, 169.
Greenbrier, Va., Militia sent to Aid in Ky., 18-26.
Greenup County, Hunnewell Station, 258.
Greenwood, disorders at, 265.
Greshman, Corp. James B., first American soldier killed in France, 341.
Gross, Adjt. Gen. Andrew J., 274.
Guard Duty within the state in 1917, 327-31.
Guerrilla measures of U.S., 213; ruthless order against, 218.
Gullion, Maj. Gen. Allen, U.S.A., 324.
Guthrie, James, 151, 170, 190.
Haldeman, Gen. William B., 317-19.
Hale, Maj. Gen. H. C., 335.
Hammond, Warden James, 361.
Hanson, Col. Roger W., 147.
Hardin, Capt. B. R., murdered, 141.
Hardin, Col. John, of Nelson, 57; killed, 67.
Hargis-Cockrell feud, 314-15.
Harlan County: disorder in, 270; troops on duty in, 351-54; 365.
Harlan, Col. John M., 174, 242.
Harlan, troops on duty in, 352, 354.
Harmar, Gen. Josiah, 53-55.
Harmar's Defeat, 55.
Harper's Ferry, Va., 154.
Hart, Col. Nathaniel, Jr., 114.
Hartsuff, Maj. Gen. Geo. L., 196.
Harrison County Confederate dead, 251.
Harrison, Maj. Gen. Wm. H., adopted into Kentucky Militia, 81, 114; President-elect visits in Kentucky, 114.
Harrod, Capt. James, 13.
Harrodsburg, 13-16; besieged by Blackfish, 17, 20; 66th anniversary, 114.
Hattiesburg, Miss., Camp Shelby, 333, 335.
Hay-Chamberlain Army Reorganization bill, 324.
Hazard: troops on duty at, 269, 272, 329-30.
Helm, Ben Hardin, 158.
Helm Guards, 250.
Helm, Gov. John L., death of, 246.
Henderson encampment, 275.
Henderson, Col. Richard, 2, 13, 14.
Henry, Col. Alexander M., 393.
Henry, Col. Jouett, 316, 332, 334.
Henry, Patrick, 17, 21.
Hewitt, Col. F. M., 250.
Hickman requests aid in 1937 flood, 356-57.
Hickman County: 251; President Taft visits, 321; requests troops, 356.
Hindman, Col. Briscoe, 316.
Hinkston's Fork, 30.
Hog Purchase order, 218-19; 224.
Holbrook-Underwood feud, 258.
Holder, Col. John, 12, 31.
Holder's Defeat, 31, 32.
Home Guards plunder stores at Bloomfield, 226; disliked, 240.
Honors earned, World War, 338-39.
Hopkinsville: night-rider raid, troops on duty in, 318.
Horse Guards, Governor's, 399.
"Horse Units," 7-8.
Houston, Gen. Sam., 112.
Howard-Baker feud, 292.
Huey, Supt. E. O., 361.
Hull's surrender, 80.
Hunt, Thomas S., executed, 220.
Impressment by U.S. Military authority, 212-14.
Indian Raids, 13-62, 67-74, 79-81.
Infantry: 75th Brig., 374; 149th, 371, Co. A, 386-88; Co. B, 388; Co. C, 389; Co. D, 389; Co. E, 390; Co. F, 390; Co. G, 391; Co. H, 392; Co. I, 393; Co. K, 393; Co. L, 394; Co. M, 394; Hdq. Co., 385; Howitzer Co., 386; Hdq. Co., 1st Battalion, 387; Hdq. Co., 2d Battalion, 390; Hdq. Co., 3d Battalion, 392; Medical Detachment, 385; Service Co., 386; 1st Regt., 378; 3d Regt., 395; lineage of 149th, 384; lineage of 149th, 2d Regt., 384.
Ingles, Lt. Thomas, 1.
Innes, Harry, Attorney General, 43.
Inspection report of 1892, 272-73.
Inventory of 2d Division for 1809, 78.
Irvine, troops on duty at, 329.
Jackson, Gen. Andrew, report of Battle of New Orleans, 97-98.
Jackson, troops on duty at, 315, 329.
Jacob, Col. Richard T., arrested for protesting military murders, 221.

Jacobin Clubs, 69.
Jefferson County Armory erected, 317.
Jefferson County Regiment, 379.
Jefferson, Thomas, orders of, 22.
Jett-White trial, 315.
Johnson, Andrew, President, 243.
Johnson, G. W., 168; Provisional Governor, 171.
Johnson, Lt. Gov. Keene, 355-56.
Johnson, Col. Richard M., 85; Cavalry Regiment organized, 88; 89-90, 92-93; dies, 141.
Johnson, Col. Robt., 48.
Johnson, Brig. Gen. W. O., 337.
Johnston, Gen. Albert Sydney, 165.
Johnston, Gen. Albert S., surrenders, 229.
Johnston, Adjt. Gen. P. P., 320.
Johnston, Adjt. Gen. J. Stoddard, 251.
Joseph, Sgt. Samuel, most wounded American in World War, 341.
Jurisdiction over Military Board curtailed, 177-78.
Kaskaskia, 21, 74.
Kavanaugh, Judge George W., 249.
Kelly, Maj. Joseph M., 361, 401.
Kelly, troops on duty at, 331.
Kendall murder trial, 295.
Kennedy, Grove C., trial, 254-56.
Kenton, Simon: first visit to Ky. 13, 24, 39-43, 46, 49.
Kentucky, a sovereign state in 1792, 62.
Kentucky admitted to Confederacy, 171-72.
Kentucky allotment of 38th Div., 348; of 75th Inf. Brig., 348.
Kentucky Association Veterans of Mexican War, 252.
Kentucky's Board of War, 55-57, 60.
Kentucky County Militia, organized 16-18, 22, 25, 379, 396.
Kentucky County, Virginia, 1, 6-7.
Knox County Volunteers, 389.
Kentucky District Convention, 36.
Kentucky "Gunboats," 31.
Kentucky Legislature adjourned to Louisville, 185-86.
"Kentucky's Militia Pig," 99-100.
Kentucky Military Institute, founded, 116, 146, 250.
Kentucky National Guard Organization 345-69.
Kentucky National Legion, 248.
Kentucky "Navy," 31.
Kentucky Rifle and Riflemakers, 101-102.
Kentucky soldiers brought home from U.S. Govt. hospitals, 286.
"Kentucky Squaw," 99.
Kentucky State Guard mobilization in 1898, 282, 327.
Kentucky State Historical Society, 288.
Kentucky troops forbidden to pursue Indians beyond state lines, 62.
Kentucky troops in Puerto Rico, 285.
Kentucky troops, tabular report of, 229-32.
Kentucky University, 244-45; Cadets, 323.
Kentucky Volunteers in U.S. hospitals, 199; cavalry in War with Spain, 288.
Kinkead, Col. Wm. B., 114.
Kinne, Howard, one of first American aviators killed in World War, 338.
Knights of the Golden Circle, 155, 234-36.
Knott County, conditions in 1890, 271-72.
Knott, Gov. J. Proctor, inaugurated, 263; 264-65; 268.
Krieger, Capt. Robert N., 319.
Ku Klux Klan, 249.
Lafayette visits Kentucky, 104-105.
Lafferty, Thornton, executed, 220, 250.
Laffoon, Gov. Ruby, proclamation of, 352-54.
Lancaster: Grove C. Kennedy trial, 254-56.
Lead mines, 6.
Lebanon, captured by Morgan and U.S. Govt. warehouse burned, 179; soldier burials, 246; nightrider raids, 319.
Lee, Henry, lieutenant of Ky. Dist. Cavalry, 47.
Lee's surrender, April 13, 1865, 229.
Legal Heritage, 1-9.
Legislature demands removal of Negro camps, 204-205.
Legislature, meets in Jefferson County Courthouse, 304.
Leitchfield, troops on duty at, 330-31.
LeMans Area, troops in, 335-36.
Leslie, Gov. P. H., 251.
Lexington: blockhouse a rendezvous 22; occupied by Morgan's men, 186; General Morgan buried in Lexington Cemetery, 216; "Clique of five persons," 221; favorite center of freed slaves, 239-40; soldier burials, 246, 248; Camp Collier, 283; Loudoun Park, 285; troops on duty at, 328.
Lexington Chasseurs, 166.
Lexington Guards, 260.
Lexington Light Infantry organized 1789, 46.
"Lexington's Regiment," 281.
Lexington Rifles, 166.
Limestone (Maysville), 8; Volunteers, 43.
Lincoln Cabin escort, 318.
Lincoln Centennial, 321.
Lincoln County Militia Regiment, 385.
Lincoln's grandfather killed, 40.
"Lincoln Guns" distributed in Ky., 155, 158-59.
Lincoln Memorial, 397.

Lindsey, Adjt. Gen. D. W., report of Ky. troops, 230-32; report, 241.
Little Mountain (Mount Sterling), 30.
Little Turtle in command of Indians, 61, 68.
Lockett, Will, execution, 349.
Logan, Col. Benjamin, 34; organizes Lincoln County Rangers, 41; Campaign against the Shawnee, 42; censure of and proceedings against, 43.
Logan, Boone, 267.
Logan County, night-rider raids, 319.
Logan's Cross Roads, soldier burials, 246.
London, state legislature adjourned to, 298, 302.
Longmire, Capt. C. W., 295, 314.
Lonz Powers, or the Regulators, excerpt from, 106-10.
Lopez expedition, 246.
Loudoun Park, Lexington, 285.
Louisiana Purchase Exposition, troops at, 316.
Louisville Legion: organized, 115; prepares for War with Mexico, 123, 125, 135, 140; revived, 257-58; ordered to Greenwood, 265; ordered to Morehead, 267; at Washington Centennial, 270, 274-75, 281-82, 284, 295, 298-99, 333, 379.
Louisville Light Artillery, prizes won, 259-61, 313.
Louisville Light Infantry, 269.
Louisville & Nashville R. R.: bridge over Rolling Fork burned, 169; railroad at Gallatin captured, 181; damage suit, L. & N. R. R. vs. Simon Bolivar Buckner, 244; troops to guard all points in Pendleton County, 328.
Louisville: erects fortifications, 186; state hospital, 229; favorite center of freed slaves, 239-40; soldier burials, 246; riot of 1877, 254; Light Artillery, 254; Exposition, 263; State Guard encampment, 263; Cyclone of 1890, 270; Armory occupied during election of 1897, 277; Citizens Central Relief commission, 282; Drum and Trumpet Corps organized, 313; Jefferson County Armory erected, 317; requests troops, 1937, 357; under Martial law, 358.
Lyon, Gen. H. B., 223-24.
Lyons, Guy, trial, 317.
McArthur, Gen. Duncan, displaces Harrison, 94.
McArthur's Raid, 95-96.
McClain, Adjt. Gen. G. Lee, 355-56, 359, 362, 363.
McClelland, John, 14.
McClure, Brig. Gen. N. P., 337.
McClure, Lt. Nathan, killed, 45.

McCook, Gen. A. M., 188.
McCreary Guards, Frankfort, 256, 260.
McCreary, Gov. James, 254; inauguration, 323.
McDonald Dragoons, 171.
McDowell, Col. James, 38.
McGary, Capt. Hugh, 28, 33.
McLean County, 341.
McMillan, Col. James, 69.
Machine Gun Battalions: 137th and 138th U.S., 335; 138th, 395.
Machine Gun Squadron: 53d, 371; 54th, 371.
Madison, Lt. Col. George, a hostage, 82.
Madisonville: troops on duty at, 330; on flood duty in, 361.
Magoffin, Gov., 147; resigned, 183.
Maine, Battleship, 281.
Mammoth Cave: instruction camp of 1896, 275; troops on duty at, 313.
Manchester, lawlessness in, 291-92.
Mansir, Maj. J. H., 274, 313, 315.
Marcum, Attorney James, killed, 315.
Marks, Nathan, executed, 226.
Marksberry murder trial, 349.
Married men mustered out, 332.
Marshall, Humphrey, on the U.S. Army bill, 143-44, 169.
Marshall, Humphrey, Jr., 210.
Marshall-Jackson duel at Port Lavaca, 131.
Marshall, Brig. Gen. Thos., 124.
Marshall's Cavalry, 130, 133, 135.
Mason County Guards, 260.
Mason County Minute Men, 39.
Massac, Fort, 70.
Mathis, Allen, trial, 317.
Maybrier, Thomas D., trial, 316.
Maysville, attack on, 210.
Medals of Honor, Congressional, awarded Kentuckians, 338, 341.
Medical Regiment, 113th, 375.
Meigs, Fort, 84-85, 90-91.
Mengel, Col. C. C., 297-99.
Meriwether, Capt. E. T., 319.
Merrill's Company of Mounted Rifles, 251.
Metcalfe, Col. Leonidas, 201.
Mexican Border: duty of 1916, 324, 372.
Mexican War Volunteers rendezvous at Louisville, 127.
Mexican War and Peace, 121-49.
Mexican War dead brought home, 136-37.
Middlesboro, 272; troops on duty at, 317, 329.
Middleton, County Attorney Elmon, killing of, 354.
Military Board of commissioners, 155, 168; Military Board jurisdiction curtailed, 177-78; abolished, 183.
Military Cemeteries, 246.
Military murders protested, 221.

Military Prisons: at Louisville, 211, 213-14; Johnson's Island, 220; Camp Douglas, 226.
Militia drafted at Lexington, 24.
Militia: enrolled, 147; reserve, 147.
Militia: garb, 80; uniform of, 116-17.
Militia: in service of U.S., 51, 176, 182; volunteers call, 196; reports, 197-98, 203, 208; law revision of 1893, 273.
Militia Laws revised, 273.
Militia Law in Myer's Supplement, 252.
Mill Springs, soldier burials, 246.
Miller, Mayor Neville, 357-59.
Mobilization of Ky. State Guard in 1898, 282.
Monarch Rifles, Owensboro, 260.
Monk, slave powder maker, 30.
Moore, Capt. Bacon L., 373.
Morehead, 267-68.
Morgan, Brig. Gen. John Hunt: 166-67, 169, 178-82; proclamation at Georgetown, 180-81; 189-91; ransom letter, 195-96; raid into Indiana and Ohio, 196; escapes from prison, 201-202; enters Ky. through Pound Gap, and captures Mount Sterling, 209; meets defeat at Mount Sterling, 210-11; death of, 215-16; reinterment in Lexington Cemetery, 248.
Morgan's Men, at Shiloh, 167; cited by Confederate Congress, 194-95.
Morgan's Squadron, 167.
Mormon uprising in Utah, 143-44.
Morris, Col. Jackson, 391.
Morrow, Lt. Col. Charles H., 386-88, 393.
Morrow, Lt. Col. Sam, 299.
Morton, Brig. Gen. Charles G., U.S.A., 325.
Mount Sterling (Little Mountain), 30; attack on, 193-94, 258, 263; captured by General Morgan, 209; Morgan defeated, 210.
Mount Vernon, troops on duty in, 349.
Mounted Riflemen, 3d Regt., 396.
Muldraugh's Hill, 189.
Mundy, Sue (Jerome Clarke), 211, 226.
Munfordville, 161; battle, 186-87.
Munitions loans: Mexican War, 123; 147, 153.
Murray, Adjt. Gen. D. R., 312-14.
Muster of 1833, 110.
National Defense Trophy, 393.
National Guard Act of 1916, 324; of 1920, 345; amendment in 1923, 346-47.
National Guard Association, 327.
National Guard Bureau, 346.
National Guard of Kentucky, 346; scope of duty during flood of 1937, 362; commendation of work of, during 1937 flood, 363-64.

National Guard, strength, 1936, 346; status, 346; maintenance of, 347; composition of, 348.
National Guard of the U.S., 1923, 346, 348.
National Legion Act of Mar. 4, 1865, 228.
Naval Officers for Ky., 8.
Neal-Craft case, 260-62; Neal and Craft convicted and executed in Catlettsburg, 263.
Negroes: recruited by agents from other states, 203-204; enrollment resented, 208; U.S. Army enlistments, 209; muster at Louisville and Camp Nelson, 212-13; substitutes, 223; status of 1861-63, 264-65; volunteers in War with Spain, 288; in World War, 342.
Nelson, Brig. Gen. Wm., 158, 184-85.
Nenoic, France, headquarters at, 335.
Neutrality, 151.
New London, soldier burials, 246.
Newport: fortified, 185; Van Voast Light Guards, 254; troops on duty in, 349-50.
Nico-Jack, 73.
Night-riders, 312, 318-20; scope of 321.
Ninth Corps area, 374.
Nuckols Guards, 260.
Nuckols, Adjt. Gen. J. P., 259-60, 263.
Oakland Racecourse, Camp Owsley, 128.
"Oaklawn," Jefferson County, Competitive Drill, 115.
Officers and men on flood duty, 1937, 365.
O'Hara, Theodore, 103; author of The Bivouac of the Dead, 137-38; taken prisoner at Encarnacion, 139; death of, 246, 252.
Ohio River patrolled, 31.
Old Chillicothe, Boone taken to, 19.
Oliver, Milton, 322.
One Hundred and Fifty-Ninth Infantry, 1st Regt. becomes, 334.
One Hundred and Forty-Ninth Inf. Regt. formed, 334, 348.
One Hundred and Thirty-Eighth Field Artillery, 159th Inf. becomes, 334.
Oniatenon sacked, 58.
Order No. 15 by General Brisbin, 242.
Ordnance Company, 113th, 374.
Organized Reserves, 346.
Ormsby, Col. Stephen, 115.
"Orphan Brigade," 159.
Owensboro, Monarch Rifles, 260.
Owsley, Governor, 121.
Packenham, Sir Edward, 96-97.
Paducah: occupied by U.S. Grant, 163; attacked, 207; Gen. Paine's occupation, 211-12; State Guard encampment, 1905, 317; troops on duty in, 330.

Paine, Gen. E. A., at Paducah, 211; arrested, 212; 224.
Palmer, Maj. Gen. John M., 227, 239.
Paris: surrender to Morgan, 180; troops on duty at, 329.
Paroles and amnesties, 241.
Patrick, Lee, killing, 323.
Patrollers, 103-104.
Patterson, Col. Robert, 14.
Peace Delegation, 151.
Pennyrile area, 283.
Perry County, conditions in 1890, 271-72.
Perry on Lake Erie, 89-90, 91, 245-46.
Perryville, soldier burials at, 246.
Pershing, Gen. John, 336, 338, 341.
Pickaway Indian towns, 91.
Pillow, Gen. J. G., 162.
Pineville, troops on duty at, 323.
Pioneer Milita garb, 12.
Pioneer Period, 11-64.
Police Company, 38th Div. Military, 372-73.
Political Turmoil and the State Guard, 295-326.
Polk, Gen. Leonidas, 160, 187.
Port Lavaca, Texas, 131.
Pottowatamie, expedition against the, 95.
Pound Gap, 216.
Powder from New Orleans, 18.
Powder grant by Virginia, 16.
Powell, Gov. L. W., 145.
Prentice, George D., 145, 158.
President McKinley refuses to interfere in Taylor-Beckham case, 309-10.
President of U.S. visits Frankfort, 263.
Preston, Lt. Col. Wm., 136.
Princeton, night-rider raid, 318.
Prison Camp (Reformatory) erected, 360.
Prisoners of War taken from Louisville to North, 211.
Prizes won in competitive drill at Nashville, Tenn., 259, 269.
Proctor Knott Guards, 263.
Provisions of First Constitution, 65.
Puckshunuble, Mingo, bruial of, 104.
Puerto Rico, troops in, 285-88.
Pulliam, Lt. Keeling, killed, 338.
Purchase area, 283.
Quartermaster Corps, State Detachment, 372.
Quota based on reduced militia population, 206.
Radford, Brig. Gen. Cyrus, 337.
Radio Station W9HDY, 387.
Raid, first into Ky. by Morgan, 179.
Rainbow Division, troops in, 336.
Raisin Massacre victims reinterred, 140.
Ranking Officers, World War, 337.
Read, H. E., 142-43.
Readjustment and Reorganization, 239-279.

Red Cross, 1937 flood, 362.
Reelfoot Lake, guard asked during 1937 flood, 356.
Refusal of Ky. to furnish Union troops, 152-53.
Regimental Districts of 1792, 65.
Regiments for intra-state duty, 241.
Regulators, 248-49, 252-53.
Report of Adjt. Gen. John W. Finnell, 176.
Reservist mobilization order, 333.
Revolutionary War Soldiers, 5, 29.
Richmond, soldier burials at, 246.
Rifle Match at Madisonville, 393.
Rifle Range at Orell, Valley Station, 323.
Rifle Regiment, 1st, 379.
Riley, Col. Thos. W., 114.
River Raisin, Battle of, 81, 251.
River Raisin dead, reinterred in Frankfort, 140.
Rockport, troops on duty at, 330.
Rodman, Rear Admiral Hugh, 341-42.
Routes to Ky., two chief, 26.
Rowan County, disorders, 264-65, 268.
Royal Spring (Georgetown), 14, 25.
Runningwatertown sacked, 73.
Russell, Capt. William, 14.
Russellville, troops sent to, 320.
Saffarans, Brig. Gen. George C., 337.
St. Clair, Maj. Gen. Arthur, U.S.A., 60.
St. Nazaire, France, 139th U.S. Engineers sent to, 336.
St. Vincents Post, 21.
Salt brought from Missouri, 20.
Salt kettles granted by Virginia, 18.
Salt-making, 18.
San Antonio, Texas, joint encampment at, 322.
Sand Cave, troops on duty at, 350.
Sandlin, Sgt. Willie, 338, 340-41.
Saufley, Richard C., killed, 338.
Saratoga cannon, 112.
Scott, Brig. Gen. (Governor) Charles, 57; expedition of 1791 against the Miami towns, 60; appeal to the Legislature for a military appropriation, 77-78.
Scott, Maj. Gen. Hugh L., 337.
Scouts of Kentucky in U.S. Service, 52, 68.
Second Regt. Infantry, officers and companies (Mexican War), 129.
Shakers and the Militia, 117.
Shelby, Gov. Isaac, Staff of, 67, 69, 70-71, 84; call for troops, 90-91; 112, 393.
Shipman, Paul R., arrested for protesting military murders, 221.
Sibert, Maj. Gen. William L., 337.
Simrall's Regiment, 93.
Six-month troops, 208.
Sixty-sixth Anniversary of First Settlement in Ky., 114.
Sixty-third Field Artillery Brigade —troops assigned to, 334, 348.

Skaggs Men, 248-49, 252.
Skirmishes in Ky., fall of 1861, 169; at Ashbridge, Nolin Station, Campbellsville, Elizabethtown, and Burkesville, 224.
Slaves imprisoned by U.S. order, 198-99.
Slaves: taken out of state, 212; runaway, 214; freed, 239.
Smith, Gen. E. Kirby, report, 184-85, 187.
Smith, Col. Sidney, 322, 348, 361.
Smith, Col. T. J., 282, 286.
Smith, Adjt. Gen. Wilbur R., 287.
Sohan, Captain, report on journey to Hazard, 269-70.
Sons of Liberty, 235-36.
Sovereignty Convention, 171.
Sparta, Wis., instruction camp at, 324.
Staff Officers of 1792, 67.
Stanley, Gov. A. O., 324.
State Arsenal burned, 111-12.
State Guard: law enacted, 146; organization of 1861, 148, 168; coroner's verdict against, 262-63; encampment at Louisville, 263; mustered out in 1898, 282.
State Military Hospital at Louisville, 229.
State Military Monument, 139.
State officials join Confederacy, 165.
State Penitentiary, 349.
State Reformatory evacuated during 1937 flood, 360.
Statehood, 65-119.
Stations: Anderson's, 68; St. Asaph's, 3, 14, 16; Benson, 321; Boiling Springs, 3, 14; Burnt, 29; Bryan, 25, 29; siege, 32, 33, 34; Brown's besieged, 28; Bowman's, 34; Boone's, 29; Baker's, 53; Carpenter's, 48; Craig's, 29; Estill's 29; Farmer's 267; Gilbert's, 26; Grant's, 68; Harmon's, 52; Hanseford's, 68; Hood's, 41, 44; Hunnewell, Greenup County, 258; Kenton's (first fort in Mason County), 39, 49; Logan's, 16; McAfee, attack on, 28; McClelland's, 28; McConnell's, attack on, 27, 32; Martin's, 24; captured by Capt. Henry Byrd, 23-24; Montgomery's, 68-69; Morgan's attacked, 68, 72; Nolin, skirmish, 224; Plake's, 68; Ruddle's, captured by Capt. Henry Byrd, 23, 24; Strode's, 34, 37, 44-45, 53, 69; Troutman's, 68.
Steele, Maj. Theophilus, 220.
Stephenson, Gov. John W., 246-47.
Stockaded stations of Fayette in 1782, 32.
Stone, Tol, trial at Bowling Green, 277.
Stites, Col. Henry J., 348.
Strohm, Maj. Victor, 338.
Strong–Callahan feud, 315.
Student Army Training Corps, units established, 337.

Substitute brokers, 226-27.
Suppressed message of Gov. Magoffin, 178.
Sue Mundy (Jerome Clarke), 211, 226.
Tabular report of Ky. troops, 229-32.
Taft, President, visits Hickman, 321.
Tank Company, 38th Div., 373.
Taylor–Beckham Case: President McKinley refuses to interfere, 309-10; U.S. Supreme Court renders decision in favor of Beckmisses Guard, 311.
Taylor, John, scout, 25.
Taylor, Gov. W. S., 296-99, 302; unseated as Gov., 304, 309; dismisses militia, 311.
Taylor, Lt. Col. W. S., 349, 388.
Taylor, Gen. (President) Zachary, 110, 121, 123-24, 133-34, 140.
Tecumseh killed, 84, 93.
Temple, John B., President Military Board, 178.
Tennessee Centennial Exposition, 277.
Texas Emigrating Society, 122.
Texas Independence, War for, 112-114, 122.
Texas Revolution, 122-23.
Thacker, Harvey, 102.
Thames, Battle of the, 90, 92, 99.
Theobald, Capt. Thos. A., pensioned, 251.
Theobald's Tavern, 25.
Third Regt. Infantry officers and companies (Mexican War), 135-36.
Thirteenth Amendment to legislature for ratification, 222; becomes operative, 239.
Thomas, Gen. George H., 168
Thomas, Maj. Gen. John, 96.
Thomas Zouaves, 250.
Thompson, Brig. Gen. J. T., 337.
Thompson, Col. M. V., 135.
Tilghman, Col. Lloyd, 147.
Todd County, 252-53.
Todd, Col. John, 16, 33.
Todd, Col. Levi, 32-34, 42-43, 71.
Todd's expedition against the Ohio Indians, 42.
Todd, Gen. Robt., 15.
Tolliver, Craig, killed, 267.
Tolliver–Martin feud, 266-68.
Tompkinsville skirmish, 179.
Tories in Ky., 11.
Transylvania Company, 2, 13.
Treason indictments, 169.
Trials: Allen Mathis, 317; Carrie Anderson, 253; Bailey Murder, 349; Dr. Baker, 121; Wm. Black, 276; Jennie Bowman, 265; Russell Browder, 319; Pearl Bryant, 276-77; Jerome Clarke (Sue Mundy), 407; George Dimming, 277; Lee Elliston, 349; W. R. Fletcher, 317; Jett-White, 315; Kendall, 295; Grove C. Ken-

nedy, 254; Guy Lyons, 317; Marksberry, 349; Thos. D. Maybrier, 316; Neal-Craft, 260-63; Tol Stone, 277.
Troop levy for Continental Army in Fayette, Jefferson and Lincoln counties, 7.
Troops at Chickamauga in 1898, 284.
Troops on duty in Oct., 1865, 243.
Troops requisitioned by U.S. in 1807, 75.
Trophies: Brig. Gen. Roger D. Williams Cup, 388; National Defense, 393.
Trotter's Regiment, 93.
Tug River disturbance, 349.
Turnpike raiders, 275-76.
Twenty-second Cavalry Division, 348.
Tyndall, Maj. Gen. Robert, 348.
Union Volunteer report for 1863, 197-98, 203.
U.S. military interference in state elections, 198.
U.S. soldiers on duty in Ky., 242.
U.S. War Dept. officials visit Ky., 170.
University of Kentucky, 244-45; Cadet Company, 323.
Upper Blue Licks, 31.
Valley Station, Orell Rifle Range, 323.
Van Rensselaer case, 100-101.
Van Voast Light Guards of Newport, 254.
Van Voorhis, Brig. Gen. Daniel, letter from, 364.
Van Wick, Dr., murder of, 172.
Vera Cruz, 128.
Vermont, raid by Lt. Bennet H. Young into, 217-18.
Vidette, The, 188, 191.
Virginia Bill of Rights, 1, 6.
Virginia Colonial line, 371.
Virginia Militia Law, 3.
Virginia Salute, 247.
Virginia State Constitution, 2.
Voltigeur Regiment, 143.
Volunteers: of 1794 under Brig. Gen. Chas. Scott, 72; under Gen. Winchester at Ft. Definance, 81; enlisted for specific purpose, 89-90; called for Seminole War, 114; in Union Army, 229.
Waddell Grays, 250.
Wagon Company, 126th, 391.
Walcutt, Capt. D. B., 296, 300.
Walker, Confederate Secretary of War, 159.
War between the States—Part I, 151-91; Part II, 193-238.
War Declared on Confederacy by Ky., 163-64.

War Declared on Mexico, 123.
Waring-Holman Duel, 103.
Ward, Sally, 135.
War with Spain, The, 281-93.
War for Texas Independence, 112-14, 122.
War of 1812, 79.
Washington Centennial celebration, 270.
Watterson, Henry, 248.
Wayne, Gen. Anthony, 67; ordered to occupy Ft. Massac, 70; 71-72.
Weir, James, Sr., portrays militia muster, 106.
West Point: Camp Young, 314; troops on duty at, 331.
Whitewater Expedition, 57.
Whitley, Col. Wm., 38; killed at Thames, 92.
Whitley's Expedition against the Southern Indians, 73.
Wickliffe, troops on duty at, 330.
Widows' and Orphans' Home of Louisville, 260.
Wilderness Road, 26; Guard, 71, 74.
Wilkinson, Gen. James, 57, 74, 79.
Williams, Col. John S. ("Cerro Gordo"), 128-30, 135-36, 165, 216.
Williams, Brig. Gen. Roger D., 292, 297-99, 302, 312, 315-17, 321, 323-24, 332, 334, 337; trophy cup, 388.
Williams, Thomas, 13.
Wilson, Col. E. J., leads regiment in Texas Rebellion, 122.
Winchester's Campaign, 94.
Winchester, troops on duty at, 331-32.
Winn, Maj. Gen. Frank Long, 337.
Winn, Brig. Gen. John S., 337.
Wolford, Col. Frank S., 174; speech at Lexington, 205; arrested, 205-207; commissioned to raise regiment, 208; relieved, 214; fourth arrest, 221; appointed Adjt. Gen., 245, 247; organizes militia for police duty, 249; resigns as Adjt. Gen., 251.
Woodfill, Capt. Samuel, awarded Congressional Medal of Honor and Crois de Guerre, 338-39.
Woodworth, Samuel, ballad, 100.
World War, 327-43.
World's Fair at Chicago, encampment of Colonel Castleman's regiment at, 273.
Worthington, Capt. Edward, 15.
Wright, Adjt. Gen. J. M., 253.
Wytheville, Tenn., lead works, 217.
Yorktown (Va.) Centennial, 260.
Young, Lt. Bennet H., raid on St. Albans, Vt., 217-18.
Zollicoffer, Brig. Gen. Felix K., 175.
Zouaves, Thomas, 250.

www.ingramcontent.com/pod-product-compliance
Lightning Source LLC
Chambersburg PA
CBHW030441090526
44586CB00044B/443